A-Z GLASGOW Deluxe Street Atlas

CONTENTS

REFERENCE

Motorway	M8
A Road	A77
Under Construction	
Proposed	
B Road	B812
Dual Carriageway	
One Way Street Traffic flow on A Roads is also indicated by a heavy line on the driver's left.	
Pedestrianized Road	
Restricted Access	
Track	
Footpath	
Residential Walkway	
Railway	Level Crossing, Station
Underground Station	
Local Authority Boundary	
Built Up Area	MILL ST.
Posttown Boundary	
Postcode Boundary Within Posttowns	
Map Continuation	86 City
Ambulance Station	
Car Park Selected	
Church or Chapel	
Cycle Route	
Fire Station	
House Numbers A and B Roads only	13 8
Information Centre	
National Grid Reference	660
Police Station (Open 24 Hours)	
Post Office	
Toilet	
with facilities for the Disabled	
Educational Establishment	
Hospital or Health Centre	H
Leisure and Recreational Facility	
Places of Interest	
Public Building	
Shopping Centre or Market	
Other Selected Buildings	

SCALES

Map Pages 6-165
1:13368 (approx 4¾ inches to 1 mile)
0 — ¼ — ½ Mile
0 — 250 — 500 — 750 Metres

Map Pages 4-5
1:6684 (approx 9½ inches to 1 mile)
0 — ⅛ — ¼ Mile
0 — 100 — 200 — 300 — 400 Metres

Geographers' A-Z Map Company Ltd.

Head Office:
Fairfield Road, Borough Green, Sevenoaks, Kent TN15 8PP
Telephone 01732 781000 (General Enquiries & Trade Sales)

Showrooms:
44 Gray's Inn Road, London, WC1X 8HX
Telephone 020 7440 9500 (Retail Sales)

www.a-zmaps.co.uk

KEY TO MAP PAGES

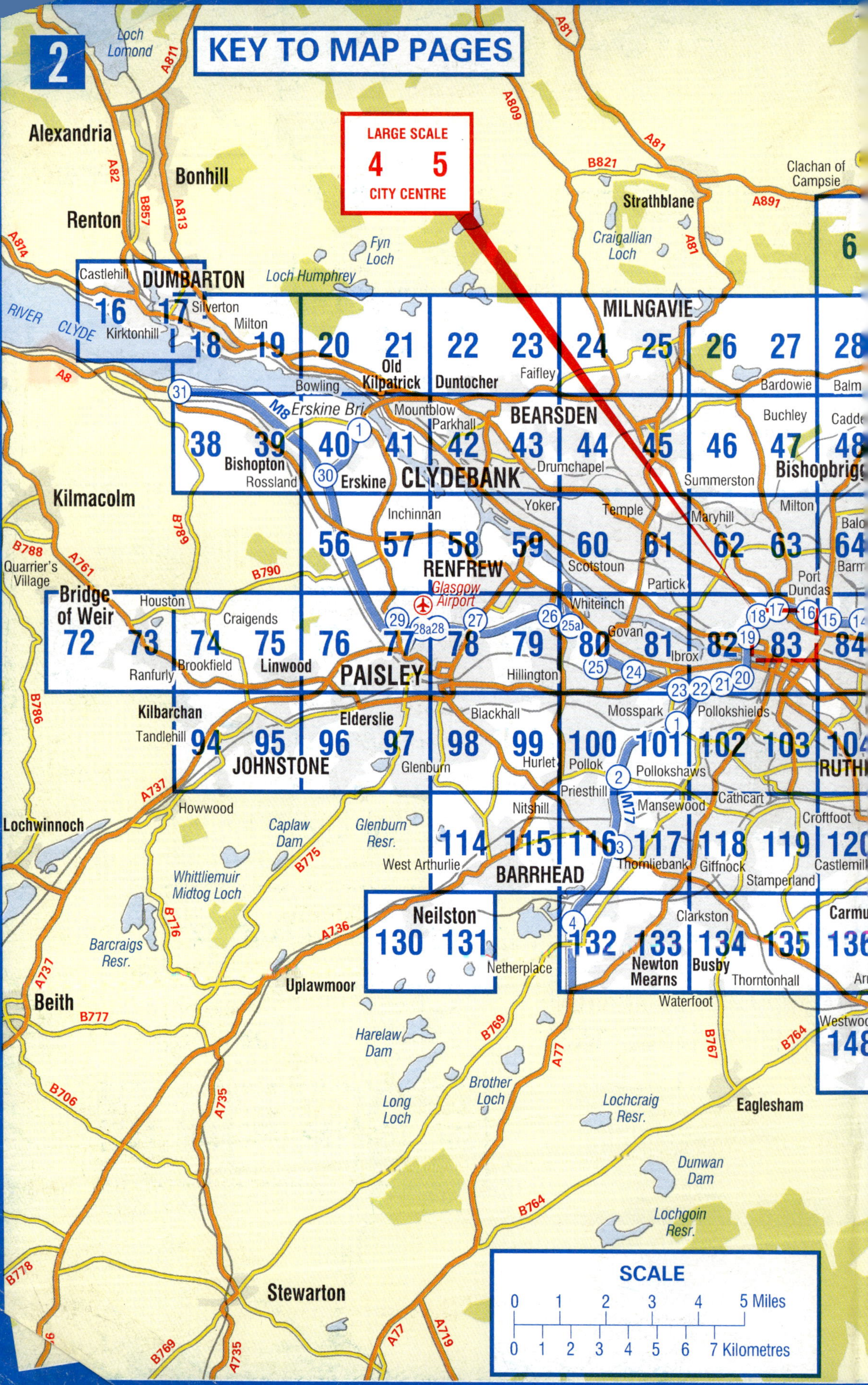

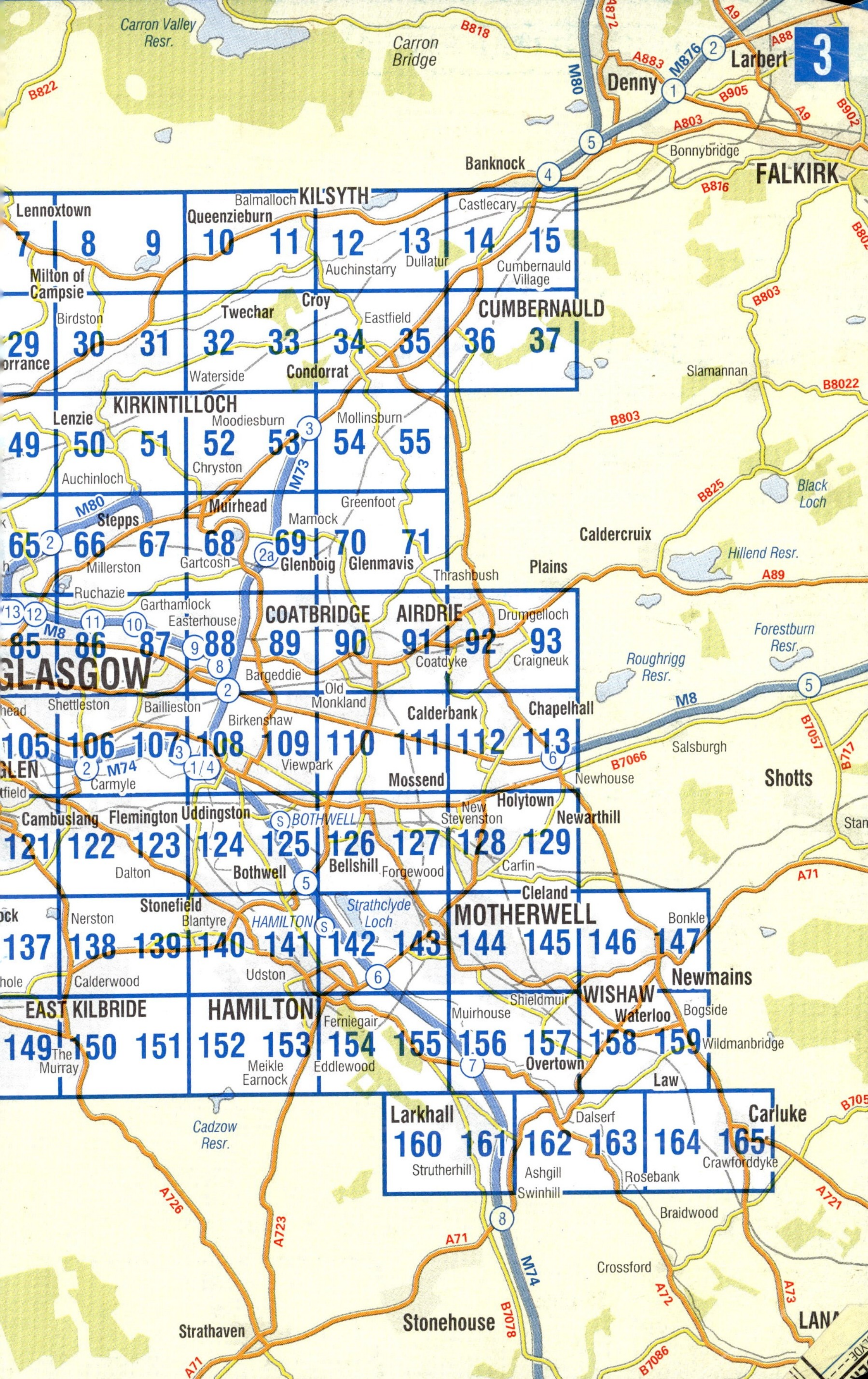
Carron Valley Resr.
Carron Bridge
B818
B822
A872
A9
A88
Denny
Larbert
M876
A883
M80
B905
B902
A803
A9
Banknock
Bonnybridge
FALKIRK
B816
B802
Balmalloch
KILSYTH
Lennoxtown
Queenzieburn
Castlecary
7
8
9
10
11
12
13
14
15
Milton of Campsie
Auchinstarry
Dullatur
Cumbernauld Village
B803
Birdston
Twechar
Croy
Eastfield
CUMBERNAULD
29
30
31
32
33
34
35
36
37
Torrance
Waterside
Condorrat
Slamannan
B8022
KIRKINTILLOCH
Lenzie
Moodiesburn
Mollinsburn
B803
49
50
51
52
53
54
55
Chryston
M73
Auchinloch
B825
Black Loch
M80
Stepps
Muirhead
Marnock
Greenfoot
65
66
67
68
69
70
71
Caldercruix
Millerston
Gartcosh
Glenboig
Glenmavis
Hillend Resr.
Thrashbush
Plains
A89
Ruchazie
Garthamlock
Easterhouse
COATBRIDGE
AIRDRIE
Drumgelloch
Forestburn Resr.
M8
85
86
87
88
89
90
91
92
93
Roughrigg Resr.
GLASGOW
Bargeddie
Coatdyke
Craigneuk
Old Monkland
Shettleston
Baillieston
Calderbank
Chapelhall
M8
B7057
Birkenshaw
105
106
107
108
109
110
111
112
113
Salsburgh
B717
M74
Viewpark
B7066
Newhouse
Shotts
Carmyle
Mossend
Holytown
Cambuslang
Flemington
Uddingston
BOTHWELL
New Stevenston
Newarthill
121
122
123
124
125
126
127
128
129
Dalton
Bothwell
Bellshill
Forgewood
Carfin
A71
Cleland
Nerston
Stonefield
Blantyre
HAMILTON
Strathclyde Loch
MOTHERWELL
Bonkle
137
138
139
140
141
142
143
144
145
146
147
Calderwood
Udston
Newmains
Shieldmuir
WISHAW
EAST KILBRIDE
HAMILTON
Ferniegair
Muirhouse
Waterloo
Bogside
149
150
151
152
153
154
155
156
157
158
159
The Murray
Meikle Earnock
Eddlewood
Overtown
Wildmanbridge
Law
Larkhall
Dalserf
Carluke
B7056
160
161
162
163
164
165
Cadzow Resr.
Strutherhill
Ashgill
Rosebank
Crawforddyke
Swinhill
A726
Braidwood
A721
A723
A71
M74
Crossford
A72
A73
Stonehouse
B7078
Strathaven
A71
B7086
LANARK

A
B
C
D
1
2
3
4
5
6
83
82
M8
Junction 17
Junction 19
Junc. 18
A804
A82
A81
DOBB
CRAIG
ST. GEORGE'S RD.
GARSCUBE RD.
NORTH
NEWTON
STREET
M8 MOTORWAY
Oakgrove Primary School
Sch.
BRAID SQ.
CORN STREET
EDGIN ST.
CIVIC STREET
STH. SPIERS WHARF
SPIERS WHARF
GLADSTONE ST.
ST. PETER'S ST.
NEW CITY ROAD
ST. GEORGE'S RD.
WEST PRINCE'S ST.
QUEEN'S CR.
ASHLEY ST.
GRANT STREET
ASHLEY LA.
CARNARVON ST.
BALIOL ST.
BALIOL LA.
WOODLANDS RD.
WOSE T.LA.
Stow College
SHAMROCK ST.
NEW CITY ROAD
WEST GRAHAM STREET
BUCCLEUCH STREET
BUCCLEUCH LANE
DUNDASVALE CT.
STEWART STREET
MAITLAND ST.
GLENMAVIS
DUNBLANE ST.
Cowcaddens
COWCADDENS
MILTON STREET
LARBERT ST.
DUNBLANE ST.
Music Sch.
McPHATER STR
Tenement Ho.
Synagogue
Nursery Sch.
GARNETHILL
DALHOUSIE
G3
St. Aloysius College
Garnethill
School of Arts
RENFREW STREET
Royal Highland Fusiliers Museum
Prim. Sch.
DENTAL HOSPITAL
Contemporary Arts Cen.
School of Art
ABC Film Cen.
Mclellan Galleries
Film Theatre
Royal Scottish Academy of Music and Drama
Theatre Royal
S.T.V. Studios
Pavilion Theatre
RENFREW
Willow Tearooms
SAUCHIEHALL ST. SHOPPING CEN.
SAUCHIEHALL LANE
SAUCHIEHALL STREET
CAMBRIDGE STREET
ROSE STREET
DALHOUSIE STREET
SCOTT STREET
GARNET STREET
BERKELEY ST.
Lib. & Theatre
KENT RD.
CLEVELAND LA.
Kings Theatre
Offs.
Charing Cross
ELMBANK CRES.
INDIA STREET
ELMBANK ST.
ELMBANK LA.
HOLLAND STREET
Police H.Q.
WEST REGENT STREET
WEST REGENT LANE
Compass Gallery
BLYTHSWOOD SQUARE
DOUGLAS LA.
BATH STREET
BATH LANE
WEST GEORGE STREET
WEST NILE STREET
Cinema
ST. VINCENT STREET
ST. VINCENT LANE
G2
Ewan Mundy Fine Art Gallery
WELLINGTON
HOPE STREET
ST. MARY'S LA.
ST. VNCT. T.
SHAFTESBURY ST.
WILLIAM ST.
WILLIAM STREET
Prim. Sch.
BISHOP LANE
BOTHWELL STREET
BOTHWELL LANE
ST. PETER'S LA.
RENFIELD LA.
DRURY ST.
WATERLOO STREET
WATERLOO LA.
GORDON STREET
GORDON LA.
WEST NILE
STOBCROSS STREET
Anderston
ANDERSTON CENTRE
WELLINGTON LA.
WELLINGTON STREET
CADOGAN STREET
Offs.
HOLM STREET
ARGYLE STREET
CENTRAL
UNION STREET
MITCHELL LA.
MITCHELL STREET
Arts Cen.
PICCADILLY ST.
BALACLAVA ST.
CRIMEA STREET
WASHINGTON STREET
McALPINE STREET
CARRICK STREET
BROWN STREET
WATT STREET
JAMES WATT LA.
YORK STREET
ROBERTSON LANE
ROBERTSON STREET
OSWALD STREET
Arches Theatre
MIDLAND STREET
JAMAICA STREET
ADAMS COURT LA.
ST. ENOCH PL.
St. Enoch
HOWARD
Divali Cinem
CHEAPSIDE ST.
ANDERSTON QUAY
BROOMIELAW
WALKWAY
258
259
665
666

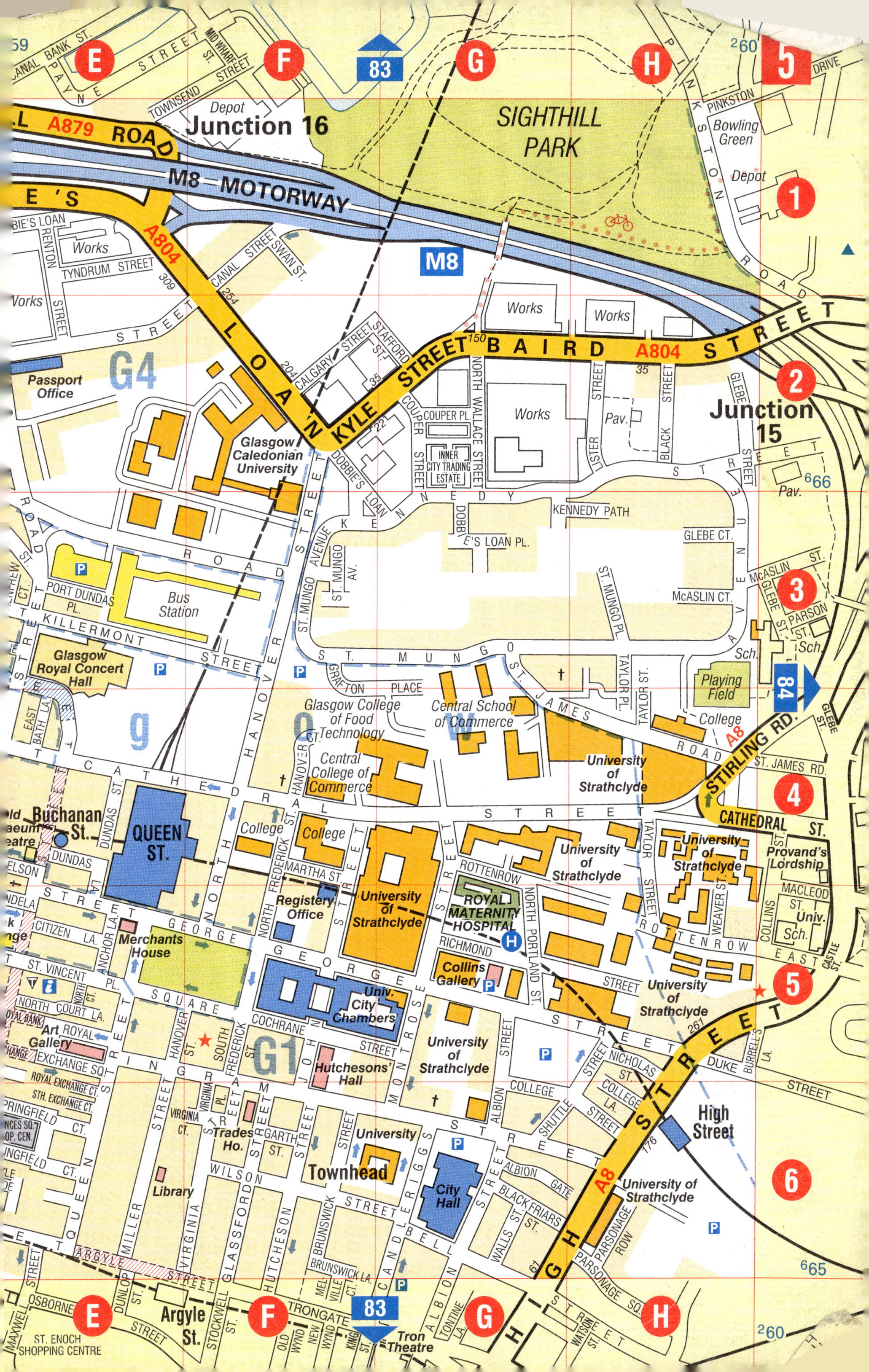

E
F
G
H
83
5
Junction 16
SIGHTHILL PARK
A879 ROAD
M8 MOTORWAY
Bowling Green
Depot
1
M8
A804
Works
TYNDRUM STREET
CANAL STREET
BAIRD STREET
A804
2
Junction 15
G4
Passport Office
Glasgow Caledonian University
KYLE STREET
INNER CITY TRADING ESTATE
KENNEDY PATH
GLEBE CT.
McASLIN CT.
3
PORT DUNDAS PL.
Bus Station
KILLERMONT STREET
Glasgow Royal Concert Hall
ST. MUNGO AVENUE
GRAFTON PLACE
Glasgow College of Food Technology
Central School of Commerce
Central College of Commerce
Playing Field
College
84
STIRLING RD.
A8
ST. JAMES ROAD
University of Strathclyde
4
CATHEDRAL STREET
Buchanan St.
QUEEN ST.
College
ROTTENROW
ROYAL MATERNITY HOSPITAL
Provand's Lordship
Univ. Sch.
Registery Office
Merchants House
GEORGE SQUARE
GEORGE STREET
Univ. City Chambers
Collins Gallery
5
Art Gallery
G1
Hutchesons' Hall
DUKE STREET
High Street
HIGH STREET
Trades Ho.
Library
Townhead
City Hall
6
INGRAM STREET
WILSON STREET
BELL STREET
ARGYLE STREET
Argyle St.
TRONGATE
Tron Theatre
ST. ENOCH SHOPPING CENTRE
E
F
83
G
H

6
260
A
B
C
D
Baillie Hill
Haughhead
Crosshouse
Kier Hill
Rosedene
Wellbank
STRATHBLANE ROAD A891
GLEN
61
KIRKTON
CASTLEVIEW
Hall
Cricket Grd.
Weir
Hall
Kilwinnet
Balcorrach
East Lodge
Finglen Burn
Kirk Burn
EAST DUN
Hole
Capieston House
Pow Burn
West Lodge
Glazert Wood
A891
Tennis Ct.
79
Bank Wood
Lovers' Leap
Ten. Cts.
Nurses Home
Football Grd.
Pavilion
LENNOX CASTLE HOSPITAL
OVAL
NETHERTON
NETHERTON HILL
678
Craigend Wood
Swimming Pool
Filter House
The White House
Campsie House
Clochcore Wood
Baldow
Reservoir
Baldow Plantation
Drum Plantation
Glen
Mounthuillie
Baldow
G l a
77
Cattle Grid
Newlands
Peathill Wood
Glenwhapp
G64
76
Waterfall
28
260
61
1
2
3
4
5
6

E
F
G
H
63
64
Rannie
79
BARTONSHIRE
CROW ROAD
B822
Burnel
Capieston
Balgrochan
Trinity House
Heatheryknowe
CAMPSIE GOLF COURSE
Club House
Ferrets
1
Maiden Castle
Bencloich Mains
LENNOXTOWN
GEELONG GDS.
CUMROCH RD.
KINCAID DR.
CROFTHEAD DR.
LENNOX ROAD
CROSSHILL ST.
St. Machan's Prim. Sch.
War Mem.
Tennis Courts
Playing Field
Pav.
2
Hall
Dam
JANEFIELD PL.
ST. MACHAN'S WY.
WHITEFIELD TERRACE
WHITEFIELD
SERVICE ST.
QUARRY LA.
Cem.
Lib.
BENCLOICH CR.
HEATHER VW.
BENCLOICH CRES.
BENCLOICH ROAD
Bencloich Farm
Dovecot Cottage
678
Stanford Cottage
Dam
Hall
WINSTON CR.
MAIN
NORTH BIRBISTON RD.
GRANGER RD.
Prim. Sch.
SCHOOL LA.
SLATEFIELD
LINDSAY TER.
PINE ST.
HOLYKNOWE CRES.
GLENWARD AV.
Glorat Ho.
3
Works
Water
STATION ROAD
VEITCH PL.
CHAPEL ST.
MILLBURN ST.
ELM ST.
Rec. Cen.
THE FELLS
GLENWARD AV.
CRAIGHTON GS.
WESTERTON RD.
LINN GLEN
Offices
WELL LA.
STREET
GREENHEAD RD.
STIRLING PL.
JAMES HEMPHILL CT.
GLORAT AV.
BENCLOICH AV.
HILLVIEW
HOLYKNOWE RD.
ASHCROFT WK.
ASHCROFT AV.
WESTERTON
MEIKLE
WARREN WK.
ARGYLE GS.
DRUMALING
Westerton Wood
8
Burnbank Cottage
Southfield
BRAE
G66
MILTON
GLAZERT MDW.
GLAZERT PK. DR.
Ferguson Park
ROAD
BENVUE
REDHILLS VIEW
BLUEBELL WY.
MURRISON
MACCABE GS.
DR.
Westerton
4
Lodge
Millgate Cottage
ROWANTREE PL.
CAMPSIE
A891
ROAD
Lennoxlea Cottage
77
S g o w
SOUTH
Dam
Sewage Works
Finniescroft Wood
Finniescroft
Gallow Hill
5
Cherry Tree Cottage
Manderston
Burn
Boyd's
Lennoxlea Farm
Reservoir (covered)
Barrhill
6
Redmoss Farm
76
Kinkell
29
62
63
64

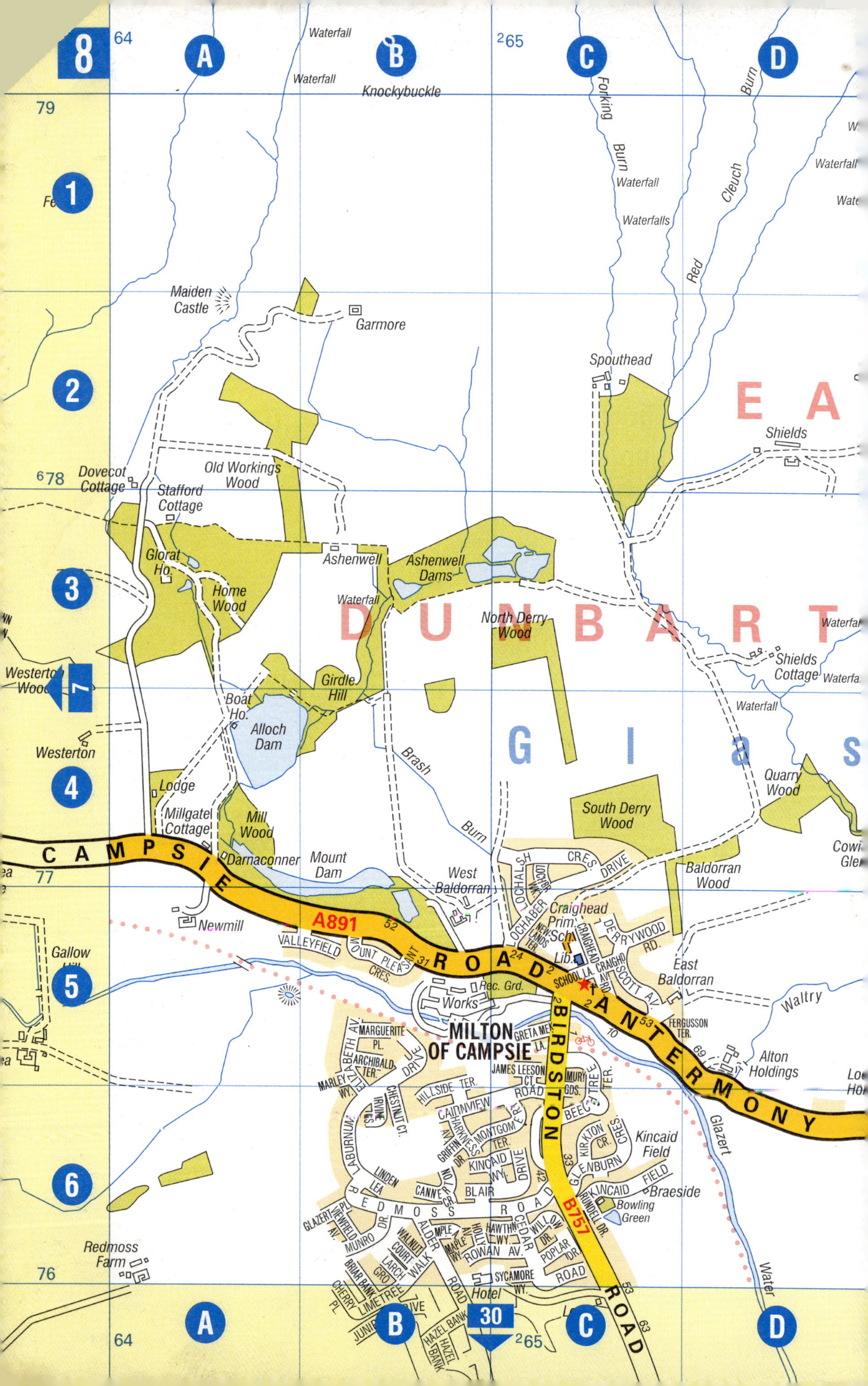
64
A
B
265
C
D
Waterfall
Waterfall
Knockybuckle
Forking
Burn
Burn
Waterfall
Waterfalls
Cleuch
Red
Waterfall
79
1
Maiden
Castle
Garmore
2
Spouthead
E A
Shields
Old Workings
Wood
Dovecot
Cottage
678
Stafford
Cottage
Glorat
Ho.
Home
Wood
Ashenwell
Ashenwell
Dams
Waterfall
3
D U N B A R T
North Derry
Wood
Shields
Cottage
Westerton
Wood
7
Girdle
Hill
Boat
Ho.
Alloch
Dam
Waterfall
Westerton
Brash
G l a s
Quarry
Wood
4
Lodge
Millgate
Cottage
Mill
Wood
South Derry
Wood
Burn
C A M P S I E
Darnaconner
Mount
Dam
West
Baldorran
Baldorran
Wood
77
Newmill
A891
52
Craighead
Prim.
Sch.
Lib.
DERRYWOOD
RD.
East
Baldorran
Gallow
Hill
VALLEYFIELD
MOUNT PLEASANT
CRES.
31
ROAD
24
ANTERMONY
5
Rec. Grd.
Works
SCHOOL LA.
SCOTT AV.
53
Waltry
FERGUSSON
TER.
MARGUERITE
PL.
MILTON
OF CAMPSIE
GRETA MEEK
LA.
BIRDSTON
ARCHIBALD
TER.
ELIZABETH AV.
DRIVE
JAMES LEESON
CT.
69
Alton
Holdings
MARLEY
WY.
HILLSIDE TER.
ROAD
CAIRNVIEW
IRVINE
CHESTNUT CT.
LABURNUM
GRIFFIN AV.
HARKNESS
MONTGOMERY
TER.
KINCAID
WY.
DRIVE
KIRKTON
CR.
CRES.
Kincaid
Field
Glazert
6
LINDEN
LEA
CANNERTON
CR.
BLAIR
GLENBURN
KINCAID
FIELD
Braeside
Bowling
Green
B757
REDMOSS
ROAD
GLAZERT PL.
WYEFIELD AV.
MUNRO
DR.
ALDER
WALNUT
COURT
HAWTHORN
WY.
CEDAR
HOLLY
MAPLE
ROWAN AV.
WILLOW
DR.
POPLAR
DR.
Redmoss
Farm
76
BRIAR BANK
GRO.
LARCH
WALK
SYCAMORE
WY.
ROAD
Hotel
CHERRY
PL.
LIMETREE
DRIVE
ROAD
A
B
30
C
D
JUNIPER
HAZEL BANK
HAZEL
BANK
64
265
63
Water

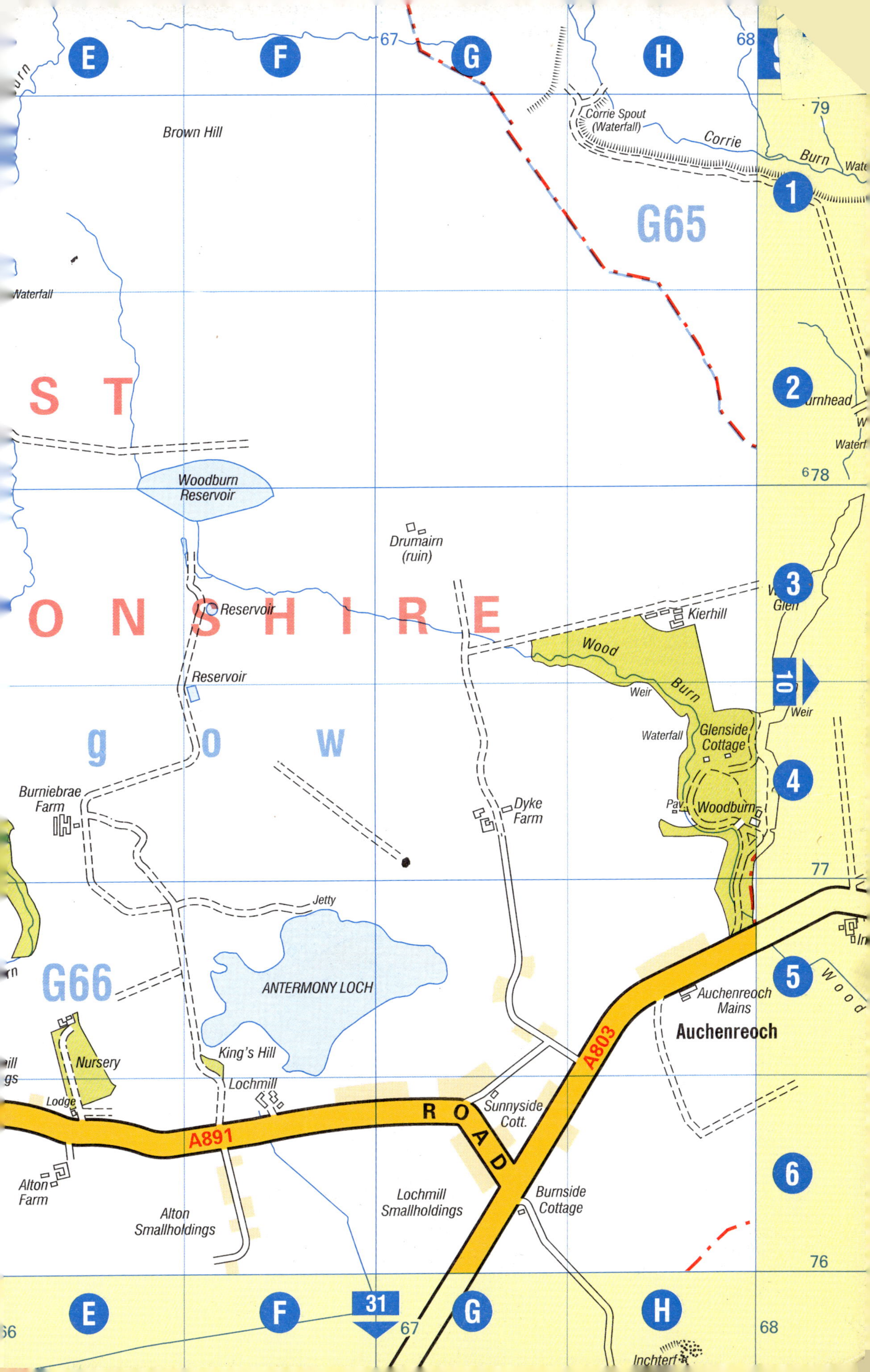
E
F
G
H
67
68
Brown Hill
Corrie Spout
(Waterfall)
Corrie
Burn
79
G65
1
2
Waterfall
STIRLINGSHIRE
Woodburn
Reservoir
678
Drumairn
(ruin)
Reservoir
Reservoir
Kierhill
Wood
Burn
Weir
Waterfall
Glenside
Cottage
3
10
Weir
4
Woodburn
Pav.
Burniebrae
Farm
Dyke
Farm
77
Jetty
G66
ANTERMONY LOCH
King's Hill
Nursery
Lodge
Lochmill
A891
ROAD
Sunnyside
Cott.
A803
Auchenreoch
Mains
Auchenreoch
5
Wood
6
Alton
Farm
Alton
Smallholdings
Lochmill
Smallholdings
Burnside
Cottage
76
31
66
Inchterf

A
B
C
D
68
69
79
78
77
76
1
2
3
4
5
6
Corrie Plantation
Corrie
Drumheldric
Corrie
Burn
Waterfall
Waterfalls
Stoneree Glen
Cairnbog
NOR
LANARK
Burnhead
Weir
Waterfall
DYKEHEAD
Dykehead
Old Place
Lossit Wood
G65
Lossit
Queenzieburn
Over Gavell
Playground
Wham Glen
Craigroot
Piggery
Kierhill
ANDERSON CR.
HILLCREST RD.
ROAD
DUMBRECK TER.
MEADOWSIDE
ROA
QUEENZIEBURN IND. EST.
9
Burn
Weir
Institute
MILL RD.
Sch.
2
Recreation Ground
Waterfall
Glenside Cottage
Gallow Hill
Queenzieburn Farm
52
Weir
Cast
Gavell Farm
Pav.
Woodburn
LOAN
WHIN
ROAD
Waterfall
Queenzie
Gavell
GAVELL
Burn
Inchwood Cottage
KILSYTH
A803
Sewage Works
Inchwood
Wood
Auchenreoch Mains
Auchenreoch
G66
Netherinch
Burn
Pav.
Kelvin
Netherinch Refuse Tip
River
Works
Twechar
Burn
32
ROAD

32

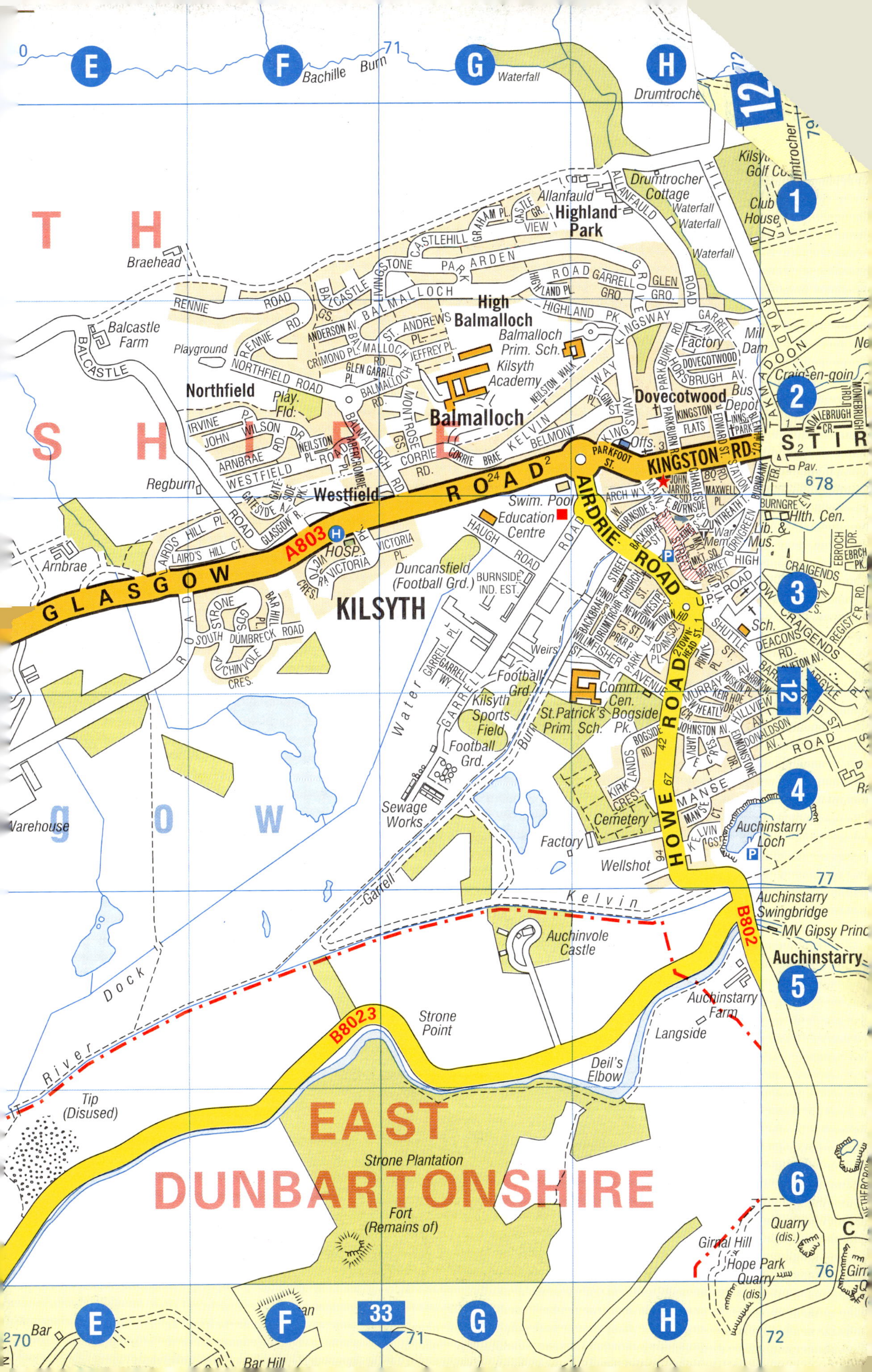
E
F
G
H
Bachille Burn
Waterfall
Drumtrocher
12
Kilsyth Golf Course
Drumtrocher
Club House
1
2
3
4
5
6
T H
S H I R E
g o w
Braehead
Balcastle Farm
BALCASTLE
Playground
Northfield
Regburn
Arnbrae
Warehouse
Allanfauld
Highland Park
Drumtrocher Cottage
Waterfall
CASTLEHILL
ARDEN
PARK
ROAD
GRAHAM PL.
CASTLE VIEW
LIVINGSTONE
BALMALLOCH
High Balmalloch
Balmalloch Prim. Sch.
Kilsyth Academy
HIGHLAND PK.
KINGSWAY
GARRELL GRO.
GLEN GRO.
GROVE
HILL ROAD
RENNIE ROAD
RENNIE RD.
NORTHFIELD ROAD
ANDERSON AV.
ST. ANDREWS PL.
JEFFREY PL.
CRIMOND PL.
GLEN GARRELL PL.
Play. Fld.
Balmalloch
MONTROSE GDS.
CORRIE RD.
CORRIE BRAE
KELVIN
BELMONT
NEILSTON WALK
ELGIN PL.
IRVINE PL.
JOHN WILSON DR.
ARNBRAE RD.
WESTFIELD
GATESIDE AV.
Westfield
GLASGOW ROAD
A803
ROAD
HOSP.
VICTORIA PL.
VICTORIA CRES.
Swim. Pool
Education Centre
HAUGH ROAD
Duncansfield (Football Grd.)
BURNSIDE IND. EST.
KILSYTH
STRONE GDS.
BAR HILL PL.
SOUTH DUMBRECK ROAD
AUCHINVOLE CRES.
LAIRD'S HILL CT.
AIRDS HILL PL.
Mill Dam
Factory
Craig-en-goin
DOVECOTWOOD
HORSBRUGH AV.
Dovecotwood
Bus Depot
KINGSTON FLATS
PARKBURN RD.
PARKFOOT ST.
KINGSTON RD.
Offs.
AIRDRIE ROAD
STIR
Pav.
Hlth. Cen.
BURNGREEN
Lib. & Mus.
War Mem.
MARKET
HIGH
CRAIGENDS
EBROCH DR.
EBROCH PK.
REGISTER RD.
DEACONS RD.
SHUTTLE ST.
Sch.
U.P. RD.
NEWTOWN ST.
BACKBRAE ST.
FINDLAY ST.
CHURCH ST.
TOWNHEAD
Weirs
Football Grd.
Kilsyth Sports Field
Football Grd.
Comm. Cen.
St. Patrick's Prim. Sch.
Bogside Pk.
GARRELL WY.
GARRELL PL.
Water
Burn
Sewage Works
HOWE ROAD
BOGSIDE RD.
KIRKLANDS CRES.
Cemetery
MANSE
MANSE CT.
KELVIN GDS.
JOHNSTON AV.
MURRAY
HILLVIEW AV.
DONALDSON AV.
ROAD
Factory
Wellshot
Auchinstarry Loch
Auchinstarry Swingbridge
MV Gipsy Princ
Auchinstarry
B802
Garrell
Kelvin
Dock
River
Auchinvole Castle
Strone Point
B8023
Auchinstarry Farm
Langside
Deil's Elbow
Tip (Disused)
EAST DUNBARTONSHIRE
Strone Plantation
Fort (Remains of)
Girnal Hill
Hope Park Quarry (dis.)
Quarry (dis.)
Bar
Bar Hill
33
71
72
76
77
78
270

A
B
C
D
1
2
3
4
5
6
73
Quarry
Beltmoss Quarry
The Strip
Stable Wood
KILSYTH LENNOX GOLF COURSE
Club House
ROAD
Waterfalls
Riskend
Colzium Castle (Rems. of)
Colzium Glen
Merryton Nursery
Colzium Ho.
North Lodge
Bandstand
Avenue Strip
Riskend Strip
Dam Wood
Boat House
Speirs Island
Colzium-Margaret Lennox Memorial Estate
Craigstone Wood
Colzium Burn
Colzium
Bank Wood
Neilston
Mill Dam
Factory
Craig-en-goin
TAK-MA-DOON ROAD
Bowl. Club
Pav.
Depot
LADESIDE DR.
MONIEBRUGH CR.
MONIEBRUGH RD.
Lodge
Castle Hill
Townhead
Weir
Currymire
STIRLING ROAD
A803
KINGSTON ROAD
KINGSTON FLATS
DOVECOTWOOD
PARKBURN RD.
Waterfall
GLEN GRO.
Factory
KILSYTH
North Barrwood
Endwood
Mill
Woodend
CADGER'S SHEUCH
Hlth. Cen.
Lib. & Mus.
BURNGREEN
HIGH ST.
MKT. SQ.
MARKET
EBROCH DR.
EBROCH PK.
COLZIUM VW.
WOODSIDE AV.
CRAIGSTONE VW.
CRAIGENDS
ANTON CRES.
REGISTER RD.
HIGH BARRWOOD RD.
HAUGHTON AV.
HAMILL DR.
Playground
ST. MIRREN'S RD.
WATSON CR.
CRONULLA PL.
COURTHILL CRES.
Barrwood
COACH CT.
COACH ROAD
L A N A R K
Colzium Plantation
SHUTTLE ST.
Sch.
DEACONS RD.
CRAIGENDS
CLIFTON AV.
BARLANDFAULD ST.
ARGYLE ST.
DONALDSON AV.
HILLVIEW AV.
EDMONSTONE DR.
JOHNSTON AV.
BARRWOOD
MID COACH PL.
STH. BARRWOOD RD.
MAL FLEMING'S BRAE
BARRPATH
COACH
MANSE ROAD
Barr
South Barrwood
Aqueduct
Craigmarloch Drawbridge
Kings Seat
Craigmarloch Wood
HOWE ROAD
Auchinstarry Loch
Kelvin
77
Auchinstarry Swingbridge
MV Gipsy Princess
Auchinstarry
Forth and Clyde Canal
Auchinstarry Farm
Langside
Langhill
G l a s
B802
Croy Hill
Nethercroy Quarry (disused)
Quarries (disused)
G65
NETHERCROY RD.
CONSTARRY ROAD
SMITHSTONE CR.
CUILMUIR VW.
HILLSIDE
Croy Quarry
Auchinbee Quarry (disused)
Quarry (dis.)
Girnal Hill
Hope Park Quarry (dis.)
76
Girnal Brae Quarry (dis.)
72
Croy
CUILMUIR TER.
34
73
Football
GLEN ORCHY
Auchinbee
11

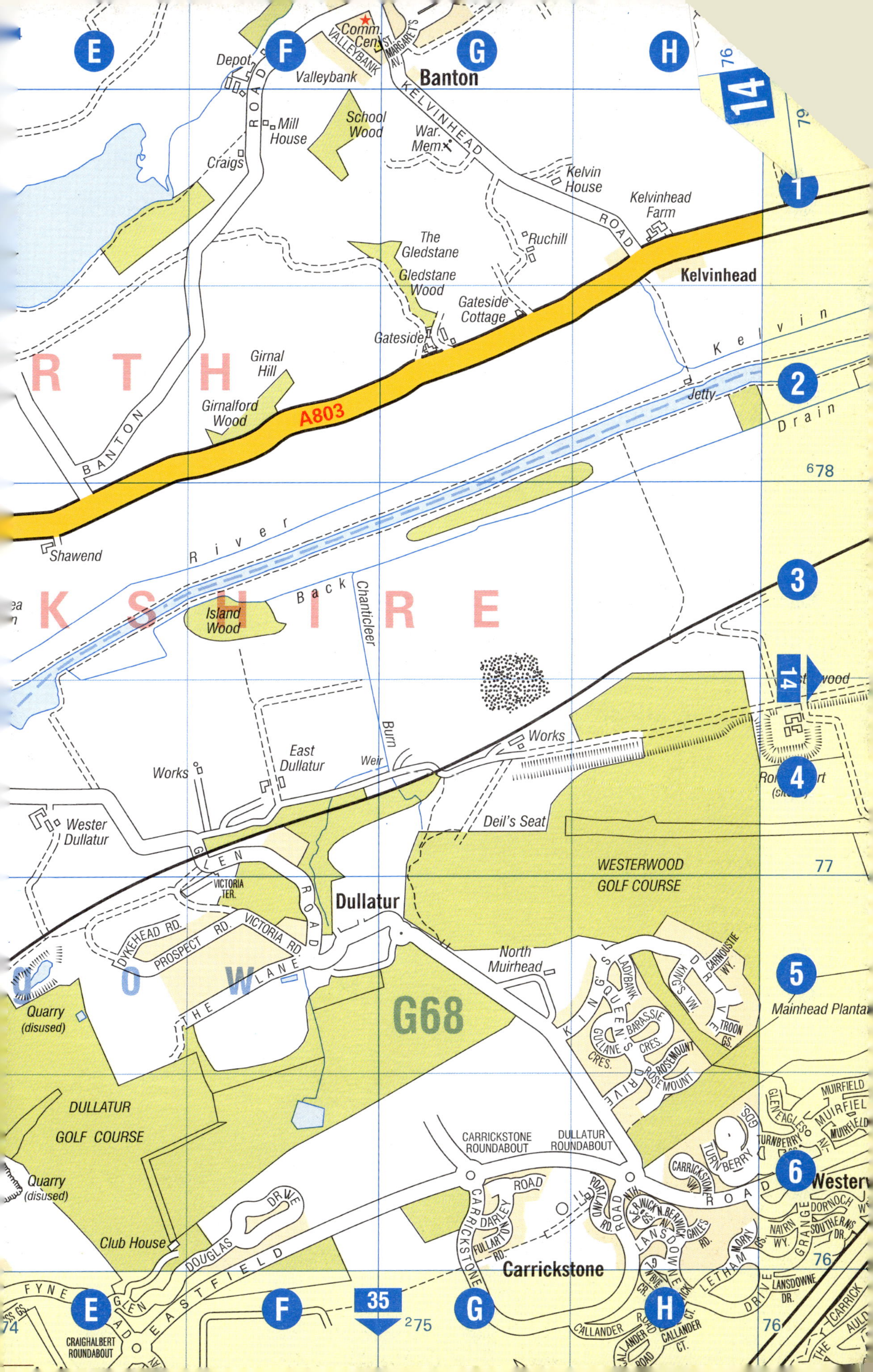
E
F
G
H
Comm. Cen.
VALLEYBANK
ST. MARGARET'S AV.
Depot
Valleybank
Banton
76
14
79
KELVINHEAD
ROAD
Mill House
School Wood
War. Mem.
Craigs
Kelvin House
Kelvinhead Farm
1
The Gledstane
Ruchill
Gledstane Wood
Kelvinhead
Gateside Cottage
Gateside
Kelvin
Girnal Hill
R T H
2
Jetty
Girnalford Wood
A803
Drain
BANTON
678
Shawend
River
3
Back
Chanticleer
Island Wood
K S H I R E
14
Burn
East Dullatur
Weir
Works
Works
4
Wester Dullatur
Deil's Seat
GLEN ROAD
VICTORIA TER.
WESTERWOOD GOLF COURSE
77
Dullatur
DYKEHEAD RD.
PROSPECT RD.
VICTORIA RD.
North Muirhead
KING'S
LADYBANK
QUEEN'S
KING'S VW.
DRIVE
CARNOUSTIE WY.
5
THE LANE
O O W
G68
Mainhead Plantat
Quarry (disused)
BARASSIE CRES.
GULLANE CRES.
ROSEMOUNT
TROON GS.
DULLATUR GOLF COURSE
GLENEAGLES AV.
MUIRFIELD
TURNBERRY
CARRICKSTONE ROUNDABOUT
DULLATUR ROUNDABOUT
CARRICKSTONE VW.
6
Wester
Quarry (disused)
DRIVE
DOUGLAS
ROAD
PORTLAND RD.
BERWICK GS.
N. BERWICK AV.
GAILES RD.
DORNOCH
NAIRN WY.
GRANGE
SOUTHERNS DR.
Club House
CARRICKSTONE
DARLEY
FULLARTON RD.
LANSDOWNE
LETHAM
MORRY GS.
76
Carrickstone
EASTFIELD
FYNE
GLEN
LANSDOWNE DR.
CARRICK
AULD
E
F
35
G
H
CALLANDER
CALLANDER CT.
CALLANDER ROAD
CRAIGHALBERT ROUNDABOUT
74
275
76
THE

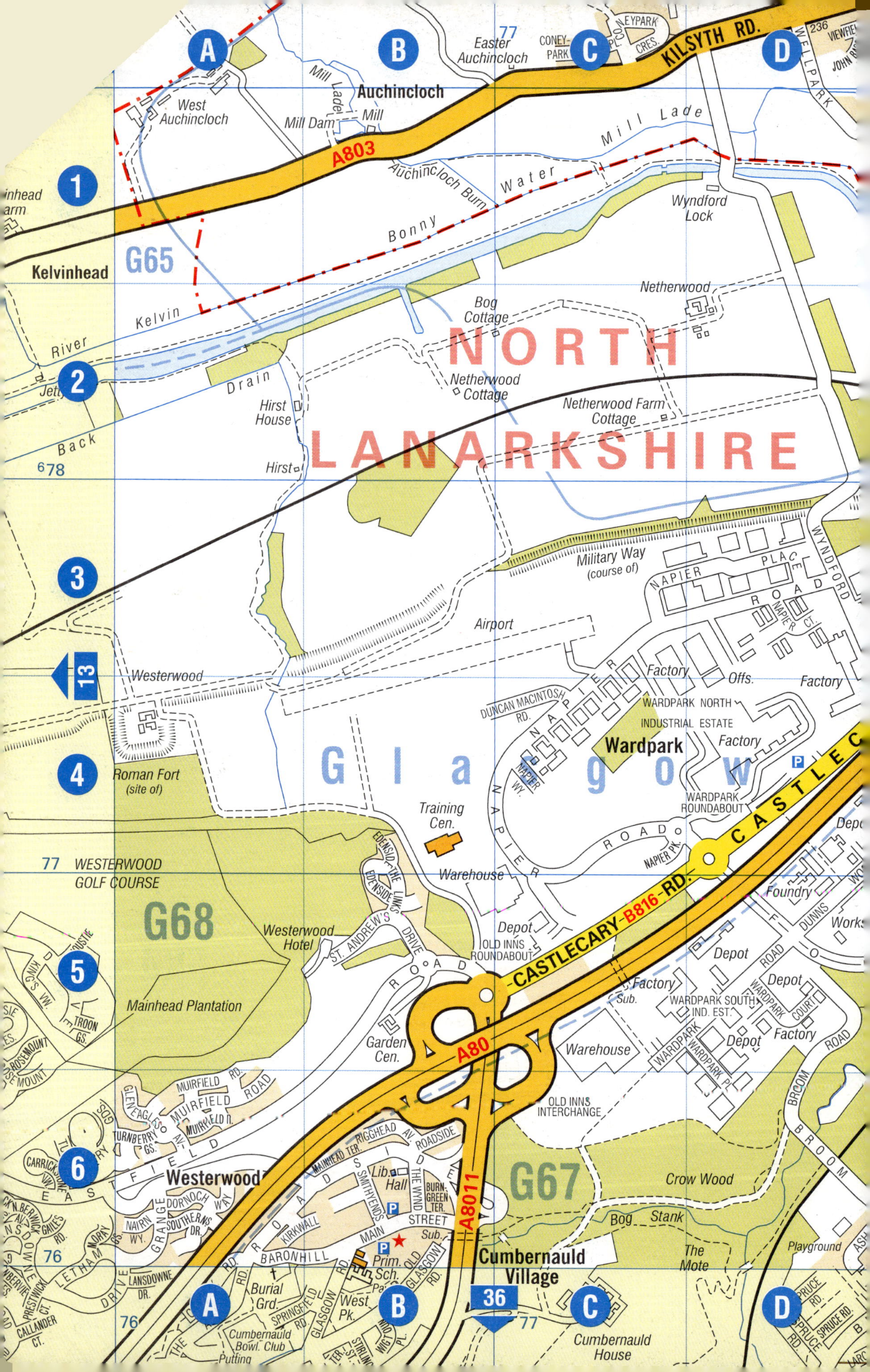

A
B
C
D
1
2
3
4
5
6
77
Easter Auchincloch
CONEY-PARK
CONEYPARK CRES.
KILSYTH RD.
236
WELLPARK
VIEWFIELD
West Auchincloch
Auchincloch
Mill Lade
Mill Dam
Mill
A803
Auchincloch Burn
Mill Lade
Bonny Water
Wyndford Lock
Kelvinhead
G65
Kelvin River
Drain
Back
678
Bog Cottage
Netherwood
NORTH LANARKSHIRE
Netherwood Cottage
Netherwood Farm Cottage
Hirst House
Hirst
Military Way (course of)
NAPIER PLACE
NAPIER ROAD
NAPIER CT.
WYNDFORD
Airport
13
Westerwood
Factory
Offs.
Factory
DUNCAN MACINTOSH RD.
WARDPARK NORTH INDUSTRIAL ESTATE
Wardpark
Factory
Roman Fort (site of)
Glasgow
NAPIER WY.
NAPIER ROAD
Training Cen.
WARDPARK ROUNDABOUT
NAPIER PK.
CASTLECARY RD.
77
WESTERWOOD GOLF COURSE
EDENSIDE
THE LINKS
Warehouse
Foundry
G68
Westerwood Hotel
ST. ANDREW'S DRIVE
ROAD
Depot
OLD INNS ROUNDABOUT
CASTLECARY-B816-RD.
DUNNS
Works
Depot
KING'S VW.
TROON GS.
Mainhead Plantation
Factory
Sub.
WARDPARK SOUTH IND. EST.
Depot
WARDPARK COURT
Factory
ROSEMOUNT
Garden Cen.
A80
Warehouse
WARDPARK
WARDPARK PL.
Depot
ROAD
MUIRFIELD RD.
MUIRFIELD ROAD
MUIRFIELD
GLENEAGLES AV.
OLD INNS INTERCHANGE
BROOM
BROOM
TURNBERRY GS.
RIGGHEAD AV.
ROADSIDE
MAINHEAD TER.
CARRICK VW.
EASTFIELD
Westerwood
Lib.
Hall
SMITHYENDS
THE WYND
BURNGREEN TER.
G67
Crow Wood
DORNOCH WAY
SOUTHERNESS DR.
GRANGE
NAIRN WY.
KIRKWALL
STREET
A8011
Bog Stank
MAIN
Sub.
N. BERWICK
GAILES RD.
LETHAM
76
BARONHILL
Prim. Sch.
OLD GLASGOW RD.
Cumbernauld Village
The Mote
Playground
LANSDOWNE DR.
DRIVE
Burial Grd.
SPRINGFIELD RD.
GLASGOW RD.
West Pk.
36
77
Cumbernauld House
SPRUCE RD.
CALLANDER CT.
PRESTWICK CT.
76
Cumbernauld Bowl. Club
Putting
STIRLING ST.

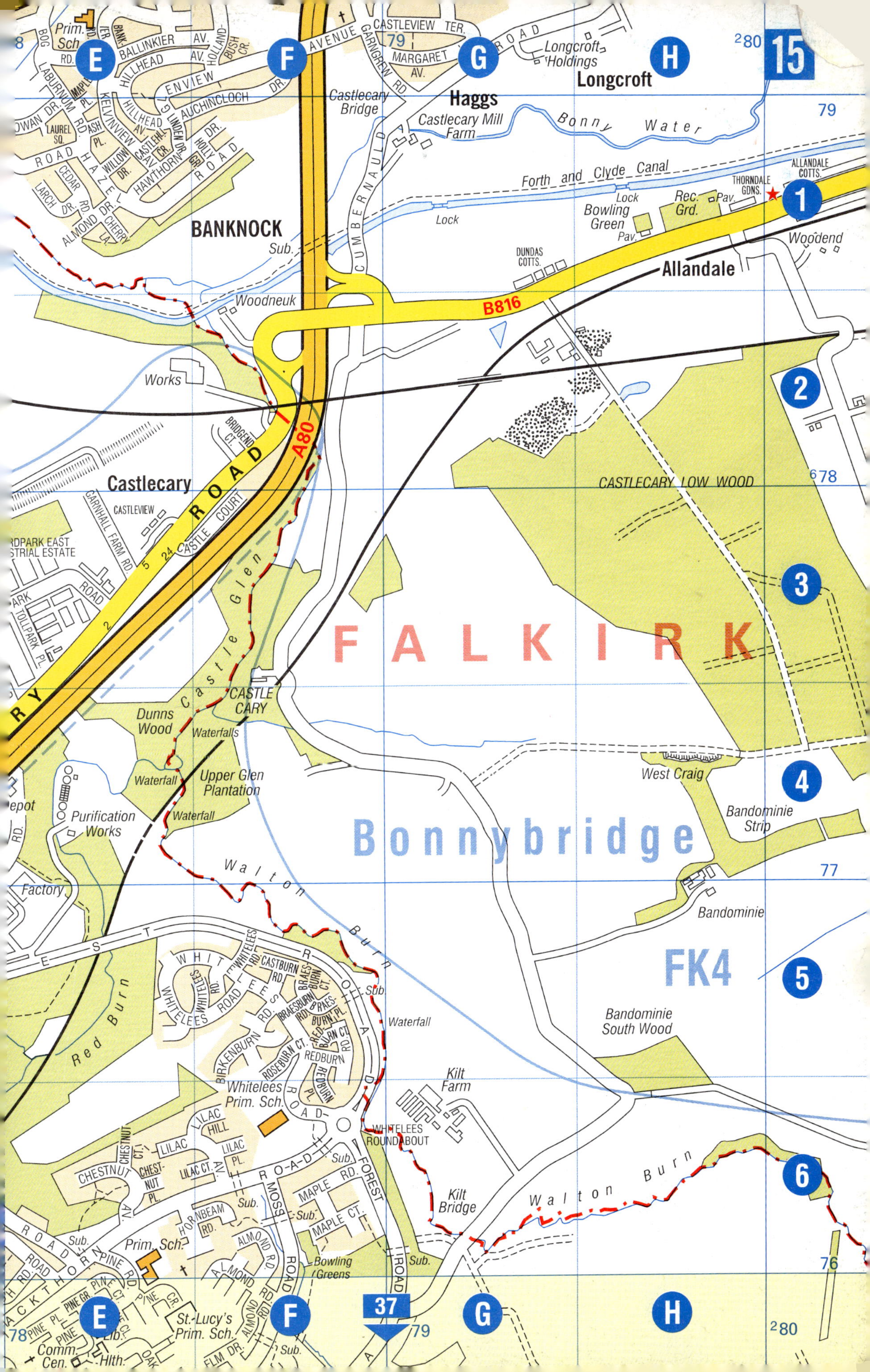
BANKNOCK
Haggs
Longcroft
Longcroft Holdings
Castlecary Bridge
Castlecary Mill Farm
Bonny Water
Forth and Clyde Canal
Lock
Bowling Green
Rec. Grd.
Pav.
THORNDALE GDNS.
ALLANDALE COTTS.
Woodend
Allandale
DUNDAS COTTS.
B816
A80
Woodneuk
Works
Sub.
BRIDGEND CT.
Castlecary
CASTLEVIEW
CARNHALL FARM RD.
CASTLE COURT
ROAD
CASTLECARY LOW WOOD
FALKIRK
Castle Glen
CASTLE CARY
Dunns Wood
Waterfalls
Waterfall
Upper Glen Plantation
Purification Works
Factory
West Craig
Bandominie Strip
Bonnybridge
Bandominie
FK4
Walton Burn
Red Burn
Bandominie South Wood
Kilt Farm
Kilt Bridge
WHITELEES ROUNDABOUT
Whitelees Prim. Sch.
REDBURN
ROSEBURN CT.
BIRKENBURN
CASTBURN RD.
BRAESBURN CT.
WHITELEES RD.
LILAC HILL
CHESTNUT CT.
MAPLE RD.
MAPLE CT.
HORNBEAM RD.
ALMOND RD.
MOSS ROAD
FOREST ROAD
Bowling Greens
Prim. Sch.
St. Lucy's Prim. Sch.
Comm. Cen.
Hlth.
Lib.
ELM DR.
OAK
PINE RD.
BALLINKIER AV.
HILLHEAD AV.
GLENVIEW
AUCHINCLOCH DR.
CASTLEVIEW TER.
MARGARET AV.
GARNGREW RD.
LABURNUM RD.
LAUREL SQ.
CEDAR RD.
LARCH DR.
ALMOND DR.
CHERRY LA.
HAWTHORN CR.
WILLOW DR.
HOLLY DR.
CUMBERNAULD ROAD
37
79
280
678
77
76
E
F
G
H
1
2
3
4
5
6

37
38
A
B
C
D
77
76
675
74
1
2
3
4
5
6
Dalmoak House
Sewage Pump Station
Works
Underpass
Dalmoak Farm
Weir
Mains Lodge
RENTON RD.
RENTON ROAD
KIPPEROCH ROAD
Whiteleys Burn
Whiteleys
DUNBAR
Perrays Wood
Lea Farm
Leabrae
Leabank
Cats Castle
CARDROSS ROAD
A814
A812
VALE
Dalreoch Prim. Sch.
Knowetop Comm Farm
Castlehill
CUMBRAE CRESCENT SOUTH
HAWTHORNHILL
CASTLEHILL ROAD
PERRAY AV.
HAZEL AV.
MAPLE AV.
DRIVE
PERRAYS
ROWAN DR.
HAWTHORN AV.
HOLLY DR.
KING'S
RATHLIN TERRACE
ARRAN WAY
KNOWE
QUARRY
QUARRY PLACE
CASTLEBRAE
SUNDERLAND AV.
BLACKBURN CR.
Dalreoch
Our Lady & St. Patricks High Sch.
Clydebank College (Dumbarton Campus)
DUMBARTON JOINT HOSP.
Mem Park
LEVEN VALLEY ENTERPRISE CEN.
DALREOCH CT.
ASHTON VIEW
WAVERLEY T.
WESTCLIFF
TALISMAN AV.
WESTFIELD
Convent
Library
ARDOCH
Sewage Works
Playing Field
Football Pitches
HAVOC
Havoc Hole
St. Michael's Prim. Sch.
Brucehill
Play. Fld.
BRUCEHILL ROAD
BONTINE
GRAHAM RD.
AVENUE
NAPIER
HILL ST.
CRESCENT
CALEDONIA TER.
GLENCAIRN
FIRTHVIEW
KEIL TERRACE
Dennystown
OXHILL
HELENSLEE
G82
Kirktonhill
Monastery
Keil Sch.
DIXON
Mean High Water Springs
Playing Field
RIVER CLYDE
Port Glasgow PA14
Timber Ponds (Disused)

E
F
G
H
240
Murroch Burn
A82
STIRLING ROAD
A813
Bellsmyre
Playing Field
St. Peter's Prim. & Nursy. Sch.
Drain
DUMBARTON COMMON
Warehouse
Warehouses
DUMBARTON GOLF COURSE
Mean High Water Springs
RIVER LEVEN
Club House
Townend
DUMBARTON COTTAGE HOSP.
Prim. Sch.
Cemetery
CARAVAN PARK
BROADMEADOW INDUSTRIAL ESTATE
Play Field
The Meadow Sports Cen.
B830
BONHILL ROAD
Bowl. Grn.
Dalreoch
Council Offs.
Police H.Q.
Council Offices
Dumbarton Central
T.A. Cen.
Clinic
Dumbarton Academy
Dumbarton F.C.
Prim. Sch.
GLASGOW ROAD
Artizan Br.
Comm. Cen.
Dumbarton Bridge
Offs.
Superstore
DUMBARTON
Silverton
BROOMFAULD IND. EST.
Civic Theatre
Court
Burgh Hall
A814
Depot
Dumbarton East
East End Park
CASTLE STREET
Scottish Maritime Museum
Tidal Basin
Distillery
Knoxland Prim. Sch.
Superstore
Church (rems.of)
LEVENGROVE PARK
Bowling Green
Tennis Courts
Sports Ground
Rec. Grd.
War Mem.
Boat Yard
Jetties
Depot
Works
Gasholder Station
Warehouse
Sewage Works
Black Lair
DUMBARTON CASTLE
Pav.
Leven Mouth
Hunter's Burn
1
2
3
4
5
6
77
76
75
74
39
41
18

A
B
C
D
17
1
2
3
4
5
6
Cemetery
DUMBARTON COTTAGE HOSP.
Prim. Sch.
Play Field
The Meadow Sports Cen.
Dumbarton Central
BON-HILL ROAD
B830
T.A. Cen.
Clinic
Dumbarton Academy
Prim. Sch.
Dumbarton F.C.
Council Offs.
Police H.Q.
Silverton
Crossley
Gruggies Burn
Weir
DUMBARTON
Lib.
Offs.
BROOMFAULD IND. EST.
Superstore
Depot
Dumbarton East
East End Park
GLASGOW ROAD
A814
STIRLING ROAD
A82
Scottish Maritime Museum
Knoxland Prim. Sch.
Superstore
Jetties
Boat Yard
RIVER LEVEN
Depot
Works
Warehouse
Gruggies Burn
DUMBARTON CASTLE
Pav.
Sewage Works
Gasholder Station
Works
Works
Pav.
Warehouses
Hotel
Hotel
Warehouses
Warehouses
Hunter's Burn
GARSHAKE ROAD
CAMPBELL AVENUE
GELLS AVENUE
DUMBUCK CRESCENT
CASTLEGREEN ST.
RIVER
Dumbuck Perch
Dumbuck Lighthouse
Long Dyke
RENFREWS
Bishopton PA7
Junction 31
M8
M8 MOTORWAY
CARAVAN PARK
FERRYHILL PLANTATION
38
74
73
240
41

E
F
G
H
Overtoun
Waterfall
Spardie Linn
43
44
Greenland Reservoir No.2
Overflow
76
Raven's Crag
Lang Craigs
Grouse Butts
Ford
1
Greenland Reservoir No.3
Barnhill
WEST
TOM'S SEAT
F.B.
Overflow
Sluice
Dumbar
MILTON
Warren Cottage
Ford
Craignair
ARTONSHIRE
Waterfall
Rigangower
Boat House
Loch Bowie
Middleton
Mast
2
Dumbowie
Boat House
Northwood
Milton Burn
Middleton Wood
Waterfall
Old Chapel of Colquhoun (remains of)
Mattockhill
75
Greenland
Riggengower
Old Mill House
Milton House
Waterfalls
3
Craigunnock
Quarry (Stone)
Auchentorlie Glen
Milton Burn
MILTON CT.
Milton
BRAE
MILTON HILL
Dumbuck
G82
LENNOX RD.
COLQUHOUN
Prim. Sch.
HILL VIEW
WHYTE CORNER
Auchentorlie Burn
20
Dumbuck Farm
CRANNOG RD.
Auchentorlie Wood
Fort
SHEEP HILL
T Wood
DUMBARTON
Depot
4
A82
Glasgow
Auchentorlie House
74
Waterfall
Weir
G60
Mean High Water Springs
ROAD
GREAT WESTERN RD.
DUMBARTON RD.
5
Milton Island
Tanks
Piers
Piers
Pier
Depot
Works
Dunglass Castle
CLYDE
HIRE
Remains of Old Causeway
6
LONGHAUGH POINT
73
E
F
39
G
H
42
43
44

A
B
C
D
LOCH HUMPHREY
(Reservoir)
Boat Shed
Dam
Overflow
Grouse Butts
Greenland Reservoir No.3
CRAIGARESTIE
F.B.
Overflow
Sluice
KILPA
Dumbarton
Rigangower
G82
675
DUNBA
Bow Linn
Waterfalls
Reservoir
Waterfall
Quarry (Disused)
Waterfall
McKellar's Wood
Auchentorlie Glen
Auchentorlie Burn
19
Lonendale Wood
Glenarbuck
T Wood
Hill of Dun
Haw Craig
Auchentorlie Cottage
Auchentorlie House
74
Dam
High Auchentorlie
East Wood
KILPA
Waterfall
Weir
Lodge
Bowling
Torwood Villa
Lodge
Waterfalls
Gavinburn Cott
GREAT WESTERN ROAD
A82
Dunarbuck Cottage
Glenarbuck House
MANSE
SCOTT AVENUE
DUMBARTON ROAD
A814
Weir
Depot
Works
Bowling
Bowling Harbour
Lodge
Jetty
Frisky Wharf
Pier
Lock
Basin
Gavinburn
Dunglass Castle
RIVER CLYDE
Jetty
Lock
DUMBARTON
Library
ROMAN CRESCENT
Chapel Hill
RENFREWSHIRE
Jetty
Bishopton PA7
Depot
PORTPATRICK
73
Donald's Quay Light
44
40
245
Napier Beacon
1
2
3
4
5
6

21
E
F
G
H
46
47
48
76
75
74
73
1
2
3
4
5
6
Dirty Leven
COCHNO HILL
TRICK HILLS
Loch Humphrey Burn
GREENSIDE RESERVOIR
WEST
RTONSHIRE
BOGAIROCH
THE SLACKS
22
Ford
Waterfall
TRICK BRAES
Cattle Grid
Mound
Craigleith
Reservoir (Covered)
Blackmailing
Blackmailing Reservoir (Covered)
Filter Beds
Waterfall
G60
Drums
Lodge
Hole Cottage
Mount Pleasant
Netherclose
A82
ROAD
Cemy.
Carleith
North Dalnottar Cemetery
Crematorium
Carleith Prim.Sch.
Old Kilpatrick
Kilpatrick
41
Halls
THISTLENEUK
MOUNT PLEASANT RD.
STA. RD.
KIRKTON CR.
GAVINBURN PL.
CRESCENT
ASHTREE
RUSSELL

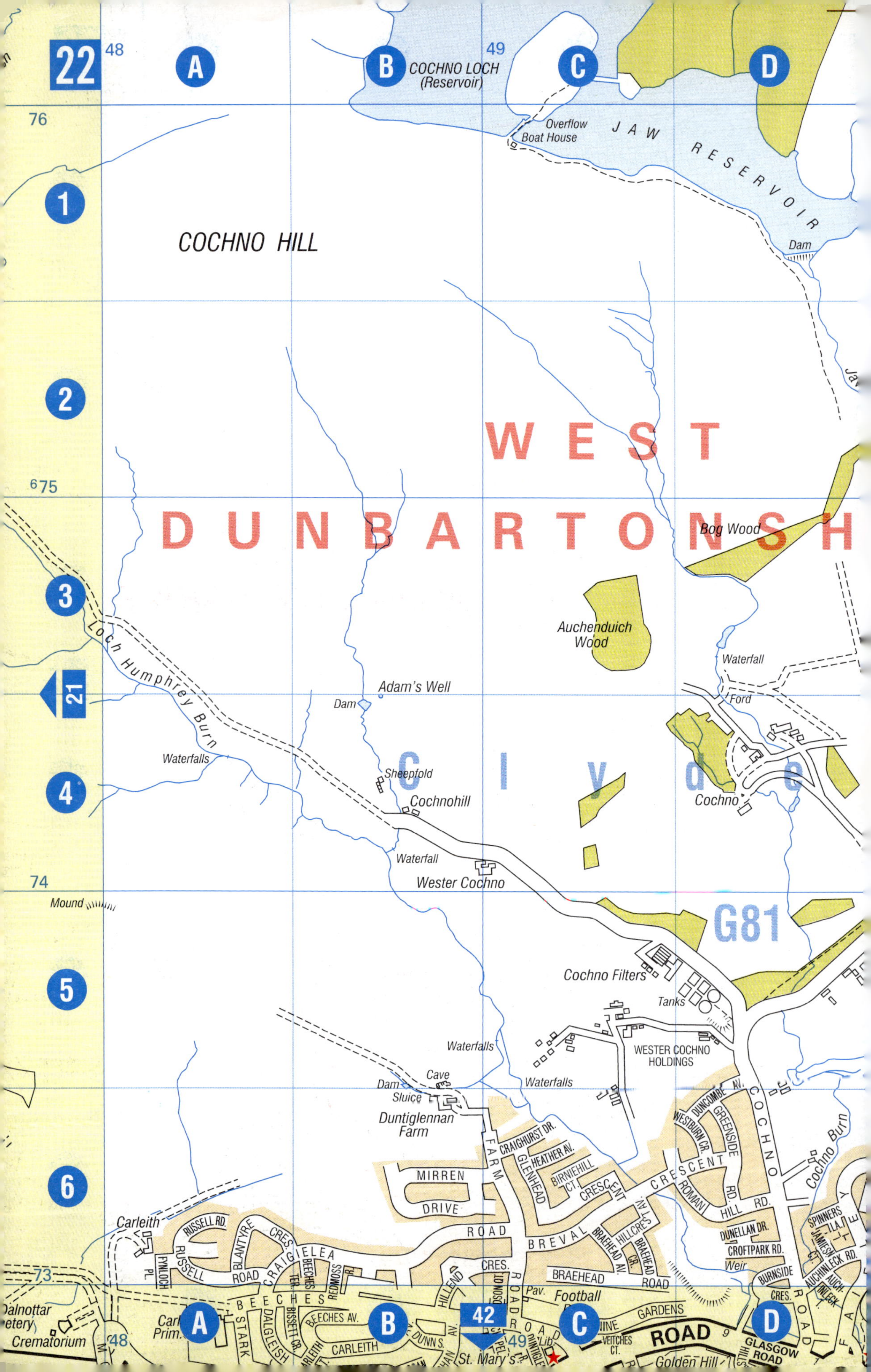
22
48
49
A
B
C
D
1
2
3
4
5
6
76
675
74
73
21
42
COCHNO LOCH
(Reservoir)
Overflow
Boat House
JAW RESERVOIR
Dam
COCHNO HILL
WEST DUNBARTONSH
Clyde
G81
Bog Wood
Auchenduich Wood
Waterfall
Ford
Cochno
Loch Humphrey Burn
Waterfalls
Adam's Well
Dam
Sheepfold
Cochnohill
Waterfall
Wester Cochno
Mound
Cochno Filters
Tanks
WESTER COCHNO HOLDINGS
Waterfalls
Cave
Dam
Sluice
Duntiglennan Farm
Cochno Burn
CRAIGHURST DR.
HEATHER AV.
GLENHEAD
BIRNIEHILL CT.
CRESCENT
FARM
MIRREN DRIVE
ROAD
BREVAL
CRESCENT
DUNCOMBE
GREENSIDE
WESTBURN CR.
COCHNO
ROMAN
HILL RD.
RD.
DUNELLAN DR.
CROFTPARK RD.
Weir
BURNSIDE
CRES.
SPINNERS LA.
JAMIESON CT.
AUCHINLECK RD.
AUCHINLECK
HILLCREST AV.
BRAEHEAD AV.
BRAEHEAD CR.
BRAEHEAD ROAD
Pav.
Football
Carleith
RUSSELL RD.
RUSSELL
PYNLOCH
PL.
BLANTYRE
CRES.
ROAD
CRAIGIELEA
TER.
BEECHES
REDMOSS
BEECHES
STARK
DALGLEISH
BISSETT CR.
BEECHES AV.
CARLEITH
DUNN S.
AV.
HILLEND
CRES.
ROAD
ROAD
Lib.
NINE
GARDENS
VEITCHES CT.
ROAD
GLASGOW ROAD
Golden Hill
St. Mary's
Dalnottar Cemetery
Crematorium
Carl Prim.

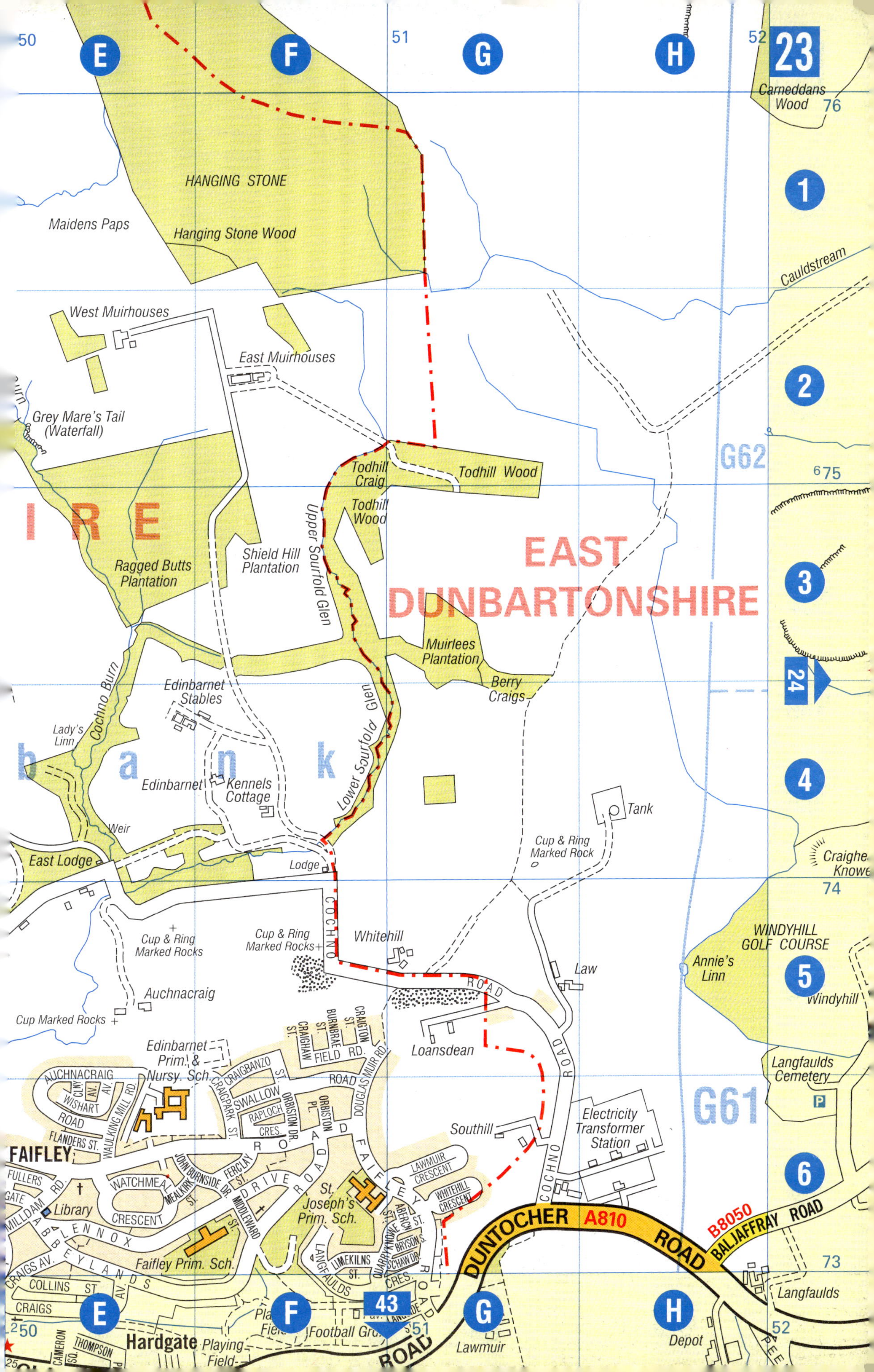

50
E
F
51
G
H
52
Carneddans Wood
76
1
HANGING STONE
Maidens Paps
Hanging Stone Wood
Cauldstream
West Muirhouses
East Muirhouses
2
Grey Mare's Tail (Waterfall)
G62
675
Todhill Craig
Todhill Wood
Todhill Wood
IRE
Upper Sourfold Glen
Shield Hill Plantation
Ragged Butts Plantation
EAST DUNBARTONSHIRE
3
Muirlees Plantation
Berry Craigs
24
Edinbarnet Stables
Cochno Burn
Lady's Linn
b a n k
Lower Sourfold Glen
4
Edinbarnet
Kennels Cottage
Tank
Weir
East Lodge
Lodge
Cup & Ring Marked Rock
Craighe Knowe
74
Cup & Ring Marked Rocks
Cup & Ring Marked Rocks
Whitehill
COCHNO
WINDYHILL GOLF COURSE
Annie's Linn
Law
5
ROAD
Windyhill
Auchnacraig
Cup Marked Rocks
Edinbarnet Prim. & Nursy. Sch.
CRAIGTON ST.
BURNBRAE ST.
CRAIGHAW ST.
FIELD RD.
Loansdean
DOUGLAS MUIR RD.
ROAD
Langfaulds Cemetery
P
AUCHNACRAIG
CLUNY AV.
WISHART
ROAD
WALKING MILL RD.
CRAIGBANZO
ST.
CRAIGPARK ST.
SWALLOW
RAPLOCH CRES.
ORBISTON DR.
ORBISTON PL.
ROAD
Electricity Transformer Station
G61
Southill
FLANDERS ST.
FAIFLEY
ROAD
FAIFLEY
COCHNO
6
FULLERS GATE
MILLDAM RD
Library
WATCHMEAL
JOHN BURNSIDE DR.
FERCLAY ST.
DRIVE
MEALKIRK ST.
LAWMUIR CRESCENT
WHITEHILL CRESCENT
St. Joseph's Prim. Sch.
DUNTOCHER
A810
ROAD
B8050
BALJAFFRAY ROAD
ABBEYLANDS
LENNOX
CRESCENT
MIDDLEWARD ST.
Faifley Prim. Sch.
ABERCORN ST.
QUARRYKNOWE ST.
BRYSON ST.
SCHAW DR.
LIMEKILNS ST.
LANGFAULDS CRES.
CRAIGS AV.
COLLINS ST
AV.
73
Langfaulds
CRAIGS
E
F
43
G
H
250
51
52
Hardgate
CAMERON SQ.
THOMPSON
Playing Field
Football Gd.
ROAD
Lawmuir
Depot

52
53
76
6 75
74
73
A
B
C
D
1
2
3
4
5
6
23
44
Carneddans Wood
Low Craigton
Craigton Cotts.
Glendorn
Bonnieview
Laighpark
Works
Dam
LOAN
The Cherry Orchard
Field Wood
Trevarrion
Braval
Carneddans
THE CARNEDDANS ROAD
Craigton
Waterfall
Cauldstream Burn
Tambowie
Dam
EAST DUNB
A809
Little Balvie
CRAIGTON
Sports Ground
Douglas Academy
Craigdhu Burn
Active Workings
DOUGLAS MUIR
Balviebank
Crossburn
DOUGLAS MUIR GS.
DOUGLAS MUIR PL.
DOUGLAS MUIR DR.
DOUGLAS MUIR DRIVE
DUNELLAN ROAD
DOUGLAS MUIR ROAD
DRUMBEG TER.
CRAIGHIRST RD.
CRAIGBARNET RD.
CASTLE
BALLAGAN PL.
DUNCOLM PL.
FALLOCH
ACHRAY
ARDLUI GS.
CORBIE
DUMBROCK RD.
DALNAIR PL.
MAINS
STOCKIEMUIR ROAD
MAINS PLANTATION
Old Mains
Reservoir (covered)
Craighead Knowe
WINDYHILL GOLF COURSE
Windyhill
Club House
Windyhill Cottage
Langfaulds Cemetery
Manse Burn
FORREST DR.
NASMYTH AV.
MOORFOOT WAY
ALSTON GS.
GREENSIDE PL.
MOORFOOT AV.
MURRAY GRO.
KILPATRICK DRIVE
FINTRY GDS.
CROMALT CR.
RUTHERFORD AV.
CULLOCH RD.
PATERSON PL.
MOORFOOT
ABERCROMBIE DRIVE
WAY
ROAD
CRAI
B8050
BALJAFFRAY ROAD
GRAMPIAN WAY
LOCHNAGAR DR.
CAIRNSMORE DR.
CORRIE GDS.
LOYAL GDS.
FINAVEN GS.
CULVAIN AV.
CLISH AV.
GDS.
KILBRECK GDS.
MENTEITH
LOWTHER AV.
WYVIS AV.
BALJAFFRAY SHOP. CEN.
Baljaffray Prim. Sch.
CLONAIG GDS.
MERRICK GDS.
MUIR HSE. PL.
THE POPLARS
CHEVIOT
VORLICH GDS.
ETTRICK DR.
LAMMERMUIR GDS.
G61
Convent of Notre Dame
Hungry Hill
St. Andrew's College
OCHIL RD.
CRUACHAN ROAD
LEDI
NEVIS
CRAIGMORE RD.
PENTLAND PL.
SIDLAW RD.
LANERS DR.
BURNSIDE
BURNSIDE CT.
ROAD
St. Andrew's Prim. Sch.
HEATHER
BAILLIE
DUMGOYNE
CAMPS
STOCKI
Bearsden Ski Club
COURTHILL
Langfaulds
Depot
DUNTOCHER RD.
CONNAUGHTON
CAIRNGORM
TINTO

E
F
G
H
255
56
76
75
74
73
54
1
2
3
4
5
6
Club Ho.
Waterfall
CRAIGALLIAN
ROAD
MUGDOCK RESERVOIR
Overflow
Pump House
Barrachan
CRAIGMADDIE RESERVOIR
ALLANDER PARK
Allander Water
Burn
Depot
Clober Dam
Works
Wks.
Factory
CLOBER GOLF COURSE
CRAWFORD
MCGRIGOR RD.
BLACKWOOD
ROAD
BIRRELL RD.
JAMES WATT RD.
STABLE RD.
BLEACHFIELD
DRUMCLOG AVENUE
Ten. Cts.
ST. EDMUNDS GRO.
MOSSPARK AV.
MOSSPARK RD.
BANK AV.
MONTROSE GDS.
Tannoch Loch
HEATHFIELD DRIVE
AVENUE
ROSELEA
BLANE DR.
DRIVE
DUNBARTONSHIRE
Club House
CLOCHBAR AV.
CLOCHBAR GS.
NORTH DUMGOYNE AV.
CLOBER
Weir
WOODLANDS GRO.
SANDFIELD AV.
THE RIGGS
WOODLANDS ST.
TANNOCH DR.
Atholl Prep. Sch.
TANNOCH
CRAIGMILLAR
DRIVE
ROAD
STRATHBLANE
MOOR RD.
CRAIGTON
KELVIN RD.
HILTON ROAD
LYLE SQ.
CRAIGEND DR. WEST
LEARMONT
GRAHAM
KIRK STREET
Clober Prim. Sch.
G62
HUNTER
MUIRLEES
BALVIE
CRESCENT
CRAIGIELEA
ASHBURN
ROAD
CARBETH
TAMBOWIE AV.
GARDENS AV.
ROAD
Lib. & Comm. Cen.
IDDESLEIGH AV.
SINCLAIR ST.
BURBANK HIGHLD. RD.
Wks.
ALLANDER RD.
BARLOCH AV.
HENDY AV.
CAIRNS DRIVE
Red Cross Cen.
HILLCREST ST.
Sch.
GRANGE AV.
Offices
BUCHANAN
KERSLAND
LADYWOOD
Art Gall.
CAMPSIE
TOWER PL.
MIDDLETON
LYNN
GLASSFORD
BALFLEURS ST.
BARLOCH RD.
ROAD
BALDERNOCK
26
FERGUSON
KNOWE
CRAIGTON
OAKBURN CRES.
GOYNE
OAKBURN
ASHBURN GARDENS
HUNTER PL.
CAULDSTREAM PL.
CAIRNLEA
Craigdow
St. Joseph's Prim. Sch.
Hall
DUMGOYNE GDNS.
B8050
ROAD
PARK
DOUGLAS ST.
STATION RD.
B8030
WAY
Milngavie
CROSSVEGGATE
SOUTH GLASSFORD ST.
BRIARWELL RD.
CONNELL CRES.
AVENUE
DOUGALSTON
GOLF COURSE
Lawn Park
CHESTNUT LANE
DRUMCARN DR.
CRAIGDHU AV.
CROSSBURN AV.
VIVIAN AV.
CAMPBELL AV.
LENNOX AV.
ASHFIELD RD.
WOODBURN
MAIN
Gavin's Mill
Lennox Park
Hall
A81
DOUGALSTON GARDENS
BRAEHEAD
PARK AV.
AVENUE
PRESTONFIELD
South Mains
SOUTH MAINS ROAD
MILNGAVIE
KEYSTONE AVENUE
Weir
A807
AUCHENHOWIE RD.
Dougalston Loch
Craighu Primary Sch.
Play. Fld.
KEYSTONE
BREADIE DR.
SHAW
DRIVE
QUADRANT
BRAE-SIDE
BRAE-FOOT
KEYSTONE ROAD
QUEEN'S CT.
Nursy.
GLASGOW
ALLANDER
Pav.
Cricket Ground
GALBRAITH
DRUMLIN
NETHERMAINS RD.
ROAD
AVENUE
West of Scotland Play. Rugby F.C. Field
WEST PARK
Sewage Works
Aqueduct
STREET
Superstore
DRIVE
Burn
WATER
Craigdhu Bus Depot
Allander Sports Complex
MILNGAVIE
QUEENSBERRY AVENUE
BRANDON DR.
BUCCLEUCH DR.
Mosshead Prim. Sch.
CROMARTY CRESCENT
MAR DRIVE
SEAFIELD AV.
AVENUE
ELGIN RD.
LOVAT
DRIVE
AVENUE
ROXBURGH DR.
HAMILTON CR.
MONTROSE
SUTHERLAND AV.
ATHOLL GS.
ARGYLE RD.
AIRLIE AV.
HUNTLY DR.
TWEEDSMUIR CR.
ROWAN
OAK AV.
HAZEL AV.
ROAD
MOSSHEAD
BEECH AVENUE
HAWTHORN AVENUE
BURNBRAE AV.
Club Ho. Playing Field
ROAD
Lower Kilmardinny
DOUGLAS PARK GOLF COURSE
NORTH GRANGE ROAD
EDGEHILL RD.
MORVEN
KILMARDINNY
45
VIEW

Barrachan
Measuring Pond
Craigash
Bankend Cottage
Craighead
Craigmaddie Lodge
MUGDOCK RESERVOIR
CRAIGMADDIE RESERVOIR
Bankell House
Bankell Farm
Craigmaddie
Burn
A81
ROAD
STRATHBLANE
AVENUE
BLANE DR.
ROSELEA
MOSSWELL
DRIVE
Tinkers Burn
Club House
DOUGALSTON GOLF COURSE
Manse
Hillend
Weir
The Kirkhouse
Baldernock House
ROAD
EAST DUNB
BACK WOOD
Saw Mill
Baldernock Mill
Baldernock
Kettlehill
CRAIGMA
DRIVE
TOWER PL.
MIDDLETON DR.
CAMPSIE
LYNN
DRIVE
BALDERNOCK
Stable Wood
Woodhouse Cottage
Tinkers Burn
Dowan
Art Gall.
GLASSFORD ST.
BALFLEURS ST.
25
SOUTH GLASSFORD ST.
BRIARWELL
BRIARWELL LA.
CONNELL CRES.
DOUGALSTON AV.
Dougalston Stables
C l a s
Craigmaddie
Boghall
GOLF COURSE
Lawn Park
DOUGALSTON
DOUGALSTON GARDENS
SOUTH CR.
Wards Wood
Ladies Ride Wood
Beech Wood
MITCHELL DR.
LAWN PK.
LAWN PARK
EWING WK.
FINLAY
FINLAY RISE
AUCHENCRUIVE
BRIDGEGAIT
OSWALDS WK.
COCHRANE CT.
VIRGINIA GS.
MURDOCH DR.
DUNMORE DR.
DOWAN ROAD
Jaw
G62
Bardowie Castle
BARDOWIE LOCH
AUCHENHOWIE
Pav.
Dougalston Loch
Weir
Sewage Works
Aqueduct
Pow Burn
Langbank Holdings
Burn
A807
Lodge
Langbank Farm
Hayhill
ALLANDER WATER
G61
ROAD
BALM
DOUGLAS PARK GOLF COURSE
Boclair
46
56
57
76
75
74
73
A B C D
1 2 3 4 5 6

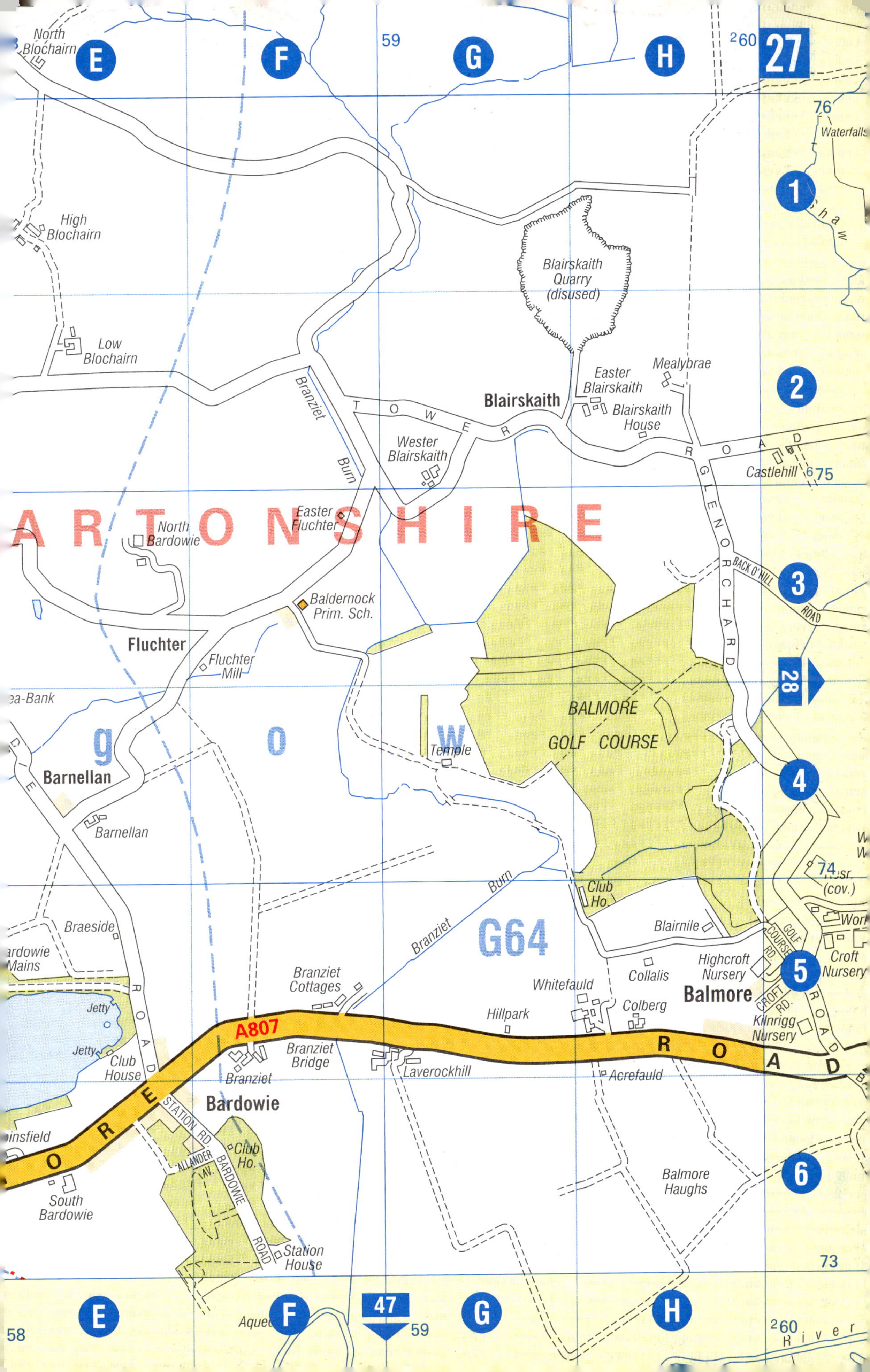
North Blochairn
High Blochairn
Low Blochairn
Blairskaith Quarry (disused)
Mealybrae
Easter Blairskaith
Blairskaith
Blairskaith House
Wester Blairskaith
TOWER ROAD
Branziet Burn
Castlehill
GLENORCHARD ROAD
BACK O' HILL ROAD
Waterfalls
DUNBARTONSHIRE
North Bardowie
Easter Fluchter
Baldernock Prim. Sch.
Fluchter
Fluchter Mill
Barnellan
Barnellan
BALMORE GOLF COURSE
Temple
Club Ho
Blairnile
GOLF COURSE RD.
Croft Nursery
Highcroft Nursery
Collalis
Whitefauld
Colberg
Balmore
CROFT RD.
Kilnrigg Nursery
Hillpark
Braeside
Bardowie Mains
Jetty
Jetty
Club House
Branziet Cottages
Branziet Burn
G64
A807
Branziet Bridge
Laverockhill
Acrefauld
Branziet
Bardowie
STATION RD.
ALLANDER AV.
BARDOWIE ROAD
Club Ho.
South Bardowie
Station House
Balmore Haughs
MOORE ROAD
Aque
River
58
59
260
76
75
74
73
47
28
E
F
G
H
1
2
3
4
5
6

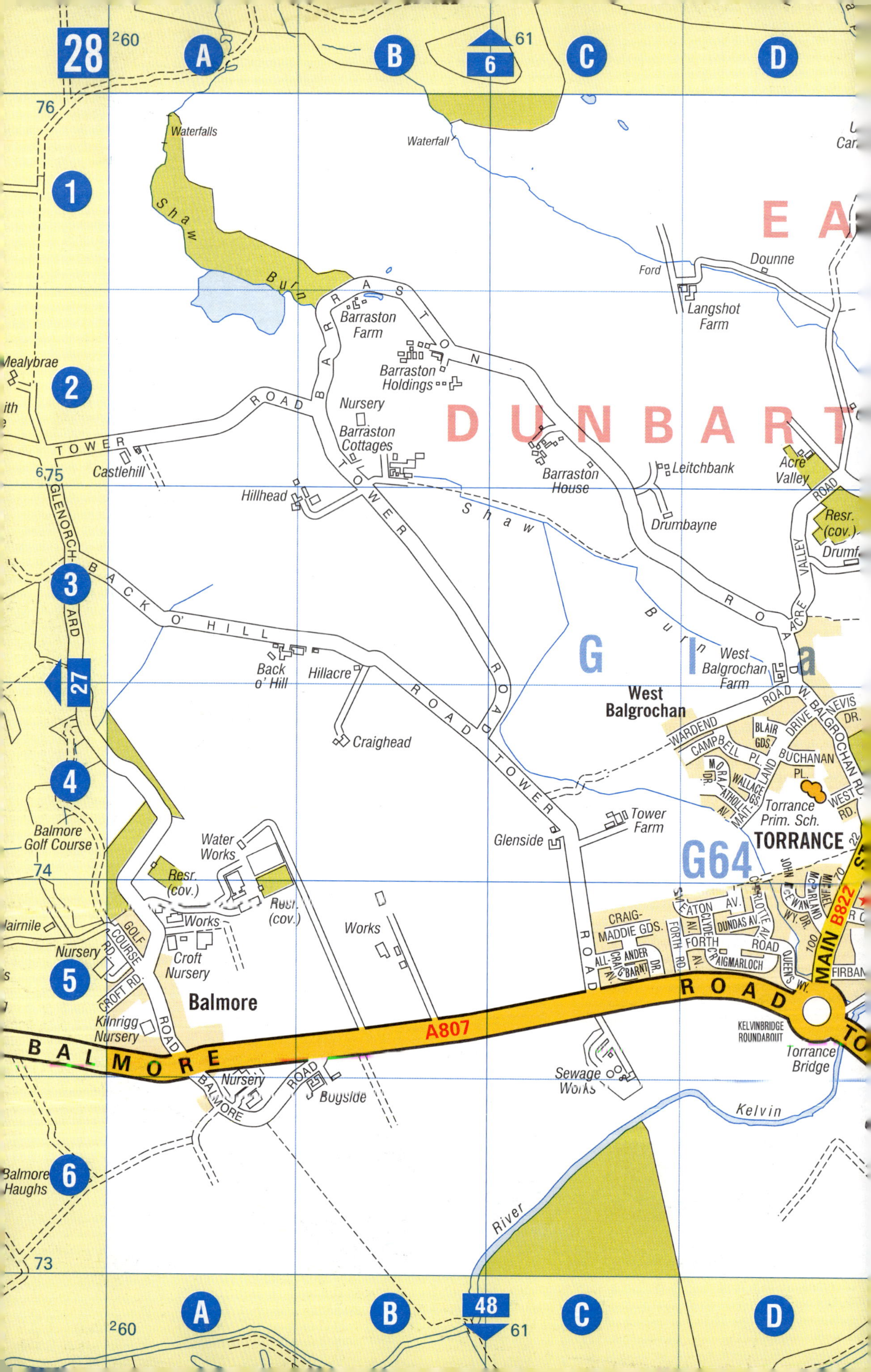

A
B
C
D
1
2
3
4
5
6
260
61
76
675
74
73
6
27
48
Waterfalls
Waterfall
Shaw Burn
BARRASTON ROAD
Barraston Farm
Barraston Holdings
Nursery
Barraston Cottages
TOWER ROAD
Castlehill
Hillhead
Ford
Dounne
Langshot Farm
DUNBARTON
EA
Barraston House
Leitchbank
Drumbayne
Acre Valley
ACRE VALLEY ROAD
Resr. (cov.)
Drumf
Mealybrae
GLENORCH ARD
BACK O' HILL ROAD
Back o' Hill
Hillacre
Craighead
Shaw Burn
G64
West Balgrochan Farm
West Balgrochan
WARDEND ROAD
BLAIR GDS.
CAMPBELL PL.
DRIVE
W. BALGROCHAN RD.
NEVIS DR.
BUCHANAN PL.
MORAY DR.
WALLACE GS.
ATHOLL AV.
MAIT-LAND
WEST RD.
Torrance Prim. Sch.
TORRANCE
Tower Farm
Glenside
Balmore Golf Course
Water Works
Resr. (cov.)
Works
Resr. (cov.)
Works
Croft Nursery
GOLF COURSE RD.
CROFT RD.
Nursery
Balmore
Kilnrigg Nursery
ROAD
Nairnile
CRAIGMADDIE GDS.
SMEATON AV.
CLYDE AV.
DUNDAS AV.
CHARLOTTE AV.
JOHN MCEWAN WY.
MICHAEL MCPARLAND DR.
FORTH RD.
FORTH ROAD
CRAIGMARLOCH
ALLANDER CRAIGBARNET AV.
DR.
QUEEN'S WY.
MAIN ST.
B822
FIRBAN
A807
BALMORE ROAD
BALMORE ROAD
Nursery
Boyside
Sewage Works
KELVINBRIDGE ROUNDABOUT
Torrance Bridge
River Kelvin
Balmore Haughs
700

E
F
G
H
7
63
64
Kinkell
Waterfall
Waterfall
ONSHIRE
Whitehill
Balquharrage Cottages
Balquharrage
Wetshod
ROAD
KIRKINTILLOCH
ROAD
B822
Craigen Glen Cottage
East Balgrochan Farm
Weir
Carlston Cottages
Carlston
East Balgrochan
West Carlestoun
Ferrymill House
Balgrochan House
Red Burn
Hayston Cottag
Hayston
30
HAYSTON GOLF COURSE
CAMPSIE
KING'S PK.
MILL CRES.
KELVINDALE
WOODMILL DR.
PARK CRES.
Playing Field
Wardhill
Meadowbank Farm
CORMACK AV.
GUTHRIE PL.
DALRIADA DR.
HEARN DR.
KELVIN VIEW
CLARK PL.
River Kelvin
Meadowbank House
Sewage Works
G66
Hayston
KELVIN
AINSLIE
ADAMSLIE CR.
Sandy Knowes
GLASGOW RD
A803
A807
Easter Cadder
Glasgow Bri.
Slipway
P
Hungryside Bridge (Drawbridge)
Forth and Clyde Canal
KIRKINTILLOCH ROAD
ROAD
Leafield
49
1
2
3
4
5
6
76
675
74
73

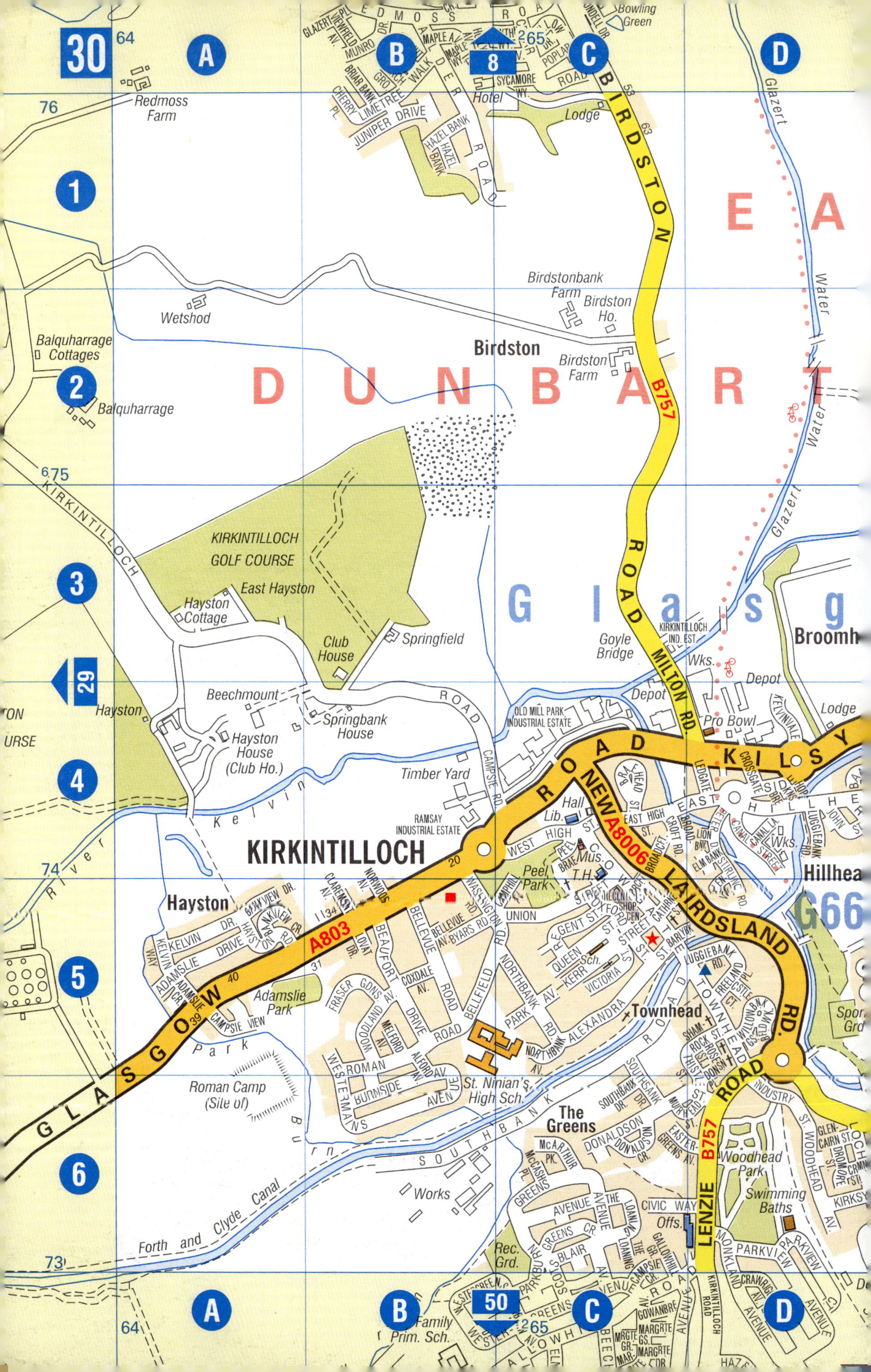

A
B
C
D
1
2
3
4
5
6
8
29
50
64
265
76
675
74
73
Redmoss Farm
REDMOSS ROAD
GLAZERT PL.
NEWFIELD AV.
MUNRO
BRIAR BANK
CHERRY PL.
LIMETREE
JUNIPER DRIVE
HAZEL BANK
MAPLE AV.
SYCAMORE WY.
POPLAR
ROAD
Hotel
Lodge
Bowling Green
BIRDSTON ROAD
Glazert Water
E A
Birdstonbank Farm
Birdston Ho.
Birdston
Birdston Farm
Wetshod
Balquharrage Cottages
Balquharrage
D U N B A R T
B757
KIRKINTILLOCH
KIRKINTILLOCH GOLF COURSE
East Hayston
Hayston Cottage
Club House
Springfield
G l a s g
Goyle Bridge
KIRKINTILLOCH IND. EST.
Wks.
Depot
Broomh
Beechmount
Springbank House
Hayston
Hayston House (Club Ho.)
OLD MILL PARK INDUSTRIAL ESTATE
Pro Bowl
Lodge
MILTON RD.
Timber Yard
CAMPSIE RD.
RAMSAY INDUSTRIAL ESTATE
River Kelvin
KIRKINTILLOCH
ROAD
KILSYTH
NEW A8006
Hall
Lib.
HIGH ST.
WEST HIGH ST.
EAST HIGH ST.
Peel Park
Mus.
T.H.
LAIRDSLAND RD.
Hillhea
G66
Hayston
A803
GLASGOW ROAD
KELVIN DR.
KELVIN WAY
ADAMSLIE DR.
Adamslie Park
CAMPSIE VIEW
BEAUFORT AV.
BELLEVUE RD.
BYARS RD.
COXDALE AV.
NORTHBANK AV.
QUEEN ST.
REGENT ST.
KERR ST.
VICTORIA ST.
ALEXANDRA
UNION ST.
Sch.
LUGGIEBANK RD.
TOWNHEAD
Townhead
Park Burn
Roman Camp (Site of)
WOODLAND AV.
MELFORD AV.
ROMAN AVENUE
BURNSIDE
WESTERMAINS AV.
St. Ninian's High Sch.
The Greens
SOUTHBANK RD.
SOUTHBANK DR.
DONALDSON CR.
INDUSTRY ST.
LENZIE ROAD
Woodhead Park
Swimming Baths
WOODHEAD AV.
Works
Forth and Clyde Canal
Rec. Grd.
CIVIC WAY
Offs.
PARKVIEW
MONKLAND AVENUE
Family Prim. Sch.
KIRKINTILLOCH ROAD
Spor Grd

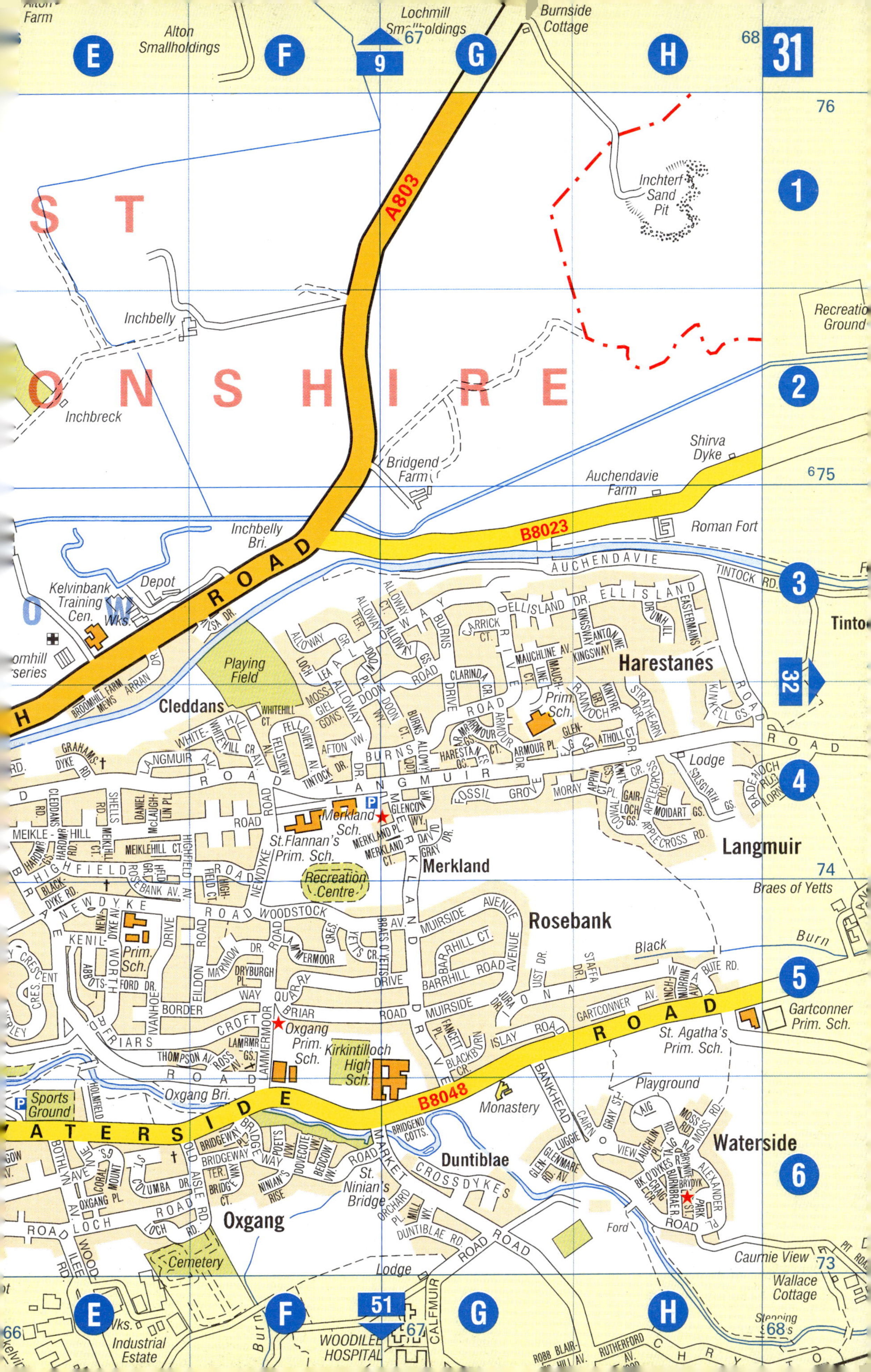
Lochmill Smallholdings
Burnside Cottage
Alton Smallholdings
9
67
68
76
Inchterf Sand Pit
A803
Inchbelly
Inchbreck
Recreation Ground
Bridgend Farm
Shirva Dyke
Auchendavie Farm
675
Roman Fort
B8023
Inchbelly Bri.
ROAD
AUCHENDAVIE
TINTOCK RD.
Kelvinbank Training Cen.
Depot
Wks.
Playing Field
Harestanes
Cleddans
Lodge
32
Merkland Sch.
St.Flannan's Prim. Sch.
Merkland
Langmuir
Recreation Centre
Rosebank
Braes of Yetts
74
Black Burn
Prim. Sch.
Gartconner Prim. Sch.
Oxgang Prim. Sch.
Kirkintilloch High Sch.
St. Agatha's Prim. Sch.
Playground
Monastery
Sports Ground
Oxgang Bri.
B8048
WATERSIDE ROAD
Duntiblae
Waterside
St. Ninian's Bridge
Oxgang
Cemetery
Ford
Caurnie View
73
Wallace Cottage
Lodge
51
Industrial Estate
WOODILEE HOSPITAL
66
CALFMUIR
Burn
ROBB BLAIR-HILL AV.
RUTHERFORD AV.
E
F
G
H
1
2
3
4
5
6
S T
O N S H I R E

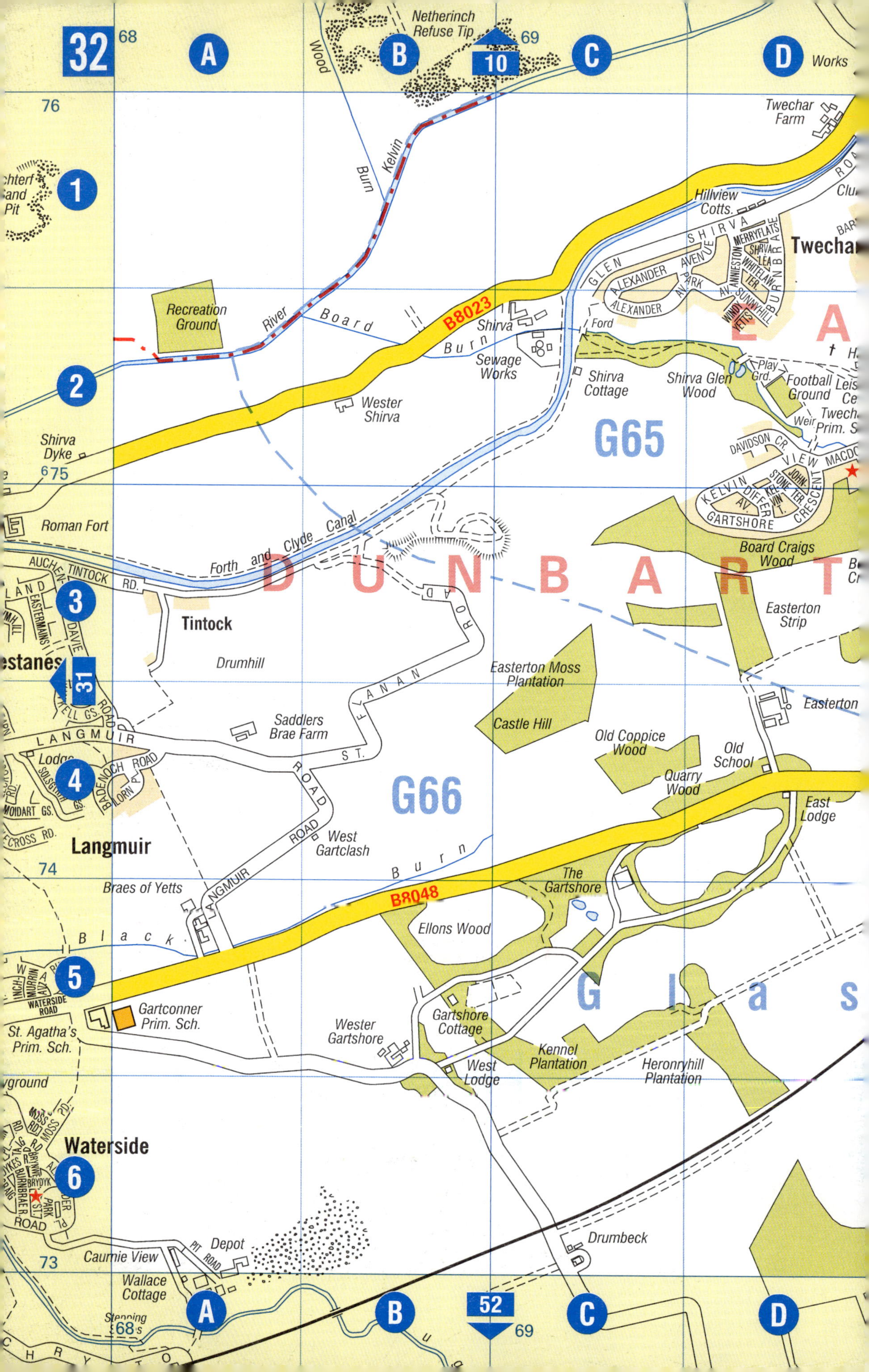

32
68
69
A
B
C
D
10
52
31
Netherinch Refuse Tip
Wood
Works
Twechar Farm
Kelvin
Burn
River
Recreation Ground
Board
B8023
Shirva
Burn
Sewage Works
Hillview Cotts.
Twechar
SHIRVA
GLEN
ALEXANDER
AVENUE
PARK
Ford
Shirva Cottage
Shirva Glen Wood
Play Grd.
Football Ground
Weir
Wester Shirva
Shirva Dyke
675
Roman Fort
Forth and Clyde Canal
G65
DAVIDSON CR.
VIEW
KELVIN AV.
GARTSHORE
CRESCENT
Board Craigs Wood
DUNBART
AUCHENTINTOCK RD.
Tintock
Drumhill
ROAD
FLANAN ST.
Easterton Moss Plantation
Castle Hill
Easterton Strip
Easterton
Old Coppice Wood
Old School
Quarry Wood
Saddlers Brae Farm
LANGMUIR
ROAD
BADENOCH ROAD
LORN
Lodge
MOIDART GS.
Langmuir
G66
West Gartclash
East Lodge
74
Braes of Yetts
LANGMUIR
Burn
B8048
The Gartshore
Ellons Wood
Black
Gartconner Prim. Sch.
WATERSIDE ROAD
St. Agatha's Prim. Sch.
Wester Gartshore
Gartshore Cottage
Glas
Kennel Plantation
Heronryhill Plantation
West Lodge
Waterside
BURNBRAE ROAD
Depot
PIT ROAD
Caurnie View
73
Wallace Cottage
Drumbeck

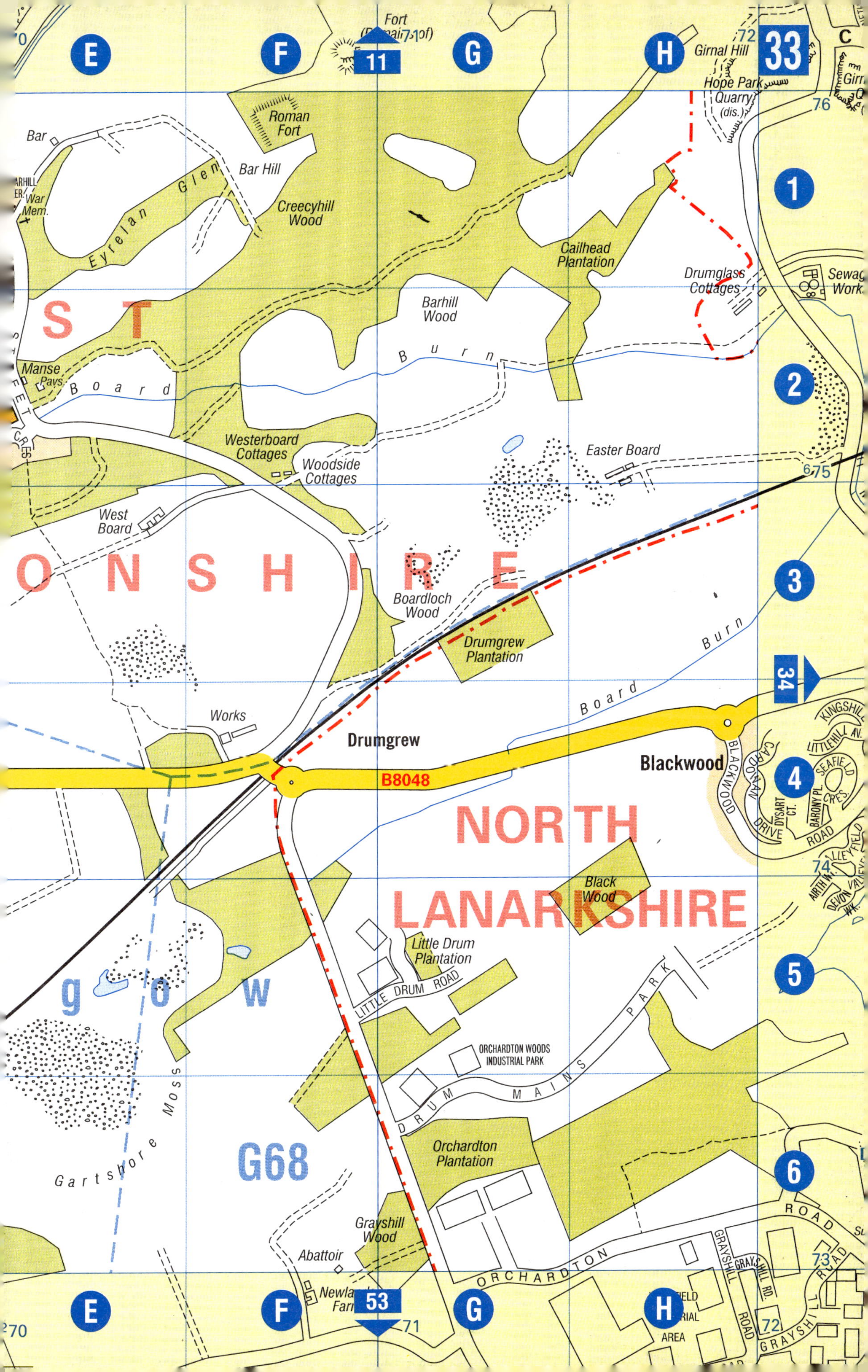
E
F
G
H
11
53
34
Fort
Girnal Hill
Hope Park Quarry (dis.)
Roman Fort
Bar
Bar Hill
Eyrelan Glen
War Mem.
Creecyhill Wood
Cailhead Plantation
Drumglass Cottages
Sewage Works
Barhill Wood
Board Burn
Manse Pavs.
Westerboard Cottages
Woodside Cottages
Easter Board
West Board
Boardloch Wood
Drumgrew Plantation
Works
Drumgrew
B8048
Blackwood
KINGSHILL AV.
LITTLEHILL
SEAFIELD CRES.
BLACKWOOD
CARDOWAN DRIVE
DYSART CT.
BARONY PL.
ROAD
VALLEYFIELD
AIRTH WY.
DEVON WK.
NORTH LANARKSHIRE
Black Wood
Little Drum Plantation
LITTLE DRUM ROAD
PARK
ORCHARDTON WOODS INDUSTRIAL PARK
DRUM MAINS ROAD
Orchardton Plantation
Grayshill Wood
Abattoir
ORCHARDTON ROAD
GRAYSHILL ROAD
GRAYSHILL RD.
AREA
Gartshore Moss
G68
S T
O N S H I R E
g o w
70
71
72
73
74
675
76

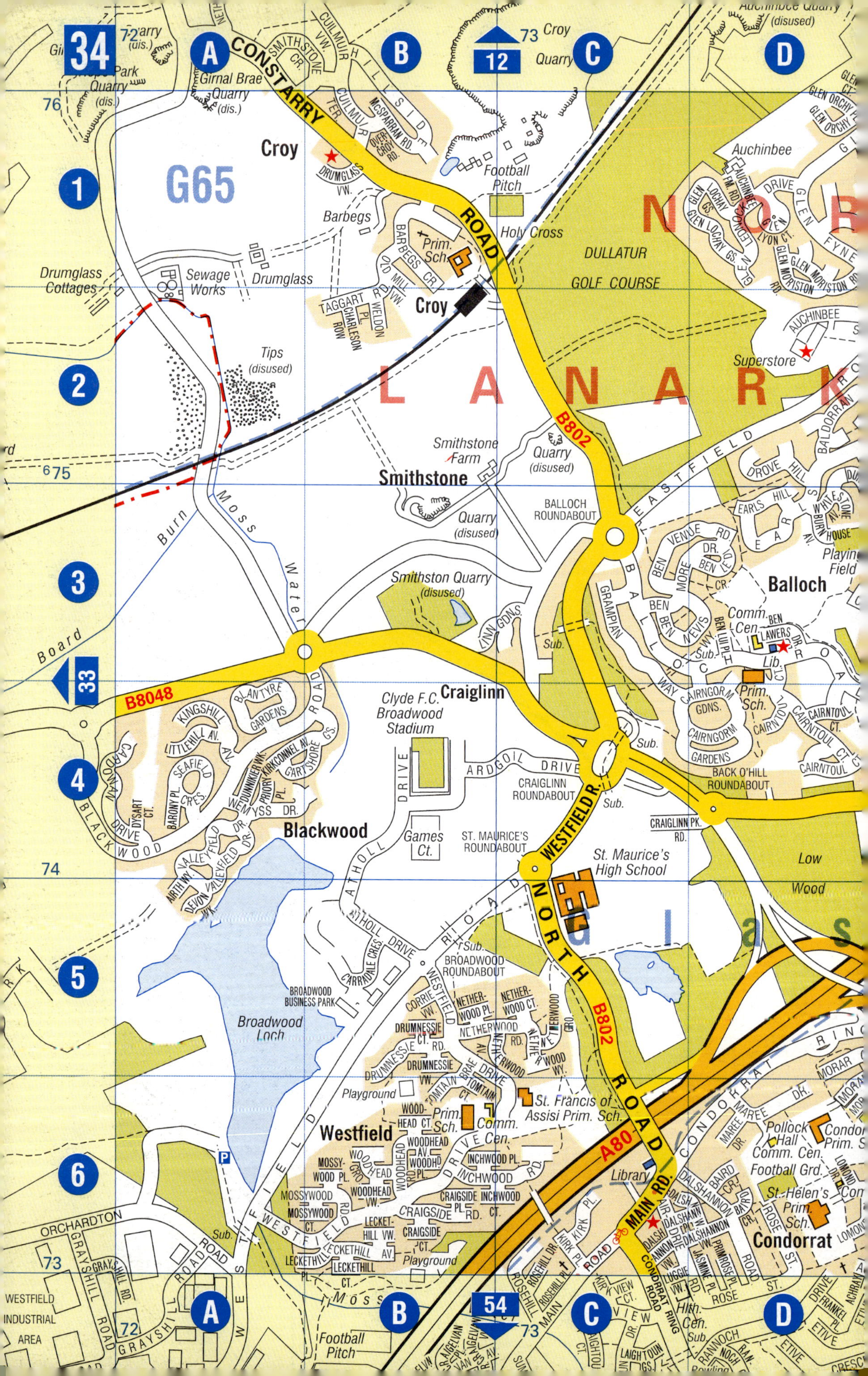
34
A
B
C
D
12
54
33
1
2
3
4
5
6
G65
Croy
Smithstone
Craiglinn
Blackwood
Westfield
Balloch
Condorrat
Auchinbee
CONSTARRY ROAD
B802
B8048
A80
NORTH ROAD
WESTFIELD R.
MAIN RD.
Girnal Brae Quarry (dis.)
Croy Quarry
Auchinbee Quarry (disused)
Drumglass Cottages
Sewage Works
Drumglass
Tips (disused)
Barbegs
Prim. Sch.
Football Pitch
Holy Cross
DULLATUR GOLF COURSE
Superstore
Smithstone Farm
Quarry (disused)
BALLOCH ROUNDABOUT
Smithston Quarry (disused)
Clyde F.C. Broadwood Stadium
ARDGOIL DRIVE
CRAIGLINN ROUNDABOUT
BACK O'HILL ROUNDABOUT
ST. MAURICE'S ROUNDABOUT
St. Maurice's High School
Games Ct.
Low Wood
BROADWOOD ROUNDABOUT
BROADWOOD BUSINESS PARK
Broadwood Loch
Playground
St. Francis of Assisi Prim. Sch.
Comm. Cen.
Library
Pollock Hall Comm. Cen.
Football Grd.
St. Helen's Prim. Sch.
Condorrat Prim. Sch.
Hlth. Cen.
WESTFIELD INDUSTRIAL AREA
ORCHARDTON ROAD
GRAYSHILL ROAD
Moss Water
Board Burn
NORTH LANARKSHIRE
Comm. Cen.
Lib.
Sub.

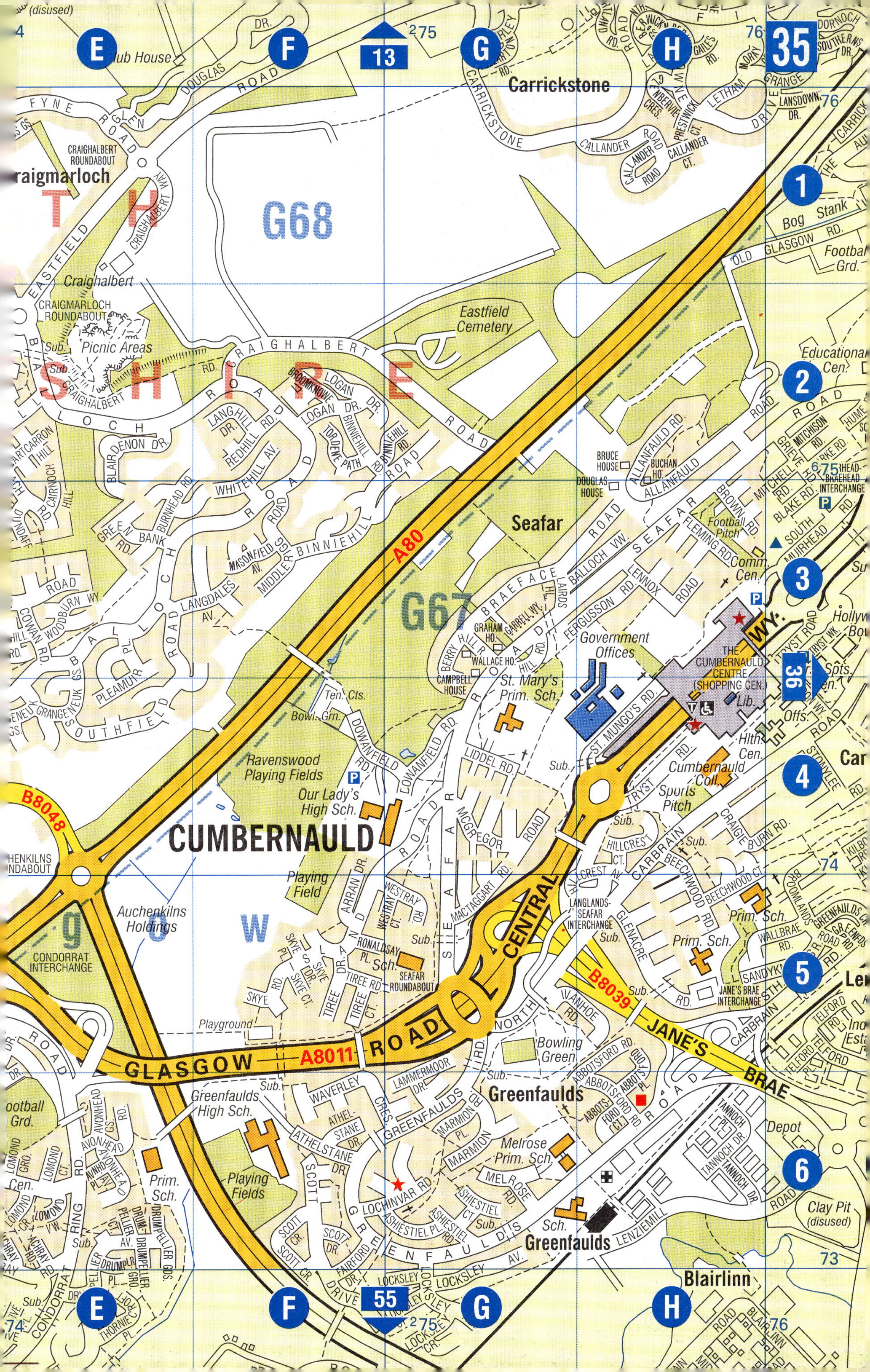
13
55
36
Carrickstone
G68
G67
Craigmarloch
Craighalbert
CRAIGHALBERT ROUNDABOUT
CRAIGMARLOCH ROUNDABOUT
Picnic Areas
Eastfield Cemetery
Seafar
CUMBERNAULD
Ravenswood Playing Fields
Our Lady's High Sch.
Government Offices
St. Mary's Prim. Sch.
THE CUMBERNAULD CENTRE (SHOPPING CEN.)
Lib.
Hlth. Cen.
Cumbernauld Coll.
Sports Pitch
Football Pitch
Comm. Cen.
Auchenkilns Holdings
AUCHENKILNS ROUNDABOUT
CONDORRAT INTERCHANGE
LANGLANDS-SEAFAR INTERCHANGE
SEAFAR ROUNDABOUT
JANE'S BRAE INTERCHANGE
BRAEHEAD INTERCHANGE
Greenfaulds
Greenfaulds High Sch.
Melrose Prim. Sch.
Bowling Green
Playing Fields
Playing Field
Prim. Sch.
Blairlinn
Clay Pit (disused)
Depot
Bog Stank
Football Grd.
Educational Cen.
A80
A8011
B8048
B8039
GLASGOW ROAD
CENTRAL WY.
JANE'S BRAE
CRAIGHALBERT RD.
BALLOCH ROAD
LOCH ROAD
SEAFAR ROAD
BRAEFACE ROAD
SOUTHFIELD ROAD
DOUGLAS ROAD
FYNE ROAD
GLEN ROAD
EASTFIELD ROAD
CARRICKSTONE DRIVE
OLD GLASGOW RD.
CARBRAIN ROAD
GREENFAULDS ROAD
LENZIEMILL ROAD
LOCKSLEY AV.
ABBOTSFORD RD.
BINNIEHILL ROAD
LOGAN DR.
ALLANFAULD RD.
MITCHELL RD.
FLEMING RD.
FERGUSSON RD.
ST. MUNGO'S RD.
TRYST ROAD
STONYLEE RD.
IVANHOE RD.
MELROSE RD.
LOCHINVAR RD.
MARMION RD.
SCOTT DR.
ATHELSTANE DR.
WAVERLEY CRES.
RING ROAD
CONDORRAT RING ROAD
E F G H
1 2 3 4 5 6
73 74 75 76
275
675

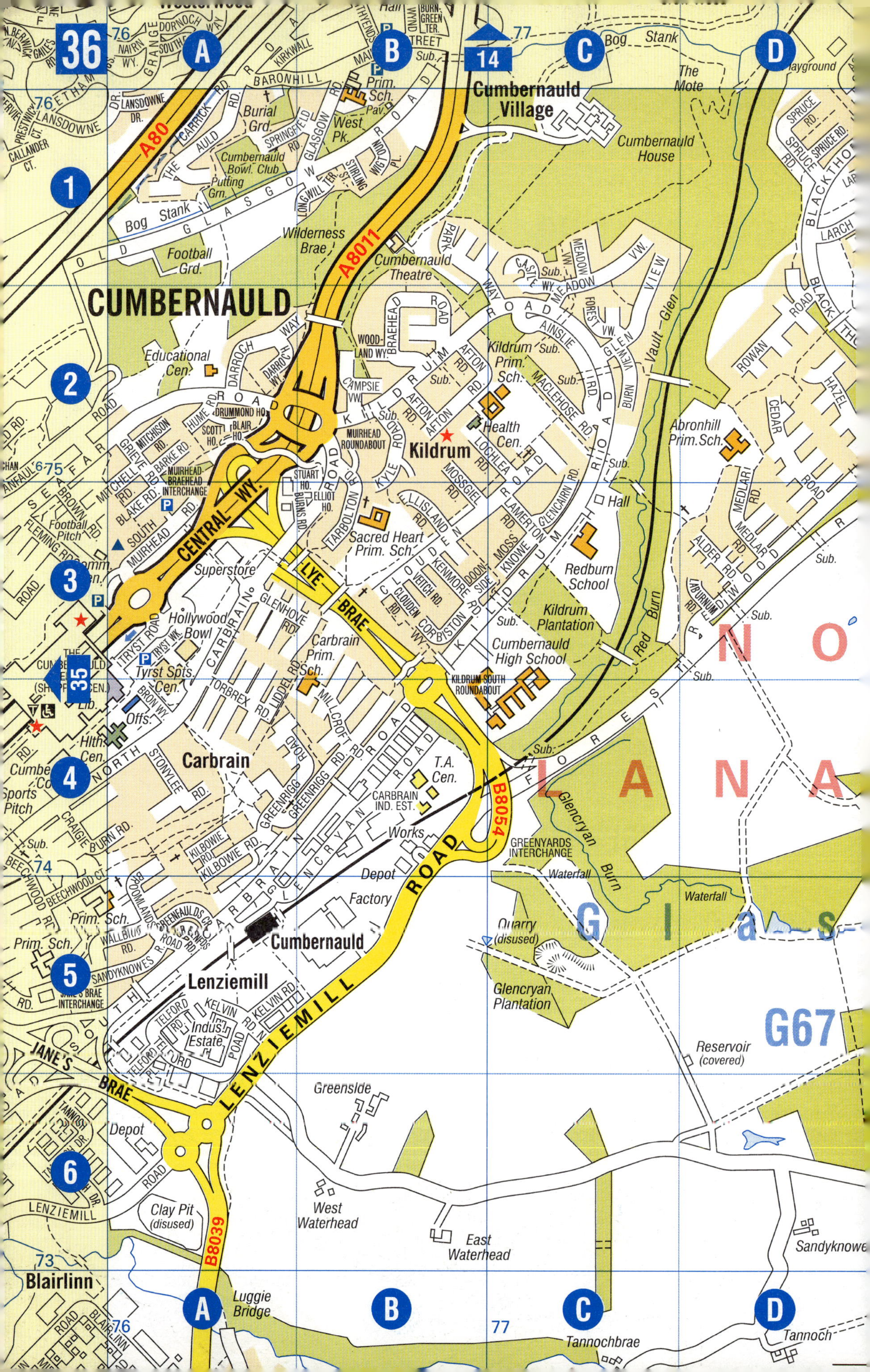

CUMBERNAULD
Cumbernauld Village
Cumbernauld House
The Mote
Bog Stank
Burial Grd.
Cumbernauld Bowl. Club
Putting Grn.
Football Grd.
Wilderness Brae
Cumbernauld Theatre
West Pk.
Prim. Sch.
Educational Cen.
Kildrum
Kildrum Prim. Sch.
Health Cen.
MUIRHEAD ROUNDABOUT
MUIRHEAD BRAEHEAD INTERCHANGE
Sacred Heart Prim. Sch.
Redburn School
Kildrum Plantation
Cumbernauld High School
KILDRUM SOUTH ROUNDABOUT
Abronhill Prim.Sch.
Hall
Vault Glen
Red Burn
Superstore
Hollywood Bowl
Tyrst Spts. Cen.
Offs.
Hlth. Cen.
Lib.
Carbrain
Carbrain Prim. Sch.
T.A. Cen.
CARBRAIN IND. EST.
Works
Depot
Factory
GREENYARDS INTERCHANGE
Glencryan Burn
Waterfall
Quarry (disused)
Glencryan Plantation
Cumbernauld
Lenziemill
Indus. Estate
JANE'S BRAE INTERCHANGE
Sports Pitch
Football Pitch
Comm. Cen.
Prim. Sch.
Greenside
West Waterhead
East Waterhead
Clay Pit (disused)
Depot
Reservoir (covered)
Sandyknowe
Blairlinn
Luggie Bridge
Tannochbrae
Tannoch
Playground
N O R T H   L A N A R K
G l a s
G67
A80
A8011
B8054
B8039
CENTRAL WY.
LYE BRAE
LENZIEMILL ROAD
JANE'S BRAE
GLASGOW ROAD
KILDRUM RING ROAD
FORREST ROAD
14
35
A B C D
1 2 3 4 5 6
75 76 77 74 73

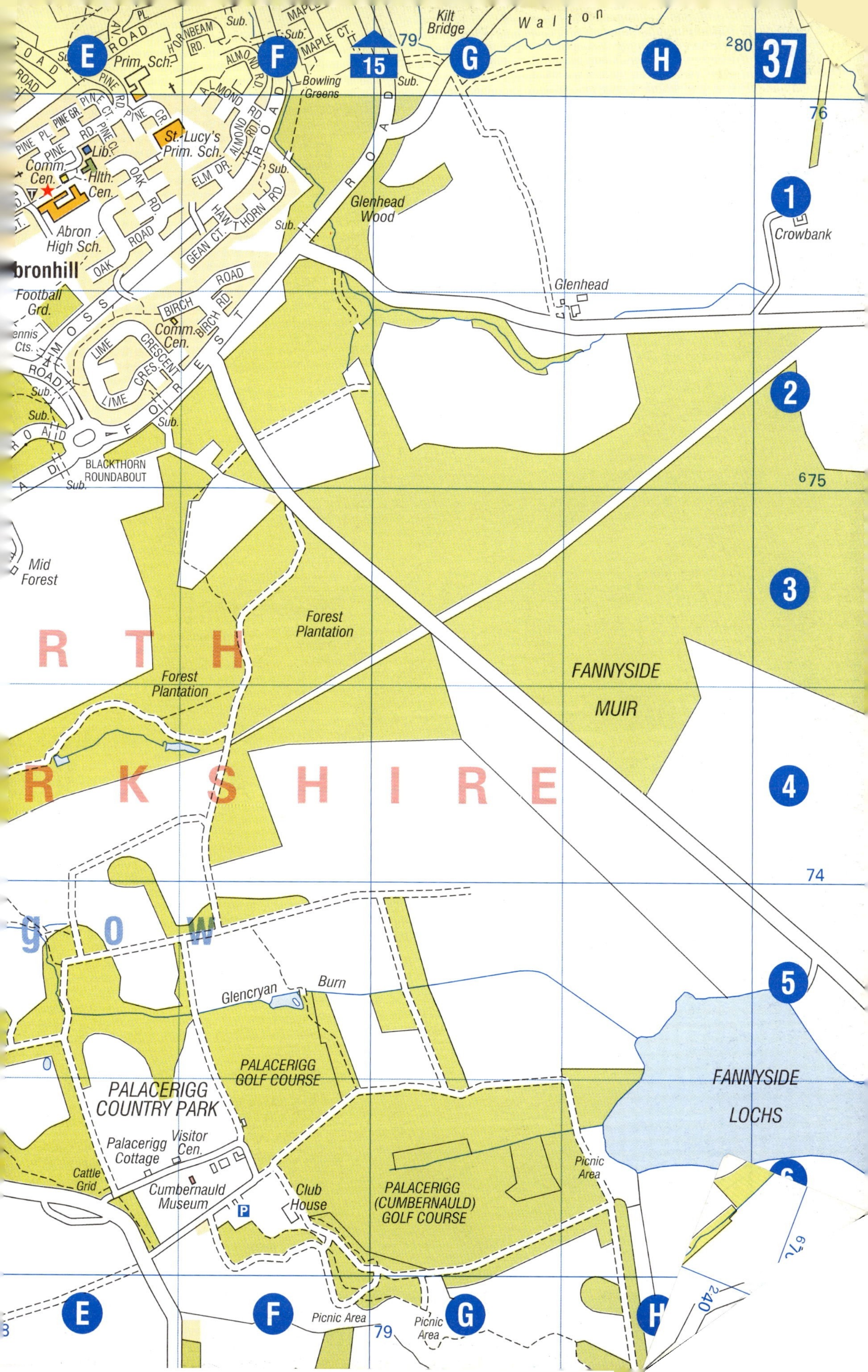

37
15
E
F
G
H
1
2
3
4
5
Walton
Kilt Bridge
Prim. Sch.
St. Lucy's Prim. Sch.
Lib.
Comm. Cen.
Hlth. Cen.
Abron High Sch.
bronhill
Football Grd.
Bowling Greens
Glenhead Wood
Crowbank
Glenhead
BLACKTHORN ROUNDABOUT
Mid Forest
Forest Plantation
Forest Plantation
FANNYSIDE MUIR
R T H
R K S H I R E
g o w
Glencryan Burn
PALACERIGG GOLF COURSE
PALACERIGG COUNTRY PARK
Palacerigg Cottage
Visitor Cen.
Cattle Grid
Cumbernauld Museum
Club House
PALACERIGG (CUMBERNAULD) GOLF COURSE
Picnic Area
FANNYSIDE LOCHS
Picnic Area
Picnic Area
FOREST ROAD
MOSS ROAD
ROAD
PINE RD.
PINE CT.
PINE GR.
PINE PL.
PINE CL.
PINE CR.
HORNBEAM RD.
MAPLE CT.
ALMOND RD.
ELM DR.
OAK RD.
OAK ROAD
HAWTHORN RD.
GEAN CT.
BIRCH RD.
BIRCH ROAD
LIME CRESCENT
LIME CRES.
280
76
675
74
79

240
41
18
A
B
C
D
RIVER
73
Junction 31
M8 MOTORWAY
M8
GREENOCK
1
FERRYHILL PLANTATION
Laigh Hatton
High Hatton
OLD GREENOCK
Convent of the Good Shepherd
A8
2
Lodge
B789
Linden Lee
Roman Fort (Site of)
72
RENFREW
Whitemoss Dam
Ingli
Cattle Grid
3
Castlehill Plantation
Drums
Whitemoss Farm
Castlehill Cottage
Port Glasgow PA14
Bishop
4
Barbeg Cottages
BARBEG HILL
71
Park Erskine
Formakin
Formakin Estate Country Park
Paddock Craig
Gatehead
PA7
Barmore Plantation
BARMORE HILL
Paddockcraig
5
HOUSTON
Formakin Mill
West Glenshinn Cottage
Parkglen Wood
Dargavel Burn
West Glenshinnoch
Nether Mill
ROAD
Johnstone PA6
6
Meiklefield
Haddockston
Boghall
BAROCHAN
REILLY
Towncroft
41
ROAD

39
E
F
G
H
1
2
3
4
5
6
LONGHAUGH POINT
19
43
44
73
72
71
70
42
RIVER CLYDE
CLYDE
M8 MOTORWAY
M8
Dove Cottage
ERSKINE GOLF COURSE
Conyston Plantation
Club House
GOLF
Freelan
Monument
Aqueduct
Burial Ground
Slateford
CHESTNUT AVENUE
CHESTNUT AV.
SHIRE
Ritchieston
B815
FERRY ROAD
BISHOPTON
West Porton
KINGSWOOD
ROAD LYLE
WRAISLAND CR.
BLANTYRE DR.
CRES.
W. PORTON PL.
DUNSMORE
ANDERSON RD.
CAIRNS R.
GLEN RD.
ROAD
GORDON AV.
BRUCE
FRASER AV.
CAMPBELL AV.
BUCHANAN
STUART AV.
CAMERON AV.
West Porton
WALLACE AV.
LESLIE AV.
SEMPLE
LENNOX AV.
BURNS AV.
QUEENS DRIVE
40
KINGSTON ROAD
OLD GREENOCK ROAD
Cemetery
Playgrd.
PORTON PL.
Lib.
CROSSGATES
GREENOCK ROAD
A8
HAMILTON CR.
NEWTON ROAD
INGLISTON DRIVE
Playing Field
BRIDGEND
THE GROVE
Prim. Sch.
CHARTWELL
RENSHAW
BRISBANE R.
CHURCHILL
FLEMING RD.
MAXWELL RD.
DARGAVEL AV.
ROAD
LAIGHPARK AV.
MARAV.
LANG AV.
SHAW AV.
KINGSTON RD.
SYRE
REDWOOD CR.
LAMONT AV.
HAY AV.
CAMPHILL
DEVON
ETIVE DR.
DUNGLASS RD.
CARRON DR.
ROSSLAND
ROSSLAND CRES.
ROSSLAND CR.
HOLMPARK
Ingliston
Easter Newton
Holmpark
Wester Rossland
Rec. Grd.
Bowling Green
Comm. Cen.
Health. Cen.
DRIVE
CASTLE CR.
KINGSTON
Kingston
CAWDOR CR.
CRAIGHEAD
ALMOND DR.
CARRICK
MORAR CR.
YARROW CRES.
RD. DR.
POPLAR CR.
POPLAR AV.
GLEDSTANE RD.
SACHELCOURT AV.
STATION RD.
ROSSLAND PL.
Nursery
Bishopton
Sewage Works
Rossland
Glen Orchy
Craigton
ROAD
ROYAL ORDNANCE FACTORY
Gladstone
Gladstone House
Bolerno
East Glenshinnoch
Easter Newton
2
21
66
69
131
132
ouse

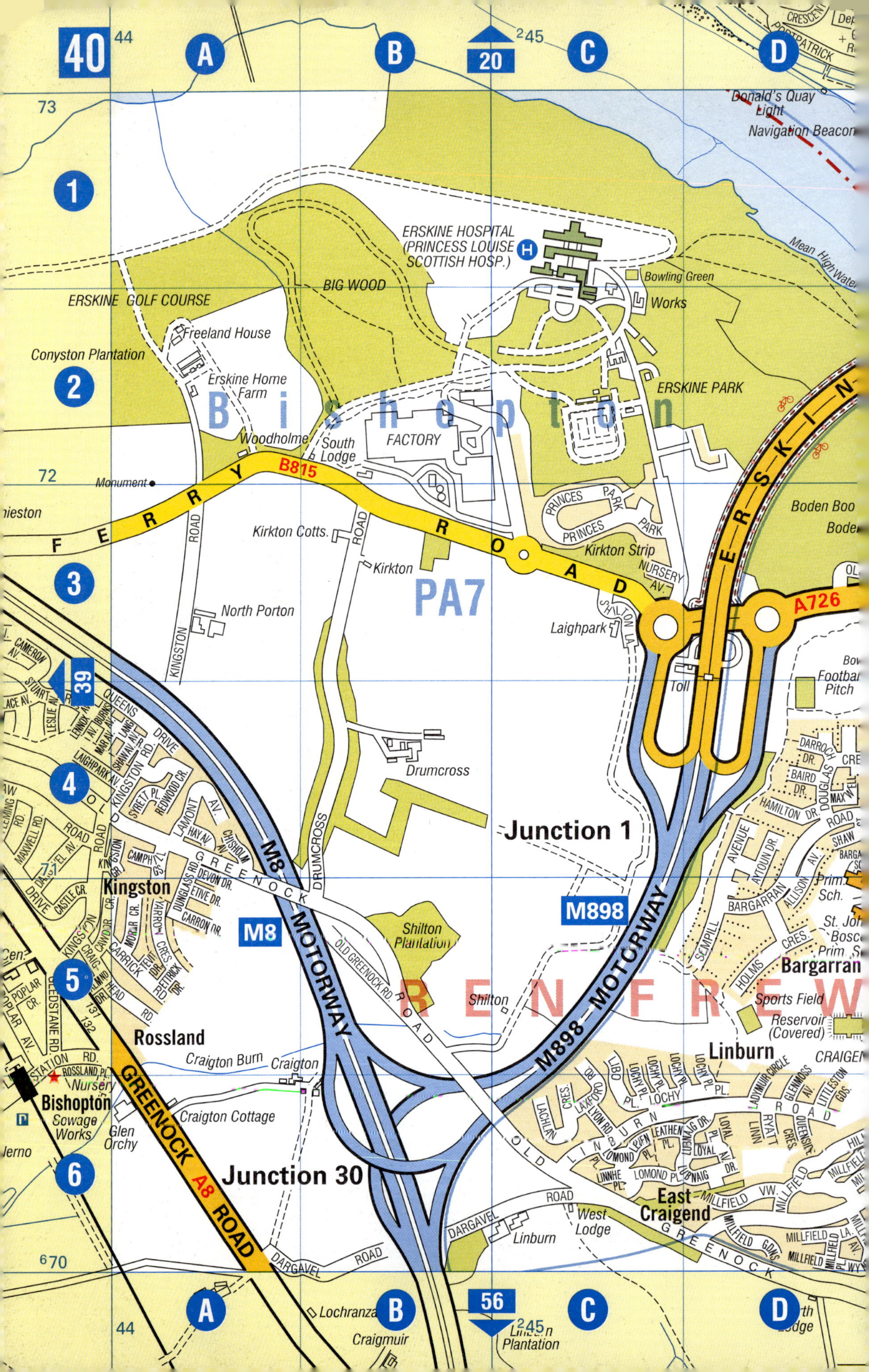

A
B
C
D
20
56
39
1
2
3
4
5
6
44
245
73
72
670
ERSKINE HOSPITAL (PRINCESS LOUISE SCOTTISH HOSP.)
Donald's Quay Light
Navigation Beacon
Mean High Water
Bowling Green
Works
BIG WOOD
ERSKINE GOLF COURSE
Freeland House
Conyston Plantation
Erskine Home Farm
ERSKINE PARK
Bishopton
Woodholme
South Lodge
FACTORY
Monument
FERRY ROAD
B815
PRINCES PARK
Kirkton Cotts.
Kirkton
Kirkton Strip
NURSERY AV.
PA7
North Porton
KINGSTON ROAD
Laighpark
SHILTON LA.
ERSKINE
A726
Boden Boo
Toll
Football Pitch
Drumcross
Junction 1
M898
M8
M8 MOTORWAY
M898 MOTORWAY
DRUMCROSS ROAD
GREENOCK ROAD
OLD GREENOCK RD.
Shilton Plantation
Shilton
RENFREW
Kingston
Rossland
Craigton Burn
Craigton
Craigton Cottage
Bishopton
Sewage Works
Nursery
STATION RD.
Glen Orchy
Junction 30
GREENOCK A8 ROAD
DARGAVEL ROAD
Linburn
West Lodge
East Craigend
Bargarran
Prim. Sch.
St. John Bosco Prim. Sch.
Sports Field
Reservoir (Covered)
Linburn
OLD LINBURN ROAD
Lochranza
Craigmuir
Plantation
QUEENS DRIVE
OLD ROAD
CAMERON AV.
STUART
LESLIE AV.
LAIGHPARK AV.
KINGSTON RD.
STREET PL.
REDWOOD CR.
LAMONT
HAY AV.
CHISHOLM
DEVON DR.
ETIVE DR.
CARRON DR.
YARROW CRES.
DUNGLASS RD.
MORAR CR.
CARRICK
ETTRICK
TEVIOT DR.
CASTLE CR.
MAXWELL RD.
POPLAR CR.
GLEDSTANE RD.
ROSSLAND PL.
HAMILTON DR.
BAIRD DR.
DARROCH DR.
DOUGLAS
MAXWELL
SHAW
AYTOUN DR.
AVENUE
BARGARRAN
ALLISON AV.
HOLMS CRES.
SEMPILL
LIBO
LOCHY PL.
LACHLAN CRES.
LAXFORD RD.
LYON RD.
LEVEN PL.
LEATHEN PL.
LOMOND PL.
LINNHE PL.
LUBNAIG DR.
LOYAL AV.
MILLFIELD VW.
MILLFIELD GDNS.
MILLFIELD LA.
LADYMUIR CIRCLE
GLENMOSS AV.
LITTLESTON GDS.
RYATT LINN
QUEENSIDE CRES.
CRAIGEND ROAD

Netherclose
21
47
48
E
F
G
H
Cemy.
Old Kilpatrick
Halls
Clinic
DUMBARTON
A814 RD
STATION
Kilpatrick
Sub.
PEACOCK PL.
HILLSIDE T.
PLEASANT RD.
A82
GREAT WESTERN ROAD
North Dalnottar Cemetery
Crematorium
Carleith Prim.Sch.
73
1
Auchentoshan Sch.
AUCHENTOSHAN ES
Lodge
Dalnottar Cemetery
Warehouses
Dam
Dalnottar Burn
Lock
A898
BRIDGE
Lusset Glen
Swing Bri.
St.Patrick's Light
Recycling Cen.
Old Kilpatrick Light
Jetty
Factory
Auchentoshan Cottages
Distillery
WEST DUNBARTONSHIRE
Wilderness
Mountblow
MOUNTBLOW ROAD
2
(CLYD
DUMBARTON ROAD
Recreation Ground
Running Track
Pav.
Ferry Lodge
Ferry Strip
Bottombow Island
RIVER CLYDE
Barhill Plantation
Erskine Harbour
G60
A814 ROAD
1003
945
874
834
72
LITTLEHOLM
3
DALMUIR
Clyde Public
Forth & Clyde Canal
Play. Field
Clydemuir Prim. Sch.
Fanum House
Hotel
Jetty
Bonded Warehouses
Our Lady of Loretto Prim. Sch.
Clydebank
4
42
Playgrd.
North Barr Sch.
Rashieburn
G81
SEWAGE PURIFICATION WORKS
Precipitation Tanks
Sluices
Depot
Works
CLYDEBANK INDUSTRIAL ESTATE
71
Duntocher Light
Wharf
BRIDGEWATER INDUSTRIAL PARK
Rashielee Light
Dalmuir Light (West)
Park
5
HEAL INTERNATIO
Erskine Pool
Liby.
BRIDGEWATER SHOPPING CENTRE
Depot
Subway
ERSKINE
SHIRE
NEWSHOT
NEWSHOT ISLAND
Recreation Ground
Rashielee Plantation
Park Mains High School
Erskine
Comm. Cen.
Health Cen.
6
Cause
West Craigend
PA8
A726
Refuse Site
670
57
Park Mains
St.Anne's Prim.Sch.
Barsail

A
B
C
D
1
2
3
4
5
6
22
41
58
48
49
Carleith
Carleith Prim. Sch.
Dalmuir Cemetery
Crematorium
GREAT WESTERN ROAD
A82
DUMBARTON ROAD
A810
Auchentoshan Sch.
Mount Blow Sch.
Auchentoshan Occupational Centre
AUCHENTOSHAN ESTATE
Ocean Field
St. Mary's Sch.
Football Park
The Antonine Sports Cen.
DUNTOCHER
Golden Hill Park
Golden Hill
Roman Fort (Site of)
Goldenhill Prim. Sch.
WEST
DUNBARTON
KILBOWIE
DALMUIR (CLYDEBANK) MUNICIPAL GOLF COURSE
Duntocher Burn
Parkhall
B814
DUNTOCHER ROAD
Club House
Putting Grn.
Bowl. Green
Bandstand
Clydebank Public Park
DALMUIR
Dalmuir
Library
Boquhanran Park
Radnor Park
Clydebank High Sch.
Playing Field
Kilbowie Prim. Sch.
Hlth. Cen.
Clydebank Coll.
Our Lady of Loretto Prim. Sch.
St. Stephen's Prim. Sch.
Sports Ground
Nursing Home
Training Cen.
G81
Singer
A8014
KILBOWIE ROAD
A814
DUMBARTON ROAD
CLYDEBANK INDUSTRIAL ESTATE
Works
Depot
HEALTH CARE INTERNATIONAL HOSPITAL
Helipad
Forth & Clyde Canal
CLYDEBANK BUSINESS PARK
RIVER CLYDE
Newshot Light
Dalmuir Light
Erskine
PA8
Mean High Water Springs
NEWSHOT ISLAND
Causeway
RENFREWSHIRE
CLYDEBANK
Clydebank District Museum
Clydebank
GLASGOW ROAD

23
44
59
E
F
G
H
1
2
3
4
5
6
DUNTOCHER
ROAD
A810
GLASGOW
Hardgate
Playing Field
Football Grd.
Faifley Prim. Sch.
St. Joseph's Prim. Sch.
Library
CRESCENT
COLLINS ST.
Lawmuir
Depot
G81
Langfauld
PEEL GLEN ROAD
Garscadden Burn
EAST DUNBARTONSHIRE
HUTCHESON HILL
Club House
CLYDEBANK AND DISTRICT GOLF COURSE
FAIRWAYS VIEW
CLEDDANS ROAD
NSHIRE
Cleddans
Braidfield
Braidfield Cottage
Cleddans Burn
NEW MUSK
LILLYBURN PL.
FASQUE PL.
ACHAMORE
LADYLOAN
AVENUE
CITY OF GLASGOW
Water Tower
Cleddens Prim. Sch.
Lochgoin
Lochgain Prim. Sch.
KINFAUNS
Drumchapel High Sch.
A82
GREAT WESTERN ROAD
St. Columba's R.C. High Sch.
KIRKOSWALD
MOSSGIEL
Sports Ground
INCHFAD
HALBEATH AV.
DUNKENNY
Rec. Grd.
LINKWOOD DRIVE
Glasgow
HECLA AVENUE
Lib.
Hlth. Cen.
ARNDALE SHOPPING CENTRE
DRUMCHAPEL
ABBOTSHALL
DRUMRY ROAD
B8055
Drumry
St. Eunan's Prim. Sch.
Braidfield High Sch.
Kilbowie Cemy.
Clydebank F.C.
VANGUARD
Comm. Cen.
Drumchapel Swim. Pool
Sports Cen.
G15
EAST GARSCADDEN RD.
Sports Ground
Works
Warehouses
DALSETTER AV.
MONTROSE
ONSLOW ROAD
Drumry
Play Fld.
Clydebank Retail Park
Clydebank Mega Bowl
GREAT WESTERN RETAIL PARK
LIVINGSTONE STREET
KIRKWOOD
ATTLEE AVENUE
Linnvale Prim. & Nursy. Sch.
Whitecrook Prim. Sch. & Cunard Sch.
Play Field
Whitecrook
Linnvale
DUNTREATH
Yoker Burn
CRAWFORD
FRUIN RD.
GARSCADDEN RD.
Sports Ground
Lock 37

44
24
43
60
A
B
C
D
1
2
3
4
5
6
52
53
73
72
71
670
DUNTOCHER ROAD
A810
A809
A82
GREAT WESTERN ROAD
Langfaulds
Depot
Garscadden Burn
Castle Hill (Roman Fort)
Castlehill
HUTCHESON HILL
Ford
GLEN ROAD
PEEL
LEDI
CAIRNGORM
BONNAUGHTON ROAD
PENTLAND PL.
SIDLAW RD.
TINTO ROAD
LAWERS DR.
NEVIS CRES.
Convent of Notre Dame
St. Andrew's College
St. Andrew's Prim. Sch.
BURNSIDE
STOCKIEMUIR ROAD
Bearsden Ski Club
COURTHILL
CASTLEHILL
ANTONINE
TIREE GDS.
LEWIS GDS.
SKYE GDS.
ROSSLYN RD.
DRYBURGH RD.
NITHSDALE
KENILWORTH CR.
ABBOTSFORD
SCOTT DR.
WHITEHURST
IAIN DR.
STIRLING
LAURENCE DR.
EAGLE CRESCENT
Prim. Sch.
FAIRWAY
WESTBOURNE
SOUTHVIEW
PARK CR.
CLIFFVIEW
MILVERTON
BEARSDEN
EAST DUN
CRESCENT
BALLAIG AV.
AVENUE
NORTH ERSKINE
SOUTH ERSKINE
CAMPBELL
COLQUHOUN
DRIVE
BEARSDEN GOLF COURSE
GARSCADDEN WOOD
Club House
UPPER
WESTBOURNE
GLENBURN
BAIRD DR.
ROAD
THORN ROAD
Public Park
Scotus College
MANNOFIELD
CAMSTRADDEN DR. WEST
CAMSTRADDEN DR. EAST
LEDCAMEROCH PK.
LEDCAMEROCH
High Sch.
LADYLOAN
AVENUE
DRUMMORE
SPRINGSIDE PL.
GROGARRY RD.
BACKMUIR RD.
SADDELL RD.
KILCLOY AV.
Sch.
SUMMERHILL
KINFAUNS
St. Pius' Prim. Sch.
Comm. Cen.
Drumchapel High Sch.
Spts Grd.
CITY OF GLASGOW
BANKGLEN RD.
NORTHMUIR RD.
PITMILLY
Drummore School
Prim. Sch.
STATION ROAD
CHESTERS
Pav.
COLQUHORN PARK
Playing Field
RYEDALE PL.
RAYNE PL.
PLACE
PILTON RD.
SHERWOOD PL.
PINEWOOD SQ.
BLACKCRAIG AV.
BARNKIRK AV.
BAYFIELD TER.
BAYFIELD AV.
CALLY AV.
ARDHU PL.
HARROW PLACE
LINKWOOD DRIVE
LINKWOOD CR.
KINCLAVEN AV.
MERRYTON AV.
JEDWORTH
ROZELLE AV.
JEDWORTH AV.
TALLANT TER.
TALLANT ROAD
GOYLE AV.
CAROLSIDE DR.
Hall
Broadholm Prim. Sch.
DRUMCHAPEL
Hlth. Cen.
DUNKENNY SQ.
GARSCADDEN RD.
SOUTHDEEN RD.
SOUTHDEEN AVENUE
CONON
ANNAN DR.
TEITH DR.
DOON
TWEED CRES.
AVENUE
Colquhoun Park Prim. Sch.
CANNIESBURN ROAD
LOCHEND
PENDICLE CRES.
PENDICLE
CANNIESBURN
ANNICK DR.
CARRON CR.
ALLANDER
FORTH RD.
TAY RD.
ESKDALE RD.
KINGLAS RD.
FALLOCH RD.
SPEY
DORNOCH RD.
TEVIOT CR.
DEVERON ROAD
WHEATFIELD RD.
DEEPDENE
MONHEIT
NORTH
Rec. Grd.
Library
Milngavie Junction
Garscadden Burn
GLENKIRK DRIVE
Stonedyke Prim. Sch.
G15
CLOAN AV.
CLOAN CRES.
DIPPLE PL.
BELSYDE AV.
GLENKIRK
BOON DR.
ARCAN CRES.
DRUMCHAPEL HOSP.
GARSCADDEN ROAD
Sports Ground
Works
DALSETTER AVENUE
DUNTREATH GS.
DUNTREATH AV.
Drumchapel
DRUMCHAPEL ROAD
ESSENSIDE AV.
MORAINE AVENUE
BLADNOCH DR.
MONKTON DR.
KIRKHOPE DR.
BLAIRDARDIE
ALMOND ROAD
Locks (Disused)
ALMOND
ROTHERWOOD AVENUE
BANNER DR.
BANNER RD.
ROTHERWOOD
TOWERHILL RD.
GLAIVE RD.
CURFEW RD.
CLOBERHILL
KNIGHTSWOOD
G13
MACE
MONKSBRIDGE
HERALD AV.
PALMER AV.
CRUSADER
MINSTREL RD.
ROWENA AV.
TEMPLAR AV.
GOWANLEA AV.
GARSCADDEN
KAYSTONE RD.
SUNNYSIDE
SUMMERHILL
KINVER DRIVE
MORAINE CIR.
KEARN PL.
Play Fields
Blairdardie Prim. Sch.
GORGET QUADRANT
GORGET AV.
CRAWFORD
FRUIN RD.
MANOR
BALVIE AV.
ROMAN
Sch.
TURRET RD.
Trinley Brae
FRIARSCOURT AVENUE
BALDWIN
IVANHOE RD.
COWDENHILL
KEAL CRESCENT
KEAL
Forth & Clyde Canal (Dis.)
Golf Course
ARCHERHILL
Sports Ground
Lock
2283
2244
2095

25
61
46
E
F
G
H
1
2
3
4
5
6
73
72
71
70
56
55
Kilmardinny Loch
Bearsden Academy Playing Fields
Kilmardinny Art Cen.
Lower Kilmardinny
DOUGLAS PARK GOLF COURSE
Club Ho.
Playing Fields
Complex
Boclair
Mausoleum
New Kilpatrick Cemetery
Library
THE LOANING
Roman Bath Ho.
Hillfoot
Depot
Furguston Muir
Manse Burn
ROMAN A808 ROAD
A809
A81
B8049
BOCLAIR ROAD
Prim. Sch.
Bearsden
Municipal Buildings
BEARSDEN SHOPPING CENTRE
G61
St. Germains Loch
Whitehill Woods
Boclair Academy
Kessington
Killermont Prim. Sch.
King George's Field
CANNIESBURN TOLL
CANNIESBURN HOSPITAL
SWITCHBACK ROAD
A739
MARYHILL ROAD
KILLERMONT GOLF COURSE
Killermont House
Club House
Home Farm
Mill
Garscube Bri.
Westerton Prim. Sch.
Westerton
Forth & Clyde Canal
Tennis Courts
Pav.
CITY OF GLASGOW
W
G20
WEST OF SCOTLAND SCIENCE PARK (Todd Campus)
WEST OF SCOTLAND SCIENCE PARK (Kelvin Campus)
UNIVERSITY OF GLASGOW
RIVER KELVIN
MARYHILL PK.
ANNIESLAND INDUS. EST.
Netherton
Dawsholm
DUNBARTONSHIRE

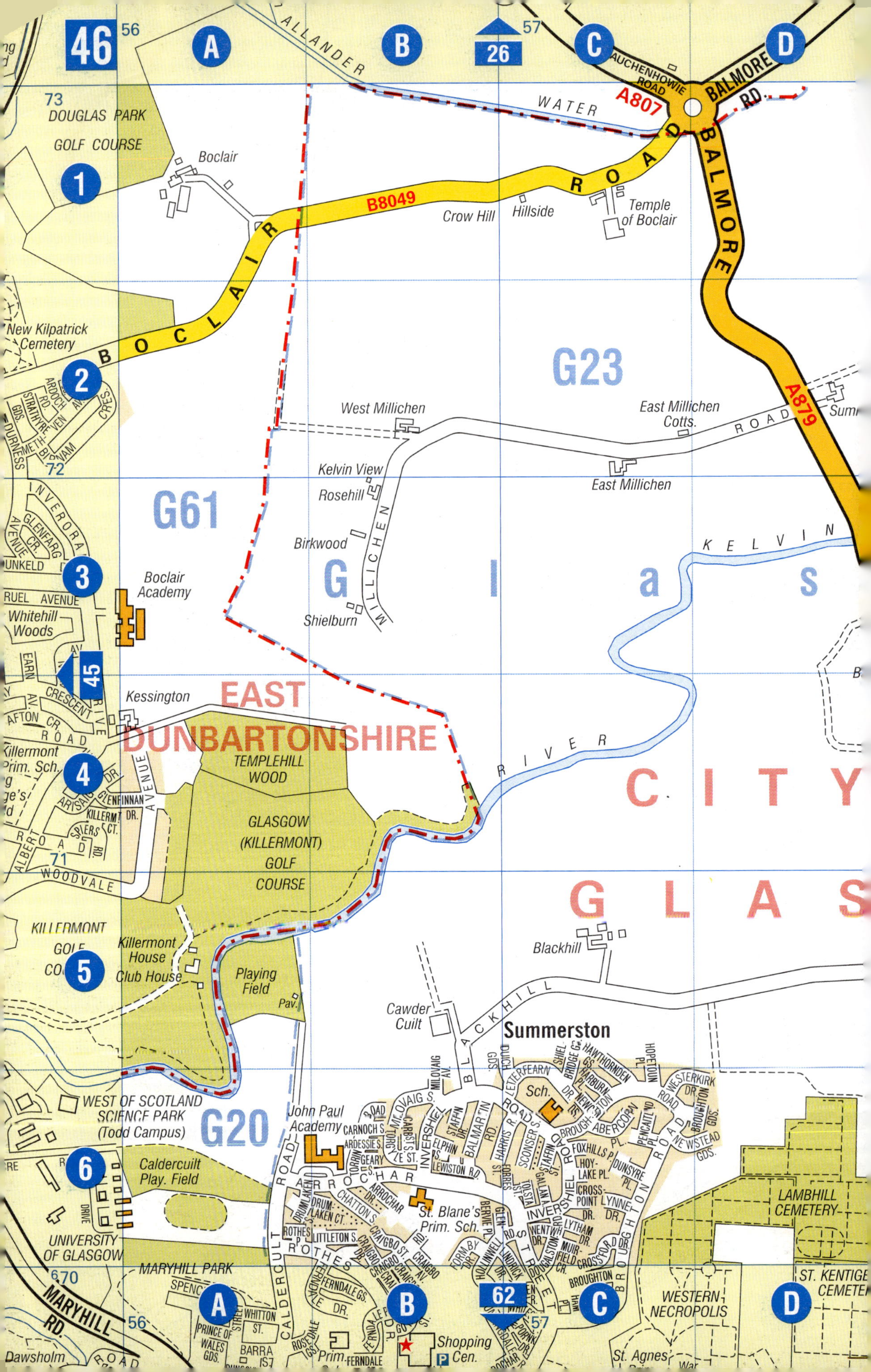
56
A
B
26
57
C
D
ALLANDER
WATER
AUCHENHOWIE ROAD
A807
BALMORE RD.
73
DOUGLAS PARK
GOLF COURSE
Boclair
1
B8049
BOCLAIR ROAD
Crow Hill
Hillside
Temple of Boclair
BALMORE
New Kilpatrick Cemetery
2
G23
A879
West Millichen
East Millichen Cotts.
ROAD
Summ
72
Kelvin View
Rosehill
East Millichen
G61
INVERORAN
GLENFARG CR.
AVENUE
DUNKELD
Birkwood
MILLICHEN
KELVIN
3
Boclair Academy
G l a s
RUEL AVENUE
Whitehill Woods
Shielburn
45
Kessington
EAST DUNBARTONSHIRE
CRESCENT
AFTON CR.
ROAD
RIVER
Killermont Prim. Sch.
4
TEMPLEHILL WOOD
C I T Y
GLENFINNAN
KILLERMONT DR.
SPIERS CT.
GLASGOW (KILLERMONT) GOLF COURSE
ALBERT ROAD
71
WOODVALE
G L A S
KILLERMONT GOLF CO
Killermont House Club House
5
Playing Field
Pav.
Blackhill
BLACKHILL
Cawder Cuilt
Summerston
WEST OF SCOTLAND SCIENCE PARK (Todd Campus)
G20
John Paul Academy
Sch.
6
Caldercuilt Play. Field
ARROCHAR
St. Blane's Prim. Sch.
LAMBHILL CEMETERY
UNIVERSITY OF GLASGOW
MARYHILL PARK
670
MARYHILL RD.
A
B
62
57
C
D
56
WESTERN NECROPOLIS
ST. KENTIGE CEMETE
Shopping Cen.
Prim.
FERNDALE
Dawsholm
ROAD
St. Agnes
PRINCE OF WALES GDS.
WHITTON ST.
BARRA ST.
CALDERCUILT ROAD
BROUGHTON ROAD
INVERSHIEL ROAD
BROUGHTON

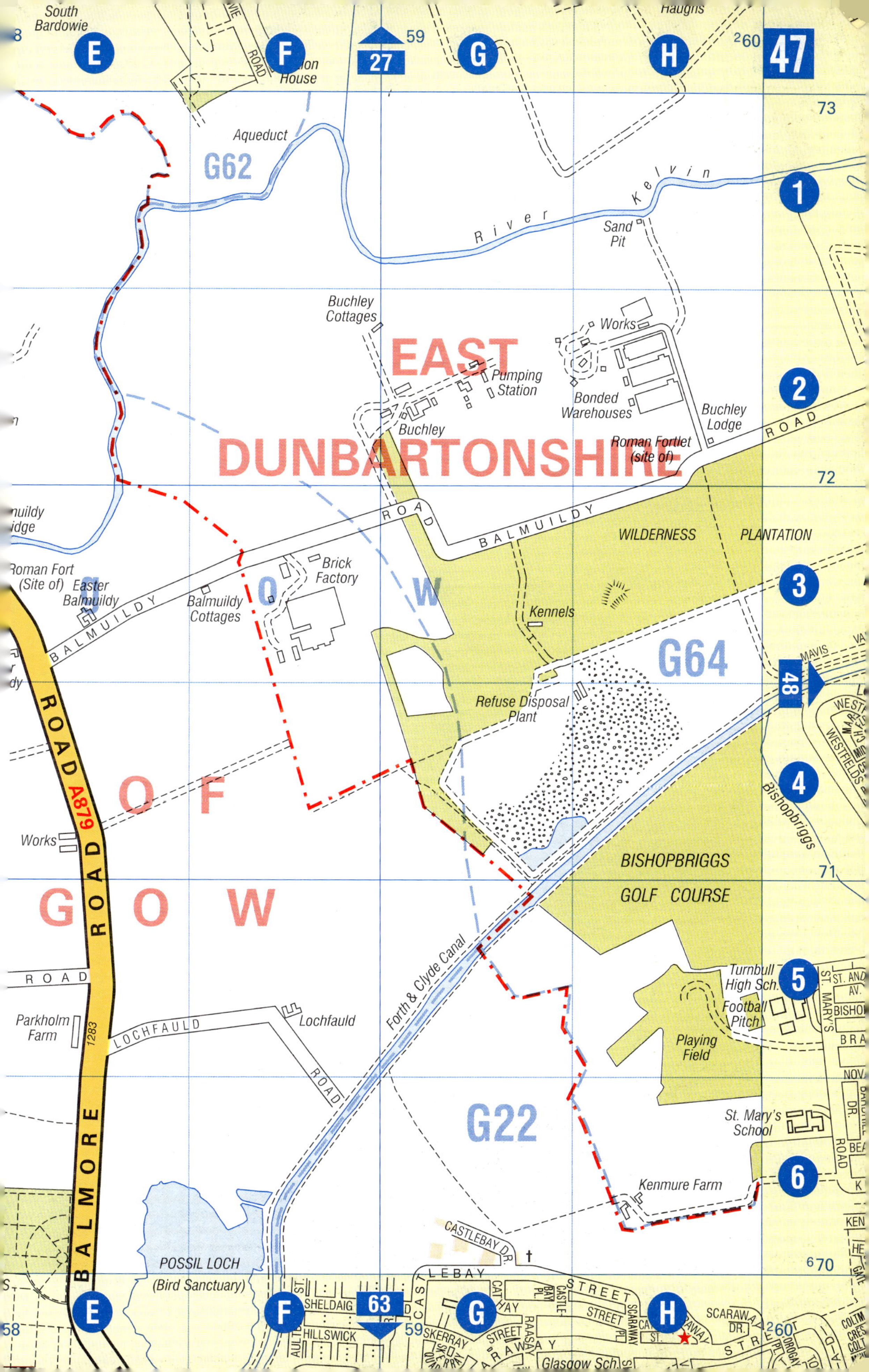
South Bardowie
Haughs
E
F
G
H
27
59
260
73
Aqueduct
G62
River Kelvin
Sand Pit
1
Buchley Cottages
Works
EAST
Pumping Station
Bonded Warehouses
Buchley
Buchley Lodge
2
ROAD
DUNBARTONSHIRE
Roman Fortlet (site of)
72
BALMUILDY ROAD
WILDERNESS
PLANTATION
Roman Fort (Site of)
Easter Balmuildy
Brick Factory
Balmuildy Cottages
Kennels
3
G64
MAVIS
48
Refuse Disposal Plant
ROAD
A879
4
Bishopbriggs
Works
O
F
BISHOPBRIGGS GOLF COURSE
71
G
O
W
Forth & Clyde Canal
Turnbull High Sch.
Football Pitch
5
ROAD
Parkholm Farm
LOCHFAULD ROAD
Lochfauld
Playing Field
St. Mary's School
G22
BALMORE ROAD
6
Kenmure Farm
CASTLEBAY DR.
POSSIL LOCH (Bird Sanctuary)
670
SHELDAIG
63
HILLSWICK
59
CASTLEBAY STREET
SKERRAY
STREET
SCARAWAY
SCARAWAY DR.
RAASAY
Glasgow Sch.
58
260

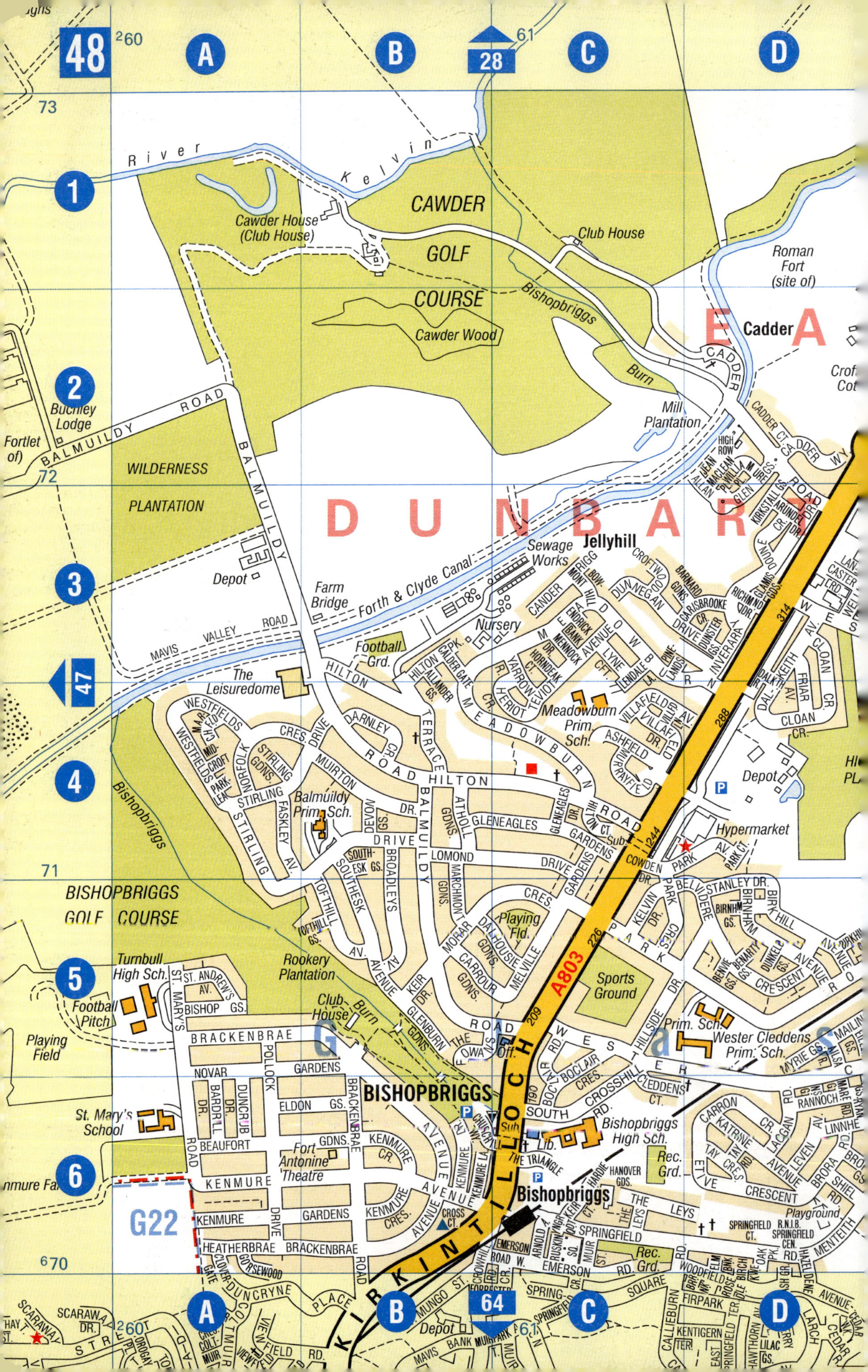
28
47
64
River Kelvin
CAWDER GOLF COURSE
Cawder House (Club House)
Club House
Cawder Wood
Bishopbriggs Burn
Roman Fort (site of)
Cadder
Mill Plantation
Buchley Lodge
BALMUILDY ROAD
WILDERNESS PLANTATION
DUNBARTON
Jellyhill
Sewage Works
Depot
Farm Bridge
Forth & Clyde Canal
MAVIS VALLEY ROAD
Football Grd.
Nursery
The Leisuredome
HILTON ROAD
MEADOWBURN
Meadowburn Prim. Sch.
Balmuildy Prim. Sch.
Hypermarket
BISHOPBRIGGS GOLF COURSE
Rookery Plantation
Club-House
Turnbull High Sch.
Football Pitch
Playing Field
Playing Fld.
Sports Ground
A803
Prim. Sch.
Wester Cleddens Prim. Sch.
BISHOPBRIGGS
St. Mary's School
Fort Antonine Theatre
Bishopbriggs High Sch.
Rec. Grd.
Bishopbriggs
KIRKINTILLOCH ROAD
G22
Playground
Depot

E
F
G
H
29
63
64
73
72
71
70
62
1
2
3
4
5
6
50
65
Hungryside Bridge (Drawbridge)
Glasgow Bri.
Slipway
Forth and Clyde Canal
TORRANCE RD.
A807
KIRKINTILLOCH ROAD
A803
Leafield
G66
Meiklehill
Works
Pav.
Playing Field
CROSSHILL
Cadder Cemetery
H.M. PRISON
Vehicle Testing Centre
Hazel Cottage
Works
Driver Testing Centre
B819
Bearhill
Park Burn
LOW MOSS PLANTATION
STRATHKELVIN RETAIL PARK
Playing Field
Industrial Estate
Sewage Works
Mid Boghead Cottage
Boghead
Wester Boghead
ROAD
Wester Boghead Holdings
Play
PINEWOOD CT.
GLENWOOD
GLENWOOD PL.
GLENWOOD RD.
GLENWOOD GS.
Football Grd.
Lochgrog
Works
Sub.
Works
Depot
MOSS
TATION
G64
Depot
Cadder Yard
Cottage
ROAD
South Loch
NORTH LANARKSHIRE
BURRA GS.
SELLA RD.
COLLA GS.
RONALDSAY PL.
WESTRAY PL.
STRONSAY PL.
DORNOCH PLACE
PENTLAND
LORNE CR.
CROMARTY AV.
MONYMUSK GS.
SPYNIE PL.
SOLWAY
KINTESSACK PL.
PITMEDDEN RD.
HARLAW GDS.
TWEEDSMUIR
BEMERSYDE
MOORFOOT
ABBOTSFORD
St. Helen's Prim. Sch.
BEAULY PL.
DR.
AVENUE
FLORA GDS.
SANDRA RD.
ELSPETH GDS.
WOODHILL
KIRRIEMUIR
Woodhill Prim. Sch.
Thomas Muir High Sch.
AVENUE
MEARNS WAY
DUNNOTTAR ST.
GRAINGER RD.
WESTERHILL
Westerhill
ROAD
Rushyhill
B812
ROBROYSTON ROAD
AUCHINAIRN ROAD
ROBROYSTON ROAD
W
THRUMS GDS.
SUNART GS.
CARNOUSTIE CRES.
OCHIL RD.
CARRADALE
ARDBEG AV.
TORR RD.
CARESTON PL.
CORTACHY PL.
DUNNICHEN GS.
MONKIE GS.
MURHEAD WY.
NEWTLE PL.
CARRICK RD.
MORAY PL.
BRECHIN
GANNOCHY DR.
CRINAN GS.
RANSON WY.
ST. CYRUS RD.
FETTERCAIRN
FINTRY CR.
MORNA
ANGUS
CERES GS.
BALMERINO PL.
FORGAN
Lumloch
Wester Lumloch
LUNDIE GS.
FALKLAND
DAIRSIE GDS.
LETHAM
LUNAN
FORFAR
GREENHILL
VALE WK.
WALK

Forth and Clyde Canal
High Gallowhill
Holy Family Prim. Sch.
Lenzie Academy
Lenzie Moss Prim. Sch.
Play. Fields
Lenzie
Lenzie Prim. Sch.
Meiklehill
Bearhill
Mid Boghead Cottage
Boghead
Wester Boghead
Playing Field
Playing Fields
CROSSHILL ROAD
B819
KIRKINTILLOCH RD.
AUCHINLOCH RD.
B757
LENZIE RD.
Loch Cottage
Loch Farm
GADLOCH
Gadloch Farm
Club House
South Loch
LENZIE GOLF COURSE
ROBROYSTON ROAD
B812
G64
Parkhillhead
Auchinloch
Auchinloch Prim. Sch.
Cardyke Plantation
Wester Auchinloch
LANGMUIRHEAD ROAD
Langmuirhead Farm
Cardyke Farm
Swimming Baths
Works
DUNBARTON
LANARK
30
49
66
64
265
73
72
71
670

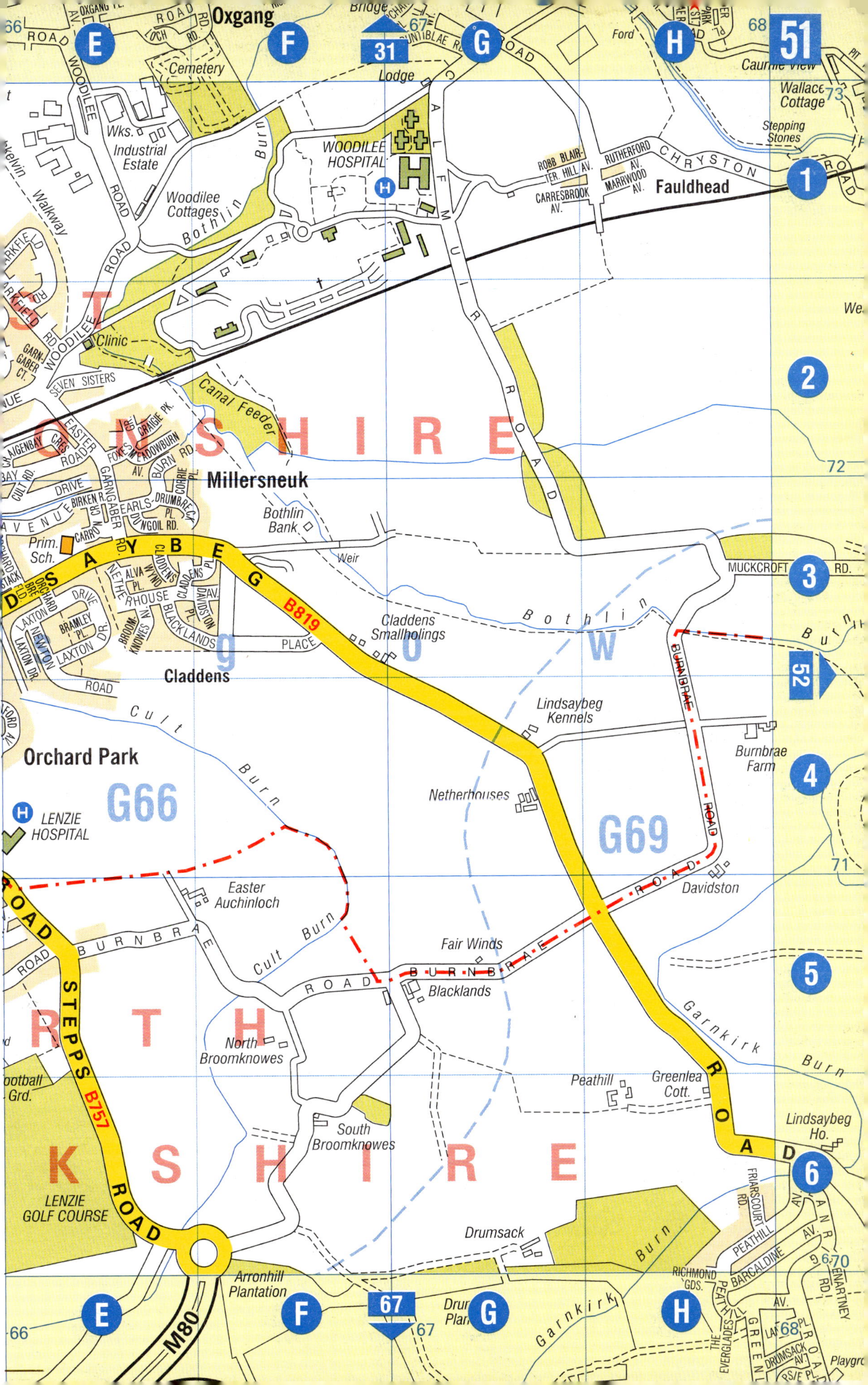
Oxgang
Cemetery
Wks.
Industrial Estate
Woodilee Cottages
WOODILEE HOSPITAL
Lodge
Fauldhead
CHRYSTON ROAD
ROBB TER.
BLAIR-HILL AV.
RUTHERFORD AV.
CARRESBROOK AV.
MARRWOOD AV.
Caurnie View
Wallace Cottage
Stepping Stones
Ford
Clinic
SEVEN SISTERS
Canal Feeder
Bothlin Burn
CALFMUIR ROAD
WOODILEE ROAD
Millersneuk
Bothlin Bank
Weir
MUCKCROFT RD.
Claddens Smallholdings
LINDSAYBEG RD.
B819
Claddens
BURNBRAE ROAD
Lindsaybeg Kennels
Burnbrae Farm
Orchard Park
G66
LENZIE HOSPITAL
Cult Burn
Netherhouses
G69
Easter Auchinloch
Davidston
Fair Winds
Blacklands
BURNBRAE ROAD
Garnkirk Burn
North Broomknowes
Peathill
Greenlea Cott.
South Broomknowes
Lindsaybeg Ho.
STEPPS ROAD
B757
LENZIE GOLF COURSE
Drumsack
Arronhill Plantation
M80
GARNKIRK ROAD
FRIARSCOURT RD.
PEATHILL AV.
BARCALDINE AV.
RICHMOND GDS.
THE EVERGLADES
Football Grd.
STIRLINGSHIRE
LANARKSHIRE
31
67
52
E F G H
1 2 3 4 5 6
66 67 68 70 71 72 73

52
68
69
A
B
C
D
32
51
68
1
2
3
4
5
6
72
73
71
70
Cawmie View
Depot
Wallace Cottage
Stepping Stones
Gambeck
Fauldhead
CHRYSTON ROAD
Luggie
EAST DUNBAR
Drumshanty
Sauchenhall
G66
Wester Bedcow
Easter Bedcow
East Muckcroft
MUCKCROFT ROAD
Glas
AUCHENGEICH ROAD
Bothlin Burn
Burn
Pav.
Football Grd.
Lodge
Sewage Works
Works
Bridgend
Burnbrae Farm
BURNBRAE ROAD
Davidston
Hill of Chryston
GARTFERRY STREET
GARTFERRY ROAD
EAST GARTFERRY RD.
Glenmanor Prim. Sch.
Play. Fld.
G69
MAILERBEG GDNS.
EDINGTON GDNS.
GLENVIEW
APPLECROSS GS.
GLENAPP PL.
TINTAGEL GS.
BODMIN GS.
HAYLE GS.
TRURO AV.
CAMBOURNE RD.
PENZANCE WAY
ST. IVES RD.
STEPPS ROAD
PORTREATH RD.
St. Michael's Prim. Sch.
PERRAN GS.
GLENMANOR AV.
DRUMVALE DR.
NORTHCROFT RD.
MEADOWHEAD AV.
GREENWOOD AV.
GARTFERRY AV.
BLACKWOOD GS.
BRAESIDE
BURNBRAE AV.
LANGDALE ROAD
Liby.
KELVIN DR.
GLENMANOR RD.
GLENCAIRN DR.
PLEAK NOWE
CASTLE GS.
GLENBURN AV.
HILLTOP RD.
EASTWOOD RD.
NETHERHILL RD.
LAVEROCK TER.
HEATHER AV.
Moodiesburn
The Glen
NORTH
Garnkirk Burn
LINDSAYBEG ROAD
Lindsaybeg Ho.
B757
Lanrigg
Chryston
LANRIGG AV.
BARGALDINE AV.
PEATHILL AV.
GLENARTNEY RD.
MAIN STREET
SOLWAY PL.
CROMARTY PL.
BEAULY PL.
DORNOCH PL.
DEAN CR.
CHRYSTON ROAD
PENTLAND ROAD
Millbrae Farm
Millbrae Nursery
Bothlin Burn
Bedlay Castle
Chryston Mains
A80
CUMBERNAULD ROAD
MAHON CT.
Bedlay Cemetery
BEECHWOOD GDNS.
Chryston Prim. Sch.
Chryston High. Sch.
CHRYSTON VALLEY BUSINESS CEN.
MORAY PL.
HILLCREST RD.
THE EVERGLADES
DRUMSACK AV.
Playground
Nicholson
Burn

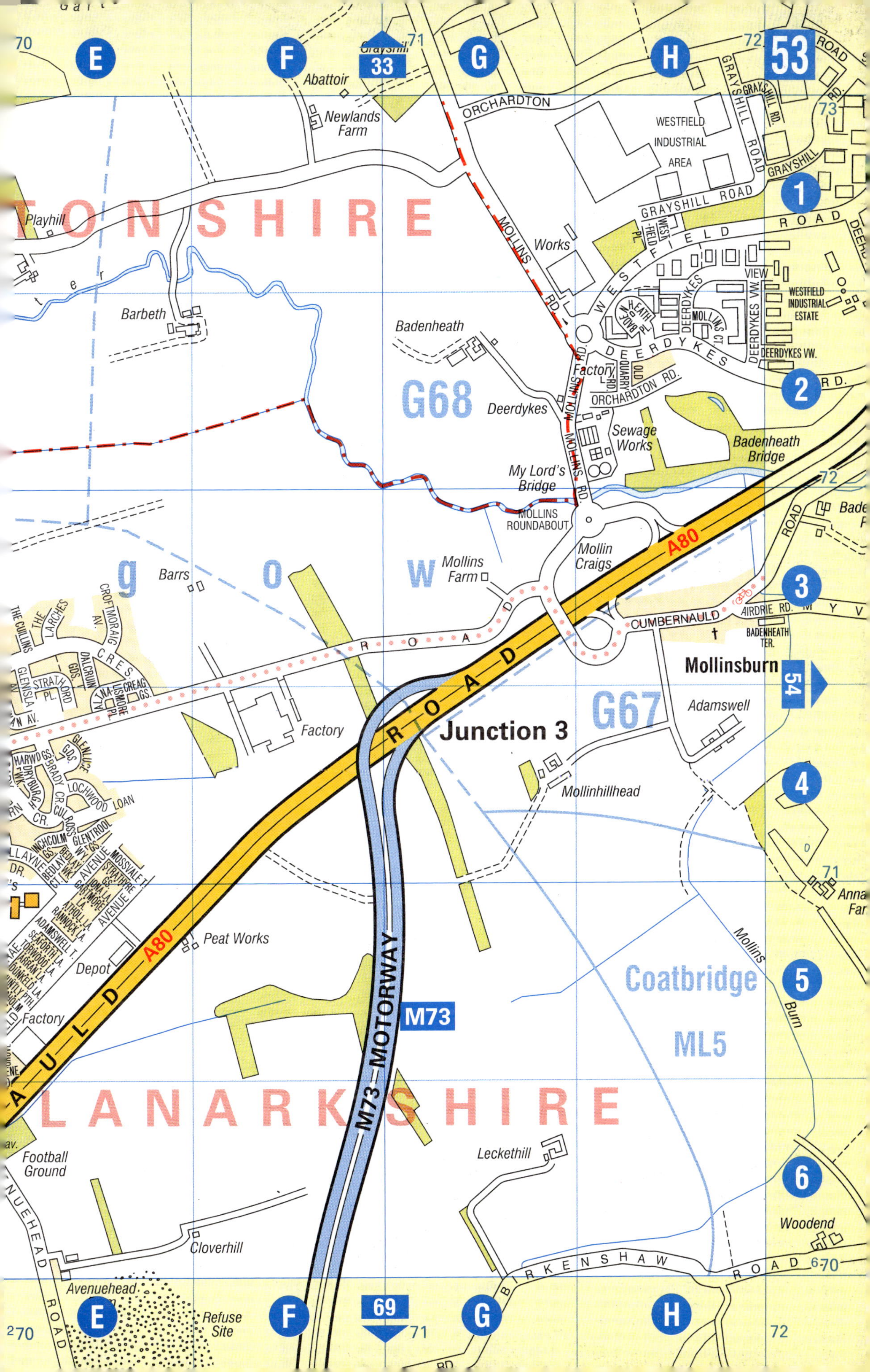

E
F
G
H
33
54
69
M73
A80
Abattoir
Newlands Farm
ORCHARDTON
WESTFIELD INDUSTRIAL AREA
GRAYSHILL ROAD
GRAYSHILL RD.
GRAYSHILL
ROAD
TONSHIRE
Playhill
Barbeth
MOLLINS RD.
Works
WESTFIELD ROAD
WESTFIELD INDUSTRIAL ESTATE
DEERDYKES RD.
DEERDYKES VW.
DEERDYKES VIEW
MOLLINS CT.
BADENHEATH PL.
QUARRY RD.
Factory
OLD ORCHARDTON RD.
Badenheath
G68
Deerdykes
Sewage Works
Badenheath Bridge
My Lord's Bridge
MOLLINS ROUNDABOUT
Mollin Craigs
Mollins Farm
Barrs
g o w
CUMBERNAULD ROAD
AIRDRIE RD.
BADENHEATH TER.
Mollinsburn
CROFTMORAIG AV.
CRES.
THE LARCHES
THE CUILLINS
GLENISLA
DALCRUIN GDS.
STRATHORD PL.
ALTNACREAG GDS.
LISMORE PL.
Factory
Adamswell
G67
Junction 3
Mollinhillhead
LOCHWOOD LOAN
GLENLUCE GDS.
HARWOOD GDS.
DRYBURGH WK.
BRADY CR.
CULROSS
GLENTROOL
INCHCOLM GDS.
BEDLAY CT.
MOSSVALE
STRATHYRE AVENUE
IONA LA.
GARTMORE LA.
ATHOLL LA.
RANNOCK LA.
SEAFORTH LA.
TORWOOD LA.
ARRAN LA.
DUNKELD LA.
ADAMSWELL T.
Peat Works
Depot
Factory
MOTORWAY
Coatbridge
ML5
Mollins Burn
LANARKSHIRE
Football Ground
Leckethill
Cloverhill
Woodend
BIRKENSHAW ROAD
Avenuehead
AVENUEHEAD ROAD
Refuse Site
70
71
72
73
1
2
3
4
5
6

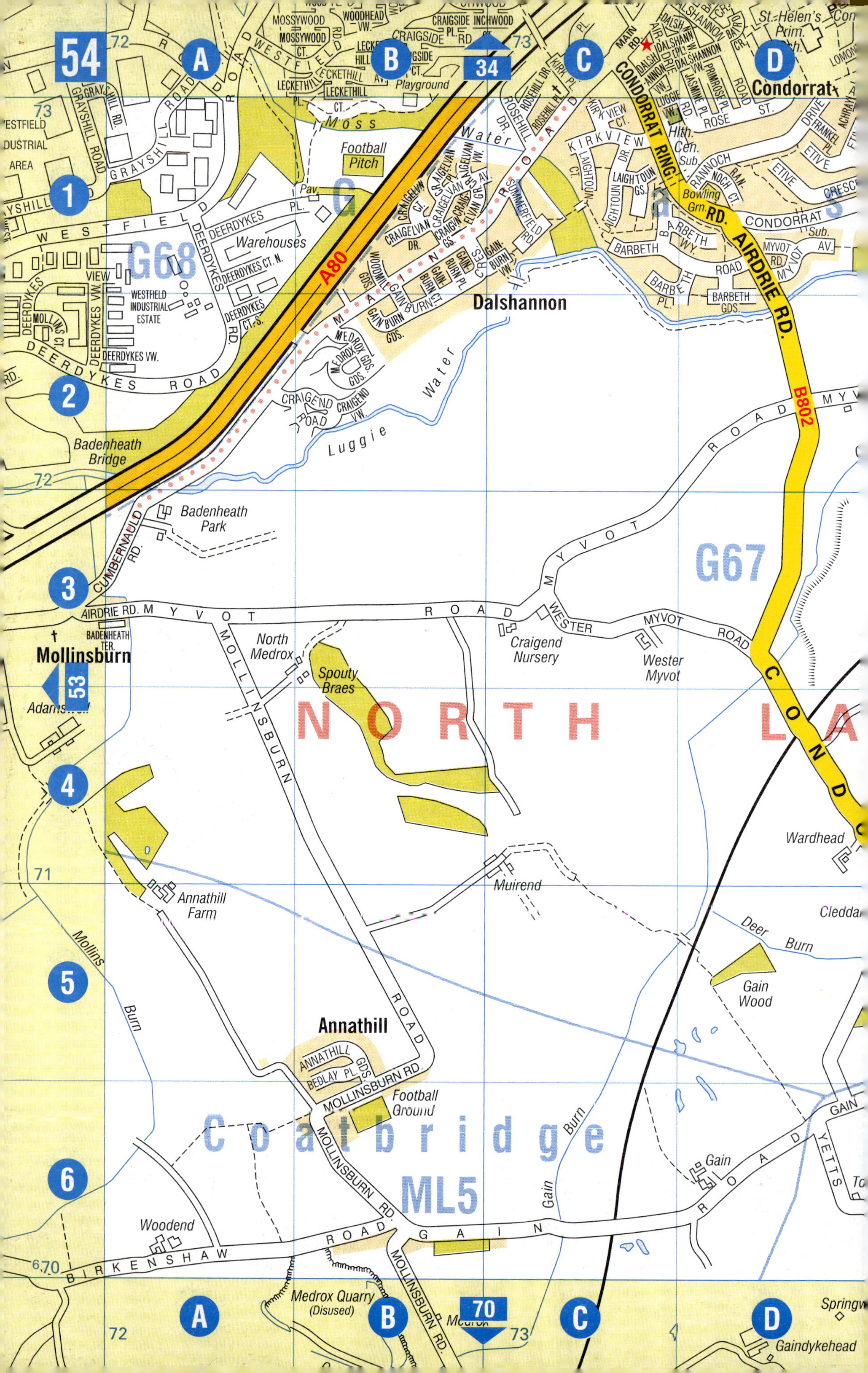
A
B
C
D
1
2
3
4
5
6
34
53
70
72
73
71
70
G68
G67
ML5
A80
B802
Condorrat
Dalshannon
Mollinsburn
Annathill
Coatbridge
NORTH LA
Westfield Industrial Area
Westfield Industrial Estate
Warehouses
Football Pitch
Pav.
Playground
Moss Water
Luggie Water
Badenheath Bridge
Badenheath Park
Badenheath Ter.
North Medrox
Spouty Braes
Craigend Nursery
Wester Myvot
Wardhead
Muirend
Annathill Farm
Mollins Burn
Deer Burn
Gain Wood
Gain Burn
Gain
Football Ground
Woodend
Medrox Quarry (Disused)
Gaindykehead
St. Helen's Prim. Sch.
Hlth. Cen.
Bowling Grn.
Sub.
Westfield Road
Grayshill Road
Grayshill Rd.
Deerdykes Road
Deerdykes Pl.
Deerdykes Ct. N.
Deerdykes Ct. S.
Deerdykes View
Deerdykes Vw.
Mollins Ct.
Cumbernauld Rd.
Airdrie Rd.
Myvot Road
Wester Myvot Road
Mollinsburn Road
Mollinsburn Rd.
Annathill Gds.
Bedlay Pl.
Birkenshaw Road
Gain Road
Yetts
Main Road
Condorrat Ring Rd.
Airdrie Rd.
Condorrat Road
Craigend Road
Craigend Vw.
Medrox Gds.
Gainburn Gds.
Gainburn Ct.
Gainburn Pl.
Gainburn Cres.
Gainburn Vw.
Woodmill Gds.
Craigelvan Ct.
Craigelvan Dr.
Craigelvan Pl.
Craigelvan Gro.
Craigelvan Vw.
Craigelvan Av.
Summerfield Rd.
Rosehill Dr.
Rosehill Pl.
Kirk Pl.
Kirkview Ct.
Kirkview Dr.
Laightoun Ct.
Laightoun Gs.
Laightoun Dr.
Barbeth Wy.
Barbeth Road
Barbeth Pl.
Barbeth Gds.
Myvot Rd.
Myvot Av.
Rannoch Dr.
Rannoch Ct.
Rose St.
Primrose Pl.
Jasmine Rd.
Dalshannon Vw.
Dalshannon Pl.
Dalshannon Way
Dalshannon Rd.
Luggie Vw.
Annon Dr.
Etive Drive
Etive Pl.
Frankel
Achray
Craigside Pl.
Craigside Rd.
Inchwood
Mossywood Rd.
Mossywood Ct.
Woodhead Vw.
Leckethill Av.
Leckethill Ct.
Leckethill Pl.
Lomond

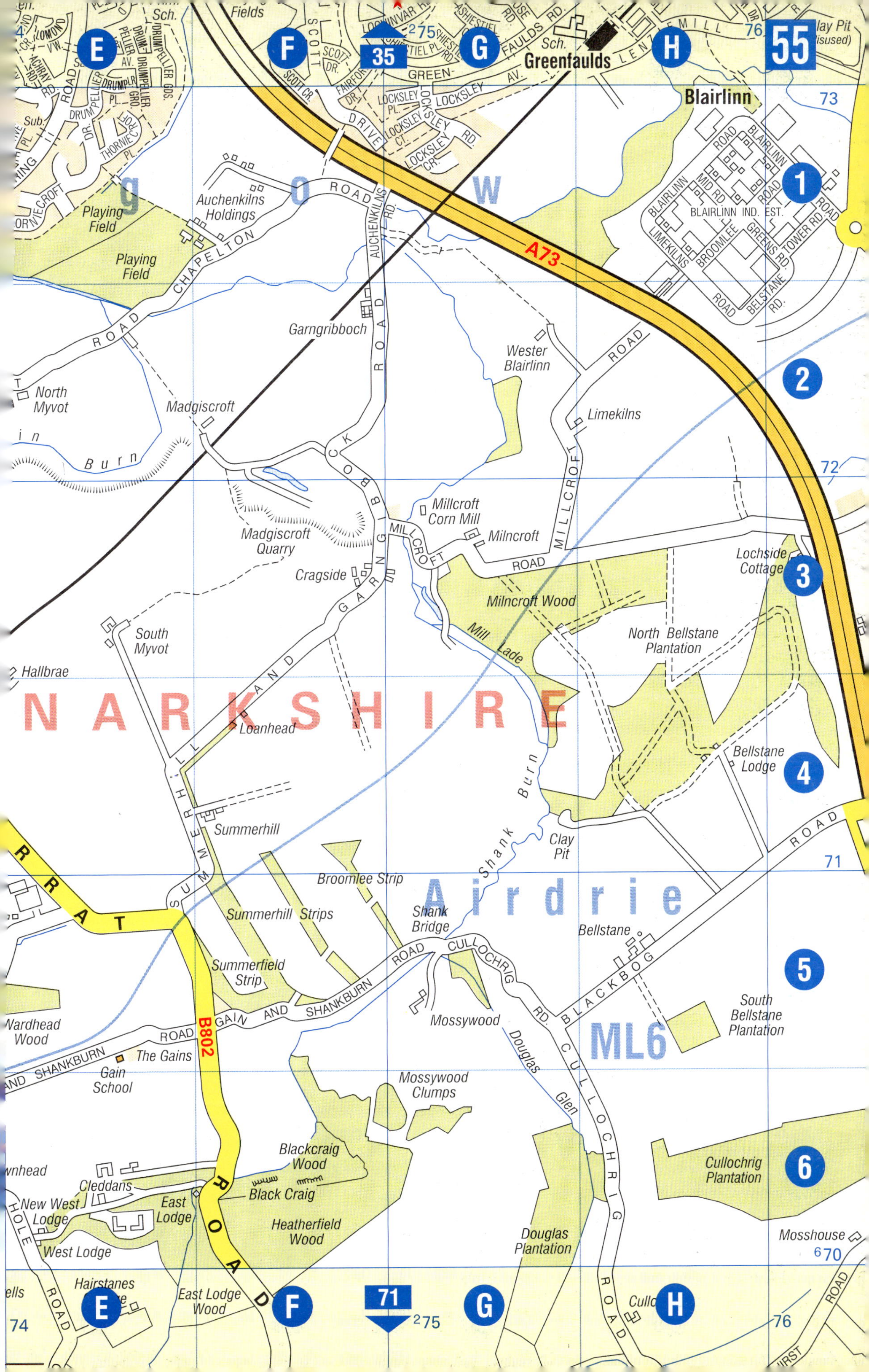

E
F
G
H
35
275
76
Greenfaulds
Sch.
FAULDS RD.
LENZIE MILL
Clay Pit (disused)
Blairlinn
73
BLAIRLINN IND. EST.
BLAIRLINN RD.
MID RD.
LIMEKILNS
BROOMLEE
GREENS RD.
TOWER RD.
BELSTANE RD.
LOCKSLEY AV.
LOCKSLEY PL.
LOCKSLEY CT.
LOCKSLEY CR.
LOCKSLEY RD.
FAIRFORD DR.
SCOTT DR.
SCOTT CR.
GREEN
Fields
DRUMPELLIER AV.
DRUMPELLIER PL.
DRUMPELLIER GDS.
THORNIECROFT PL.
Sch.
Sub.
Playing Field
Playing Field
Auchenkilns Holdings
ROAD
CHAPELTON ROAD
AUCHENKILNS RD.
g o w
A73
1
2
3
4
5
6
Garngribboch
Wester Blairlinn
Limekilns
North Myvot
Madgiscroft
Burn
72
Millcroft Corn Mill
Milncroft
MILLCROFT ROAD
Madgiscroft Quarry
Cragside
Lochside Cottage
Milncroft Wood
Mill Lade
North Bellstane Plantation
South Myvot
Hallbrae
GARNGIBBOCK
HILL AND GARNGIBBOCK ROAD
LANARKSHIRE
Loanhead
Bellstane Lodge
Shank Burn
Summerhill
Clay Pit
71
Broomlee Strip
Airdrie
Summerhill Strips
Shank Bridge
Bellstane
Summerfield Strip
GAIN AND SHANKBURN ROAD
CULLOCHRIG RD.
BLACKBOG ROAD
B802
Mossywood
ML6
South Bellstane Plantation
Wardhead Wood
The Gains
Gain School
Douglas Glen
Mossywood Clumps
Blackcraig Wood
Black Craig
Cullochrig Plantation
Cleddans
New West Lodge
East Lodge
Heatherfield Wood
Douglas Plantation
Mosshouse
670
West Lodge
Hairstanes
East Lodge Wood
71
275
74
76
CULLOCHRIG ROAD
ROAD

Junction 30
40
Dargavel Road
Linburn
West
East Craigend
Old Greenock Road
Millfield
Lochranza
Craigmuir
Greenock
M8 Motorway
Linburn Plantation
North Lodge
Southbar House
M8
A8
Lin Burn
Tappock Clu
Renfre
Nether Southbar
Bishopton
North Commonside
PA7
Hareshaw
Lin Burn
Re
East Fulwood
Johnstone
Georgetown
M8
Houston Road
Dargavel Burn
B790
Dargavel Bridge
Barnhill
Netherfield
PA6
Selvieland
Paisley
River Gryfe
Moss
Fulwood
PA3
Fulwood Mains Cottages
Road
Birkenhead
76
Fulwood Bridge

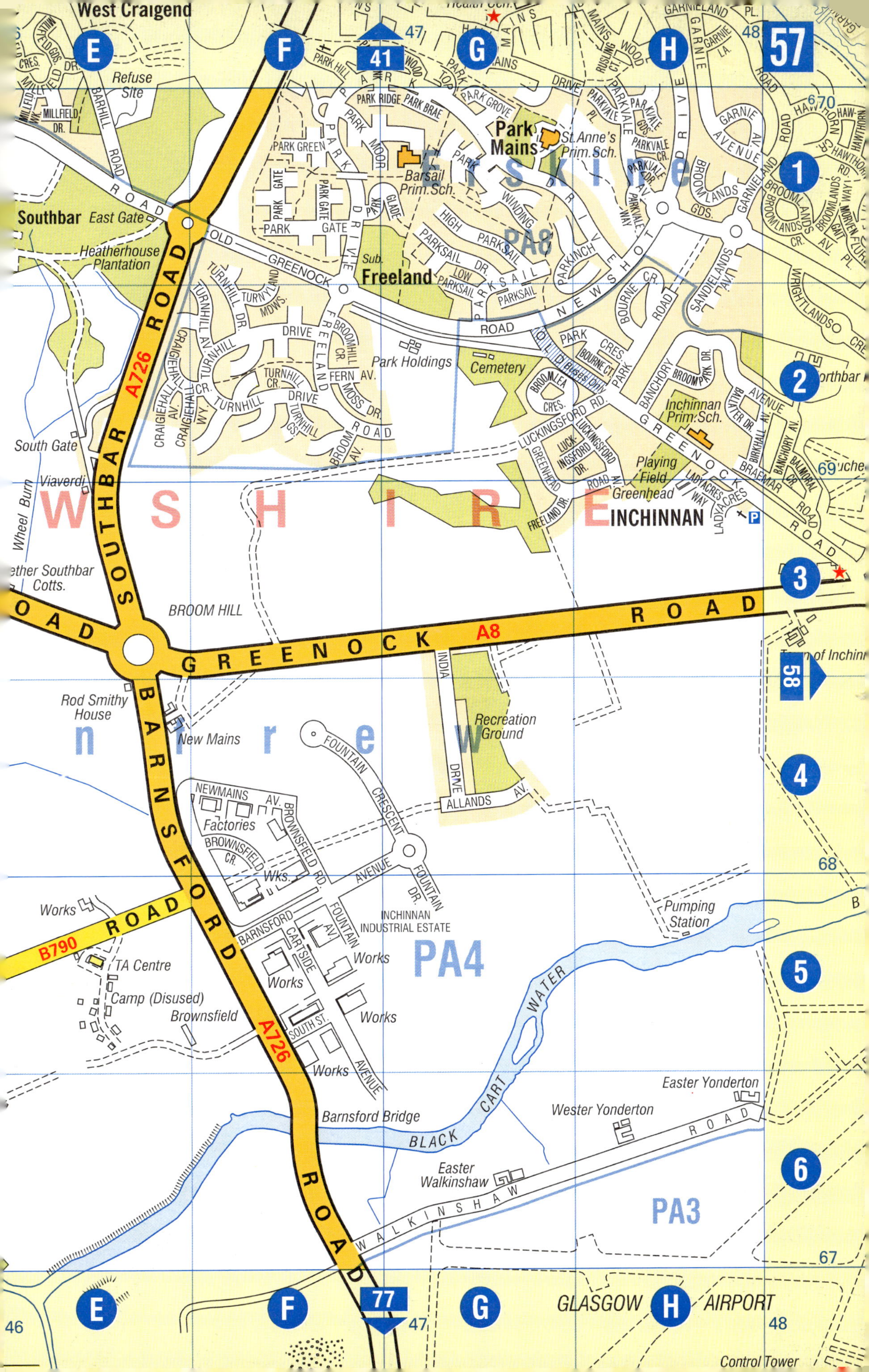
West Craigend
Refuse Site
MILLFIELD DR.
BARHILL ROAD
Southbar
East Gate
Heatherhouse Plantation
SOUTHBAR ROAD
A726
OLD GREENOCK ROAD
PARK RIDGE
PARK BRAE
PARK GROVE
PARK GREEN
PARK GATE
PARK MOOR
PARK DRIVE
PARK GLADE
Barsail Prim.Sch.
Park Mains
St.Anne's Prim.Sch.
Erskine
PA8
HIGH PARKSAIL
PARKSAIL DR.
LOW PARKSAIL
WINDING PARK
PARKINCH
PARKVALE DR.
PARKVALE CR.
PARKVALE WAY
MAINS DRIVE
MAINS WOOD
RUSLING CT.
GARNIELAND RD.
GARNIE AVENUE
GARNIE LA.
GARNIE PL.
NEWSHOT DRIVE
BROOMLANDS GDS.
BROOMLANDS CR.
BROOMLANDS AV.
BROOMLANDS WAY
SANDIELANDS AV.
WRIGHTLANDS CRES.
HAWTHORN CR.
Sub.
Freeland
TURNHILL DR.
TURNHILL AV.
TURNHILL CR.
TURNHILL DRIVE
TURNHILL GS.
TURNYLAND MDWS.
CRAIGIEHALL AV.
CRAIGIEHALL CR.
CRAIGIEHALL WY.
FREELAND DRIVE
BROOMHILL CR.
FERN AV.
MOSS DR.
BROOM ROAD
BROOM AV.
Park Holdings
Cemetery
BROOMLEA CRES.
BOURNE CT.
BOURNE CRES.
BOURNE CR.
PARK ROAD
BANCHORY AVENUE
BROOMPARK DR.
BALLATER DR.
BIRKHALL AV.
BANCHORY AV.
BALMORAL CR.
BRAEMAR ROAD
Inchinnan Prim.Sch.
Playing Field
LUCKINGSFORD RD.
LUCKINGSFORD DR.
LUCKINGSFORD AV.
GREENHEAD ROAD
Greenhead
FREELAND DR.
LADYACRES WAY
LADYACRES
INCHINNAN
GREENOCK ROAD
South Gate
Viaverdi
Wheel Burn
RENFREWSHIRE
Nether Southbar Cotts.
BROOM HILL
GREENOCK ROAD
A8
Rod Smithy House
BARNSFORD ROAD
New Mains
INDIA DRIVE
Recreation Ground
ALLANDS AV.
FOUNTAIN CRESCENT
NEWMAINS AV.
Factories
BROWNSFIELD CR.
BROWNSFIELD RD.
Wks.
FOUNTAIN AVENUE
FOUNTAIN DR.
INCHINNAN INDUSTRIAL ESTATE
PA4
Works
B790
TA Centre
Camp (Disused)
Brownsfield
CARTSIDE AV.
SOUTH ST.
Pumping Station
BLACK CART WATER
Barnsford Bridge
Easter Yonderton
Wester Yonderton
Easter Walkinshaw
WALKINSHAW ROAD
PA3
GLASGOW AIRPORT
Control Tower
Town of Inchinnan
Northbar
Bouche
41
77
58

Causeway
42
CLYDEBANK
Clydebank District Museum
Clydebank
Lib.
HALL ST.
BRUCE ST.
CENTENARY CT.
WALLACE ST.
CHALMERS
ABBOTSFORD RD.
HUME ST.
BELMONT ST.
CANAL ST.
Bus Stat.
ARGYLL
CART ST.
ATLAS RD.
CUNARD CT.
Works
Dock
R I V E R C
Erskine PA8
GARNIE AVENUE
GARNIE AV.
GARNIELAND ROAD
HAWTHORN CR.
HAWTHORN AV.
HAWTHORN WAY
BROOMLANDS CR.
BROOMLANDS AV.
BROOMLANDS RD.
MORVEN WAY
GAIT PL.
FLURES AV.
FLURES DRIVE
FLURES CRES.
FLURES PL.
BROOM GDS.
SANDIELANDS AV.
WRIGHTLANDS CRES.
Sandieland Wood
BANCHORY DR.
BROOM PARK DR.
Northbar House
AVENUE
Inchinnan Prim. Sch.
BIRKHALL AV.
BANCHORY AV.
BALMORAL CR.
BRAEMAR RD.
Teucheen Wood
Florish Cottage
Works
Pump House
Old Mains
OLD GREENOCK ROAD
LADYACRES WAY
LADYACRES
INCHINNAN
R E N F R E W S H I R E
Depot
BEARDMORE COTTAGES
Florish
G R E E N O C K ROAD
A8
Town of Inchinnan
Colin's Isle
RENFREW GOL
57
Portnauld
R e n
BLACK CART WATER
Inchinnan Bridge
Swing Bridge
Depot
Club Ho.
GRYFFE AV.
AVENUE
Hotel
WEST LODGE RD.
ARGYLL
Warehouses
24
INCHINNAN
Pumping Station
White Cart Bridge
ROAD
KIRKLANDNEUK CR.
KIRKLANDNEUK
SUNART AV.
LAGGAN TER.
MORAR PL.
RD.
CRERAN DR.
MOIDART AV.
VENNACHER ROAD
LEVEN SQ.
NESS RD.
KIRKLANDNEUK ROAD
ARD
Kirklandneuk
Pavs.
Kirklandneuk Park
MCCLUE AV.
Easter Yonderton
ROAD
Paisley PA3
ABBOTSINCH ROAD
WHITE CART WATER
NETHERGREEN WYND
PORTERFIELD ROAD
Netherton
GLASGOW AIRPORT
Works
CLARK ST.
VICTORIA DR.
BROWN ST.
Prim. Sch.
Porterfield
78
Works
Rec. Grd.
Control Tower
FRENCH ST.
MOORPARK SQ.
Factory
A B C D
1 2 3 4 5 6
48 49
67 68 69 670

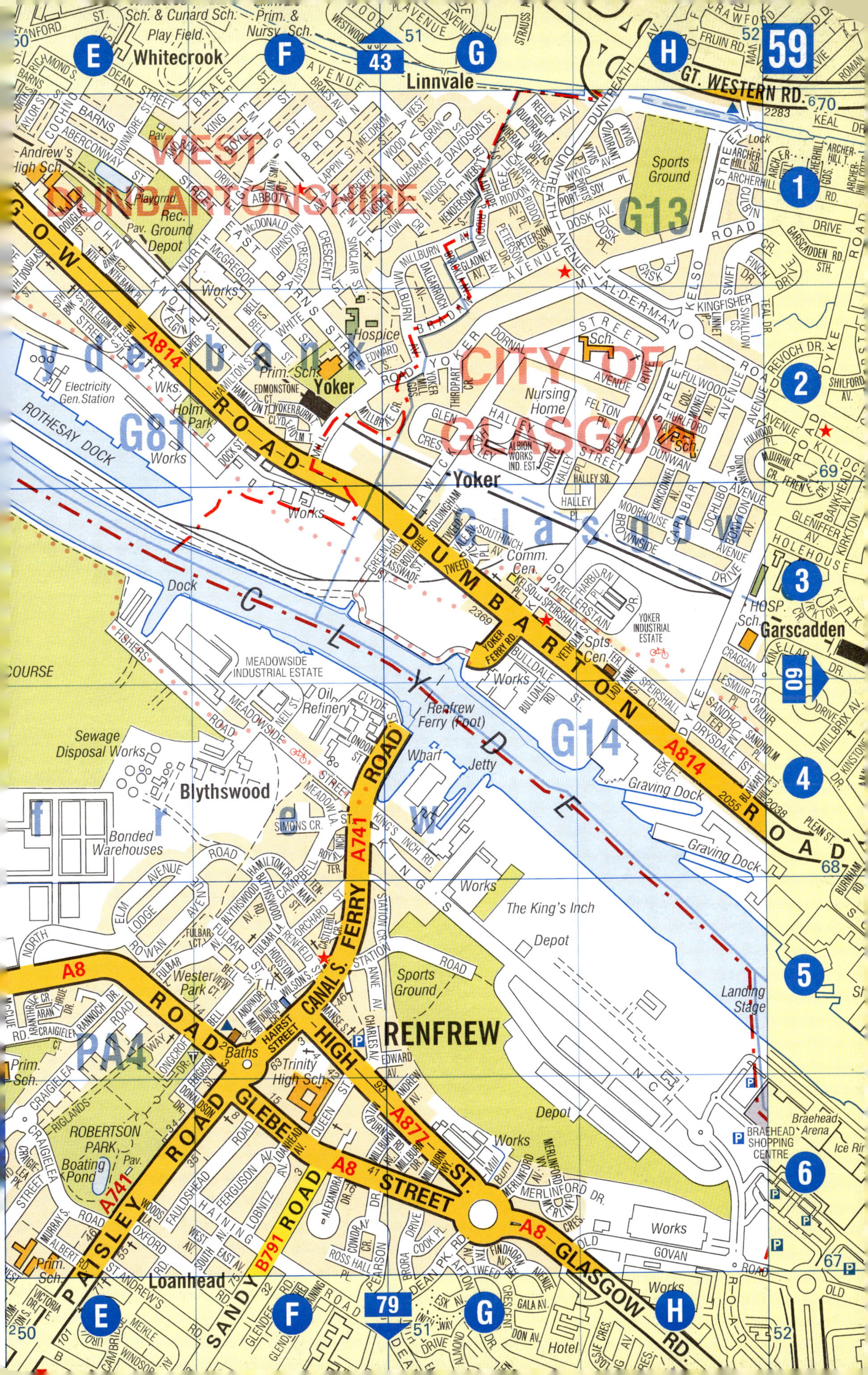

E
F
G
H
43
51
52
Linnvale
Whitecrook
Play Field
Sch. & Cunard Sch.
Prim. & Nursy. Sch.
GT. WESTERN RD.
670
2283
Lock
Sports Ground
G13
WEST DUNBARTONSHIRE
CITY OF GLASGOW
Clydebank
Glasgow
Renfrew
Playgrnd.
Rec. Ground
Pav.
Depot
Andrew's High Sch.
Works
Hospice
Prim. Sch.
Yoker
Nursing Home
Sch.
Electricity Gen. Station
Wks.
Holm Park
G81
ROTHESAY DOCK
Dock
A814
DUMBARTON ROAD
GLASGOW ROAD
DUNTREATH AVENUE
ALDERMAN ROAD
KELSO STREET
YOKER MILL ROAD
HALLEY STREET
Comm. Cen.
Spts. Cen.
YOKER INDUSTRIAL ESTATE
HOSP.
Sch.
Garscadden
60
69
68
2369
2055
2038
CLYDE
MEADOWSIDE INDUSTRIAL ESTATE
Oil Refinery
Renfrew Ferry (Foot)
Wharf
Jetty
G14
Graving Dock
Sewage Disposal Works
Blythswood
Bonded Warehouses
The King's Inch
Depot
Landing Stage
KING'S INCH ROAD
A741
FERRY ROAD
Sports Ground
RENFREW
A8
PAISLEY ROAD
Westerview Park Ct.
PA4
Baths
Trinity High Sch.
HIGH STREET
GLEBE STREET
A877
Prim. Sch.
ROBERTSON PARK
Boating Pond
Pav.
Works
Depot
BRAEHEAD SHOPPING CENTRE
Braehead Arena
Ice Rink
GOVAN ROAD
Works
Hotel
Loanhead
SANDY ROAD
B791
79
51
50
52
67
1
2
3
4
5
6

A
B
C
D
44
53
52
1
2
3
4
5
6
59
68
69
67
80
GREAT WESTERN RD.
A82
DUMBARTON ROAD
A814
VICTORIA PARK DRIVE
Forth & Clyde Canal (Dis.)
High Knightswood
Knightswood
KNIGHTSWOOD GOLF COURSE
Playing Field
Club House
Running Track
Knightswood Park
Garscadden Burn
G15
G13
G14
G51
KNIGHTSWOOD HOSPITAL
Garscadden
Scotstounhill
Scotstoun
Scotstoun Showground
Scotstoun Leisure Centre
Whiteinch
UNIVERSITY STRATHCLYDE (Jordanhill Campus)
Hostels
Playing Fields
Shipbuilding Yard
Works
RIVER CLYDE
Landing Stage
Braehead Arena
Ice Rinks
BRAEHEAD SHOPPING CENTRE
Maritime Heritage Centre
Retail Park
Graving Dock
Fossil Grove
Rec. Grd.
Comm. Cen.
Lib.
Blairdardie Prim. Sch.
Shieldhall
Depot

E
F
G
H
45
81
62
1
2
3
4
5
6
University of Glasgow
West of Scotland Science Park (Kelvin Campus)
Maryhill
A81
University of Glasgow (Veterinary Medicine)
G61
Dawsholm Park
Playing Fields
Dawsholm Bri.
Refuse Destructors
Dalsholm Industrial Estate
G20
Netherton
Sports Ground
Temple
Temple Swim. Pool
Forth & Clyde Canal
Works
Skaethorn Rd.
A739
Bearsden Road
Westerlands Glasgow Univ. Athletic Ground
Superstore
Anniesland
Glasgow High/ Kelvinside Rugby F.C.
The High Sch. of Glasgow
Glasgow Academicals Rugby F.C.
Great Western Road
A82
Anniesland Coll.
Kelvinside Academy War Mem. Grd.
Kelvindale
Cleveden Sec. Sch.
Kelvinside
Pond
G12
Whiteinch North Junction
Jordanhill
Gartnavel Royal Hospital
Gartnavel General Hospital
Cleveden Hosp.
Halls of Res.
Hyndland
Broomhill
G11
Crow Road
Balshagray Av.
Play. Fields
Victoria Park
Broomlea Sch.
Cross Park
Partickhill
Dowanhill
Partick
Expressway South

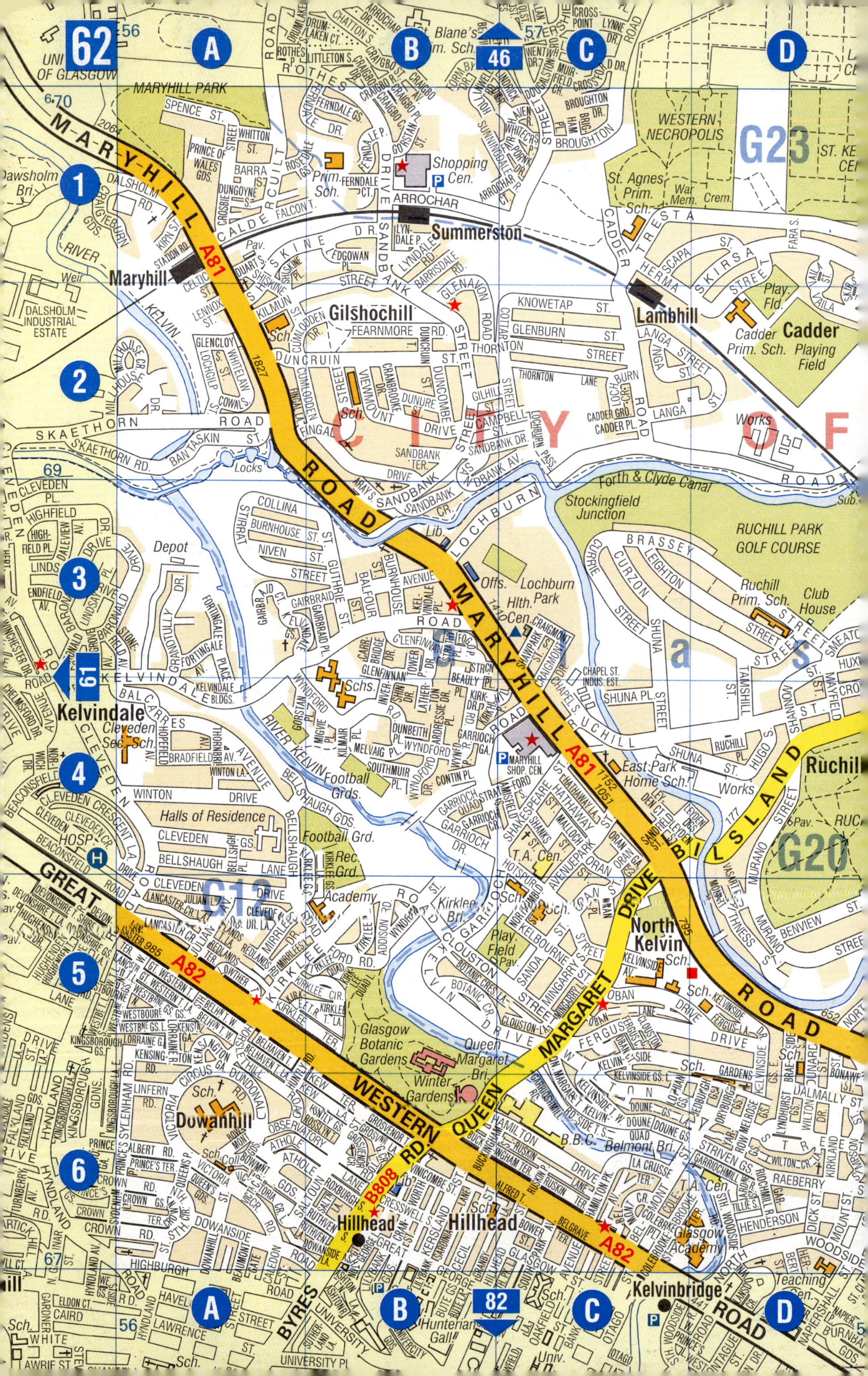

46
82
61
MARYHILL PARK
UNIV. OF GLASGOW
MARYHILL ROAD
A81
Dawsholm Bri.
DALSHOLM INDUSTRIAL ESTATE
RIVER KELVIN
Maryhill
Summerston
Shopping Cen.
Gilshochill
Lambhill
WESTERN NECROPOLIS
G23
St. Agnes Prim. Sch.
War Mem.
Crem.
Cadder
Cadder Prim. Sch.
Playing Field
CITY OF
SKAETHORN ROAD
Locks
Forth & Clyde Canal
Stockingfield Junction
RUCHILL PARK GOLF COURSE
Ruchill Prim. Sch.
Club House
Lochburn Park
Depot
Kelvindale
Cleveden Sec. Sch.
MARYHILL SHOP. CEN.
East Park Home Sch.
Ruchill
BILSLAND DRIVE
G20
Halls of Residence
Football Grd.
Rec. Grd.
Academy
G12
HOSP.
GREAT WESTERN RD.
A82
North Kelvin
Glasgow Botanic Gardens
Winter Gardens
Queen Margaret Bri.
QUEEN MARGARET DRIVE
Dowanhill
B808
Hillhead
B.B.C.
Belmont Bri.
Glasgow Academy
Kelvinbridge
Teaching Cen.
Hunterian Gall.
Univ.
BYRES ROAD
UNIVERSITY PL

E
F
G
H
47
59
260
670
83
1
2
3
4
5
6
64
69
68
67
POSSIL LOCH
(Bird Sanctuary)
Forth & Clyde Canal
BALMORE
A879
BALMORE INDUSTRIAL ESTATE
GLASGOW
Lambhill
Lambhill Bridge
Milton
Colston
Library
Milton Park
Milton Sch.
Glasgow Sch. for the Deaf
St. Augustine's Prim. & Sec. Schs.
Playing Fields
Chirnsyde Prim. Sch.
G22
Possilpark & Parkhouse
Ashfield
Our Lady of the Assumption Prim. Sch.
RUCHILL HOSPITAL
DRIVE
B808
HAWTHORN
STREET
POSSIL PARK TRADING CEN.
DENMARK STREET INDUS. CENTRE
Possil Park
Saracen Park
Keppoch Park
Hawthorn Prim. Sch.
Cowlairs West Junc.
COWLAIRS INDUSTRIAL ESTATE
Cowlairs
Partick Thistle F.C. (Firhill Park)
Wester Common Prim. Sch.
Firhill
Hamiltonhill
SARACEN ST.
St. Teresa's Prim. Sch.
COWLAIRS PARK (Rec. Grd.)
G21
Sighthill Prim. Sch.
SIGHTHILL CEMETERY
GARSCUBE ROAD
A81
OAKBANK INDUS. EST.
Warehouse
G4
KEPPOCHHILL
PORT DUNDAS INDUS. EST.
M8 FOOD PARK
CRAIGHALL RD.

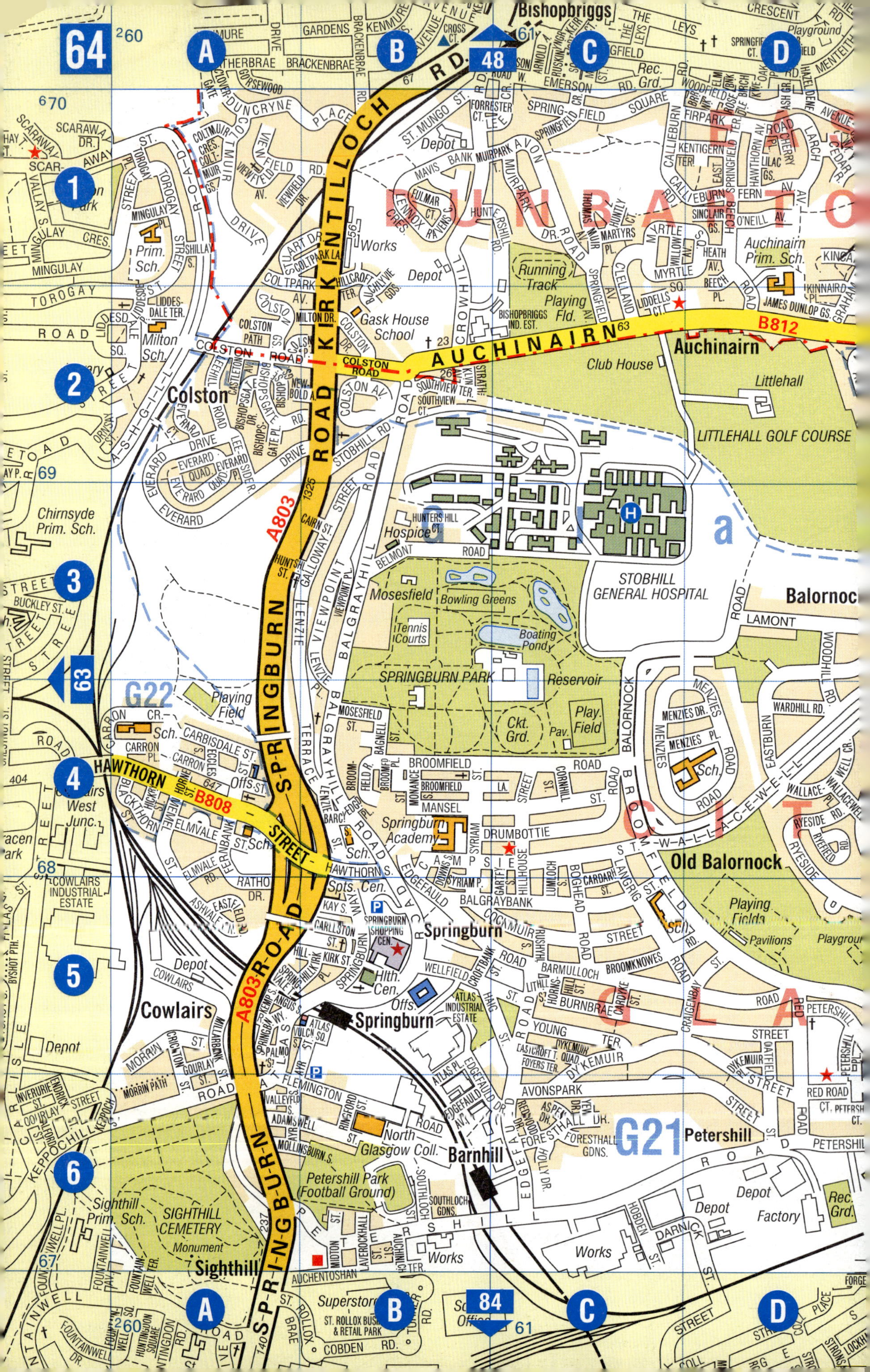

A B C D
1 2 3 4 5 6
48
61
63
84

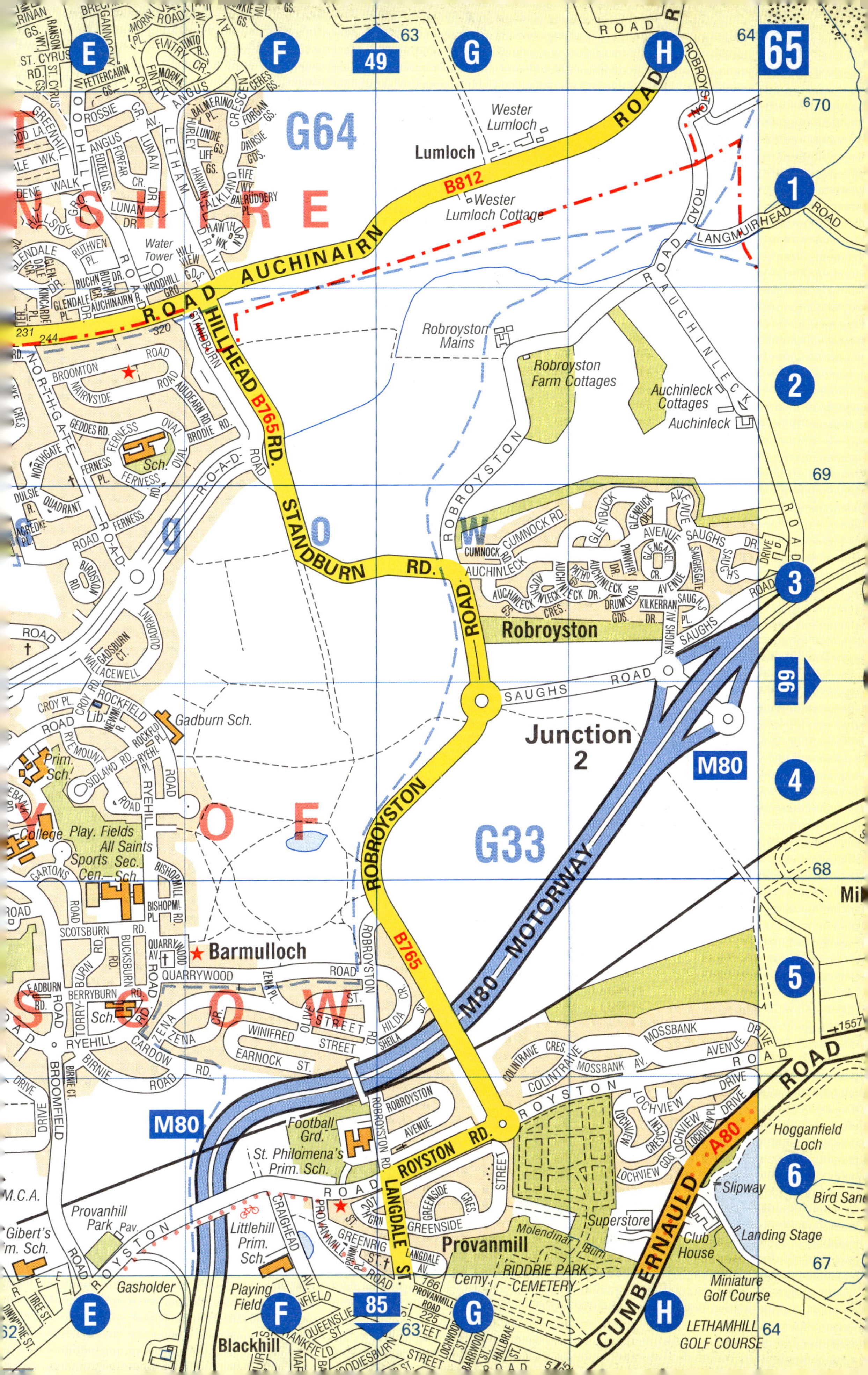
E
F
G
H
49
63
64
670
1
2
3
4
5
6
69
68
67
99
85
G64
G33
Lumloch
Wester Lumloch
Wester Lumloch Cottage
B812
AUCHINAIRN ROAD
ROBROYSTON ROAD
LANGMUIRHEAD ROAD
Robroyston Mains
Robroyston Farm Cottages
Auchinleck Cottages
Auchinleck
AUCHINLECK ROAD
HILLHEAD RD.
B765
STANDBURN RD.
STANDBURN
Robroyston
SAUGHS ROAD
Junction 2
M80
M80 MOTORWAY
ROBROYSTON ROAD
B765
Gadburn Sch.
Lib.
Prim. Sch.
College
Play. Fields
All Saints Sec. Sch.
Sports Cen.
Barmulloch
QUARRYWOOD ROAD
WINIFRED STREET
EARNOCK ST.
OLIVE STREET
Sch.
Football Grd.
St. Philomena's Prim. Sch.
ROYSTON RD.
ROYSTON ROAD
LANGDALE ST.
Provanmill
Superstore
RIDDRIE PARK CEMETERY
Cemy.
Molendinar Burn
A80
CUMBERNAULD ROAD
Hogganfield Loch
Slipway
Bird Sanc
Landing Stage
Club House
Miniature Golf Course
LETHAMHILL GOLF COURSE
MOSSBANK DRIVE
MOSSBANK AVENUE
MOSSBANK AV.
COLINTRAIVE CRES.
LOCHVIEW DRIVE
LOCHVIEW GDS.
LOCHVIEW CRES.
Provanhill Park
Pav.
Littlehill Prim. Sch.
CRAIGHEAD AV.
Gasholder
Playing Field
Blackhill
Gilbert's Sch.
M.C.A.
BROOMFIELD ROAD
RYEHILL ROAD
BISHOPMILL RD.
SCOTSBURN RD.
BUCKSBURN RD.
BERRYBURN RD.
NORTHGATE ROAD
BROOMTON ROAD
NAIRNSIDE ROAD
GEDDES RD.
FERNESS OVAL
FERNESS PL.
FERNESS RD.
AULDEARN RD.
BRODIE RD.
QUADRANT RD.
GADSBURN CT.
WALLACEWELL ROAD
ROCKFIELD RD.
RYEMOUNT RD.
SIDLAND RD.
CROY PL.
CROY RD.
GARTONS RD.
Water Tower
WOODHILL RD.
LUNAN DR.
LETHAM DR.
RUTHVEN PL.
GLENDALE PL.
Sch.
Mil
1557
N S H I R E
G O
O F
S G O W

A
B
C
D
50
64
265
670
69
68
67
1
2
3
4
5
6
65
86
LENZIE GOLF COURSE
Langmuirhead Farm
LANGMUIRHEAD ROAD
Cardyke Farm
G66
Cult Burn
Hillview Farm
Auchengree Farm
NORTH
ROBROYSTON ROAD
AUCHINLECK ROAD
Auchinleck Cottages
Auchinleck
M80 MOTORWAY
M80
SAUGHS DR.
SAUGHS ROAD
SAUGHS AV.
SAUGHS PL.
SAUGHSGATE
Saughs
SAUGHS ROAD
BOGSIDE ROAD
G
l
a
LENZIE ROAD
BOTHLIN DR.
Whitehill Farm
WHITEHILL FARM ROAD
ALEXANDRA AV.
CHURCH AV.
ANNIESDALE AV.
Rec.
VICTORIA RD.
WEST AV.
STATION RD
STEPPS
Garnkirk Burn
Junction 2
A80
G33
MILLERSNEUK CRES.
DUNALASTAIR
INGLENEUK AV.
LOCHEARNHEAD RD.
ST. FILLANS RD.
ALMOND DRIVE
BALLAIG CRESCENT
LAUNDRY LA.
LOCH ROAD
STATION ROAD
MILLERSNEUK
CESSNOCK ROAD
LOUDON RD.
COSHNEUK
FOURTH AV.
FIRST AV.
SECOND AV.
THIRD AV.
LEDNOCK RD.
COMRIE
STEPPSHILL TER.
Works
Millerston
CUMBERNAULD ROAD
1819
1790
1739
1650
1557
ROWALLAN TER.
The Tower
Ogilvie Athletic Ground
Running Track
Playing Field
Games Court
Pav.
Molendinar Burn
Playing Fields
Frankfield Loch
Craigendmuir Park
BLANEVIEW
CRAIGENDMUIR CARAVAN SITE
MOSSBANK DRIVE
MOSSBANK AVENUE
CITY OF
CARDOWAN MOSS
Hogganfield Loch
Bird Sanctuary
Landing Stage
Club House
Hogganfield Park
Miniature Golf Course
LETHAMHILL GOLF COURSE
Hogganfield
Ashcraig School
MOSSVALE
CARDRONA ST.
POWRIE ST.
Sch.
Football Grd.
GLENRAITH WLK.
MOSSVALE PATH
Craigend
CRAIGEND ROAD
MOSSVALE ROAD
GLENRAITH RD.
AVENUE END ROAD
Football Ground
GILBERTFIELD PATH
BIGTON ST.
BANFF ST.
BINNS ROAD
BAVELAW ST.
COLLESSIE DR.
CAMBUSKENNETH

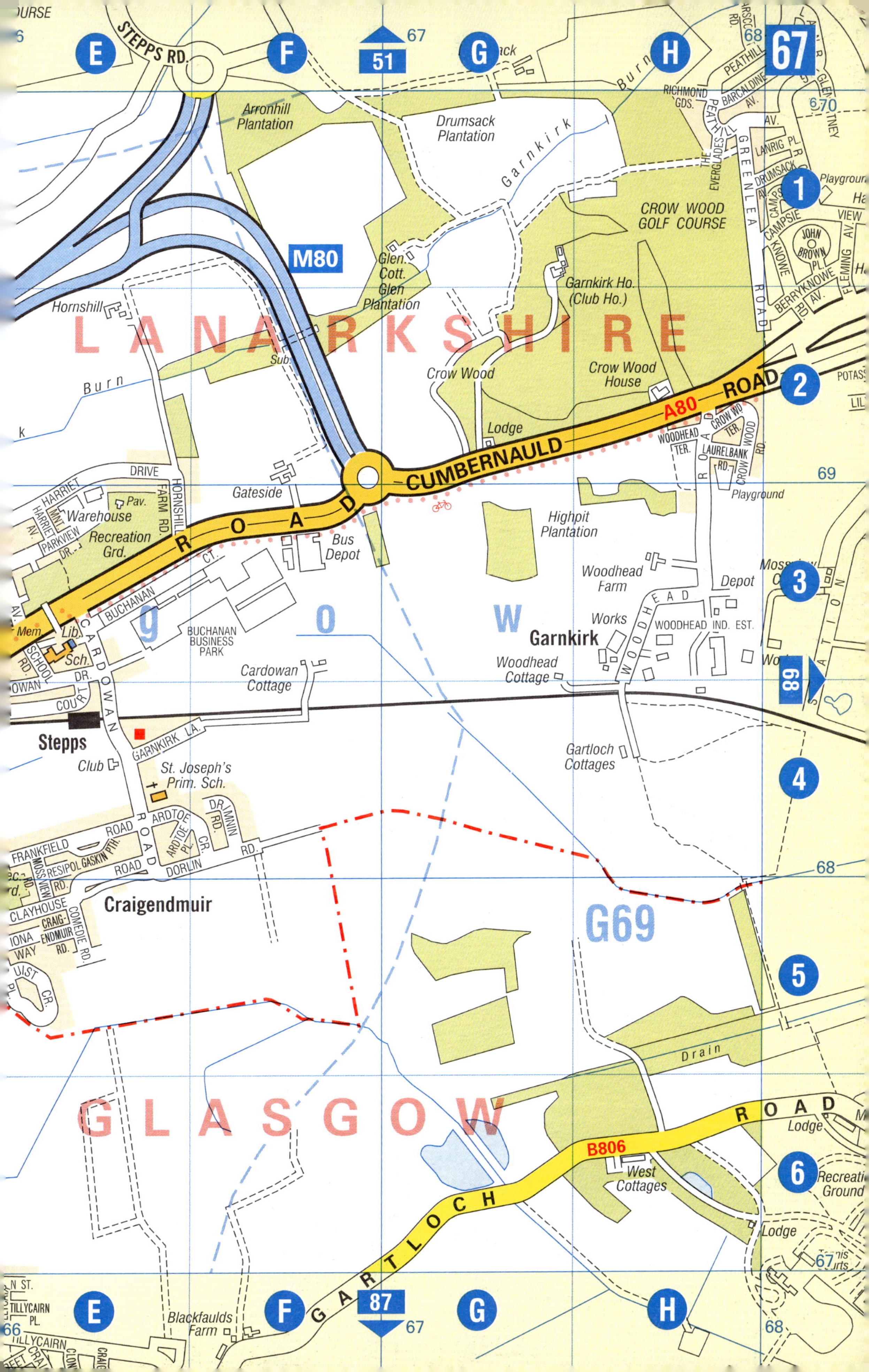
51
67
87
E
F
G
H
1
2
3
4
5
6
68
69
670
STEPPS RD.
Arronhill Plantation
Drumsack Plantation
Garnkirk Burn
M80
Glen Cott.
Glen Plantation
Hornshill
LANARKSHIRE
Sub.
Burn
Crow Wood
CROW WOOD GOLF COURSE
Garnkirk Ho. (Club Ho.)
Crow Wood House
Lodge
CUMBERNAULD ROAD
A80
Gateside
Pav.
Warehouse
Recreation Grd.
Bus Depot
Highpit Plantation
Woodhead Farm
Depot
Works
Garnkirk
WOODHEAD IND. EST.
WOODHEAD RD.
Woodhead Cottage
BUCHANAN BUSINESS PARK
BUCHANAN CT.
Cardowan Cottage
CARDOWAN RD.
Lib.
Sch.
Mem.
Stepps
Club
GARNKIRK LA.
St. Joseph's Prim. Sch.
Gartloch Cottages
Craigendmuir
G69
FRANKFIELD ROAD
DORLIN RD.
ARDTOE CR.
DRIMNIN RD.
CLAYHOUSE
CRAIGENDMUIR RD.
COMEDIE RD.
IONA WAY
UIST CR.
Drain
GLASGOW
GARTLOCH ROAD
B806
West Cottages
Lodge
Recreation Ground
Blackfaulds Farm
TILLYCAIRN PL.
RICHMOND GDS.
PEATHILL
BARCALDINE AV.
GREENLEA ROAD
THE EVERGLADES
LANRIG PL.
DRUMSACK
CAMPSIE VIEW
JOHN BROWN PL.
BERRYKNOWE AV.
FLEMING AV.
Playground
WOODHEAD TER.
LAURELBANK RD.
CROW WOOD TER.
CROW WOOD RD.
POTASSA
STATION
HARRIET DRIVE
HORNSHILL FARM RD.
PARKVIEW DR.
SCHOOL RD.
COURT
Cardowan DR.
RESIPOL
GASKIN PTH.
MOSS VIEW RD.
68

Chryston
Lindsay Road
B757
Main
Chryston Prim. Sch.
Chryston High. Sch.
Chryston Valley Business Cen.
Cloverhill Pl.
Lib.
Bothlyn Rd.
Moray Pl.
Millbrae
Pentland Road
Hillcrest
South Loan
Iain Nicholson Rec. Cen.
Chryston Rd.
Chryston Mains
Bedlay Castle
Bedlay Cemetery
Bothlin Burn
Holms
A80
Cumbernauld Road
Muirhead
Glaudhall Farm
North L
Playground
Hall
Park Rd.
Football Grd.
War Mem.
Bowl. Grns.
John Brown Pl.
Berryknowe
Fleming Av.
Stenho. Av.
Station R.
Church Rd.
Elmira Rd.
St. Barbara's Prim. Sch.
Slakiewood
Potassels
Lilybank Av.
Drumcavel Road
A752
Lochend Road
Drumcavel
Coronation Pl.
Holms Pl.
Woodlands Av.
Queensbank Av.
Greenhill Av.
Southview Pl.
Mount Ellen
Football Grd.
Pav.
Lochend House
Lochend Nursery
Garnkirk Moss
Mossvale Nurseries
Neuk Av.
Crow Wood Rd.
Laurelbank Rd.
Woodhead Ter.
Woodhead Ind. Est.
Mossview Cotts.
Heathfield Moss
Heathfield Farm
Works
Station Cott.
Johnston Loch
Mowbray
Jardine
Manor
Kirkhill
Neuk
Lochview Ter.
G69
Gartcosh
Old Gartloch Road
Depot
Allison Pl.
Drain
Gartloch Road
B806
Mid Cotts.
Gartloch Cotts.
Lochview Cottages
City of Glasgow
Rec. Grd.
Lodge
Gartloch Hospital
Tennis Courts
Bothlin Burn
M73 Motorway
Bishop Loch
52
67
88

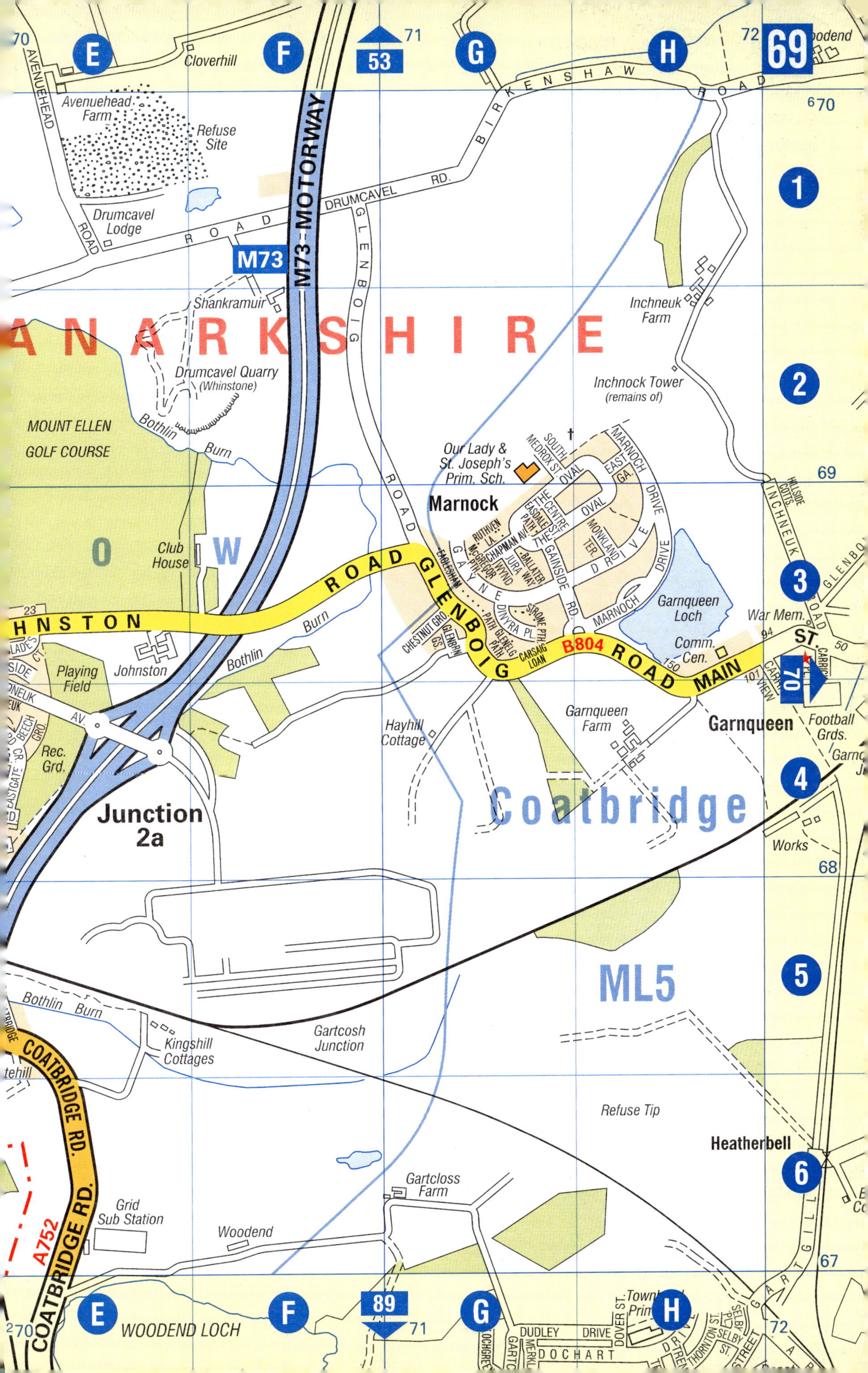

53
71
72
E
F
G
H
Cloverhill
AVENUEHEAD ROAD
Avenuehead Farm
Refuse Site
BIRKENSHAW ROAD
670
Woodend
1
2
3
4
5
6
Drumcavel Lodge
DRUMCAVEL ROAD
RD.
M73
M73 MOTORWAY
Shankramuir
LANARKSHIRE
GLENBOIG ROAD
Inchneuk Farm
Drumcavel Quarry (Whinstone)
Inchnock Tower (remains of)
MOUNT ELLEN GOLF COURSE
Bothlin Burn
Our Lady & St. Joseph's Prim. Sch.
Marnock
SOUTH MEDROX ST.
OVAL
EAST GA.
MARNOCH DRIVE
THE CENTRE
EASDALE PATH
OVAL
MONKLAND TER.
RUTHVEN LA.
CHAPMAN AV.
McGREGOR PTH.
JURA WYND
BALLATER WAY
THE GAINSIDE
GAYNE DRIVE
69
INCHNEUK ROAD
HILLSIDE COTTS.
Club House
O
W
JOHNSTON ROAD
23
EAGLESHAM PATH
GLENELG PATH
DINYRA PL.
STROME PTH.
GAINSIDE RD.
MARNOCH DRIVE
Garnqueen Loch
War Mem.
MAIN ST.
GLENBOIG
50
94
CARRICK
Comm. Cen.
B804 MAIN ROAD
150
101
CARRICK VIEW
70
Bothlin Burn
Playing Field
Johnston
CHESTNUT GRO.
GLENBRAE GS.
CARSAIG LOAN
Hayhill Cottage
Garnqueen Farm
Garnqueen
Football Grds.
Garnq
INCHNEUK AV.
Rec. Grd.
BEECH GRO.
EASTGATE
Junction 2a
Coatbridge
Works
68
ML5
Bothlin Burn
Kingshill Cottages
Gartcosh Junction
COATBRIDGE RD.
tehill
Refuse Tip
Heatherbell
A752
Grid Sub Station
Gartcloss Farm
Woodend
GARTGILL ROAD
67
89
E
F
G
H
270
WOODEND LOCH
71
DUDLEY DRIVE
DOVER ST.
Town Prim
DOCHART DRIVE
THORNTON ST.
SELBY PL.
SELBY ST.
STREET
72

Birkenshaw Road
Wooden
Mollinsburn Road
Gain Burn
Medrox Quarry (Disused)
Medrox
Spring
Gaindykehead
Shawlands
Glenboig Farm
Greenfoot Siding
Bus Depot
Greenfoot
Greenside
Blackbrae Cottage
Castlehill
NORTH LA
Farm Road
Hawthorn Cottage
Castlepails
Inchneuk Road
Hillside Cotts
Glenboig Road
Glenboig
New Glenboig
Haggmuir
Garnqueen Loch
War Mem.
Comm. Cen.
Main St.
B804
Carrick Pl.
Carrick View
Gartverrie Wood
Garnqueen
Football Grds.
Ramoan
Coatbridge Road
Garnqueen North Junction
Gartsherrie Av.
View-Bank St.
Whitelaw Av.
Ramoan House
Glenboig Prim. Sch.
Works
Muirdyke Road
Hole Road
Burnlip Road
Coatbridge
Burnlip
Gartverrie Burn
Gartliston
Gartliston Rd.
Palace
ML5
Ford
Gartverrie Farm
Road
Gartsherrie Holm Farm
Gartverrie Cottage
Copse Wood
Yetts
Heatherbell
Gartcolt Cottages
Gartverrie Burn
Cromlet
Gartgill
Beech Cottage
Coltswood House
Gartliston Road
Yetts Hole
Gartsherrie Wood
Thornton St.
Selby St.
Selby Street
Works
Kennels
Burn
Braeside
North Burn
54
69
90
72
73
70
69
68
67

E
F
G
H
55
275
76
1
2
3
4
5
6
670
69
68
67
Cleddans
New West Lodge
East Lodge
West Lodge
Black Craig
Douglas Plantation
CULLOCHRIG
Cullochrig
Hairstanes Cottage
East Lodge Wood
HOLE RD.
ROAD
CONDORRAT ROAD
B802
Foot o' Loan Wood
East Gartmillan
Shank Burn
Glenmill
BRACKENHIRST ROAD
West Gartmillan
Glenmill Wood
LANARKSHIRE
Arderyth
Drumbowie
Mainhurst Cottage
Firknowe
INSBURN ROAD
Airdrie
BRACKENHIRST ST
Ryding
Reservoir (covered)
Brackenhirst
Gas Storage Depot
Quarry (dis.)
Ryden Mains
Laverock Knowe
New Monkland
Cemetery
ML6
New Monkland Prim. Sch.
DRAEBOG ROAD
B803
CRATHIE DRIVE
Norwood
Rochsoles
Crowhill Plantation
ARRAN DR.
BALMORAL GS.
STRATHYRE GS.
GRANTOWN AV.
DUNNET DR.
BANCHORY AV.
CULZEAN
IRVINE ST.
HAWKWD. RD.
DUNIGN
WINDSOR
MELDRUM MAINS
APPIN WY.
LOCHBUIE LA.
MELDRUM
MAINS
CLEDDANS VW.
QUARRYSIDE ST.
MAINS AV.
RYDEN
WADDELL
Comm. Cen.
KIRKSTYLE PL.
MACARTHUR AV.
GLENVIEW ST.
GLENWELL ST.
GLENMAVIS
AIRDRIE GOLF COURSE
Blackwalk Plantation
Playground
Football Ground
Bowl. Grn.
GLENMAVIS ROAD
Roughcraig Glen
Dryflat
Braidenhill
COATBRIDGE ROAD
South Lodge
STRATHSPEY CRES.
STRATHBLANE CR.
STRATHTUMMEL CRES.
STRATHCONON CR.
DRIVE
PARK
Club Ho.
Golfhill
91
Virtuewell Glen
BLUEBELL WAY
LOCHEARN CR.
TUMMEL
GARELOCH
STAINEY BRAES PL.
STRATHAVEN CRES.
STRATHPEFFER
Cemy.
RINGHOLM
DYKE

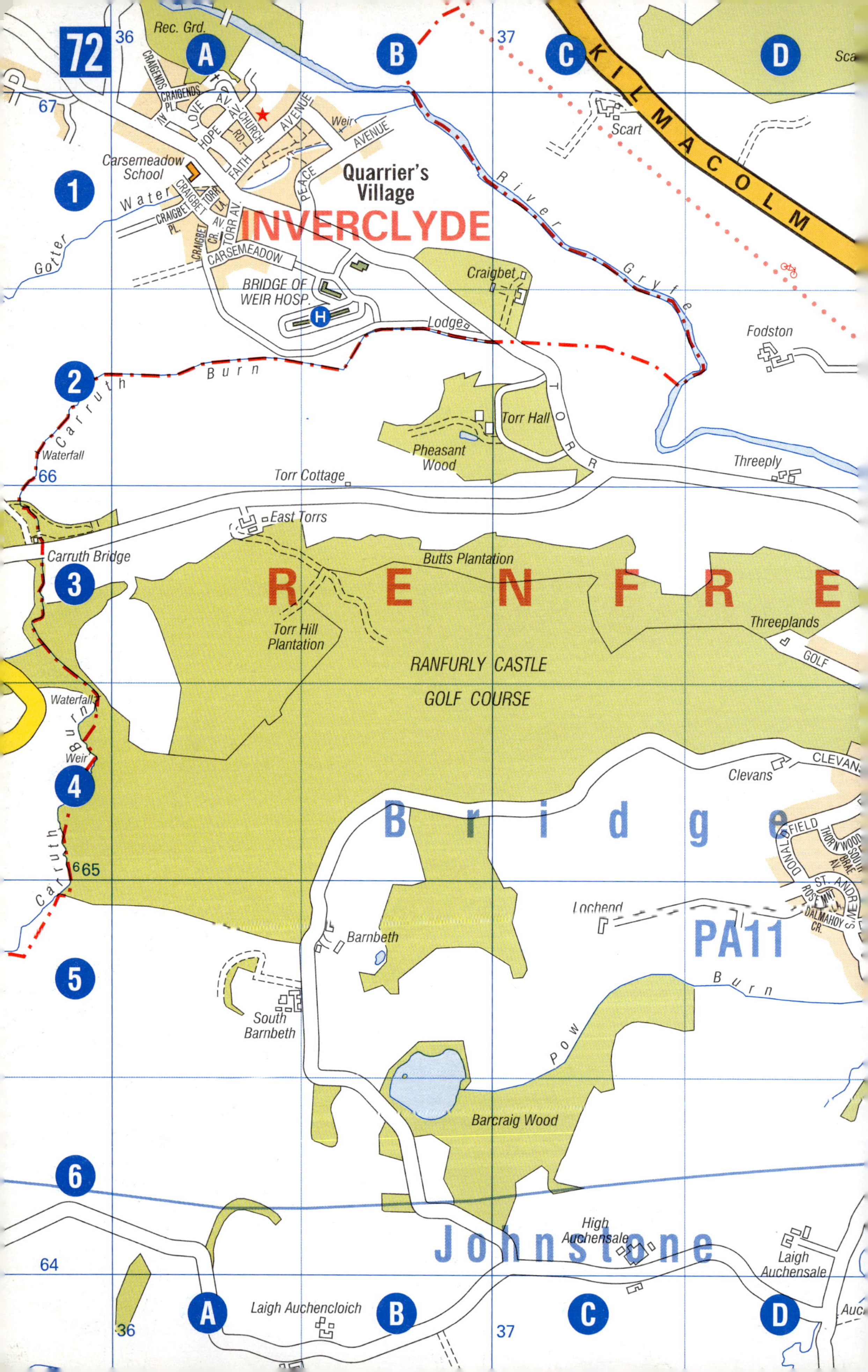
A
B
C
D
1
2
3
4
5
6
36
37
67
66
65
64
Rec. Grd.
CRAIGENDS
CRAIGENDS PL.
LOVE AV.
HOPE AV.
CHURCH RD.
FAITH AV.
AVENUE
PEACE AVENUE
Weir
Carsemeadow School
Quarrier's Village
INVERCLYDE
Gotter Water
CRAIGBET PL.
CRAIGBET CR.
CRAIGBET AV.
TORR LA.
TORR AV.
CARSEMEADOW
BRIDGE OF WEIR HOSP.
Craigbet
Lodge
KILMACOLM
Scart
River Gryfe
Fodston
Carruth Burn
Waterfall
Torr Hall
Pheasant Wood
TORR
Threeply
Torr Cottage
East Torrs
Carruth Bridge
Butts Plantation
RENFRE
Torr Hill Plantation
Threeplands
GOLF
RANFURLY CASTLE GOLF COURSE
Waterfall
Burn
Weir
CLEVANS
Clevans
Bridge
DONALDFIELD
THORN AV.
WOODSIDE BRAE
ST. ANDREWS
ROSEMNT
DALMAHOY CR.
Lochend
PA11
Barnbeth
Burn
South Barnbeth
Pow
Barcraig Wood
High Auchensale
Johnstone
Laigh Auchensale
Laigh Auchencloich
Auc

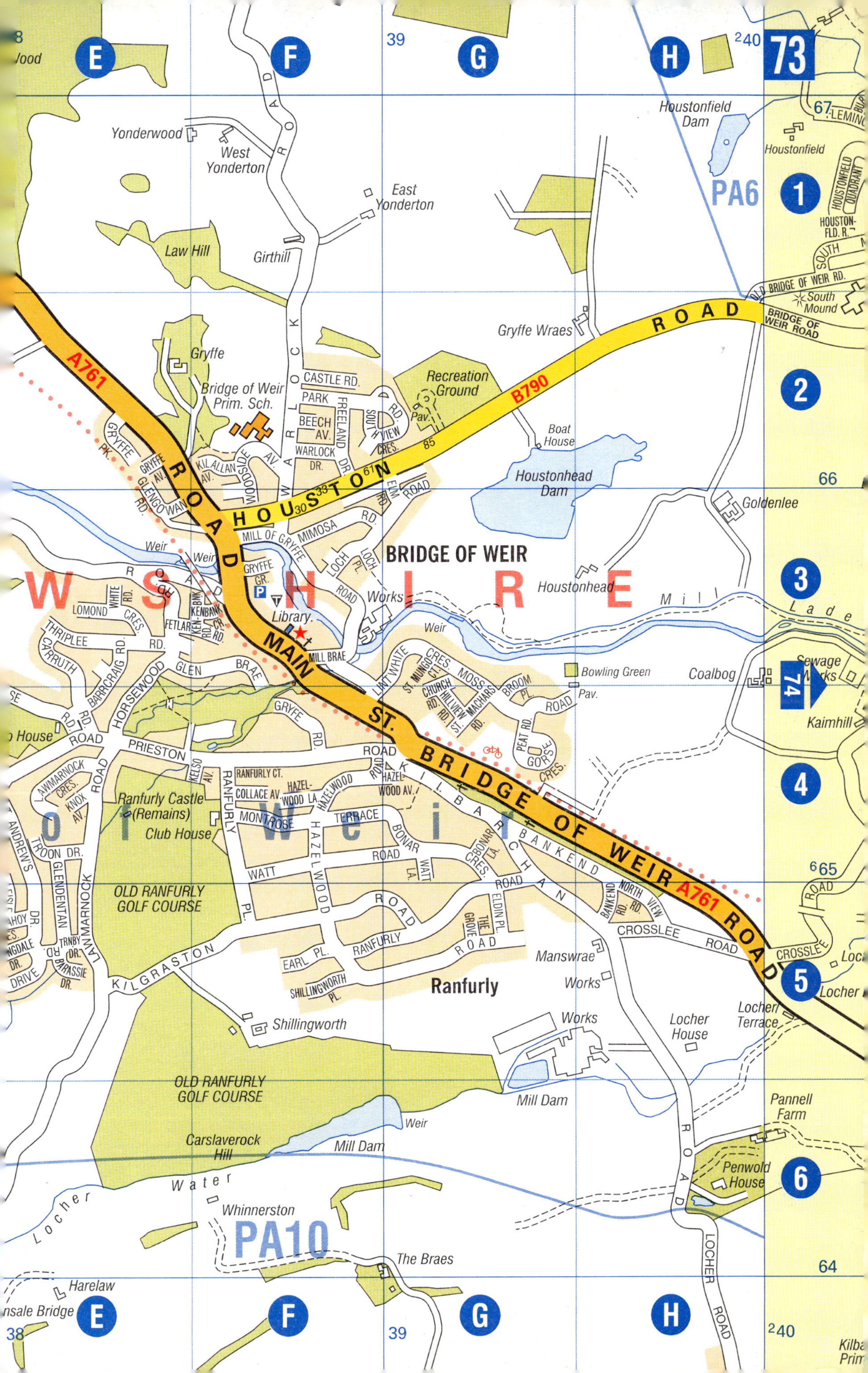
E
F
G
H
39
240
Yonderwood
West Yonderton
East Yonderton
Houstonfield Dam
Houstonfield
PA6
HOUSTONFIELD QUADRANT
HOUSTON-FLD. R.
SOUTH
OLD BRIDGE OF WEIR RD.
South Mound
BRIDGE OF WEIR ROAD
Law Hill
Girthill
Gryffe Wraes
ROAD
WARLOCK ROAD
A761
Gryffe
Bridge of Weir Prim. Sch.
CASTLE RD.
PARK
BEECH AV.
FREELAND DR.
SOUTH VIEW CRES.
RD.
WARLOCK DR.
Recreation Ground
Pav.
B790
85
Boat House
Houstonhead Dam
66
Goldenlee
GRYFFE PK.
GRYFFE AV.
KILALLAN AV.
WOODSIDE AV.
GLENGOWAN RD.
HOUSTON ROAD
30
33
61
ELM RD.
ROAD
MILL OF GRYFFE
MIMOSA RD.
LOCH ROAD
LOCH PL.
BRIDGE OF WEIR
Weir
GRYFFE GR.
Library
Works
Houstonhead
Mill Lade
WHITE RD.
LOMOND CRES.
KENBANK CR.
FETLAR RD.
THRIPLEE RD.
CARRUTH
BARRCRAIG RD.
HORSEWOOD
GLEN BRAE
MILL BRAE
MAIN ST.
LINTWHITE
ST. MUNGO CT.
CHURCH RD.
HILLVIEW RD.
ST. MACHARS RD.
CRES.
MOSS
BROOM PL.
ROAD
Pav.
Bowling Green
Coalbog
Sewage Works
74
Kaimhill
House
ROAD
PRIESTON ROAD
GRYFFE RD.
PEAT RD.
GORSE CRES.
BRIDGE OF WEIR ROAD
LAWMARNOCK CRES.
KNOX AV.
KELSO AV.
RANFURLY CT.
COLLACE AV.
HAZELWOOD LA.
HAZELWOOD AV.
KILBARCHAN ROAD
Ranfurly Castle (Remains)
Club House
MONTROSE TERRACE
BONAR LA.
CROONAR CRES.
BANKEND
ST. ANDREW'S DR.
TROON DR.
GLENDENTAN RD.
LAWMARNOCK ROAD
WATT ROAD
WATT LA.
HAZELWOOD ROAD
RANFURLY PL.
ROAD
NORTH VIEW RD.
BANKEND RD.
A761
665
OLD RANFURLY GOLF COURSE
TRNBY DR.
BRASSIE DR.
DRIVE
KILGRASTON ROAD
EARL PL.
SHILLINGWORTH PL.
RANFURLY ROAD
THE GROVE
ELDIN PL.
CROSSLEE ROAD
CROSSLEE
Manswrae
Works
Ranfurly
Locher
Locher Terrace
Locher House
Shillingworth
Works
Mill Dam
Pannell Farm
OLD RANFURLY GOLF COURSE
Weir
Carslaverock Hill
Mill Dam
Locher Water
Whinnerston
PA10
Penwold House
The Braes
LOCHER ROAD
64
Harelaw
E
F
G
H
38
39
240
1
2
3
4
5
6
WEIR

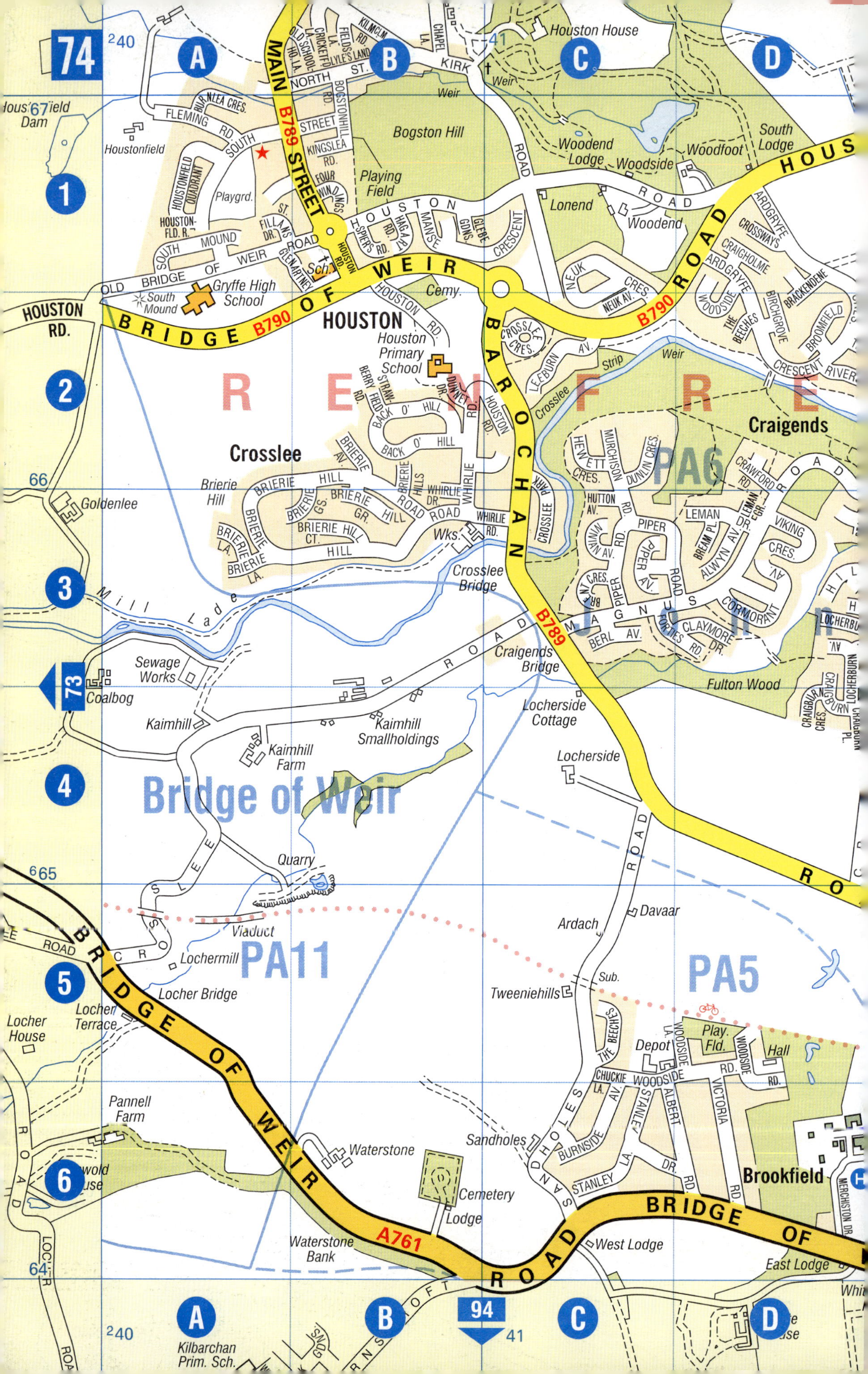
A
B
C
D
1
2
3
4
5
6
240
41
67
66
665
64
Houston House
Kirk
Chapel La.
Kilmclm Rd.
Lyle's Land
Fields La.
Cricketfld La.
Old School Hd. La.
North St.
Bogstonhill Rd.
Main Street B789
Weir
Houstonfield Dam
Fleming Rd.
Burnlea Cres.
South Street
Kingslea Rd.
Bogston Hill
Woodend Lodge
Woodside
Woodfoot
South Lodge
Houstonfield
Houstonfield Quadrant
Playgrd.
Four Windings
Playing Field
Houston Road
Lonend
Woodend
Houston-Fld. R.
South Mound
Fillans Dr.
St.
Road
Speirs Rd.
Hagart Rd.
Manse
Glebe Gdns.
Crescent
Neuk Cres.
Neuk Av.
Ardgryffe
Crossways
Craigholme
Ardgryffe
Brackendene
Woodside
The Beeches
Birchgrove
Broomfield
Crescent
River
Glenartney
Sch.
Houston Rd.
Old Bridge of Weir Rd.
Gryffe High School
Houston Rd.
Bridge of Weir Road B790
B790
Cemy.
Houston
Houston Primary School
Houston Rd.
Crosslee Cres.
Leeburn Av.
Strip
Weir
Renfrew
Barochan Road B789
Crosslee
Craigends
PA6
Strawberry Field Rd.
Back O' Hill
Dunnet Dr.
Houston Rd.
Crosslee
Brierie Hill
Brierie Av.
Brierie Hill
Brierie Gs.
Brierie Gr.
Brierie Hills
Brierie Hill Ct.
Whirlie Dr.
Whirlie Road
Whirlie Rd.
Wks.
Brierie La.
Crosslee Park
Hewett Cres.
Murchison Rd.
Dunlin Cres.
Hutton Av.
Crawford Rd.
Road
Leman
Leman Dr.
Leman Gr.
Bream Pl.
Alwyn Av.
Viking Cres.
Piper Rd.
Piper Av.
Ninian Av.
Brent Cres.
Road
Cormorant Av.
Magnus Cres.
Berl Av.
Forties Rd.
Claymore Dr.
Locherburn
Locherburn Av.
Goldenlee
Mill Lade
Crosslee Bridge
Craigends Bridge
Fulton Wood
Craigburn Cres.
Craigburn Pl.
Sewage Works
73
Coalbog
Kaimhill
Road
Kaimhill Smallholdings
Locherside Cottage
Kaimhill Farm
Locherside
Bridge of Weir
Road
Quarry
Crosslee Road
Viaduct
Davaar
Ardach
Road
PA11
PA5
Lochermill
Sub.
Locher Bridge
Tweeniehills
Bridge of Weir Road
Locher Terrace
Locher House
The Beeches
Depot
Woodside La.
Play. Fld.
Woodside Rd.
Hall
Rd.
Chuckie La.
Woodside Av.
Stanley Dr.
Albert Rd.
Victoria Rd.
Pannell Farm
Sandholes
Burnside
Stanley La.
Sandholes
Brookfield
Merchiston Dr.
Waterstone
Cemetery
Lodge
A761
Bridge of Weir Road
Waterstone Bank
West Lodge
East Lodge
Locher Rd.
Road
94
Kilbarchan Prim. Sch.

E
F
G
H
North Mains
43
Loanhead Cottages
Fulwood
44
ROAD
B790
South Mains Cotts.
Wester Fulwood Cottages
Wester Fulwood
Fulwood Mains Cottages
67
River Gryfe
Fulwood Bridge
1
South Mains
Lodge
Ardgryfe
Knowes
ROAD
Ford
Nether Craigends
Auchans Cottages
2
LINWOODMOSS WOOD
Auchans
66
GRYFEBANK CR.
LOCHER AV.
LOCHER WY.
LOCHER GS.
CRESCENT
FULTON GS.
DRIVE
AUCHANS
3
NETHERBURN AV.
CLIPPENS
stone
LINWOOD MOSS
76
Paisley
East Fulton Holdings
West Fulton
ROAD
RICHMOND DR.
4
Linwood Moss Sports Complex
PA3
Tennis Courts
ROWAN
BERWICK CRES.
CRAIG
IRVINE DR.
East Fulton
HOLM PL.
SEMPLE PL.
SPIERS PL.
65
Clippens Sch.
Clippens
LINWOOD
KINNAIRD DR.
CAIRN DR.
DARLUITH
GILMARTIN
ROAD
EDMISTON DR.
Comm. Cen.
East Fulton Holdings
BRAIDWOOD PL.
RUSSELL PL.
ROAD
CLIPPENS
BRIDGE OF WEIR
BAROCHAN
LOANHEAD AV.
LOANHEAD RD.
ATHOLL PL.
KILBRENNAN RD.
AVON DR.
OXFORD DR.
MOSS RD.
5
East Fulton
GILMARTIN
ALFORD PL.
East Fulton Prim. Sch.
DRIVE
MORAY PL.
ARRAN PL.
MONTROSE PL.
CLAIR PL.
ERSKINE FAULD
GREEN FARM RD.
FULWOOD AV.
BRYDSON PL.
NORTH DR.
SOUTH DR.
ROAD
BRIDGE ST.
DUNLOP
Windyhill
MOORBURN PL.
Linwood High Sch.
WEEPLE DR.
VERNON DR.
CARRADALE PL.
WOODFORD PL.
MILL PL.
WATSON AV.
MOSS AV.
BLACKSTOUN AV.
Comm. Cen.
GREENHILL CRES.
GREENHILL DR.
Sch.
Sch.
STREET
ARMOUR PL.
Sub.
ROAD
STIRLING
KINLOCH AV.
PENTLAND DR.
WILSON AV.
BLACKWOOD AV.
DR.
LAUDER DR.
REID AV.
COTTON AV.
HART
MERCHISTON DR.
LISMORE AV.
CALDWELL AV.
ELLIOT DR.
OGDEN AV.
Club
ABERNETHY DR.
BRIDGE
SHAW PL.
LOCHEAD AV.
PEARSON PL.
MELROSE AV.
ARDLAMONT SQ.
Hlth. Cen.
STIRLING DR.
KILNSCARFE FINLAY DR.
MUIRHEAD DR.
COWAL DR.
ARDGOUR DR.
MORVEN DR.
MORAR DR.
ROAD
MILLFORD DR.
LAGHOLM DR.
6
A761
B789
ROAD
ERCHISTON HOSPITAL
Sub.
ROAD
A761
LORNE DR.
KINTYRE AV.
CLIPPENS RD.
AVENUE
Rec. Grd.
KINTYRE
BY-PASS
64
WEIR
House
JOHNSTONE HOSPITAL
JOHNSTONE
95
43
LYON ROAD
44
LINWOOD INDUSTRIAL
E
F
G
H
42
Newfield

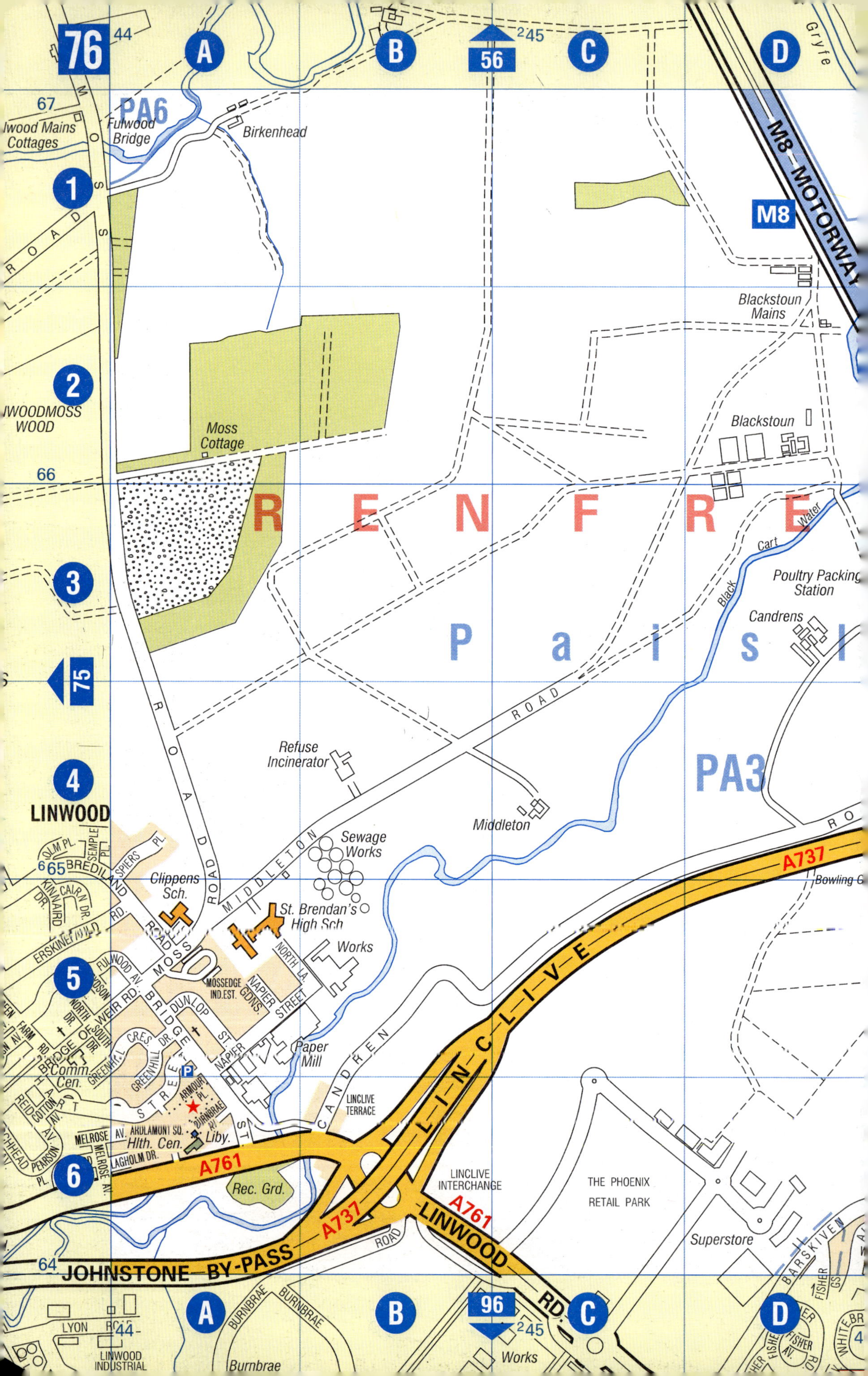
A
B
C
D
56
75
96
44
245
67
66
65
64
1
2
3
4
5
6
PA6
PA3
Fulwood Bridge
lwood Mains Cottages
Birkenhead
lwoodmoss Wood
Moss Cottage
Blackstoun Mains
Blackstoun
M8 MOTORWAY
M8
Gryfe
RENFREW
Paisley
Poultry Packing Station
Candrens
Black Cart Water
Refuse Incinerator
Middleton
MIDDLETON ROAD
MOSS ROAD
LINWOOD
Sewage Works
Clippens Sch.
St. Brendan's High Sch
Works
MOSSEDGE IND.EST.
NAPIER GDNS.
NAPIER STREET
NORTH LA.
Paper Mill
CANDREN ROAD
LINCLIVE TERRACE
LINCLIVE
LINCLIVE INTERCHANGE
A737
A761
Rec. Grd.
LINWOOD RD.
JOHNSTONE BY-PASS
THE PHOENIX RETAIL PARK
Superstore
BARSKIVEN
FISHER AV.
FISHER GS.
FISHER RD.
Bowling G
BREDILAND RD.
SPIERS PL.
SEMPLE PL.
ELM PL.
KINNAIRD DR.
CAIRN DR.
ERSKINE VIEW
FULWOOD AV.
WEIR RD.
BRIDGE OF WEIR RD.
NORTH DR.
SOUTH DR.
DUNLOP ST.
GREENHILL CRES.
GREENHILL DR.
BRIDGE ST.
NAPIER ST.
HART ST.
Comm. Cen.
ARMOUR PL.
BURNBRAE PL.
ARDLAMONT SQ.
Hlth. Cen.
Liby.
MELROSE AV.
LAGHOLM DR.
PEARSON PL.
REID AV.
COTTON AV.
BURNBRAE
Burnbrae
LYON ROAD
LINWOOD INDUSTRIAL
Works

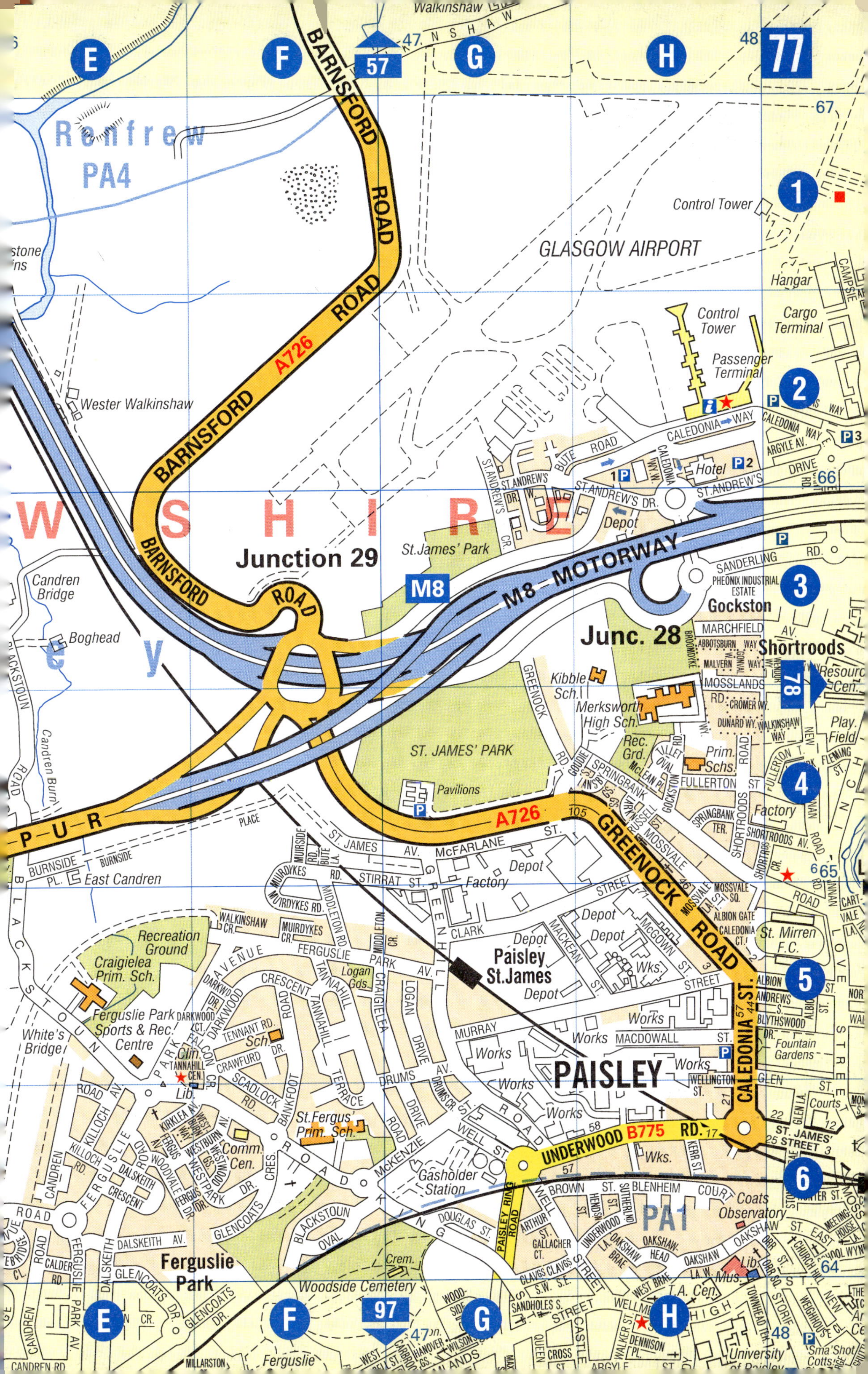

Walkinshaw
57
47
48
67
66
65
64
E
F
G
H
1
2
3
4
5
6
Renfrew
PA4
Control Tower
GLASGOW AIRPORT
Hangar
Cargo Terminal
Passenger Terminal
CALEDONIA WAY
BARNSFORD ROAD
A726
Wester Walkinshaw
BUTE ROAD
ST. ANDREW'S DR.
Hotel
Depot
SHIRE
Junction 29
St. James' Park
M8
M8 MOTORWAY
SANDERLING RD.
PHEONIX INDUSTRIAL ESTATE
Gockston
Junc. 28
Candren Bridge
Boghead
MARCHFIELD AV.
Shortroods
MOSSLANDS
Kibble Sch.
Merksworth High Sch.
78
Resourc. Cen.
Play. Field
ST. JAMES' PARK
Rec. Grd.
Prim. Schs.
FULLERTON ST.
Pavilions
SPRINGBANK
Candren Burn
Factory
GREENOCK ROAD
105
MOSSVALE
SHORTROODS AV.
BURNSIDE PL.
East Candren
ST. JAMES AV.
McFARLANE ST.
Depot
STIRRAT ST.
Factory
MUIRDYKES RD.
St. Mirren F.C.
WALKINSHAW
Recreation Ground
Craigielea Prim. Sch.
FERGUSLIE PARK AV.
CLARK
Paisley St.James
Depot
Logan Gdns.
BLACKSTOUN ROAD
Ferguslie Park Sports & Rec. Centre
White's Bridge
Sch.
Works
MACDOWALL ST.
CALEDONIA ST.
Fountain Gardens
Clin.
TANNAHILL CEN.
Lib.
CRAWFURD
SCADLOCK RD.
DRUMS AV.
PAISLEY
WELLINGTON ST.
GLEN ST.
Comm. Cen.
St. Fergus' Prim. Sch.
UNDERWOOD B775 RD.
ST. JAMES' ST.
Gasholder Station
Wks.
Coats Observatory
PA1
PAISLEY RING ROAD
DOUGLAS ST.
OAKSHAW
Lib.
Mus.
T.A. Cen.
HIGH
DALSKEITH AV.
Ferguslie Park
Crem.
Woodside Cemetery
97
GLENCOATS DR.
CANDREN RD.
Ferguslie
MILLARSTON
University of Paisley
Sma'Shot Cotts.

A
B
C
D
1
2
3
4
5
6
Netherton 58
77
98
GLASGOW AIRPORT
Control Tower
Hangar
Cargo Terminal
Passenger Terminal
Rec. Grd.
Altwood House
Storage Depot
Jetty
WHITE CART WATER
Works
Mill
Depot
Sewage Works
Abbatoir
Factory
Porterfield
Moorpark
Knockhill Park
M8-MOTORWAY
M8
PAISLEY ROAD
A741
COCKELS B791
PA4
PA3
The David Club
Junction 27
Gockston
Liby. H.Q.
Resource Cen.
Shortroods
Play Field
New Harbour
NETHERCOMMON INDUSTRIAL ESTATE
PHEONIX INDUSTRIAL ESTATE
AIRLINK IND. EST.
NETHERCOMMON IND. EST.
Warehouses
Depot
RENFREW
Gallowhill
Reid Kerr College
Laigh Park
St. Catherine's Prim. Sch.
St. Mirren F.C.
ABERCORN IND. EST.
Fountain Gardens
RENFREW ROAD
GX Superbowl
GREENLAW INDUS. EST.
Whitehaugh
Ckt. Grd.
PAISLEY
Paisley Gilmour St.
County Courts
Coats Observatory
Lib. & Mus.
T.A. Cen.
University of Paisley
Clinic
Abbey
Mun. Bldgs.
Leisure Cen.
GLASGOW ROAD A761
Williamsburgh
East End Park
Superstore
Playing Field
St. John Ogilvie Running Track
Arkleston Ho.
A726
ST. JAMES' STREET
OLD SNEDDON STREET
GAUZE ST.
CALEDONIA ST.

E
F
G
H
59
99
80
1
2
3
4
5
6
50
51
52
64
65
66
67
Loanhead
Dean Park
Renfrew High School
Running Track
King George V Mem. Play. Fields
Newmains
Prim. Sch.
Hlth. Cen.
Arkleston Prim. Sch.
Hotel
Works
GLASGOW A8 ROAD
RENFREW ROAD
Sports Grnd.
M8 MOTORWAY
Junc. 26
DEANSIDE TRANSIT DEPOT
HILLINGTON ROAD
Hillington Industrial Estate
HILLINGTON INDUSTRIAL ESTATE
Glasgow
G52
Training Cen.
Mus.
Hillington West
Arkleston
COCKLESHILL PARK
North Arkleston
Lodge
Arkleston Cemetery
East Arkleston
South Arkleston
ARKLESTON ROAD
QUEEN ELIZABETH AVENUE
SHIRE
BYRES HILL
HONEYBOG HILL
BARSHAW (MUNICIPAL) GOLF COURSE
PA1
Club House
BARSHAW PARK
Putting Green
CITY OF GLASGOW
Penilee Sec. Sch.
Rec. Grd.
Penilee
Ralston Prim. Sch.
Playing Field
Oldhill
Prim. Sch.
A761
PAISLEY ROAD
SANDWOOD ROAD
SANDY ROAD
B791
PENILEE ROAD
MOSSLAND ROAD
LINBURN ROAD
HONEYBOG ROAD
BARSHAW ROAD
CORSE ROAD
GLEDDOCH ROAD
CRAIGMUIR ROAD
KELHEAD AVENUE
Comm. Cen.
Football Grd.
Ralston

BRAEHEAD SHOPPING CENTRE
Retail Park
Works
60
53
52
A
B
C
D
Whiteinch
OLD RENFREW ROAD
BONDED WAREHOUSES
M8
King George V Dock
Shieldhall Riverside Quay
RIVER CLYDE
Factory
Depot
JORDANVALE
DEHOLM
G14
DUMBARTON
NORTHINCH
CURLE ST.
Sewage Works
Linthouse Burn
Works
1
2
3
4
5
6
67
66
665
64
RENFREW A8 ROAD
Junc. 26
DEANSIDE TRANSIT DEPOT
Superstore
Junc. 25a
Warehouses
RENFREWSHIRE
M8 MOTORWAY
HILLINGTON ROAD
Hillington Ind. Est.
CARLYLE
79
GOVAN ROAD
BOGMOOR PL.
BOGMOOR RD.
RENFREW ROAD
CITY
GLASGOW
SOUTHERN GENERAL HOSPITAL
Play Field
Helipad
SHIELDHALL
Warehouse
Timber Yard
SHIELDHALL ROAD
HARDGATE DR.
LANGLANDS
A739
A736
North Cardonald
AINSLIE ROAD
HEPBURN RD.
NASMYTH RD.
QUEEN ELIZABETH AV.
CARNEGIE RD.
FIFTY PITCHES RD.
CARDONALD PARK
Works
Junc. 25
Cardonald Pk.
West Drumoyne
MOUNTGARRIE RD.
MOREFIELD RD.
MEIKLEWOOD RD.
A8
CHIRNSIDE RD.
Hillington East
HILLINGTON
HARTLAW CRES.
QUEENSLAND DRIVE
KINGSLAND DRIVE
REDPATH DR.
LAMBERTON DRIVE
CARHAM DRIVE
Cardonald
G52
Crematorium
CRAIGTON CEMETERY
Monument
CRAIGTON
War Mem.
BERRYKNOWES ROAD
SANDWOOD ROAD
ALLANTON
INVERGYLE
CARDONALD
WEDDERLEA
TWEEDSMUIR
DRYBURN
BOWFIELD
KELHEAD
PAISLEY ROAD
CROOKSTON
100
HATTON

E
F
G
H
61
101
82
1
2
3
4
5
6
PARTICK
Partickhill
Partick
Kelvinhall
GOVAN
Govan
LINTHOUSE
IBROX
Ibrox
BELLAHOUSTON
Junction 24
Junc. 23
CLYDESIDE EXPRESSWAY
A814
A739
BEITH STREET
B808
DUMBARTON ROAD
CASTLEBANK STREET
RIVER CLYDE
Merklands Quay
Meadowside Quay
Shipbuilding Yard
Football Ground
CLYDE TUNNEL
ELDER PARK
St. Anthony's Prim. Sch.
GOVAN ROAD
Govan Fun Pool
POINTHOUSE RD.
QUEEN MOTHERS MAT. HOSP.
ROYAL SICK
EDMISTON DRIVE
A8
M8 MOTORWAY
PAISLEY ROAD WEST
A761
BROOMLOAN RD.
B768
DUMBRECK RD.
RANGERS F.C. (Ibrox Stadium)
Moore Park
Tinto Park Football Ground
Superstore
Govan High Sch.
Drumoyne Prim. Sch.
Langlands Sch.
Pirie Pk.
House for an Art Lover
Bellahouston Sports Centre
BELLAHOUSTON PARK
G11
G51
G41
G3
Ckt. Grd.
Depot
Works
Gasholder

A
B
C
D
62
102
81
1
2
3
4
5
6
Hillhead
Kelvinbridge
Kelvinhall
Kelvingrove
Kelvingrove Park
University of Glasgow
Hunterian Mus.
Hunterian Gall.
Visitors Cen.
Western Infirmary
Kelvin Hall (Mus.)
Kelvingrove Mus. & Art Gallery
Kelvin Statue
War Mem.
Roberts Mem.
Roller Skating Rink
Royal Hosp. for Sick Children
Queen Mothers Mat. Hosp.
Yorkhill Park
Kelvinhaugh
Summit Cen. Ice Rink
Exhibition Cen.
Finnieston
Cranston Hill
Anderston
Scottish Exhibition & Conference Cen.
Glasgow Heliport
Hotel
Bell's Bridge
Finnieston Crane
River Clyde
Stobcross Quay
Plantation Quay
Yorkhill Quays
Prince's Dock
North Quay
West Quay
West Basin
Mavisbank Quay
Lancefield Quay
General Terminus Quay
P.S. Waverley
Springfield Quay
Plantation
Festival Park
Cessnock
Ibrox
Kinning Pk.
Kinning Park
Shields Rd.
School Museum
Junc. 20
Junc. 21
Junc. 22
M8 Motorway
M77
Paisley Road West
Pointhouse Road
Stobcross Road
Lancefield Quay
Anderston Quay
Clydeside Expressway
Argyle St.
Sauchiehall St.
Dumbarton Road
Byres Road
Western Road
University Avenue
Beith St.
Kelvin Way
St. Vincent St.
Berkeley St.
North Street
Glasgow Academy
Teaching Cen.
Woodside Sec. Sch.
Academy
G11
G12
G3
G51
G41
A814
A8
A82
B808
M8

E
F
G
H
63
103
1
2
3
4
5
6
84
Port Dundas
PORT DUNDAS INDUS. EST.
M8 FOOD PARK
Sports Field
Sighthill Cemetery
SIGHTHILL PARK
CITY OF GLASGOW
G20
G21
G4
G2
G1
G5
G40
Junc. 15
Junc. 16
Junc. 17
Junc. 18
Junc. 19
St. Georges Cross
CRAIGHALL RD.
A879
A81
A804
A8
A77
A814
A74
M8 MOTORWAY
DOBBIE'S LOAN
BAIRD ST.
Cowcaddens
Garnethill
GLASGOW CALEDONIAN UNIVERSITY
Charing Cross
Academy
T.V. Studios
Bus Sta.
Royal Concert Hall
Buchanan St.
QUEEN ST.
GLASGOW
Cathedral
Univ.
City Chambers
Gallery
Townhead
High Street
Ladywell Sch.
Anderston
ANDERSTON CENTRE
CENTRAL
St. Enoch
ST. ENOCH SHOPPING CEN.
Argyle St.
BROOMIELAW
Broomielaw Quay Gdns.
Windmillcroft Quay
Clyde Place Quay
Harbour
Upper Harbour
Quay Gdns.
KINGSTON ST.
NELSON ST.
MORRISON ST.
Bridge St.
Court
Mosque
Coll.
Coll. Play. Fld.
Citizens Theatre
SALTMARKET
GALLOWGATE
LONDON RD.
BALLATER ST.
Tradeston
West St.
Glasgow Parcels Sta.
Kingston
Laurieston
GORBALS
River Clyde
Weir
Monument
People's Palace (Museum)
Suspension Bridge
Glasgow Green
Bowl. Green
Courts
TRADESTON IND. EST.
TEMPLETON BUSINESS CEN.
EGLINTON ST.
GORBALS ST.
LAURIESTON ROAD
CROWN STREET
HIGH STREET

A
B
C
D
1
2
3
4
5
6
64
104
83
5
Petershill Park (Football Ground)
Sighthill
Sighthill Cemetery
Superstore
St. Rollox Business & Retail Park
Sorting Office
Works
Depot
G21
Glenconner Park
Germiston
Sighthill Park
Junc. 15
Royston
Glasgow Fruit Market
Glasgow Fish Market
Junction 14
City of
M8 Motorway
Burial Grd.
Alexandra Parade
Springburn Road
A803
A804
Baird St.
Castle St.
A8
Royal Infirm.
St. Mungo's Cath.
Cemetery
Milnbank
Dennistoun
Brewery
Abbatoir
Cathedral St.
Univ.
High St.
High Street
Duke Street
G4
G31
G1
Calton
Bellgrove
Gallowgate
A89
Camlachie
Cumbernauld Road
B763
Millerston St.
Crownpoint Sports Park
St. Mungo's Academy
G40
London Road
A749
Monument
People's Palace (Museum)
Suspension Bridge
Glasgow Green
Leisure Cen.
Bridgeton
A74
Fielden St.
Barrow Field
Celtic Park
Biggar St.

Provanhill
Blackhill
Junction 1 (M80)
M80 MOTORWAY
M80
Gasholder
Gas Works
Playing Field
Provanmill
Provanmill Cemy.
RIDDRIE PARK CEMETERY
PROVANMILL B765 RD
Superstore
Club House
Miniature Golf Course
LETHAMHILL GOLF COURSE
Junction 12
GARTLOCH B765 ROAD
Hogganfield Reservoir
M8 MOTORWAY
Riddrie
St. Thomas's Prim. Sch.
Football Ground
G33
H.M.PRISON
GLASGOW
Junction 13 (M8)
Alexandra Park Golf Course
ALEXANDRA PARK
Tennis Court
Model Yacht Pond
Kennyhill Sch.
Alexandra Sports Hall
Riddrie Knowes
CUMBERNAULD ROAD
A80
GARTCRAIG ROAD
EDINBURGH ROAD
A8
Offices
Hagill
Carntyne
CARNTYNE INDUSTRIAL ESTATE
Football Ground
Running Track
Recreation Ground
G32
Works (Disused)
Carntyne
Depot
Parkhead
THE FORGE SHOPPING CENTRE
Virgin Cinema
SHETTLESTON ROAD
A89
Sports Cen.
Eastern Necropolis
St. Michael's Prim. Sch.
Factory
College
Rec. Grd.
St. Mark's Prim. Sch.
Football Grounds
TOLLCROSS PARK
Helenvale Park
Caravan Site
65
105
86

A
B
C
D
1
2
3
4
5
6
66
85
106
Bird Sanctuary
Landing Stage
Hogganfield Loch
Hogganfield Park
Ashcraig School
Football Ground
Craigend
Hogganfield
Miniature Golf Course
LETHAMHILL GOLF COURSE
Hogganfield Reservoir
Reservoir (Covered)
GARTLOCH ROAD
B765
B806
CITY OF
STEPPS ROAD
Sch.
Play. Field
Water Towers
Resr.
Croftcroighn Park
Tennis Ct.
Craigend House
Ruchazie
Play. Fld.
M8 MOTORWAY
M8
Junction 11
Football Ground
G33
Queenslie Prim. Sch.
Queenslie Ind. Estate
Factory
Works
Wks.
Cranhill
Cranhill Park
Miniature Golf Course
Comm. Cen.
EDINBURGH ROAD
A8
SPRINGBOIG ROAD
B765
Lightburn
St. Andrew's Sec. Sch.
Play. Field
HOSP.
Springboig St. John's Sch.
Barlanark Rec. Grd.
Running Track
Recreation Ground
Play. Fld.
Bowling Greens
Pav.
Greenfield
Springboig
Eastmuir Sch.
Prim. Sch.
Educ. Cen.
Lib.
Comm. Cen.
Play. Fld.
SANDYMOUNT CEMETERY
GARTOCHER ROAD
Caravan Site
Greenfield Pk. Hlth. Cen.
Shettleston
Works
Depot
Indus. Est.
G32
Eastbank Prim. Sch.
SHETTLESTON ROAD
A89
Sports Cen.
Sports Grd.
Coll.
Shettleston
Academy
LESTON HOSP.
Liby.
BAILLIESTON ROAD

E
F
G
H
67
1
2
3
4
5
6
Cottages
Tennis Courts
Blackfaulds Farm
B806
ROAD
G69
Garthamlock
Club
CRAIGIEVAR ST.
CLONBEITH ST.
CRAIGNEIL ST.
INCHOCH ST.
GARTHAMLOCK RD.
AUCHINLEA ROAD
GLASGOW
Provan Hall
AUCHINLEA PARK
Easterhouse Sports Centre
CONISBOROUGH
CONISBOROUGH PTH.
BALCURVIE
BALFLUIG ST.
GARDNE ST.
WAITSIDE ST.
DUFFUS ST.
Provanhall Prim. Sch.
BRUNSTANE
DROCHIL ST.
Craigend Wood
Easterhouse
LOCHEND ROAD
DUBTON ST.
FORGLEN ST.
AVOCH ST.
DUBTON PATH
BALDRAGON
COLFIN ST.
St. Leonard's Sec. Sch.
CAIRNBROOK IND. EST.
Lochend Secondary Sch.
Junction 10
AUCHINLEA RETAIL PARK
Health Cen.
EASTERHOUSE TOWNSHIP CEN.
Lib.
Offs.
College
School
Playing Fields
Pav.
Ten. Cts.
Blairtummock Prim. Sch.
Blairtummock
WESTERHOUSE
SHANDWICK ST.
BOGBAIN RD.
Swim. Pool
ABERDALGIE
DUNTARVIE
ERROGIE ST.
BOYNDIE ST.
BALDINNIE
BUCHLYVIE
REUCHIE ST.
M8 MOTORWAY
M8
MABEN RD.
DUMMOCK RD.
EASTER QUEENSLIE RD.
Refuse Destructor
STREET
ARNISDALE
KILDERMORIE RD.
NIGG PL.
ARMADALE PL.
STRUIE ST.
WELLHOUSE
BALDOVAN CRES.
BALDOVAN PTH.
TRONDRA PL.
LANGBAR
TORRAN RD.
Easthall Prim. Sch.
HALLIBURTON
LOCHBRIDGE RD.
EDDLEWOOD RD.
EDERTON
WARDIE
STEPFORD
GEORGE PL.
Sch.
Schs.
NEWHILLS
RIGG PL.
KILTEARN RD.
AULTMORE RD.
WELLHOUSE CRESCENT
GARTHAMLOCK
A8
EDINBURGH ROAD
Junction 9
WHAMFLET AV.
65
Lib.
Prim. Sch.
BALARNARK
GARVEL RD.
BRESSAY RD.
Barlanark Prim. Sch.
BARLANARK RD.
Playing Field
EAST HALLHILL RD.
Swinton
HALLHILL ROAD
SPRINGCROFT
SPRINGCROFT DR.
SPRINGCROFT AVENUE
MICKLEHOUSE
QUEENSBY
BARONY DR.
Barlanark
Comm. Cen.
Sandaig Prim. Sch.
Glenduffhill Cemetery
BURNMOUTH RD.
PENDEEN
GARTLOCH
Wks.
Depot
Depots
Garrowhill
B7058
BARRACHNIE
MILLBEG PL.
USMORE PL.
UIG PL.
SANDAIG
Halls
Garrowhill Prim. Sch.
THORNBRIDGE
BAKEWELL RD.
BENTS RD.
HATHERSAGE DR.
CAMP
RYECROFT DR.
DOLAN ST.
GREENSHIELDS RD.
Football Grd.
BUCHANAN ST.
Sch.
SWINTON RD.
DYKE ST.
MARTIN CR.
EASTERHOUSE RD.
Football Ground
VIEWFIELD DR.
GLENDUFFHILL
GORDON AV.
SPRINGHILL
HILLSBOROUGH
HILARY DR.
DOUGLAS AV.
MAXWELL AV.
COATS CR.
BEECH AV.
WHIRLOW
Garrowhill
Barrachnie
BAILLIESTON RD.
BARRACHNIE
WEIRWOOD
AVENUE
BAILLIESTON ROAD
107
GLASGOW ROAD
MAIN ST.
CHURCH ST.
ROWANDALE AV.
ROSEDALE DR.
JUNIPER
BIRCHWOOD PL.
Rec. Grd.
HUNTINGTOWER
MILLER ST.
68
64
66
88

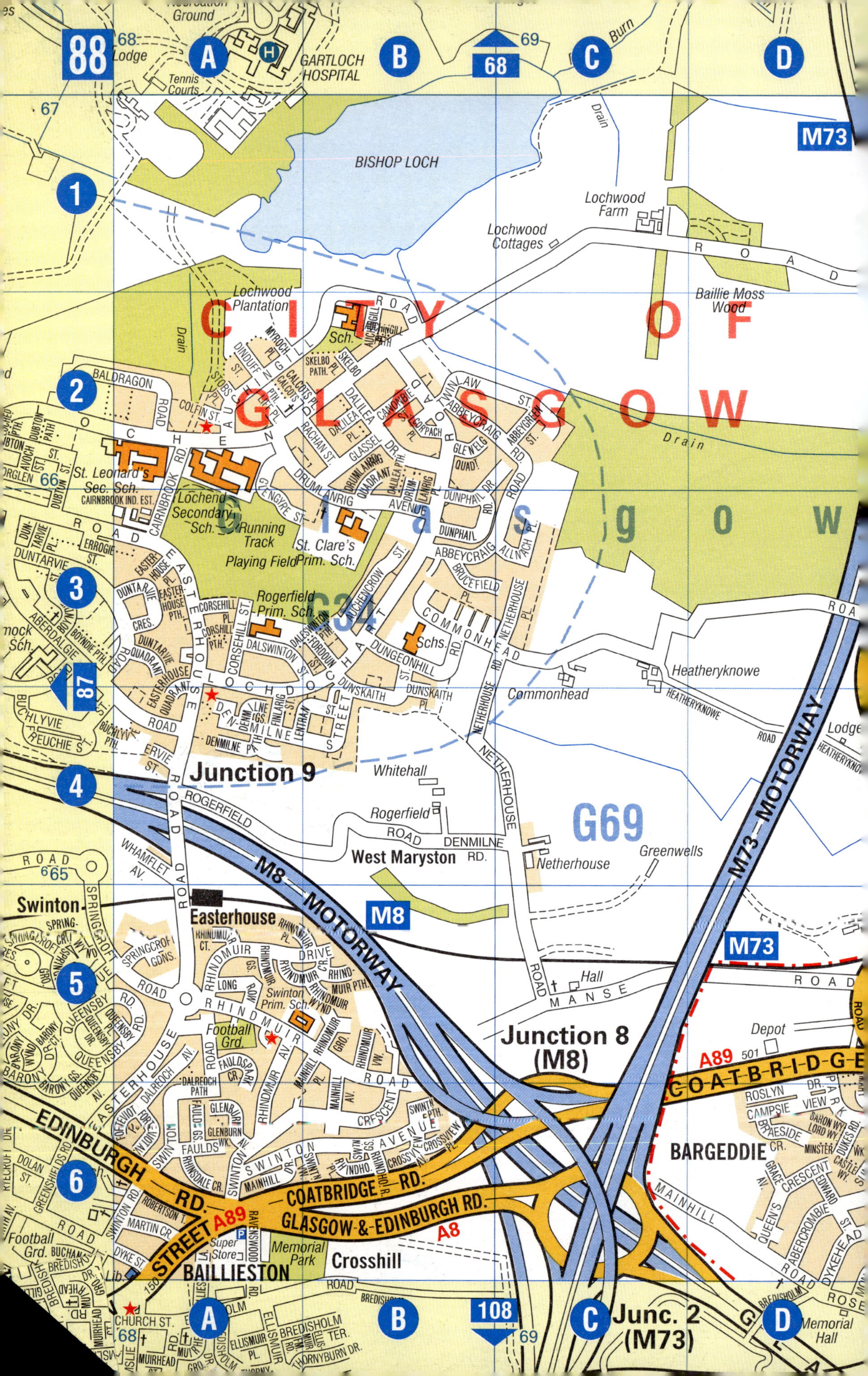
A
B
C
D
1
2
3
4
5
6
68
69
67
66
65
M73
M8
GARTLOCH HOSPITAL
Lodge
Tennis Courts
BISHOP LOCH
Burn
Drain
Lochwood Farm
Lochwood Cottages
ROAD
Baillie Moss Wood
Lochwood Plantation
CITY OF GLASGOW
Glasgow
Sch.
St. Leonard's Sec. Sch.
CAIRNBROOK IND. EST.
Lochend Secondary Sch.
Running Track
Playing Field
St. Clare's Prim. Sch.
Rogerfield Prim. Sch.
G34
Schs.
COMMONHEAD
Commonhead
Heatheryknowe
HEATHERYKNOWE ROAD
Lodge
BALDRAGON ROAD
COLFIN ST.
LOCHEND
DUNTARVIE
EASTERHOUSE ROAD
CORSEHILL ST.
DALSWINTON ST.
DUNGEONHILL
DUNSKAITH ST.
DENMILNE
BUCHLYVIE
REUCHIE ST.
ERVIE ST.
Junction 9
Whitehall
Rogerfield
ROGERFIELD ROAD
DENMILNE RD.
West Maryston
NETHERHOUSE ROAD
Netherhouse
G69
Greenwells
M73 MOTORWAY
M8 MOTORWAY
Swinton
Easterhouse
RHINDMUIR
Swinton Prim. Sch.
Football Grd.
MANSE ROAD
Hall
Junction 8 (M8)
Depot
A89
501
COATBRIDGE ROAD
BARGEDDIE
MAINHILL
EDINBURGH RD.
COATBRIDGE RD.
GLASGOW-&-EDINBURGH RD.
A8
STREET
Super Store
Memorial Park
Crosshill
BAILLIESTON
Football Grd.
Lib.
CHURCH ST.
BREDISHOLM
Junc. 2 (M73)
Memorial Hall
108
87

69
90
109
E
F
G
H
1
2
3
4
5
6
70
71
72
67
66
65
64
NORTH LANARKSHIRE
Coatbridge
ML5
Grid Sub Station
Woodend
Farm
COATBRIDGE RD.
GARTCOSH RD.
GARTCOSH ROAD
A752
WOODEND LOCH
COATBRIDGE GOLF COURSE
Townhead
Lochend Cotts.
TOWNHEAD
Visitor Centre
LOCHEND LOCH
Club House
Driving Range
DRUMPELLIER COUNTRY PARK
Playing Fields
Comm. Cen.
Gilmourneuk
Garnheath Wood
Townhead Prim. Sch.
DUDLEY DRIVE
DOVER ST.
DOCHART
DERWENT DRIVE
TEVIOT
WILTON
THORNTON ST.
SELBY PL.
SELBY ST.
GARTGILL RD.
LOCHGREEN PL.
GARTCLOSS RD.
MERKLAND RD.
LOCHVIEW RD.
LOMOND DRIVE
WITCHWOOD CT.
LOMOND RD.
Witch Wood
DEE ST.
KATRINE PL.
ALMOND PL.
WYE CR.
LEVEN ROAD
DEVERON
TAY ST.
Sch.
BELMONT STREET
CRINAN CRES.
CRINAN PL.
IONA PL.
Prim. Sch.
TANTALLON
ACHRAY PL.
RANNOCH AV.
DUNVEGAN AV.
AVON PL.
LEVEN STREET
MORAR
CARRON PL.
DOUNE TERRACE
LOMOND PL.
COLT AV.
Freightliner Terminal
Depot
MOSSPARK RD.
ESPIESIDE CR.
ESPIESIDE CRES.
BLAIRPARK AV.
MUIRDYKE RD.
HOSP.
ROAD
Blairhill
Drumpellier Home Farm
Monkland Canal
Bishop Burn
DRUMPELLIER
WOODLANDS
CARRICK PL.
CARRICK DR.
GOLFVIEW
DAVAAR DR.
DRIVE
GOLFVIEW PL.
SINCLAIR DR.
RYEFIELD AV.
HILLFOOT
Burnhouse DRIVE
Blair Bridge
Burn
AVENUE
PARKVIEW
MUIR
ALBANY S.
TORRISDALE ST.
TORRISDALE PL.
KING
BLAIR ROAD
Drumpellier
DRUMPELLIER GOLF COURSE
Club House
Ckt. Grd.
West Lodge
West Pub. Par.
War Mem.
Sch.
Bargeddie Prim. Sch.
STEWART DR.
725
730
609
GLASGOW ROAD
A89
Drumpark
Drumpark School
Hall
Sewage Works
LANGMUIR ROAD
Saw Mills
Works
Depot
LANGMUIR WAY
Luggie Glen
Luggie Burn
Viaduct
Kirkwood
Waterfall
BURNSIDE
KIRKWOOD
LANG
BURNSIDE WK.
ANNERLEY CT.
ANNERLEY PL.
PLACE
STREET
TORRIDON ST.
TORRIDON CT.
MILLBRAE CT.
GLEN CT.
RAMSAY PL.
PEEL PL.
ALLAN STREET
MITCHELL STREET
RENFREW ST.
WELLINGTON PL.
CRAIGEND DR.
CUMBERLAND PLACE
AVENUE
WOODSIDE
CUPARHEAD
MARSH
NELSON
CULLEAN
KIRKWOOD
Playgrd.
SHARP
Kirkwood Prim. Sch.
EDZELL
DUNBAR
St. James Prim. Sch.
SWINTON CRES.
DRIVE
CRAIGEND
DUNNACHIE
DRUM
RHINDS
CROSSHILL
AITKENHEAD
PARK
School
Factory
Football Grds.
TERRACE
VIEW CRES.
BREDISHOLM
LUGGIE BANK PL.
OLD CHURCH GDNS.
GAIRBRAID TER.
151
206
297
257

70
110
68
GARTSHERRIE WOOD
Gartsherrie
NORTH LA
Greenhill
Sunnyside
Coatbridge Sunnyside
Summerlee Heritage Trust
Summerlee Heritage Park
Coatbridge Central
Blairhill
Dunbeth
COATBRIDGE
ML5
Langloan
Whifflet
Barrowfield
Dundyvan
Kirkwood
Coltswood House
Beech Cottage
Kennels
Braeside
Blacklands
North Burn
Gartsherrie Burn
Witch Wood
Hollandhurst
Freightliner Terminal
Depot
GARTSHERRIE INDUSTRIAL ESTATE
COATBRIDGE IND. EST.
Factory
Works
Football Grounds
Gas Works
ALEXANDER HOSPITAL
Comm. Cen.
Bowl. Grn.
Sch.
Lib.
Hornock Cotts.
Heritage Trust
The Time Capsule
West End Public Park
War Mem.
Bowling Greens
Blair Bridge
Coatbridge Outdoor Sports Complex
Luggie Burn
Saw Mills
Health Cen.
CENTRE PARK CT.
FARADAY RETAIL PARK
QUADRANT SHOP. CEN.
Whifflet Junction
Langloan Junction
Foundry
Ind. Est.
Playing Field
Whifflet Public Park
St. James Prim. Sch.
Sprts. Cen.
GARTLISTON RD.
COLTSWOOD ROAD
B804
B803
A89
A725
B753
BURNBANK ST.
WAVERLEY
DUNBETH ROAD
SUNNYSIDE RD.
MAIN ST.
STH. CIRCULAR RD.
BANK STREET
GLASGOW RD.
DUNDYVAN ROAD
COATBANK ST.
WHIFFLET ST.
GARTSHERRIE ROAD
GARTGILL ROAD
HORNOCK ROAD
HOLLANDHURST ROAD
CORSEWALL ST.
MUIR STREET
LEFROY STREET
KING STREET
WEST CANAL ST.
ALEXANDER STREET
CALDEAN
YETTS

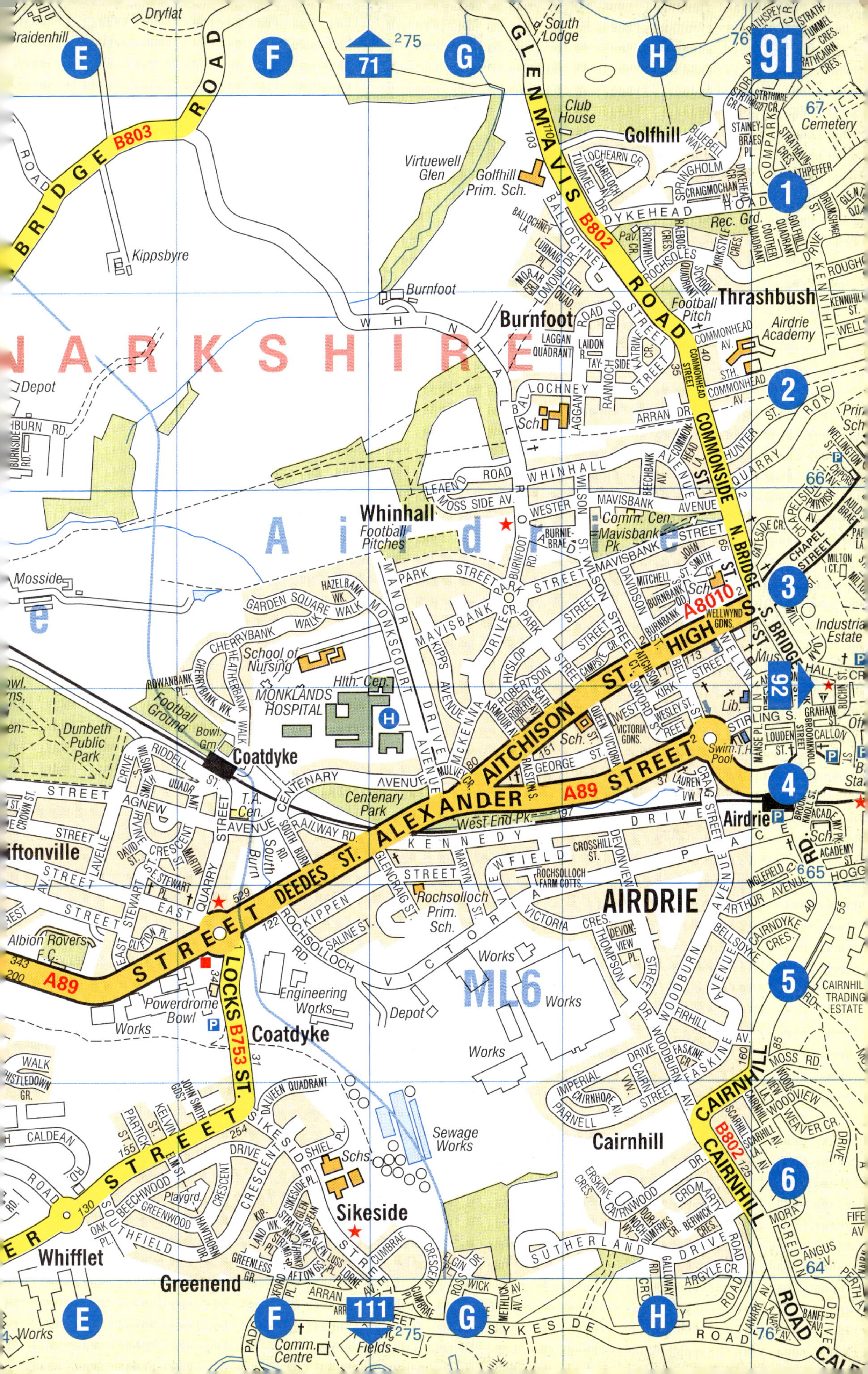
71
111
92
E
F
G
H
1
2
3
4
5
6
Dryflat
Braidenhill
South Lodge
BRIDGE ROAD
B803
Kippsbyre
Virtuewell Glen
Golfhill Prim. Sch.
Burnfoot
Club House
Golfhill
GLENMAVIS ROAD
B802
Cemetery
DYKEHEAD ROAD
Rec. Grd.
Thrashbush
Football Pitch
Airdrie Academy
Burnfoot
WHINHALL ROAD
NARKSHIRE
Depot
LOCHNEY
COMMONSIDE STREET
Airdrie
Whinhall
Football Pitches
Comm. Cen.
Mavisbank Pk.
N. BRIDGE ST.
S. BRIDGE ST.
Industrial Estate
Mosside
GARDEN SQUARE WALK
School of Nursing
Hlth. Cen.
MONKLANDS HOSPITAL
A8010
HIGH ST.
Mus.
Lib.
Dunbeth Public Park
Football Ground
Bowl. Grn.
Coatdyke
CENTENARY AVENUE
Centenary Park
AITCHISON ST.
ALEXANDER ST.
DEEDES ST.
A89
STREET
Swim. Pool
West End Pk.
Airdrie
KENNEDY DRIVE
iftonville
Albion Rovers F.C.
Rochsolloch Prim. Sch.
AIRDRIE
VICTORIA PLACE
ML6
Works
Engineering Works
Depot
Powerdrome Bowl
Coatdyke
LOCKS ST.
B753
CAIRNHILL TRADING ESTATE
Sewage Works
Cairnhill
CAIRNHILL ROAD
Sikeside
Schs.
Whifflet
Greenend
SUTHERLAND DRIVE
SYKESIDE ROAD
Comm. Centre
Fields
Works

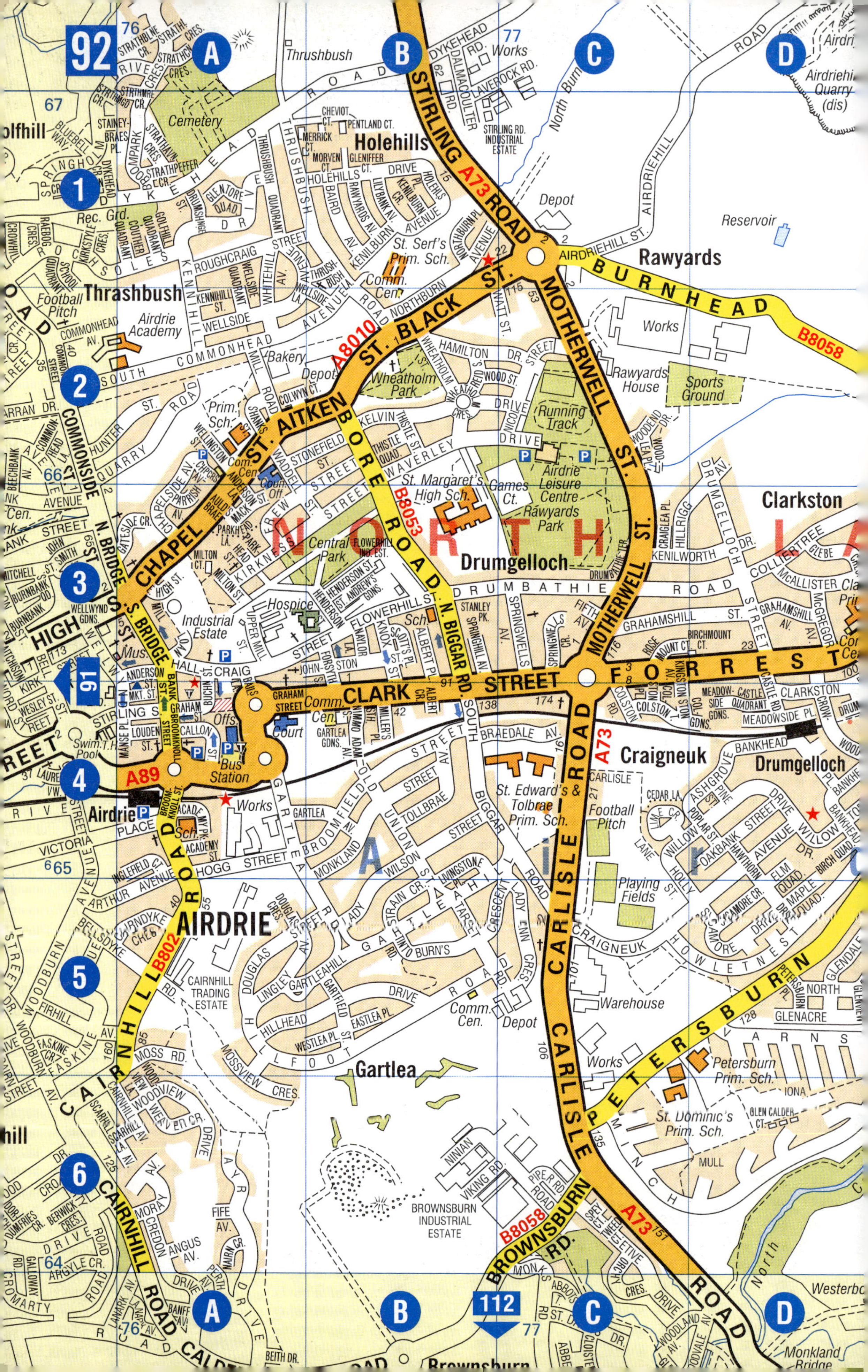

A
B
C
D
1
2
3
4
5
6
76
77
67
66
65
64
Thrushbush
Works
Airdrie
Airdriehill Quarry (dis)
Cemetery
Holehills
STIRLING RD. INDUSTRIAL ESTATE
STIRLING ROAD
A73
North Burn
Depot
Reservoir
Rawyards
BURNHEAD
B8058
AIRDRIEHILL ST.
Thrashbush
Rec. Grd.
Football Pitch
Airdrie Academy
St. Serf's Prim. Sch.
Comm. Cen.
BLACK ST.
A8010
AITKEN ST.
Wheatholm Park
Rawyards House
Sports Ground
Running Track
Airdrie Leisure Centre
Rawyards Park
MOTHERWELL ST.
COMMONHEAD
SOUTH COMMONHEAD
COMMONSIDE
HUNTER ST.
QUARRY
CHAPEL ST.
BORE ROAD
B8053
St. Margaret's High Sch.
Games Ct.
NORTH LA
Clarkston
Drumgelloch
DRUMBATHIE ROAD
Central Park
Hospice
Industrial Estate
N. BRIDGE ST.
S. BRIDGE ST.
HIGH ST.
HALLCRAIG
GRAHAM STREET
Comm. Cen.
Court
CLARK STREET
FORREST ST.
N. BIGGAR RD.
Offs.
Bus Station
A89
Swim.T.H. Pool
Airdrie
Works
91
GRAHAMSHILL ST.
Craigneuk
St. Edward's & Tolbrae Prim. Sch.
Football Pitch
Playing Fields
CARLISLE ROAD
Drumgelloch
VICTORIA PLACE
HOGG STREET
AIRDRIE
B802
CAIRNHILL TRADING ESTATE
CAIRNHILL
Gartlea
Comm. Cen.
Depot
Warehouse
Works
PETERSBURN
Petersburn Prim. Sch.
St. Dominic's Prim. Sch.
CARLISLE
BROWNSBURN INDUSTRIAL ESTATE
B8058
BROWNSBURN RD.
A73
ROAD
112
CAIRNHILL ROAD
Westerbo
Monkland Bridge

PLAINS
Playing Fields
Playing Flds.
Club Ho.
BALLOCHNEY RD.
MEADOWHEAD
ARBUCKLE RD.
WALLACE ST.
JARVIE AVENUE
BRUCE ST.
VICTOR ST.
MAIN STREET
A89
ROAD
AIRDRIE
ST.
Sch.
St. David's Primary School
Depots
BROWNIESIDE ROAD
STATION RD.
Weir
Waterfall
Sewage Farm
Hillhead
EASTER MOFFAT GOLF COURSE
Club Ho.
Greystones
St. Phillip's School
CONNOR ST.
CHURCH CR.
Depot
Katherine Cottage
Play. Fld.
Katherine Pk.
LANARKSHIRE
TOWERS ROAD
STATION RD.
WESTER MOFFAT HOSPITAL
Wester Moffat Farm
Dunrobin
North Calder Water
Caldervale High Sch.
Caldervale Forge
Ponds
DUNROBIN ROAD
B8058
ROAD
TOWERS WAY
Warehouses
Dunrobin Prim. Sch.
Weir
Burn Wood
Warehouses
STEPENDS ROAD
Recreation Ground
Petersburn
Moffat Mills
Bowl. Grn.
ML6
Comm. Cen.
ISLAY
ROUGHRIGG ROAD
Gimmerscroft
Weir
Water
CRAIGENS ROAD
Kameyknowe Cottage
Knowehead
Glenview
Mill Farm
GARTNESS DRIVE
Gartness
Bowhouse
BOWHOUSEBRAE
BOWHOUSE ROAD
Damhead Farm
Clattering Burn
DUNISTON ROAD
Easter Dunsyston
CALDERVALE
E
F
G
H
1
2
3
4
5
6
67
66
665
64
280
79
113

74
Lodge
Waterstone Bank
West Lodge
BRIDGE OF
East Lodge
White House
Barrhill Wood
Barr Hill
Tower
LOCHER ROAD
SHUTTLE ST.
FOREHO. RD.
Forehouse
Kilbarchan Prim. Sch.
GLENTYAN AV.
VICTORY DR.
MONTGMRY DR.
MEADSIDE RD.
WEST RD.
THE GROVE
WHEATLANDS
EAST RD.
WHEATLANDS DRIVE
WHEATLANDS FM. RD.
PARK VW.
PARK GDNS.
BARNSCROFT
MEADSIDE RD.
TAYLOR AV.
STREET
LOOM WLK.
NEW ST.
GATESIDE PL.
Public Park
Pav.
KILBARCHAN
Weaver's Cott.
MERCHANTS CL.
ST.
STEEPLE ST.
THE CROSS
STEEPLE SQ.
BARN GRN.
EWING ST.
WELL RD.
FULTON CR.
Liby.
CRAIGENDS DR.
CUNNINGHAME RD.
CRESCENT
Burn
CHURCH ST.
CEDAR CT.
Football Grd.
HIGH BARHOLM
CHURCHILL DR.
Bank Brae
KIBBLESTON ROAD
LANGSIDE DR.
LANGSIDE PK.
HUNTER PL.
MACLAY AV.
STATION RD.
STATION WYND
ROCK DR.
LOW BARHOLM
BARRHILL
LEWIS CRES.
TOPPERSFLD.
QUARRYBANK
MILLIKEN DR.
MILLIKEN RD.
Kilbarchan
Black Cart Water
JOHNSTONE
EASWALD BANK
BURNSIDE GDNS.
BARCHAN'S RD.
SMITH
LADY- ROAD
Foremount House
DALHOUSIE RD.
RAMSAY AV.
CLOCHODERICK AV.
TROUBRIDGE CR.
RHUMOR AV.
LISMORE GDNS.
KILBARCHAN RD.
WATERSIDE LA.
MILLIKEN
MACKENZIE DR.
TROUBRIDGE AV.
Abbanoy
J
Johnstone
Mill
KILBARCHAN
JUBILEE TER.
CARTSIDE AV.
BEECH RD.
RYEFIELD AV.
McLAURIN
LADESIDE DR.
PA10
Auchenames Cottage
Tandlehill
Mosside
Wardend
TANDLEHILL
Burnbrae
BY-PASS
PARK
MELFORD
GLENCART GR.
COCHRANEMILL ROAD
B787
LONGMEAD
ARRAN DR.
BUTE DR.
FLD. PL.
HUNTERSFIELD
Cartside
Bus Depot
Millikenpark
HIGHCRAIG AV.
Prim. Sch.
CRAIGVIEW TER.
GREENEND
CRAIGBOG
DUNDONALD AV.
DUNCANCRAG
Sch.
Muirfaulds Cottage
RENFREWSHIRE
Cartside
Kibbleston
Faulds
CLYDE PL.
DEE PL.
FORTH PL.
TAY PL.
ETTRICK
TWEED PL.
CRAIGVIEW
Playing Fields
Johnstone High Sch.
Fordbank Prim. Sch.
CORSEFORD
NESS AV.
DON PL.
SPEY PL.
NITH PL.
ANNAN PL.
TEVIOT
AUCHENGREOCH
Red House
A737
Cart Water
Corseford
AVENUE
PALMERSTON PL.
WALPOLE PL.
GLADSTONE AV.
ROAD
HALLHILL RD.
CHURCH
Fordbank Stables
St. Cuthbert's High Sch.
St. Anthony's Prim. Sch.
Liby.
FINCH PL.
HERON PL.
KESTREL PL.
SWIFT PL.
THRUSH PL.
FALCON RD.
SWAN PL.
PLOVER PL.
LINNET AV.
MARTLET DR.
CURLEW PL.
SPATESTON RD.
Spateston
Corseford School
PA9
Midtown Burn
ROAD
MIDTON
Stables
Piggery
Thirdpart Hall
Black Cart
Warbowie
BEITH
West Corsefield Farm
TERN PL.
WREN PL.
SHELDRAKE PL.
NIGHTINGALE PL.
FULMAR PL.
SANDERLING PL.
SPATESTON ROAD
ROAD

JOHNSTONE
Johnstone
Johnstone Castle
Quarrelton
Elderslie
Cochrane Castle
PA3
PA5
A737
B789
75
96
JOHNSTONE HOSPITAL
HIGH STREET
THORN BRAE
MAIN ROAD
GRAHAM ST.
BY-PASS
BAROCHAN RD.
Newfield House
Gowanlea Gardens
Barbush
LOMONDVIEW IND. EST.
LINWOOD INDUSTRIAL ESTATE
Sewage Works
Paisley
Cemetery
Abbey Cemetery
Football Ground
Thomas Shanks Park
Wee Wood
Nurseries
Rannoch Quarry (disused)
Craigston Wood
Craigbog
Craigenfeoch Quarry (dis.)
Highcraig Wood
High Craig
High Craig Quarry
Wester Craigenfeoch
High Craigenfeoch
Windyhill
Woodhill
COCHRANE CASTLE GOLF COURSE
Club House
Auchenlodment Prim. Sch.
Glenpatrick Building
Auchingreoch Riding School
E F G H
1 2 3 4 5 6
42 43 44
61 62 63 64

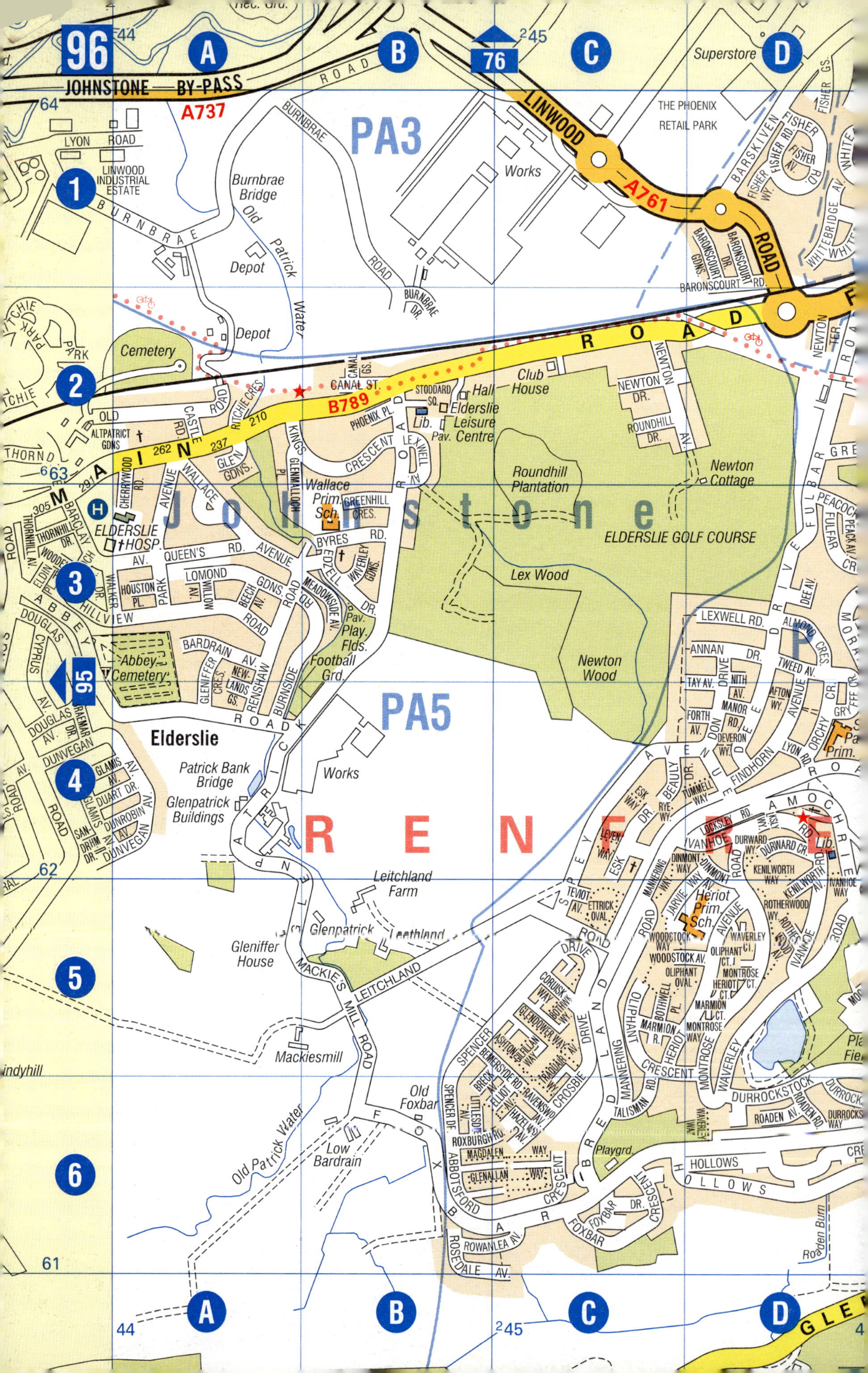
A
B
C
D
76
95
1
2
3
4
5
6
44
245
64
63
62
61
JOHNSTONE BY-PASS
A737
ROAD
LYON ROAD
LINWOOD INDUSTRIAL ESTATE
BURNBRAE
Burnbrae Bridge
Old Patrick Water
Depot
PA3
Works
BURNBRAE ROAD
BURNBRAE DR.
LINWOOD
A761
ROAD
Superstore
THE PHOENIX RETAIL PARK
BARSKIVEN
FISHER RD.
FISHER AV.
FISHER WY.
FISHER GS.
WHITEBRIDGE AV.
BARONSCOURT GDNS.
BARONSCOURT DR.
BARONSCOURT RD.
NEWTON TER.
Cemetery
RITCHIE PARK
OLD
ALTPATRICK GDNS
THORN
CASTLE RD.
ROAD
RITCHIE CRES.
CANAL ST.
CANAL GS.
B789
210
262
237
291
305
MAIN ROAD
STODDARD SQ.
Hall
PHOENIX PL.
Lib.
Elderslie Leisure Centre
Pav.
Club House
NEWTON DR.
NEWTON AV.
ROUNDHILL DR.
Roundhill Plantation
Newton Cottage
GLEN GDNS.
KINGS PL.
GLENMALLOCH
CRESCENT
LEXWELL AV.
Wallace Prim. Sch.
GREENHILL CRES.
Johnstone
ELDERSLIE GOLF COURSE
CHERRYWOOD RD.
AVENUE
WALLACE
BARCLAY
THORNHILL AV.
THORNHILL DR.
ELDERSLIE HOSP.
H
QUEEN'S RD.
AVENUE
BYRES RD.
EDZELL DR.
WAVERLEY GDNS.
Lex Wood
HOUSTON PL.
PARK
LOMOND AV.
WILLOW
BEECH AV.
GDNS.
ROAD
MEADOWSIDE AV.
Pav.
Play. Flds.
Football Grd.
ABBEY
HILLVIEW
DOUGLAS
CYPRUS AV.
Abbey Cemetery
BARDRAIN AV.
GLENIFFER CRES.
NEWLANDS GS.
RENSHAW
BURNSIDE
ROAD
PA5
Newton Wood
LEXWELL RD.
ALMOND CRES.
ANNAN DR.
DRIVE
TAY AV.
NITH AV.
TWEED AV.
AFTON WY.
FORTH AV.
MANOR RD.
DON
DEVERON WY.
DEE
FINDHORN
LYON RD.
ORCHY
AVENUE
FULBAR
PEACOCK
FULFAR
DEE AV.
Prim.
Elderslie
DOUGLAS AV.
BRAEMAR DR.
DUNVEGAN
GLAMIS AV.
DUART DR.
DUNROBIN AV.
SANDRINGHAM DR.
DUNVEGAN AV.
ROAD
Patrick Bank Bridge
Glenpatrick Buildings
Works
PATRICK
GLEN
RENFREW
ESK WAY
BEAULY DR.
TUMMEL WAY
RYE WY.
LEVEN WAY
ESK
LOCKSLEY RD.
IVANHOE
DURWARD WY.
DURWARD CR.
KENILWORTH WAY
Lib.
SPEY AVENUE
TEVIOT AV.
ETTRICK OVAL
DINMONT WAY
MANNERING WAY
JARVIE WAY
Heriot Prim. Sch.
ROTHERWOOD WY.
IVANHOE WAY
Leitchland Farm
Glenpatrick
Leethland
Gleniffer House
MACKIE'S MILL ROAD
LEITCHLAND
ROAD
WOODSTOCK WAY
WOODSTOCK AV.
OLIPHANT OVAL
OLIPHANT CT.
WAVERLEY CT.
MONTROSE CT.
HERIOT CT.
MARMION CT.
MONTROSE WAY
BOTHWELL PL.
MARMION R.
HERIOT
OLIPHANT CRESCENT
WAVERLEY
Mackiesmill
CORUISK WAY
GLENDOWER WAY
TRAQUAIR AV.
SPENCER
ASHTON WAY
DRIVE
CROSBIE
BREDILAND
MANNERING
TALISMAN RD.
DURROCKSTOCK
ROADEN AV.
ROADEN RD.
DURROCK WAY
Old Foxbar
SPENCER DR.
LITTLESIDE AV.
ROXBURGH RD.
MAGDALEN WAY
GLENALLAN WAY
ABBOTSFORD
CRESCENT
Playgrd.
HOLLOWS
FOXBAR DR.
CRESCENT
FOXBAR ROAD
ROWANLEA AV.
ROSEDALE AV.
Roden Burn
Low Bardrain
Old Patrick Water
indyhill
GLEN

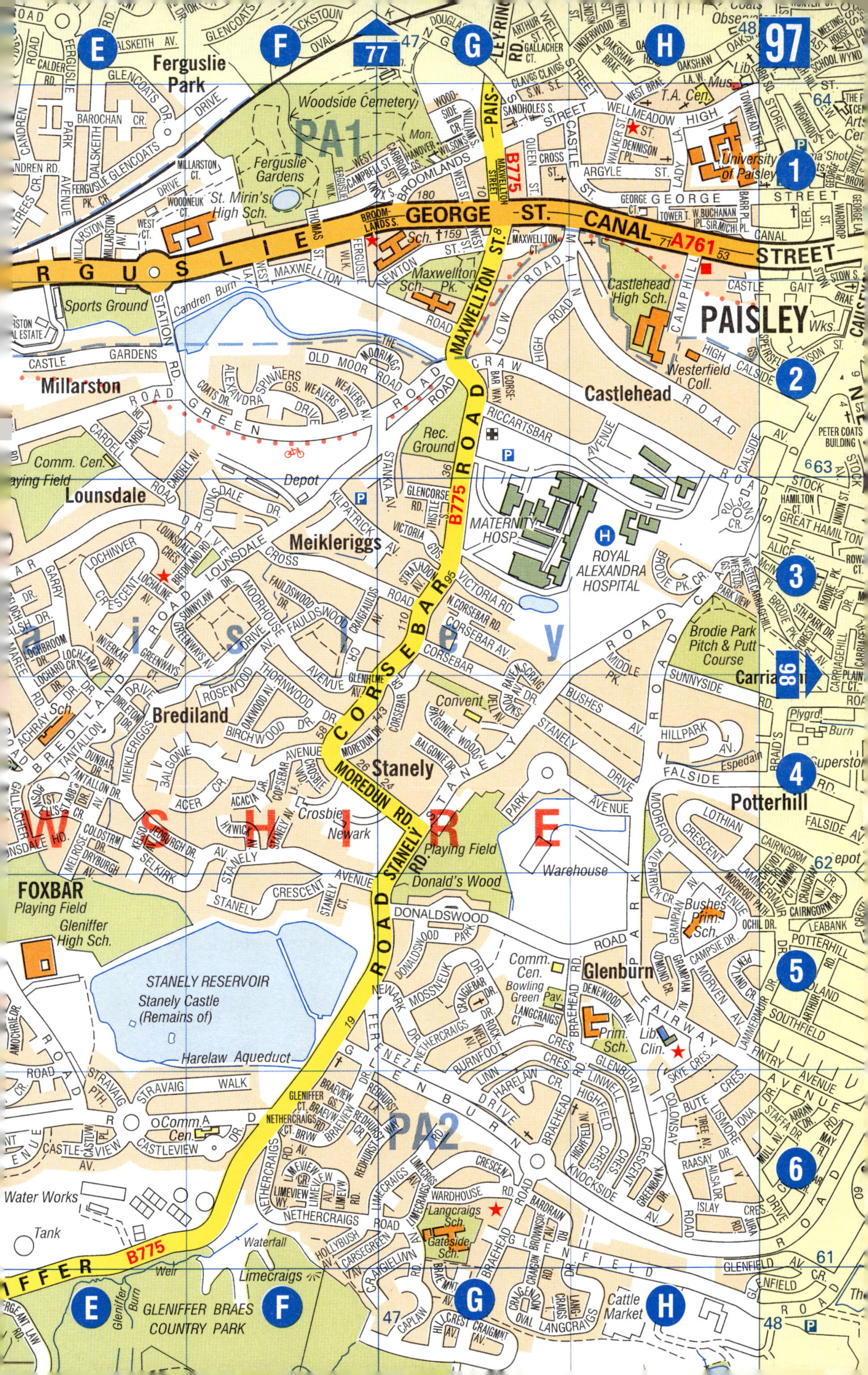
E
F
G
H
1
2
3
4
5
6
77
47
48
64
63
62
61
86
Ferguslie Park
Woodside Cemetery
PA1
Ferguslie Gardens
St. Mirin's High Sch.
GEORGE ST.
CANAL
A761
STREET
FERGUSLIE
B775
University of Paisley
T.A. Cen.
Mus.
Lib.
Observatory
PAISLEY
Castlehead High Sch.
Maxwellton Sch.
Maxwellton Pk.
Sports Ground
Candren Burn
Millarston
CASTLE GARDENS
Castlehead
Westerfield Coll.
Rec. Ground
MATERNITY HOSP.
ROYAL ALEXANDRA HOSPITAL
Comm. Cen.
Playing Field
Lounsdale
Depot
Meikleriggs
CORSEBAR ROAD
Brodie Park Pitch & Putt Course
Brediland
Convent
Stanely
MOREDUN RD.
Crosbie
Newark
Playing Field
Donald's Wood
Warehouse
Potterhill
FOXBAR
Playing Field
Gleniffer High Sch.
STANELY RESERVOIR
Stanely Castle (Remains of)
Harelaw Aqueduct
Glenburn
Comm. Cen.
Bowling Green
Pav.
Prim. Sch.
Bushes Prim. Sch.
Lib.
Clin.
FAIRWAY
PA2
Langcraigs Sch.
Gateside Sch.
Water Works
Tank
Waterfall
Limecraigs
Weir
Gleniffer Burn
GLENIFFER BRAES COUNTRY PARK
GLENIFFER
Cattle Market
GLENFIELD
Superstore
Plygrd.
Burn
Espedair
PETER COATS BUILDING
Carriagehill

PAISLEY
Paisley Canal
Saucel Hill
Saucelhill Park
Williamsburgh
Seedhill
Seedhill Playing Fields
Running Track
Hawkhead
Auchentorlie
BLACKHALL
Blackhall (Rems.of)
Hunterhill Tutorial Cen.
Millstream
Mills
Abbey
Leisure Cen.
East End Park
Arts Cen.
Superstore
CHARLESTON
Carriagehill
Brodie Park
Pitch & Putt Course
Lochfield
Potterhill
Hunterhill
Blackhall Hill
Hunters Hill
Dykebar
Dykebar Hill
Thornly Park
Shaw Wood
UNIVERSITY OF PAISLEY (Campus)
Games Courts
Playing Field
Thorscrag
Hollybush
DYKEBAR HO
Bowling Green
Play. Field
Tod Burn
Depot
Prim. Sch.
St. Charles's Prim.Sch.
RENFREWSH
PA1
PA2
A761
A726
B774
CANAL ST.
MILL STREET
LONEND
BARRHEAD ROAD
NEILSTON ROAD
CAUSEYSIDE ST.
CAPLETHILL ROAD
GLASGOW ROAD
HIGH ST.
GEORGE STREET
GORDON ST.
SEEDHILL ROAD
ANCHOR AV.
BLACKHALL ST.
CALSIDE AV.
STOCKHOLM CRES.
BARTERHOLM RD.
GREAT HAMILTON ST.
ROWAN ST.
LOCHFIELD ROAD
HUNTLY TERRACE
TODHOLM TERRACE
FALSIDE ROAD
THORNLY PARK AVENUE
SOUTH AVENUE
78
97
114
A
B
C
D
1
2
3
4
5
6
48
49
61
62
63
64

79
115
100
E
F
G
H
1
2
3
4
5
6
50
51
52
61
62
63
64
Oldhill
Putting Green Pav.
DUNCHURCH
ROFFEY
AUCHM
GARTARTAN RD.
KELHEAD
TINWALD AVENUE
BIRKHALL
A761
ROAD
PAISLEY RD.
CROOKS
HATTON
STRATHMORE
DRUMMOND DR.
DARVEL
CORRIE DR.
CRESCENT
Ralston
AVENUE
NEWNHAM RD.
WOODEND DR.
ROTHERWICK DR.
BATHGO
Club House
Lib.
ALLANTON
Comm. Cen.
Football Grd.
Pav.
Playing Field
MARCHBANK GDS.
MARCH
BANK GDS.
ALTON ROAD
GOLF DR.
ROSSHALL AV.
CROOKSTON DR.
NETHERDALE DR.
KILLEARN
DUCHRAY DRIVE
RALSTON
RALSTON DR.
RALSTON PL.
RALSTON PATH
RALSTON CT.
CROOKSTON
DRIVE
LOCHMABEN RD
G52
Crookston
CAIRNHILL
CRONBERRY QUADRANT
CIRCUS
BATHGO HILL
RALSTON GOLF COURSE
Depots
SCOTT'S ROAD
Rosshall Cottage
ROAD
Rosshall
HAWKHEAD CEMETERY
Hawkhead
The Mary Russell Sch.
Hawkhead Bri.
HAWKHEAD HOSPITAL
Playing Field
White Cart Water
Howford Bridge
Bonnyh Prim. S
Play. Fields
Rosshall Estate Gds.
Ross 63 Park
CROOKSTON
A736
Howford School
Bowl. Green
Blacksey
Glasgow
Pav.
LEVERNDALE HOSPITAL
Burn
Hawkhead Farm
BEN LAWERS DRIVE
BEN HOPE AV.
BEN LOYAL AV.
BEN LEDI AV.
BEN MORE DRIVE
BEN VENUE WAY
BEN BUIE WAY
BEN ALDER DRIVE
BEN NEVIS
BEN LUI DR.
BEN VANE AV.
BEN WYVIS DR.
Nurses Home
St. Andrew's Academy
Hawkhead Burn
Kersland School
Hawkhead House Farm
BULL WOOD
G53
HURLET
BULLWOOD GDNS.
BULLWOOD PL.
BULLWOOD AV.
BULLWOOD CT.
LEVERNDALE INDUSTRIAL CENTRE
RAESWOOD GDNS.
RAESWOOD
CITY OF GLASGOW
TEMPLE HILL
GRAHAMSTON PL.
GRAHAMSTON CR.
GRAHAMSTON COURT
CRESCENT
Oldbarhills Bridge
Tongues Hill
Hurlethill Plantation
A726
MULBEN CRES.
MINMOIR RD
KINARVIE
FASKIN CR.
KINARVIE CR.
GAMRIE RD
CROVIE RD.
SANDEND
Low Oldbar
Oldbar Burn
Oldbar Hills
Hurlet Hill
Roughmussel
Hurlet
BARRHEAD ROAD
A736
Works
B771
GRAHAMSTON
West Hurlet
Levern Bridge
LEVERN ROAD
Depot
Hurlet Cottages
Bowl. Green
PRESTWICK ST.

CARDONALD
CRAIGTON
Craigton Cemetery
CROOKSTON
PAISLEY ROAD
A761
BERRYKNOWES
South Cardonald
Convent
Lourdes Sec. Sch.
Cardonald Cemetery
Cardonald College
Crookston
Cardonald Place Farm
Mosspark
Crookston Wood
Bonnyholm Prim. Sch.
Play. Fields
ROSS HALL HOSPITAL
Rosshall
Rosshall Park
Howford Bridge
Howford School
CROOKSTON WOOD
McGill Prim. Sch.
Lochar Park
Bowl. Green
Corkerhill
Crookston Castle (Remains of)
Crookston Castle Sec. Sch.
Running Track
Play. Field
White Cart Water
LEVERNDALE HOSPITAL
CROOKSTON ROAD
A736
G53
G52
CITY OF
Leithland Prim. Sch.
Comm. Cen.
St. Edmund's Prim. Sch.
POLLOK
Haugh Hill
M77
M77 MOTORWAY
Junc. 2
BARRHEAD ROAD
B762
Levern Water
Househillwood
Househill Park
Swim. Pool
Hlth. Cen.
POLLOK TOWNSHIP CENTRE (SHOPPING CEN.)
PRIESTHILL
Bellarmine Secondary School
Recreation Ground
COWGLEN HOSPITAL
Levern Bridge
Works
80
99
116

M8 MOTORWAY
Junc. 23
81
255
BELLAHOUSTON
House for an Art Lover
Bellahouston Sports Centre
BELLAHOUSTON PARK
Glasgow Ski Centre
Nursery
Lodge
Pitch & Putt Course
Running Track
A761
Mosspark
Dumbreck
DUMBRECK ROAD
B768
M77 MOTORWAY
Junction 1
Club House
M77
Rugby Football Club Playing Fields
Dumbreck Riding Sch.
Engine Shed
HAGGS CASTLE GOLF COURSE
G41
NORTH WOOD
POLLOK COUNTRY PARK
Corkerhill
Lochinch Sports Field
Burrell Collection Museum
Knowehead Cottage
GLASGOW
White Cart Water
NETHER POLLOK PLAYING FIELDS
Works
Pollok House
Weir
Tennis Courts
Cricket Ground
G43
Pollokshaws
Pollokshaws West
POLLOK GOLF COURSE
Hippingstones
South Lodge
BARRHEAD ROAD
B762
Broompark Farm
Club House
Bowling Greens
B769
POLLOKSHAWS ROAD
NETHER AULDHOUSE RD.
COWGLEN GOLF COURSE
117
Pollok Wood
Busby
KENNISHEAD
102
Playing Fields
Warehouse
SHAWBRIDGE INDUSTRIAL EST.
AULDHOUSE RETAIL PARK
E
F
G
H
1
2
3
4
5
6

Junc. 22
Junc. 21
Kinning Park
Shields Junc.
Depots
Sikh Temple
Shields Rd.
School Museum
M77
Dumbreck
Academy
POLLOKSHIELDS
Craigholme Sch.
Maxwell Park
Burgh Hall
Maxwell Pk.
Pollokshields
Pollokshields West
Crossmyloof
Cricket Grd.
Haggs Castle
Srathbungo
Shawlands
Shawlands Academy
Waverley Pk.
Camphill House
QUEEN'S
Camp Hill
Langside
Nursery
Pollokshaws
Pollokshaws West
Pollokshaws East
Superstore
Football Grd.
Warehouse
Works
Bowling Greens
Albert Park
Millbrae Bri.
Langside
NETHER POLLOK PLAYING FIELDS
Playing Fields
Lodge
Tennis Courts
CITY OF
G41
G43
DUMBRECK RD. B768
TITWOOD RD.
HAGGS ROAD B769
POLLOKSHAWS ROAD A77
LANGSIDE AVENUE B768
KILMARNOCK ROAD
DARNLEY RD. B763
MINARD ROAD
NITHSDALE ROAD
MAXWELL DRIVE
SHIELDS ROAD
SPRINGKELL AVENUE
SHAWMOSS RD.
AULDHOUSE RD.
CAMPHILL AVENUE
RIVERSIDE
CORROUR ROAD
101
82
118
A
B
C
D
1
2
3
4
5
6

E
F
G
H
1
2
3
4
5
6
West St.
Glasgow Parcels Sta.
Laurieston
83
59
BALLATER
COMMERCIAL CT.
Palace (Museum)
Leisure Cen.
GORBALS
Hutchesontown
CALEDONIA ROAD
A730
A74 STREET
KING'S BRIDGE
CLYDE
RIVER
Glasgow Green
Tennis Courts
Polmadie Bridge
PLAYING FIELDS
Port Dundas
Training Cen.
Works
Gasholder Station
EGLINTON
A77
ROAD
Freightliner Terminal
Cemetery
CATHCART
A728
RUTHERGLEN ROAD
G5
GLASGOW
Bus Depot
Govanhill
Gushetfaulds Junction
DIXONS BLAZES INDUSTRIAL ESTATE
John Bosco Sec. Sch.
AIKENHEAD
POLMADIE
Park
CALDER STREET
B763
Swim. Pool
Lib.
Hlth. Cen.
Works
Factory
Depots
Oatlands
POLMADIE INDUSTRIAL ESTATE
104
Crosshill
G42
Polmadie Marshalling Yard
WORKS
QUEEN MARY AVENUE
Holyroad Sec. Sch.
MYRTLE
Crosshill
Football Grounds
Recreation Ground
Miniature Golf Course
Hangingshaw
Cathkin Park
TORYGLEN PARK
Playing Fields
Community Centre
PROSPECTHILL ROAD
B768
VICTORIA INFIRMARY
Mt. Florida
Battlefield
Coll.
B766
Depot
Playing Fields
Prim. Sch.
Play. Fld.
Hampden Sch.
Toryglen
Comm. Cen.
Football Grd.
HAMPDEN PARK
QUEEN'S PARK F.C.
Mount Florida
CURLING
Public Park
G44
MONTFORD AVENUE
CASTLEMILK ROAD
KING'S PK. RD.
Rec. Grd.
Works
119
King's Park
Schs.
Lib.
King's Pk.

104
A
B
C
D
84
120
103
1
2
3
4
5
6
Bridgeton
Bridgeton Cross
Barrow Field
CITY OF
Glasgow Green
Suspension Bridge
Tennis Courts
PLAYING FIELDS
Polmadie Bridge
Richmond Park
Model Yacht Pond
Polmadie Burn
Shawfields Stadium
SHAWFIELD IND. EST.
Training Cen.
Dalmarnock
DALMARNOCK
Caravan Park
Works
G40
G5
G42
G73
G44
Oatlands
Depots
POLMADIE INDUSTRIAL ESTATE
Polmadie Marshalling Yard
Warehouse
Shawfield
Shawfield Ind. Est.
Southcroft Park
Sewage Works
Bridgeton Bank
Trading Estate
RUTHERGLEN IND. EST.
Rutherglen
Rutherglen Mus.
Community Centre
Burnhill Sports Cen.
Rec. Grd.
Toryglen
Clincarthill
LANARK
Bankhead
Overtoun Park
Public Pk.
King's Park
Public Park
HOSP.
Hlth. Cen.
KING'S DR.
JAMES ST.
LONDON ROAD
A74
DALMARNOCK ROAD
A749
DUNN ST.
B763
RUTHERGLEN ROAD
A730
GLASGOW ROAD
PROSPECTHILL RD.
B768
BURNHILL ST.
MAIN ST.
MILL ST.
STONELAW RD.
FARMELOAN RD.
POLMADIE ROAD
SHAWFIELD DR.
CLYDESIDE RD.
RIVER CLYDE
KINGSBRIDGE DRIVE
KINGSHEATH

GLASGOW
G31
G32
G72
RUTHERGLEN
THE SHIRE
85
121
106
63
64
62
61
E
F
G
H
1
2
3
4
5
6
TOLLCROSS PARK
SHETTLESTON DAY HOSP.
BELVIDERE HOSPITAL
Celtic Sports Grd.
Westthorn Rec. Grd.
Helenvale Park
Braidfauld
Dalbeth
Cemetery
Bonded Stores
Depot
Factory
Works
Sand Pit
Cuningar
RIVER CLYDE
Clyde Workshops
Junc. 1
Hamilton Farm
Farme Cross
Gallowflat
Eastfield
Trinity High Sch.
Playing Field
Recreation Ground
CAMBUSLANG IND. PARK
Silverbank
Somervell Park
St. Paul's Prim. Sch.
St. Mark's Prim. Sch.
Football Grounds
College
Nursery
Bowling Greens
Comm. Cen.
Bus Garage
Burial Grd.
Ind. Est.
A74
A724
LONDON ROAD
BUSLANG
STREET
COUNTY ROAD
GLASGOW RD.
CAMBUSLANG ROAD
BOGLESHOLE RD.
DRUMHEAD RD.
FULLARTON
CLYDESMILL RD.
DUKE'S RD.

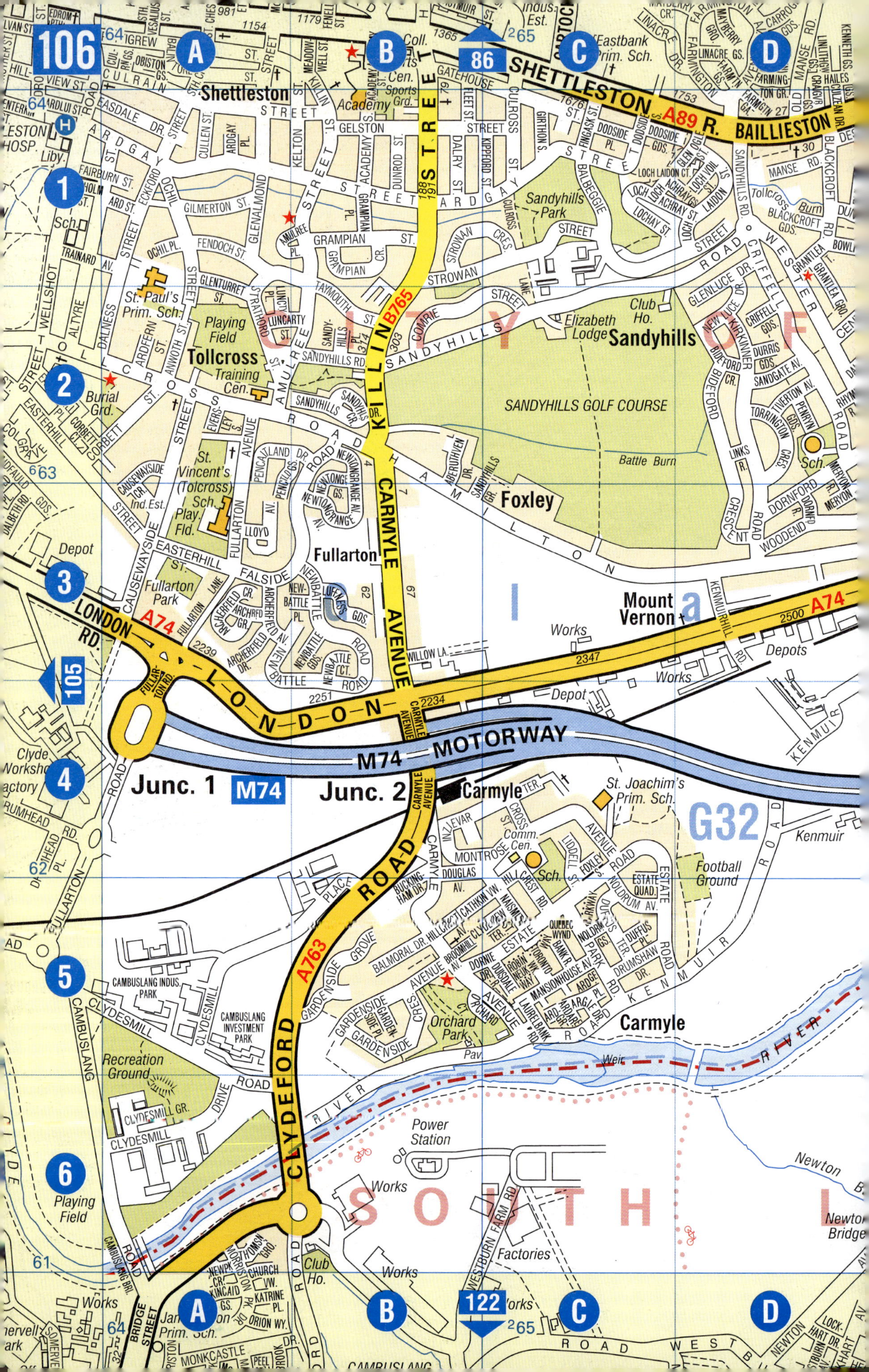

Shettleston
SHETTLESTON R.
A89
BAILLIESTON
86
Eastbank Prim. Sch.
Academy
Sports Grd.
Coll.
Tollcross
St. Paul's Prim. Sch.
Playing Field
Tollcross Training Cen.
Burial Grd.
Sandyhills Park
Sandyhills
Elizabeth Lodge
Club Ho.
SANDYHILLS GOLF COURSE
Battle Burn
Foxley
Fullarton
St. Vincent's (Tolcross) Sch.
Play. Fld.
Fullarton Park
Depot
Mount Vernon
Works
Depots
KILLIN STREET
B765
CARMYLE AVENUE
HAMILTON ROAD
LONDON RD.
A74
LONDON
105
M74 MOTORWAY
Junc. 1
M74
Junc. 2
Carmyle
St. Joachim's Prim. Sch.
G32
Kenmuir
Football Ground
Comm. Cen.
Sch.
CLYDEFORD ROAD
A763
Orchard Park
Carmyle
KENMUIR ROAD
RIVER
Weir
CAMBUSLANG INDUS. PARK
CAMBUSLANG INVESTMENT PARK
Recreation Ground
Clyde Workshops
Factory
Power Station
Works
SOUTH
Newton
Newton Bridge
Factories
Playing Field
Club Ho.
WESTBURN FARM RD
122
BRIDGE STREET
Prim. Sch.
CAMBUSLANG
A B C D
1 2 3 4 5 6

E
F
G
H
87
67
68
Barrachnie
Baillieston
Muirhead
Mount Vernon
Broomhouse
GLASGOW
LANARKSHIRE
GLASGOW ROAD
MAIN ST.
A89
B7058
VERNON AVENUE
MOUNT VERNON AVENUE
HAMILTON ROAD
A74
Bannerman High Sch.
Prim. Sch.
Sch.
Hlth. Cen.
Lib.
Rec. Grd.
Running Track
Lodge
Pav.
Hall
Playing Field
Mount Vernon Sports Stadium
Boghall
Works
GLASGOW ZOO
Junction 3
M74
M74 MOTORWAY
G69
G71
G72
Wester Daldowie
Orchard Cottage
Kenmuir Hill
Kenmuirhill
Kenmuir Wood
CLYDE
Sewage Works
Dovecote
Chuckie Hill
Daldowie Crematorium
Newton Farm
West Haughhead
Clydeway Golf Driving Range
Honeyhill Plantation
Waterfall
Newton Bridge
Westburn
Gowanbank
NEWTON FARM RD.
123
Playground
Calder Bri.
ROUNDKNOWE
108
1
2
3
4
5
6
61
62
63
64
Junc
CHURCH ST.
MILLER ST.
NELSON
GEORGE ST.
MUIRSIDE ST.
SCOTT STREET
SOUTH SCOTT ST.
CALDER PLACE
LOANCROFT PL.
LOANCROFT HO.
MUIRHEAD ROAD
BAILLIESTON ROAD
DRUMPELLIER
CALDEDONIA
CALEDONIA
ROWANDALE AV.
ROSEDALE DR.
HUNTINGTOWER RD.
HAIG
BOWES RD.
SHERBURN GDS.
BURNTBROOM
GREENTREE
OAKHILL AV.
ORCHARD DRIVE
CASTLE ST.
ALBION ST.
TUDOR ST.
MOSS PATH
CALDERPARK AV.
LUSSHILL TER.
MANSIONHOUSE RD.
CARRICK DRIVE
KENMUIR AV.
WEIRWOOD AV.
WHIRLOW AV.
BUCHANAN ST.
ROBERTSON

A
B
C
D
88
124
107
1
2
3
4
5
6
68
69
64
63
62
61
Baillieston
Crosshill
Muirhead
Junction 2
(M73)
Junction 1
(M73)
Junction 4
(M74)
Cattle Grid
G69
CITY OF GLASGOW
M73
M74
M73 MOTORWAY
M74 MOTORWAY
Waterfall
Newlands Glen
Thornyburn
Calderbank
House
Woodhead
Farm
Newlands
Farm
Ellismuir
Glasgow
NORTH
Station
Park
Memorial
Park
Memorial
Hall
GLASGOW ZOO
CALDERBRAES
GOLF COURSE
North Calder Water
Club House
Roundknowe
ROUNDKNOWE RD.
Calder
Bri.
HAMILTON RD. A721 GLASGOW
GLASGOW & EDINBURGH RD.
A8
Daldowie
Crematorium
Calderbraes
OLD EDINBURGH ROAD
B7001
EDINBURGH ROAD
Birkenshaw
Recreation
Grd.
Birkenshaw
Sports
Hall
Aitkenhead
Prim. Sch.
Warehouses
Depots
Powburn
NEW EDINBURGH
A721
HOLMBRAE RD.
GLASGOW ROAD
B7071
FARM ROAD
BLANTYRE
B758
RIVER CLYDE
West
Haughhead
East
Haughhead
Clydeway
Golf Driving
Range
Works
Waterfall
SOUTH
LANARKSHIRE
Kylepark
Uddingston
Meadowbank
Playing
Fields
Myers

E
F
G
H
89
71
72
64
1
2
3
4
5
6
63
62
61
110
125
70
Bargeddie
Factory
Braehead Piggery
Braehead
Works Depot
LANGMUIR WAY
LANGMUIR A752 RD.
Viaduct
Football Grds.
Kirkwood Sports Barn
Kirkwood
Prim. Sch.
St. Monica's Prim. Sch.
St. James Prim. Sch.
Coatbridge
Showcase Cinema
Old Monkland Cemetery
EDINBURGH ROAD
A8
Rosebank
Luggie Bri.
Calder Water
North
Thistlebank Cott.
Bankhead
ML5
Kirkstyle Cotts.
KIRKSHAWS
Aitkenhead
Ravel Burn
A752
Chemical Works
LANARKSHIRE
Crowflat Wood
The Wilderness
Craighead Belt
Grove Wood
Red Burn
Playing Fields
Tannochside
TANNOCHSIDE PARK
G71
Superstore
Running Track
Tannochside Prim. Sch.
Playing Fields
Burnhead Prim. Sch.
St. Gabriel's Prim. Sch.
PUBLIC PARK
Bowling Grn.
Hlth. Cen.
Liby.
Comm. Cen.
THE BIRCHWOOD COURTYARDS
Comm. Centre
OLD EDINBURGH ROAD
B7001
Viewpark
St. Columba's Prim. Sch.
ML4
Depot
Warehouse
Bellshill
VIEWPARK SHOP. CEN.
Works
Viewpark Gdns.
Fallside
Warehouses
LABURNUM ROAD
MYRTLE ROAD
BURNHEAD STREET
AITKENHEAD ROAD

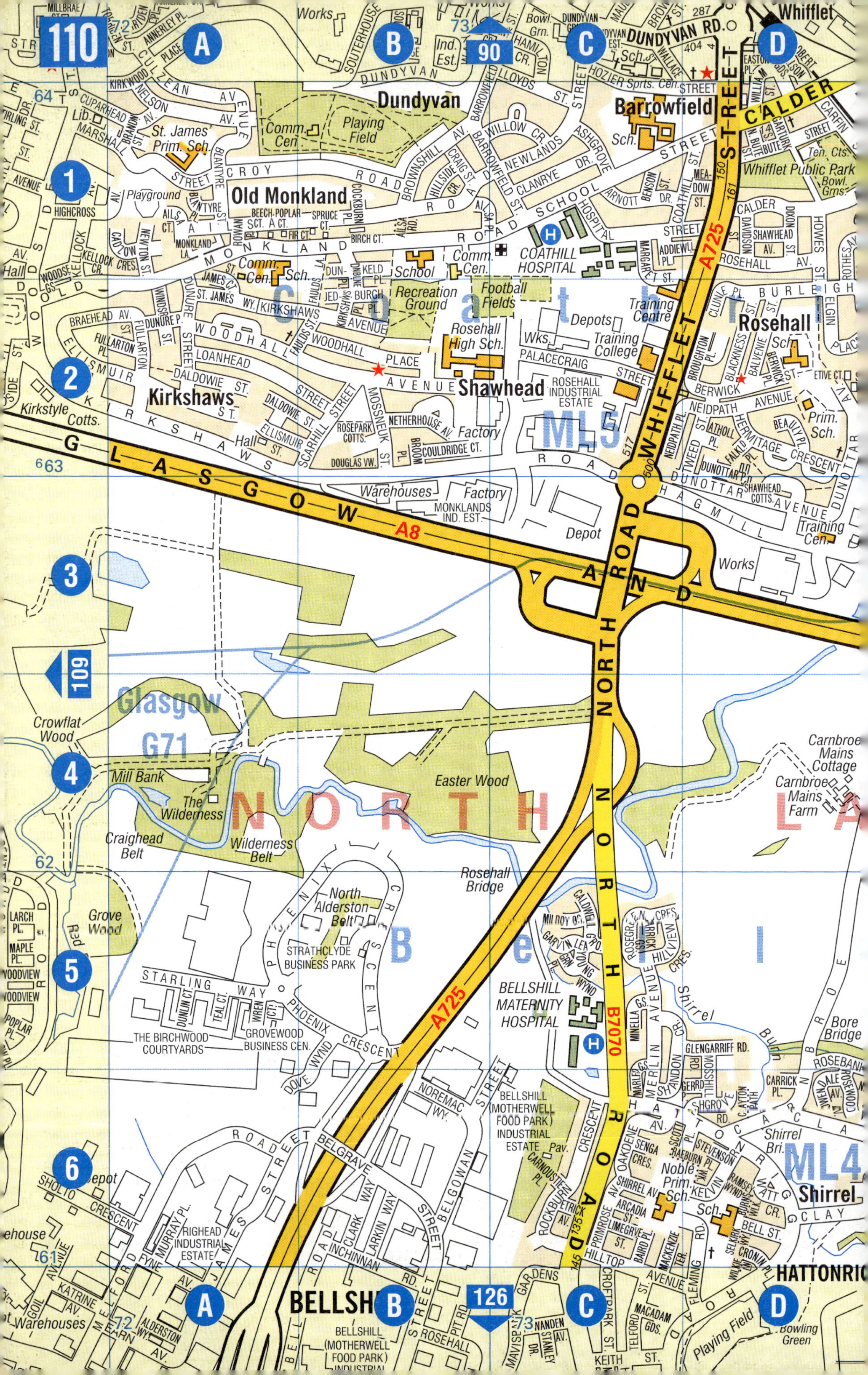
A
B
C
D
1
2
3
4
5
6
90
109
126
Dundyvan
Barrowfield
Whifflet
Old Monkland
Kirkshaws
Shawhead
Rosehall
ML5
Glasgow
G71
NORTH LA
Bellshill
ML4
Shirrel
HATTONRIG
DUNDYVAN RD.
CALDER STREET
WHIFFLET STREET
A725
A8
GLASGOW ROAD
NORTH ROAD
B7070
CROY ROAD
MONKLAND ROAD
SCHOOL ROAD
WOODHALL AVENUE
KIRKSHAWS ROAD
HAGMILL ROAD
COATHILL HOSPITAL
Playing Field
Comm. Cen.
Recreation Ground
Football Fields
Rosehall High Sch.
ROSEHALL INDUSTRIAL ESTATE
Training College
Training Centre
Depots
Factory
Warehouses
MONKLANDS IND. EST.
Depot
Works
Kirkstyle Cotts.
Crowflat Wood
Mill Bank
The Wilderness
Craighead Belt
Wilderness Belt
Easter Wood
Rosehall Bridge
Carnbroe Mains Cottage
Carnbroe Mains Farm
North Alderston Belt
STRATHCLYDE BUSINESS PARK
STARLING WAY
PHOENIX CRESCENT
THE BIRCHWOOD COURTYARDS
GROVEWOOD BUSINESS CEN.
BELLSHILL MATERNITY HOSPITAL
BELLSHILL (MOTHERWELL FOOD PARK) INDUSTRIAL ESTATE
Grove Wood
Shirrel Burn
Bore Bridge
Noble Prim. Sch.
Shirrel Bri.
BELGRAVE STREET
JAMES STREET
RIGHEAD INDUSTRIAL ESTATE
Warehouses
Playing Field
Bowling Green

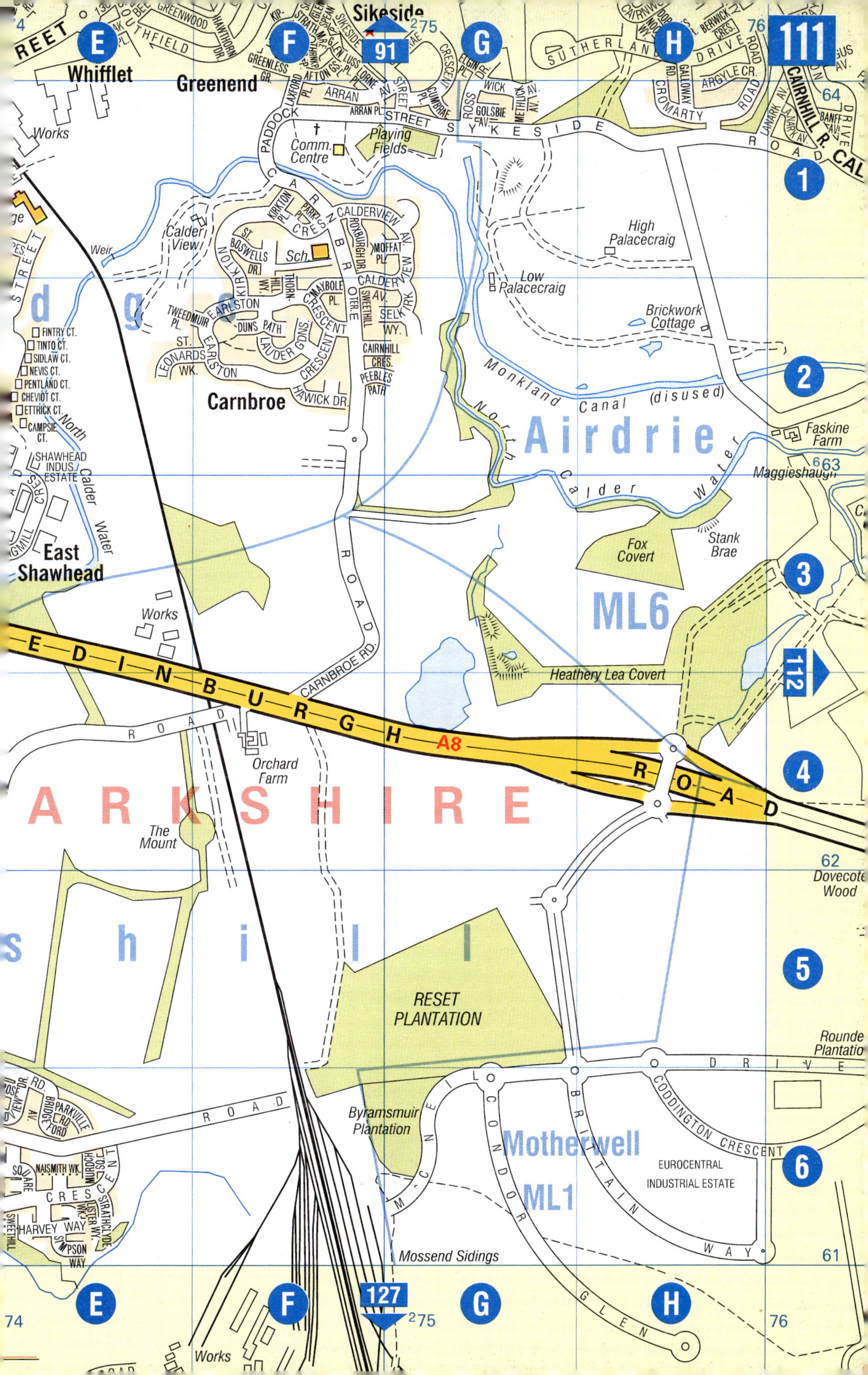

Whifflet
Greenend
Sikeside
91
275
76
Works
Comm. Centre
Playing Fields
SYKESIDE STREET
SUTHERLAND DRIVE
CAIRNHILL R.
High Palacecraig
Low Palacecraig
Brickwork Cottage
Calder View
Weir
Sch.
Carnbroe
Monkland Canal (disused)
Airdrie
North Calder Water
Faskine Farm
Maggieshaugh
63
Fox Covert
Stank Brae
East Shawhead
SHAWHEAD INDUS. ESTATE
ML6
Works
Heathery Lea Covert
112
EDINBURGH ROAD
A8
CARNBROE RD.
Orchard Farm
LANARKSHIRE
The Mount
62
Dovecote Wood
RESET PLANTATION
Rounde Plantatio
Byramsmuir Plantation
Motherwell
ML1
EUROCENTRAL INDUSTRIAL ESTATE
CODDINGTON CRESCENT
BRITAIN WAY
CONDOR GLEN
DRIVE
Mossend Sidings
61
127
74
275
76
Works

A
B
C
D
1
2
3
4
5
6
BROWNSBURN INDUSTRIAL ESTATE
92
111
128
CALDERBANK B802 RD.
BROWNSBURN B8058
Brownsburn
CALDERBANK B802 RD.
MAIN ST.
WOODHALL MILL B802 ROAD
CAIRNHILL ROAD
SYKESIDE ROAD
CARLISLE A73 ROAD
Monkland Bridge
Westerbo
CHAPELHALL INDUSTRIAL ESTATE
Depot
NORTH L
Hillhead
(disused)
Faskine Farm
CALDERBANK
Maggieshaugh
Cricket Grd.
Stank Brae
Calderbank Prim. Sch.
Manse
Playing Field
Sch.
Bowl. Grn.
Playground
Dam
North Calder Water
Chapelhall Prim. Sch.
Crogalglen
Kennel Burn
Football Ground
WOODHALL COTTAGE ROAD
Woodhall Cottage
GLASGOW A8 AND EDINBU-
Dovecote Wood
Blacklands Plantation
NEWHOUSE INDUSTRIAL ESTATE
Roundel Plantation
McNEIL DRIVE
CRESCENT
CODDINGTON
EUROCENTRAL IND. EST.
B799
BO'NESS ROAD
WOODHALL ROAD
ROWANTREE AVENUE
EDINBURGH ROAD
Bowling Green
Pav.
Motherwell
76
77
64
63
62
61

Gartness
Bowhouse
GARTNESS DRIVE
BOWHOUSE ROAD
CRAIGENDS
Damhead Farm
93
79
Clattering Burn
280
Easter Dunsyston
64
DUNISTON ROAD
Craigends
CALDERVALE ST.
BOWHOUSEBRAE ROAD
Works
Sauchenbog Bridge
Shotts Burn
Gartness Farm
GARTNESS ROAD
NARKSHIRE
BURNIEBRAE
MILL ROAD
LAWHOPE MILL
Wester Dunsyston
63
MAIN ST.
LAUCHOPE ST.
B799
Comm. Cen.
ROBERTON ST.
NISBETT ST.
ASHER RD.
RUSSELL ST.
Football Ground
St. Aloysius Prim. Sch.
CHAPELHALL
MAIN STREET
BELLSIDE ROAD
A73
Bailside Farm
Budshaw
Waterfall
ABBOTSFORD RD.
McPHERSON CRES.
ARRANVIEW ST.
CRESCENT
BIGGAR ROAD
TURNBERRY CRES.
ML6
Junction 6
M8
M8 MOTORWAY
62
Sandyford Farm
A8
BELLSIDE RD.
Reservoir
B7066
GLASGOW AND EDINBURGH ROAD
Newhouse
Motel
Pollockshill
BIGGAR RD.
A775
NICKLAUS WAY
BODDEN SQUARE
315
ML1
Greenside
B7066
MOTHERWELL RD.
CARLISLE ROAD
A73
61
EGBRANNOCK RD.
78
129
79
280
Burn
E
F
G
H
1
2
3
4
5
6

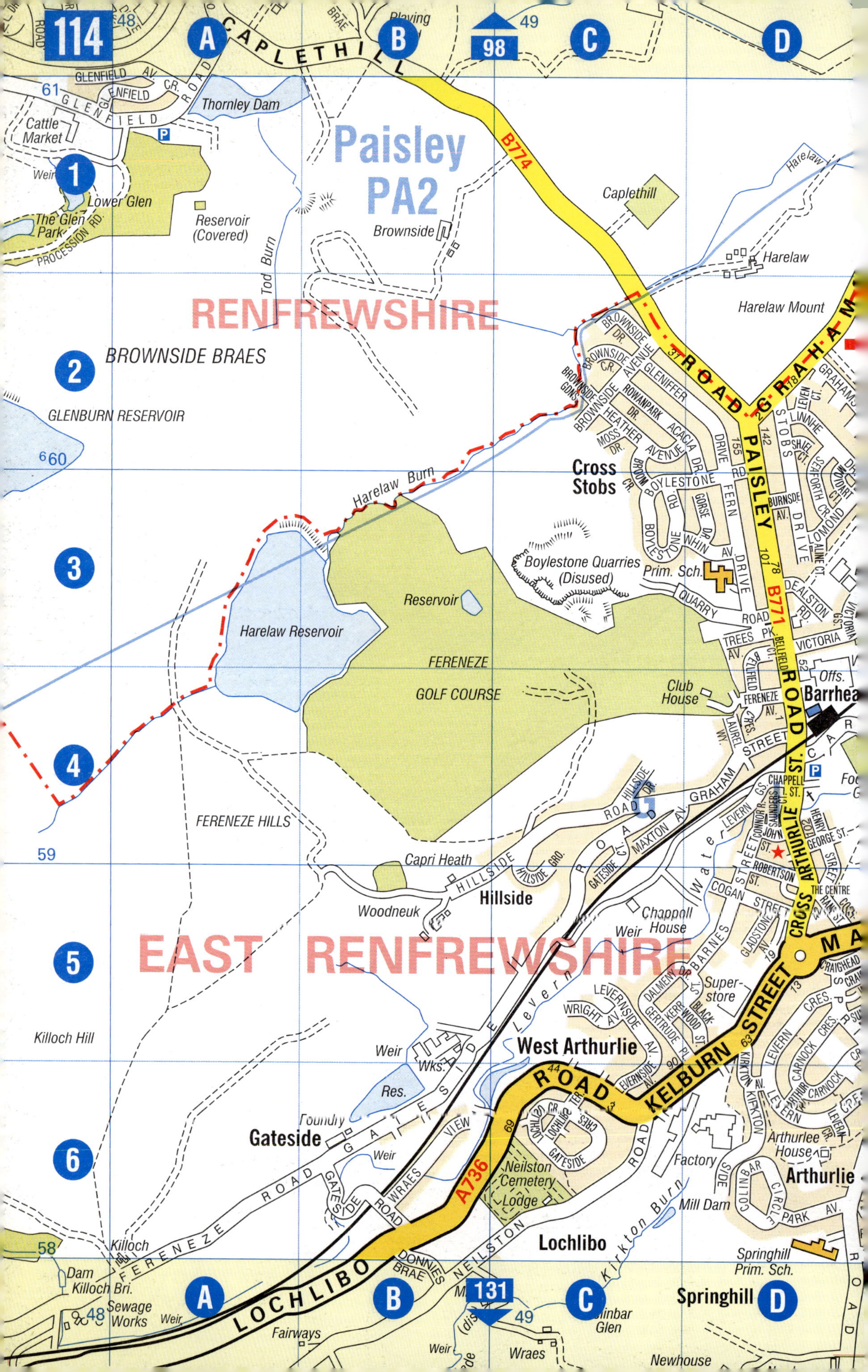
A
B
C
D
1
2
3
4
5
6
98
131
49
48
61
60
59
58
CAPLETHILL
Playing
BRAE
GLENFIELD AV.
GLENFIELD CR.
GLENFIELD ROAD
Cattle Market
Thornley Dam
Paisley PA2
B774
Weir
Lower Glen
The Glen Park
PROCESSION RD.
Reservoir (Covered)
Tod Burn
Brownside
Caplethill
Harelaw
Harelaw Mount
RENFREWSHIRE
BROWNSIDE BRAES
GLENBURN RESERVOIR
BROWNSIDE DR.
BROWNSIDE CR.
BROWNSIDE GDNS.
BROWNSIDE AVENUE
GLENIFFER
ROWANPARK DR.
HEATHER AVENUE
MOSS DR.
ACACIA DR.
BROOM CR.
BOYLESTONE RD.
BOYLESTONE
GORSE DR.
WHIN AV.
FERN DRIVE
ROAD GRAHAM
PAISLEY RD
LEVEN CT.
LINNHE CT.
STOBS DRIVE
SHIEL CT.
SEAFORTH CR.
BURNSIDE AV.
LOMOND
ALLINE CT.
DEALSTON RD.
B771
Cross Stobs
Harelaw Burn
Boylestone Quarries (Disused)
Prim. Sch.
QUARRY ROAD
TREES PK.
AV.
BELLFIELD CT.
VICTORIA
Offs.
Barrhead
Harelaw Reservoir
Reservoir
FERENEZE GOLF COURSE
Club House
FERENEZE AV.
CRES.
LAUREL WY.
STREET
ROAD
CAR
FERENEZE HILLS
HILLSIDE DR.
ROAD
GRAHAM
MAXTON AV.
LEVERN
CONNOR R.
SAUNDERS
CHAPPELL ST.
ST.
JOHN ST.
HENRY
GEORGE ST.
Water
ROBERTSON ST.
COGAN STREET
THE CENTRE
CROSS ARTHURLIE ST.
Capri Heath
HILLSIDE
HILLSIDE GRO.
GATESIDE CT.
Hillside
Woodneuk
Chappell House
Weir
EAST RENFREWSHIRE
BARNES ST.
GLADSTONE AV.
Super-store
MAIN
CRAIGHEAD
SPRINGHILL
LEVERNSIDE AV.
WRIGHT AV.
DALMENY
GERTRUDE PL.
KERR ST.
WOOD ST.
BLACK
STREET
KELBURN
ROAD
Levern
West Arthurlie
EVERNSIDE AV.
KIRKTON AV.
LEVERN CRES.
CARNOCK CRES.
ARTHURLIE
Killoch Hill
Weir
Wks.
Res.
GATESIDE
Foundry
Gateside
Weir
VIEW
WRAES
GATESIDE ROAD
A736
LOCHLIBO CR.
LOCHLIBO TER.
GATESIDE CRES.
Neilston Cemetery
Lodge
Factory
KIRKTON SIDE
Arthurlee House
Arthurlie
COLINBAR CIRCLE
PARK AV.
Mill Dam
Kirkton Burn
FERENEZE ROAD
Killoch
Dam
Killoch Bri.
Sewage Works
Weir
LOCHLIBO
DONNIES BRAE
NEILSTON
Lochlibo
Springhill Prim. Sch.
Springhill
Colinbar Glen
Fairways
Wraes
Newhouse

E
F
99
51
G
H
52
Roughmussel
Hurlet
West Hurlet House
BARRHEAD RD.
NITSHILL
Levern Bridge
Depot
Hurlet Cottages
A726
A736
LEVERN ROAD
Harelaw Burn
Raes Wood
Tinto House
Logansraes
Waterside
Cemetery
Salterland Bridge
Blackbyres
BLACKBYRES
PINMORE
SEAMILL
St. Bernard's Prim. Sch.
NITSHILL
Nitshill
G53
Sports Ground
Depot
Sewage Works
WOODHEAD ROAD
Works
CITY OF GLASGOW
Weir
Factory
Prim. Sch.
Works
Crossmill
Bowerwalls
Water
WILLOWFORD ROAD
WHITACRES RD.
CROSSMILL
Parkhouse
PARKHOUSE ROAD
Works
St. John's Prim. Sch.
Dovecothall
Levern
Adult Training Cen.
116
Raisdale
Redhall
B773
DARNLEY ROAD
Tower Rais
Comm. Cen.
Weir
GLASGOW STREET
War Memorial
Carlibar Prim. Sch.
COWAN PARK
Bandstand
Barrhead Sports Cen.
Barrhead High Sch.
Aurs
Dubbs
Health Cen.
Playing Fields
Burn
59
Lib.
Mus.
Offs.
Aurs Bridge
Convent
BARRHEAD
G78
Sch.
North Brae
Sch.
Auchenback
58
Waterfall Weirs
St. Luke's High Sch.
Lyoncross
250
51
52
1
2
3
4
5
6
61
60

116
A
B
C
D
100
132
115
52
53
61
60
59
58
1
2
3
4
5
6
Works
Levern Bridge
GLENLORA
HARTSTON RD.
PRIESTHILL
Prim. Sch.
Bowl. Green
PRESTWICK ST.
NEWFIELD SQUARE
BANKBRAE AV.
OVERTOWN AV.
JOHNSBURN RD.
GLENTYAN TER.
HOUSEHILLWOOD
HOUSEHILLMUIR ROAD
HOUSEHILLMUIR
DUNSIDE DR.
CITY OF
RAVENSCRAIG DRIVE
LINNHEAD DRIVE
GLENMUIR
Comm. Cen.
Sch.
PRIESTHILL
BROCK ROAD
BROCK OVAL
FREELAND DR.
MUIRSHIEL
Bellarmine Secondary School
Recreation Ground
Comm. Cen.
COWGLEN HOSPITAL
M77
M77 MOTORWAY
St. Robert's Prim. Sch.
PRIESTHILL CRESCENT
Kennishead Wood
Burnbrae Prim. Sch.
Burn
MUIRSHIELL CRESCENT
ELLISTON AV.
ELLISTON DR.
NEILSTON AV.
Brock Burn
NITSHILL
NITSHILL ROAD
SEAMILL ST.
St. Bernard's Prim. Sch.
CLEEVES ROAD
QUADRANT ROAD
Nitshill
Playground
Priesthill & Darnley
DRIVE
Works
Depot
WOODHEAD
Works
Factory
Prim. Sch.
South Nitshill
WOODNEUK ROAD
WELBECK RD.
DARNLEY INDUS. ESTATE
Nursing Home
KENNISHEAD ROAD
GLEN CONA DR.
GLEN AFFRIC AV.
GLEN AFFRIC DRIVE
Play. Fields
Lib.
Sch.
A726
WHITEHAUGH ROAD
WHITACRES ROAD
WOODFOOT ROAD
PARKHOUSE ROAD
B773
CRAIGFLOWER ROAD
COLWOOD AVENUE
BRUNTSFIELD AV.
MILLVIEW PL.
Mill
Superstore
G53
Superstore
ARDEN
Prim. Schools
KILBEG T.
KYLEAKIN TER.
WAUKGLEN DRIVE
WAUKGLEN CRESCENT
WAUKGLEN AVENUE
HABERLEA AV.
CORSELET ROAD
Junc. 3
A726
INVEREWE
Jenny Lind
INVERGARRY
Burn
Waukmill Glen
Upper Darnley
Works
M77 MOTORWAY
M77
G78
G77
Works
Waterfall
Weirs
WAULKMILL GLEN RESERVOIR
Patterton
Patterton
ROAD

GLASGOW
EAST RENFREWSHIRE
COWGLEN GOLF COURSE
Pollok Wood
Pollokwood House
Kennishead
KENNISHEAD
King George's Field
Thornliebank
Carnwadric
Auldhouse Playing Field
Eastwood Cemy.
Cemetery
Sewage Works
Orchard Park
Playing Fields
Woodfarm High Sch.
Giffnock
St. Ninian's High Sch.
Eastwood Park
Recreation Cen.
Municipal Offices
Rouken Glen Park
Miniature Golf Course
DEACONSBANK GOLF COURSE
Busby Junction
Auldhouse Burn
Mansewood
Industrial Est.
THORNLIEBANK INDUSTRIAL ESTATE
BARRHEAD ROAD
NETHER AULDHOUSE RD.
THORNLIEBANK ROAD
MAIN STREET
SPIERSBRIDGE ROAD
STEWARTON ROAD
ROUKEN GLEN ROAD
FENWICK RD.
AYR RD.
EASTWOODMAINS ROAD
B769
A726
A77
G43
G46
101
118
133

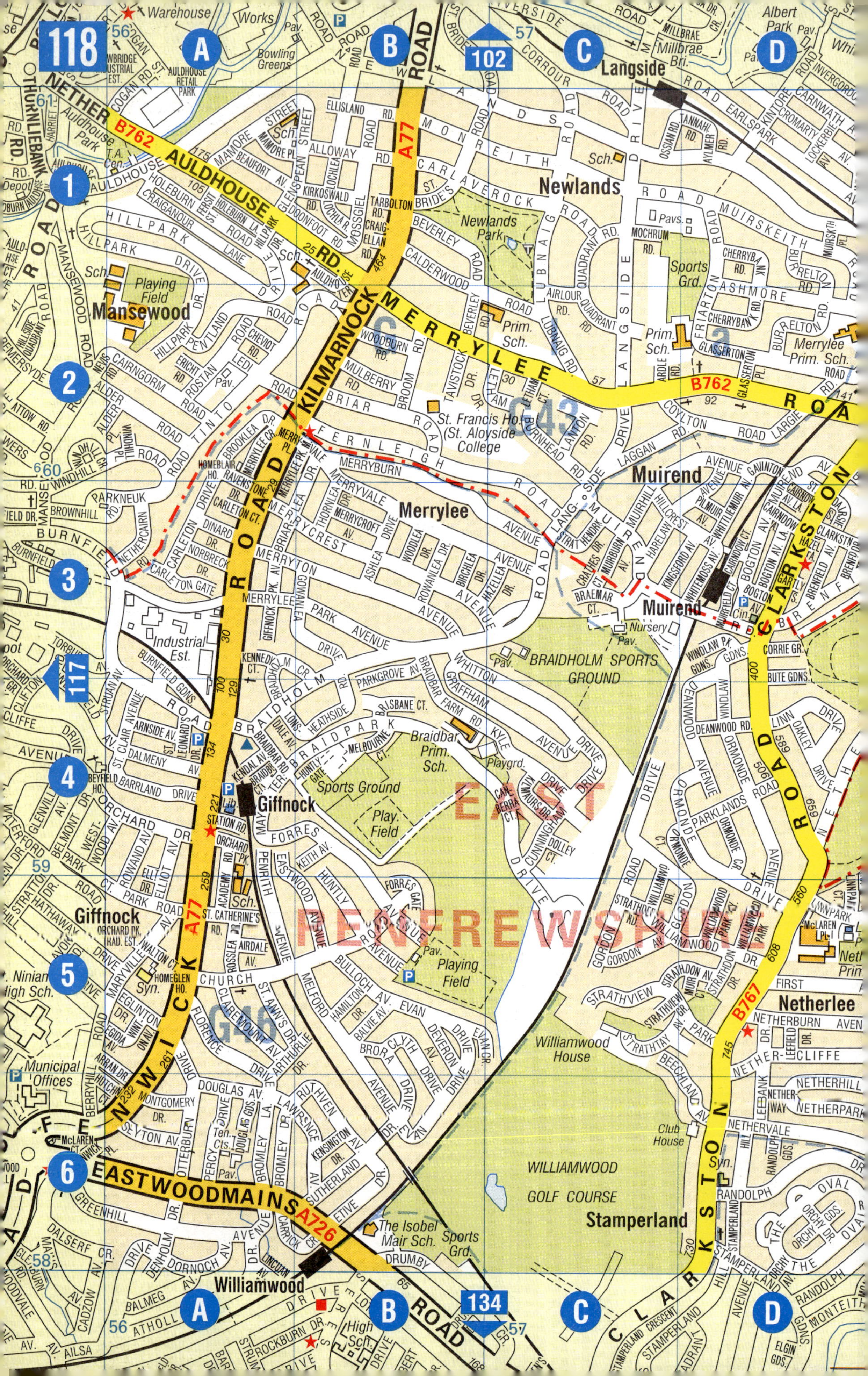
118
A
B
C
D
1
2
3
4
5
6
102
117
134
Langside
Newlands
Newlands Park
Mansewood
Playing Field
Merrylee
Muirend
Giffnock
Netherlee
Stamperland
Williamwood
Williamwood House
WILLIAMWOOD GOLF COURSE
BRAIDHOLM SPORTS GROUND
Sports Ground
Play. Field
Playing Field
Industrial Est.
St. Francis Hosp. (St. Aloyside College
Braidbar Prim. Sch.
The Isobel Mair Sch.
Municipal Offices
Club House
EAST RENFREWSHIRE
NETHER AULDHOUSE RD.
AULDHOUSE RD.
KILMARNOCK ROAD
MERRYLEE ROAD
FERNLEIGH ROAD
BRAIDPARK
FENWICK RD.
EASTWOODMAINS ROAD
CLARKSTON ROAD
B762
B767
A77
A726
Warehouse
Works
Bowling Greens
Sports Grd.
Pavs.
Prim. Sch.
Merrylee Prim. Sch.
Sch.
Nursery
Pav.
Playgrd.
Syn.
High Sch.

E
F
G
H
103
135
120
1
2
3
4
5
6
King's Park
Croftfoot
Castlemilk
Cathcart
King's-Pk.
KING'S PARK AVENUE
B762
KING'S PARK RD.
AIKENHEAD ROAD
MENOCK RD.
MANSE BRAE
DELVIN ROAD
OLD CASTLE STREET
New Bri.
CARMUNNOCK ROAD
B766
CROFTFOOT ROAD
CARMUNNOCK BY-PASS
KING'S PARK
Aikenhead House
KING'S PARK GOLF COURSE
Club House
Playing Fields
Bowling Green
Castle (rems. of)
Court Knowe
Old Bri.
LINN PARK
Mansion House
Putting Green
LINN PARK GOLF COURSE
Crematorium
Cemetery
St. Raymond's School
LINNPARK INDUSTRIAL ESTATE
Depot
Factory
Works
Netherton Prim. Sch.
St. Margaret Mary's Prim. Sch.
St. Margaret Mary's Sec. Sch.
Castleton Prim. Sch.
Windlaw Prim. Sch.
Simshill Prim. Sch.
St. Mirin's Prim. Sch.
Mid Netherton
NETHERTON BRAES
CITY OF GLASGOW
G44
G45
G76
CROFTPARK AVENUE
CARNA DRIVE
SIMSHILL ROAD
RAITHBURN AVENUE
DRAKEMIRE DRIVE
LAINSHAW DRIVE
CROFTON AVENUE
ARNPRIOR ROAD
DOUGRIE ROAD
DOWNCRAIG ROAD
BIRGIDALE ROAD
DUNAGOIL ROAD
CROFTFOOT ROAD
CARMUNNOCK ROAD
KINGSACRE ROAD
Public Park
Lib.
Sch.
Schs.
Tennis Cts.
Pavs.
Grave Yards
Rec. Grd.
Works
Comm. Cen.
Hlth. Cen.
Bowl. Grn.
58
59
60
260
262

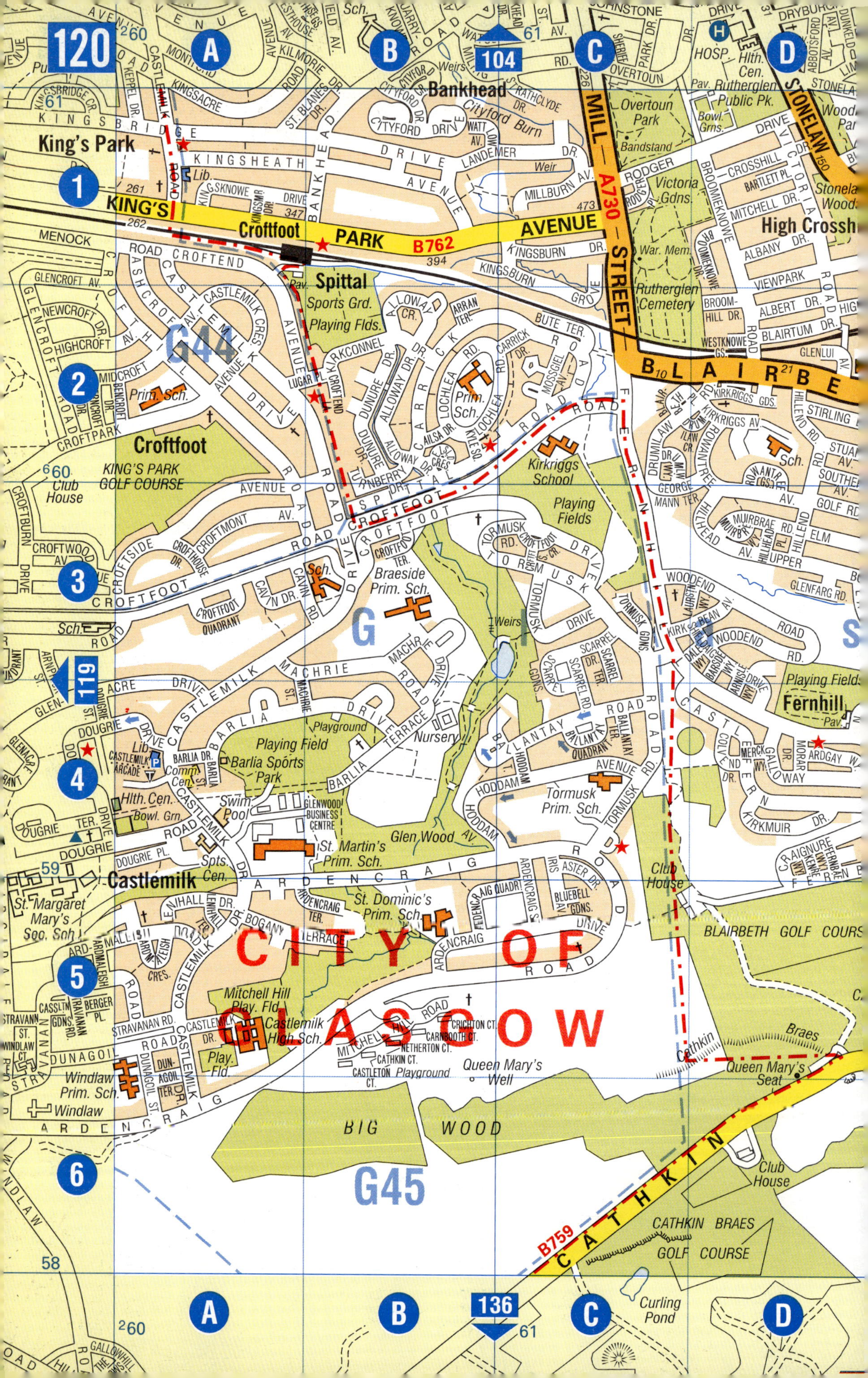

104
136
119
A
B
C
D
1
2
3
4
5
6
King's Park
Bankhead
KING'S PARK AVENUE
B762
Croftfoot
Spittal
Sports Grd.
Playing Flds.
Overtoun Park
Bandstand
Victoria Gdns.
War. Mem.
Rutherglen Cemetery
MILL STREET
A730
High Crosshill
BLAIRBETH
G44
G45
Croftfoot
KING'S PARK GOLF COURSE
Club House
Prim. Sch.
Kirkriggs School
Playing Fields
Braeside Prim. Sch.
Barlia Sports Park
Playing Field
Playground
Nursery
Tormusk Prim. Sch.
St. Martin's Prim. Sch.
Glen Wood
Castlemilk
St. Dominic's Prim. Sch.
CITY OF GLASGOW
Mitchell Hill Play. Fld.
Castlemilk High Sch.
Windlaw Prim. Sch.
Queen Mary's Well
Queen Mary's Seat
Cathkin Braes
BLAIRBETH GOLF COURSE
BIG WOOD
CATHKIN
B759
CATHKIN BRAES GOLF COURSE
Club House
Curling Pond
Fernhill
Playing Fields
Hosp.
Rutherglen Public Pk.
Stonelaw

Eastfield
105
63
Trinity High Sch.
Works
Playing Field
64
E
F
G
H
Recreation Grd.
Calderwood Prim. Sch.
BULLIONSLAW
COLVILLE DR.
OVERLEA AV.
Silverbank
GLASGOW RD.
A724
Somervell Park
Cambuslang
MAIN ST.
James Prim. Sch.
1
GREYSTONE
SOUTHHILL
DUKE'S ROAD
B762
124
73
GLENSIDE
BALMORAL DR.
MILTON AV.
CAMBUSLANG
WELLSHOT
HAMILTON DR.
CADZOW DR.
2
Burnside
EAST KILBRIDE ROAD
A749
A730
ROAD
WESTBURN
Burnside Sports Ground
STEWARTON
West Coats Prim. Sch.
Kirkhill
60
GRENVILLE
DOUGLAS DRIVE
3
LANGLEA
High Burnside
St. Anthony's Prim. Sch.
Loch Prim. Sch.
Springhall
Cathkin High School
Holmhills Wood
Holmhills Farm
122
WESTERN ROAD
KILBRIDE
4
CATHKIN
ST. STEPHEN'S
Cathkin Prim. Sch.
G73
SKYE ROAD
BY PASS
Nursery Sch.
Whitlawburn
G72
Fernhill Sch.
Playing Field
B759
EAST
59
Club House
GREENLEES
TROSSACHS
SOUTH
Cathkin House
Cathkin
East Farm
5
CATHKIN BRAES PARK
The Mid Gardens
West Greenlees Cottage
KIRKHILL GOLF COURSE
LANARKSHIRE
Motte
Cathkin Quarry
Easthills
GLASGOW
6
Greenleeshill
Turnlaw Cotts.
58
South Cathkin Farm
137
63
Kirk Burn
CAIRNMUIR RD.
62
64

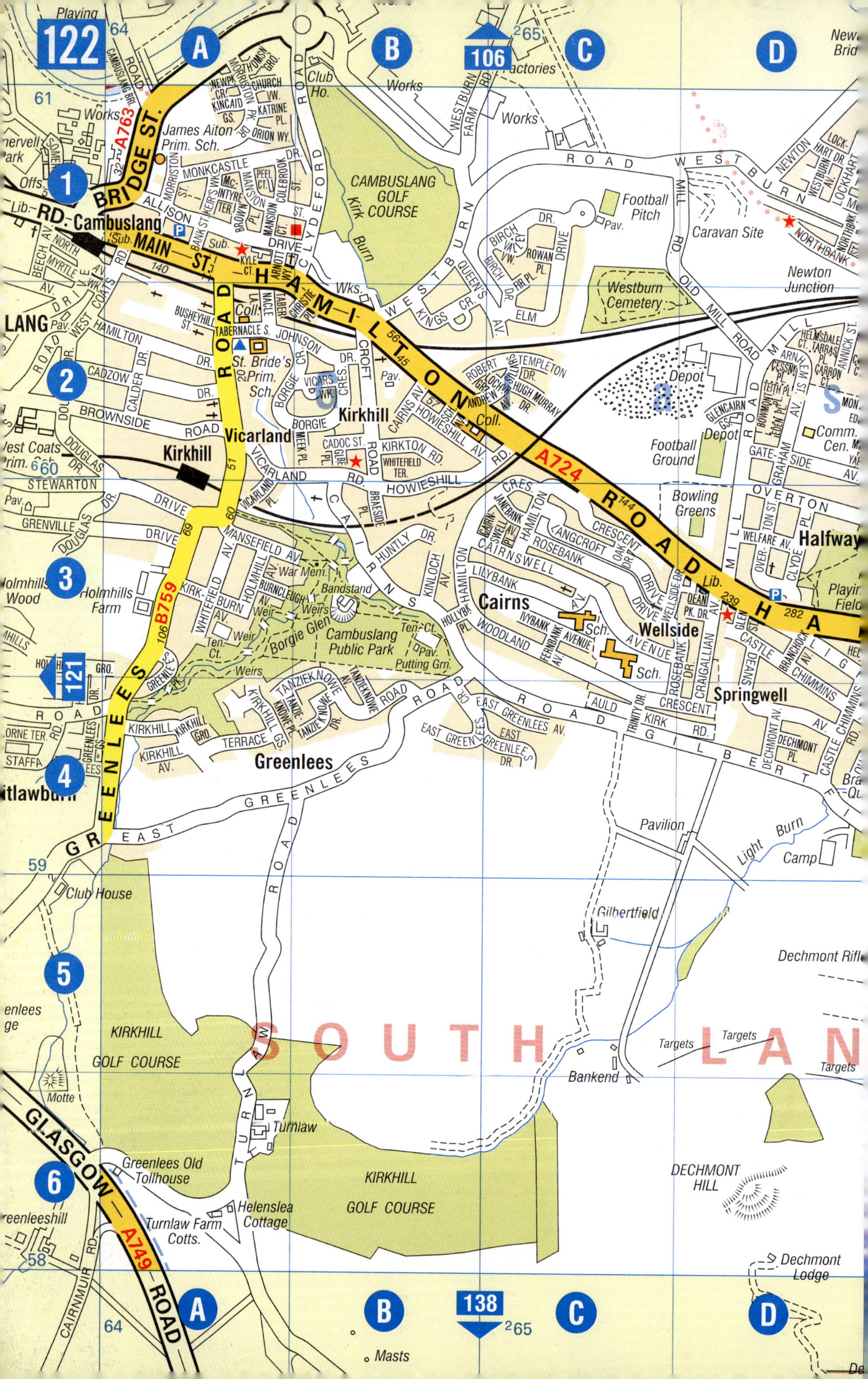

A
B
C
D
106
138
121
1
2
3
4
5
6
Cambuslang
James Aiton Prim. Sch.
BRIDGE ST.
A763
MAIN ST.
HAMILTON ROAD
A724
CAMBUSLANG GOLF COURSE
Kirk Burn
Works
Factories
Club Ho.
WESTBURN ROAD
WESTBURN FARM RD.
Football Pitch
Pav.
Caravan Site
Newton Junction
Westburn Cemetery
Depot
Football Ground
Bowling Greens
Halfway
Comm. Cen.
OLD MILL ROAD
MILL ROAD
St. Bride's Prim. Sch.
Coll.
Kirkhill
Vicarland
VICARLAND RD.
HOWIESHILL RD.
CAIRNS RD.
Cairns
Wellside
Springwell
Sch.
Lib.
GILBERTFIELD
Cambuslang Public Park
Borgie Glen
Bandstand
War Mem.
Weirs
Ten. Ct.
Putting Grn.
Holmhills Farm
Holmhills Wood
B759
GREENLEES RD.
EAST GREENLEES RD.
Greenlees
KIRKHILL AV.
KIRKHILL TERRACE
Club House
KIRKHILL GOLF COURSE
Motte
GLASGOW ROAD
A749
Greenlees Old Tollhouse
Turnlaw Farm Cotts.
Helenslea Cottage
Turnlaw
TURNLAW ROAD
CAIRNMUIR RD.
SOUTH LAN
Pavilion
Light Burn
Camp
Gilbertfield
Dechmont Rifle
Targets
Bankend
DECHMONT HILL
Dechmont Lodge
Masts
Playing Field

E
F
G
H
107
67
68
61
Gowanbank
Football Ground
Playground
Westburn
Newton
St. Charles' Prim. Sch.
NEWTON FARM ROAD
REDLAWOOD PL.
REDLAWOOD RD.
NEWTON BRAE
WESTBURN ROAD
EASTWOOD VW.
RIVERSIDE PL.
DUNLOP ST.
Rotten Calder
Redlees
Brackenbrae
Hallside Newhouse Farm
Bogend
CALDER RD.
Redlees Bridge
Hamilton Junction
Light Burn
HALLSIDE DR.
HALLSIDE AV.
HALLSIDE CR.
WORKS AV.
VILLAGE ROAD
BOWLING GRN. VW.
1
2
3
4
5
6
60
59
58
Hallside Prim. Sch.
NEWTON STATION RD.
Hallside
West Hallside
East Hallside
HALLSIDE ROAD
Knowetop Cottages
Back O'Hill
BLANTYRE FARM RD.
Calderglen Nursing Home
124
CALDERGLEN AV.
Depots
FLEMINGTON
FLEMINGTON IND. EST.
LOGAN TOWER
HUTCHINSON PL.
414
461
HAMILTON ROAD
Depot
G72
Hallside Farm
Spittal Burn
Works
Piggery
DECHMONT COTTAGES
LETTERICKHILLS CRES.
Hallside Manse
Spittalhill
Cairnsmore
Dalton School
A724
GLASGOW ROAD
Works
Flemington Farm Cottage
Flemington House
Spittal
LANARKSHIRE
Targets
Quarry Wood
FLEMINGTON ROAD
LOANEND COTTAGES
Lodge
Priory Bri.
CALLAGHAN WYND
Caldergrove
Bardykes
LOCHALSH PL.
SANQUHAR GDNS.
KYLEAKIN GS.
DALCRAIG CR.
MOSSGEIL TER.
GORDON TER.
ANNFIELD GS.
DECHMONT GS.
BURNS GS.
BURNS CR.
HELMSDALE AV.
KIRKWALL AV.
TARBERT AV.
JURA AVENUE
CRESCENT
BALMORAL GS.
MONTROSE GS.
KINNIE GS.
LAUDER GS.
NAIRN AV.
LINNHE PL.
NORTHWAY
BLANTYRE
SOUTH
497
HERBERTSON GRO.
CYPRESS AV.
SPRUCE AV.
HAZELWOOD DR.
POPLAR
LOUDHOWE
JAR PL.
FERNS
Calder House
SYCAMORE GRO.
Queen Mary's Well (site of)
139
67
68

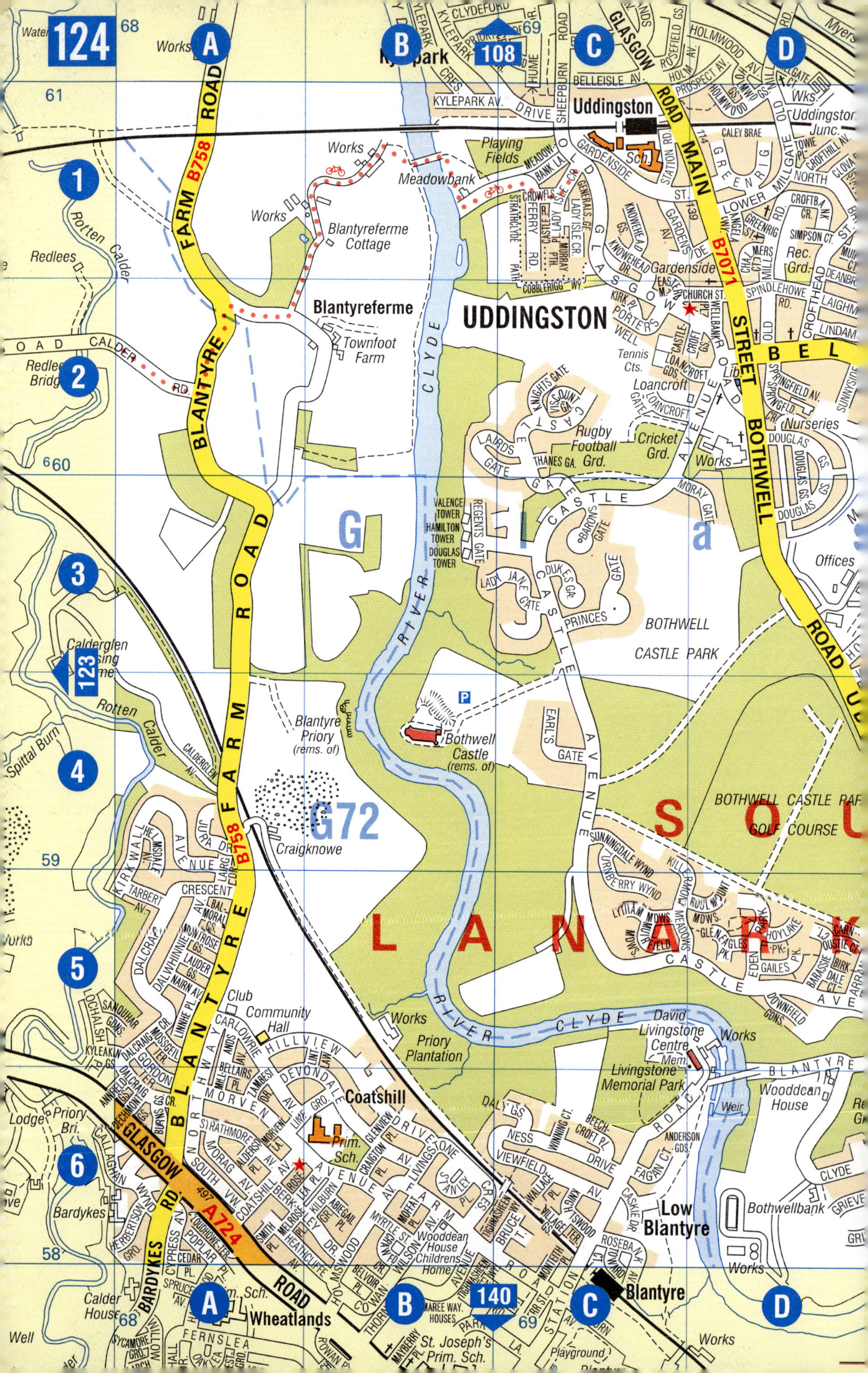

A
B
C
D
108
140
123
1
2
3
4
5
6
68
69
61
60
59
58
Kylepark
Uddingston
UDDINGSTON
Uddingston Junc.
Blantyreferme
Blantyreferme Cottage
Townfoot Farm
Meadowbank
Playing Fields
Works
Redlees
Redlees Bridge
Rotten Calder
Calder
Spittal Burn
Calderglen
BLANTYRE FARM ROAD
B758
GLASGOW ROAD
MAIN STREET
BOTHWELL ROAD
B7071
A724
RIVER CLYDE
Gardenside
Loancroft
Rugby Football Grd.
Cricket Grd.
Nurseries
Tennis Cts.
Rec. Grd.
BOTHWELL CASTLE PARK
Bothwell Castle (rems. of)
Blantyre Priory (rems. of)
Craigknowe
G72
BOTHWELL CASTLE PARK GOLF COURSE
SOUTH LANARK
CASTLE AVENUE
Offices
Community Hall
Club
Coatshill
Prim. Sch.
Priory Plantation
David Livingstone Centre
Livingstone Memorial Park
Wooddean House
Weir
Low Blantyre
Blantyre
Bothwellbank
Bardykes
Priory Bri.
Lodge
Calder House
Wheatlands
St. Joseph's Prim. Sch.
Wooddean House Childrens Home
Playground
NORTHWAY
SOUTH VW.
Sch.

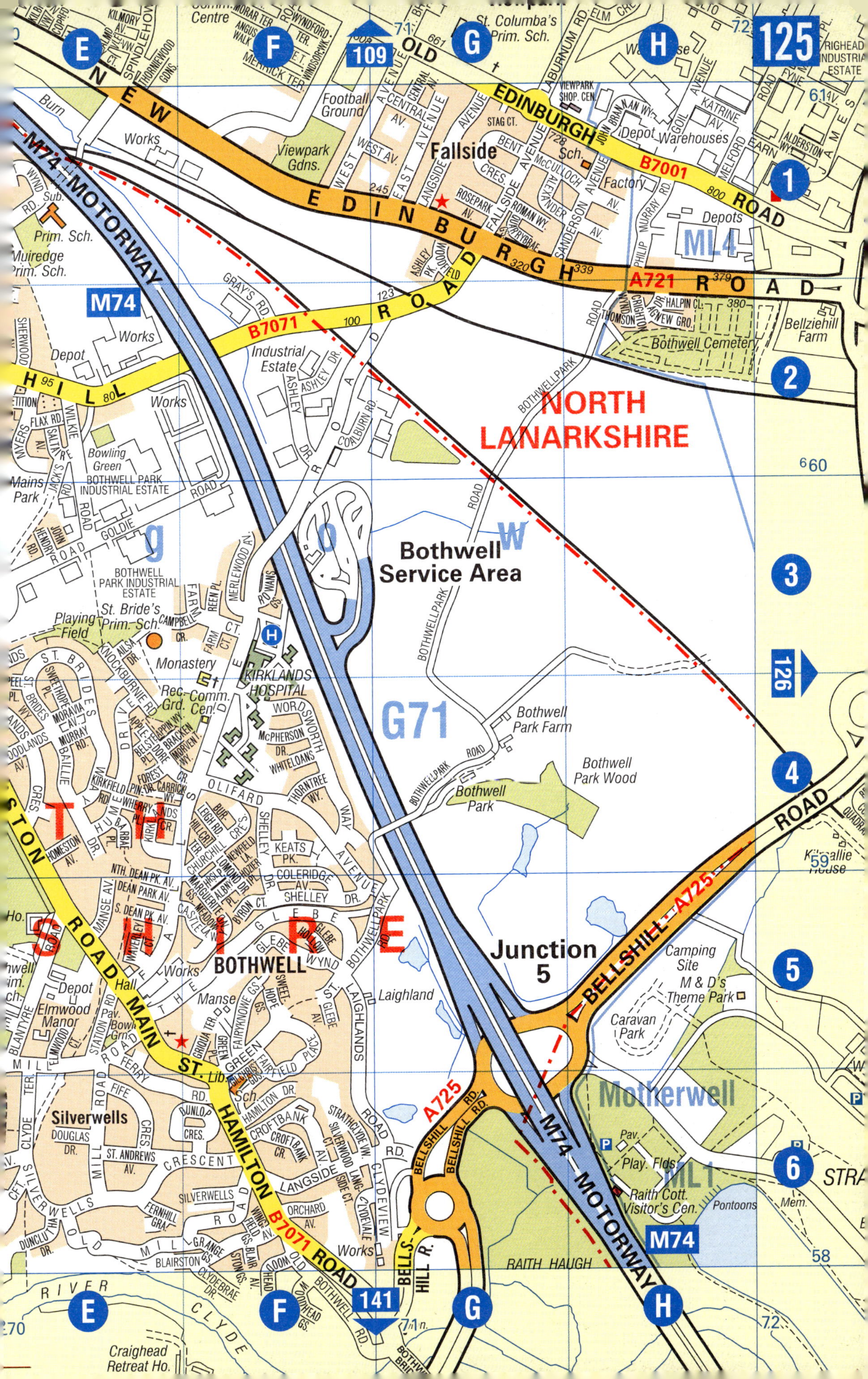
E
F
G
H
109
141
126
1
2
3
4
5
6
NEW EDINBURGH ROAD
OLD EDINBURGH ROAD
B7001
A721
M74 MOTORWAY
M74
B7071
HILL ROAD
Fallside
Football Ground
Viewpark Gdns.
St. Columba's Prim. Sch.
Works
Depots
Depot Warehouses
Factory
ML4
Bellziehill Farm
Bothwell Cemetery
NORTH LANARKSHIRE
Industrial Estate
Bowling Green
BOTHWELL PARK INDUSTRIAL ESTATE
Mains Park
Muiredge Prim. Sch.
Prim. Sch.
Bothwell Service Area
G71
Playing Field
St. Bride's Prim. Sch.
Monastery
KIRKLANDS HOSPITAL
Rec. Comm. Grd. Cen.
Bothwell Park Farm
Bothwell Park Wood
Bothwell Park
Junction 5
BELLSHILL ROAD
A725
Camping Site
M & D's Theme Park
Caravan Park
Motherwell
ML1
Play. Flds.
Raith Cott. Visitor's Cen.
Pontoons
RAITH HAUGH
BOTHWELL
Laighland
Elmwood Manor
Silverwells
MAIN ST.
HAMILTON ROAD
RIVER CLYDE
Craighead Retreat Ho.
BELLS HILL R.
NORTH LANARKSHIRE
SOUTH LANARKSHIRE

A
B
C
D
1
2
3
4
5
6
110
142
125
BELLSHILL
HATTONRIGG
NORTH LANARKSHIRE
Bellshill (Motherwell Food Park) Industrial Estate
Works
Warehouses
Depots
OLD EDINBURGH RD.
B7001
A721
NEW EDINBURGH RD.
A725
GARTCOSH WALK
A775
CAMPBELL ST.
NORTH ROAD
B7070
NORTH RD.
MAIN STREET
MOTHERWELL ROAD
A721
HAMILTON ROAD
B7070
BELLSHILL ROAD
Bellziehill Farm
Bothwell Cemetery
Sir Matt Busby Sports Comp.
Cardinal Newman High Sch.
Bellshill
Bellshill Academy
Comm. Cen.
Clinic
Cultural Cen. & Lib.
Government Offices
Playing Field
Playing Fields
Bowling Green
Playground
Bowling Greens
Orbiston
Public Park
Sacred Heart Prim. Sch.
Comm. Cen.
Lawmuir Prim. Sch.
Viewfield
Kilmallie House
Mary Rae's Well
Douglas Park Cottages
Rec. Grd.
Fairways
Club House
Corby Craig
BELLSHILL GOLF COURSE
ML4
G71
Camping Site
M & D's Theme Park
Works
STRATHCLYDE COUNTRY PARK
Bothwellhaugh Plantation
Bothwellhaugh
STRATHCLYDE FUN PARK
BOTHWELLHAUGH RD.
South Calder Water
Mem.
Pontoons
Flds.
Roman Bath Ho. (site of)
Football Pitch
St. Bernadette's Prim. Sch.
Playing Fields
North
WATLING ST.
Motherwell
58
59
60
61
72
73

111
Mossend Sidings
Works
Mossend
Depot
Wester Holytown
Rec. Grd.
Keir Hardie Sports Cen.
Playing Field
STREET A775 HOLYTOWN RD.
King George's Field
Woodend
Thankerton
Mossend West Junction
Fullwood Junction
Foundry
CALDER RD.
CLYDESDALE B7029 RD. CLYDESDALE STREET
Prim. Sch.
Milnwood Junction
Depot
Works
Clydesdale
CORONATION
Bus. Cen.
Milnwood
Playgrd.
Playground
Kirklee Cottage
Biggins
Works
Cemetery
St. Patrick's School
Jerviston Junction
Rec. Grd.
Dam
Holm Forge Bridge
BELLSHILL ROAD A721
Riccardjohnston
ML1
Gilly's Burn
COBBLETON
JERVISTON ROAD
COLVILLE PARK GOLF COURSE
Sports Field
Jerviston House
Club Ho.
New Jerviston House
Burial Ground
Rec. Grd.
Forgewood
Braidhurst Sports Barn
Braidhurst High Sch.
BRAIDHURST INDUSTRIAL ESTATE
Depot
Playing Field
Works
143
128
Lodge

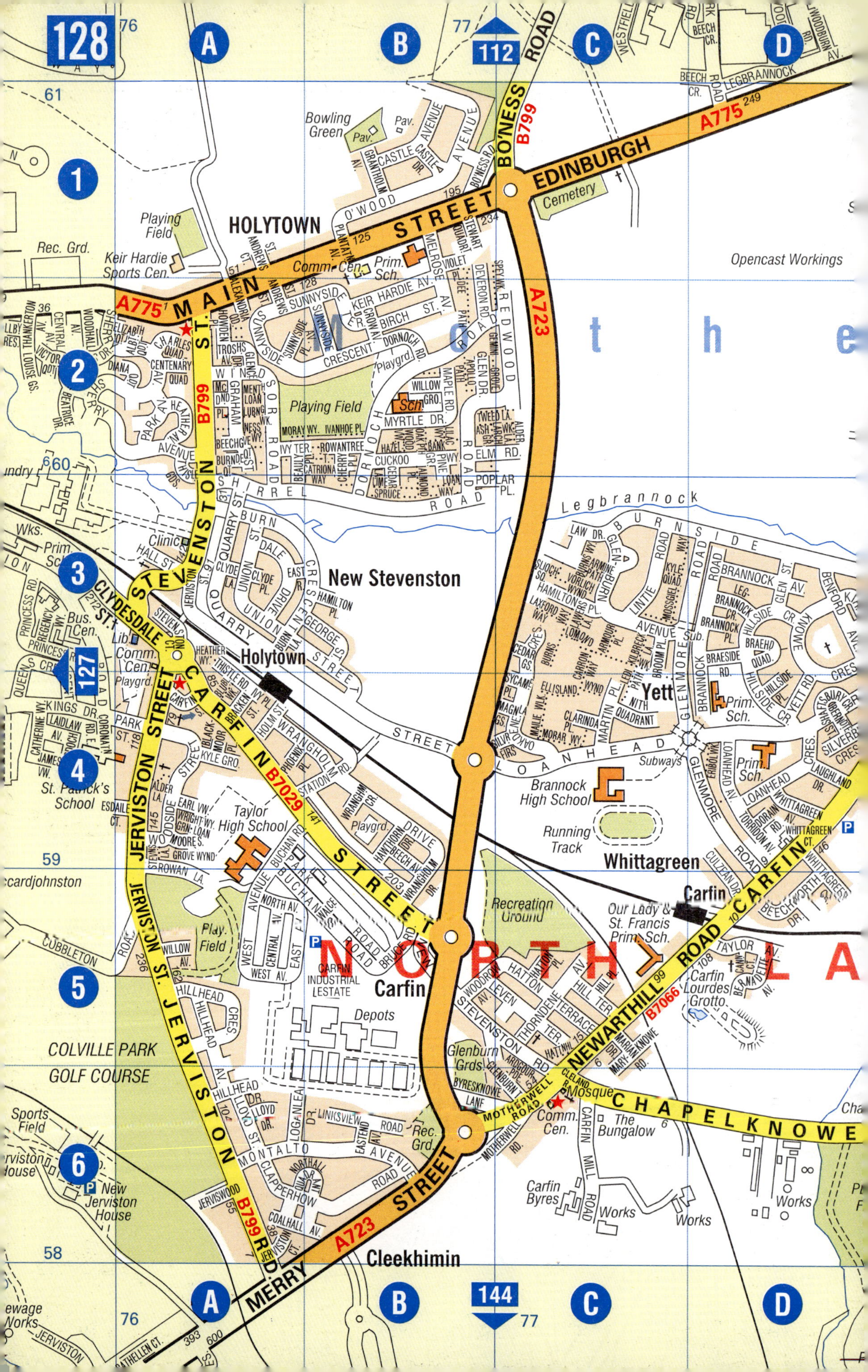

112
144
127
A
B
C
D
1
2
3
4
5
6
76
77
61
60
59
58
HOLYTOWN
MAIN STREET
EDINBURGH
A775
A723
B799
B7029
B7066
BO'NESS ROAD
Bowling Green
Pav.
Playing Field
Rec. Grd.
Keir Hardie Sports Cen.
Comm. Cen.
Prim. Sch.
Cemetery
Opencast Workings
Motherwell
NORTH LANARKSHIRE
STEVENSTON ST.
KEIR HARDIE AV.
SUNNYSIDE CRESCENT
BIRCH ST.
DORNOCH RD.
REDWOOD ROAD
MYRTLE DR.
SHIRREL ROAD
Legbrannock
BURNSIDE
New Stevenston
Holytown
QUARRY ST.
UNION ST.
CLYDESDALE ST.
CARFIN STREET
HAMILTON PL.
GEORGE ST.
LOANHEAD STREET
Yett
Brannock High School
Running Track
Whittagreen
Carfin
Our Lady & St. Francis Prim. Sch.
Taylor High School
Recreation Ground
Play Field
Carfin Industrial Estate
Depots
Glenburn Grds.
NEWARTHILL ROAD
CARFIN ROAD
CHAPELKNOWE
Mosque
Comm. Cen.
The Bungalow
Carfin Lourdes Grotto
Carfin Byres
Works
JERVISTON STREET
JERVISTON ST.
COLVILLE PARK GOLF COURSE
Sports Field
New Jerviston House
Cleekhimin
MERRY STREET
MONTALTO AVENUE
St. Patrick's School
Clinic
Prim. Sch.
Bus. Cen.
Lib.
Playgrd.
Wks.
Sewage Works

113
145
E
F
G
H
1
2
3
4
5
6
280
61
660
59
58
79
CARLISLE ROAD
A73
MOTHERWELL ROAD
B7066
BIGGAR ROAD
Burn
Mossband
Legbrannock
LEGBRANNOCK ROAD
Stane Cottage
Biggar Road
Pickerstonhill
Tillan
Works
Omoa
Biggarford Bridge
Biggarford
Newarthill
Gowkhall
Football Ground
Running Track
Rec. Grd.
Newarthill Prim. Sch.
HIGH STREET
SPALEHALL DR.
TILLANBURN ROAD
TOWNHEAD DR.
Townhead
CLELAND STREET
ML1
Ford
Knownoblehill
Knownoble
LANARKSHIRE
CHURCH ST.
Depot
MOSSHALL ST.
GOWKHALL AV.
CROSSGATES AV.
WINDYEDGE & HARESHAW RD.
Playgrd.
FRASER STREET
FOUNDRY RD.
Chapel Knowe
Westerfield
B7029
OMOA ROAD
Omoa Cottage
Football Ground
Public Park
Cleland
Cleland Prim. Sch.
MAIN ST.
Lib.
Sch.
Whitecraighead
Playing Fields
Running Track
Cleland House
Niebald Plantation
Knowenoble
WISHAW ROAD
STATION RD.
RAVENSHILL DR.
LITHGOW DRIVE

A
B
C
D
46
47
58
57
56
55
1
2
3
4
5
6
Killoch Water
Burn
Witch
Waterfall
Waterfalls
Killoch Glen
Waterfall
Dam
Killoch Bri.
Auchentiber
FERENEZE ROAD
FERENEZE
Foreside
STA. BRAE
Works
LOW BROADLIE
ROBERTSON CRES.
BROADLIE
HOLEHOUSE
Mill (Dis.)
Res.
Prim. Sch.
BANK RD.
HILL SIDE
HILL SIDE CR.
LEA AV.
STATHERS PL.
BRAEHEAD AV.
BRAEHEAD QUAD.
BRAE
KIRKSTYLE
STATION R
Crofthead Cottages
MILLVIEW MDWS.
MILLVIEW TER.
Lodge
Weir
Dam
Holehouse Farm
High Crofthead House
Holehouse
Sidney Cottage
Neilston
Playing Field
LOCHLIBO
A736
Cowdon Burn
Smiddyhill
Brimstone Bridge
Lodge
Football Grd.
HARELAW AV.
KINGSTON AV.
EDGE
ROAD
COMMORE PL.
GLENLIVET R.
GLEN ORRIN WY.
GLEN CRERAND
GLEN TARBET DR.
KINGSTON AV.
LOANFOOT AV.
CRAIG
Water
UPLAWMOOR ROAD
Crumyards Cottage
Crumyards
EAST RENF
GLENDOLL ROAD
GLEN FINLET RD.
GLEN MARK RD
GLEN MAIR RD.
LYON RD.
GLEN ROY DR.
GLEN FALLOCH CR.
GLEN ISLA AV.
SHEE
Levern
Kilburn
Water Works
Midgehole Glen
Neilstonside Cottage
MUIRHEAD
Jaapston Farm
ROAD
Neilstonside Bridge
Levern
Neilstonside Hill
KINGSTON
Water Works
G
Craig Cottage
Craig Wood
Craig of Neilston
Barr
Braeface Farm
Links of Levern
Neilstonside
MUIRHEAD ROAD
Waterside
Aboon the Brae
Levern Water
Boat House
Overflow
CRAIGHALL DAM
NEILSTON PAD

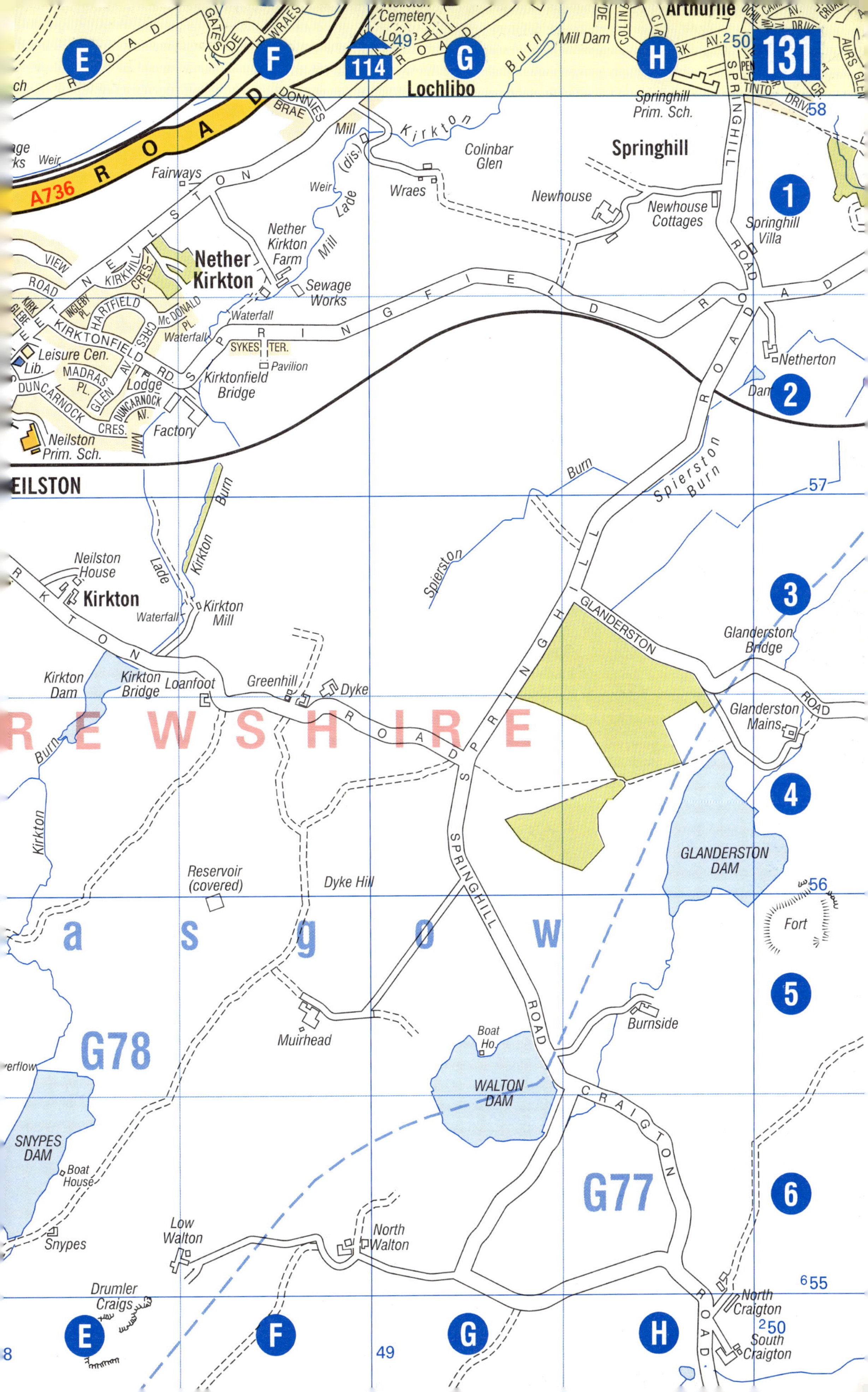
Cemetery
Lochlibo
Arthurlie
Mill Dam
Springhill Prim. Sch.
Springhill
Colinbar Glen
Kirkton Burn
Wraes
Newhouse
Newhouse Cottages
Springhill Villa
A736 ROAD
DONNIES BRAE
Fairways
NEILSTON ROAD
Weir
Mill Lade (dis.)
Nether Kirkton Farm
Nether Kirkton
Sewage Works
Waterfall
SPRINGFIELD ROAD
SYKES TER.
Pavilion
Kirktonfield Bridge
KIRKTONFIELD RD.
HARTFIELD CRES.
McDONALD PL.
INGLEBY PL.
KIRKHILL
Leisure Cen.
Lib.
MADRAS PL.
GLEN AV.
Lodge
DUNCARNOCK CRES.
DUNCARNOCK AV.
Factory
Neilston Prim. Sch.
NEILSTON
Netherton
Dam
Spierston Burn
Spierston
Kirkton Burn
Lade
Neilston House
Kirkton
Kirkton Mill
Waterfall
KIRKTON ROAD
Kirkton Dam
Kirkton Bridge
Loanfoot
Greenhill
Dyke
SPRINGHILL ROAD
GLANDERSTON ROAD
Glanderston Bridge
Glanderston Mains
GLANDERSTON DAM
RENFREWSHIRE
Reservoir (covered)
Dyke Hill
Fort
Glasgow
G78
Muirhead
Boat Ho.
WALTON DAM
Burnside
CRAIGTON ROAD
G77
SNYPES DAM
Boat House
Overflow
Snypes
Low Walton
North Walton
Drumler Craigs
North Craigton
South Craigton
E F G H
1 2 3 4 5 6
114
49
55 56 57 58

116
A
B
C
D
1
2
3
4
5
6
52
53
58
57
56
55
Works
Waterfall
Weirs
CORSELET RD.
WAULKMILL GLEN
RESERVOIR
Littleton Reservoir
G78
M77
RYAT LINN RESERVOIR
Ryat
Junction 4
Weir
Waterfall
Pier
AURS
CROOKFUR RD.
Greenlaw
Pollock Lodge
DODSIDE ROAD
B769
M77 MOTORWAY
ROAD
West Lodge
Polloktown
FINGALTON RD.
DODSIDE
Patterton
B769 ROAD
Thornliebank
Towerwood
Thornhill Ho.
Craigend
MORAR PL.
LOMOND
EARN RD.
LAGGAN
RANNOCH AV.
WOLFE AV.
WESTRAY AV.
WEMYSS AV.
WEAVER AV.
WYLIE AV.
WICKHAM AV.
WORSLEY
WIGTON AV.
CORROUR
CORRAN AV.
WALTON AV.
WARNOCK
KINLOCH RD.
FOWLIS DR.
ABERCORN
LOGAN AV.
KINTYRE
DAVAAR PL.
CRESCENT
Crookf
G77
CAPELRIG
WELLMEADOW
WELLMEADOW GREEN
THE LAURELS
MEADOWBURN AV.
MEADOWBANK PL.
TEAWELL
TORMEADOW
HARRIS CL.
JURA DR.
SHUNA PL.
LEWIS PL.
TIREE
RAMSAY
LISMORE PL.
GLANDERSTON AV.
ERSTON GATE
RYAT DRIVE
RYAT GRN.
LANGTON PL.
LANGTON GATE
CRAIGTON
CRES.
ISLAY
COLONSAY DR.
COLONSAY
ERISKAY
ERISKAY AV.
SKAY CRES.
GREENFARM
EASDALE
GOODFELLOW
CRAIG PL.
CARSWELL
BALGRAY RD.
INVEREWE WY.
BARRHEAD ROAD
St. Cadoc's Prim. Sch.
LAMBIE
BARR PL.
GREENLAW CRESCENT
AVENUE
RODGER
CRAIG GDS.
GREENLAW DR.
WATERSIDE DR.
NEWTON MEARNS
ROBSHILL CT.
FORDYCE CT.
Playgrd.
GLEBE
Sch.
Lib.
THE AVENUE (SHOP. CEN.)
Rec. Grd.
RENFREWSHIRE
Glasgow
Capelrig Burn
Fords
Netherplace Farm
Netherplace
Works
Res.
Netherplace Cottage
Netherplace House
NETHERPLACE
Lodge Bridge
Lofts
M77
ANDERSON DR.
WILLIAM MANN DR.
ALLISON PL.
WILSON PL.
KNOX PL.
CLARK PL.
GEMMEL PL.
CASTLE
POLLOCK RD.
RUSSELL GDS.
HILL AV.
MOORHILL
TOWNHEAD RD.
FAIRWEATHER PL.
ST. VIGEANS
NETHERPLACE CR.
ASHTREE GRO.
AVENUE
MAPLE
LIMETREE
EAGLESHAM
BEECH
GILMOURTON
ARTHURLIE DR.
RAESIDE AV.
FORD RD.
PALDMYRE
PAIDMYRE ROAD
MOORCROFT RD.
EDDINGTON DR.
LAUDERDALE DR.
CHEVIOT
DRIVE
LANGRIG
NEWTON
MEARNSKIRK HOSPITAL
East Malletsheugh
Malletsheugh
MALLETSHEUGH ROAD
A77
AYR ROAD
Lodge
LANGRIG
Faside House

DEACONSBANK GOLF COURSE
Course
117
Rouken Glen Park
Boat Ho.
Boating Lake
Dam
DAVIELAND
MILVERTON
TREEMAIN
TORRINGTON
LANGTREE AV.
AVENUE
DALSERF CR.
DORNOCH
BALMEG AV.
ATHOLL
THE GROVE
WOODVALE
REDBURN AV.
AILSA
DORIAN DR.
KILPATRICK
FERENEZE
CAMPSIE
LOMONDSIDE
A77
ROAD
DRIVE
Sewage Works
Whitecraigs
Depot
Aqueduct
Barcapel Flats
Barcapel Holm Farm
Eastwood High Sch.
Capelrig
Playing Fields
Capelrig Burn
G46
Auldhouse Burn
Club House
WHITECRAIGS GOLF COURSE
CATHCART CASTLE GOLF COURSE
G76
Whitecraigs
DERAMORE AV.
GREENBANK AV.
LOANING
CRAIGNETHAN
LETHINGTON
ELPHINSTONE
METHVEN RD.
ERSKINE
BURNSIDE
KENMURE RD.
NEIDPATH ROAD WEST
NETHERTON CT.
RODDINGHEAD
BROOMFLD. RD.
NEIDPATH ROAD
HERNDON CT.
BROOMCROFT
Greenbank Lodge
Greenbank
134
Greenbank Gardens
LESLIE
CAMERON DR.
CAMPBELL CRES.
CHISHOLM DR.
GORDON CR.
FRUIN
FRASER
DOUGLAS
STEWART AV.
ARISDALE
CRESCENT
KILMORY
THE BEECHES
CAPEL AV.
ELMWOOD AV.
WESTBRAE
LOCHBROOM
SANDRINGHAM AVENUE
Sch.
BROOM ROAD
DUNVEGAN DR.
FALKLAND
Broom
SANDRINGHAM CT.
MATHERTON AV.
KIRKVALE CR.
NETHERDALE
TEVIOTDALE
LANGDALE
KIRKSTONE
ESKDALE
KIRKDENE
Sch.
SUNNINGDALE
CAVENDISH
KINFAUNS DR.
GLAMIS
BROOMVALE
WINDSOR
DUNBLANE DR.
DUNBEATH AV.
Pav. Playing Field
BROOMFARM
KINNAIRD
DUART DRIVE
GALSTON
CROY AV.
DARVEL DR.
TURNBERRY DR.
HILLCREST
KIRKHILL
AYR ROAD
RYSLAND CR.
KNOWES AV.
ARCHFIELD
FIRWOOD
DOUNE CR.
CEDRWD AV.
OAKWOOD
Broom Burn
DUNURE
MAIDENS AV.
CULZEAN CR.
ALLOWAY
MAYBOLE GR.
PRESTWICK
MONKTON
TROON PL.
GLENEAGLES DR.
Kirkhill House
KIRKHILL GA.
ARKAIG
Kirkhill
NETHERCAIRN PL.
NAPROCH PL.
BROADMOSS AV.
BYRESTONE AV.
LAWFIELD AV.
LANGLEES AV.
KATRINE DR.
TORRIDON GDS.
HAZELWOOD
EDZELL AVENUE
NEWTONLEA
CEDARWOOD
BLACKHOUSE AV.
BROOMBURN
BROOMHILL AV.
G77
Playground
BALLANTRAE CRES.
Castle Farm
Mearns Castle High Sch.
Barrance
WATERFOOT ROAD
BROOM ROAD
SHAWWOOD CRESCENT
SHAWHILL CR.
KIRKVIEW CRESCENT
CRAIGIE DR.
BROOMFIELD
CASTLETON
BLACKWOOD
MANOT GA.
KING'S GDS.
BROOMBURN DR.
CASTLETON CT.
BROOM CLIFF
CASTLE GA.
Mearns Castle
Hall
Manse
ROLAND CRES.
CROFTHEAD
MEARNSCROFT
RUCHAN DR.
HUMBIE
Mearns
White Hill
Mearns Cemetery
Burnhouse
E
F
G
H
1
2
3
4
5
6
255
56
57
58
655

134
118
133
A
B
C
D
1
2
3
4
5
6
56
57
58
655
GOLF COURSE
Stamperland
Williamwood
Clarkston
CATHCART CASTLE
GOLF COURSE
Club
House
Greenbank
Greenbank
Gardens
East
Lodge
Flenders
Ravenswood
Newford
Housecraigs
Millerston
Barrance
Waterfoot
Farm
Waterfoot
Bridge
Dripps
Mill
Letham
Waterfoot
Earn
Bridge
Hill of
Birches
Meikle
Dripps
Townhead
of Dripps
Cartside
Busby
Glen
Park
Weir
Works
Warehouse
Rec.
Grd.
St.
Joseph's
Prim. Sch.
Prim. Sch.
High
Sch.
Lib.
Halls
Pav.
G46
G45
G77
EASTWOOD MAINS ROAD
A726
CLARKSTON ROAD
B767
BUSBY ROAD
EAGLESHAM ROAD
GLASGOW RD.
MAIN
FLENDERS ROAD
HIGH FLENDERS ROAD
LOW FLENDERS ROAD
WATERFOOT ROAD
RAVENSWOOD ROAD
GREENWOOD DRIVE
HILLVIEW
MANSEFIELD CRESCENT
CRAIGHILL DRIVE
BEECHLANDS
HILLEND
STAMPERLAND
E A S T
R E N F R E W S H I R E
G l a

CITY OF GLASGOW
SOUTH LANARKSHIRE
CARMUNNOCK
Busby
BUSBY
Thorntonhall
Braehead
NETHERTON BRAES
CARMUNNOCK BY-PASS
B766
BUSBY ROAD
B759
CARMUNNOCK ROAD
CARMUNNOCK
EAST KILBRIDE ROAD
A726
KILBRIDE RD.
G76
G74
Carnbooth House
Kittoch Water
Clyth House
Kittoch Bridge
Castle Hill
The Peel
Lodge
Bystone
Busbyside
Bystone Farm Cottage
Electricity Switching Station
Thorntonhill Burn
Laigh Braehead
Braehead Court
Kingsknowe
Craigpark
Sewage Wks.
North Hill of Dripps
Birkwood
Pedmyre Nurseries
PEDMYRE LANE
Waterside
Stepends Bridge
Cemetery
Picketlaw
Prim. Sch.
Rec. Grd.
Works
Parklea
Playground
Easter Busby
PRINTERS LAND
THE AULDKIRK
THE CRESCENT
EASTER RD.
GLENVILLE GA.
WOODHOUSE CT.
BELLCRAIG CT.
RUSSELL PL.
KIPPEN
LISTER GDS.
AVENUE DRIVE
SOUTH ROAD
STATION ROAD
SILVAN PL.
WESTERTON CT.
WESTERTON LANE
EASTERTON
CARMUNNOCK ROAD
WINDLAW
WATERSIDE RD.
WATERBANK ROAD
WATERSIDE ROAD
WESTERFIELD ROAD
PICKETLAW FARM RD.
PICKETLAW DR.
WOODSIDE GDNS.
WOODLAND GDNS.
CRAIGSHEEN AV.
WATERSIDE GDNS.
BANKHEAD RD.
STUART RD.
PLAYFIELD RD.
HILLCREST
OLD RD.
KIRK RD.
PATHHEAD RD.
GLEBE AV.
SYCAMORE WAY
MANSE R.
CRAGWELL PARK
KITTOCHSIDE RD.
PARKLEE DR.
CAMERON CRES.
CATHKIN RD.
GREEN BEECHES
FAIR OAK
HIGH
GALLOWHILL RD.
THE WILLOWS
BRAEHEAD ROAD
OSBORNE CR.
BISHOPS PK.
WELLKNOWE RD.
WELLKNOWE
PARK PL.
PARK DRIVE
THORNTON AV.
RAVENSCOURT
BISHOPS GATE
GILMOUR AV.
Mid Netherton
CROMARTY GDS.
ALYTH GDS.
E F G H
1 2 3 4 5 6
58 57 56 55
259 260
119
136

A
B
C
D
120
135
148
CITY OF GLASGOW
G45
G76
SOUTH LANARKSHIRE
Glasgow
CATHKIN ROAD
B759
CATHKIN BRAES GOLF COURSE
Curling Pond
Muir Farm
CARMUNNOCK
Works
BUSBY RD.
Prim. Sch.
KITTOCHSIDE ROAD
Parklea
Braefoot
Rockcrest
Bellcraig
Highflat Farm
Wester Kittochside
Kittochside
Kittochside Farm
CAIRNMUIR
KITTOCHSIDE RD.
CARMUNNOCK
Eastend
Dykehead Farm
Waterbank
Sewage Works
Stepends Bridge
Cemetery
Mill Cottage
Philipshill
Kittochside
GLEN RD
WARTFIELD ROAD
CASTLEGLEN ROAD
Castleglen
Castle Hill
Kittoch Water
Rough Hill
Government Offices
Hotel
EAST KILBRIDE ROAD
A726
QUEENSWAY
Kingsknowe
Braehead Court
Industrial Estate
PEEL PARK IND. EST.
REDWOOD DRIVE
REDWOOD CRESCENT
BARBANA ROAD
GLENBURN WY.
GLENBURN
HAWBANK ROAD
RENNIE PL.
JAMES WATT PLACE
DIXON PLACE
WESTGARTH PLACE
SPRINGBURN PL.
College Milton
FARROTSHOLE ROAD
MACFIE PL.
MACNEILL GS.
MACLEAN
McCALLUM AVENUE
MACDONALD
McKAY PL.
MACKENZIE GDNS.
MAC IVOR
McEWAN GS.
McCLAREN GR.
MACNICOL PK.
Superst.
Comm. Cen.
West Mains
260
61
58
57
56
MILTON

E
F
G
H
121
63
64
Easthills
South Cathkin Farm
G73
Kirk Burn
GLASGOW ROAD
58
1
2
57
3
4
56
5
6
55
T H
K S H I R E
Works
CAIRNMUIR ROAD
ROAD
Nerston
West Nerston Farm
West Nerston
NERSTON ROAD
Rogerton
East Rogerton
West Rogerton
Barley Well
MARKETHILL ROAD
Ardoch Ho.
KINGSGATE RETAIL PARK
Allanvale
138
g o W
High Mains
MAINS ROAD
STEWARTFIELD WAY
Training Cen.
PLACE
Lee's Burn
Law Knowe
Laigh Mains
Mains Castle
Heritage Cen
James Hamilton Heritage Park
Stewartfield
STEWARTFIELD WAY
LAW RNDBT
Nerston
Recreation Ground
MAVOR ROUNDABOUT
MARKETHILL ROUNDABOUT
Pav.
Burial Gound
G74
DUNLIN DRIVE
EAST MAINS
B783
Art Cen.
COACH ROAD
HOWARD
Industr Estate
WILSON
AVENUE
Sch.
Halfmerke Sch. & West Mains Sch.
School
Cambus Coll.
Depot
Show Park
149
63
64
MAINS
East

KIRKHILL GOLF COURSE
Helenslea Cottage
Dechmont Lodge
122
150
137
A
B
C
D
1
2
3
4
5
6
64
265
58
57
56
55
GLASGOW ROAD
A749
MUIR ROAD
Masts
S O U T H
L A N A R K
G l a s
G73
G74
Cocks Burn
Crookedshields
CROOKEDSHIELDS ROAD
Nerston Residential School
East Nerston
Scottsmuir Nursery
Letterickhills Cotts.
Letterickhills
Nerston
West Nerston Farm
West Nerston
NERSTON RD.
CHAPELSIDE ROAD
EAST KILBRIDE GOLF COURSE
Club House
Chapelside
Ardoch Ho.
Allanvale
KINGSGATE RETAIL PARK
STEWARTFIELD WY.
KINGSWAY
STONEYMEADOW ROAD
HAMILTON ROAD
A725
Lee's
Weir
Training
MAVOR AV.
PLACE
LAW
HOWARD AV.
HOWARD
AVENUE
Industrial Estate
Works
BRAE VIEW
STONEYMEADOW RD.
BOSWORTH
THORNDYKE
EDMUND KEAN
REDGRAVE
ASHCROFT
TEWKESBURY
STRATFORD
Prim. Sch.
OTHELLO
HAMLET
FALSTAFF
ALBANY
BOLINGBROKE
ORLANDO
NEVILLE ROAD
PEMBROKE
SALISBURY
BARRIE
CANONGATE
IVANHOE
MOWBRAY
Mus.
Calderwood
Playing Fields
Miniature Golf Course
Bowl. Grns.
BLACKBRAES
RUNCIMAN PL.
ORCHARD GRN.
BAILLIE
RAEBURN
LAUDER
WINGATE DR.
WINGATE CRESCENT
MAXWELLTON
MORRISHALL
STOBO
Brankumhall
BRANKUMHALL RD.
Playing Fields
Sch.
ST. LEONARDS ROAD
ALLOWAY
BALLOCHMYLE
MAINS ROAD
B783
LEESBURN
The GATEWAY
NILSON
Playgrd.
Burial Ground
CALDERWOOD ROAD
AVENUE
PARK
Art Cen.
KELSO
LOGIE
ROSSLYN
GLAMIS
ELGIN
COACH
Sch.
Halfmerke Sch. & West Mains Sch.
Show Park
East
AYTON
GORDON DR.
POLLOK LA.
Hlth. Cen.
Lib.
ALISON
Football Pitch
DRIVE
SUTHERLAND
KINCARDINE PL.
GALLOWAY RD.
Maxwellton Sch.
Greenburn Sch.
Hunter Prim. School
Hunter High School
ABERCROMBY
CAPELRIG
GLEN

E
F
G
H
123
67
68
Caldergrove
Bardykes
Calder House
Queen Mary's Well (site of)
Rotten Calder
Barnhill
BARDYKES
Malcolmwood
Dechmont Farm Cott.
Spy Wood
FLEMINGTON ROAD
T H
S H I R E
g o w
Mid Lettrick
Mid Lettrick Farm Cott.
Weir
HUNTHILL
B758
Prim. Sch.
Playing Field
Playing Fields
Rotten Calder
Crossbow Ho.
Greenhall Estate
Crossbasket
Spring
West Lodge
East Lodge
Dam
Lodge
General's Bridge
Allers
Allers Cotts.
Burn
HAMILTON ROAD
B7012
ROAD
Greenhall View
ARMOUR CT.
ELLISLAND DR.
AFTON GDS.
CRAIGMUIR GDS.
CRAIGMUIR RD.
Mem.
MAIN ST.
Kirkton Park
140
A725
ROAD
G72
HILLHOUSE RD.
HAMILTON DR.
BRAE
Sewage Works
Cambuslang College (Allers Cen.)
Rotten Calder
Calder Glen
Basket
Craigmuir
Newhouse
SYDES
ROAD
Craigneith Castle (Ruins)
LAMMERMOOR
CRAIGNEITH CT.
CALDERWOOD GDS.
Saw Mill
AUCHENTIBBER ROAD
Auchentibber Farm
Auchentibber
Clyde Cottage
Park Farm
Blantyre Park Farm
Park House
Red Burn
CALDERSIDE
Calderside
Pit (disused)
Waterfalls
Springbank
War Mem.
PARKN
151
56
57
58
55
66
1
2
3
4
5
6

140
A
B
C
D
1
2
3
4
5
6
124
152
139
Low Blantyre
Bothwellbank
Works
Blantyre
Wheatlands
Prim. Sch.
Calder House
Barnhill
BARDYKES RD.
HUNTHILL RD.
St. Joseph's Prim. Sch.
Wooddean House Childrens Home
Maree Way Houses
Playground
Blantyre Public Park
Stonefield
Blantyre Sports Cen.
Ind. Est.
Football Grd.
Craighead Park Football Ground
Depot
GLASGOW ROAD
A724
Y.M.C.A.
Comm. Cen.
Gov. Offs.
Health Cen.
Blantyre High Sch.
Clydeview Shopping Cen.
Lib.
Prim. Sch.
Indoor Bowl Rink
Playing Field
Iona Path
Hall
BLANTYRE
Auchinraith
Springwells
Play Area
Blantyre Cemy.
War Mem.
Kirkton Park
Broompark Av.
HAMILTON RD.
MAIN STREET
B7012
B758
DOUGLAS ST.
High Blantyre
KIRKTON
A725
Cemetery
Hamilton International Technology Park
Priestfield Industrial Estate
Blantyre Industrial Estate
Training Centre
Burnbrae
G72
Red Burn
Park Farm
Park House
Blantyre Park Farm
Blantyre Park House
Udston Cottage
Dykehead
John Ogilvie High Sch.
Udston Hospital
Bowling Green
Udston Prim. Sch
Hillhouse
Jock Stein Sports Barn
St. Ninian's Prim. Sch.
Civic Cen.
Townhill Prim. Sch.
EARNOCK

125
153
142
E
F
G
H
1
2
3
4
5
6
70
71
72
55
56
57
58
G71
ML3
RIVER CLYDE
M74 MOTORWAY
M74
A725
A724
A72
B7071
B755
Raith Cott. Visitor's Cen.
RAITH HAUGH
Craighead Retreat Ho.
Craighead
Manresa
STATION RD.
BELLSHILL RD.
BOTHWELL BRIDGE
BOTHWELL RD.
Craighead Sch.
Training Cen.
Works
Sewage Works
Bothwell Bridge Animal Home (RSPCA)
Barmichael Plantation
Duchess Bridge
Stables
Fire Brigade H.Q.
Gow's Linn
Black Muir Plantation
Auchinraith Gardens
STRATHCLYDE COUNTRY PARK
Grandstand
HAMILTON PARK RACE COURSE
WHISTLEBERRY INDUSTRIAL PARK
St. Paul's Prim. Sch.
Whitehill
Football Pitches
Rec. Grd.
Public Park
War Mem.
Bandstand
STRATHCLYDE PARK GOLF COURSE
PARK BURN INDUSTRIAL ESTATE
Sports Barn
Lib.
Burnbank
Beckford Prim. Sch.
Hamilton College
Playing Field
BURNBANK RD.
BURNBANK ROAD
Hamilton West
Council Offices
Bell College
Court
Water Palace
Holy Cross High Sch.
ALMADA ST.
UNION ST.
MUIR ST.
CLYDESDALE STREET
PEACOCK CROSS
Udston
HILLHOUSE PK. INDUSTRIAL EST.
WELLHALL RD.
Well Hall
Millar Park
Wellhall Bri.
West Cemetery
St. Mary's Prim. Sch.
Hamilton Grammer Sch.
Hamilton Grammar Sch.
AUCHINGRAMONT RD.
HAMILTON
CHANTINGHALL RD.
Chantinghall
Chantinghall Bridge
Bent Cemetery
St. John's Prim. Sch.
Rec. Grd.
Superstore
Factory
Hamilton Central
Gasholder Sta.
Office

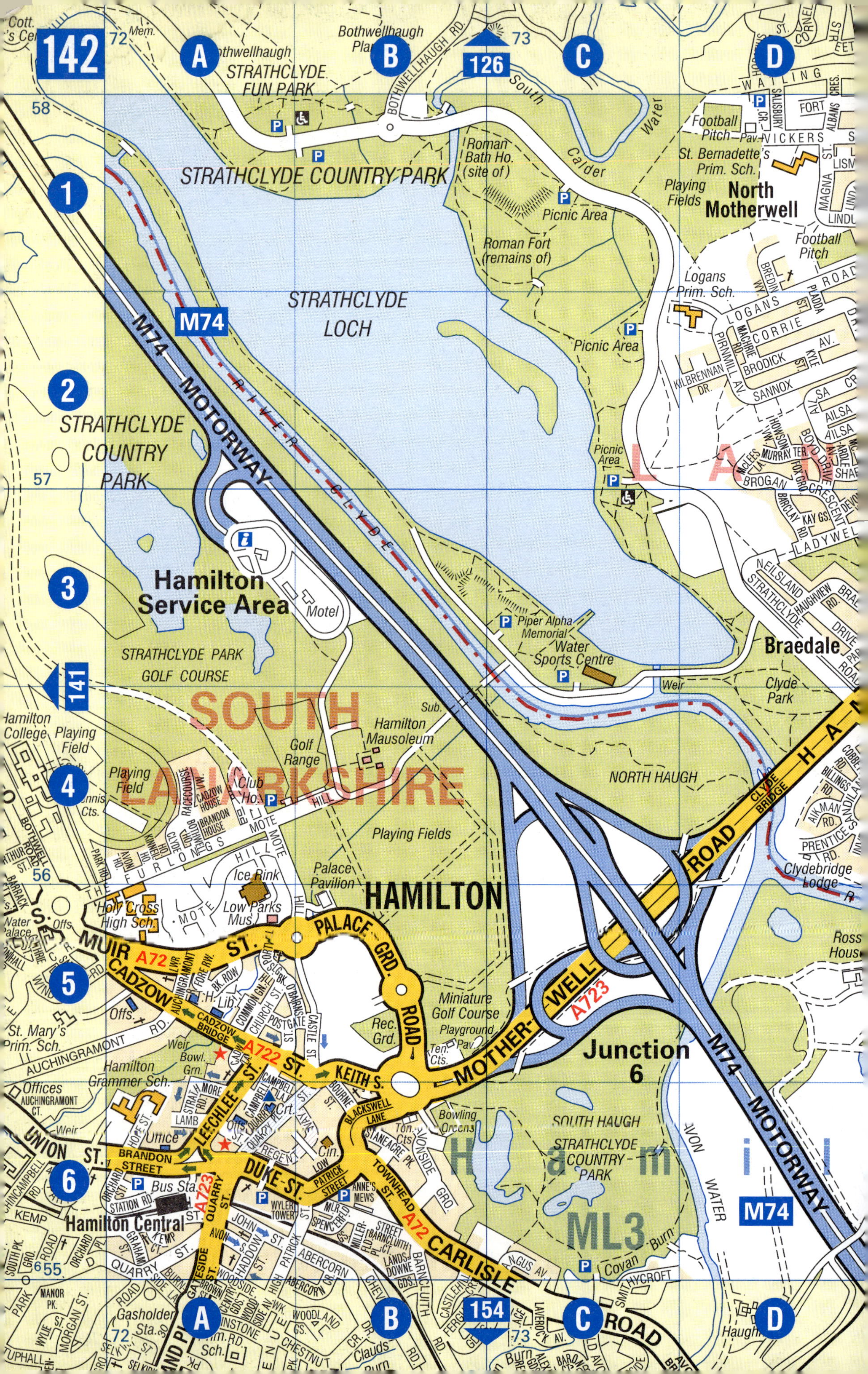

126
141
154
A
B
C
D
1
2
3
4
5
6
STRATHCLYDE FUN PARK
STRATHCLYDE COUNTRY PARK
Bothwellhaugh Pl.
BOTHWELLHAUGH RD.
South Calder Water
Roman Bath Ho. (site of)
Picnic Area
Roman Fort (remains of)
STRATHCLYDE LOCH
M74
M74 MOTORWAY
RIVER CLYDE
Football Pitch
St. Bernadette's Prim. Sch.
Playing Fields
North Motherwell
Logans Prim. Sch.
LOGANS RD.
CORRIE
BRODICK AV.
SANNOX
KILBRENNAN DR.
PIRNMILL AV.
MACHRIE RD.
KYLE ST.
PLADDA ST.
BREDIN WY.
AILSA
MURRAY TER.
BROGAN
BARCLAY RD.
KAY GS.
LADYWELL
McLEES LA.
BOYD ST.
CRESCENT
FORT
VICKERS
WATLING
SALISBURY
MAGNA ST.
ALBANS CRES.
STRATHCLYDE COUNTRY PARK
Hamilton Service Area
Motel
Piper Alpha Memorial
Water Sports Centre
NEILSLAND
STRATHCLYDE
HAUGHVIEW RD.
Braedale
Clyde Park
Weir
STRATHCLYDE PARK GOLF COURSE
SOUTH LANARKSHIRE
Hamilton College
Playing Field
Golf Range
Hamilton Mausoleum
Sub.
NORTH HAUGH
CLYDE BRIDGE ROAD
BILLINGS RD.
AIKMAN RD.
PRENTICE RD.
Clydebridge Lodge
Club Ho.
Tennis Cts.
MOTE HILL
FURLONGS
RACECOURSE VW.
CADZOW HOUSE
BRANDON HOUSE
BOTHWELL ROAD
Ice Rink
Palace Pavilion
HAMILTON
Playing Fields
Holy Cross High Sch.
Low Parks Mus.
Water Palace
Offs.
MUIR ST.
A72
CADZOW ST.
PALACE GRD. ROAD
AUCHINGRAMONT RD.
T.H.
Lib.
CASTLE ST.
Rec. Grd.
Miniature Golf Course
Playground
Pav.
Ten. Cts.
MOTHERWELL ROAD
A723
Junction 6
Ross House
St. Mary's Prim. Sch.
Hamilton Grammer Sch.
Bowl. Grn.
Weir
CADZOW BRIDGE
A722
KEITH ST.
BLACKSWELL LANE
LEECHLEE ST.
Bowling Greens
SOUTH HAUGH
STRATHCLYDE COUNTRY PARK
AVON WATER
UNION ST.
Offices
BRANDON STREET
Office
Cin.
DUKE ST.
TOWNHEAD ST.
ANNE'S MEWS
PATRICK STREET
Bus Sta.
Hamilton Central
QUARRY ST.
A723
A72
CARLISLE ROAD
ML3
Covan Burn
Gasholder Sta.
Clauds Burn
Haugh
GATESIDE ST.
ABERCORN
WOODLAND GS.
CHESTNUT
Sch.
KEMP ST.
STATION RD.

127
155
144
E
F
G
H
1
2
3
4
5
6
MOTHERWELL
NORTH LANARKSHIRE
Motherwell
Knowetop
Airbles
North Lodge
ML1
Bellshill Road
Muir St.
A721
A723
Merry Street
Menteith Rd.
Hamilton Road
Windmillhill St.
Brandon St.
Airbles Road
B754
Camp Road
Ladywell Road
Crawford St.
Strathclyde Hospital
Playing Field
Sewage Works
South Calder Water
Football Ground
Calder Park
Coursington Bri.
Ladywell Prim. Sch.
Sports Grd.
Heritage Cen.
Lib.
The Aquatic
High Sch.
War Mem.
Civ. Cen.
Concert Hall & Thtre.
Y.M.C.A.
Airbles Burial Ground
Camp Road Cotts.
Works and Depot
Play. Fld.
Motherwell F.C.
Firpark Sch.
Stewart Hall
Motherwell College
Our Lady's High Sch.
Cricket Ground
Barons Haugh RSPB Nature Reserve
Sow Bri.
Dalzell Gardens
The Old Manse
Graveyard
Dalzell House
Waterfall
Bus Depot
River Clyde

A
B
C
D
1
2
3
4
5
6
128
143
156
Cleekhimin
JERVISTON RD.
MERRY STREET
A723
B 799
Lodge
HIGHFIELD CRES.
Football Ground
Calder Park
Calder Water
Coursington Bri.
WILSON
DRAFFEN
ALLAN TWR.
Works
STREET
ROAD
Todhole Burn
Carfin Byres
Works
NORTH LANARK
SOUTH
RAVENSCRAIG STEEL WORKS (SITE OF)
Motherwell
ML1
ORBISTON
MEADOW
Works
WINDMILLHILL ST.
CRAIGNEUK
A721
College (Annexe)
Craigneuk
Flemington
Offs.
Depot
RANGE ROAD INDUSTRIAL ESTATE
ETNA INDUSTRIAL ESTATE
SHIELDMUIR ST.
Shieldmuir
GLASGOW
Prim. Sch.
Motherwell F.C.
Firpark Sch.
Stewart Hall
Motherwell College
Our Lady's High Sch.
DALZELL AVENUE
Cricket Ground
SHIELDS RD.
B754
Whinny Burn
Shields Glen Public Pk.
RANGE ROAD
Ind. Estate
Comm. Cen.
Play. Fld.
Lib.
Timber Yd.
Cuckoo Bridge
Dalzell House
Waterfall
Sow Bri.
NETHERHALL
CANYON
Factory

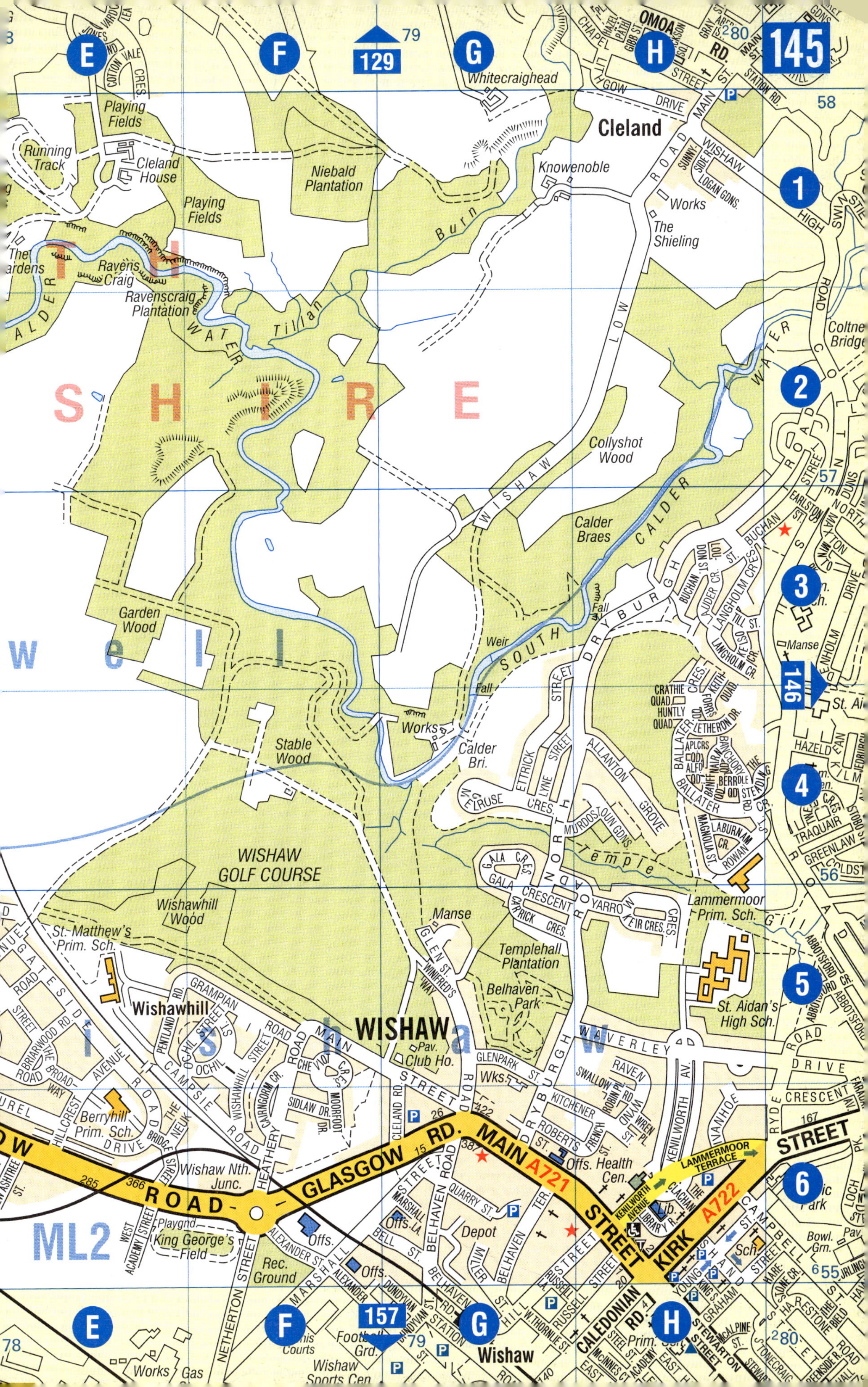
E
F
G
H
129
79
157
146
Whitecraighead
Cleland
Knowenoble
Works
The Shieling
Playing Fields
Running Track
Cleland House
Niebald Plantation
Burn
Ravens Craig
Ravenscraig Plantation
The Gardens
Tillan
WATER
CALDER
S H I R E
w e l l
Garden Wood
Collyshot Wood
Calder Braes
Weir
Fall
Works
Calder Bri.
Stable Wood
WISHAW GOLF COURSE
Wishawhill Wood
St. Matthew's Prim. Sch.
Wishawhill
WISHAW
Pav. Club Ho.
Manse
Templehall Plantation
Belhaven Park
Lammermoor Prim. Sch.
St. Aidan's High Sch.
Coltness Bridge
Berryhill Prim. Sch.
Wishaw Nth. Junc.
Playgnd.
King George's Field
Rec. Ground
Offs.
Depot
Offs. Health Cen.
Lib.
Sch.
Bowl. Grn.
Wishaw
Wishaw Sports Cen.
Football Grd.
Works
Gas
ML2
GLASGOW RD.
MAIN STREET
KIRK STREET
A721
A722
LAMMERMOOR TERRACE
WAVERLEY ROAD
WISHAW LOW ROAD
SOUTH DRYBURGH ROAD
NORTH DRYBURGH ROAD
GALA CRESCENT
CARRICK CRES.
YARROW CRES.
FIR CRES.
ALLANTON GROVE
ETTRICK CRES.
LYNE STREET
MELROSE CRES.
MURDOSTOUN GDNS.
Temple
BALLATER CR.
LABURNAM CR.
ROWAN
MAGNOLIA ST.
CRATHIE QUAD
HUNTLY QUAD
FORRES QUAD
KEITH QUAD
LANGHOLM CRES.
LANGHOLM CR.
TILL ST.
KELSO QUAD
BUCHAN ST.
ABBOTSFORD RD.
ABBOTSFORD CR.
GLEN ST.
WINIFRED'S WAY
GLENPARK ST.
KITCHENER ST.
ROBERTS ST.
FRENCH ST.
SWALLOW RD.
RAVEN WYND
ROBIN PL.
WREN PL.
KENILWORTH AV.
IVANHOE
RYDE CRESCENT
DRIVE
STREET
CALEDONIAN RD.
STEWARTON STREET
CAMPBELL STREET
YOUNG ST.
GRAHAM
HARESTONE RD.
RUSSELL STREET
BELHAVEN TER.
BELHAVEN ROAD
QUARRY ST.
MILLER ST.
BELL ST.
MARSHALL LA.
MARSHALL ST.
ALEXANDER ST.
NETHERTON STREET
HEATHERY ROAD
CLELAND RD.
CAIRNGORM CR.
SIDLAW DR.
MOORFOOT DR.
CHEVIOT CRES.
WISHAWHILL STREET
GRAMPIAN RD.
PENTLAND RD.
OCHIL STREET
CAMPSIE ROAD
THE NEUK
BRIDGE STREET
BERRYHILL ROAD
GATESIDE STREET
BRIARWOOD RD.
THE BROADWAY
HILLCREST AVENUE
ROAD
WEST ACADEMY STREET
COTTON VALE
CHAPEL ST.
GIBB ST.
OMOA RD.
LITHGOW DRIVE
STATION RD.
MAIN ST.
WISHAW HIGH ROAD
SUNNYSIDE CR.
LOGAN GDNS.
HAZELDEAN CRES.
TRAQUAIR
GREENLAW
58
57
56
55
1
2
3
4
5
6
280
78
79
80
285
366
387
422
167
15
26
140
Manse
St. Ai

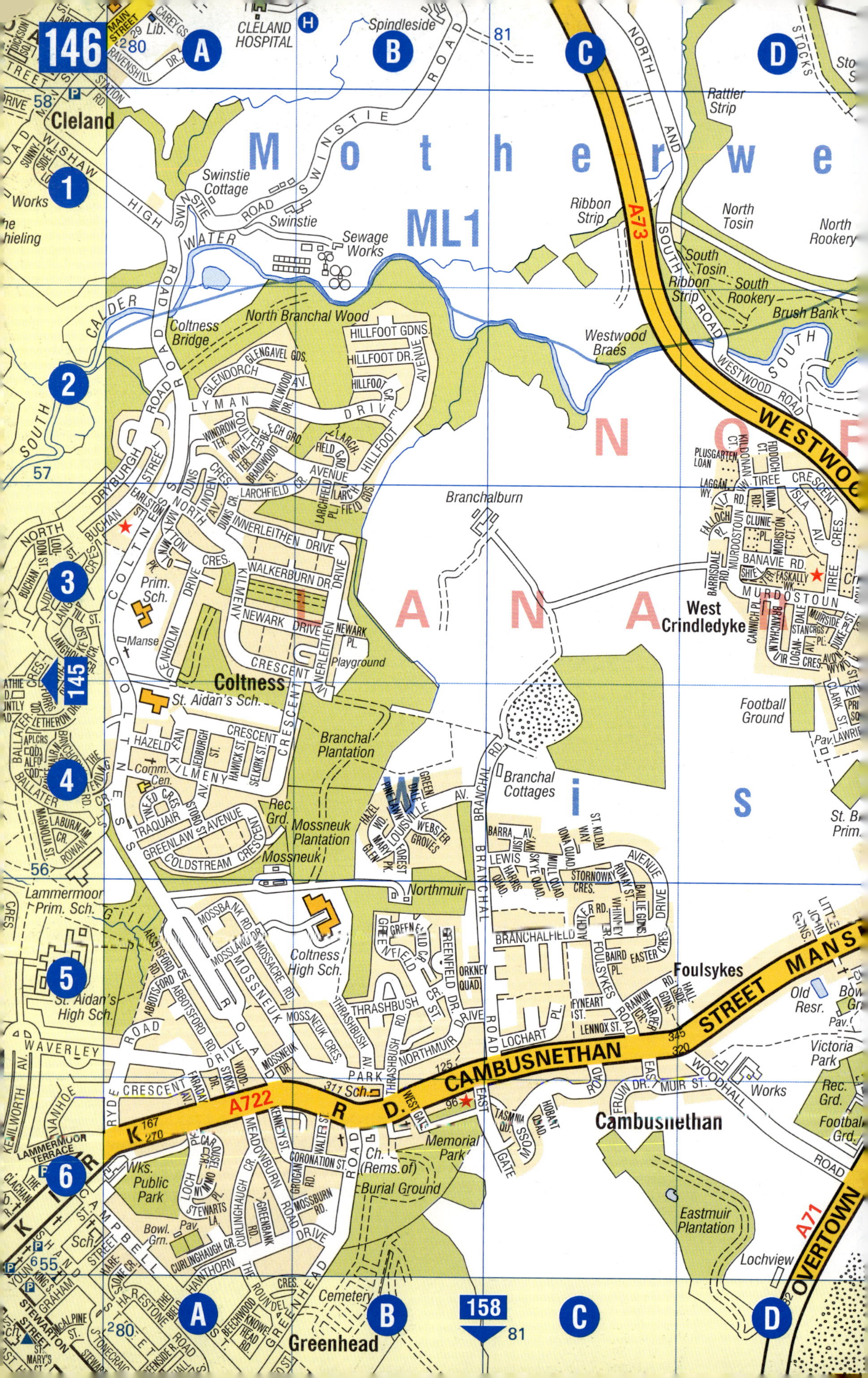
Cleland
Cleland Hospital
Spindleside
Swinstie Road
Swinstie Cottage
Swinstie
Sewage Works
Motherwell
ML1
Rattler Strip
Ribbon Strip
North Tosin
North Rookery
South Tosin
Ribbon Strip
South Rookery
Brush Bank
North and South Road
A73
Westwood Braes
Westwood Road
Calder Water
High Road
Wishaw Road
Works
Coltness Bridge
North Branchal Wood
Hillfoot Gdns.
Hillfoot Dr.
Hillfoot Avenue
Lyman Drive
Glendorch
Glengavel Gds.
Larchfield Cr.
Innerleithen Drive
Walkerburn Dr.
Newark Drive
Kilmeny Crescent
Playground
Coltness Road
Coltness
St. Aidan's Sch.
Prim. Sch.
Manse
Branchalburn
West Crindledyke
Murdostoun Cres.
Football Ground
Branchal Plantation
Branchal Cottages
Branchal Rd.
Mossneuk Plantation
Mossneuk
Rec. Grd.
Comm. Cen.
Greenlaw Avenue
Coldstream Crescent
Traquair Cres.
Northmuir
Coltness High Sch.
Mossneuk Road
Branchalfield
Foulsykes
Foulsykes Road
Mansel Street
Old Resr.
Victoria Park
Rec. Grd.
Football Grd.
Woodhall Road
Works
Cambusnethan Street
Cambusnethan
A722
Kirk Road
Memorial Park
Burial Ground
Ch. (Rems. of)
Eastmuir Plantation
Lochview
Overtown Road
A71
Wks.
Public Park
Bowl. Grn.
Pav.
Cemetery
Greenhead
Lammermoor Prim. Sch.
St. Aidan's High Sch.
Waverley
Stewarton Street
Campbell St.
St. Brendan's Prim.
145
158

Muiredge Wood
BIG WOOD
Pine Strip
Mill
Easterhouse Cottages
Bolt Strip
Glenhead Wood
Cuckoo Strip
MURDOSTOUN
Murdostoun Home Farm
South Rookery
Fountainhead Wood
Calder Water
Jay Wood
Tennis Court
Stable Glen
Crow Hill
Lodge
Water Splash
South
ALLANTON ROAD
Mill
CALDER
Lion Cleugh
Murdostoun Castle
Garden Glen
Weir
WATER
Kennel Knowe Wood
Murdostoun Bridge
South Plantation
Rec. Ground
Brownhill Wood
DEVINE GR.
McCARRISON RD.
McMAHON RD.
East Crindledyke
CHURCH ROAD
CAIRNEY PL.
West Croft
Falls
Bonkle
Pav.
BROWNHILL VW.
Brownhill Wood
EASTWOOD
CALDER AV.
KILMICHAEL AV.
East Crindledyke
BOLEYN CT.
BONDS
BROOKING WY.
DR.
WOODSIDE
CRESCENT
MEADOWFIELD PL.
Woodside
A73
FIRTREE RD.
ALCATH
ROAD
NORTHWOOD DR.
DRIVE
ABERNETHYN
FIRTREE PL.
WOODSIDE CR.
BONKLE
VIEW
BAILLIS-MUIR PL.
EASTWOOD DR.
MUIRHOUSE
Whitestripe
RD.
LYNWOOD RD.
HAWTHORN AV.
MAVIS-BANK ST.
Sharnothshield Small Holdings
STREET
STEWART
TAY LA.
WEST PL.
CR.
CRINDLEDYKE
CRESCENT
AVENUE
AUCHTER CR.
BONKLE GS.
BRAEDALE PL.
AUCHTER AV.
BRAE DALE CRES.
BRAEDALE
Water
ROAD
Football Ground
PARK DR.
NEWMAINS
GODDARD PL.
Crindledyke
A71
Cathburn
PARK
DRIVE
BONKLE
Convent
Auchter Water
NEWTON CR.
TOLL PARK
Lintmill Kennels
Cathburn Holdings
Hlth. Cen.
MORNINGSIDE ROAD
A722 RD.
War Mem.
Lib.
HOPE ST.
BROWN ST.
PARK VIEW CR.
SCHOOL
Sch.
STREET
Works
Lintmill
CATHBURN
ROAD
ROAD
Works
Cathburn Cottage
ML2
VICTORIA ST.
A73
MAIN
Morningside Prim. Sch.
MORNINGSIDE
Morningside Farm
Torbush
SCHOOL RD.
Works
Works
Play Ground
Woodside Farm
RD.
MAIN
Morningside
MILL
WOODHALL ROAD
A73
STREET
Auchter
ROAD
Oakbank
Water
Depot
E
F
G
H
1
2
3
4
5
6
82
83
84
55
56
57
58
159

Craigpark
Industrial Estate
Offices
136
61
Industrial Estate
College Milton
West Mains
HAWBANK ROUNDABOUT
ARROTSHOLE ROAD
A726
B761
QUEENSWAY
WEST MAINS ROAD
PEEL PARK IND. EST.
REDWOOD CRESCENT
REDWOOD DRIVE
BARBANA ROAD
G74
Peel Park
LINWOOD AVENUE
TENNANT AVENUE
MILTON AVENUE
Works
BROOKLANDS
Hairmyres
B764
EAGLESHAM ROAD
Millbrae
Government Offices
HAIRMYRES ROUNDABOUT
Lodge
Ten. Cts.
WESTPORT
DUNEDIN DRIVE
WINDWARD
Play. Flds.
Duncanrig Sec. Sch.
Duncanrig Sports Cen.
Playground
Rec. Ground
Pav.
Westwood
HAIRMYRES HOSPITAL
Hairmyres
MOSSNEUK DRIVE
WELLESLEY DRIVE
WELLESLEY CRESCENT
INGLEWOOD CRESCENT
PITCAIRN CRESCENT
GLEN ROAD
Canberra Prim. Sch.
BELMONT DRIVE
ROCKHAMPTON
Playing Field
School
Comm. Cen.
G75
Mossneuk
EDEN DRIVE
NEWLANDS ROAD
Gardenhall
SOUTH LANARKSHIRE
NEWLANDSMUIR ROAD
Newlandsmuir
GREENHILLS ROAD
Greenhills
Comm. Cen.
Lib.
Hlth Cen.
Castlefield Prim. Sch.
Crosshouse Prim. Sch.
CROSSHOUSE ROAD
Newlands Farm
Dunrobin
Dorniebank
Trunlehill
JACKTON RD.
NEWLANDS
NETHERTON RD.
Netherton Lodge
St. Vincent's Primary School
Ballerup High School
Water Tower
260
655
54
53
52
61
1
2
3
4
5
6
A
B
C
D

137
150
EAST KILBRIDE
East Kilbride
East Mains
Kirktonholme Park
Kirktonholme Prim. Sch.
Cambuslang Coll.
Village Theatre
Football Grd
The Show Park
Halfmerke Sch. & West Mains Sch.
Town Centre Park
Dollan Aqua Cen.
Civic Centre
Hlth. Cen.
Atholl Ho.
St. Bride's High Sch.
THE PLAZA (SHOP. CEN.)
OLYMPIA (SHOP. CEN.)
Ice Rink
Lib.
Kittoch Bridge
THE MURRAY ROUNDABOUT
BIRNIEHILL ROUNDABOUT
Birniehill
Gov. Offs.
N.E.L. TECHNOLOGY PARK
Headhouse Greenway
Murray Prim. Sch.
The Murray
E. Milton Prim. Sch.
HOSP.
St. Louise's Prim. Sch.
Heathery Knowe Prim. Sch.
Robert Owen Centre
South Park Prim. Sch.
Sports Cen.
St. Andrew's High Sch.
Hostel
Greenhills Prim. Sch.
Playing Fields
Whitehills
Industrial Estate
Kelvin
KELVIN SOUTH BUSINESS PARK
Kittoch Water
G74
LANARKSHIRE
MAINS ROAD
B761
EAST MAINS RD.
B783
QUEENSWAY
A726
WHITEMOSS AV.
KINGSWAY
STROUD ROAD
KELVIN ROAD
GREENHILLS ROAD
WHITEHILLS
CORNWALL ST.
CALEDONIAN CT.
RIGHEAD ROUNDABOUT
THE CENTRE ROUNDABOUT
E
F
G
H
1
2
3
4
5
6
52
53
54
55
62
63
64

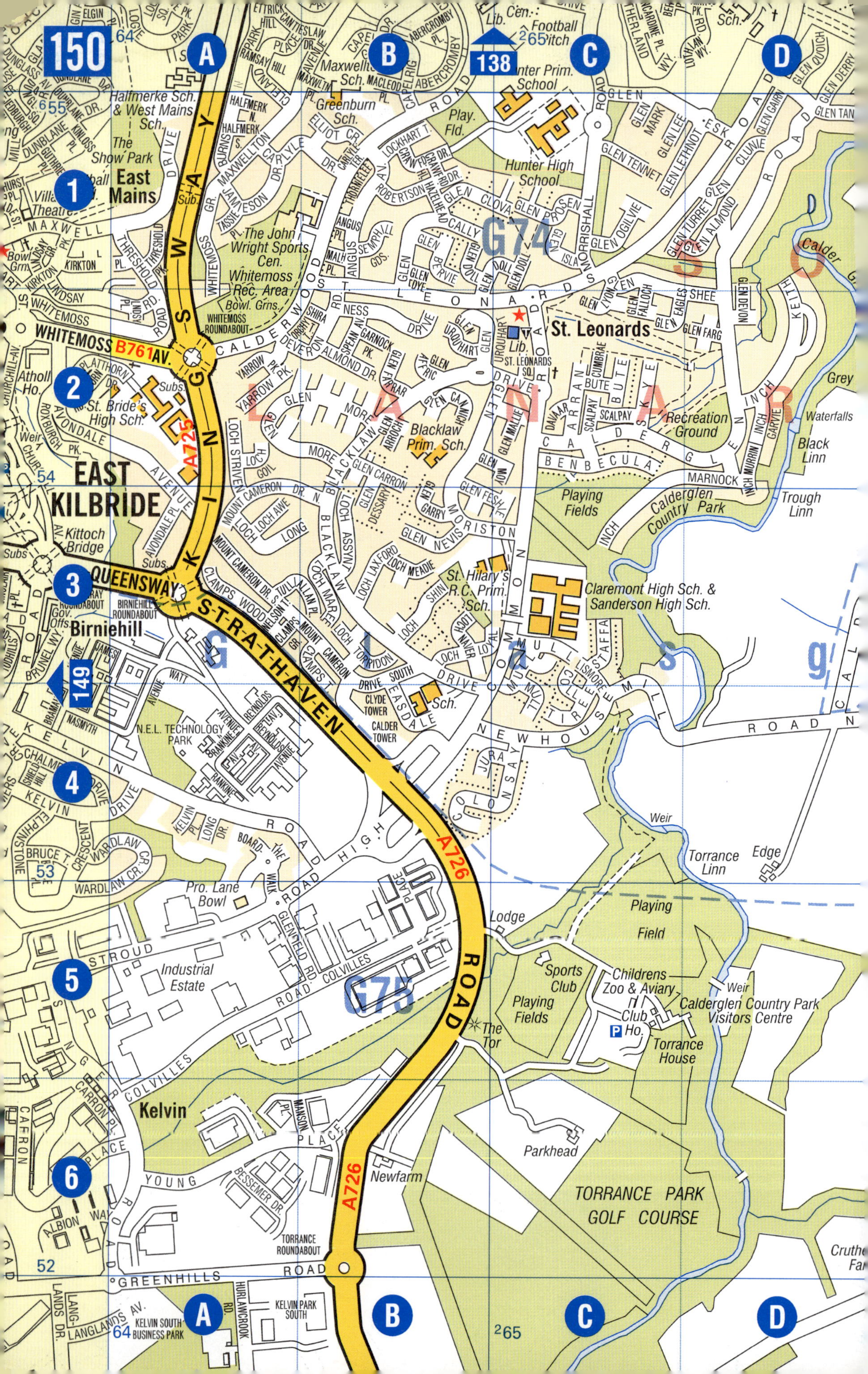
138
149
A
B
C
D
1
2
3
4
5
6
64
265
55
54
53
52
G74
G75
EAST KILBRIDE
East Mains
St. Leonards
Birniehill
Kelvin
KINGSWAY
QUEENSWAY
STRATHAVEN ROAD
A725
A726
B761
WHITEMOSS AV.
WHITEMOSS ROUNDABOUT
BIRNIEHILL ROUNDABOUT
TORRANCE ROUNDABOUT
ST. LEONARDS ROAD
CALDERWOOD RD.
MAXWELL DR.
KELVIN DRIVE
KELVIN ROAD
HIGH ROAD
COLVILLES ROAD
YOUNG PLACE
GREENHILLS ROAD
NEWHOUSE MILL ROAD
BLACKLAW DR.
MORISTON DRIVE
MOUNT CAMERON DR.
BENBECULA
INCH GARVIE
GLEN OGILVIE
GLEN CLOVA
MORRISHALL ROAD
Halfmerke Sch. & West Mains Sch.
The Show Park
Village Theatre
Greenburn Sch.
Maxwellton Sch.
Hunter High School
Hunter Prim. School
Football Pitch
Play. Fld.
The John Wright Sports Cen.
Whitemoss Rec. Area
Bowl. Grns.
St. Bride's High Sch.
Atholl Ho.
Blacklaw Prim. Sch.
St. Hilary's R.C. Prim. Sch.
Claremont High Sch. & Sanderson High Sch.
Recreation Ground
Playing Fields
Calderglen Country Park
Black Linn
Trough Linn
Waterfalls
Torrance Linn
Edge
Weir
Kittoch Bridge
Gov. Offs.
N.E.L. TECHNOLOGY PARK
Pro. Lane Bowl
Industrial Estate
Lodge
Playing Field
Sports Club
Childrens Zoo & Aviary
Club Ho.
Calderglen Country Park Visitors Centre
Torrance House
The Tor
Parkhead
Newfarm
TORRANCE PARK GOLF COURSE
KELVIN PARK SOUTH
KELVIN SOUTH BUSINESS PARK
CLYDE TOWER
CALDER TOWER
LANARKS
Glasgow

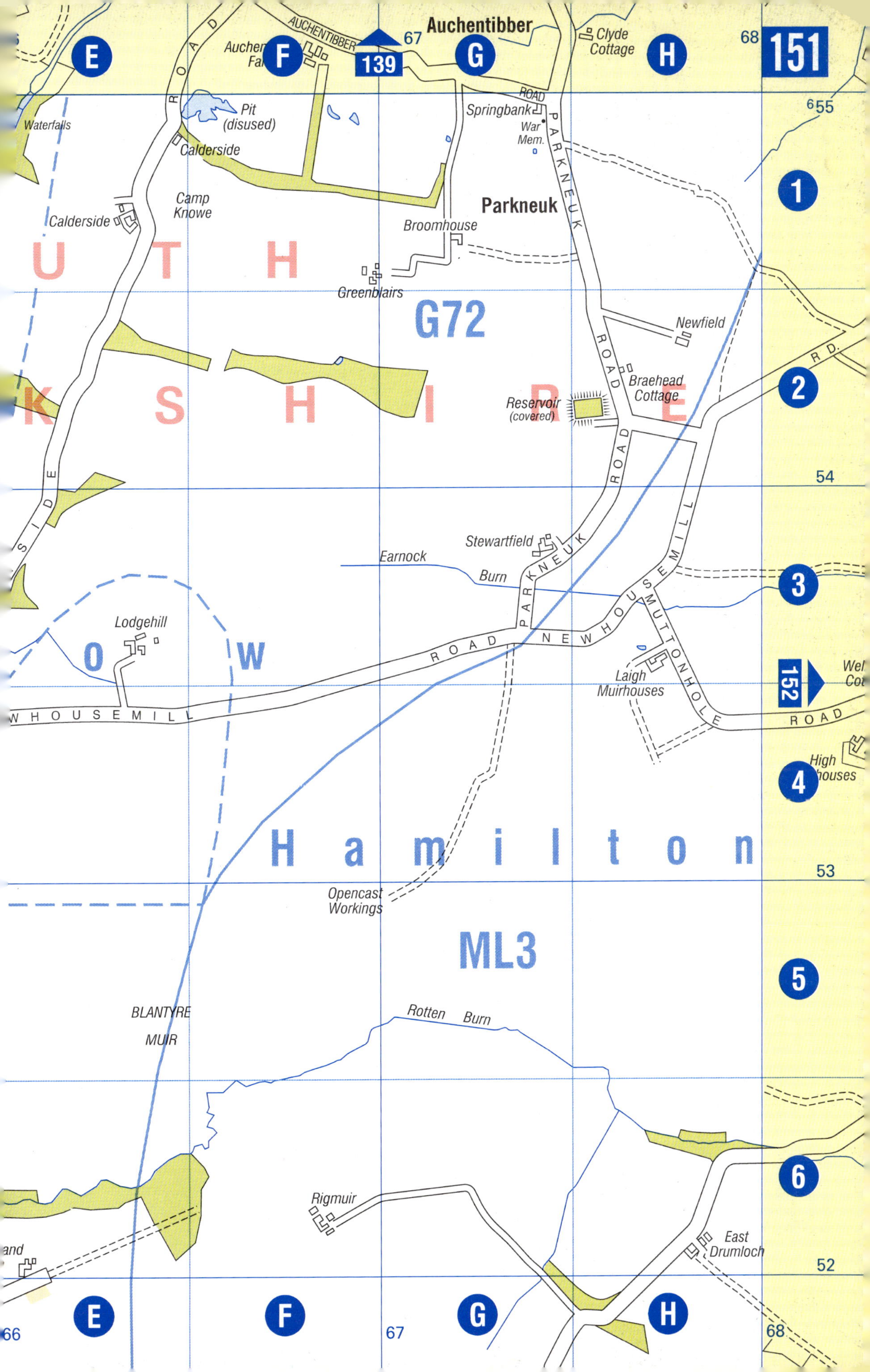

E
F
G
H
Auchentibber
AUCHENTIBBER
139
67
68
Clyde Cottage
ROAD
Pit (disused)
Waterfalls
Calderside
Springbank
War Mem.
PARKNEUK
655
1
Camp Knowe
Parkneuk
Calderside
Broomhouse
Greenblairs
G72
Newfield
RD.
2
ROAD
Braehead Cottage
Reservoir (covered)
ROAD
54
CALDERSIDE
Stewartfield
PARKNEUK
MILL
Earnock
Burn
3
Lodgehill
NEWHOUSEMILL ROAD
MUTTONHOLE ROAD
Laigh Muirhouses
152
NEWHOUSEMILL
High houses
4
Hamilton
53
Opencast Workings
ML3
5
BLANTYRE MUIR
Rotten Burn
6
Rigmuir
East Drumloch
52
66
67
68

140
151
A
B
C
D
1
2
3
4
5
6
68
69
655
54
53
52
Udston Cottage
Dykehead
Dykehead House
Reservoir (covered)
Newfield
Muirmains
Earnock
EARNOCK ROAD
NEWHOUSEMILL
Townhill Prim. Sch.
TOWNHILL
CLARKWELL
MELFORT
BALFRON
SHANDON TER.
GILMOUR
BALFRON CR.
CORRIE CT.
TORWOOD BRAE
POMONA PL.
LUSS
LOMOND VW.
FRUIN
RISE
ERISKAY AV.
REDERECH
LANGORETH AV.
ISLAY CT.
DALTON HILL
DUNSCORE BRAE
CORSOCK AV.
BORELAND
DALRY GS.
STRAITON DR.
MUIRKIRK DR.
DUNURE DR.
DAVINGTON DR.
TURNBERRY DR.
MAUCHLINE CT.
ALLOWAY GDS.
BARNHILL DR.
BOLE GDS.
DALFOOT GS.
RICK GS.
TYNRON CT.
CUMNOCK DR.
AILSA CT.
DURISDEER
DRIVE
TORRANYARD TER.
KILWINNING CR.
OCHILTREE
COYLTON CR.
PATNA
CRAIGELL CT.
AQUA CT.
AQUA AV.
BOURTREE
CAMPSIE VW.
SWIFT
BANK
IONA
RIDGE
WELLHALL ROAD
Earnock Burn
Weir
L A N A R
S O U
St. Mark Prim. Sch.
Kennedies
Wellbrae Cottage
MUTTON HOLE
High Muirhouses
HIGHSTONEHALL ROAD
ML3
Dykend
Electricity Sub Station
Mast
Sherriff Faulds
Beechfield House
MEIKLE
H a m i
Devonhill
Earnockmuir
Earnockmuir Cottage
East Drumloch
Cadzow Burn
Haspielaw
Muirha
Torhe Lak

141
154
E
F
G
H
1
2
3
4
5
6
70
71
72
55
54
53
52
Chantinghall
Chantinghall Bridge
Playing Field
Bent Cemetery
Prim. Sch.
Rec. Grd.
Earnock High Sch.
Works
Factory
Earnock Burn
Laighstonehall
Weir
Cadzow Burn
MILL ROAD
B755
Hall
Comm. Cen.
Prim. Sch.
St. Peter's Prim. Sch.
Football Grd.
Little Earnock
Lib.
NEILSLAND SQUARE
Neilsland Park
Woodhead Green
Woodhead Prim. Sch.
Fairhill
Bowling Green
Rec. Grd.
LOW WATERS ROAD
A723
Low Waters
CADZOW INDUSTRIAL ESTATE
Gasholder Sta.
Eddlewood
Play Field
Games Crt.
Eddlewood Sports Barn
Meikle Earnock
MEIKLE EARNOCK ROAD
Eddlewood Fm.
Brackenhill
EARNOCK
Cadzow Burn
Whitecraigs
Broomknowe
Oaklea
Annsfield
Chapel
Simpsonland
Simpsonland Glen
CARSCALLAN
STRATHAVEN ROAD
A723
Hillcrest
Depot
Cornhills
Blue Waters Cottage
Blackbog
Blackbog Glen
Waterfall
LANARKSHIRE
Hamilton

A
B
C
D
142
73
153
72
1
2
3
4
5
6
55
54
53
52
Central
Station Rd.
Wylie St.
Morgan St.
Gasholder Sta.
Portland Pl.
Portland Rd.
Burnblea St.
Quarry St.
Johnstone Rd.
Prim. Sch.
Abercorn St.
Cheviot Dr.
Carlisle A72 Rd.
Covan Burn
Smithycroft
Haughhead
Avon Bridge
Avon Mill
Avon Mill Ho.
Avon Mill Cottage
Nursery
Rec. Grd.
Old Avon Bridge
Weir
Barncluith Lodge
Silvertonhill
Ferniegair
Monument
Chatelherault Country Park
Chatelherault
Chatelherault Prim. Sch.
Low Waters
A723
Waters Rd.
Low Waters Rd.
Laverock Hill
Meikle Burn
Cattle Grid
Cadzow Industrial Estate
Cadzow Castle (remains of)
Cave
Waterfall
Avon Water
Cadzow House
Old Oaks
Eddlewood
Eddlewood Glen
Games Crt.
Eddlewood Sports Barn
Pav.
High Parks Farm
Hamilton High Parks
LANARK
SOUTH LANARKSHIRE
Hamilton
ML3
Clydesdale Av.
Simpsonland
Simpsonland Glen
Thorney Glen
Ramsay's Plantation
Divoty Wood
Carscallan Road
Carscallan
Blue Waters Cottage
Blackbog
Blackbog Glen
Clover Cottage
Annax Lodge

E
F
G
H
143
275
76
Cricket
Bow Bri.
Dalzell
The Old Manse
Gardens
MANSE ROAD
ROAD
Barons Haugh RSPB Nature Reserve
M74
NORTH LANARKSHIRE
Burn
Dalzell House
Wate.
55
Graveyard
Dalzell
Motherwell
ML1
RIVER
CLYDE
Weir
1
2
3
4
5
6
Depot
Hall
162
PARK DR.
FAIR-HOLM AV.
ROSS TER.
AVENUE
CASTLEHILL CR.
CLYDE
Sewage Works
Saw Mill
Allanton
M74 MOTORWAY
54
Garden Centre
Allanton Ter.
M74
A72
Club House
S H I R E
COURSE
156
Merryton
ROAD
BELVIDERE PLANTATION
Merryton Farm Cotts.
LANARK RD. END
LANARK
A72
ROAD
53
CARLISLE
Garden Centre
ROAD
Go-Kart
Avon Braes
Larkhall
B7078
Dykehead Cottage
MERRYTON
High Merryton
ROAD
ML9
Lodge
25
HAMILTON RD.
DAVE BARRIE AV.
WEST FAIRHOLM ST.
SUMMERLEE
ROAD
MAPLE
BEECH
WOOD
BIRCH GRO.
ELM W
TREE
CHESTNUT
BROOM DR.
52
HAMILTON ST.
Lodge
Fairholm Bridge
BEATON ST.
SUNNYSIDE ST.
MERRYTON STREET
War Mem.
GLEN-VIEW
CLYDESDALE ST.
34
DOUGLAS ST.
CADZOW ST.
NORTH ST.
Merryton Braes
AVON WATER
Sewage Works
Playground
LONDON
160
275
74
76

A
B
C
D
1
2
3
4
5
6
76
77
55
54
53
52
144
155
161
Cricket Ground
Waterfall
Dalzell House
Motherwell
Muirhouse
ML1
Easterbraes Plantation
Pumping Station
Adders' Gill
Adders' Gill Wood
Weir
GALLACHER CT.
SHIELDS RD.
NETHERWOOD TWR.
MERRYTON TWR.
GRANGE TOWER
Prim. Sch.
BARONS RD.
MERRYTON ROAD
MUIRHOUSE DRIVE
CLYDE TER.
ROAD
B754
EXCELSIOR
STREET
NETHERHALL
CANYON RD.
Factory
ROWAN CT.
BOURHILL CT.
NETHERTON
ATTERCLIFFE AV.
COVENANT ST.
PRIORY TER.
Playgrd.
INGLIS ST.
THOMSON AV.
STENT
STENTON PL.
CLYDESDALE AV.
AVENUE
KIRKNETHAN
Depot
ST. MICHAEL RD.
Muirhouse Farm
Upper Muirhouse Farm
Kirkhill Orchard
KIRKHILL ROAD
LANARK
Netherton
Monument
Graveyard
Sewage Works
CARBARNS ROAD
Randalls Orchard
Carbarns Orchard
Carbarnswood
Carbarns Wood
Lower Carbarns
W
Hamilton ML3
RIVER
CLYDE
Larkhall
M74
Hall Gill
Tammy's Burn
Upper Carbarns
Junction 7
LANARK ROAD
A72
MOTORWAY
Go-Kart Track
Dykehead Cottage
Highlees
Prince's Lodge
ML9
Whittrick Burn
Skelly Gill
SOUTH LANARKSHIRE
Sewage Works
Tilework Cottage
Cemetery
EAST STATION INDUSTRIAL ESTATE
Rec. Grd.
HAMILTON RD.
HAMILTON ST.
CHERRY
BEECHWOOD
BIRCH GRO.
ELM WY.
WILLOW BANK
TREE CRESCENT
MAPLE DR.
CHESTNUT
SUMMERLEE ROAD
DUKE ST.
War Mem.
Playground

145
162
158
Wishaw
Pather
Gowkthrapple
OVERTOWN
ML2
Netherton Comm. Cen.
Netherton Prim. Sch.
NETHERTON IND. EST.
King George's Field
Playgnd.
Tennis Courts
Football Grd.
Wishaw Sports Cen.
Spts. Grd.
Wishaw Greyhound Stadium
Football Ground
St. Thomas' Prim. Sch.
Community Centre
Prim. Sch.
Play. Field
Presby
Playing Field
Works
Gas Sta.
Factory
Depot
Bowling Green
Cattle Grids
Electricity Sub Station
Castlehill Prim. Sch.
GARRION BUSINESS PARK
Clyde Valley High Sch.
Gowkthrapple Burn
Lodge
Castlehill
Durhambank
Mausoleum
Highmainshead Wood
Lucindabank
Wemysshill Orchard
Wemysshill
West Belmont
East Belmont
Pathhead Orchard
Laurelbank
Trotterbank
Stewartbank
Nursery
Nursy.
Ford
RIVER CLYDE
Upper Callender
Lower Callender
Horsleyhead
Blairs Orchard
Pather Farm
CALEDONIAN ROAD
CASTLEHILL ROAD
CASTLEHILL
NETHERTON ROAD
STEWARTON ROAD
MAIN ST.
HORSLEY BRAE
MAIN
A72 ROAD
B754
B7032
A721
A71
STREET

A
B
C
D
1
2
3
4
5
6
146
157
163
Greenhead
Cemetery
Waterloo
Dimsdale
Pather Farm
Recreation Ground
Rec. Ground
PARK
OPENCAST WORKINGS
Works
ML2
Overtown Prim. Sch.
Bowling Green
Garriongill Junction
Garrion Burn
Playing Field
Hall
Comm. Cen.
Depot
Castlehill
OVERTOWN
Rosebank
Ford Gill
Wemyssbank
Horsleyhead Nursy.
Blairs Orchard
Upper Callender
Lower Callender
Shawgill
Birks
Nursery
Play. Field
Eastmuir Plantation
Lochview
Lanniem
STEWARTON STREET
WISHAW RD.
OVERTOWN ROAD
WISHAW ROAD
OVERTOWN STREET
MAIN STREET
CASTLEHILL RD.
HORSLEY BRAE
BROWNLEE ROAD
GREENHEAD STREET
CAMPBELL STREET
DIMSDALE ROAD
HOSPITAL RD.
A721
A71
B754
B7011
NORTH LANARKSHIRE
SOUTH LANARKSHIRE
Wishaw
Carluke

E
F
G
H
147
83
84
HALL ROAD
MAIN ST.
Oakbank
Auchter Water
War Mem.
MORNINGSIDE ROAD
Depot
Chapel
CHAPEL ROAD
Holmhill
ROAD
Herdshill
A73
1
2
3
4
5
6
655
54
53
52
Bogside Farm
Bogside
A721 ROAD
517
Twelve Acre Plantation
89
Wildmanbridge
Works
Subway
LAW HOSPITAL
Gillhead
B7011
Wildman Bridge
WILDMAN ROAD
STATION PL.
Nursery
103
Waterlands Nursery
OLD WISHAW ROAD
DOBBIES CT.
BUCHANAN DR.
126
STATION ROW
Depot
Waterlands
PATTERSON DR.
LAW
Garrion Burn
Old Toll House
BRACKENHILL RD.
Brackenhill
STRATH CARRON
NAIRN
STRATHDEARN
STRATHALLADALE
Works
Castlehill Bridge
Football Ground
AIRDRIE RD.
Works
ML8
Law Primary Sch.
BLACKHILL VW.
MANSE CT.
CASTLEHILL CRES.
Castlehill
164

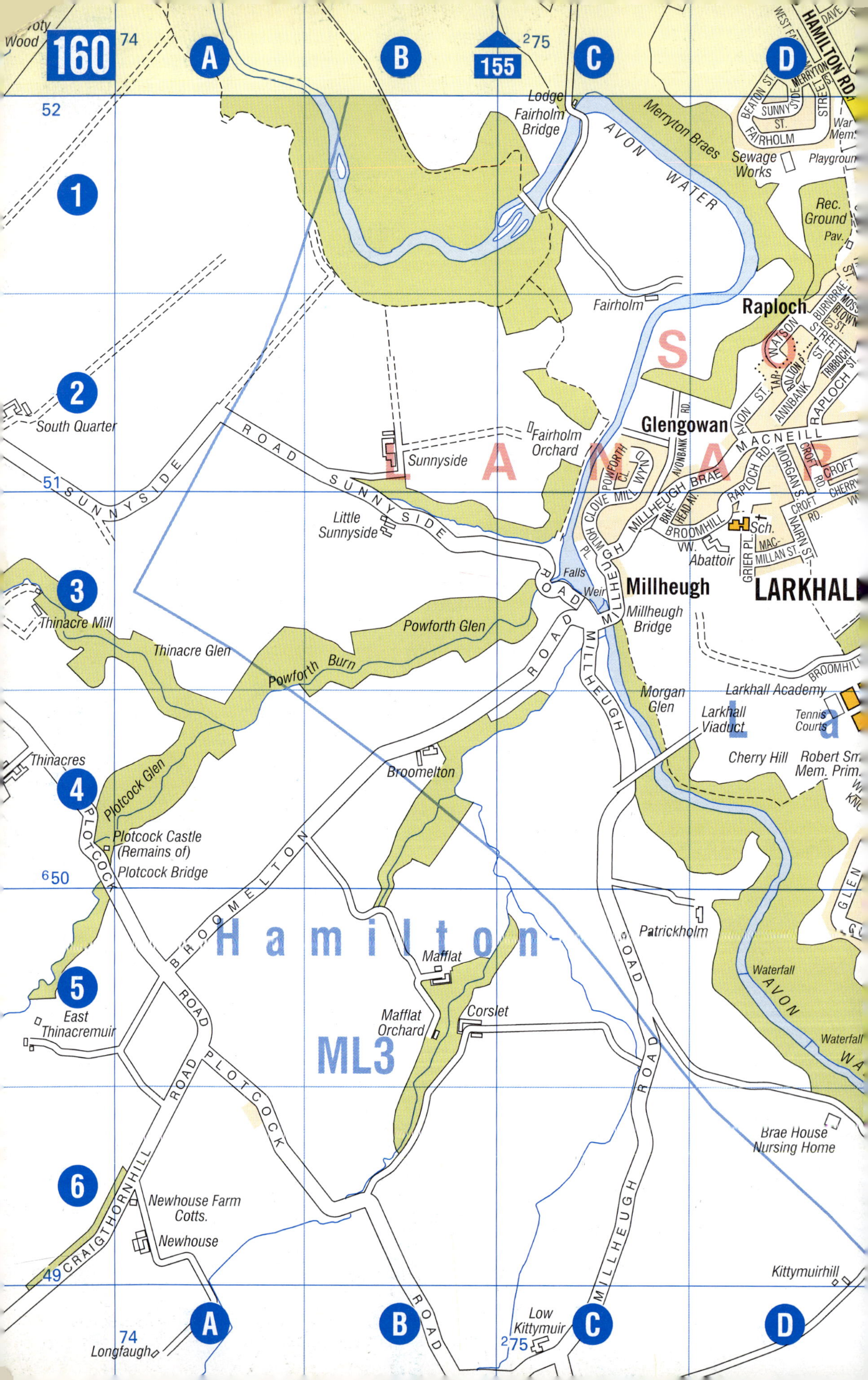

A
B
C
D
155
74
275
52
51
650
49
1
2
3
4
5
6
Lodge
Fairholm Bridge
Merryton Braes
AVON WATER
HAMILTON RD
BEATON ST.
SUNNYSIDE ST.
FAIRHOLM
MERRYTON
STREET
War Mem.
Sewage Works
Playground
Rec. Ground
Pav.
Fairholm
Raploch
BURNBRAE
WATSON
STREET
RAPLOCH ST.
TRIBBOCH ST.
BOLTON P.
TAR-
ANNBANK
AVON ST.
S
South Quarter
SUNNYSIDE ROAD
Sunnyside
Fairholm Orchard
Glengowan
AVONBANK RD.
POWFORTH CL.
WYND
CLOVE MILL
MILLHEUGH BRAE
MACNEILL
RAPLOCH RD.
MORGAN S.
CROFT RD.
CROFT
CHERRY
L A N A R
Little Sunnyside
HOLM PL.
HEAD AV.
BRAE
BROOMHILL
VW.
Sch.
Abattoir
GRIER PL.
MAC-MILLAN ST.
NAIRN ST.
CROFT RD.
Falls
Weir
Millheugh
LARKHALL
Thinacre Mill
Thinacre Glen
Powforth Glen
Powforth Burn
ROAD
MILLHEUGH
Millheugh Bridge
Morgan Glen
Larkhall Academy
BROOMHILL
Larkhall Viaduct
Tennis Courts
Cherry Hill
Robert Sm Mem. Prim.
La
Thinacres
Plotcock Glen
Broomelton
Plotcock Castle (Remains of)
Plotcock Bridge
PLOTCOCK
BROOMELTON ROAD
Hamilton
Patrickholm
Mafflat
Waterfall
AVON
East Thinacremuir
Mafflat Orchard
Corslet
ML3
PLOTCOCK ROAD
Waterfall
WA
Brae House Nursing Home
CRAIGTHORNHILL ROAD
Newhouse Farm Cotts.
Newhouse
MILLHEUGH ROAD
Kittymuirhill
Low Kittymuir
Longfaugh
GLEN

156
162
M74
MOTORWAY
Sewage Works
Firework Cottage
EAST STATION INDUSTRIAL ESTATE
Cemetery
Rec. Grd.
MILTON ST.
DRYGATE ST.
UNION ST.
B7078
Meadowhill
Skelly Bridge
Skellyton Wood
Skelly Gill
LARKHALL GOLF COURSE
Burnhead
BURNHEAD ROAD
B7019
Club Ho.
Millburn Cottage
Millburn
Machanhill Prim. Sch.
Offs.
Lib.& Hlth. Cn.
Hareleeshill
HARELEESHILL ROAD
JOHN STREET
MACHAN ROAD
CHURCH ST.
Running Track
Park
Prim. Sch.
Shawsburn
Shawsburn House
Nursery
Shawsrigg
ML9
Machan Industrial Estate
Harehills Sports Barn
Games Courts
Works
LARKHALL INDUSTRIAL ESTATE
Nursing Home
STRUTHERHILL INDUSTRIAL ESTATE
CARLISLE ROAD
Strutherhill
Craigbank Prim. Sch.
Struther Farm
Hall
Pav.
Football Grd.
Foundry
Birkenshaw
Birkenshaw Farm
Ringsdale Castle
Shaws
Little Shaws
AYR ROAD
A71
Hills Farm Cottage
Bogside
Football Ground
Swinhill
Hailstonemyre
Mill Burn
E
F
G
H
1
2
3
4
5
6
52
51
50
49
76
77
78

A
B
C
D
1
2
3
4
5
6
78
79
52
51
50
49
157
161
LANARK
A72
A71
NORTH LANARKSHIRE
Wishaw
ML2
Larkhall
ML9
SOUTH LANARKSHIRE
Nursy.
Nursery
Trotterbank
Stewartbank
Skellyton
RIVER CLYDE
Garrionhaugh Farm
Erskine-bank
BRAE
HORSLEY
BR
Cardies Bridge
Depot
Weir
Cornsilloch Lodge
Castlehill
Millburn Glen
Mill Burn
CORNSILLOCH BRAE
ROAD
Cornsilloch
The Beeches
Garrion Bridge
Garrionhurst
Garrion Farm Tower
Clyde Valley Farm Park
Stewart Gill Bridge
Old Mill
Stewart Gill
Millburn
BURNHEAD RD.
Shawsburn
AYR ROAD
ASHGILLHEAD ROAD
Dalserf
Milburn House
Works
GARRION PL.
GRAHAM PL.
STEWART GILL PL.
Ashgillhead
Rec. Grd.
Pav.
MILLBURN
CRAIGBURN CT.
Ashgill
Auldton
AULDTON DR.
RORISON PL.
DOUGLAS CR.
CENTRAL DR.
Dalserf Prim. Sch.
PROSPECT RD.
Whinknowe
WHINKNOWE
NURSERY DR.
AILSA AV.
RD.
BOGSIDE
ROSSLYN
MAULDSLIE PL.
ASHKIRK DR.
DUNLOP PL.
Over Dalserf
NETHERBURN ROAD
MANSE BRAE
Meadowbank
Shawsburn House
Hills Farm Cottage
Hills
VIEW
Woodside House
Over Dalserf Cottages
Burn
Regill
Bogside
Overwood
Dunaird
Woodside Cottage
CANDERMILL & MARLAGE ROAD
Hailstonemyre
LINTO
Millburn Cottage

163
158
164
Blairs Orchard
Shawgill
Jollyfield
B7011
BROWNLEE ROAD
West Brownlee
Brownlee House
Bowmanhirst
Castlehill
Nursery
Binniesbrig
MAULDSLIE ROAD
BIRKS ROAD
Birks
STRAVENHOUSE ROAD
Law of Mauldslie
Comm. Cen.
QUARRY RD.
Stravenhouse Farm
Carluke
Gill
Rams
RIVER CLYDE
Dalserf House
Mauldslie Mains
Mauldslie Stables
ML8
East Lodge
Mauldslie Cottage
Works
Mauldslie Bridge
Mauldslie House
LANARK ROAD
A72
LANARKSHIRE
JOCK'S GILL WOOD
Jock's Burn
Mauldslie View
Hotel
Haugh Hill
Nurseries
Gillbank
Rosebank
Annsfield
Dalpatrick
Nursery
Milton-Lockhart Farm
Hazelwood Cottage
Overton Wood
Carcain Gill
Milton Lockhart Bri.
Waterfall
Sandilandgate
Townhead
Primary Sch.
BRAEFOOT
SHAWGILL
WESTFIELD CT.
BIRKS CT.
MANSE CT.
SWAN WY.
MURRAY RD.
WATLDS
KINGSHAW HILL VW.
ANSTRUTHER CT.
CARMICHAEL WY.
Nursery
E
F
G
H
1
2
3
4
5
6
80
81
82
49
50
51
52

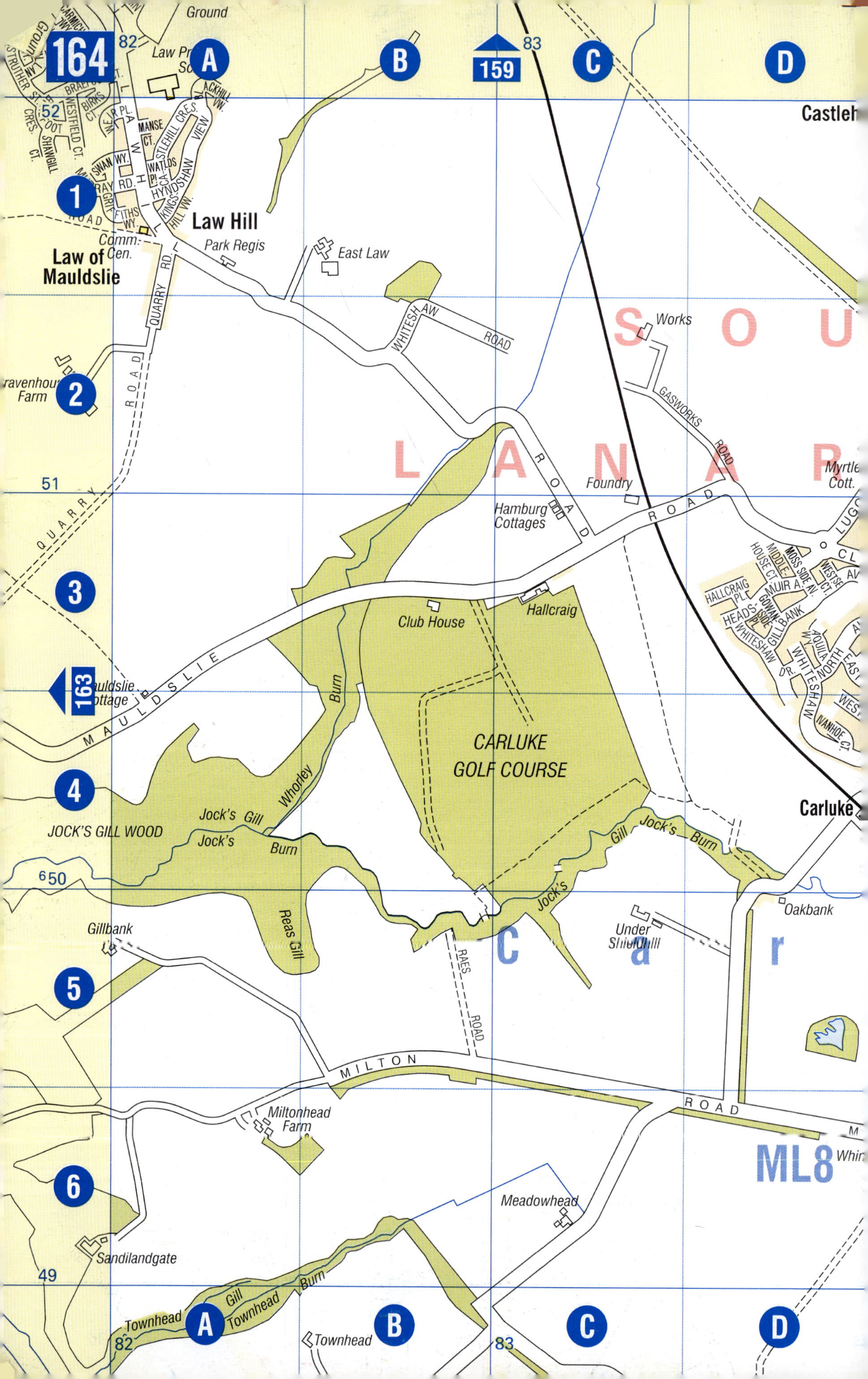

Ground
Law Pr
Sc
159
A
B
C
D
82
83
52
51
49
650
Castleh
LAW
STRUTHER ST.
CRES.
SHAWGILL CT.
BRAEFOOT
WESTFIELD CT.
BIRKS CT.
WEIR PL.
MANSE CT.
LAW HILL
STLEHILL CRES.
BLACKHILL VW.
VIEW
HYNDSHAW
WATLDS PL.
SWAN WY.
MURRAY RD.
GRIFFITHS WY.
KINGS HILL VW.
ROAD
Law Hill
Comm. Cen.
Law of Mauldslie
Park Regis
East Law
QUARRY RD.
WHITESHAW ROAD
ROAD
Cravenhouse Farm
Works
GASWORKS ROAD
S O U
L A N A R
Myrtle Cott.
Foundry
Hamburg Cottages
ROAD
QUARRY
MOSS SIDE AV.
MIDDLE HOUSE CT.
HALLCRAIG PL.
MUIR A
WESTSE CT.
GOWAN SIDE PL.
HEADS
GILLBANK
WHITESHAW
AQUILA WY.
NORTH
WHITESHAW DR.
IVANHOE CT.
Hallcraig
Club House
MAULDSLIE
Mauldslie Cottage
163
Burn
Whorley
CARLUKE GOLF COURSE
Carluke
JOCK'S GILL WOOD
Jock's Gill
Jock's
Burn
Jock's Burn
Gill
Jock's
Reas Gill
Gillbank
Oakbank
Under Shieldhill
C a r
RAES ROAD
MILTON
ROAD
Miltonhead Farm
ML8
Whir
Meadowhead
Sandilandgate
Townhead
Gill
Townhead
Burn
Townhead
1
2
3
4
5
6

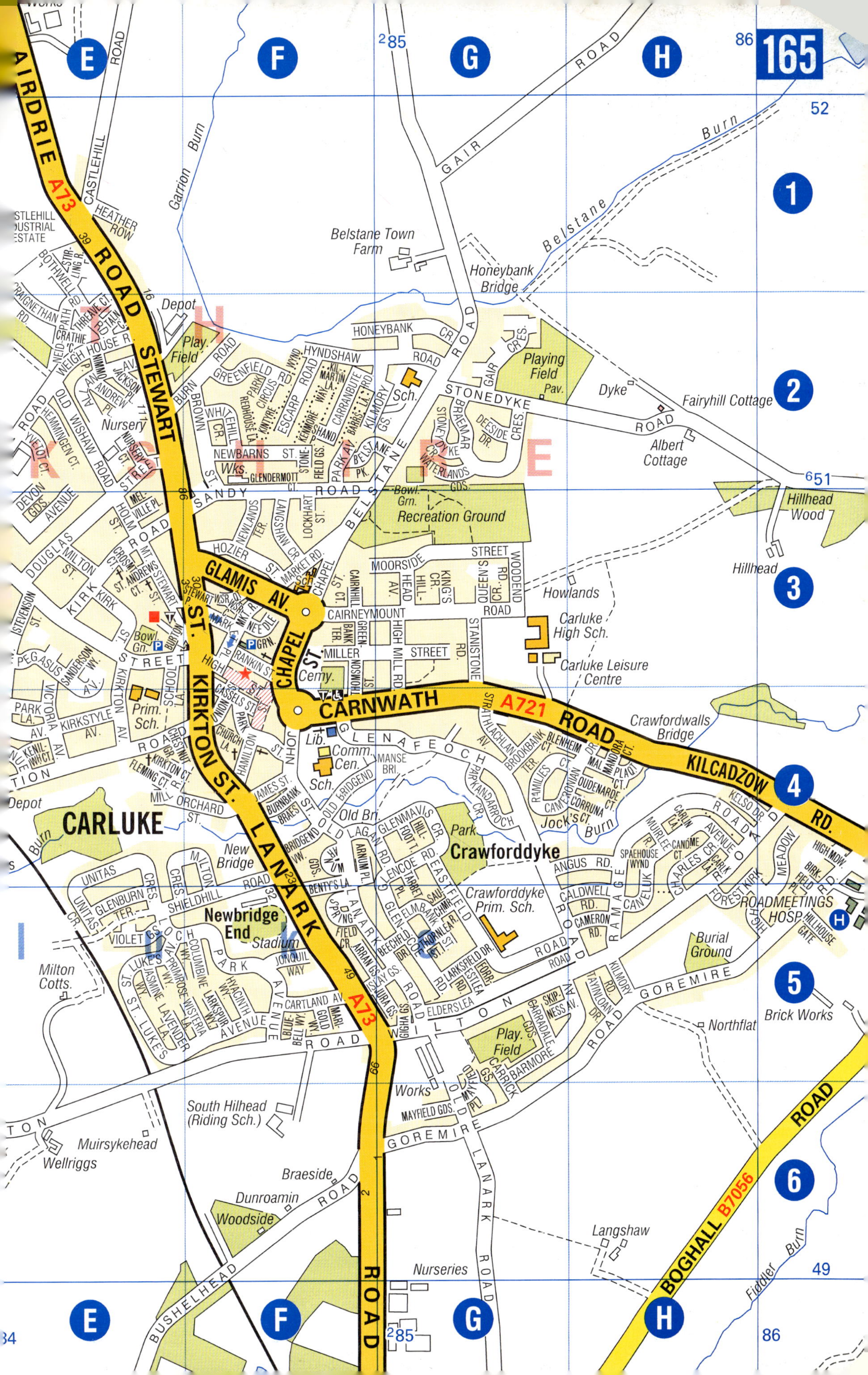

CARLUKE
AIRDRIE ROAD
A73
STEWART ROAD
KIRKTON ST.
LANARK ROAD
GLAMIS AV.
CHAPEL ST.
CARNWATH ROAD
A721
KILCADZOW RD.
GAIR ROAD
STONEDYKE ROAD
BELSTANE ROAD
SANDY ROAD
HIGH ST.
GOREMIRE ROAD
BOGHALL ROAD
B7056
BUSHELHEAD ROAD
MILTON ROAD
RAMAGE ROAD
SHIELDHILL ROAD
Belstane Town Farm
Honeybank Bridge
Belstane Burn
Garrion Burn
Playing Field
Pav.
Dyke
Fairyhill Cottage
Albert Cottage
Hillhead Wood
Hillhead
Howlands
Carluke High Sch.
Carluke Leisure Centre
Crawfordwalls Bridge
Recreation Ground
Bowl. Grn.
Cemy.
Lib.
Comm. Cen.
Sch.
Prim. Sch.
Play. Field
Depot
Nursery
Wks.
Old Bri.
New Bridge
Newbridge End
Stadium
Crawforddyke
Park
Crawforddyke Prim. Sch.
Jock's Burn
Burial Ground
ROADMEETINGS HOSP.
Brick Works
Northflat
Milton Cotts.
South Hilhead (Riding Sch.)
Works
Muirsykehead
Wellriggs
Braeside
Dunroamin
Woodside
Nurseries
Langshaw
Fiddler Burn
CASTLEHILL INDUSTRIAL ESTATE
E
F
G
H
1
2
3
4
5
6
285
86
52
651
49
84

INDEX TO STREETS

HOW TO USE THIS INDEX

1. Each street name is followed by its Postal District (or, if outside the Glasgow Postal District, by its Posttown or Postal Locality), and then by its map reference; e.g. Abbeycraig Rd. *G34* —2B **88** is in the Glasgow 34 Postal District and is to be found in square 2B on page **88**. The page number being shown in bold type.
A strict alphabetical order is followed in which Av., Rd., St., etc. (though abbreviated) are read in full and as part of the street name; e.g. Abbey Dri. appears after Abbeydale Way but before Abbeyfield Ho.

2. Streets and a selection of Subsidiary names not shown on the Maps, appear in the index in *Italics* with the thoroughfare to which it is connected shown in brackets; e.g. *Abbey Wlk. Bail —6D **88** (off Abercrombie Cres.)*

3. Railway stations appear in the index in CAPITALS and are referenced to the actual building and not to the station name; e.g. AIRBLES STATION. *Moth* —4G **143**.

4. The page references shown in brackets indicate those streets that appear on the large scale map pages 4 & 5; e.g. Albion Ga. *G1* —4H **83** (6G **5**) appears in square 4H on page **83** and also appears in the enlarged section in square 6G on page **5**.

5. With the now general usage of Postcodes for addressing mail, it is not recommended that this index is used for such a purpose.

GENERAL ABBREVIATIONS

All : Alley
App : Approach
Arc : Arcade
Av : Avenue
Bk : Back
Boulevd : Boulevard
Bri : Bridge
B'way : Broadway
Bldgs : Buildings
Bus : Business
Cvn : Caravan
Cen : Centre
Chu : Church
Chyd : Churchyard
Circ : Circle
Cir : Circus
Clo : Close
Comn : Common
Cotts : Cottages
Ct : Court
Cres : Crescent
Dri : Drive
E : East
Embkmt : Embankment
Est : Estate
Gdns : Gardens
Ga : Gate
Gt : Great
Grn : Green
Gro : Grove
Ho : House
Ind : Industrial
Junct : Junction
La : Lane
Lit : Little
Lwr : Lower
Mnr : Manor
Mans : Mansions
Mkt : Market
M : Mews
Mt : Mount
N : North
Pal : Palace
Pde : Parade
Pk : Park
Pas : Passage
Pl : Place
Quad : Quadrant
Rd : Road
S : South
Sq : Square
Sta : Station
St : Street
Ter : Terrace
Trad : Trading
Up : Upper
Vs : Villas
Wlk : Walk
W : West
Yd : Yard

POSTTOWN AND POSTAL LOCALITY ABBREVIATIONS

Abb : Abbotsinch
Air : Airdrie
Alla : Allandale
Anna : Annathill
Ashg : Ashgill
B'rig : Bishopbriggs
B'ton : Bishopton
Bail : Baillieston
Balm : Balmore
Bank : Banknock
Bant : Banton
Bard : Bardowie
Barg : Bargeddie
Barr : Barrhead
Bear : Bearsden
Bell : Bellshill
Bell I : Bellshill Ind. Est.
Blan : Blantyre
Bog : Bogside
Both : Bothwell
Bowl : Bowling
Brdwd : Braidwood
Bri W : Bridge of Weir
Brkfld : Brookfield
Broad I : Broadmeadow Ind. Est.
C'bnk : Calderbank
C'crx : Caldercruix
C'cry : Castlecary
C'lee : Crosslee
Cam G : Campsie Glen
Camb : Cambuslang
Carf : Carfin
Carl : Carluke
Carm : Carmyle
Cast : Castlehead
Chap : Chapelhall
Chry : Chryston
Clar : Clarkston
Cle : Cleland
Clyd : Clydebank
Clyd B : Clydebank Bus. Pk.
Coat : Coatbridge
Crmck : Carmunnock
Croy : Croy
Cumb : Cumbernauld
Dalm : Dalmuir
Dals : Dalserf
Dix B : Dixon Blazes Ind. Est.
Drum : Drumchapel
Dull : Dullatur
Dumb : Dumbarton
Dun : Duntocher
Eag : Eaglesham
E Kil : East Kilbride
Eld : Elderslie
Ersk : Erskine
G'csh : Gartcosh
Giff : Giffnock
Glas A : Glasgow Airport
Glenb : Glenboig
Glenm : Glenmavis
H'hse I : Hillhouse Ind. Est.
H'ton I : Hillington Ind. Est.
Hag : Haggs
Ham : Hamilton
Hard : Hardgate
Holy : Holytown
Hous : Houston
Inch : Inchinnan
John : Johnstone
Kilb : Kilbarchan
Kils : Kilsyth
Kirk : Kirkintilloch
Lark : Larkhall
Law : Law
Len : Lennoxtown
Lenz : Lenzie
Lin : Linwood
Lin I : Linwood Ind. Est.
Longc : Longcroft
Mill P : Milliken Park
Mille : Millerston
Miln : Milngavie
Milt : Milton
Milt C : Milton of Campsie
Mood : Moodiesburn
Morn : Morningside
Moth : Motherwell
Mt V : Mount Vernon
Muir : Muirend
Muirh : Muirhead
N'hill : Newarthill
N'hse : Newhouse
Neil : Neilston
New S : New Stevenston
Newm : Newmains
Newt M : Newton Mearns
Old K : Old Kilpatrick
Over : Overtown
Pais : Paisley
Plain : Plains
Quar H : Quarrier's Homes
Queen : Queenzieburn
Renf : Renfrew
Rig I : Righead Ind. Est.
Rigg : Riggend
Ruth : Rutherglen
St R : St Rollox Bus. & Retail Pk.
Shaw : Shawsburn
Spri : Springboig
Step : Stepps
Stra B : Strathclyde Bus. Pk.
Stru I : Strutherhill Ind. Est.
T'bnk : Thornliebank
T'hall : Thorntonhall
Torr : Torrance
Twe : Twechar
Udd : Uddingston
Ward E : Wardpark East
Ward N : Wardpark North
Ward S : Wardpark South
Waterl : Waterloo
Waters : Waterside
White : Whiteinch
Wis : Wishaw

INDEX TO STREETS

Abbey Clo. *Pais* —1A **98**
Abbeycraig Rd. *G34* —2B **88**
Abbeydale Way. *Ruth* —4E **121**
Abbey Dri. *G14* —5E **61**
Abbeyfield Ho. *Giff* —4H **117**
Abbeygreen St. *G34* —2C **88**
Abbeyhill St. *G32* —4G **85**
Abbeylands Rd. *Clyd* —6E **23**
Abbey Pl. *Air* —1C **112**
Abbey Rd. *Eld* —3H **95**
*Abbey Wlk. Bail —6D **88***
(off Abercrombie Cres.)
*Abbey Wlk. Lark —1F **161***
(off Duncan Graham St.)
Abbotsburn Way. *Pais* —3H **77**
Abbotsford. *B'rig* —5E **49**
Abbotsford Av. *Ham* —3F **141**
Abbotsford Av. *Lark* —4E **161**
Abbotsford Av. *Ruth* —6D **104**
Abbotsford Brae. *E Kil* —6G **137**
Abbotsford Ct. *Cumb* —6H **35**
Abbotsford Cres. *Ham* —3F **141**
Abbotsford Cres. *Pais* —6B **96**
Abbotsford Cres. *Wis* —5A **146**
Abbotsford Dri. *Kirk* —5E **31**
Abbotsford La. *Bell* —1B **126**
Abbotsford Pl. *G5* —1F **103**
(in two parts)
Abbotsford Pl. *Cumb* —6H **35**
*Abbotsford Pl. Moth —2A **128***
(off Ivy Ter.)
Abbotsford Rd. *Bear* —1C **44**
Abbotsford Rd. *Chap* —4E **113**
Abbotsford Rd. *Clyd* —6D **42**
Abbotsford Rd. *Cumb* —6H **35**
Abbotsford Rd. *Ham* —3E **141**
Abbotsford Rd. *Wis* —5A **146**
Abbotshall Av. *G15* —4G **43**
Abbotsinch Rd. *Pais & Renf* —2A **78**
Abbotsinch Rd. *Renf* —6A **58**
Abbots Ter. *Air* —1C **112**
Abbot St. *G41* —4C **102**
Abbot St. *Pais* —5B **78**
Abbott Cres. *Clyd* —1F **59**
Aberconway St. *Clyd* —1E **59**
Abercorn Av. *G52* —3G **79**
Abercorn Cres. *Ham* —1B **154**
Abercorn Dri. *Ham* —6B **142**
Abercorn Ind. Est. *Pais* —5B **78**
Abercorn Pl. *G23* —6C **46**
Abercorn Rd. *Newt M* —3C **132**
Abercorn St. *Clyd* —6G **23**
Abercorn St. *Pais* —6A **78**
Abercrombie Cres. *Bail* —6D **88**
Abercrombie Dri. *Bear* —5B **24**
Abercrombie Pl. *Kils* —2F **11**
Abercromby Cres. *E Kil* —6B **138**
Abercromby Dri. *G40* —5B **84**
Abercromby Pl. *E Kil* —6B **138**
*Abercromby Sq. G40 —5B **84***
(off Millroad Dri.)
Abercromby St. *G40* —6A **84**
*Aberdalgie Path. G34 —3H **87***
(off Aberdalgie Rd.)
Aberdalgie Rd. *G34* —3H **87**
Aberdeen Rd. *Chap* —1D **112**
Aberdour St. *G31* —4E **85**
Aberfeldy Av. *Plain* —1F **93**
Aberfeldy St. *G31* —4E **85**
Aberfoyle St. *G31* —4E **85**
Aberlady Rd. *G51* —4E **81**
Aberlady St. *Cle* —6H **129**
Abernethy Dri. *Lin* —6G **75**
Abernethyn Rd. *Newm* —3E **147**
Abernethy Pk. *E Kil* —1F **149**
Abernethy St. *G31* —5E **85**
Aberuthven Dri. *G32* —2B **106**
Abiegail Pl. *Blan* —6B **124**
Aboukir St. *G51* —3E **81**
Aboyne Dri. *Pais* —4B **98**
Aboyne St. *G51* —5F **81**
Acacia Dri. *Barr* —2C **114**
Acacia Dri. *Pais* —4F **97**
Acacia Pl. *John* —5G **95**
Academy Ct. *Coat* —4C **90**
Academy Pk. *G51* —1A **102**
Academy Pk. *Air* —4A **92**
Academy Rd. *Giff* —5A **118**
Academy St. *G32* —1B **106**
(in three parts)
Academy St. *Air* —4A **92**
Academy St. *Coat* —4C **90**
Academy St. *Lark* —2E **161**
Academy Ter. *Bell* —2D **126**
Acer Cres. *Pais* —4E **97**
Achamore Rd. *G15* —3G **43**
Achnasheen Rd. *Air* —5G **93**
Achray Dri. *Pais* —4E **97**
Achray Pl. *Coat* —2H **89**
Achray Pl. *Miln* —2D **24**
Achray Rd. *Cumb* —6D **34**
Acorn Ct. *G40* —1B **104**
Acorn St. *G40* —1B **104**
Acredyke Cres. *G21* —2E **65**
Acredyke Pl. *G21* —3E **65**
Acredyke Rd. *G21* —2D **64**
Acredyke Rd. *Ruth* —5B **104**
Acre Rd. *G20* —6H **45**
Acres, The. *Lark* —3F **161**
Acre Valley Rd. *Torr* —3D **28**
Adam Av. *Air* —4B **92**
Adams Ct. La. *G1* —5F **83** (6D **4**)
Adams Dri. *G32* —3B **106**
Adamslie Cres. *Kirk* —5A **30**
Adamslie Dri. *Kirk* —5A **30**
Adamson St. *Bell* —2F **127**
Adams Pl. *Kils* —3H **11**
Adamswell St. *G21* —6A **64**
Adamswell Ter. *Chry* —5E **53**
Addie St. *Moth* —1H **143**
Addiewell Pl. *Coat* —1C **110**
Addison Gro. *T'bnk* —3F **117**
Addison Pl. *T'bnk* —3F **117**
Addison Rd. *G12* —5B **62**
Addison Rd. *T'bnk* —3E **117**
Adelaide Ct. *Clyd* —2H **41**
Adelaide Rd. *E Kil* —4D **148**
Adele St. *Moth* —5H **143**
Adelphi St. *G5* —6G **83**
(in two parts)
Admiral St. *G41* —6C **82**
Admiralty Gdns. *Old K* —2F **41**
Admiralty Gro. *Old K* —2F **41**
Admiralty Pl. *Old K* —2F **41**
Advie Pl. *G42* —5F **103**
Affric Av. *Plain* —1G **93**
Affric Dri. *Pais* —4D **98**
Afton Cres. *Bear* —4H **45**
Afton Dri. *Renf* —6G **59**
Afton Gdns. *Blan* —3H **139**
Afton Gdns. *Coat* —6F **91**
Afton Rd. *Cumb* —2B **36**
Afton St. *G41* —5C **102**
Afton St. *Lark* —3G **161**
Afton View. *Kirk* —4F **31**
Afton Way. *Pais* —4D **96**
Agamemnon St. *Clyd* —5B **42**
*Agate Ter. Bell —3C **126***
(off Diamond St.)
Agnew Av. *Coat & Air* —4E **91**
Agnew Gro. *Bell* —2H **125**
Agnew La. *G42* —4E **103**
Aikenhead Rd. *G42* —2F **103**
Aikenhead Rd. *G44* —1G **119**
Aikman Pl. *E Kil* —5B **138**
Aikman Rd. *Moth* —4D **142**
*Ailart Loan. Newm —3D **146***
(off Tiree Cres.)
Ailean Dri. *G32* —1E **107**
Ailean Gdns. *G32* —1E **107**
Ailort Av. *G44* —2E **119**
Ailport Pl. *E Kil* —6G **137**
Ailsa Av. *Ashg* —5B **162**
Ailsa Av. *Moth* —2D **142**
Ailsa Ct. *Coat* —1A **110**
Ailsa Ct. *Ham* —2B **152**
Ailsa Cres. *Moth* —2D **142**
Ailsa Dri. *G42* —6D **102**
Ailsa Dri. *Clyd* —1E **43**
Ailsa Dri. *Giff* —1H **133**
Ailsa Dri. *Kirk* —3F **31**
Ailsa Dri. *Pais* —6H **97**
Ailsa Dri. *Ruth* —2B **120**
Ailsa Dri. *Udd* —3E **125**
Ailsa Pl. *Coat* —1B **110**
Ailsa Rd. *B'rig* —5D **48**
Ailsa Rd. *Coat* —1A **110**
Ailsa Rd. *Renf* —1E **79**
Ailsa Tower. *Camb* —4G **121**
Ainslie Rd. *Cumb* —2C **36**
Ainslie Rd. *H'ton I* —4A **80**
(in two parts)
Airbles Cres. *Moth* —4F **143**
Airbles Dri. *Moth* —4F **143**
Airbles Farm Rd. *Moth* —4E **143**
Airbles Rd. *Moth* —4E **143**
AIRBLES STATION. *Moth* —4G **143**
Airbles St. *Moth* —4G **143**
Airbles Tower. *Moth* —4G **143**
Airdale Av. *Giff* —5A **118**
Airdriehill Rd. *Air* —1C **92**
Airdriehill St. *Air* —1C **92**
Airdrie Rd. *C'crx* —2F **93**
Airdrie Rd. *Carl* —6H **159**
Airdrie Rd. *Cumb* —3H **53**
(Mollinsburn)
Airdrie Rd. *Cumb* —6C **34**
(in two parts)
Airdrie Rd. *Kils* —2H **11**
AIRDRIE STATION. *Air* —4A **92**
*Aird's La. G1 —5G **83***
(off Bridgegate)
Airgold Dri. *G15* —3H **43**
Airgold Pl. *G15* —4H **43**
Airlie Av. *Bear* —6E **25**
Airlie Dri. *Bell* —1C **126**
Airlie Gdns. *Ruth* —3F **121**
Airlie La. *G12* —6H **61**
Airlie Rd. *Bail* —2G **107**
Airlie St. *G12* —6G **61**
Airlink Ind. Est. *Pais* —3A **78**
Airlour Rd. *G43* —2C **118**
Airth Ct. *Moth* —6F **127**
Airth Dri. *G52* —2F **101**
Airth La. *G52* —2F **101**
*Airth Pl. G52 —2F **101***
(off Airth La.)
*Airthrey Av. G14 —5E **61***
(off Mitre Rd.)
*Airthrey La. G14 —5E **61***
(off Airthrey Av.)
Airth Way. *Cumb* —5A **34**
Aitchison Ct. *Air* —3H **91**
Aitchison St. *Air* —4G **91**
Aitkenbar Circ. *Dumb* —2H **17**
Aitkenbar Dri. *Dumb* —1H **17**
Aitkenhead Av. *Coat* —1F **109**
Aitkenhead Rd. *Chap* —3D **112**
Aitkenhead Rd. *Udd* —5E **109**
Aitken Rd. *Ham* —4A **154**
Aitken St. *G31* —4D **84**
Aitken St. *Air* —2A **92**
Aloodair Ct. *Barr* —5E **115**
Albans Cres. *Moth* —1D **142**
Albany. *E Kil* —5C **138**
Albany Av. *G32* —5C **86**
Albany Dri. *Ruth* —1D **120**
Albany Pl. *Both* —5F **125**
Albany Quad. *G32* —5C **86**
Albany Rd. *Ham* —4G **153**
Albany St. *G40* —1C **104**
Albany St. *Coat* —4A **90**
Albany Ter. *Camb* —4G **121**
Albany Way. *Pais* —3A **78**
*Albany Wynd. Lark —1F **161***
(off Carrick Pl.)
Alba Way. *Ham* —5G **153**
*Alba Way. Lark —4G **161***
(off Donaldson Rd.)

Alberta Av. Coat —3B 90
Alberta Av. E Kil —3D 148
Alberta Cres. E Kil —3E 149
Alberta Pk. E Kil —3F 149
Alberta Pl. E Kil —3F 149
Albert Av. G42 —4D 102
Albert Bri. G5 —6G 83
Albert Cres. Air —4B 92
Albert Cross. G41 —2D 102
Albert Dri. G41 —3A 102
Albert Dri. Bear —4H 45
Albert Dri. Lark —3F 161
Albert Dri. Ruth —2D 120
Albert Pl. Air —3B 92
Albert Quad. Moth —2A 128
Albert Rd. G12 —6H 61
Albert Rd. G42 —4E 103
Albert Rd. Brkfld —6C 74
Albert Rd. Clyd —4B 42
Albert Rd. Lenz —4C 50
Albert Rd. Renf —6E 59
Albert St. Coat —4C 90
(in two parts)
Albert St. Ham —3F 141
Albert St. Moth —2H 143
Albert Ter. Ham —3E 141
Albion Ct. Coat —5E 91
(off Clifton Pl.)
Albion Ga. G1 —4H 83 (6G 5)
Albion Ga. Pais —5H 77
Albion St. G1 —5H 83 (6G 5)
Albion St. Bail —2F 107
Albion St. Coat —4D 90
Albion St. Moth —4G 143
Albion St. Pais —5A 78
Albion Tower. Moth —4G 143
Albion Way. E Kil —6H 149
Albion Works Ind. Est. G13 —2G 59
Alcaig Rd. G52 —3E 101
Alcath Rd. Newm —3F 147
Alclutha Av. Dumb —4H 17
Alder Av. Ham —2A 154
Alder Av. Kirk —2B 50
Alder Bank. Udd —4G 109
Alder Ct. Barr —6E 115
Alder Ct. E Kil —6E 149
Alder Cres. E Kil —6E 149
Alder Gro. Coat —5D 90
Alder La. Holy —2C 128
Alder La. New S —4A 128
Alderman Pl. G13 —3C 60
Alderman Rd. G13 —2H 59
Alder Pl. G43 —2A 118
Alder Pl. E Kil —6E 149
Alder Pl. John —4G 95
Alder Rd. G43 —2H 117
Alder Rd. Broad I —3E 17
Alder Rd. Clyd —2B 42
Alder Rd. Cumb —3D 36
Alder Rd. Milt C —6B 8
Alderside Gdns. Udd —6C 108
Alderstocks. E Kil —6G 149
Alderston Pl. Bell —3A 126
Alderston Way. Rig I —1A 126
Aldersyde Av. Wis —5D 144
Aldersyde Pl. Blan —6A 124
Alexander Av. Kils —2C 32
Alexander Av. Udd —1G 125
Alexander Balfour Gdns. Ham —2H 153
Alexander Gdns. Ham —1C 154
Alexander Pl. Kirk —6H 31
Alexander St. Air —4G 91
Alexander St. Clyd —6D 42
Alexander St. Coat —3D 90
Alexander St. Dumb —3G 17
Alexander St. Wis —6F 145
Alexander Ter. Neil —3C 130
Alexandra Av. Lenz —3C 50
Alexandra Av. Step —3D 66
Alexandra Ct. G31 —3D 84
Alexandra Dri. Pais —2F 97
Alexandra Dri. Renf —6F 59
Alexandra Gdns. Kirk —3C 50
Alexandra Pde. G31 —3A 84
ALEXANDRA PDE. STATION. G31 —3D 84
Alexandra Pk. Kirk —3C 50
Alexandra Pk. St. G31 —3D 84
Alexandra Rd. Lenz —3C 50
Alexandra St. Kirk —5C 30
Alford Av. Kirk —5B 30
Alford Pl. Lin —5E 75
Alford Quad. Wis —4H 145
Alford St. G21 —6H 63
Alfred La. G12 —6C 62
(off Cecil St.)
Alfred Ter. G12 —6C 62
Algie St. G41 —5D 102
Algoma Pl. E Kil —3D 148
Alice Av. Bell —3C 126
Alice St. Pais —3A 98
Aline Ct. Barr —3D 114
Alison Lea. E Kil —6B 138
Allan Av. Carl —2E 165
Allan Av. Renf —2G 79
Allan Ct. E Kil —4A 148
Allan Cres. Dumb —1H 17
Allandale Av. Moth —2F 129
Allandale Cotts. Alla —1H 15
Allander Av. Bard —6E 27
Allander Dri. Torr —5C 28
Allander Gdns. B'rig —3B 48
Allander Ho. Cumb —3H 35
(off Cumbernauld Cen., The)
Allander Rd. Miln —3G 25
Allander St. G22 —5G 63
Allander Wlk. Cumb —3H 35
(off Cumbernauld Cen., The)
Allands Av. Inch —4G 57
Allanfauld Rd. Cumb —3H 35
Allanfauld Rd. Kils —1H 11
Allan Glen Gdns. B'rig —3D 48
Allan Pl. G40 —3D 104
Allan Pl. Dumb —3G 17
Allan Pl. E Kil —4A 148
Allanshaw Gdns. Ham —6F 141
Allanshaw Gro. Ham —1F 153
Allanshaw Ind. Est. Ham —6G 141
Allanshaw St. Ham —6G 141
Allan St. G40 —3D 104
Allan St. Coat —6H 89
Allan St. Moth —2H 143
Allanton Av. Pais —1G 99
Allanton Dri. G52 —6B 80
Allanton Gro. Wis —4H 145
Allanton Lea. Ham —3G 153
Allanton Pl. Ham —2A 154
Allanton Rd. Newm —2H 147
Allanton Ter. Ham —3E 155
Allan Tower. Moth —2H 143
Allbany Cres. Moth —2H 127
Allendale. E Kil —6E 137
Allender Rd. Bear —4D 44
Allerdyce Dri. G15 —6G 43
Allershaw Pl. Wis —3F 157
Allershaw Rd. Wis —3F 157
Allershaw Tower. Wis —3F 157
Allerton Gdns. Bail —1F 107
Alleysbank Rd. Ruth —4D 104
Allison Av. Ersk —5D 40
Allison Dri. Camb —1A 122
Allison Pl. G42 —3E 103
Allison Pl. G'csh —5C 68
Allison Pl. Newt M —5C 132
Allison St. G42 —3E 103
Allnach Pl. G34 —3C 88
Alloway Av. Pais —5D 98
Alloway Ct. Kirk —3G 31
Alloway Cres. Pais —5D 98
Alloway Cres. Ruth —2B 120
Alloway Dri. Clyd —4E 43
Alloway Dri. Kirk —3F 31
Alloway Dri. Newt M —5G 133
Alloway Dri. Pais —5D 98
Alloway Dri. Ruth —2B 120
Alloway Gdns. Ham —1B 152
Alloway Gdns. Kirk —3G 31
Alloway Gro. Kirk —3F 31
Alloway Quad. Kirk —4G 31
Alloway Rd. G43 —1B 118
Alloway Rd. Air —3F 93
Alloway Rd. E Kil —5D 138
Alloway St. Lark —3G 161
Alloway Ter. Kirk —3F 31
Alloway Wynd. Moth —3E 129
Almada Gro. Ham —5H 141
Almada La. Ham —5H 141
Almada St. Ham —5G 141
Alma St. G40 —6D 84
Almond Av. Renf —1G 79
Almond Bank. Bear —5C 44
Almond Cres. Pais —3D 96
Almond Dri. Bank —1E 15
Almond Dri. B'ton —5H 39
Almond Dri. E Kil —2B 150
Almond Dri. Kirk —2B 50
Almond Pl. Coat —2H 89
Almond Pl. Moth —3B 128
Almond Rd. G33 —4C 66
Almond Rd. Bear —5D 44
Almond Rd. Cumb —6F 15
Almond St. G33 —2F 85
Almond Vale. Udd —6E 109
Almond Way. Moth —6G 143
Alness Cres. G52 —2E 101
Alness St. Ham —2H 153
Alness Ter. Ham —1H 153
Alpine Gro. Udd —6D 108
Alsatian Av. Clyd —5F 43
Alsh Ter. Ham —2E 153
Alston Av. Coat —3D 90
Alston Gdns. Bear —5B 24
Altnacreag Gdns. Chry —4E 53
Alton Ct. Kirk —5E 31
(off Highfield Rd.)
Alton Rd. Pais —1E 99
Altpatrict Gdns. Eld —2H 95
Altyre St. G32 —2H 105
Alva Gdns. G52 —3E 101
Alva Gdns. Bear —6D 24
Alva Ga. G52 —2E 101
Alva Pl. Lenz —3E 51
Alwyn Av. Hous —3D 74
Alwyn Ct. E Kil —6G 137
Alyssum Cres. Moth —1F 143
Alyth Cres. Clar —1E 135
Alyth Gdns. G52 —2E 101
Alyth Gdns. Clar —1E 135
Ambassador Way. Renf —2F 79
Amber Ter. Bell —3C 126
Ambleside. E Kil —5B 148
Amethyst Av. Bell —3C 126
Amisfield St. G20 —4C 62
Amochrie Dri. Pais —5E 97
Amochrie Rd. Pais —4D 96
Amochrie Way. Pais —4D 96
(off Amochrie Rd.)
Amulree Pl. G32 —1A 106
Amulree St. G32 —2A 106
Ancaster Dri. G13 —3F 61
Ancaster La. G13 —3F 61
Anchor Av. Pais —1C 98
Anchor Cres. Pais —2C 98
Anchor Dri. Pais —1C 98
Anchor La. G2 —4G 83 (5E 5)
Anchor Wynd. Pais —1C 98
Ancroft St. G20 —6E 63
Andersen Ct. E Kil —5G 149
Anderside. E Kil —6G 149
Anderson Av. Kils —2F 11
Anderson Ct. Bell —2D 126
Anderson Cres. Kils —3C 10
Anderson Dri. Newt M —5C 132
Anderson Dri. Renf —5F 59
Anderson Gdns. Blan —6C 124
Anderson La. Air —3A 92
Anderson Rd. B'ton —3G 39
Anderson St. G11 —1H 81
Anderson St. Air —3A 92
Anderson St. Ham —4D 140
Anderson St. Moth —4G 143
Anderson Tower. Moth —3G 143
Anderston Cen. G2 —4E 83 (5A 4)
Anderston Quay. G3 —5D 82
ANDERSTON STATION. G2 —4E 83 (5A 4)
Andrew Av. Lenz —4D 50
Andrew Av. Renf —6G 59
Andrew Dri. Clyd —1E 59
Andrew Pl. Carl —2E 165
Andrew Sillars Av. Camb —2B 122
Andrews St. Pais —5A 78
Andrew St. E Kil —2H 149
Anford Pl. Blan —2C 140
Angela Way. Udd —1D 124
Angle Ga. G14 —5D 60
Angus Av. G52 —2C 100
Angus Av. Air —6A 92
Angus Av. B'rig —1E 65
Angus Av. E Kil —1B 150
Angus Av. Ham —6C 142
Angus Av. Moth —1E 143
Angus Gdns. Udd —5D 108
Angus Oval. G52 —1B 100
Angus Pl. G52 —1B 100
Angus Pl. E Kil —1B 150
Angus Rd. Carl —4G 165
Angus St. G21 —5A 64
Angus St. Clyd —1G 59
Angus Wlk. Udd —6F 109
Annan Av. E Kil —4A 148
Annan Ct. Coat —5B 90
(off Kirk St.)
Annan Cres. Chap —4D 112
Annandale St. G42 —2F 103
Annan Dri. Bear —4C 44
Annan Dri. Pais —3D 96
Annan Dri. Ruth —6F 105
Annan Glade. Moth —6A 144
Annan Gro. Moth —6A 144
Annan Ho. Cumb —3H 35
(off Cumbernauld Cen., The)
Annan Pl. John —5C 94
Annan St. G42 —5E 103
Annan St. Moth —6A 144
Annathill Gdns. Anna —5B 54
Annbank St. G31 —5B 84
Annbank St. Lark —2D 160
Ann Ct. Ham —4E 141
Anne Av. Renf —5F 59
Anne Cres. Lenz —4D 50
Annerley Ct. Coat —6A 90
Annerley Pl. Coat —6A 90
Annes Ct. G40 —1A 104
Anne's M. Ham —6B 142
Annette St. G42 —3E 103
Annfield Gdns. Blan —6A 124
Annfield Pl. G31 —4B 84
Annick Dri. Bear —4C 44
Annick St. G32 —6B 86
Annick St. Camb —2D 122
Anniesdale Av. Step —3D 66
Annieshill View. Plain —1G 93
Anniesland Cres. G14 —4A 60
Anniesland Ind. Est. G13 —1E 61
Anniesland Rd. G14 & G13 —4A 60
ANNIESLAND STATION. G13 —3F 61
Annieston. Twe —1D 32
Anniversary Av. E Kil —4E 149
Annsfield Rd. Ham —4G 153
Ann St. Ham —4E 141
Ann St. John —2G 95
Ansdell Av. Blan —2A 140
Anson St. G40 —6B 84
Anson Way. Renf —2E 79
Anstruther Ct. Law —6D 158
Anstruther St. G32 —6H 85
Anstruther St. Law —6D 158
Antermony Rd. Milt C —5C 8
Antigua Way. E Kil —2C 148
Anton Cres. Kils —3A 12
Antonine. Kirk —3H 31
Antonine Av. Moth —1E 143
Antonine Gdns. Clyd —1C 42
Antonine Rd. Bear —1B 44
Antrim La. Lark —1F 161
Anwoth St. G32 —2A 106
Apollo Path. Moth —2B 128
Appin Ct. Kirk —4H 31
Appin Rd. G31 —4D 84
Appin Ter. Ham —5C 140
Appin Ter. Ruth —3F 121
Appin Way. Both —4E 125
Appin Way. Glenm —5H 71
Appleby Clo. E Kil —5B 148
Appleby St. G22 —6F 63
Applecross Gdns. Chry —4D 52
Applecross Quad. Wis —4H 145
Applecross Rd. Kirk —4H 31
Applecross St. G4 —6F 63
Appledore Cres. Both —4E 125
Apsley La. G11 —1G 81
Apsley St. G11 —1G 81
Aqua Av. Ham —1C 152
Aqua Ct. Ham —1C 152
Aquila Way. Carl —3D 164
Araburn Dri. E Kil —6G 149
Aranthrue Cres. Renf —5E 59
Aranthrue Dri. Renf —5E 59
Aray St. G20 —3B 62
Arbroath Av. G52 —1B 100
Arbroath Gro. Ham —1F 153
Arbuckle Pl. Plain —1G 93
Arbuckle Rd. Plain —1H 93
Arcadia St. G40 —6A 84
Arcadia St. Bell —6C 110
Arcan Cres. G15 —5B 44
Archerfield Av. G32 —3A 106
Archerfield Cres. G32 —3A 106
Archerfield Dri. G32 —3A 106
Archerfield Gro. G32 —3A 106
Archerhill Av. G13 —1A 60
Archerhill Cotts. G13 —1A 60
Archerhill Cres. G13 —1B 60
Archerhill Gdns. G13 —1A 60
Archerhill Rd. G13 —1H 59
Archerhill Sq. G13 —1H 59
Archerhill Ter. G13 —1A 60
Archibald Ter. Milt C —5B 8
Archiebald Pl. Bell —3F 127
Arch Way. Kils —2H 11
Ardargie Dri. G32 —5C 106
Ardargie Gro. G32 —5C 106
Ardargie Pl. G32 —5C 106
Ardbeg Av. B'rig —6E 49
Ardbeg Av. Ruth —4G 121
Ardbeg La. G42 —3E 103
(off Calder St.)
Ardbeg St. G42 —3E 103
Ardconnel St. T'bnk —3F 117
Arden Av. T'bnk —5E 117
Ardenclutha Av. Ham —5F 141
Arden Ct. Air —3F 91
(off Monkscourt Av.)
Arden Ct. Ham —2H 153
Ardencraig Cres. G45 —6G 119
Ardencraig Dri. G45 —5B 120
Ardencraig La. G45 —6G 119
Ardencraig Quad. G45 —5B 120
Ardencraig Rd. G45 —6G 119
Ardencraig St. G45 —4C 120
Ardencraig Ter. G45 —5B 120
Arden Dri. Giff —5H 117
Arden Gro. Kils —1G 11
Ardenlea. Udd —6D 108
Ardenlea St. G40 —2D 104
Arden Pl. T'bnk —5E 117
Arden Rd. Ham —1G 153
Arden St. Plain —1G 93
Arden Ter. Ham —1G 153
Ardery St. G11 —1G 81
Ardessie St. G23 —6B 46
Ardfern Rd. Air —5F 93
Ardfern St. G32 —2A 106
Ardgay Pl. G32 —1A 106
Ardgay St. G32 —1A 106
Ardgoil Dri. Cumb —4B 34
Ardgour Ct. Blan —3D 140
Ardgour Dri. Lin —6G 75
Ardgour Pde. Moth —6C 128
Ardgowan Av. Pais —2B 98
Ardgowan Ct. Pais —2D 98
Ardgowan Dri. Udd —6D 108
Ardgowan St. Pais —3B 98
Ardgowan Ter. La. G3 —2B 82
(off Radnor St.)
Ardgryfe Cres. Hous —1D 74
Ardholm St. G32 —6A 86
Ardhu Pl. G15 —3A 44
Ardlamont Sq. Lin —6A 76
Ardlaw St. G51 —5F 81
Ardle Rd. G43 —2C 118
Ard Loan. Moth —2A 128
(off Howden Pl.)
Ardlui Gdns. Miln —2D 24
Ardlui St. G32 —1H 105
Ardmaleish Cres. G45 —5A 120
Ardmaleish Rd. G45 —5H 119
Ardmaleish St. G45 —5H 119
Ardmay Cres. G44 —6G 103
Ardmillan St. G33 —3H 85
Ardmory Av. G42 —6H 103
Ardmory La. G42 —6A 104
Ardmory Pl. G42 —6A 104
Ardnahoe Av. G42 —5H 103
Ardnahoe Pl. G42 —5H 103
Ardneil Rd. G51 —5F 81
Ardnish St. G51 —4E 81
Ardoch Cres. Dumb —3D 16
Ardoch Gdns. Camb —1H 121
Ardoch Gro. Camb —1H 121
Ardoch Path. Newm —3D 146
(off Tiree Cres.)
Ardochrig. E Kil —6G 149
Ardoch Rd. Bear —2H 45
Ardoch St. G22 —5F 63
Ardoch Way. Chry —5D 52
Ardo Gdns. G51 —6G 81
Ardressie Pl. G20 —4B 62
Ard Rd. Renf —5D 58
Ardshiel Rd. G51 —4E 81
Ardsloy La. G14 —5A 60
Ardsloy Pl. G14 —5A 60
Ard St. G32 —1A 106
Ardtoe Cres. G33 —4E 67
Ardtoe Pl. G33 —4E 67
Arduthie Rd. G51 —4E 81
Ardwell Rd. G52 —2E 101
Argosy Way. Renf —2E 79
Argus Av. Chap —3C 112
Argyle Arc. G1 —6D 4
Argyle Av. Glas A —2A 78
Argyle Cres. Air —6H 91
Argyle Cres. H'hse I —6D 140
Argyle Dri. Ham —5E 141
Argyle Gdns. Lark —2F 161
Argyle Gdns. Len —4G 7
Argyle Pl. Kils —3A 12
Argyle Rd. Bear —6E 25
Argyle St. G1 —4G 83
Argyle St. G2 —4E 83 (6A 4)
Argyle St. G3 —2B 82
Argyle St. Pais —1H 97
ARGYLE ST. STATION. G1 —5G 83
Argyll Av. Dumb —1C 18
Argyll Av. Renf —5D 58
Argyll Pl. Bell —5B 126
Argyll Pl. Dumb —1C 18
Argyll Pl. E Kil —6C 138
Argyll Rd. Clyd —1D 58
Arisaig Dri. G52 —2D 100
Arisaig Dri. Bear —4H 45
Arisaig Pl. G52 —2E 101
Arisdale Cres. Newt M —3E 133
Arkaig Av. Plain —1F 93
Arkaig Pl. Newt M —5H 133
Arkaig St. Wis —2H 157
Ark La. G31 —4B 84
Arkleston Ct. Pais —3D 78
Arkleston Cres. Pais —4D 78
Arkleston Rd. Pais —5D 78
Arkleston Rd. Renf —3D 78
Arkle Ter. Camb —4G 121
Arklet Rd. G51 —5E 81
Arlington St. G3 —2D 82
Armadale Ct. G31 —3C 84
Armadale Path. G31 —3C 84
Armadale Pl. G31 —3C 84
Armadale St. G31 —4C 84
Armine Path. Moth —3C 128
Armour Av. Air —4G 91
Armour Ct. Blan —3H 139
Armour Ct. Kirk —4G 31
Armour Dri. Kirk —4G 31
Armour Gdns. Kirk —4G 31
Armour Gro. Moth —5A 144
Armour Pl. John —2G 95
Armour Pl. Kirk —4G 31
Armour Pl. Lin —6A 76
Armour Pl. Moth —3C 128
Armour St. G4 —5A 84
Armour St. John —2G 95
Armstrong Cres. Udd —5E 109
Armstrong Gro. E Kil —4F 149
Arnbrae Rd. Kils —2F 11
Arndale Shopping Cen. G15 —4H 43
Arngask Rd. G51 —4E 81
Arnhall Pl. G52 —2E 101
Arnhem St. Camb —2D 122
Arnholm Pl. G52 —2E 101
Arnisdale Pl. G34 —3G 87
Arnisdale Rd. G34 —3G 87
Arnisdale Way. Ruth —3D 120
Arniston St. G32 —4H 85
Arnold Av. B'rig —6C 48
Arnold St. G20 —3E 63
Arnol Pl. G33 —4F 87
Arnott Dri. Coat —1C 110
Arnott Quad. Moth —6E 127
Arnott Way. Camb —1A 122
Arnprior Gdns. Bail —5D 52
Arnprior Quad. G45 —3H 119
Arnprior Rd. G45 —3H 119
Arnprior St. G45 —3H 119
Arnside Av. Giff —4A 118
Arnum Gdns. Carl —4F 165
Arnum Pl. Carl —4F 165
Arnwood Dri. G12 —4G 61
Aron Ter. Camb —4H 121
Aros Dri. G52 —2D 100
Aros La. G52 —2D 100
Arran. E Kil —2C 150
Arran Av. Coat —1F 111
Arran Av. Dumb —2D 16

Arran Av. Glas A —2A 78
Arran Dri. G52 —2F 101
Arran Dri. Air —2H 91
Arran Dri. Cumb —5F 35
Arran Dri. Giff —5A 118
Arran Dri. Glenm —4H 71
Arran Dri. John —4D 94
Arran Dri. Kirk —3E 31
Arran Dri. Pais —6A 98
Arran Gdns. Carl —5F 165
Arran Gdns. Ham —2A 154
Arran La. Chry —5E 53
Arran Path. Lark —4G 161
(off Donaldson Rd.)
Arran Pl. Clyd —5E 43
Arran Pl. Coat —1F 111
Arran Pl. Lin —5G 75
Arran Rd. Moth —2E 143
Arran Rd. Renf —1F 79
Arran Tower. Camb —4G 121
Arran View. Kils —3H 11
Arranview St. Chap —4E 113
Arran Way. Both —5D 124
Arran Way. Ruth —2B 120
Arrochar Ct. G23 —1B 62
Arrochar Dri. G23 —6B 46
Arrochar Path. G23 —6B 46
(off Arrochar Rd.)
Arrochar St. G23 —6B 46
Arrol Pl. G40 —1D 104
Arrol St. G52 —4G 79
(in two parts)
Arrotshole Rd. E Kil —1D 148
Arrotside Ct. E Kil —6D 136
Arrowsmith Av. G13 —1D 60
Arthur Av. Air —5H 91
Arthur Av. Barr —6D 114
Arthurlie Av. Barr —5E 115
Arthurlie Dri. Giff —5A 118
Arthurlie Dri. Newt M —6D 132
Arthurlie St. G51 —4F 81
Arthurlie St. Barr —5E 115
Arthur Pl. Clar —3C 134
Arthur Rd. Pais —5A 98
Arthur St. G3 —2B 82
Arthur St. Clar —3C 134
Arthur St. Ham —4H 141
Arthur St. Pais —6G 77
Arundel Dri. G42 —6E 103
Arundel Dri. B'rig —3D 48
Ascaig Cres. G52 —3E 101
Ascog Rd. Bear —5F 45
Ascog St. G42 —3E 103
Ascot Av. G12 —3F 61
Ascot Ct. G12 —3G 61
Ash Av. E Kil —5E 149
Ashburn Gdns. Miln —4E 25
Ashburn Loan. Lark —1F 161
Ashburn Rd. Miln —3E 25
Ashburton La. G12 —3H 61
(off Ashburton Rd.)
Ashburton Pk. E Kil —4C 148
Ashburton Rd. G12 —3H 61
Ashby Cres. G13 —6E 45
Ash Ct. E Kil —5E 149
Ashcroft. E Kil —4D 138
Ashcroft Av. Len —4G 7
Ashcroft Dri. G44 —1A 120
Ashcroft Wlk. Len —4G 7
Ashdale Dri. G52 —2E 101
Ashdene St. G22 —2F 63
Asher Rd. Chap —3E 113
Ashfield. B'rig —4C 48
Ashfield Rd. Clar —3C 134
Ashfield Rd. Law —5D 158
Ashfield Rd. Miln —4G 25
ASHFIELD STATION. G22 —4G 63
Ashfield St. G22 —5G 63
(in two parts)
Ashgillhead Rd. Ashg —4A 162
Ashgill Pl. G22 —3G 63
Ashgill Rd. G22 —2F 63
Ashgrove. Air —4D 92
Ash Gro. B'rig —1D 64
Ashgrove. Coat —1C 110
Ash Gro. Kirk —2B 50
Ash Gro. Law —5D 158
Ashgrove. Mood —6D 52
Ash Gro. Udd —5F 109
Ashgrove Rd. Bell —6D 110
Ashgrove St. G40 —3C 104
Ashiestiel Ct. Cumb —6G 35
Ashiestiel Pl. Cumb —6G 35
Ashiestiel Rd. Cumb —6G 35
Ashkirk Dri. G52 —2E 101
Ashkirk Dri. Ashg —5D 102
Ashland Av. Ham —5H 153
Ashlea Dri. Giff —3B 118
Ashley Dri. Both —2F 125
Ashley Pk. Udd —1G 125
Ashley Pl. Blan —1A 140
Ashley St. G3 —2D 82
Ashmore Rd. G43 & G44 —2D 118
Ash Pl. Bank —1E 15
Ash Pl. E Kil —5E 149
Ash Pl. John —4G 95
Ash Rd. Bail —2G 107
Ash Rd. Broad I —3F 17
Ash Rd. Clyd —2B 42
Ash Rd. Cumb —6D 14
(in two parts)
Ashton Grn. E Kil —1G 149
Ashton La. G12 —6B 62
Ashton La. N. G12 —1B 82
Ashton Rd. G12 —1B 82
Ashton Rd. Ruth —4C 104
Ashton St. Moth —5F 127
Ashton View. Dumb —3B 16
Ashton Way. Pais —5C 96
Ashtree Ct. Old K —1F 41
Ashtree Gro. Newt M —6C 132
Ashtree Rd. G43 —5A 102
Ashvale Cres. G21 —5A 64
Ash Wlk. Moth —2B 128
Ash Wlk. Ruth —4E 121
Ashworth Ter. Ham —5E 141
Aspen Dri. G21 —6C 64
Aspen Pl. John —4G 95
Aspen Way. Ham —1A 154
Asquith Pl. Bell —2F 127
Aster Dri. G45 —4C 120
Aster Gdns. G53 —4C 116
Aster Gdns. Moth —4G 143
Athelstane Dri. Cumb —6F 35
Athelstane Rd. G13 —2C 60
Athena Way. Udd —6E 109
Athole Gdns. G12 —6A 62
Athole La. G12 —6A 62
Atholl Av. G52 —3G 79
(in two parts)
Atholl Av. Torr —4D 28
Atholl Ct. Blan —3D 140
Atholl Ct. Kirk —4H 31
Atholl Cres. Pais —5G 79
Atholl Dri. Cumb —5B 34
Atholl Dri. Giff —1A 134
Atholl Gdns. Bear —6E 25
Atholl Gdns. B'rig —4B 48
Atholl Gdns. Ruth —3G 121
Atholl La. Chry —5E 53
Atholl Pl. Coat —2D 110
Atholl Pl. Lin —5G 75
Atholl St. Ham —3F 141
Atholl Ter. Udd —4D 108
Atlas Ind. Est. G21 —5B 64
Atlas Pl. G21 —5B 64
Atlas Rd. G21 —6A 64
Atlas Sq. G21 —5B 64
Atlas St. Clyd —1D 58
Attercliffe Av. Wis —1C 156
Attlee Av. Clyd —6F 43
Attlee Pl. Clyd —6G 43
Attow Rd. G43 —2H 117
Auburn Dri. Barr —6F 115
Auchans Rd. Hous —3F 75
Auchencrow St. G34 —3B 88
Auchencruive. Miln —5A 26
Auchendavie Rd. Kirk —3G 31
Auchengeich Rd. Mood —3B 52
Auchengilloch. E Kil —6G 149
Auchenglen Dri. Chry —5D 52
Auchengreoch Av. John —5D 94
Auchengreoch Rd. John —5D 94
Auchenkilns Rd. Cumb —1F 55
Auchenkilns Roundabout. Cumb —4E 35
Auchenlodment Rd. John —3H 95
Auchenowie Rd. Miln —5H 25
Auchenreoch Av. Dumb —1H 17
Auchentibber Rd. Blan —6F 139
Auchentorlie Quad. Pais —1D 98
Auchentorlie St. G11 —1F 81
Auchentoshan Av. Clyd —1B 42
Auchentoshan Est. Clyd —1A 42
Auchentoshan Ter. G21 —1B 84
Auchinairn Rd. B'rig —2B 64
Auchinbee Farm Rd. Cumb —1D 34
Auchinbee Way. Cumb —2D 34
Auchincampbell Rd. Ham —6H 141
Auchincloch Dri. Bank —1F 15
Auchingill Path. G34 —2B 88
(off Auchingill Pl.)
Auchingill Pl. G34 —2B 88
Auchingill Rd. G34 —2A 88
Auchingramont Ct. Ham —6H 141
Auchingramont Rd. Ham —5H 141
Auchinlea Retail Pk. G34 —3F 87
Auchinlea Rd. G34 —1F 87
Auchinleck Av. G33 —3G 65
Auchinleck Cres. G33 —3G 65
Auchinleck Dri. G33 —3G 65
Auchinleck Gdns. G33 —3G 65
Auchinleck Rd. G33 —2H 65
Auchinleck Rd. Clyd —6D 22
Auchinleck Ter. Clyd —6D 22
Auchinloch Rd. Lenz —3D 50
Auchinloch St. G21 —6B 64
Auchinraith Av. Ham —3F 141
Auchinraith Rd. Blan —3B 140
Auchinraith Ter. Blan —3C 140
(in two parts)
Auchintibber Ct. Blan —4C 140
Auchinvole Cres. Kils —3F 11
Auchmannoch Av. Pais —6G 79
Auchnacraig Rd. Clyd —5E 23
Auchter Av. Newm —4G 147
Auchter Rd. Wis —5C 146
Auckland Pk. E Kil —3C 148
Auckland Pl. Clyd —3H 41
Auckland St. G22 —6F 63
Auldbar Rd. G52 —2F 101
Auldbar Ter. Pais —3C 98
Auldburn Pl. G43 —1H 117
Auldburn Rd. G43 —1H 117
Auldearn Rd. G21 —2E 65
Auldgirth Rd. G52 —2F 101
Auldhame St. Coat —3A 90
Auldhouse Av. G43 —1H 117
Auldhouse Ct. G43 —1H 117
Auldhouse Gdns. G43 —1H 117
Auldhouse Retail Pk. G43 —6A 102
Auldhouse Rd. G43 —1H 117
Auldhouse Rd. E Kil —6F 149
Auldhouse Ter. G43 —1B 118
Auld Kirk Rd. Camb —4C 122
Auldkirk, The. Clar —4E 135
Auld Rd., The. Cumb —1A 36
Auld's Brae. Air —3A 92
Auld St. Dalm —4A 42
Auldton Ter. Ashg —4B 162
Aultbea St. G22 —1F 63
Aultmore Rd. G33 —4F 87
Aursbridge Cres. Barr —5F 115
Aursbridge Dri. Barr —5F 115
Aurs Cres. Barr —5F 115
Aurs Dri. Barr —6F 115
Aurs Glen. Barr —6E 115
Aurs Pl. Barr —5G 115
Aurs Rd. Barr —4F 115
Aurs Rd. Newt M —3A 132
Austen La. G13 —4E 61
Austen Rd. G13 —4E 61
Austine Dri. Ham —4A 154
Avenel Rd. G13 —6E 45
Avenue End Rd. G33 —5B 66
Avenuehead Rd. Chry —6D 52
Avenuepark St. G20 —5C 62
Avenue St. G40 —6C 84
Avenue St. Ruth —4D 104
Avenue, The. Newt M —5D 132
Aviemore Gdns. Bear —2H 45
Aviemore Rd. G52 —2E 101
Avoch St. G34 —2H 87
Avon Av. Bear —4H 45
Avon Av. Carl —3E 165
Avonbank Cres. Ham —3A 154
Avonbank Rd. Lark —2C 160
Avonbank Rd. Ruth —6B 104
Avonbrae Cres. Ham —3A 154
Avon Bri. Ham —1C 154
Avondale Av. E Kil —2H 149
Avondale Dri. Pais —5D 78
Avondale Pl. E Kil —3A 150
Avondale St. G33 —2A 86
Avon Dri. Bell —3E 127
Avon Dri. Lin —5H 75
Avonhead. E Kil —6G 149
Avonhead Av. Cumb —6E 35
Avonhead Gdns. Cumb —6E 35
Avonhead Pl. Cumb —6E 35
Avonhead Rd. Cumb —6E 35
Avon Ho. Ham —4A 142
Avon Pl. Coat —2H 89
Avon Pl. Lark —6F 161
Avon Rd. B'rig —1C 64
Avon Rd. Giff —5H 117
Avon Rd. Lark —5E 161
Avonside Gro. Ham —6B 142
Avonspark St. G21 —6C 64
Avon St. Ham —6A 142
Avon St. Lark —2D 160
Avon St. Moth —4F 143
Avon Tower. Moth —4G 143
Avon Wlk. Cumb —3H 35
(off Cumbernauld Cen., The)
Avon Wynd. Newm —3D 146
Aylmer Rd. G43 —1D 118
Ayr Dri. Air —6A 92
Ayr Rd. Newt M —6A 132
Ayr Rd. Shaw —6H 161
Ayr St. G21 —5B 64
Ayton Pk. N. E Kil —6B 138
Ayton Pk. S. E Kil —6B 138
Aytoun Dri. Ersk —4D 40
Aytoun Rd. G41 —1B 102

Babylon Av. Bell —4C 126
Babylon Dri. Bell —4C 126
Babylon Pl. Bell —5C 126
Babylon Rd. Bell —4C 126
Backbrae St. Kils —3H 11
(in two parts)
Bk. Causeway. G31 —6F 85
Backmuir Cres. Ham —3F 141
Backmuir Rd. G15 —3B 44
Backmuir Rd. Ham —3F 141
Bk. o'Barns. Ham —5A 142
Bk. o'Dykes Rd. Kirk —6H 31
Back o' Hill. C'lee —2B 74
Bk. o'Hill Roundabout. Cumb —4D 34
Back Row. Ham —5A 142
Bk. Sneddon St. Pais —6A 78
Badenheath Pl. Cumb —2H 53
Badenheath Ter. Cumb —3H 53
Badenoch Rd. Kirk —4H 31
Bagnell St. G21 —4B 64
Bahamas Way. E Kil —2C 148
Bailie Dri. Bear —6D 24
Bailie Fyfeway. Over —4H 157
Baillie Dri. Both —4E 125
Baillie Dri. E Kil —5B 138
Baillie Gdns. Wis —5C 146
Baillie Pl. E Kil —5C 138
Baillies La. Air —4A 92
Bailliesmuir Pl. Wis —3E 147
Baillieston Rd. G32 —1D 106
BAILLIESTON STATION. Bail —2H 107
Baillie Wynd. Udd —5E 109
Bainsford St. G32 —5H 85
Bain St. G40 —5A 84
Baird Av. G52 —3G 79
Baird Av. Air —1B 92
Baird Av. Stru I —5F 161
Baird Brae. G4 —6F 63
Baird Ct. Clyd —5C 42
Baird Cres. Cumb —6D 34
(in two parts)
Baird Dri. Bear —2D 44
Baird Dri. Ersk —4D 40
Baird Hill. E Kil —3F 149
Baird Pl. Bell —6C 110
Baird Pl. Wis —5C 146
Bairds Cres. Ham —6G 141
Bairdsland View. Bell —2D 126
Baird St. G4 —2H 83 (2G 5)
Baird St. Coat —4C 90
Baker Rd. Udd —5F 109
Baker St. G41 —4C 102
Bakewell Rd. Bail —6G 87
Balaclava St. G3 —4E 83 (6A 4)
Balado Rd. G33 —4E 87
Balanark Pl. G33 —4E 87
Balbeggie St. G32 —1C 106
Balbeg St. G51 —5E 81
Balblair Rd. G52 —3F 101
Balcarres Av. G12 —4A 62
Balcastle Gdns. Kils —1F 11
Balcastle Rd. Kils —2E 11
Balcomie St. G33 —2A 86
Balcomie Ter. Ham —3F 153
Balcurvie Rd. G34 —1G 87
Baldernock Rd. Miln —4H 25
Baldinnie Rd. G34 —3H 87
Baldorran Cres. Cumb —2D 34
Baldovan Cres. G33 —3F 87
Baldovan Path. G33 —4F 87
Baldovie Rd. G52 —1C 100
Baldragon Rd. G34 —2H 87
Baldric Rd. G13 —3C 60
Baldwin Av. G13 —2D 60
Balerno Dri. G52 —2E 101
Balfleurs St. Miln —3H 25
Balfluig St. G34 —2F 87
Balfour St. G20 —3B 62
Balfour Ter. E Kil —4H 149
Balfour Wynd. Lark —4F 161
Balfron Cres. Ham —6D 140
Balfron Rd. G51 —4E 81
Balfron Rd. Pais —6F 79
Balgair Dri. Pais —6D 78
Balgair St. G22 —4F 63
Balgair Ter. G32 —6B 86
Balglass St. G22 —5F 63
Balgonie Av. Pais —4E 97
Balgonie Dri. Pais —4G 97
Balgonie Rd. G52 —1E 101
Balgonie Woods. Pais —4G 97
Balgownie Cres. T'bnk —5G 117
Balgraybank St. G21 —5B 64
Balgray Cres. Barr —5G 115
Balgrayhill Rd. G21 —3B 64
Balgray Rd. Newt M —4A 132
Balintore St. G32 —6A 86
Baliol St. G3 —2D 82
Baljaffray Rd. Bear —6H 23
Baljaffray Shopping Cen. Bear —5G 24
Ballagan Pl. Miln —3D 24
Ballaig Av. Bear —2D 44
Ballaig Cres. Step —4C 66
Ballantay Quad. G45 —4C 120
Ballantay Rd. G45 —4C 120
Ballantay Ter. G45 —4C 120
Ballantine Av. G52 —4A 80
Ballantrae. E Kil —1F 149
Ballantrae Cres. Newt M —5G 133
Ballantrae Dri. Newt M —5G 133
Ballantrae Rd. Blan —4C 140
Ballantrae Wynd. Moth —2A 128
(off Beauly Pl.)
Ballater Cres. Wis —4H 145
Ballater Dri. Bear —5F 45
Ballater Dri. Inch —2H 57
Ballater Dri. Pais —4B 98
Ballater Pl. G5 —1H 103
Ballater St. G5 —6G 83
Ballater Way. Glenb —3G 69
Ballayne Dri. Chry —4E 53
Ballerup Ter. E Kil —5G 149
Ballieston Rd. Udd —2H 107
Ballindalloch Dri. G31 —3C 84
Ballindalloch La. G31 —3C 84
Ballinkier Av. Bank —1E 15
Balliol La. G3 —2D 82
(off Woodlands Rd.)
Balloch Gdns. G52 —2F 101
Ballochmill Rd. Ruth —5F 105
Ballochmyle. E Kil —5D 138
Ballochney La. Air —1G 91
Ballochney Rd. Air —1E 93
Ballochney St. Air —2G 91
Ballochnie Dri. Plain —1F 93
Balloch Rd. Air —5G 93
Balloch Rd. Cumb —3C 34
Balloch Roundabout. Cumb —3C 34
Balloch View. Cumb —3H 35
Ballogie Rd. G44 —6F 103
Balmalloch Rd. Kils —2F 11
Balmartin Rd. G23 —6B 46
Balmedie. Ersk —5E 41
Balmeg Av. Giff —1A 134
Balmerino Pl. B'rig —1F 65
Balmoral Av. Glenm —4H 71
Balmoral Cres. Coat —1H 109
Balmoral Cres. Inch —2A 58
Balmoral Dri. G32 —5B 106
Balmoral Dri. Bear —5G 45
Balmoral Dri. Camb —1G 121
Balmoral Gdns. Blan —5A 124
Balmoral Gdns. Udd —4D 108
Balmoral Path. Lark —4G 161
(off Donaldson Rd.)
Balmoral Pl. E Kil —2E 149
Balmoral Rd. Eld —5H 95
Balmoral St. G14 —6B 60
Balmore Dri. Ham —3E 153
Balmore Ind. Est. G22 —1F 63
Balmore Pl. G22 —3F 63
Balmore Rd. G23 & G22 —1D 46
Balmore Rd. Balm —5H 27
Balmore Sq. G22 —4F 63
Balmuildy Rd. G23 —3E 47
Balmuildy Rd. B'rig —3G 47
Balornock Rd. G21 & B'rig —4C 64
Balruddery Pl. B'rig —1F 65
Balshagray Av. G11 —6F 61
Balshagray Cres. G14 —1E 81
Balshagray Dri. G11 —6F 61
Balshagray La. G11 —6F 61
Balshagray Pl. G11 —6F 61
Baltic Ct. G40 —2C 104
Baltic La. G40 —2C 104
Baltic Pl. G40 —1C 104
Baltic St. G40 —1C 104
Balure St. G31 —4E 85
Balvaird Cres. Ruth —6C 104
Balvaird Dri. Ruth —6C 104
Balvenie St. Coat —2D 110
Balveny St. G33 —1D 86
Balvicar Dri. G42 —4D 102
Balvicar St. G42 —3D 102
Balvie Av. G15 —6A 44
Balvie Av. Giff —5B 118
Balvie Cres. Miln —3F 25
Balvie Rd. Miln —3E 25
Banavie Rd. G11 —6G 61
Banavie Rd. Newm —3D 146
Banbury Path. E Kil —5F 137
Banchory Av. G43 —2H 117
Banchory Av. Glenm —4H 71
Banchory Av. Inch —2H 57
Banchory Cres. Bear —5G 45
Banchory Rd. Wis —4H 145
Banff Av. Air —1A 112
Banff Pl. E Kil —3E 149
Banff Quad. Wis —4H 145
Banff St. G33 —1B 86
Bangorshill St. T'bnk —3F 117
Bank Av. Miln —2G 25
Bankbrae Av. G53 —1A 116
Bankend. Bri W —4G 73
Bankend Rd. Bri W —5H 73
Bankend Rd. Dumb —3F 17
Bankend St. G33 —2A 86
Bankfield Dri. Ham —4H 153
Bankfoot Dri. G52 —6B 80
Bankfoot Rd. G52 —1B 100
Bankfoot Rd. Pais —6F 77
Bankglen Rd. G15 —3B 44
Bankhall St. G42 —3F 103
Bankhead Av. G13 —3A 60
Bankhead Av. Air —4D 92
Bankhead Av. Bell —4D 126
Bankhead Av. Coat —1G 109
Bankhead Dri. Ruth —6C 104
Bankhead Pl. Air —4D 92
Bankhead Pl. Coat —1G 109
Bankhead Rd. Crmck —2H 135
Bankhead Rd. Kirk —6G 31
Bankhead Rd. Ruth —1B 120
Bankholm Pl. Clar —4D 134
Bankier Rd. Bank —1E 15
Banknock St. G32 —5G 85
Bank Pk. E Kil —3F 149
Bank Rd. G32 —5C 106
Bankside Av. John —2F 95
Banks Rd. Kirk —4D 30
Bank St. G12 —1C 82
Bank St. Air —4A 92
Bank St. Barr —5E 115
Bank St. Camb —1A 122
Bank St. Coat —5A 90
Bank St. Neil —2D 130
Bank St. Pais —1B 98
(in two parts)
Banktop Pl. John —2F 95
Bank View. Chap —3D 112
Bankview Cres. Kirk —5A 30
Bankview Dri. Kirk —5A 30
Bank Way. Lark —1F 161
(off Carrick Pl.)
Bannatyne Av. G31 —4D 84

Bannercross Av. *Bail* —6G **87**
Bannercross Dri. *Bail* —5G **87**
Bannercross Gdns. *Bail* —6G **87**
Banner Dri. *G13* —6C **44**
Bannerman Dri. *Bell* —2F **127**
Bannerman Pl. *Clyd* —5D **42**
Banner Rd. *G13* —6C **44**
Bannockburn Dri. *Lark* —4G **161**
Bantaskin St. *G20* —2A **62**
Banton Pl. *G33* —4G **87**
Banton Rd. *Kils* —2E **13**
Banyan Cres. *Udd* —4H **109**
Barassie. *E Kil* —6F **137**
Barassie Ct. *Both* —5D **124**
Barassie Cres. *Cumb* —5H **13**
Barassie Dri. *Bri W* —5E **73**
Baraston Rd. *B'rig* —2B **28**
Barbados Grn. *E Kil* —2C **148**
Barbana Rd. *E Kil* —1A **148**
Barbegs Cres. *Kils* —1B **34**
Barberry Av. *G53* —5B **116**
Barberry Gdns. *G53* —5B **116**
Barberry Pl. *G53* —5C **116**
Barbeth Gdns. *Cumb* —1D **54**
Barbeth Pl. *Cumb* —1C **54**
Barbeth Rd. *Cumb* —1C **54**
Barbeth Way. *Cumb* —1C **54**
Barbor St. *Chap* —3D **112**
Barbrae Pl. *Udd* —4E **125**
Barcaldine Av. *Chry* —1H **67**
Barcapel Av. *Newt M* —2E **133**
Barchan's Rd. *Mill P* —3B **94**
Barclay Av. *Eld* —3H **95**
Barclay Ct. *Old K* —1F **41**
Barclay Rd. *Moth* —3D **142**
Barclay Sq. *Renf* —2D **78**
Barclay St. *G21* —4B **64**
Barclay St. *Old K* —2F **41**
Barcraigs Dri. *Pais* —5B **98**
Bard Av. *G13* —1B **60**
Bardowie Rd. *Miln* —6F **27**
Bardowie St. *G22* —5F **63**
(in three parts)
Bardrain Av. *Eld* —3A **96**
Bardrain Rd. *Pais* —6G **97**
Bardrill Dri. *B'rig* —6A **48**
Bardykes Rd. *Blan* —1H **139**
Barefield St. *Lark* —1E **161**
Barfillan Dri. *G52* —6E **81**
Bargaran Rd. *G53* —2B **100**
Bargarran Rd. *Ersk* —5D **40**
Bargarran Sq. *Ersk* —4E **41**
Bargarron Dri. *Pais* —4C **78**
BARGEDDIE STATION. *Barg* —1E **109**
Bargeddie St. *G33* —1F **85**
Barhill La. *Twe* —1D **32**
Bar Hill Pl. *Kils* —3F **11**
Barhill Rd. *Ersk* —3E **41**
Barhill Ter. *Twe* —1E **33**
Barholm Sq. *G33* —1D **86**
Barke Rd. *Cumb* —2A **36**
Barkly Ter. *E Kil* —3E **149**
Barlanark Av. *G32* —4C **86**
Barlanark Cres. *G33* —4D **86**
Barlanark Pl. *Spri* —5D **86**
Barlanark Rd. *G33* —4D **86**
Barlandfauld St. *Kils* —3A **12**
Barleybank. *Kirk* —5C **30**
Barlia Dri. *G45* —4A **120**
Barlia St. *G45* —4A **120**
Barlia Ter. *G45* —4B **120**
Barloan Cres. *Dumb* —2G **17**
Barloan Pl. *Dumb* —2G **17**
Barloch Av. *Miln* —3G **25**
Barloch Rd. *Miln* —3H **25**
Barloch St. *G22* —5G **63**
Barlogan Av. *G52* —6E **81**
Barlogan Quad. *G52* —6E **81**
Barmore Av. *Carl* —5G **165**
Barmulloch Rd. *G21* —5C **64**
Barnard Gdns. *B'rig* —3C **48**
Barnbeth Rd. *G53* —3B **100**
Barncluith Ct. *Ham* —6B **142**
Barncluith Rd. *Ham* —6B **142**
Barnes Rd. *G20* —3E **63**
Barnes St. *Barr* —5D **114**
Barnflat St. *Ruth* —4D **104**
Barn Grn. *Kilb* —2A **94**
Barnhill Dri. *Ham* —1B **152**
Barnhill Rd. *Dumb* —2C **18**
BARNHILL STATION. *G21* —6B **64**
Barnkirk Av. *G15* —4A **44**
Barnscroft. *Kilb* —1B **94**
Barnsford Av. *Inch* —5F **57**
Barnsford Rd. *Inch* —4E **57**
Barnsford Rd. *Pais* —3E **77**
Barns St. *Clyd* —6E **43**
Barnton St. *G32* —4G **85**
Barnwell Ter. *G51* —4E **81**
Barochan Cres. *Pais* —1E **97**
Barochan Rd. *G53* —2B **100**
Barochan Rd. *Hous* —2C **74**
Baronald Dri. *G12* —3H **61**
Baronald Ga. *G12* —3H **61**
Baronald St. *Ruth* —4D **104**
Baron Ct. *Ham* —1C **154**
Barone Dri. *Clar* —1A **134**
Baronhall Dri. *Blan* —1A **140**
Baronhill. *Cumb* —6A **14**
Baron Rd. *Pais* —5C **78**
Baronscourt Dri. *Pais* —1D **96**
Baronscourt Gdns. *Pais* —1D **96**
Baronscourt Rd. *Pais* —1D **96**
Barons Ga. *Both* —3C **124**
Barons Rd. *Moth* —1B **156**
Barons Tower. *Moth* —6B **144**
Baron St. *Renf* —1E **79**
Baron Way. *Bail* —6D **88**
Barony Ct. *Bail* —5H **87**
Barony Dri. *Bail* —5H **87**
Barony Gdns. *Bail* —6H **87**
Barony Pl. *Cumb* —4A **34**
Barony Wynd. *Bail* —5H **87**
Barra Av. *Renf* —2E **79**
Barra Av. *Wis* —4C **146**
Barrachnie Ct. *Bail* —5F **87**
Barrachnie Cres. *Bail* —6F **87**
Barrachnie Rd. *Bail* —1F **107**
Barrack St. *G4* —5A **84**
Barrack St. *Ham* —5H **141**
Barra Cres. *Old K* —2G **41**
Barra Dri. *Air* —5E **93**
Barra Gdns. *Old K* —2G **41**
Barra Rd. *Old K* —2G **41**
Barra St. *G20* —1A **62**
Barr Av. *Neil* —1E **131**
Barrcraig Rd. *Bri W* —4E **73**
Barr Cres. *Clyd* —2D **42**
Barr Gro. *Udd* —5E **109**
Barrhead Rd. *G53 & G43* —1H **115**
Barrhead Rd. *Newt M* —4A **132**
Barrhead Rd. *Pais* —2B **98**
BARRHEAD STATION. *Barr* —4D **114**
Barrhill. *Twe* —1D **32**
Barrhill Ct. *Kirk* —5G **31**
Barrhill Cres. *Kilb* —3B **94**
Barrhill Rd. *Kirk* —5G **31**
Barriedale Av. *Ham* —6F **141**
Barrie Quad. *Clyd* —3C **42**
Barrie Rd. *G52* —4A **80**
Barrie Rd. *E Kil* —4D **138**
Barrie St. *Moth* —3G **143**
Barrington Dri. *G4* —1D **82**
Barrisdale Rd. *G20* —2B **62**
Barrisdale Rd. *Newm* —3D **146**
Barrisdale Way. *Ruth* —3D **120**
Barrland Dri. *Giff* —4A **118**
Barrland St. *G41* —2E **103**
Barrmill Rd. *G43* —2G **117**
Barrowfield St. *G40* —6C **84**
Barrowfield St. *Coat* —1B **110**
Barrpath. *Kils* —4B **12**
Barr Pl. *Newt M* —4C **132**
Barr Pl. *Pais* —1H **97**
Barrs La. *Carl* —2F **165**
Barr St. *G20* —6E **63**
Barr St. *Moth* —1G **143**
Barr Ter. *E Kil* —1G **149**
Barrwood Pl. *Udd* —5E **109**
Barrwood St. *G33* —1G **85**
Barry Gdns. *Blan* —3A **140**
Barscube Ter. *Pais* —3C **98**
Barshaw Dri. *Pais* —5C **78**
Barshaw Pl. *Pais* —6F **79**
Barshaw Rd. *G52* —5G **79**
Barskiven Rd. *Pais* —1D **96**
Barterholm Rd. *Pais* —3A **98**
Bartholomew St. *G40* —2C **104**
Bartiebeith Rd. *G33* —4D **86**
Bartlett Sq. *Barr* —5E **115**
Bartonhall Rd. *Wis* —2B **158**
Barty's Rd. *Bell* —2E **127**
Barwood Hill. *Dumb* —1H **17**
Bassett Av. *G13* —1B **60**
Bassett Cres. *G13* —1B **60**
Bathgate St. *G31* —5C **84**
Bathgo Av. *Pais* —1G **99**
Bath La. *G2* —3E **83** (3A **4**)
Bath St. *G2* —3E **83** (3A **4**)
Batson St. *G42* —3F **103**
Battlefield Av. *G42* —6E **103**
Battlefield Gdns. *G42* —5E **103**
Battlefield Rd. *G42* —5D **102**
*Battle Pl. G41 —5D **102***
(off Algie St.)
Bavelaw St. *G33* —1D **86**
Bayfield Av. *G15* —4A **44**
Bayfield Ter. *G15* —4A **44**
Beaconsfield Rd. *G12* —4H **61**
Beard Cres. *G'csh* —4E **69**
Beardmore Cotts. *Inch* —3A **58**
Beardmore Pl. *Clyd* —4A **42**
Beardmore St. *Clyd* —4H **41**
Beardmore Way. *Clyd* —5H **41**
Bearford Dri. *G52* —6B **80**
Bearsden Rd. *G13* —3F **61**
Bearsden Shopping Cen. *Bear* —3G **45**
BEARSDEN STATION. *Bear* —3E **45**
Beaton Rd. *G41* —3C **102**
Beaton St. *Lark* —1D **160**
Beatrice Dri. *Moth* —2H **127**
Beatrice Gdns. *Hous* —3D **74**
Beatson Wynd. *Udd* —4E **109**
Beattock St. *G31* —6F **85**
Beattock Wynd. *Ham* —6E **141**
Beatty St. *Clyd* —4A **42**
Beaufort Av. *G43* —1A **118**
Beaufort Dri. *Kirk* —5B **30**
Beaufort Gdns. *B'rig* —6A **48**
Beauly Dri. *Pais* —4C **96**
Beauly Pl. *G20* —4B **62**
Beauly Pl. *B'rig* —5F **49**
Beauly Pl. *Chry* —6B **52**
Beauly Pl. *Coat* —2D **110**
Beauly Pl. *E Kil* —1F **149**
Beauly Pl. *Moth* —2A **128**
Beauly Rd. *Bail* —2G **107**
Beaumont Ga. *G12* —6A **62**
Bedale Rd. *Bail* —1F **107**
Bedcow View. *Kirk* —6F **31**
Bedford Av. *Clyd* —5F **43**
Bedford La. *G5* —6F **83**
Bedford St. *G5* —6F **83**
Bedlay Ct. *Chry* —4E **53**
Bedlay Pl. *Anna* —5B **54**
Bedlay View. *Udd* —4F **109**
Bedlay Wlk. *Chry* —4E **53**
Beech Av. *G41* —1H **101**
(in two parts)
Beech Av. *Bail* —6G **87**
Beech Av. *Bear* —6G **25**
Beech Av. *Bri W* —2F **73**
Beech Av. *Camb* —1H **121**
Beech Av. *Eld* —3A **96**
Beech Av. *Lark* —3H **161**
Beech Av. *Moth* —4B **128**
Beech Av. *Newt M* —5D **132**
Beech Av. *Pais* —4C **98**
Beech Av. *Ruth* —3E **121**
Beechbank Av. *Air* —2H **91**
Beech Ct. *Coat* —1A **110**
Beech Cres. *Moth* —6D **112**
Beech Cres. *Newt M* —6E **133**
Beechcroft Pl. *Blan* —6C **124**
Beech Dri. *Clyd* —2C **42**
Beeches Av. *Clyd* —1B **42**
Beeches Rd. *Clyd* —1A **42**
Beeches Ter. *Clyd* —6B **22**
Beeches, The. *Brkfld* —5C **74**
Beeches, The. *Hous* —2D **74**
Beeches, The. *Newt M* —3F **133**
Beechfield Dri. *Carl* —5G **165**
Beech Gdns. *Bail* —6G **87**
Beechgrove. *Chry* —5D **52**
Beech Gro. *E Kil* —5D **148**
Beech Gro. *G'csh* —4E **69**
Beech Gro. *Law* —5D **158**
Beech Gro. *Wis* —2A **146**
Beechgrove Av. *Udd* —6G **109**
Beechgrove Quad. *Moth* —2A **128**
Beechgrove St. *G40* —3D **104**
Beechland Av. *G44* —5C **118**
Beechlands Dri. *Clar* —3A **134**
Beechmount Rd. *Lenz* —3C **50**
Beech Pl. *B'rig* —1D **64**
Beech Pl. *Blan* —2C **140**
Beech Rd. *B'rig* —1D **64**
Beech Rd. *John* —4D **94**
Beech Rd. *Lenz* —1C **50**
Beech Rd. *Moth* —6C **112**
Beech Ter. *Lark* —4F **161**
Beechtree Ter. *Milt C* —6C **8**
Beechwood. *Lark* —6A **156**
Beechwood Av. *Clar* —3A **134**
Beechwood Av. *Ham* —3F **153**
Beechwood Av. *Ruth* —1E **121**
Beechwood Ct. *Bear* —4F **45**
Beechwood Ct. *Cumb* —5H **35**
Beechwood Cres. *Wis* —1A **158**
Beechwood Dri. *G11* —5F **61**
Beechwood Dri. *Coat* —6E **91**
Beechwood Dri. *Renf* —2D **78**
Beechwood Gdns. *Bell* —3E **127**
Beechwood Gdns. *Mood* —6D **52**
Beechwood Gro. *Barr* —6E **115**
Beechwood Pl. *G11* —5F **61**
Beechwood Pl. *Bell* —3E **127**
Beechwood Rd. *Cumb* —4F **35**
Beechworth Dri. *Moth* —5D **128**
Beith Dri. *Air* —1A **112**
Beith Rd. *How & John* —6A **94**
Beith St. *G11* —2G **81**
Belgrave St. *Bell* —6B **110**
Belgrave Ter. *G12* —6C **62**
Belhaven Rd. *Ham* —6C **140**
Belhaven Rd. *Wis* —6G **145**
Belhaven Ter. *G12* —5A **62**
Belhaven Ter. *Wis* —6G **145**
Belhaven Ter. La. *G12* —5A **62**
Belhaven Ter. W. *G12* —5A **62**
Belhaven Ter. W. La. *G12* —5A **62**
Bellahouston Dri. *G52* —2E **101**
Bellairs Pl. *Blan* —6A **124**
Bellas Pl. *Plain* —1G **93**
Bellcraig Ct. *Clar* —4F **135**
Bell Dri. *G13* —2H **59**
Belleisle Av. *Udd* —6C **108**
Belleisle Cres. *Bri W* —5E **73**
Belleisle St. *G42* —4F **103**
Bellevue Av. *Kirk* —5B **30**
Bellevue Rd. *Kirk* —5B **30**
Bellfield Ct. *Barr* —3D **114**
Bellfield Cres. *Barr* —3D **114**
Bellfield Dri. *Wis* —1A **158**
Bellfield Rd. *Kirk* —5B **30**
Bellfield St. *G31* —5C **84**
Bellflower Ct. *E Kil* —6E **137**
Bellflower Gdns. *G53* —4C **116**
Bellflower Gro. *E Kil* —5E **137**
Bell Grn. E. *E Kil* —3H **149**
Bell Grn. W. *E Kil* —3G **149**
BELLGROVE STATION. *G31* —5B **84**
Bellgrove St. *G40* —5B **84**
Bellisle Ter. *Ham* —4F **153**
Bellrock Ct. *G33* —3B **86**
Bellrock Cres. *G33* —3A **86**
Bellrock Path. *G33* —3B **86**
Bellrock St. *G33* —3A **86**
Bellscroft Av. *Ruth* —6B **104**
Bellsdyke Rd. *Air* —5H **91**
Bellsfield Dri. *Blan* —3B **140**
Bellshaugh Gdns. *G12* —4A **62**
Bellshaugh La. *G12* —4A **62**
Bellshaugh Pl. *G12* —4A **62**
Bellshaugh Rd. *G12* —4A **62**
Bellshill Ind. Est. *Bell* —1B **126**
Bellshill Rd. *Both* —1G **141**
Bellshill Rd. *Moth* —4E **127**
Bellshill Rd. *Udd* —2D **124**
BELLSHILL STATION. *Bell* —2C **126**
Bellside Rd. *Chap* —3E **113**
Bellsmyre Av. *Dumb* —1G **17**
Bell St. *G1 & G4* —4H **83** (6G **5**)
Bell St. *Air* —3H **91**
Bell St. *Bell* —6D **110**
Bell St. *Clyd* —2F **59**
Bell St. *Renf* —5F **59**
Bell St. *Wis* —6F **145**
Belltrees Cres. *Pais* —1E **97**
Bell View Ct. *Renf* —5F **59**
Bellvue Cres. *Bell* —3A **126**
Bellwood St. *G41* —6C **102**
Belmont Av. *Udd* —6C **108**
*Belmont Ct. Kirk —5D **30***
(off Willowbank Gdns.)
Belmont Cres. *G12* —6C **62**
Belmont Dri. *Barr* —6F **115**
Belmont Dri. *E Kil* —3D **148**
Belmont Dri. *Giff* —4H **117**
Belmont Dri. *Ruth* —6D **104**
*Belmont La. G12 —6C **62***
(off Gt. Western Rd.)
Belmont Rd. *G21* —3B **64**
Belmont Rd. *Camb* —4G **121**
Belmont Rd. *Pais* —5C **78**
Belmont St. *G12 & G20* —6C **62**
Belmont St. *Clyd* —1B **58**
Belmont St. *Coat* —2G **89**
Belmont St. *Kils* —2G **11**
Belmont St. *Wis* —5H **157**
Belses Dri. *G52* —6C **80**
Belstane Pk. *Carl* —2F **165**
Belstane Pl. *Udd* —4E **125**
Belstane Rd. *Carl* —3F **165**
Belstane Rd. *Cumb* —2H **55**
Belsyde Av. *G15* —5A **44**
Beltane St. *G3* —3D **82**
Beltane St. *Wis* —1G **157**
Beltrees Av. *G53* —4A **100**
Beltrees Cres. *G53* —4A **100**
Beltrees Rd. *G53* —4A **100**
Belvidere Cres. *Bell* —3D **126**
Belvidere Cres. *B'rig* —5D **48**
Belvidere Rd. *Bell* —3C **126**
Belvoir Pl. *Blan* —1B **140**
Bemersyde. *B'rig* —5E **49**
Bemersyde Av. *G43* —2H **117**
Bemersyde Pl. *Lark* —4E **161**
Bemersyde Rd. *Pais* —5B **96**
Ben Alder Dri. *Pais* —4F **99**
Benalder St. *G11* —2A **82**
Benarty Gdns. *B'rig* —5D **48**
Benbecula. *E Kil* —2C **150**
Benbow Rd. *Clyd* —5B **42**
Ben Buie Way. *Pais* —4F **99**
Bencloich Av. *Len* —3G **7**
Bencloich Cres. *Len* —2G **7**
Bencloich Rd. *Len* —3G **7**
Bencroft Dri. *G44* —2A **120**
Benford Av. *Moth* —3D **128**
Benford Knowe. *Moth* —3E **129**
Bengairn St. *G31* —4E **85**
Bengal Pl. *G43* —6A **102**
Bengal St. *G43* —6A **102**
Benhar Pl. *G33* —4H **85**
Benholm St. *G32* —2H **105**
Ben Hope Av. *Pais* —3F **99**
Ben Lawers Dri. *Cumb* —3D **34**
Ben Lawers Dri. *Pais* —3F **99**
Ben Ledi Av. *Pais* —3F **99**
Ben Ledi Cres. *Cumb* —3D **34**
Ben Loyal Av. *Pais* —3F **99**
Ben Lui Dri. *Pais* —4E **99**
Ben Lui Pl. *Cumb* —3D **34**
Ben More Dri. *Cumb* —3C **34**
Ben More Dri. *Pais* —3F **99**
Benmore Tower. *Camb* —4G **121**
Bennan Sq. *G42* —3G **103**
Ben Nevis Rd. *Pais* —4E **99**
Ben Nevis Way. *Cumb* —3C **34**
Benny Lynch Ct. *G5* —6G **83**
Benson St. *Coat* —1C **110**
Benston Pl. *John* —4E **95**
Benston Rd. *John* —4E **95**
Bent Cres. *Udd* —1G **125**
Bentfoot Rd. *Wis* —5A **158**
Benthall St. *G5* —1H **103**
Bentinck St. *G3* —2C **82**
Bent Rd. *Chap* —2D **112**
Bent Rd. *Ham* —1G **153**
Bents Rd. *Bail* —6H **87**
Benty's La. *Carl* —4F **165**
Ben Vane Av. *Pais* —4E **99**
Ben Venue Rd. *Cumb* —3C **34**
Ben Venue Way. *Pais* —4F **99**
Benvie Gdns. *B'rig* —5D **48**
Benview Rd. *Clar* —2C **134**
Benview St. *G20* —5D **62**
Benview Ter. *Pais* —3D **98**
Benvue Rd. *Len* —4G **7**
Ben Wyvis Dri. *Pais* —4E **99**
Berelands Cres. *Ruth* —6A **104**
Berelands Pl. *Ruth* —6A **104**
Beresford Av. *G14* —5E **61**
Berger Ct. *G45* —3D **118**
Berkeley St. *G3* —3C **82**
Berkley Dri. *Blan* —6A **124**
*Berkley Ter. La. G3 —3D **82***
(off Granville St.)
Berl Av. *Hous* —3C **74**
Bernadette Av. *Moth* —5D **128**
Bernadette St. *Moth* —4D **128**
*Bernard Path. G40 —1C **104***
(off Bernard Ter.)
Bernard St. *G40* —1C **104**
Bernard Ter. *G40* —1C **104**
Berneray St. *G22* —2G **63**
Berridale Av. *G44* —2E **119**
Berriedale. *E Kil* —3A **148**
Berriedale Av. *Bail* —1G **107**
Berriedale Quad. *Wis* —4H **145**
Berryburn Rd. *G21* —5E **65**
Berry Dyke. *Kirk* —6H **31**
Berryhill Dri. *Giff* —5H **117**
Berry Hill Rd. *Cumb* —3G **35**
Berryhill Rd. *Giff* —6H **117**
Berryknowe. *Kirk* —6H **31**
Berryknowe Av. *Chry* —2A **68**
Berryknowes Av. *G52* —6C **80**
Berryknowes La. *G52* —6C **80**
Berryknowes Rd. *G52* —1C **100**
Bertram St. *G41* —4C **102**
Bertram St. *Ham* —3E **141**
Bertram St. *Lark* —4G **161**
Bervie St. *G51* —5F **81**
Berwick Cres. *Air* —6H **91**
Berwick Cres. *Lin* —4F **75**
Berwick Dri. *G52* —1B **100**
Berwick Dri. *Ruth* —6F **105**
Berwick Pl. *Coat* —2D **110**
Berwick Pl. *E Kil* —6C **138**
Berwick St. *Coat* —2D **110**
Berwick St. *Ham* —4F **141**
Bessemer Dri. *E Kil* —6A **150**
Betula Dri. *Clyd* —2C **42**
Bevan Gro. *John* —3E **95**
Beveridge Ter. *Bell* —3F **127**
Beverley Rd. *G43* —1B **118**
Bevin Av. *Clyd* —6F **43**
Bideford Cres. *G32* —2D **106**
Bield, The. *Wis* —1A **158**
Biggar Rd. *Chap* —4E **113**
Biggar Rd. *Moth* —6F **113**
Biggar St. *G31* —5D **84**
Bigton St. *G33* —1B **86**
Billings Rd. *Moth* —4D **142**
Bilsland Ct. *G20* —4F **63**
Bilsland Dri. *G20* —4D **62**
Binend Rd. *G53* —5C **100**
Binniehill Rd. *Cumb* —2F **35**
Binnie Pl. *G40* —6A **84**
Binns Rd. *G33* —1C **86**
Birch Av. *Clar* —3D **134**
Birch Brae. *Ham* —2A **154**
Birch Ct. *Coat* —1B **110**
Birch Cres. *Clar* —3D **134**
Birch Cres. *John* —4G **95**
Birch Dri. *Camb* —1C **122**
Birch Dri. *Lenz* —2D **50**
Birchfield Dri. *G14* —5B **60**
Birchfield Rd. *Ham* —6F **141**
Birchgrove. *Hous* —2D **74**
Birch Gro. *Lark* —6A **156**
Birch Gro. *Udd* —6F **109**
Birch Knowe. *B'rig* —6D **48**
Birchlea Dri. *Giff* —3B **118**
Birchmount Ct. *Air* —3D **92**
Birch Pl. *Blan* —1B **140**
Birch Quad. *Air* —4D **92**
Birch Rd. *Clyd* —3C **42**
Birch Rd. *Cumb* —2E **37**
Birch Rd. *Dumb* —3F **17**
Birch St. *G5* —1H **103**
Birch St. *Moth* —2B **128**
Birch View. *Bear* —2G **45**
Birchview Dri. *Clar* —5D **134**
Birchwood Av. *G32* —1E **107**
Birchwood Courtyards, The. *Bell* —5A **110**
Birchwood Dri. *Pais* —4F **97**
Birchwood Pl. *G32* —1E **107**
Birdsfield Ct. *Ham* —3D **140**
Birdsfield Dri. *Blan* —3B **140**
Birdsfield St. *Ham* —3D **140**
Birdston Rd. *G21* —3E **65**
Birdston Rd. *Milt C* —5C **8**
Birgidale Av. *G45* —6H **119**
Birgidale Rd. *G45* —5H **119**
Birgidale Ter. *G45* —5H **119**
Birkdale. *E Kil* —6E **137**
Birkdale Ct. *Both* —5D **124**
Birkenburn Rd. *Cumb* —5F **15**

Birken Rd. *Lenz* —3E 51
Birkenshaw Rd. *G'csh* —1G 69
Birkenshaw St. *G31* —4D 84
Birkenshaw Way. Pais —3A 78 (off Mosslands Rd.)
Birkfield Pl. *Carl* —4H 165
Birkhall Av. *G52* —1H 99
Birkhall Av. *Inch* —2H 57
Birkhall Dri. *Bear* —5F 45
Birkhill Av. *B'rig* —5D 48
Birkhill Gdns. *B'rig* —5D 48
Birkhill Rd. *Ham* —4H 153
Birkmyre Rd. *G51* —5F 81
Birks Ct. *Law* —1H 163
Birkshaw Brae. *Wis* —3G 157
Birkshaw Pl. *Wis* —3G 157
Birkshaw Tower. *Wis* —3F 157
Birks Rd. *Lark* —6F 161
Birks Rd. *Law* —1G 163
Birkwood St. *G40* —3D 104
Birmingham Rd. *Renf* —2D 78
Birnam Cres. *Bear* —2H 45
Birnam Pl. *Ham* —6C 140
Birnam Rd. *G32* —2F 105
Birness Dri. *G43* —5B 102
Birnham Av. *B'rig* —5D 48
Birnham Gdns. *B'rig* —5D 48
Birnie Ct. *G21* —5E 65
Birniehill Ct. *Clyd* —6C 22
Birniehill Roundabout. *E Kil* —3A 150
Birnie Rd. *G21* —5E 65
Birnock Av. *Renf* —2G 79
Birrell Rd. *Miln* —2F 25
Birrens Rd. *Moth* —1E 143
Birsay Rd. *G22* —2F 63
Bishopbriggs Ind. Est. *B'rig* —2C 64
BISHOPBRIGGS STATION. *B'rig* —6C 48
Bishopdale. *E Kil* —6E 137
Bishop Gdns. *B'rig* —5A 48
Bishop Gdns. *Ham* —4A 154
Bishop La. *G2* —4E 83 (5A 4)
Bishopmill Pl. *G21* —5E 65
Bishopmill Rd. *G21* —4E 65
Bishops Ga. *E Kil* —6G 135 (in two parts)
Bishopsgate Dri. *G21* —2A 64
Bishopsgate Gdns. *G21* —2A 64
Bishopsgate Pl. *G21* —2A 64
Bishopsgate Rd. *G21* —2A 64
Bishops Pk. *T'hall* —6F 135
BISHOPTON STATION. *B'ton* —6H 39
Bisset Ct. John —4E 95 (off Tannahill Cres.)
Bissett Cres. *Clyd* —1A 42
Blackadder Pl. *E Kil* —4A 148
Blackbog Rd. *Rigg* —5H 55
Blackbraes Rd. *E Kil* —5B 138
Blackburn Ct. *G51* —5B 82
Blackburn Cres. *Dumb* —3D 16
Blackburn Cres. *Kirk* —5G 31
Blackburn Sq. *Barr* —6F 115
Blackbyres Ct. *Barr* —3F 115
Blackbyres Rd. *Barr* —1E 115
Blackcraig Av. *G15* —4A 44
Blackcroft Av. *Air* —6E 93
Blackcroft Gdns. *G32* —1D 106
Blackcroft Rd. *G32* —1D 106
Blackdyke Rd. *Kirk* —5E 31
Blackfarm Rd. *Newt M* —5F 133
Blackfaulds Rd. *Ruth* —5A 104
Blackford Rd. *Pais* —3C 98
Blackfriars St. *G1* —4H 83 (6G 5)
Blackhall Ct. *Pais* —2D 98
Blackhall La. *Pais* —2B 98
Blackhall St. *Pais* —2B 98
Blackhill Pl. *G33* —1F 85
Blackhill Rd. *G23* —5B 46
Blackhill View. *Law* —6E 159
Blackhouse Av. *Newt M* —5F 133
Blackhouse Gdns. *Newt M* —5F 133
Blackhouse Rd. *Newt M* —5F 133
Blackie St. *G3* —2B 82
Blacklands Pl. *Lenz* —3E 51
Blacklands Rd. *E Kil* —2F 149
Blacklaw Dri. *E Kil* —2B 150
Blacklaw La. *Pais* —6A 78
Blackmoor Pl. *Moth* —4A 128
Blackmoss Dri. *Bell* —3B 126
Blackmuir Pl. *Ham* —3F 141
Blackness St. *Coat* —2D 110
Blackstone Av. *G53* —5C 100
Blackstone Cres. *G53* —4C 100
Blackstoun Av. *Lin* —5H 75
Blackstoun Oval. *Pais* —6F 77
Blackstoun Rd. *Pais* —3E 77
Black St. *G4* —2H 83 (2H 5)
Black St. *Air* —2B 92
Blackswell La. *Ham* —6B 142
Blackthorn Av. *Kirk* —2A 50
Blackthorn Gro. *Kirk* —2B 50
Blackthorn Rd. *Cumb* —1D 36
Blackthorn Rd. *Udd* —5G 109
Blackthorn Roundabout. *Cumb* —2E 37
Blackthorn St. *G22* —4A 64
Blackwood. *E Kil* —6F 149
Blackwood Av. *Lin* —6G 75
Blackwood Av. *Newt M* —6F 133
Blackwood Gdns. *Moth* —6E 127
Blackwood Rd. *Cumb* —4H 33
Blackwood Rd. *Miln* —1F 25
Blackwoods Cres. *Bell* —3E 127
Blackwoods Cres. *Mood* —5D 52
Blackwood St. *G13* —2E 61
Blackwood St. *Barr* —5D 114
Bladda La. *Pais* —1B 98
Blades Ct. *G'csh* —3E 69
Bladnoch Dri. *G15* —5C 44
Blaeloch Av. *G45* —6G 119
Blaeloch Dri. *G45* —6F 119
Blaeloch Ter. *G45* —6F 119
Blaeshill Rd. *E Kil* —3A 148
Blairathol Av. *G11* —6G 61
Blairathol Gdns. *G11* —6G 61
Blair Atholl Dri. *Lark* —4G 161
Blairbeth Dri. *G44* —6F 103
Blairbeth Pl. *Ruth* —2C 120
Blairbeth Rd. *Ruth* —2C 120
Blairbeth Ter. *Ruth* —2E 121
Blair Ct. *Clyd* —5D 42
Blair Cres. *Bail* —2G 107
Blairdardie Rd. *G15 & G13* —6B 44
Blairdenan Av. *Chry* —4E 53
Blairdenon Dri. *Cumb* —2E 35
Blair Dri. *Milt C* —6B 8
Blair Gdns. *Torr* —4D 28
Blairgowrie Rd. *G52* —1C 100
Blairgrove Ct. *Coat* —5A 90
Blairhall Av. *G41* —5D 102
Blairhill Av. *Kirk* —1G 51
Blairhill Pl. *Coat* —4A 90
BLAIRHILL STATION. *Coat* —3A 90
Blairhill St. *Coat* —4A 90
Blairholm Dri. *Bell* —4D 126
Blair Ho. *Cumb* —2A 36
Blairlinn Ind. Est. *Cumb* —1H 55
Blairlinn Rd. *Cumb* —1H 55
Blairlogie St. *G33* —2B 86
Blairpark Av. *Coat* —3A 90
Blair Path. *Moth* —4H 143
Blair Rd. *Coat* —4A 90
Blair Rd. *Pais* —6G 79
Blairston Av. *Both* —6E 125
Blairston Gdns. *Both* —6F 125
Blair St. *G32* —6H 85
Blairtum Dri. *Ruth* —2D 120
Blairtummock Rd. *G33* —3C 86 (in three parts)
Blake Rd. *Cumb* —3A 36
Blane Dri. *Miln* —2H 25
Blane St. *Coat* —3C 90
Blaneview. *Step* —5D 66
Blantyre Ct. *Ersk* —4E 41
Blantyre Cres. *Clyd* —6A 22
Blantyre Dri. *B'ton* —3G 39
Blantyre Farm Rd. *Blan* —6A 124
Blantyre Gdns. *Cumb* —4A 34
Blantyre Ind. Est. *Blan* —4C 140
Blantyre Mill Rd. *Both* —5D 124
Blantyre Pl. *Coat* —1A 110
Blantyre Rd. *Both* —5E 125
BLANTYRE STATION. *Blan* —1C 140
Blantyre St. *G3* —2B 82
Blantyre St. *Coat* —1A 110
Blaven Ct. *Bail* —1A 108
Blawart Hill St. *G14* —4H 59
Bleachfield. *Miln* —2F 25
Bleasdale Ct. *Clyd* —5D 42
Blenheim Av. *E Kil* —4E 149
Blenheim Av. *Step* —3D 66
Blenheim Ct. *Carl* —4G 165
Blenheim Ct. *Kils* —2H 11
Blenheim Ct. *Pais* —6H 77
Blochairn Rd. *G21* —2C 84
Bluebell Gdns. *G45* —5C 120
Bluebell Gdns. *Moth* —5F 127
Bluebell Wlk. *Moth* —4A 128
Bluebell Way. *Air* —1H 91
Bluebell Way. *Carl* —5F 165
Bluebell Way. *Len* —4H 7
Blueknowes Rd. *Law* —6C 158 (in two parts)
Bluevale St. *G31* —5C 84
Blyth Pl. *G33* —5D 86
Blyth Rd. *G33* —5E 87
Blythswood Av. *Renf* —5F 59
Blythswood Dri. *Pais* —5A 78
Blythswood Rd. *Renf* —5F 59
Blythswood Sq. *G2* —3E 83 (4B 4)
Blythswood St. *G2* —4E 83 (5B 4)
Boardwalk, The. *E Kil* —4A 150
Boclair Av. *Bear* —3F 45
Boclair Cres. *Bear* —3G 45
Boclair Cres. *B'rig* —6C 48
Boclair Rd. *G23* —1B 46
Boclair Rd. *Bear* —3G 45
Boclair Rd. *B'rig* —6C 48
Boclair St. *G13* —1E 61
Bodden Sq. *Moth* —6E 113
Boden Ind. Est. *G40* —1C 104
Boden Quad. *Moth* —5D 126
Boden St. *G40* —1C 104
Bodmin Gdns. *Chry* —4D 52
Bogany Ter. *G45* —5A 120
Bogbain Rd. *G34* —3G 87
Boggknowe. *Udd* —5B 108
Boghall Rd. *Brdwd* —6H 165
Boghall Rd. *Udd* —3G 107
Boghall St. *G33* —2B 86
Boghead Av. *Dumb* —3H 17
Boghead Rd. *G21* —4C 64
Boghead Rd. *Dumb* —3G 17
Boghead Rd. *Kirk* —3A 50
Bogleshole Rd. *Camb* —6G 105
Bogmoor Pl. *G51* —2C 80
Bogmoor Rd. *G51* —3B 80
Bog Rd. *Bank* —1E 15
Bogside Rd. *G33* —3A 66
Bogside Rd. *Ashg* —5B 162
Bogside Rd. *Kils* —4H 11
Bogside St. *G40* —1D 104
Bogstonhill Rd. *Hous* —1B 74
Bogs View. *Bell* —4B 126
Bogton Av. *G44* —3D 118
Bogton Av. La. *G44* —3D 118
Boleyn Ct. *Wis* —3F 147
Boleyn Rd. *G41* —3C 102
Bolingbroke. *E Kil* —5C 138
Bolivar Ter. *G42* —5G 103
Bolton Dri. *G42* —5F 103
Bolton Ter. *Len* —3G 7
Bon Accord Rd. *Clar* —3D 134
Bon Accord Sq. *Clyd* —1D 58
Bonar Cres. *Bri W* —4G 73
Bonar La. *Bri W* —4G 73
Bonawe St. *G20* —5D 62
Bond M. *Ruth* —4G 121
Bonds Dri. *Newm* —3F 147
Bo'ness Rd. *Moth* —1C 128
Boness St. *G40* —1D 104
Bonhill Rd. *Dumb* —3G 17
Bonhill St. *G22* —6F 63
Bonkle Gdns. *Newm* —4F 147
Bonkle Rd. *Newm* —4F 147
Bonnar St. *G40* —2C 104
Bonnaughton Rd. *Bear* —1B 44
Bonnyholm Av. *G53* —2A 100
Bonnyrigg Dri. *G43* —2G 117
Bonnyton La. *Ham* —4F 153
Bontine Av. *Dumb* —3D 16
Bonyton Av. *G13* —3H 59
Boon Dri. *G15* —5B 44
Boquhanran Pl. *Clyd* —4C 42
Boquhanran Rd. *Clyd* —5B 42 (in three parts)
Borden La. *G13* —4E 61
Borden Rd. *G13* —4E 61
Border Way. *Kirk* —5E 31
Boreland Dri. *G13* —2A 60
Boreland Dri. *Ham* —1C 152
Boreland Pl. *G13* —3B 60
Bore Rd. *Air* —2B 92
Borgie Cres. *Camb* —2A 122
Borland Dri. *Lark* —5F 161
Borland Rd. *Bear* —4G 45
Borron St. *G4* —6G 63
Borrowdale. *E Kil* —6B 148
Borthwick Dri. *E Kil* —4A 148
Borthwick St. *G33* —2B 86
Bosfield Corner. *E Kil* —6H 137
Bosfield Pl. *E Kil* —6H 137
Bosfield Rd. *E Kil* —6G 137
Boswell Ct. *G42* —6D 102
Boswell Dri. *Blan* —2B 140
Boswell Pk. *E Kil* —5C 138
Boswell Sq. *G52* —4H 79
Bosworth Rd. *E Kil* —5B 138
Botanic Cres. *G20* —5B 62
Botanic Cres. La. *G20* —5B 62
Bothlin Dri. *Step* —3D 66
Bothlyn Av. *Kirk* —6E 31
Bothlyn Cres. *G'csh* —2D 68
Bothlyn Rd. *Chry* —1B 68
Bothwell Bri. *Ham* —1G 141
Bothwellhaugh Quad. *Bell* —4B 126
Bothwellhaugh Rd. *Moth* —6B 126
Bothwell Ho. *Ham* —4A 142
Bothwell La. *G2* —4E 83 (5D 4)
Bothwell La. G12 —1C 82 (off Glasgow St.)
Bothwell Pk. Ind. Est. *Udd* —2E 125
Bothwellpark Rd. *Both* —5F 125
Bothwell Pl. *Coat* —4B 90
Bothwell Pl. *Pais* —5C 96
Bothwell Rd. *Carl* —1E 165
Bothwell Rd. *Ham* —1G 141
Bothwell Rd. *Udd* —2D 124
Bothwell St. *G2* —4E 83 (5B 4)
Bothwell St. *Camb* —1G 121
Bothwell St. *Ham* —4G 141
Bothwick Way. *Pais* —5C 96
Bourhill Ct. *Wis* —1D 156
Bourne Ct. *Inch* —2H 57
Bourne Cres. *Inch* —2H 57
Bourne St. *Ham* —6B 142
Bourock Sq. *Barr* —6F 115
Bourtree Rd. *Ham* —1C 152
Bouverie St. *G14* —3G 59
Bouverie St. *Ruth* —6B 104
Bowden Dri. *G52* —5B 80
Bowden Pk. *E Kil* —3E 149
Bower St. *G12* —6C 62
Bowerwalls St. *Barr* —3F 115
Bowes Cres. *Bail* —1F 107
Bowfield Av. *G52* —5H 79
Bowfield Cres. *G52* —5H 79
Bowfield Dri. *G52* —5H 79
Bowfield Path. *G52* —5H 79
Bowfield Pl. *G52* —5H 79
Bowhousebrae Rd. *Air* —1E 113
Bowhouse Rd. *Air* —6E 93
Bowie St. *Dumb* —4E 17
Bowling Grn. La. G14 —6D 60 (off Westland Dri.)
Bowling Grn. Rd. *G44* —2E 119
Bowling Grn. Rd. *Chry* —1B 68
Bowling Grn. Rd. *Mt V* —1D 106
Bowling Grn. Rd. *White* —6D 60
Bowling Grn. St. *Bell* —2D 126
Bowling Grn. View. *Camb* —3F 123
BOWLING STATION. *Bowl* —5A 20
Bowling St. *Coat* —4B 90
Bowmanflat. *Lark* —2E 161
Bowman St. *G42* —3E 103
Bowmont Gdns. *G12* —6A 62
Bowmont Hill. *B'rig* —3C 48
Bowmont Pl. *Camb* —2D 122
Bowmont Pl. *E Kil* —4A 148
Bowmont Ter. *G12* —6A 62
Bowmore Gdns. *Ruth* —4G 121
Bowmore Gdns. *Udd* —5C 108
Bowmore Rd. *G52* —6E 81
Bowyer Vennel. *Bell* —1B 126
Boyd Dri. *Moth* —2D 142
Boydstone Pl. *T'bnk* —2G 117
Boydstone Rd. *G53, G43 & T'bnk* —1E 117
Boyd St. *G42* —4F 103
Boylestone Rd. *Barr* —3C 114
Boyle St. *Clyd* —1F 59
Boyndie Path. *G34* —3H 87
Boyndie St. *G34* —3H 87
Brabloch Cres. *Pais* —5B 78
Bracadale Dri. *Bail* —1B 108
Bracadale Gdns. *Bail* —1B 108
Bracadale Gro. *Bail* —1A 108
Bracadale Rd. *Bail* —1A 108
Brackenbrae Av. *B'rig* —5A 48
Brackenbrae Rd. *B'rig* —6B 48
Brackendene. *Hous* —2D 74
Brackenhill Dri. *Ham* —4F 153
Brackenhill Rd. *Law* —5E 159
Brackenhirst Rd. *Glenm* —3F 71
Brackenhurst St. *Dumb* —1H 17
Brackenrig Rd. *T'bnk* —5E 117
Bracken St. *G22* —3F 63
Bracken St. *Moth* —4A 128
Bracken Ter. *Both* —4E 125
Bracken Way. Lark —4G 161 (off Donaldson Rd.)
Brackla Av. *Clyd* —1G 59
Bradan Av. *Clyd* —2G 59
Bradda Av. *Ruth* —3E 121
Bradfield Av. *G12* —4A 62
Bradshaw Cres. *Ham* —6C 140
Brady Cres. *Mood* —4E 53
Braedale. *Ham* —6E 141
Braedale Av. *Air* —4B 92
Braedale Av. *Moth* —3D 142
Braedale Cres. *Newm* —4F 147
Braedale Pl. *Newm* —4G 147
Braeface Rd. *Cumb* —3G 35
Braefield Dri. *T'bnk* —4G 117
Braefoot Av. *Miln* —5G 25
Braefoot Ct. *Law* —6D 158
Braefoot Cres. *Law* —1H 163
Braefoot Cres. *Pais* —6B 98
Braehead. *Blan* —3B 140
Braehead Av. *Clyd* —6C 22
Braehead Av. *Coat* —2H 109
Braehead Av. *Lark* —3C 160
Braehead Av. *Miln* —4F 25
Braehead Av. *Neil* —2D 130
Braehead Cres. *Clyd* —6C 22
Braehead Dri. *Bell* —3B 126
Braehead Loan. Carl —5H 165 (off Charles Cres.)
Braehead Pl. *Bell* —3B 126
Braehead Quad. *Moth* —3D 128
Braehead Quad. *Neil* —2D 130
Braehead Rd. *Clyd* —6C 22
Braehead Rd. *Cumb* —2B 36
Braehead Rd. *Pais* —6G 97
Braehead Rd. *T'hall* —6G 135
Braehead St. *G5* —2H 103
Braehead St. *Kirk* —4C 30
Braemar Av. *Clyd* —3B 42
Braemar Ct. *G44* —3C 118
Braemar Cres. *Carl* —2G 165
Braemar Cres. *Pais* —4B 98
Braemar Dri. *Eld* —4H 95
Braemar Rd. *Inch* —2H 57
Braemar Rd. *Ruth* —4G 121
Braemar St. *G42* —6D 102
Braemar St. *Ham* —3F 141
Braemar View. *Clyd* —2B 42
Braemount Av. *Pais* —6G 97
Braes Av. *Clyd* —6F 43
Braesburn Ct. *Cumb* —5F 15
Braesburn Pl. *Cumb* —5F 15
Braesburn Rd. *Cumb* —5F 15
Braeside Av. *Chry* —5D 52
Braeside Av. *Miln* —5G 25
Braeside Av. *Ruth* —6E 105
Braeside Cres. *Bail* —6D 88
Braeside Cres. *Barr* —6G 115
Braeside Dri. *Barr* —6F 115
Braeside Dri. *Dumb* —2H 17
Braeside Gdns. *Ham* —3A 154
Braeside La. Lark —1F 161 (off Carrick Pl.)
Braeside Pl. *Camb* —3B 122
Braeside Rd. *Moth* —3D 128
Braeside St. *G20* —5D 62
Braeside Way. Lark —4F 161 (off Keir Hardie Rd.)
Braes o'Yetts. *Kirk* —5G 31
Braeview Av. *Pais* —6F 97
Braeview Dri. *Pais* —6F 97
Braeview Gdns. *Pais* —6F 97
Brae View Pl. *E Kil* —5B 138
Braeview Rd. *Pais* —6F 97
Braidbar Ct. *Giff* —4A 118
Braidbar Farm Rd. *Giff* —3B 118
Braidbar Rd. *Giff* —4A 118
Braidcraft Pl. *G53* —5C 100
Braidcraft Rd. *G53* —4C 100
Braidcraft Ter. *G53* —4D 100
Braidfauld Gdns. *G32* —2H 105
Braidfauld Pl. *G32* —3H 105
Braidfauld St. *G32* —3H 105
Braidfield Gro. *Clyd* —2D 42
Braidfield Rd. *Clyd* —2D 42
Braidholm Cres. *Giff* —4A 118
Braidholm Rd. *Giff* —4A 118
Braidhurst Ind. Est. *Moth* —6F 127
Braidhurst St. *Moth* —1G 143
Braidley Cres. *E Kil* —6G 149
Braidpark Dri. *Giff* —4B 118
Braid Sq. *G4* —1E 83
Braid's Rd. *Pais* —4A 98
Braid St. *G4* —1E 83
Braidwood Pl. *Lin* —5F 75
Braidwood St. *Wis* —2A 146
Bramah Av. *E Kil* —4H 149
Bramar Cres. *Bear* —5F 45
Brambling Ct. *Wis* —2F 157
Bramley Pl. *Lenz* —3E 51
Brampton. *E Kil* —5B 148
Branchalfield Dri. *Wis* —5C 146
Branchalmuir Cres. *Newm* —3D 146
Branchal Rd. *Wis* —4B 146
Branchock Av. *Camb* —3D 122
Brancumhall Rd. *E Kil* —6D 138
Brandon Arc. *Moth* —3G 143
Brandon Ct. *Ham* —5G 141
Brandon Dri. *Bear* —6E 25
Brandon Gdns. *Camb* —2G 121
Brandon Ho. *Ham* —4A 142
Brandon Pde. E. *Moth* —2G 143
Brandon Pde. S. *Moth* —3G 143
Brandon Pl. *Bell* —4A 126
Brandon St. *G31* —5B 84
Brandon St. *Coat* —1A 110
Brandon St. *Ham* —6A 142
Brandon St. *Moth* —3H 143
Brandon Way. *Coat* —1H 109
Brand St. *G51* —5A 82
Brankholm Brae. *Ham* —5B 140
Brannock Av. *Moth* —3D 128
Brannock Pl. *Moth* —3D 128
Brannock Rd. *Moth* —4D 128
Brassey St. *G20* —3C 62
Breadalbane Cres. *Moth* —6F 127
Breadalbane Gdns. *Ruth* —3F 121
Breadalbane St. *G3* —3D 82
Breadie Dri. *Miln* —5F 25
Breamish Pl. *E Kil* —5B 148
Bream Pl. *Hous* —3D 74
Brechin Rd. *B'rig* —6E 49
Brechin St. *G3* —3C 82
Breck Av. *Pais* —6B 96
Brediland Rd. *Lin* —5G 75
Brediland Rd. *Pais* —6C 96
Bredin Way. *Moth* —1D 142
Bredisholm Cres. *Udd* —4G 109
Bredisholm Dri. *Bail* —1A 108
Bredisholm Rd. *Bail* —1A 108 (in four parts)
Bredisholm Ter. *Bail* —1A 108
Bremners Cotts. *Clyd* —1B 42
Brenfield Av. *G44* —3D 118
Brenfield Dri. *G44* —3D 118
Brenfield Rd. *G44* —3D 118
Brent Av. *T'bnk* —2F 117
Brent Ct. *E Kil* —6G 137
Brent Cres. *Hous* —3C 74
Brent Dri. *T'bnk* —2F 117
Brent Rd. *E Kil* —6G 137
Brent Rd. *T'bnk* —2F 117
Brentwood Av. *G53* —3A 116
Brentwood Dri. *G53* —3B 116
Brentwood Sq. *G53* —3B 116
Brereton St. *G42* —4G 103
Bressay. *E Kil* —6G 137
Bressay Rd. *G33* —5E 87
Bressay Wynd. Newm —3D 146 (off Tiree Cres.)
Breval Cres. *Clyd* —6C 22
Brewery St. *John* —2F 95
Brewster Av. *Pais* —4C 78
Briar Bank. *Milt C* —6B 8
Briarbush Way. *Blan* —1A 140
Briar Dri. *Clyd* —3D 42
Briarlea Dri. *Giff* —3A 118
Briar Neuk. *B'rig* —1D 64
Briar Rd. *G43* —2B 118
Briar Rd. *Kirk* —5F 31
Briarwell La. *Miln* —4H 25
Briarwell Rd. *Miln* —4H 25
Briarwood Ct. *G32* —3E 107
Briarwood Gdns. *G32* —3E 107

Briarwood Rd. Wis —5E 145
Brick La. Pais —6B 78
Bridgebar St. Barr —3G 115
Bridgeburn Dri. Chry —5C 52
Bridgeford Av. Bell —6E 111
Bridgegait. Miln —5A 26
Bridgegate. G1 —5G 83
Bridgend. B'ton —4G 39
Bridgend Cotts. Kirk —6G 31
Bridgend Ct. C'cry —2F 15
Bridgend View. Carl —4F 165
Bridge of Weir Rd. Bri W —4G 73
Bridge of Weir Rd. Brkfld & Lin —6C 74
Bridge of Weir Rd. Hous —2A 74
Bridge St. G5 —5F 83
Bridge St. Camb —1A 122
Bridge St. Clyd —4A 42
Bridge St. Dumb —4E 17
Bridge St. Ham —1G 153
Bridge St. Lin —5A 76
Bridge St. Pais —1A 98
Bridge St. Wis —6E 145
BRIDGE ST. STATION. G5 —6F 83
Bridgeton Bus. Cen. G40 —6B 84
Bridgeton Cross. G40 —6B 84
BRIDGETON STATION. G40 —1B 104
Bridgewater Ind. Pk. Ersk —5F 41
Bridgewater Shopping Cen. Ersk —5F 41
Bridgeway Ct. Kirk —6F 31
Bridgeway Pl. Kirk —6F 31
Bridgeway Rd. Kirk —6F 31
Bridgeway Ter. Kirk —6F 31
Bridie Ter. E Kil —5C 138
Brierie Av. C'lee —2B 74
Brierie Gdns. C'lee —3B 74
Brierie Hill Ct. C'lee —3B 74
Brierie Hill Gro. C'lee —3B 74
Brierie Hill Rd. C'lee —3A 74
Brierie Hills. C'lee —2B 74
Brierie La. C'lee —3A 74
Brigbrae Av. Bell —4E 127
Brigham Pl. G23 —1C 62
Brighton Pl. G51 —5H 81
Brighton St. G51 —5H 81
Brightside Av. Udd —2D 124
Brig o'Lea Ter. Neil —3C 130
Brigside Gdns. Ham —1C 154
Brisbane Ct. Giff —4B 118
Brisbane Rd. B'ton —4H 39
Brisbane St. G42 —6E 103
Brisbane St. Clyd —3H 41
Brisbane Ter. E Kil —4E 149
Britannia Way. Clyd —5D 42
Britannia Way. Renf —2E 79
Briton St. G51 —4H 81
Brittain Way. Moth —6H 111
Broadcroft. Kirk —4C 30
(in two parts)
Broadcroft Rd. Kirk —4C 30
Broadford St. G4 —1G 83
Broadholm St. G22 —3F 63
Broadleys Av. B'rig —4B 48
Broadlie Ct. Neil —2D 130
Broadlie Dri. G13 —3A 60
Broadlie Rd. Neil —2C 130
Broadloan. Renf —1E 79
Broadmeadow Ind. Est. Dumb —3F 17
Broadmoss Av. Newt M —5A 134
Broad Sq. Houses. Blan —1A 140
Broad St. G40 —6B 84
Broadway, The. Wis —5E 145
Broadwood Bus. Pk. Cumb —5B 34
Broadwood Dri. G44 —1F 119
Broadwood Roundabout. Cumb —5B 34
Brockburn Cres. G53 —5B 100
Brockburn Rd. G53 —3A 100
Brockburn Ter. G53 —5C 100
Brocklinn Pk. E Kil —4A 148
Brock Oval. G53 —1C 116
Brock Pl. G53 —6C 100
Brock Rd. G53 —1B 116
Brock Ter. G53 —1C 116
Brockville St. G32 —5H 85
Brodick Av. Moth —2D 142
Brodick Dri. E Kil —6F 137
Brodick Sq. B'rig —1E 65
Brodick St. G21 —2C 84
Brodie Pk. Av. Pais —3A 98
Brodie Pk. Cres. Pais —3H 97
Brodie Pk. Gdns. Pais —3A 98
Brodie Pl. E Kil —6F 137
Brodie Rd. G21 —2F 65
Brogan Cres. Moth —2D 142
Bromley Dri. Giff —6A 118
Bromley La. Giff —6A 118
Bron Way. Cumb —4A 36
Brookbank Ter. Carl —4G 165
Brooklands. E Kil —2C 148
Brooklands Av. Udd —6C 108
Brooklea Dri. Giff —2A 118
Brooklime Gdns. E Kil —5E 137
Brooklime Gro. E Kil —5E 137
Brooklyn Pl. Wis —5H 157
Brookside St. G40 —6C 84
Brook St. G40 —6B 84
Brook St. Clyd —3B 42
Broom Av. Ersk —2F 57
Broomburn Dri. Newt M —5F 133
Broom Cliff. Newt M —6F 133
Broom Cres. Barr —2C 114
Broom Cres. E Kil —6F 149
Broomcroft Rd. Newt M —3G 133
Broom Dri. Clyd —3C 42
Broom Dri. Lark —6A 156
Broomdyke Way. Pais —3H 77
Broomelton Rd. Ham —5A 160
Broomfauld Gdns. Dumb —3G 17
Broomfauld Ind. Est. Dumb —4F 17
Broomfield. Hous —2D 74
Broomfield Av. Camb —6F 105
Broomfield Av. Newt M —6F 133
Broomfield La. G21 —4B 64
Broomfield Pl. G21 —4B 64
Broomfield Rd. G21 —4B 64
Broomfield Rd. Giff —3G 133
Broomfield Rd. Lark —5F 161
Broomfield St. Air —4B 92
Broomfield Ter. Udd —4D 108
Broomfield Wlk. Kirk —5D 30
Broom Gdns. Kirk —1B 50
Broomhill Av. G11 —1F 81
Broomhill Av. Carm —5B 106
Broomhill Av. Newt M —5F 133
Broomhill Cres. Bell —4B 126
Broomhill Cres. Ersk —2F 57
Broomhill Dri. G11 —6F 61
Broomhill Dri. Dumb —2H 17
Broomhill Dri. Ruth —2D 120
Broomhill Farm M. Kirk —4E 31
Broomhill Gdns. G11 —6F 61
Broomhill Gdns. Newt M —5F 133
Broomhill Ga. Lark —3E 161
Broomhill La. G11 —6F 61
Broomhill Path. G11 —6F 61
Broomhill Pl. G11 —1F 81
Broomhill Rd. Lark —3D 160
Broomhill Ter. G11 —1F 81
Broomhill View. Lark —3C 160
Broomieknowe Dri. Ruth —1D 120
Broomieknowe Rd. Ruth —1D 120
Broomielaw. G1 —5E 83
Broomknoll St. Air —4A 92
Broomknowe. Cumb —2F 35
Broomknowes Av. Kirk —3E 51
Broomknowes Rd. G21 —5C 64
Broomlands Av. Ersk —1A 58
Broomlands Cres. Ersk —1A 58
Broomlands Gdns. Ersk —1H 57
Broomlands Rd. Cumb —5A 36
Broomlands St. Pais —1F 97
Broomlands Way. Ersk —1A 58
Broomlea Cres. Inch —2G 57
Broomlee Rd. Cumb —1H 55
Broomloan Ct. G51 —6G 81
Broomloan Pl. G51 —5G 81
Broomloan Rd. G51 —5G 81
Broompark Av. Blan —3A 140
Broompark Cir. G31 —4B 84
Broompark Cres. Air —1A 92
Broompark Dri. G31 —4B 84
Broompark Dri. Inch —2H 57
Broompark Dri. Newt M —4G 133
Broompark La. G31 —4B 84
Broompark Rd. Blan —2A 140
Broompark Rd. Wis —5D 144
Broompark St. G31 —4B 84
Broom Path. Bail —2F 107
Broom Pl. Bri W —4G 73
Broom Pl. Coat —2B 110
Broom Pl. Moth —3C 128
Broom Rd. G43 —2B 118
Broom Rd. Cumb —6D 14
Broom Rd. Newt M —3G 133
Broom Rd. E. Newt M —6G 133
Broomside Cres. Moth —5G 143
Broomside St. Moth —5G 143
Broomstone Av. Newt M —6F 133
Broom Ter. John —4F 95
Broomton Rd. G21 —2E 65
Broomvale Dri. Newt M —4F 133
Broomward Dri. John —2H 95
Brora Cres. Ham —3D 152
Brora Dri. Bear —3H 45
Brora Dri. Giff —5B 118
Brora Dri. Renf —6G 59
Brora Gdns. B'rig —6D 48
Brora Rd. B'rig —6D 48
Brora St. G33 —2F 85
Broughton. E Kil —6G 149
Broughton Dri. G23 —1C 62
Broughton Gdns. G23 —6D 46
Broughton Pl. Coat —2D 110
Broughton Pl. Ham —6E 141
Broughton Rd. G23 —1C 62
Brouster Ga. E Kil —2H 149
Brouster Hill. E Kil —2G 149
Brouster Pl. E Kil —2G 149
Brown Av. Clyd —1F 59
Brown Av. Dumb —1C 18
Brownhill Rd. G43 —3H 117
Brownhill View. Wis —3H 147
Brownieside Pl. Plain —1G 93
Brownieside Rd. Plain —1H 93
Brownlee Rd. Wis —1D 162
Brownlie St. G42 —5F 103
Brown Pl. Camb —1A 122
Brown Rd. Cumb —3H 35
Brownsburn Ind. Est. Air —6B 92
Brownsburn Rd. Air —1B 112
Brownsdale Rd. Ruth —6B 104
Brownsfield Cres. Inch —4F 57
Brownsfield Rd. Inch —4F 57
Brownshill Av. Coat —1B 110
Brownside Av. Barr —2C 114
Brownside Av. Camb —2G 121
Brownside Av. Pais —6G 97
Brownside Cres. Barr —2C 114
Brownside Dri. G13 —3H 59
Brownside Dri. Barr —2C 114
Brownside Gdns. Barr —2C 114
Brownside M. Camb —2G 121
Brownside Rd. Ruth —2F 121
Brown's La. Pais —1A 98
Brown St. G2 —4E 83 (6B 4)
Brown St. Carl —2F 165
Brown St. Coat —6C 90
Brown St. Ham —1A 154
Brown St. Lark —1E 161
Brown St. Moth —1H 143
Brown St. Newm —5E 147
Brown St. Pais —6G 77
Brown St. Renf —1D 78
Bruar Way. Newm —3D 146
(off Tiree Cres.)
Bruce Av. John —5E 95
Bruce Av. Moth —2F 143
Bruce Av. Pais —4C 78
Bruce Ct. Air —3E 93
Brucefield Pl. G34 —3B 88
Brucehill Rd. Dumb —3C 16
Bruce Ho. Cumb —2H 35
Bruce Loan. Wis —5A 158
Bruce Pl. E Kil —4H 149
Bruce Rd. G41 —1C 102
Bruce Rd. B'ton —3G 39
Bruce Rd. Moth —5B 128
Bruce Rd. Pais —5C 78
Bruce Rd. Renf —2C 78
Bruce's Loan. Lark —4G 161
(off Donaldson Rd.)
Bruce St. Bell —2D 126
Bruce St. Clyd —6D 42
Bruce St. Coat —3D 90
Bruce St. Dumb —5G 17
Bruce St. Plain —1G 93
Bruce Ter. Blan —6C 124
Bruce Ter. E Kil —4H 149
Brunel Way. E Kil —3H 149
Brunstane Rd. G34 —2G 87
Brunswick La. G1 —4G 83 (6F 5)
Brunswick St. G1 —4G 83 (6F 5)
Brunton St. G44 —2D 118
Brunton Ter. G44 —3E 119
Bruntsfield Av. G53 —4B 116
Bruntsfield Gdns. G53 —4B 116
Bryan St. Ham —4F 141
Bryce Gdns. Lark —1E 161
Bryce Pl. E Kil —5E 149
Brydson Pl. Lin —5H 75
Bryson Ct. Ham —4H 153
Bryson St. Clyd —6G 23
Buccleuch Av. G52 —3G 79
Buccleuch Av. Clar —2B 134
Buccleuch Dri. Bear —6E 25
Buccleuch La. G3 —2E 83 (2B 4)
Buccleuch St. G3 —2E 83 (2A 4)
Buchanan Av. B'ton —3H 39
Buchanan Bus. Pk. Step —3F 67
Buchanan Ct. G33 —3E 67
Buchanan Cres. B'rig —1E 65
Buchanan Cres. Ham —1F 153
Buchanan Dri. Bear —3G 45
Buchanan Dri. B'rig —1E 65
Buchanan Dri. Camb —1G 121
Buchanan Dri. Law —5E 159
Buchanan Dri. Lenz —4D 50
Buchanan Dri. Newt M —2E 133
Buchanan Dri. Ruth —1D 120
Buchanan Gro. Bail —6H 87
Buchanan Pl. Torr —4D 28
Buchanan St. G1 —4F 83 (6D 4)
Buchanan St. Air —4A 92
Buchanan St. Bail —1H 107
Buchanan St. Coat —5B 90
Buchanan St. Dumb —5G 17
Buchanan St. John —3E 95
Buchanan St. Miln —3H 25
BUCHANAN ST. STATION. G1 —3G 83 (4E 5)
Buchandyke Rd. E Kil —5B 138
Buchanen Gdns. G32 —3E 107
Buchan Ga. E Kil —6B 138
Buchan Ho. Cumb —2H 35
Buchan Rd. Moth —4A 128
Buchan St. Ham —3G 153
Buchan St. Wis —3H 145
Buchan Ter. Camb —4G 121
Buchlyvie Gdns. B'rig —2B 64
Buchlyvie Path. G34 —4H 87
Buchlyvie Rd. Pais —6G 79
Buchlyvie St. G34 —4H 87
Buckie. Ersk —4E 41
Buckie Wlk. Bell —1C 126
Buckingham Ct. Ham —5C 140
Buckingham Dri. G32 —5B 106
Buckingham Dri. Ruth —6F 105
Buckingham St. G12 —6B 62
Buckingham Ter. G12 —6B 62
Bucklaw Gdns. G52 —1C 100
Bucklaw Pl. G52 —1C 100
Bucklaw Ter. G52 —1C 100
Buckley St. G22 —3H 63
Bucksburn Rd. G21 —5E 65
Buckthorne Pl. G53 —4B 116
Buddon St. G40 —1E 105
Budhill Av. G32 —6B 86
Budshaw Av. Chap —3C 112
Bulldale Rd. G14 —4G 59
Bulldale St. G14 —3G 59
Bullionslaw Dri. Ruth —1F 121
Bulloch Av. Giff —5B 118
Bull Rd. Clar —3D 134
Bullwood Av. G53 —5H 99
Bullwood Ct. G53 —5A 100
Bullwood Dri. G53 —4H 99
Bullwood Gdns. G53 —4H 99
Bullwood Pl. G53 —4H 99
Bunbury Ter. E Kil —3F 149
Bunessan St. G52 —6F 81
Bunhouse Rd. G3 —2A 82
Burbank Highland Rd. Miln —3G 25
Burghead Dri. G51 —3E 81
Burghead Pl. G51 —3E 81
Burgher St. G31 —6E 85
Burgh Hall St. G11 —1H 81
Burgh La. G12 —6B 62
(off Cresswell St.)
Burleigh Rd. Both —4F 125
Burleigh St. G51 —3G 81
Burleigh St. Coat —2D 110
Burley Pl. E Kil —1B 148
Burlington Av. G12 —3H 61
Burmola St. G22 —5F 63
Burnacre Gdns. Udd —6C 108
Burnbank Braes. Carl —4F 165
Burnbank Cen. Ham —4E 141
Burnbank Dri. Barr —6E 115
Burnbank Gdns. G20 —1D 82
Burnbank Gdns. Ham —4E 141
(off Burnbank Rd.)
Burnbank Pl. G20 —1E 83
Burnbank Quad. Air —3H 91
Burnbank Rd. Ham —4E 141
Burnbank St. Air —3H 91
Burnbank St. Coat —3D 90
Burnbank Ter. G20 —1D 82
Burnbank Ter. Kils —2H 11
Burnblea Gdns. Ham —1A 154
Burnblea St. Ham —1H 153
Burn Brae. Clyd —1C 42
Burnbrae. Twe —2D 32
Burnbrae Av. Bear —6G 25
Burnbrae Av. Lin —6A 76
Burnbrae Av. Mood —5D 52
Burnbrae Dri. Lin —2B 96
Burnbrae Dri. Ruth —2F 121
Burnbrae Pl. E Kil —1E 149
Burnbrae Rd. Blan —2A 140
Burnbrae Rd. Kirk & Chry —5E 51
Burnbrae Rd. Lin I —1H 95
Burnbrae Rd. Waters —6H 31
Burnbrae St. G21 —5C 64
Burnbrae St. Clyd —5F 23
Burnbrae St. Lark —2D 160
Burncleugh Av. Camb —3A 122
Burn Cres. Chap —3D 112
Burn Cres. Moth —3A 128
Burncrooks Av. E Kil —1E 149
Burncrooks Ct. Clyd —1B 42
Burndyke Ct. G51 —4H 81
Burndyke Sq. G51 —4A 82
Burnet Rose Ct. E Kil —5E 137
Burnet Rose Gdns. E Kil —5E 137
Burnet Rose Pl. E Kil —5E 137
Burnett Rd. G33 —4E 87
Burnfield Av. T'bnk —3H 117
Burnfield Cotts. T'bnk —3H 117
Burnfield Dri. G43 —3H 117
Burnfield Gdns. Giff —3A 118
Burnfield Rd. G43 & T'bnk —2G 117
Burnfoot Cres. Pais —5G 97
Burnfoot Cres. Ruth —2F 121
Burnfoot Dri. G52 —6B 80
Burnfoot Rd. Air —3G 91
Burngreen. Kils —3H 11
Burngreen Ter. Cumb —6B 14
Burnhall Pl. Wis —2B 158
Burnhall Rd. Wis —1A 158
Burnhall St. Wis —2B 158
Burnham Rd. G14 —5A 60
Burnhaven. Ersk —5E 41
Burnhead Rd. G43 —2C 118
Burnhead Rd. Air —1C 92
Burnhead Rd. Cumb —3E 35
Burnhead Rd. Lark —2F 161
Burnhead St. Udd —5F 109
Burnhill Quad. Ruth —5B 104
Burnhill St. Ruth —5B 104
Burnhouse Av. Cumb —3D 34
Burnhouse Cres. Ham —2F 153
Burnhouse Rd. Ham —2F 153
Burnhouse St. G20 —3A 62
(in two parts)
Burniebrae. Air —3G 91
Burniebrae Rd. Chap —2E 113
Burn La. Moth —3A 128
Burnlea Cres. Hous —1A 74
Burnlip Rd. Air —5C 70
Burnmouth Ct. G33 —5F 87
Burnmouth Rd. G33 —5F 87
Burnock Pl. E Kil —4A 148
Burnpark Av. Udd —6B 108
Burn Pl. Camb —6G 105
Burn Rd. Carl —2F 165
Burns Av. B'ton —4H 39
Burns Ct. Kirk —4G 31
Burn's Cres. Air —5B 92
Burns Dri. John —5E 95
Burns Dri. Kirk —3G 31
Burns Gdns. Blan —6A 124
Burns Gro. T'bnk —5G 117
Burnside. Bear —6C 24
Burnside Av. Barr —3D 114
Burnside Av. Bell —3E 127
Burnside Av. Brkfld —6C 74
Burnside Av. C'bnk —3B 112
Burnside Av. Kirk —6B 30
Burnside Ct. Bear —1C 44
Burnside Ct. Coat —5B 90
(off Kirk St.)
Burnside Ct. Moth —5B 144
Burnside Ct. Ruth —2E 121
Burnside Cres. Blan —3C 140
Burnside Cres. Clyd —6D 22
Burnside Gdns. Clar —2B 134
Burnside Gdns. Mill P —3B 94
Burnside Ga. Ruth —2E 121
Burnside Gro. John —3E 95
Burnside Ind. Est. Kils —3G 11
Burnside La. Ham —1A 154
Burnside Pl. Dumb —5H 17
Burnside Pl. Lark —2F 161
Burnside Pl. Pais —4E 77
(in two parts)
Burnside Quad. Moth —2A 128
Burnside Rd. Coat —2E 91
Burnside Rd. Eld —4A 96
Burnside Rd. Giff —3H 133
Burnside Rd. Moth —3C 128
Burnside Rd. Ruth —2E 121
BURNSIDE STATION. Ruth —2E 121
Burnside St. Dumb —5H 17
Burnside St. Moth —5B 144
Burnside Ter. Dumb —4H 17
(off Burnside Pl.)
Burnside Tower. Moth —5A 144
(off Burnside Ct.)
Burnside View. Coat —6A 90
Burnside Wlk. Coat —6A 90
Burns La. Chap —2D 112
Burns Loan. Lark —1F 161
(off Carrick Pl.)
Burns Pk. E Kil —1A 150
Burns Rd. Chap —1D 112
Burns Rd. Cumb —3B 36
Burns Rd. Kirk —4F 31
Burns St. G4 —1F 83
Burns St. Clyd —4A 42
Burns St. Ham —1H 153
Burns Wlk. Bell —6D 110
Burns Way. Moth —3C 128
Burntbroom Dri. Bail —2F 107
Burntbroom Gdns. Bail —2F 107
Burntbroom Rd. Udd —3F 107
Burntbroom St. G33 —3D 86
Burn Ter. Camb —6G 105
Burn View. Cumb —2C 36
Burnwood Dri. Air —5G 93
Burra Gdns. B'rig —5F 49
Burrell Ct. G41 —3A 102
Burrell's La. G4 —4A 84 (5H 5)
Burrelton Rd. G43 —1D 118
Burton La. G42 —4E 103
Burton La. Carl —3E 165
Busby Rd. Bell —4B 126
Busby Rd. Crmck —3G 135
Busby Rd. Clar —1C 134
BUSBY STATION. Clar —4E 135
Bush Cres. Wis —1A 158
Bushelhead Rd. Brdwd —6E 165
Bushes Av. Pais —4H 97
Busheyhill St. Camb —2A 122
Bute. E Kil —2C 150
Bute Av. Moth —2E 143
Bute Av. Renf —2F 79
Bute Cres. Bear —5F 45
Bute Cres. Pais —6H 97
Bute Dri. John —4D 94
Bute Gdns. G12 —1B 82
Bute Gdns. Muir —3D 118
Bute La. G12 —1B 82
Bute La. Pais —4F 77
Bute Rd. Glas A —2G 77
Bute Rd. Kirk —5H 31
Bute St. Coat —1D 110
Bute St. Ham —3F 141
Bute Ter. Ruth —2C 120
Bute Ter. Udd —6F 109
Bute Tower. Camb —4G 121
Butler Wynd. Bell —2B 126
Butterbiggins Rd. G42 —2E 103
Butterburn Pk. St. Ham —2H 153
Butterfield Pl. G42 —2E 103
Buttermere. E Kil —6B 148
Byars Rd. Kirk —5B 30
Byrebush Rd. G53 —4C 100
Byres Av. Pais —5C 78
Byres Cres. Pais —5C 78

Byresknowe La. Moth —6B 128
Byres Rd. G11 & G12 —1A 82
Byres Rd. Eld —3B 96
Byres Rd. Moth —3E 129
Byrestone Av. Newt M —5A 134
Byron Ct. Both —5F 125
Byron St. G11 —1E 81
Byron St. Clyd —3C 42
Byshot Path. G22 —5H 63
Byshot St. G22 —5H 63

Cable Depot Rd. Clyd —5B 42
Cadder Ct. B'rig —2D 48
Cadder Gro. G20 —2C 62
Cadder Pl. G20 —2C 62
Cadder Rd. G23 —1C 62
Cadder Rd. B'rig —2D 48
Cadder Way. B'rig —2D 48
Cadell Gdns. E Kil —4D 138
Cadger's Sheuch. Kils —3D 12
Cadoc St. Camb —2B 122
Cadogan St. G2 —4E 83 (5B 4)
Cadzow Av. Giff —1H 133
Cadzow Bri. Ham —5A 142
Cadzow Cres. Coat —1A 110
Cadzow Dri. Bell —3F 127
Cadzow Dri. Camb —2H 121
Cadzow Grn. E Kil —1F 149
Cadzow Ho. Ham —4A 142
Cadzow Ind. Est. Ham —3H 153
Cadzow La. Ham —5A 142
Cadzow St. Ham —5A 142
Cadzow St. Lark —1E 161
Cadzow St. Moth —3F 143
Caird Dri. G11 —1H 81
Caird Gdns. Ham —4G 141
Caird Pk. Ham —4H 141
Caird St. Ham —4G 141
Caird Ter. Bear —6D 24
(off Grampian Way)
Cairhill Trad. Est. Air —5A 92
Cairn Av. Renf —2G 79
Cairnbairn Ct. Carl —2F 165
(off Carranbute Rd.)
Cairnban St. G51 —5D 80
Cairnbrook Ind. Est. G34 —3A 88
Cairnbrook Rd. G34 —3A 88
Cairn Ct. E Kil —5G 137
Cairn Ct. Moth —4H 143
Cairncraig St. G40 —1E 105
Cairndow Av. G44 —3D 118
Cairndow Av. La. G44 —3D 118
Cairndow Ct. G44 —3D 118
Cairn Dri. Lin —5H 75
Cairndyke Cres. Air —5A 92
Cairneymount Rd. Carl —3F 165
Cairney Pl. Newm —3H 147
Cairngorm Cres. Barr —6E 115
Cairngorm Cres. Bear —1B 44
Cairngorm Cres. Pais —4A 98
Cairngorm Cres. Wis —6F 145
Cairngorm Gdns. Cumb —4D 34
Cairngorm Rd. G43 —2A 118
Cairnhill Av. Air —6A 92
Cairnhill Cir. G52 —2H 99
Cairnhill Ct. Carl —3F 165
Cairnhill Cres. Coat —2F 111
Cairnhill Dri. G52 —2H 99
Cairnhill Pl. G52 —2H 99
Cairnhill Rd. Air —6H 91
Cairnhill Rd. Bear —6F 45
Cairnhope Av. Air —6H 91
Cairnlea Dri. G51 —5H 81
Cairnlea Gdns. Bell —4D 126
Cairnlea Rd. Miln —4E 25
Cairnmuir Rd. Clar —4C 136
Cairnmuir Rd. E Kil —3F 137
Cairnoch Hill. Cumb —3E 35
Cairn Pl. E Kil —5G 137
Cairnryan. E Kil —6F 137
Cairns Av. Camb —2B 122
Cairns Dri. Miln —3G 25
Cairnsmore Dri. Bear —6B 24
Cairnsmore Rd. G15 —5G 43
Cairns Rd. B'ton —3G 39
Cairns Rd. Camb —3B 122
Cairns St. Moth —3G 143
Cairn St. G21 —3B 64
Cairnswell Av. Camb —3C 122
Cairnswell Pl. Camb —3C 122
Cairntoul Ct. Cumb —4D 34
Cairntoul Dri. G14 —3A 60
Cairntoul Pl. G14 —4A 60
Cairn View. Air —5H 91
Cairn View. Kirk —6H 31
Cairnview Rd. Milt C —6B 8
Cairnwood Dri. Air —6H 91
Caithness Rd. E Kil —6D 138
Caithness St. G4 —1F 83
Caithness St. G20 —5D 62
Caithness St. Blan —3A 140
Cala Sona Ct. Wis —3E 157
Calcots Path. G34 —2A 88
Calcots Pl. G34 —2B 88
Caldarvan St. G22 —6F 63
Caldean Rd. Coat —6D 90
Calder Av. Barr —6E 115
Calder Av. Coat —1D 110
Calder Av. Newm —3E 147
Calderbank Rd. C'bnk —1A 112
Calderbank Ter. Moth —2H 143
Calderbank View. Bail —1A 108
Calderbraes Av. Udd —4C 108
Calder Ct. Coat —1D 110
(off Whifflet St.)
Caldercuilt Rd. G20 —1A 62
Calder Dri. Bell —3E 127
Calder Dri. Camb —2A 122
Calder Ga. B'rig —3B 48
Calderglen Av. Camb —4A 124
Calderglen Rd. E Kil —2C 150
Caldergrove. Moth —1G 143
Calderpark Av. Udd —3H 107
Calderpark Cres. Udd —3H 107
Calder Pl. Bail —1H 107
Calderrigg Pl. Air —4E 93
Calder Rd. Bell —2E 127
Calder Rd. Camb —2H 123
Calder Rd. Pais —6E 77
Calder Rd. Udd —4H 109
Calderside Rd. E Kil —3D 150
Calder St. G42 —3E 103
Calder St. Blan —1B 140
Calder St. C'bnk —3C 112
Calder St. Coat —1D 110
Calder Tower. E Kil —4B 150
Calder Tower. Moth —4G 143
Caldervale St. Air —1E 113
Calder View. Ham —3F 153
Calder View. Moth —2H 143
Calderview Av. Coat —1F 111
Calderwood Av. Bail —2G 107
Calderwood Dri. Bail —2G 107
Calderwood Dri. Blan —3B 140
Calderwood Gdns. Bail —2G 107
Calderwood Gdns. E Kil —6E 139
Calderwood Rd. G43 —1B 118
Calderwood Rd. E Kil —2A 150
Calderwood Rd. Ruth —6E 105
Calderwoon Sq. E Kil —6B 138
(off Pollok Pl.)
Caldwell Av. G13 —3A 60
Caldwell Av. Lin —6F 75
Caldwell Gro. Bell —5C 110
Caldwell Quad. Moth —4E 143
Caldwell Rd. Carl —5H 165
Caledonia Av. G5 —2G 103
Caledonia Av. Ruth —5D 104
Caledonia Ct. Pais —5H 77
Caledonia Dri. Bail —2H 107
Caledonia Dri. Moth —3E 129
Caledonian Av. Bell —3B 126
Caledonian Ct. E Kil —3G 149
Caledonian Cres. G12 —1C 82
(off Otago St.)
Caledonian Rd. Lark —2E 161
Caledonian Rd. Wis —2G 157
Caledonia Rd. G5 —1G 103
Caledonia Rd. Bail —2G 107
Caledonia St. G5 —2G 103
Caledonia St. Clyd —4B 42
Caledonia St. Pais —6H 77
Caledonia Ter. Cumb —4C 16
Caledonia Way. Glas A —2H 77
Caledonia Way E. Glas A —2A 78
Caledonia Way W. Glas A —2H 77
Caledon La. G12 —1A 82
(off Highburgh Rd.)
Caledon St. G12 —1A 82
Caley Brae. Udd —1D 124
Calfhill Rd. G53 —2B 100
Calfmuir Rd. Kirk —6G 31
Calgary Pk. E Kil —3F 149
Calgary Pl. E Kil —3F 149
Calgary St. G4 —2G 83 (2F 5)
Callaghan Wynd. Blan —6H 123
Callander Ct. Cumb —1H 35
Callander Rd. Chap —4D 112
Callander Rd. Cumb —1H 35
Callander St. G20 —6E 63
Callieburn Rd. B'rig —1C 64
Callon St. Air —4A 92
Cally Av. G15 —4A 44
Calside. Pais —3H 97
Calside Av. Pais —2H 97
Calton Entry. G40 —5A 84
(off Stevenson St.)
Calvay Cres. G33 —4D 86
Calvay Rd. G33 —4D 86
Cambell Pl. E Kil —4G 149
Cambourne Rd. Chry —4D 52
Cambridge Av. Clyd —4D 42
Cambridge Rd. Renf —1E 79
Cambridge St. G3 & G2 —3F 83
Camburn St. G32 —6H 85
Cambusdoon Rd. G33 —1C 86
Cambuskenneth Gdns. G32 —6D 86
Cambuskenneth Pl. G33 —1C 86
Cambuslang Bri. Camb —6A 106
Cambuslang Ind. Pk. G32 —5A 106
Cambuslang Investment Pk. G32 —5A 106
Cambuslang Rd. G32 —5H 105
Cambuslang Rd. Camb —5G 105
Cambuslang Rd. Ruth —4D 104
CAMBUSLANG STATION. Camb —1H 121
Cambusmore Pl. G33 —1C 86
Cambusnethan St. Wis —5C 146
Cambus Pl. G33 —1C 86
Camden St. G5 —1G 103
Camelon Cres. Blan —2B 140
Camelon St. G32 —5H 85
Cameron Av. B'ton —3H 39
Cameron Ct. Air —3E 93
Cameron Ct. Ruth —6C 104
Cameron Cres. Crmck —2A 136
Cameron Cres. Ham —6F 141
Cameron Dri. Bear —4G 45
Cameron Dri. Newt M —2E 133
Cameron Dri. Udd —5E 109
Cameronian Dri. Carl —4G 165
Cameronian Pl. Bell —4B 126
Cameronian Way. Lark —4G 161
Cameron Path. Lark —4G 161
(off Donaldson Rd.)
Cameron Rd. Carl —5H 165
Cameron Sq. Clyd —1E 43
Cameron St. G52 —4G 79
Cameron St. Coat —3D 90
Cameron St. Moth —3F 143
Camlachie St. G31 —6D 84
Campbell Av. B'ton —3H 39
Campbell Av. Dumb —1C 18
Campbell Av. Miln —4G 25
Campbell Cres. Both —3E 125
Campbell Cres. Newt M —3E 133
Campbell Dri. Barr —5E 115
Campbell Dri. Bear —2D 44
Campbell Dri. Dumb —1C 18
Campbell Ho. Cumb —4G 35
Campbell La. Ham —6A 142
Campbell Pl. Torr —4D 28
Campbell St. G20 —2B 62
Campbell St. Bell —2C 126
Campbell St. Ham —6A 142
Campbell St. John —3F 95
Campbell St. Renf —5F 59
Campbell St. Wis —6H 145
Campbell Ter. Dumb —1C 18
Camphill. Pais —2H 97
Camphill Av. G41 —5C 102
Camphill Av. Kirk —5C 30
Camphill Gdns. B'ton —4A 40
Camphill Ho. G41 —4D 102
Campion Rd. Moth —1G 143
Camp Rd. Bail —6H 87
Camp Rd. Moth —5G 143
Camp Rd. Ruth —3B 104
Camps Cres. Renf —1G 79
Campside Gdns. Clar —1A 134
Campsie Av. Barr —6E 115
Campsie Ct. Coat —2E 111
Campsie Cres. Air —3H 91
Campsie Cres. Kirk —1C 50
Campsie Dri. Abb —1A 78
Campsie Dri. Bear —6D 24
Campsie Dri. Miln —3H 25
Campsie Dri. Pais —5H 97
Campsie Dri. Renf —3C 78
Campsie Pl. Chry —1A 68
Campsie Rd. Kirk —4B 30
Campsie Rd. Milt C —4H 7
Campsie Rd. Torr —4E 29
Campsie Rd. Wis —5E 145
Campsie St. G21 —4B 64
Campsie View. G33 —5D 66
Campsie View. Bail —6D 88
Campsie View. Chry —1A 68
Campsie View. Cumb —2B 36
Campsie View. Ham —1D 152
Campsie View. Kirk —5A 30
Campsie View. Udd —5E 109
Campston Pl. G33 —2B 86
Camp St. Moth —4G 143
Camstradden Dri. E. Bear —3C 44
Camstradden Dri. W. Bear —3C 44
Camus Pl. G15 —3H 43
Canal Av. John —3G 95
Canal Gdns. Eld —2B 96
Canal La. Kirk —4D 30
Canal Rd. John —3F 95
Canal St. G4 —2G 83 (1F 5)
Canal St. Clyd —1D 58
Canal St. Eld —2B 96
Canal St. John —2G 95
Canal St. Kirk —4D 30
Canal St. Pais —1H 97
Canal St. Renf —5F 59
Canal Ter. Pais —1A 98
Canberra Av. Clyd —3H 41
Canberra Ct. Giff —4C 118
Canberra Dri. E Kil —3E 149
Candermill & Marlage Rd. Ashg —6B 162
Canderrigg. B'rig —3C 48
Cander St. Lark —5F 101
Candimilne Ct. Carl —4H 165
Candleriggs. G1 —4H 83 (6G 5)
Candren Rd. Lin —6B 76
Candren Rd. Pais —6E 77
Caneluk Av. Carl —5H 165
Canmore Pl. G31 —1F 105
Canmore St. G31 —1F 105
Cannerton Cres. Milt C —6B 8
Cannich Dri. Pais —4D 98
Cannich Pl. Newm —3D 146
Canniesburn Rd. Bear —5C 44
Canniesburn Sq. Bear —5F 45
Canniesburn Toll. Bear —4F 45
Canniesbury Rd. Bear —4D 44
Canonbie St. G34 —2B 88
Canon Ct. Moth —5D 128
Canongate. E Kil —5D 138
Canterbury. E Kil —5D 148
Cantieslaw Dri. E Kil —6A 138
Canton Way. G51 —4A 82
Canyon Rd. Wis —1D 156
Capel Av. Newt M —3F 133
Capel Gro. E Kil —6B 138
Capelridge Dri. E Kil —1B 150
Capelrig Dri. Newt M —1D 132
Capelrig La. Newt M —3D 132
Capelrig Rd. Newt M —1D 132
Capelrig St. T'bnk —3F 117
Caplaw Pl. Wis —3F 157
Caplaw Rd. Pais —6G 97
Caplaw Tower. Wis —3F 157
Caplethill Rd. Pais —6A 98
Caprington St. G33 —2A 86
Cara Dri. G51 —3E 81
Caravelle Way. Renf —2F 79
Carbarns. Wis —2D 156
Carbarns E. Wis —2D 156
Carbarns Rd. Wis —3C 156
Carbarns W. Wis —2D 156
Carberry Rd. G41 —3B 102
Carbeth Rd. Miln —4F 25
Carbeth St. G22 —5F 63
Carbisdale St. G22 —4A 64
Carbost St. G23 —6B 46
Carbrach Loan. Newm —3D 146
(off Tiree Cres.)
Carbrain Ind. Est. Cumb —4B 36
Carbrook St. G21 —2C 84
Carbrook St. Pais —1G 97
Cardarrach St. G21 —5C 64
Cardean Rd. Bell —1G 127
Cardell Av. Pais —2E 97
Cardell Cres. Chap —3D 112
Cardell Dri. Pais —2E 97
Cardell Rd. Pais —2E 97
Cardonald Dri. G52 —1A 100
Cardonald Gdns. G52 —1B 100
Cardonald Pk. G52 —4B 80
Cardonald Pl. Rd. G52 —1B 100
CARDONALD STATION. G52 —5D 80
Cardowan Dri. Cumb —4A 34
Cardowan Dri. Step —4D 66
Cardowan Pk. Udd —4F 109
Cardowan Rd. G32 —5H 85
Cardowan Rd. Step —3E 67
Cardow Rd. G21 —5E 65
Cardrona St. G33 —6B 66
Cardross Ct. G31 —4B 84
Cardross Rd. Dumb —2A 16
Cardross St. G31 —4B 84
Cardwell St. G41 —1E 103
Cardyke St. G21 —5C 64
Careston Pl. B'rig —6F 49
Carey Gdns. Cle —6H 129
Carfin Ind. Est. Carf —5B 128
Carfin Mill Rd. Moth —6C 128
Carfin Rd. Moth —5D 128
Carfin Rd. Wis —5C 144
CARFIN STATION. Carf —5D 128
Carfin St. G42 —3F 103
Carfin St. Coat —1D 110
Carfin St. Moth —4A 128
Carfrae St. G3 —3A 82
Cargill Sq. B'rig —1E 65
Cargill St. G31 —1G 105
Carham Cres. G52 —6C 80
Carham Dri. G52 —6C 80
Caribou Grn. E Kil —3D 148
Carillon Rd. G51 —6A 82
Carinthia Sq. Clyd —5D 42
Carisbrooke Cres. B'rig —3D 48
Carlaverock Rd. G43 —1B 118
Carleith Av. Clyd —1B 42
Carleith Quad. G51 —4D 80
Carleith Ter. Clyd —1B 42
Carleston St. G21 —5B 64
Carleton Ct. Giff —3A 118
Carleton Dri. Giff —3A 118
Carleton Ga. Giff —3A 118
Carlibar Av. G13 —3H 59
Carlibar Dri. Barr —4E 115
Carlibar Gdns. Barr —4E 115
Carlibar Rd. Barr —4D 114
Carlile Pl. Pais —5A 78
Carlin La. Carl —4H 165
Carlisle La. Air —4C 92
Carlisle Rd. Air —5C 92
Carlisle Rd. Ham —6B 142
Carlisle St. G21 —6H 63
Carlock Wlk. G32 —5C 86
Carlouk La. Carl —4H 165
Carlowrie Av. Blan —5A 124
Carlton Ct. G5 —5F 83
Carlton Pl. G5 —5F 83
CARLUKE STATION. Carl —4D 164
Carlyle Av. G52 —3H 79
Carlyle Dri. E Kil —1A 150
Carlyle Ter. E Kil —1B 150
Carlyle Ter. Ruth —4D 104
Carmaben Rd. G33 —3E 87
Carman View. Dumb —1G 17
Carment Dri. G41 —5B 102
Carmichael Path. Glenb —3G 69
(off Oval, The)
Carmichael Pl. G42 —6D 102
Carmichael St. G51 —5H 81
Carmichael St. Law —6D 158
Carmichael Way. Law —6D 158
Carmunnock By-Pass. Clar —6G 119
Carmunnock Rd. G44 & G45 —6F 103
Carmunnock Rd. Crmck —4C 136
Carmunnock Rd. Clar —4E 135
Carmunnock Rd. E Kil —1F 149
Carmyle Av. G32 —3B 106
CARMYLE STATION. Carm —4B 106
Carna Dri. G44 —2G 119
Carnarvon St. G3 —2D 82
Carnbooth Ct. G45 —5B 120
Carnbroe Rd. Bell —6D 110
Carnbroe Rd. Coat —1F 111
Carneddans Rd. Miln —1C 24
Carnegie Pl. E Kil —3F 149
Carnegie Rd. G52 —4A 80
Carney Hill. E Kil —3F 149
Carnoch St. G23 —6B 46
Carnock Cres. Barr —6D 114
Carnock Gdns. Miln —3E 25
Carnock Rd. G53 —5C 100
Carnoustie Ct. Both —5D 124
Carnoustie Cres. B'rig —6E 49
Carnoustie Cres. E Kil —5C 148
Carnoustie Pl. G5 —6D 82
Carnoustie Pl. Bell —6C 110
Carnoustie St. G5 —6D 82
Carnoustie Way. Cumb —5H 13
Carntynehall Rd. G32 —4H 85
Carntyne Ind. Est. G32 —5G 85
Carntyne Path. G32 —4F 85
Carntyne Pl. G32 —4F 85
Carntyne Rd. G31 & G32 —5E 85
CARNTYNE STATION. G32 —5H 85
Carnwadric Rd. T'bnk —3E 117
Carnwath Av. G43 —1D 118
Carnwath Rd. Carl —4F 165
Caroline St. G31 —6G 85
Carolside Av. Clar —2C 134
Carolside Dri. G15 —4B 44
Carolside Gdns. Clar —2C 134
Carousel Cres. Wis —6A 146
Carradale Cres. Cumb —5B 34
Carradale Gdns. B'rig —6E 49
Carradale Gdns. Carl —5G 165
Carradale Pl. Lin —5G 75
Carradale St. Coat —4B 90
(in two parts)
Carranbute Rd. Carl —2F 165
Carrbridge Dri. G20 —3B 62
Carresbrook Av. Kirk —1G 51
Carriagehill Av. Pais —3A 98
Carriagehill Dri. Pais —4A 98
Carrickarden Rd. Bear —4F 45
Carrick Ct. Kirk —3G 31
Carrick Cres. Giff —6A 118
Carrick Cres. Wis —5G 145
Carrick Dri. G32 —1E 107
Carrick Dri. Coat —4H 89
Carrick Dri. Ruth —2C 120
Carrick Gdns. Bell —5C 110
Carrick Gdns. Blan —3B 140
Carrick Gdns. Carl —5G 165
Carrick Gdns. Ham —1C 152
Carrick Gro. G32 —1E 107
Carrick Pl. Bell —6D 110
Carrick Pl. Coat —4H 89
Carrick Pl. Glenb —3A 70
Carrick Pl. Lark —1F 161
Carrick Rd. B'rig —6E 49
Carrick Rd. B'ton —5A 40
Carrick Rd. Cumb —1A 36
Carrick Rd. E Kil —6H 137
Carrick Rd. Ruth —2B 120
Carrickstone Rd. Cumb —6G 13
Carrickstone Roundabout. Cumb —6G 13
Carrickstone View. Cumb —6H 13
Carrick St. G2 —4E 83 (6B 4)
Carrick St. Lark —3G 161
Carrick Ter. Dumb —3B 16
Carrick View. Glenb —3A 70
Carrick Way. Both —4E 125
Carriden Path. G33 —4E 87
(off Langbar Cres.)
Carrington St. G4 —1D 82
Carroglen Gdns. G32 —6D 86
Carroglen Gro. G32 —6D 86
Carron Ct. Camb —2D 122
Carron Ct. Ham —2F 153
Carron Cres. G22 —4H 63
Carron Cres. Bear —4C 44
Carron Cres. Lenz —3E 51
Carron Dri. B'ton —5A 40
Carron Ho. Cumb —3H 35
(off Cumbernauld Cen., The)
Carron Pl. G22 —4A 64
Carron Pl. Coat —2H 89
Carron Pl. E Kil —6H 149
Carron St. G22 —4A 64
Carron St. Wis —2H 157
Carron Way. Cumb —3H 35
(off Cumbernauld Cen., The)
Carron Way. Moth —3C 128
Carron Way. Pais —4C 78
Carrour Gdns. B'rig —5B 48
Carrow Cres. B'rig —6D 48
Carruth Rd. Bri W —3E 73

Carsaig Dri. G52 —6E 81
Carsaig Loan. Glenb —3G 69
Carscallan Rd. Ham —5H 153
Carsegreen Av. Pais —6F 97
Carsemeadow. Bri W —1A 72
Carse View Dri. Bear —1G 45
Carstairs St. G40 —3B 104
Carswell Gdns. G41 —3C 102
Carswell Pl. Newt M —4B 132
Cartcraigs Rd. G43 —1H 117
Carter Dri. Udd —4E 125
Cartha Cres. Pais —2C 98
Cartha St. G41 —6C 102
Cartland Av. Carl —5F 165
Cart La. Pais —5A 78
Cartsbridge Rd. Clar —3C 134
Cartside Av. Inch —5F 57
Cartside Av. John —4D 94
Cartside Dri. Clar —3E 135
Cartside Pl. Clar —4D 134
Cartside Quad. G42 —6E 103
Cartside Rd. Clar —4D 134
Cartside St. G42 —6D 102
Cart St. Clyd —1D 58
Cartvale La. Pais —5A 78
Cartvale Rd. G42 —6D 102
Cartview Ct. Clar —3D 134
Caskie Dri. Blan —6C 124
Cassells St. Moth —1G 143
Cassels Gro. Moth —6E 127
Cassels St. Carl —4F 165
Cassels St. Moth —1G 143
Cassiltoun Gdns. G45 —5H 119
Cassley Av. Renf —1H 79
Castburn Rd. Cumb —5F 15
Castle Av. Eld —4H 95
Castle Av. Moth —1B 128
Castle Av. Udd —3C 124
Castle Bank Ct. G13 —3E 61
Castlebank Cres. G11 —2G 81
Castle Bank Gdns. G13 —3E 61
Castlebank St. G11 —2F 81
Castle Bank Vs. G13 —3E 61
Castlebay Dri. G22 —6G 47
Castlebay Pl. G22 —1G 63
Castlebay St. G22 —1G 63
Castlebrae. Dumb —2C 16
Castlecary Rd. C'cry —5C 14
Castle Chimmins Av. Camb —3D 122
Castle Chimmins Rd. Camb —4D 122
Castle Ct. C'cry —3F 15
Castle Ct. Kirk —5D 30
Castle Cres. B'ton —5H 39
Castlecroft Gdns. Udd —2D 124
Castle Dri. Moth —1B 128
Castlefern Rd. Ruth —4D 120
Castlefield Gdns. E Kil —6D 148
Castle Gait. Pais —2H 97
Castle Gdns. Chry —5D 52
Castle Gdns. Pais —2E 97
Castle Ga. Newt M —6G 133
Castle Ga. Udd —2C 124
Castleglen Rd. E Kil —5B 136
Castlegreen Cres. Dumb —5H 17
Castlegreen La. Dumb —5G 17
Castlegreen St. Dumb —5G 17
Castle Gro. Kils —1G 11
Castlehill Cres. Bank —1E 15
Castlehill Cres. Ham —1B 154
Castlehill Cres. Ham —2F 155 (Allanton)
Castlehill Cres. Law —1A 164
Castlehill Cres. Renf —5F 59
Castlehill Dri. Newt M —5F 133
Castlehill Grn. E Kil —5B 136
Castlehill Ind. Est. Carl —1E 165
Castlehill Quad. Dumb —2C 16
Castlehill Rd. Bear —1B 44
Castlehill Rd. Carl —1E 165
Castlehill Rd. Dumb —2C 16
Castlehill Rd. Over —3F 157
Castlehill View. Kils —1G 11
Castlelaw Gdns. G32 —5B 86
Castlelaw St. G32 —5B 86
Castle Mains Rd. Miln —3D 24
Castlemilk Arc. G45 —4A 120
Castlemilk Cres. G44 —2A 120
Castlemilk Dri. G45 —4A 120
Castlemilk Rd. G44 —6A 104
Castlemount Av. Newt M —6F 133
Castle Pl. Udd —1C 124
Castle Quad. Air —4D 92
Castle Rd. Air —4D 92
Castle Rd. Bri W —2F 73
Castle Rd. Dumb —5G 17
Castle Rd. Eld —2A 96
Castle Rd. Newt M —5C 132
Castle Sq. Clyd —4A 42
Castle St. G4 —3A 84
Castle St. G11 —2A 82
Castle St. Bail —2G 107
Castle St. Chap —3D 112
Castle St. Clyd —4A 42
Castle St. Dumb —4F 17
Castle St. Ham —5B 142
Castle St. Pais —1H 97
Castle St. Ruth —5C 104
Castle Ter. Bri W —4G 73 (off Kilbarchan Rd.)
Castleton Av. B'rig —2A 64
Castleton Av. Newt M —6F 133
Castleton Ct. G45 —5B 120
Castleton Ct. Newt M —6F 133
Castleton Cres. Newt M —6F 133
Castleton Dri. Newt M —6F 133
Castleton Gro. Newt M —6F 133
Castleview. Cam G —1B 6
Castle View. Clyd —4D 42
Castleview. Cumb —3E 15
Castle View. Wis —3E 147
Castleview Av. Pais —6E 97
Castleview Dri. Pais —6E 97
Castleview Pl. Pais —6E 97
Castleview Ter. Hag —1G 15
Castle Way. Bail —6D 88
Castle Way. Cumb —1C 36
Castle Wynd. Both —5F 125
Cathay St. G22 —1G 63
Cathburn Rd. Wis —5F 147
Cathcart Cres. Pais —2C 98
Cathcart Pl. Ruth —6B 104
Cathcart Rd. G42 —6E 103
Cathcart Rd. Ruth —6B 104
CATHCART STATION. G44 —1E 119
Cathedral Sq. G4 —4A 84
Cathedral St. G1 & G4 —3G 83 (4E 5)
Catherine St. Kirk —5C 30
Catherine St. Moth —5G 143
Catherines Wlk. Blan —3A 140
Catherine Way. Moth —4H 127
Cathkin Av. Camb —1G 121
Cathkin Av. Ruth —6E 105
Cathkin By-Pass. Ruth —4F 121
Cathkin Ct. G45 —5B 120
Cathkin Gdns. Udd —4C 108
Cathkin Pl. Camb —1G 121
Cathkin Rd. G42 —6D 102
Cathkin Rd. Clar & Ruth —1A 136
Cathkin Rd. Udd —4C 108
Cathkin View. Carm —5B 106
Cathkinview Pl. G42 —6F 103
Cathkinview Rd. G42 —6E 103
Catrine. E Kil —1F 149
Catrine Cres. Moth —6A 144
Catrine St. Lark —3G 161
Catriona Way. Moth —2B 128
Catter Gdns. Miln —2E 25
Cauldstream Pl. Miln —4E 25
Causewayside Cres. G32 —2A 106
Causewayside St. G32 —3A 106
Causeyside St. Pais —2A 98 (in two parts)
Causeystanes. Blan —2A 140 (off Burnbrae Rd.)
Cavendish Ct. G5 —1F 103
Cavendish Dri. Newt M —3F 133
Cavendish Pl. G5 —1F 103
Cavendish St. G5 —1F 103
Cavin Dri. G45 —3A 120
Cavin Rd. G45 —3A 120
Cawdor Cres. B'ton —5H 39
Cawdor Way. E Kil —6F 137
Cayton Gdns. Bail —1F 107
Cecil St. G12 —6D 62
Cecil St. Clar —2C 134
Cecil St. Coat —6C 90
Cedar Av. Clyd —3H 41
Cedar Av. John —5F 95
Cedar Av. Udd —5F 109
Cedar Ct. G20 —1E 83
Cedar Ct. E Kil —6E 149
Cedar Ct. Kilb —2A 94
Cedar Cres. Ham —2A 154
Cedar Dri. E Kil —6E 149
Cedar Dri. Lenz —2C 50
Cedar Dri. Udd —5G 109
Cedar Gdns. Law —5D 158
Cedar Gdns. N'hill —3C 128
Cedar Gdns. Ruth —3E 121
Cedar La. Air —4C 92
Cedar La. Moth —3B 128
Cedar Pl. Barr —6E 115
Cedar Pl. Blan —6A 124
Cedar Pl. E Kil —6E 149
Cedar Rd. Bank —1E 15
Cedar Rd. B'rig —1D 64
Cedar Rd. Cumb —2D 36
Cedar Rd. Milt C —6C 8
Cedar St. G20 —1E 83
Cedar Wlk. B'rig —1D 64
Cedarwood Av. Newt M —5F 133
Cedric Pl. G13 —2D 60
Cedric Rd. G13 —2D 60
Celtic St. G20 —1A 62
Cemetery Rd. G52 —1D 100
Cemetery Rd. Blan —3A 140
Centenary Av. Air —4F 91
Centenary Ct. Clyd —6D 42
Centenary Gdns. Coat —6C 90
Centenary Gdns. Ham —1A 154
Centenary Quad. Moth —2A 128
Central Av. G11 —1F 81
Central Av. Blan —4C 140
Central Av. Camb —1H 121
Central Av. Clyd B —5C 42
Central Av. Holy —2H 127
Central Av. Moth —5A 128
Central Av. Mt V —2D 106
Central Av. Udd —1G 125
Central Cres. Ashg —5B 162
Central Path. G32 —2E 107
Central Rd. Pais —6A 78
CENTRAL STATION. G2 —4F 83
Central Way. Cumb —5G 35
Central Way. Pais —6A 78
Centre Pk. Ct. Coat —5C 90
Centre Roundabout, The. E Kil —2H 149
Centre St. G5 —6E 83
Centre St. Chap —3D 112
Centre St. Glenb —3G 69
Centre, The. Barr —5D 114
Ceres Gdns. B'rig —6F 49
Cessnock Pl. Camb —2D 122
CESSNOCK STATION. G51 —5A 82
Cessnock St. G51 —5A 82
Chalmers Ct. G40 —5A 84 (off Chalmers St.)
Chalmers Ct. Udd —1D 124
Chalmers Cres. E Kil —4H 149
Chalmers Dri. E Kil —4H 149
Chalmers Ga. G40 —5A 84 (off Claythorn St.)
Chalmers Pl. G40 —5A 84 (off Claythorn St.)
Chalmers St. G40 —5A 84
Chalmers St. Clyd —6D 42
Chamberlain La. G13 —4E 61
Chamberlain Rd. G13 —3E 61
Chancellor St. G11 —1H 81
Chantinghall Rd. Ham —6F 141
Chantinghall Ter. Ham —6F 141
Chantree Ct. Moth —4C 128
Chapel Ct. Ruth —5B 104
Chapelcross Av. Air —2A 92
Chapelhall Ind. Est. Chap —1D 112
Chapelhill Rd. Pais —3C 98
Chapelknowe Rd. Moth —6C 128
Chapel La. Hous —1B 74
Chapel Rd. Clyd —1C 42
Chapel Rd. Wis —2F 159
Chapelside Av. Air —3A 92
Chapelside Rd. E Kil —3A 138
Chapel St. G20 —4C 62
Chapel St. Air —3A 92
Chapel St. Carl —3F 165
Chapel St. Cle —6H 129
Chapel St. Len —3F 7
Chapel St. Ruth —5B 104
Chapel St. Ind. Est. G20 —4C 62
Chapelton Av. Bear —3F 45
Chapelton Av. Dumb —2G 17
Chapelton Gdns. Bear —3F 45
Chapelton Gdns. Dumb —2G 17
Chapelton Rd. Cumb —1E 55
Chapelton St. G22 —3F 63
Chaplet Av. G13 —1C 60
Chapman Av. Glenb —3G 69
Chapman St. G42 —3E 103
Chappell St. Barr —4D 114
Charing Cross. Lark —2E 161
Charing Cross La. G3 —3D 82 (off Granville St.)
CHARING CROSS STATION. G2 —3E 83
Charles Av. Renf —5F 59
Charles Cres. Carl —4H 165
Charles Cres. Lenz —4D 50
Charleson Row. Kils —2B 34
Charles Path. Chap —4D 112
Charles Quad. Moth —2A 128
Charles St. G21 —2A 84
Charles St. Kils —2H 11
Charles St. Wis —5C 144
Charlotte Av. Torr —5D 28
Charlotte Path. Lark —3E 161
Charlotte Pl. Pais —3A 98
Charlotte St. G1 —5H 83
Charlotte St. Dumb —3D 16
Chartwell Rd. B'ton —4H 39
Chassels St. Coat —3C 90
Chateau Gro. Ham —1C 154
Chatelherault Av. Camb —2G 121
Chatelherault Cres. Ham —2A 154
Chatelherault Wlk. Ham —2A 154
Chatham. E Kil —4E 149
Chatton St. G23 —6B 46
Cheapside St. G3 —4D 82
Chelmsford Dri. G12 —4H 61
Cherry Bank. Kirk —2B 50
Cherrybank Rd. G43 —1D 118
Cherrybank Wlk. Air —3F 91
Cherry Cres. Clyd —3C 42
Cherryhill View. Lark —2D 160
Cherry La. Bank —1E 15
Cherry Pl. B'rig —1D 64
Cherry Pl. John —4G 95
Cherry Pl. Milt C —1B 30
Cherry Pl. Moth —2B 128
Cherry Pl. Udd —6H 109
Cherry Tree Cres. Lark —6A 156
Cherry Wlk. Moth —6G 143
Cherrywood Rd. Eld —3A 96
Chesterfield Av. G12 —4G 61
Chesters Cres. Moth —1E 143
Chesters Pl. Ruth —6B 104
Chesters Rd. Bear —3C 44
Chester St. G32 —6A 86
Chestnut Av. B'ton —2F 39
Chestnut Av. Cumb —6E 15
Chestnut Ct. Cumb —6E 15
Chestnut Ct. Milt C —6B 8
Chestnut Cres. E Kil —5E 149
Chestnut Cres. Ham —1A 154
Chestnut Cres. Udd —6H 109
Chestnut Dri. Clyd —2B 42
Chestnut Dri. Kirk —1B 50
Chestnut Gro. Blan —1A 140
Chestnut Gro. Carl —4E 165
Chestnut Gro. Glenb —3G 69
Chestnut Gro. Lark —6A 156
Chestnut Gro. Moth —4F 143
Chestnut La. Miln —4E 25
Chestnut Pl. Cumb —6E 15
Chestnut Pl. John —5G 95
Chestnut St. G22 —4H 63
Cheviot Av. Barr —5E 115
Cheviot Ct. Air —1B 92
Cheviot Ct. Coat —2E 111
Cheviot Cres. Wis —5F 145
Cheviot Dri. Newt M —6C 132
Cheviot Gdns. Bear —6D 24
Cheviot Rd. G43 —2A 118
Cheviot Rd. Ham —1B 154
Cheviot Rd. Lark —3G 161
Cheviot Rd. Pais —4A 98
Cheviot St. Blan —2A 140
Chillin Pl. Lark —2G 161
Chirnside Ct. Blan —4C 140
Chirnside Pl. G52 —5A 80
Chirnside Rd. G52 —5A 80
Chisholm Av. B'ton —4A 40
Chisholm Dri. Newt M —3E 133
Chisholm St. G1 —5H 83
Chisholm St. Coat —3D 90
Chrighton Grn. Udd —5E 109
Chriss Av. Ham —4H 153
Christchurch Pl. E Kil —4D 148
Christian St. G43 —5A 102
Christie La. Pais —6A 78
Christie Pl. Camb —2B 122
Christie St. Bell —2F 127
Christie St. Pais —6B 78
Christopher St. G21 —2C 84
Chryston Rd. Chry —1B 68
Chryston Rd. Kirk —1H 51
Chryston Valley Bus. Cen. Bail —1A 68
Chuckie La. Brkfld —5C 74
Church Av. G33 —3D 66
Church Av. Newm —5D 146
Church Av. Ruth —2E 121
Church Ct. Dumb —4F 17
Church Cres. Air —2E 93
Church Cres. Ham —5H 153
Church Dri. Kirk —1C 50
Church Hill. Pais —6A 78
Churchill Av. E Kil —2H 149
Churchill Av. John —6C 94
Churchill Cres. Both —4F 125
Churchill Dri. G11 —5F 61
Churchill Dri. B'ton —4H 39
Churchill Dri. Kilb —2A 94
Churchill Pl. Barr —2E 131
Churchill Way. B'rig —6B 48
Church La. Carl —4F 165
Church La. Coat —4C 90
Church La. Kils —3H 11 (off Church St.)
Church Pl. Old K —1E 41
Church Rd. Bri W —4G 73
Church Rd. Clar —3D 134
Church Rd. Muirh —2A 68
Church Rd. Quar H —1A 72
Church Rd. Wis —2H 147
Church St. G11 —1A 82
Church St. Bail —1A 108
Church St. Blan —2C 140
Church St. Clyd —4D 42
Church St. Coat —4C 90
Church St. Dumb —4F 17
Church St. Ham —5A 142
Church St. John —2F 95
Church St. Kilb —2A 94
Church St. Kils —3H 11
Church St. Lark —2E 161
Church St. Moth —3F 129
Church St. Udd —2D 124
Church View. Camb —6A 106
Church View. Coat —4C 90
Church View Ct. Len —2F 7
Church View Gdns. Bell —2C 126
Circus Dri. G31 —4B 84
Circus Pl. G31 —4B 84
Circus Pl. La. G31 —3B 84
Citadel Pl. Moth —1E 143
Citizen La. G2 —4G 83 (5E 5)
Citrus Cres. Udd —5G 109
Cityford Cres. Ruth —6B 104
Cityford Dri. Ruth —1B 120
Civic Sq. Moth —4H 143 (off Camp St.)
Civic St. G4 —1F 83 (1C 4)
Civic Way. Kirk —6C 30
Clachan Dri. G51 —3E 81
Clachan, The. Wis —6H 145
Claddens Pl. Lenz —3E 51
Claddens Quad. G22 —3G 63
Claddens St. G22 —3F 63
Claddens Wynd. Kirk —3E 51
Cladence Gro. E Kil —6H 149
Claire St. Newm —4E 147
Clairinch Gdns. Renf —2E 79
Clairmont Gdns. G3 —2D 82
Clair Rd. B'rig —6F 49
Clamp Rd. Wis —5C 144
Clamps Gro. E Kil —3A 150
Clamps Ter. E Kil —3B 150
Clamps Wood. E Kil —3A 150
Clanrye Dri. Coat —1C 110
Clapperhow Rd. Moth —6A 128
Claremont Av. Kirk —5B 30
Claremont Dri. Miln —4G 25
Claremont Gdns. Miln —4G 25
Claremont Pl. G3 —2D 82 (off Lynedoch Ter.)
Claremont St. G3 —3C 82 (in two parts)
Claremont Ter. G3 —2D 82
Claremont Ter. La. G3 —2D 82 (off Clifton St.)
Claremount Av. Giff —5A 118
Clarence Dri. G11 & G12 —6G 61
Clarence Dri. Pais —6C 78
Clarence Gdns. G11 —6G 61
Clarence La. G12 —6H 61 (off Hyndland Rd.)
Clarence St. Clyd —4D 42
Clarence St. Pais —6C 78
Clarendon Pl. G20 —1E 83
Clarendon Rd. Wis —2E 157
Clarendon St. G20 —1E 83
Clare St. G21 —2C 84
Clarinda Cres. Kirk —3G 31
Clarinda Pl. Moth —4C 128
Clarion Cres. G13 —1A 60
Clarion Rd. G13 —2A 60
Clark Pl. Newt M —5B 132
Clark Pl. Torr —5E 29
Clarkston Av. G44 —3D 118
Clarkston Dri. Air —4D 92
Clarkston Rd. G44 —3D 118
Clarkston Rd. Clar —1C 134
CLARKSTON STATION. Clar —2C 134
Clark St. Air —4B 92
Clark St. Clyd —3B 42
Clark St. John —2F 95
Clark St. Newm —4D 146
Clark St. Pais —5G 77
Clark St. Renf —6D 58
Clark Ter. Newt M —5G 133
Clark Way. Bell I —6B 110
Clarkwell Rd. Ham —1C 152
Clarkwell Ter. Ham —6D 140
Clathic Av. Bear —3G 45
Claude Av. Camb —3E 123
Claude St. Lark —2E 161
Claud Rd. Pais —5C 78
Clavens Rd. G52 —5G 79
Claverhouse Pl. Pais —2C 98
Claverhouse Rd. H'ton I —4H 79
Clavering St. E. Pais —6G 77
Clavering St. W. Pais —6G 77
Clay Cres. Bell —6D 110
Clayhouse Rd. G33 —5E 67
Claymore Dri. Hous —3D 74
Claypotts Pl. G33 —2A 86
Claypotts Rd. G33 —2A 86
Clay Rd. Bell —6D 110
Clayslaps Rd. G3 —2B 82
Claythorn Av. G40 —5A 84
Claythorn Ct. G40 —5A 84 (off Claythorn St.)
Claythorn Pk. G40 —6A 84
Claythorn St. G40 —5A 84
Claythorn Ter. G40 —5A 84
Clayton Cir. G40 —5A 84
Clayton Path. Bell —6D 110
Clayton Ter. G31 —4B 84
Clearfield Av. Ham —5F 141
Cleddans Cres. Clyd —1E 43
Cleddans Rd. Clyd —2E 43
Cleddans Rd. Kirk —4E 31
Cleddans View. Clyd —3E 43
Cleddans View. Glenm —5G 71
Cleddens Ct. Air —3F 91 (off Monkscourt Av.)
Cleddens Ct. B'rig —6C 48
Cleeves Quad. G53 —2A 116
Cleeves Rd. G53 —2A 116
Cleghorn St. G22 —6F 63
Cleland La. G5 —6G 83
Cleland Pl. E Kil —6A 138
Cleland Rd. Moth —6C 128
Cleland Rd. N'hill —4F 129
Cleland Rd. Wis —6G 145
Cleland St. G5 —6G 83
Clelland Av. B'rig —1C 64
Clem Atlee Gdns. Lark —3F 161
Clerwood St. G32 —5F 85
Cleuch Gdns. Clar —1B 134
Clevans Rd. Bri W —4D 72
Cleveden Cres. G12 —4H 61
Cleveden Cres. La. G12 —4H 61
Cleveden Dri. G12 —4H 61
Cleveden Dri. Ruth —1E 121
Cleveden Dri. La. G12 —5A 62
Cleveden Gdns. G12 —4A 62
Cleveden La. G12 —3H 61 (off Northampton Dri.)
Cleveden Pl. G12 —3H 61
Cleveden Rd. G12 —4H 61

Cleveden Rd. G20 —2H 61
Cleveland La. G3 —3D 82
(off Kent Rd.)
Cleveland St. G3 —3D 82
Cliesh Av. Bear —5C 24
Clifford Gdns. G51 —6H 81
Clifford La. G51 —6B 82
Clifford Pl. G51 —6B 82
(off Clifford La.)
Clifford St. G51 —6H 81
Cliff Rd. G3 —1D 82
Clifton Ct. Clar —1H 135
Clifton Pl. G3 —2C 82
(off Clifton St.)
Clifton Pl. Coat —5E 91
Clifton Rd. Giff —4H 117
Clifton St. G3 —2C 82
Clifton Ter. Camb —4G 121
Clifton Ter. John —3G 95
Cliftonville Ct. Coat —5E 91
(off Clifton Pl.)
Clincarthill Rd. Ruth —6C 104
Clincart Rd. G42 —5F 103
Clippens Rd. Hous —3E 75
Clippens Rd. Lin —6H 75
Cloan Av. G15 —5B 44
Cloan Cres. B'rig —3D 48
Clober Farm La. Miln —2E 25
Cloberfield. Miln —1F 25
Cloberfield Gdns. Miln —2F 25
Cloberhill Rd. G13 —6C 44
Clober Rd. Miln —2F 25
Clochbar Av. Miln —2F 25
Clochbar Gdns. Miln —3F 25
Clochoderick Av. Mill P —3B 94
Cloch St. G33 —3A 86
Clockerhill Pl. Moth —3E 129
Clock Sq. Cumb —3H 35
(off Cumbernauld Cen., The)
Cloister Av. Air —1C 112
Clonbeith St. G33 —1E 87
Closeburn St. G22 —4G 63
Cloth St. Barr —5E 115
Clouden Rd. Cumb —3B 36
Cloudhowe Ter. Blan —6A 124
Clouston Ct. G20 —5C 62
Clouston La. G20 —5C 62
Clouston St. G20 —5B 62
Clova Pl. Udd —1D 124
Clova St. T'bnk —3F 117
Clove Mill Wynd. Lark —3C 160
Clovend Dri. Ruth —4D 120
Cloverbank St. G21 —2C 84
Clovergate. B'rig —6A 48
Cloverhill Pl. Chry —1A 68
Cloverhill Ter. E Kil —2G 149
Cloverhill View. E Kil —2F 149
Clunie Pl. Coat —2D 110
Clunie Pl. Wis —3D 146
Clunie Rd. G52 —1E 101
Cluny Av. Bear —5G 45
Cluny Av. Clyd —6E 23
Cluny Dri. Bear —5G 45
Cluny Dri. Pais —5C 78
Cluny Gdns. G14 —5E 61
Cluny Gdns. Bail —1G 107
Cluny Vs. G14 —5E 61
Clutha Pl. E Kil —4C 148
Clutha St. G51 —5B 82
Clyde Av. Barr —6F 115
Clyde Av. Both —6D 124
Clyde Av. Ham —2E 155
Clyde Av. Torr —5D 28
Clydebank Bus. Pk. Clyd —5C 42
Clydebank Ind. Est. Clyd —5H 41
Clydebrae Dri. Both —1F 141
Clydebrae St. G51 —3H 81
Clyde Bri. Ham —4D 142
Clyde Ct. Clyd —2A 42
Clyde Ct. Coat —5E 91
(off Clifton Pl.)
Clyde Ct. Dumb —3E 17
Clyde Dri. Bell —3E 127
Clydeford Dri. G32 —2G 105
Clydeford Dri. Udd —6B 108
Clydeford Rd. G32 —6A 106
Clydeford Rd. Camb —1B 122
Clydeholm Rd. G14 —1D 80
Clydeholm Ter. Clyd —2F 59
Clyde Ho. Ham —4A 142
Clyde La. Moth —3A 128
Clydeneuk Dri. Udd —6B 108
Clyde Pl. G5 —5E 83
Clyde Pl. Camb —3D 122
Clyde Pl. John —5C 94
Clyde Pl. Moth —3A 128
Clyde Rd. Pais —4D 78
Clydesdale Av. Ham —5H 153
Clydesdale Av. Pais —2C 78
Clydesdale Av. Wis —2D 156
Clydesdale Pl. Ham —5H 153
Clydesdale St. Bell —3F 127
Clydesdale St. Ham —5G 141
Clydesdale St. Lark —1E 161
Clyde Shopping Cen. Clyd —5D 42
Clydeshore Rd. Dumb —5E 17
Clydeside Expressway. G14 —6D 60
Clydeside Ind. Est. G14 —1D 80
Clydeside Rd. Ruth —3B 104
Clydesmill Dri. G32 —6A 106
Clydesmill Gro. G32 —6A 106
Clydesmill Pl. G32 —5A 106
Clydesmill Rd. G32 —5H 105
Clyde Sq. Cumb —3H 35
(off Cumbernauld Cen., The)
Clyde St. Carl —3D 164
Clyde St. Clyd —1E 59
Clyde St. Coat —4E 91
Clyde St. Renf —4F 59
Clyde Ter. Both —6E 125
Clyde Ter. Moth —1C 156
Clyde Tower. E Kil —4B 150
Clyde Tower. Moth —4G 143
(off Airbles Rd.)
Clyde Tunnel. G51 —2E 81
Clydevale. Both —6F 125
Clyde Valley Av. Moth —5G 143
Clydeview. Both —6G 125
Clyde View. Dumb —5E 17
Clyde View. Ham —2F 153
Clyde View. Pais —3D 98
Clyde View Ct. Bowl —5A 20
Clydeview Shopping Cen. Blan —2C 140
Clydeview Ter. G32 —5C 106
Clyde Wlk. Cumb —3H 35
(off Cumbernauld Cen., The)
Clyde Wlk. Newm —3E 147
Clyde Way. Cumb —3H 35
(off Cumbernauld Cen., The)
Clyde Way. Pais —4D 78
Clydeway Ind. Est. G3 —3C 82
(off Finnieston Sq.)
Clynder St. G51 —5H 81
Clyth Dri. Giff —5B 118
Coach Clo. Kils —3C 12
Coach Pl. Kils —4A 12
Coach Rd. Kils —4B 12
Coalburn Rd. Both —2F 125
Coalhall Av. Moth —6A 128
Coatbank St. Coat —6D 90
Coatbank Way. Coat —5D 90
COATBRIDGE CENTRAL STATION. Coat —4B 90
Coatbridge Ind. Est. Coat —2C 90
Coatbridge Rd. Bail —6B 88
Coatbridge Rd. G'csh —1E 89
Coatbridge Rd. Glenb —1E 91
Coatbridge Rd. Glenm —4B 70
COATBRIDGE SUNNYSIDE STATION. Coat —3C 90
COATDYKE STATION. Coat —4F 91
Coathill St. Coat —1C 110
Coats Cres. Bail —6G 87
Coats Dri. Pais —2F 97
Coatshill Av. Blan —6A 124
Coats St. Coat —5D 90
Cobbett Rd. Moth —4D 142
Cobblerigg Way. Udd —2C 124
Cobbleton Rd. Moth —5H 127
Cobden Rd. St R —1B 84
Cobington Pl. G33 —2B 86
Cobinshaw St. G32 —5A 86
Coburg St. G5 —6F 83
(in two parts)
Cochno Rd. Clyd —5F 23
Cochno Rd. Hard —6D 22
Cochno St. Clyd —1E 59
Cochrane Ct. Miln —5A 26
Cochranemill Rd. John —4C 94
Cochrane St. G1 —4G 83 (5F 5)
Cochrane St. Barr —5D 114
Cochrane St. Bell —2B 126
Cochran St. Pais —1B 98
Cockburn Pl. Coat —1B 110
Cockels Loan. Renf —2D 78
Cockenzie St. G32 —6A 86
Cockmuir St. G21 —5C 64
Coddington Cres. Moth —6H 111
Cogan Rd. G43 —1A 118
Cogan St. G43 —6A 102
Cogan St. Barr —5D 114
Colbert St. G40 —1B 104
Colbreggan Ct. Clyd —1E 43
Colbreggan Gdns. Clyd —1E 43
Colbreggan Pl. Clyd —1E 43
Colchester Dri. G12 —3G 61
Coldingham Av. G14 —3G 59
Coldstream Cres. Wis —4A 146
Coldstream Dri. Pais —4E 97
Coldstream Dri. Ruth —6F 105
Coldstream Pl. G21 —6G 63
Coldstream Rd. Clyd —6D 42
Coldstream St. Blan —2B 140
Cole. E Kil —3C 150
Colebrooke Pl. G12 —6C 62
Colebrooke St. G12 —6C 62
Colebrooke Ter. G12 —6C 62
Colebrook St. Camb —1A 122
Coleridge. E Kil —4C 148
Coleridge Av. Both —5F 125
Colfin St. G34 —2A 88
Colgrain St. G20 —3E 63
Colgrave Cres. G32 —2H 105
Colinbar Circ. Barr —6D 114
Colinslee Av. Pais —4B 98
Colinslee Cres. Pais —4B 98
Colinslee Dri. Pais —4B 98
Colinslie Rd. G53 —5D 100
Colinton Pl. G32 —4B 86
Colintraive Av. G33 —6G 65
Colintraive Cres. G33 —5G 65
Collace Av. Bri W —4F 73
Colla Gdns. B'rig —5F 49
Coll Av. Renf —2F 79
College La. G1 —4H 83 (6H 5)
College St. G1 —4H 83 (6G 5)
College St. Dumb —4F 17
College Way Shopping Cen. Dumb —4F 17
Collessie Dri. G33 —1C 86
Collier St. John —2F 95
Colliertree Rd. Air —3D 92
Collina St. G20 —3A 62
Collins St. G4 —4A 84
Collins St. Clyd —1E 43
Coll Pl. G21 —1D 84
Coll St. G21 —1D 84
Coll St. Wis —3D 146
Collylinn Rd. Bear —3E 45
Colmonell Av. G13 —2H 59
Colonsay. E Kil —4B 150
Colonsay Av. Renf —2E 79
Colonsay Dri. Newt M —4B 132
Colonsay Rd. G52 —6E 81
Colonsay Rd. Pais —6H 97
Colquhoun Av. G52 —4A 80
Colquhoun Ct. G41 —1A 102
Colquhoun Dri. Bear —2D 44
Colquhoun Rd. Milt —4E 19
Colquhoun St. Dumb —3G 17
Colston Av. B'rig —2B 64
Colston Dri. B'rig —2B 64
Colston Gdns. Air —4C 92
Colston Gdns. B'rig —2A 64
Colston Path. B'rig —2A 64
Colston Pl. Air —4C 92
Colston Pl. B'rig —2A 64
Colston Rd. Air —4C 92
Colston Rd. B'rig —2A 64
Colston Ter. Air —4C 92
Colt Av. Coat —3A 90
Coltmuir Cres. B'rig —1A 64
Coltmuir Dri. B'rig —1A 64
Coltmuir Gdns. B'rig —1A 64
Coltmuir St. G22 —3F 63
Coltness Dri. Bell —3D 126
Coltness La. G33 —4C 86
Coltness Rd. Wis —3A 146
Coltness St. G33 —3C 86
Coltpark Av. B'rig —1A 64
Coltpark La. B'rig —1B 64
Colt Pl. Coat —3C 90
Coltsfoot Dri. G53 —4B 116
Coltswood Ct. Coat —3C 90
Coltswood Rd. Coat —2C 90
Colt Ter. Coat —3C 90
Columba Cres. Moth —5F 127
Columba St. G51 —4H 81
Columbia Path. Blan —1A 140
Columbia Pl. E Kil —4D 148
Columbia Way. E Kil —3D 148
Columbine Way. Carl —5F 165
Colvend St. G40 —2B 104
Colville Dri. Ruth —1F 121
Colvilles Pl. E Kil —5B 150
Colvilles Rd. E Kil —6A 150
Colwood Av. G53 —3A 116
Colwood Gdns. G53 —4A 116
Colwood Path. G53 —3A 116
Colwood Pl. G53 —4A 116
Colwood Sq. G53 —4A 116
Colwyn Ct. Air —2A 92
Colzium View. Kils —3A 12
Combe Quad. Bell —4A 126
Comedie Rd. G33 —5E 67
Comely Bank. Ham —6D 140
Comelybank La. Dumb —3D 16
Comelybank Rd. Dumb —3D 16
Comelypark Pl. G31 —5C 84
(off Comelypark St.)
Comleypark St. G31 —5B 84
Commerce St. G5 —6F 83
Commercial Ct. G5 —6H 83
Commercial Rd. G5 —1G 103
Commercial Rd. Barr —4E 115
Common Grn. Ham —5A 142
Commonhead Av. Air —2H 91
Commonhead La. Air —2H 91
Commonhead Rd. G34 —3B 88
Commonhead St. Air —2H 91
Commonside St. Air —2H 91
Commore Av. Barr —6F 115
Commore Dri. G13 —2A 60
Commore Pl. Neil —3C 130
Community Av. Bell —5C 126
Community Pl. Bell —4D 126
Community Rd. Bell —4B 126
Comrie Cres. Ham —6B 140
Comrie Rd. G33 —4C 66
Comrie St. G32 —2B 106
Conan Ct. Camb —2D 122
Cona St. Giff —3E 117
Condor Glen. Holy —6G 111
Condorrat Interchange. Cumb —5E 35
Condorrat Ring Rd. Cumb —6C 34
Condorrat Rd. Cumb —4D 54
Condorrat Rd. Glenm —5F 55
Coneypark Cres. Bank —1C 14
Coneypark Pl. Bank —1C 14
Congress Rd. G3 —4B 82
Conifer Pl. Kirk —1B 50
Conisborough Path. G34 —1F 87
Conisborough Rd. G34 —1F 87
Coniston. E Kil —6B 148
Coniston Dri. Bell —4D 126
Conistone Cres. Bail —1F 107
Connal St. G40 —2D 104
Connell Cres. Miln —4A 26
Conniston St. G32 —4G 85
Connor Rd. Barr —4D 114
Connor St. Air —2E 93
Conolly's Land. Clyd —1C 42
(off Dumbarton Rd.)
Conon Av. Bear —4C 44
Consett La. G33 —3C 86
Consett St. G33 —3C 86
Constable Cres. E Kil —6F 137
Constarry Rd. Croy —6A 12
Contin Pl. G20 —4B 62
Convair Way. Renf —2F 79
Cook St. G5 —6E 83
Cook St. E Kil —6B 138
Coolgardie Grn. E Kil —4E 149
Coolgardie Pl. E Kil —4E 149
Co-operative Ter. John —2G 95
Cooper's Well St. G11 —2A 82
Copenhagen Av. E Kil —5G 149
Copland Pl. G51 —5H 81
Copland Quad. G51 —5H 81
Copland Rd. G51 —6H 81
Coplaw St. G42 —2E 103
Copperfield La. Udd —6E 109
Coral Mt. Gdns. Kirk —6E 31
Corbett Ct. G32 —2H 105
Corbett St. G32 —2H 105
Corbie Pl. Miln —3D 24
Corbiston Way. Cumb —3B 36
Cordiner St. G44 —6F 103
Corkerhill Gdns. G52 —1E 101
Corkerhill Pl. G52 —3D 100
Corkerhill Rd. G52 —2D 100
Corkerhill Rd. G53 —4D 100
CORKERHILL STATION. G52 —3D 100
Corlaich Av. G42 —6A 104
Corlaich Dri. G42 —6A 104
Cormack Av. Torr —4E 29
Cormorant Av. Hous —3D 74
Cornaig Rd. G53 —5B 100
Cornalee Gdns. G53 —5A 100
Cornalee Pl. G53 —5A 100
(in two parts)
Cornalee Rd. G53 —5B 100
Cornelian Ter. Bell —3C 126
Cornelia St. Moth —6D 126
Cornhill Dri. Coat —3A 90
Cornhill St. G21 —4C 64
Cornish Ct. Coat —3B 90
Cornock Cres. Clyd —4D 42
Cornock St. Clyd —4D 42
Cornsilloch Brae. Lark —2C 162
Corn St. G4 —1F 83
Cornwall Av. Ruth —2F 121
Cornwall Ct. E Kil —2H 149
Cornwall St. G41 —6B 82
Cornwall St. E Kil —2F 149
Cornwall St. S. G41 —6B 82
Cornwall Way. E Kil —2H 149
Coronation Av. Lark —5E 161
Coronation Cres. Ham —5E 161
Coronation Pl. G'csh —2C 68
Coronation Pl. Lark —5F 161
Coronation Rd. Moth —3H 127
Coronation Rd. E. Moth —4H 127
Coronation St. Wis —6B 146
Coronation Way. Bear —5F 45
Corpach Pl. G34 —2B 88
Corra Linn. Ham —6E 141
Corran Av. Newt M —3C 132
Corran St. G33 —3H 85
Correen Gdns. Bear —6B 24
Corrie Brae. Kils —2G 11
Corrie Ct. Ham —1D 152
Corrie Dri. Moth —2D 142
Corrie Dri. Pais —1G 99
Corrie Gro. G44 —3D 118
Corrie Pl. Lenz —3E 51
Corrie Rd. Kils —2G 11
Corrie View. Cumb —5B 34
Corrie View Cotts. Kils —1C 32
(off Alexander Av.)
Corrie Way. Lark —3F 161
Corrour Rd. G43 —6B 102
Corrour Rd. Newt M —3C 132
Corruna Ct. Carl —4H 165
Corsebar Av. Pais —3G 97
Corsebar Cres. Pais —4G 97
Corsebar Dri. Pais —3G 97
Corsebar La. Pais —4F 97
Corsebar Rd. Pais —4F 97
Corsebar Way. Pais —2G 97
Corseford Av. John —5C 94
Corsehill Path. G34 —3A 88
Corsehill Pl. G34 —3A 88
Corsehill St. G34 —3A 88
Corselet Rd. G53 —4A 116
Corselet Rd. Barr —1A 132
Corse Rd. G52 —5G 79
Corsewall Av. G32 —2E 107
Corsewall St. Coat —4A 90
Corsford Dri. G53 —1C 116
Corsock Av. Ham —1C 152
Corsock St. G31 —4D 84
Corston St. G33 —3F 85
Cortachy Pl. B'rig —6F 49
Coruisk Dri. Clar —1B 134
Coruisk Way. Pais —5C 96
Corunna St. G3 —3C 82
Coshneuk Rd. G33 —4B 66
Cosy Neuk. Lark —4G 161
Cottar St. G20 —2C 62
Cotton Av. Lin —6H 75
Cotton St. G40 —3C 104
Cotton St. Pais —1B 98
Cotton Vale. Moth —6E 129
Couldridge Gdns. Ham —5C 140
Coulter Av. Coat —3A 90
Coulter Av. Wis —2A 146
Countess Way. Bail —6E 89
(off Princess Dri.)
County Av. Camb —6F 105
County Pl. Pais —6A 78
County Sq. Pais —6A 78
Couper Pl. G4 —2H 83 (2G 5)
Couper St. G4 —2H 83 (2G 5)
Coursington Cres. Moth —2A 144
Coursington Gdns. Moth —2H 143
Coursington Pl. Moth —2H 143
Coursington Rd. Moth —2H 143
(in two parts)
Coursington Tower. Moth —2H 143
(off Coursington Rd.)
Courthill. Bear —1D 44
Courthill Av. G44 —2F 119
Courthill Cres. Kils —3A 12
Coustonholm Rd. G43 —6B 102
Couther Quad. Air —1A 92
Covanburn Av. Ham —2B 154
Covenant Cres. Lark —3F 161
Covenanters Way. Wis —5A 158
Covenant St. Wis —1C 156
Coventry Dri. G31 —3D 84
Cowal Cres. Kirk —4H 31
Cowal Dri. Lin —6G 75
Cowal St. G20 —2A 62
Cowal View. Clyd —4D 42
Cowan Cres. Barr —4F 115
Cowan La. G12 —1C 82
(off Glasgow St.)
Cowan Rd. Cumb —3D 34
Cowan St. G12 —1C 82
Cowan Wilson Av. Blan —1B 140
Cowan Wynd. Wis —4A 158
Cowcaddens Rd. G4 —2F 83 (2C 4)
COWCADDENS STATION. G4 —2F 83 (2C 4)
Cowcaddens St. G2 —3F 83 (3D 4)
Cowden Dri. B'rig —4C 48
Cowdenhill Cir. G13 —1D 60
Cowdenhill Pl. G13 —1D 60
Cowdenhill Rd. G13 —1C 60
Cowden St. G51 —4D 80
Cowdray Cres. Renf —6F 59
Cowgate. Kirk —4C 30
Cowglen Rd. G53 —6C 100
Cowlairs Ind. Est. G21 —5H 63
Cowlairs Rd. G21 —5A 64
Coxdale Av. Kirk —5B 30
Coxhill St. G21 —6H 63
Coxton Pl. G33 —2D 86
Coylton Cres. Ham —2C 152
Coylton Rd. G43 —2C 118
Crabb Quad. Moth —6E 127
Cragdale. E Kil —6E 137
Craggan Dri. G14 —3H 59
Crags Av. Pais —4B 98
Crags Cres. Pais —3B 98
Crags Rd. Pais —4B 98
Cragwell Pk. Crmck —2A 136
Craigallan Av. Camb —3D 122
Craigallian Av. Miln —1F 25
Craiganour La. G43 —1A 118
Craigard Pl. Ruth —4F 121
Craigash Quad. Miln —2E 25
Craigash Rd. Miln —3E 25
Craigbank Dri. G53 —1A 116
Craigbank Rd. Lark —5E 161
Craigbank St. Lark —4E 161
Craigbanzo St. Clyd —5F 23
Craigbarnet Av. Torr —5C 28
Craigbarnet Rd. Miln —3D 24
Craigbet Av. Quar H —1A 72
Craigbet Cres. Quar H —1A 72
Craigbet Pl. Quar H —1A 72
Craigbo Av. G23 —6B 46
Craigbo Ct. G23 —1B 62
Craigbo Dri. G23 —6B 46
Craigbog Av. John —4D 94
Craigbog Rd. John —5F 95
Craigbo Pl. G23 —1B 62
Craigbo Rd. G23 —1B 62
Craigbo St. G23 —6B 46
Craigburn Av. Hous —3D 74
Craigburn Ct. Ashg —4B 162
Craigburn Cres. Hous —4D 74
Craigburn Pl. Hous —4D 74
Craigburn St. Ham —3H 153
Craig Cres. Kirk —6H 31
Craigdhu Av. Air —4E 93
Craigdhu Av. Miln —4F 25
Craigdhu Cres. Air —4E 93
Craigdhu Rd. Bear —5D 24
Craigdonald Pl. John —2F 95

Craigellan Rd. G43 —1B 118
Craigelvan Av. Cumb —1B 54
Craigelvan Ct. Cumb —1B 54
Craigelvan Dri. Cumb —1B 54
Craigelvan Gdns. Cumb —1B 54
Craigelvan Gro. Cumb —1B 54
Craigelvan Pl. Cumb —1B 54
Craigelvan View. Cumb —1B 54
Craigenbay Cres. Lenz —2E 51
Craigenbay Rd. Lenz —3D 50
Craigenbay St. G21 —5D 64
Craigencart Ct. Clyd —1B 42
Craigend Cres. Miln —3F 25
Craigend Dri. Coat —1G 109
Craigend Dri. W. Miln —3E 25
Craigendmuir Cvn. Site. Step —5D 66
Craigendmuir Rd. G33 —5E 67
Craigendmuir St. G33 —1F 85
Craigendon Oval. Pais —6G 97
Craigendon Rd. Pais —6G 97
Craigend Pl. G13 —3E 61
Craigend Rd. Cumb —2B 54
Craigends Av. Quar H —1A 72
Craigends Dri. Kilb —2A 94
Craigends Pl. Quar H —1A 72
Craigends Rd. Hous —4D 74
Craigend St. G13 —3E 61
Craigend View. Cumb —2B 54
Craigenfeoch Av. John —4D 94
Craigens Rd. Air —6F 93
Craigfaulds Av. Pais —3F 97
Craigfell Ct. Ham —1C 152
Craigflower Av. G53 —3A 116
Craigflower Gdns. G53 —3A 116
Craigflower Rd. G53 —4A 116
Craig Gdns. Newt M —5C 132
Craighalbert Rd. Cumb —2E 35
(in two parts)
Craighalbert Roundabout. Cumb —1E 35
Craighalbert Way. Dull —1E 35
Craighall Quad. Neil —3D 130
Craighall Rd. G4 —1F 83 (1D 4)
Craighaw St. Clyd —5F 23
Craighead Av. G33 —6F 65
Craighead Av. Milt C —5C 8
Craighead Rd. B'ton —5H 39
Craighead Rd. Milt C —5C 8
Craighead St. Air —3E 93
Craighead Way. Barr —5D 114
(in two parts)
Craig Hill. E Kil —4E 149
Craighill Dri. Clar —3B 134
Craighill Gro. Clar —3B 134
Craighirst Rd. Miln —3D 24
Craigholme. Hous —1D 74
Craighouse St. G33 —2A 86
Craighton Gdns. Len —3H 7
Craighurst Dri. Clyd —6C 22
Craigiebar Dri. Pais —5G 97
Craigieburn Gdns. G20 —1H 61
Craigieburn Rd. Cumb —4H 35
Craigie Dri. Newt M —6E 133
Craigiehall Av. Ersk —2E 57
Craigiehall Cres. Ersk —2E 57
Craigiehall Pl. G51 —5B 82
Craigiehall St. G51 —5B 82
Craigiehall Way. Ersk —2E 57
Craigie La. Lark —1F 161
(off Duncan Graham St.)
Craigielea Ct. Renf —5E 59
Craigielea Cres. Miln —3E 25
Craigielea Dri. Pais —5F 77
Craigielea Pk. Renf —6E 59
Craigielea Rd. Clyd —6A 22
Craigielea Rd. Renf —6E 59
Craigielea St. G31 —3C 84
Craigielinn Av. Pais —6F 97
Craigie Pk. Lenz —2E 51
Craigie St. G42 —3E 103
Craigievar St. G33 —1E 87
Craiglea Pl. Air —3C 92
Craiglea Ter. Plain —1F 93
Craiglee. E Kil —6G 149
Craigleith St. G32 —5G 85
Craiglinn Pk. Rd. Cumb —4C 34
Craiglinn Roundabout. Cumb —4C 34
Craiglockhart St. G33 —1D 86
Craigmaddie Gdns. Torr —5C 28
Craigmaddie Rd. Bard —3D 26
Craigmaddie Ter. La. G3 —2C 82
(off Derby St.)
Craigmarloch Av. Torr —5D 28
Craigmarloch Roundabout. Cumb —2E 35
Craigmillar Av. Miln —3H 25
Craigmillar Rd. G42 —6E 103
Craigmochan Av. Air —1H 91
Craigmont Dri. G20 —3C 62
Craigmont St. G20 —3C 62
Craigmore Rd. Bear —6B 24
Craigmore St. G31 —5E 85
Craigmount Av. Pais —6G 97
Craigmount St. Kirk —6D 30
Craigmuir Cres. G52 —5H 79
Craigmuir Gdns. Blan —3H 139
Craigmuir Pl. G52 —5G 79
Craigmuir Rd. G52 —5G 79
Craigmuir Rd. Blan —3H 139
Craigneil St. G33 —1E 87
Craigneith Ct. E Kil —5E 139
Craignethan Rd. Carl —2E 165
Craignethan Rd. Giff —2G 133
Craigneuk Av. Air —5C 92
Craigneuk St. Moth & Wis —4B 144
Craignure Cres. Air —4E 93
Craignure Rd. Ruth —4D 120
Craigpark. G31 —4C 84
Craigpark Dri. G31 —4C 84
Craigpark St. Clyd —6F 23
Craigpark Way. Udd —6E 109
Craig Pl. Newt M —4B 132
Craig Rd. G44 —2E 119
Craig Rd. Lin —4F 75
Craig Rd. Neil —3D 130
Craigs Av. Clyd —1E 43
Craigsheen Av. Crmck —2H 135
Craigside Ct. Cumb —6B 34
Craigside Pl. Cumb —6B 34
Craigside Rd. Cumb —6B 34
Craigson Pl. Air —5F 93
Craigstone View. Kils —3B 12
Craigston Pl. John —3F 95
Craigston Rd. John —3E 95
Craig St. Air —4H 91
Craig St. Blan —3C 140
Craig St. Coat —1B 110
Craigthornhill Rd. Ham —6A 160
Craigton Av. Barr —6G 115
Craigton Av. Miln —3F 25
Craigton Clo. Newt M —4B 132
Craigton Dri. G51 —5F 81
Craigton Dri. Barr —6G 115
Craigton Dri. Newt M —4C 132
Craigton Gdns. Miln —2E 25
Craigton Ind. Est. G52 —6E 81
Craigton Pl. G51 —5E 81
Craigton Pl. Blan —6B 124
Craigton Rd. G51 —5F 81
Craigton Rd. Miln —2C 24
Craigton Rd. Newt M —6H 131
Craigton St. Clyd —5F 23
Craigvicar Gdns. G32 —6D 86
Craigview Av. John —5D 94
Craigview Rd. Moth —1H 143
Craigview Ter. John —4D 94
Craigwell Av. Ruth —1F 121
Crail St. G31 —6F 85
Craithie Ct. G11 —1G 81
Crammond Av. Coat —1G 109
Cramond Av. Renf —1G 79
Cramond St. G5 —3H 103
Cramond Ter. G32 —6B 86
Cranborne Rd. G12 —4G 61
Cranbrooke Dri. G20 —2B 62
Crannog Rd. Milt —4E 19
Cranston St. G3 —4D 82
Cranworth La. G12 —6B 62
(off Gt. George St.)
Cranworth St. G12 —6B 62
Crarae Av. Bear —5E 45
Crathes Ct. G44 —3C 118
Crathie Ct. Carl —2E 165
Crathie Dri. G11 —1G 81
Crathie Dri. Glenm —5H 71
Crathie Quad. Wis —4H 145
Crauchlan Av. Pais —5A 98
Crawford Av. Lenz —4D 50
Crawford Cres. Blan —6B 124
Crawford Cres. Udd —6C 108
Crawford Dri. G15 —6H 43
Crawford Dri. E Kil —1B 150
Crawford Hill. E Kil —1B 150
Crawford La. G11 —1G 81
(off Crawford St.)
Crawford Path. G11 —1G 81
(off Crawford St.)
Crawford Rd. Hous —2D 74
Crawford Rd. Miln —1F 25
Crawford Rd. Ruth —3D 120
Crawford St. G11 —1G 81
Crawford St. Ham —4E 141
Crawford St. Moth —3E 143
Crawfurd Dri. Pais —5F 77
Crawfurd Gdns. Ruth —3E 121
Crawriggs Av. Kirk —1D 50
Craw Rd. Pais —2G 97
Creamery Rd. Wis —2B 158
Crebar Dri. Barr —5E 115
Crebar St. T'bnk —3E 117
Credon Dri. Air —6A 92
Credon Gdns. Ruth —3E 121
Cree Av. B'rig —6F 49
Cree Gdns. G32 —6H 85
Cree Pl. E Kil —2D 148
Creighton Gro. E Kil —2G 149
Creran Ct. Ham —2E 153
Creran Dri. Renf —5D 58
Creran Path. Newm —3D 146
(off Tiree Cres.)
Crescent Ct. Clyd —4A 42
(off Crescent, The)
Crescent Rd. G14 & G13 —4B 60
Crescent, The. Clar —4E 135
Crescent, The. Clyd —4A 42
Cresswell La. G12 —6B 62
(off Cresswell St.)
Cresswell St. G12 —6B 62
Cressy St. G51 —3E 81
Crest Av. G13 —1B 60
Crestlea Av. Pais —5A 98
Crichton Ct. G45 —5B 120
Crichton St. G21 —5A 64
Crichton St. Coat —3C 90
Cricketfield La. Hous —1B 74
Criffell Gdns. G32 —2D 106
Criffell Rd. G32 —1D 106
Criffel Pl. Moth —4C 128
(off Clarinda Pl.)
Crighton Wynd. Bell —2H 125
Crimea St. G2 —4E 83 (6A 4)
Crimond Pl. Kils —2F 11
Crinan Cres. Coat —2H 89
Crinan Gdns. B'rig —6E 49
Crinan Pl. Bell —3D 126
Crinan Pl. Coat —2H 89
Crinan Rd. B'rig —6E 49
Crinan St. G31 —3D 84
Crindledyke Cres. Newm —3F 147
Cripps Av. Clyd —6F 43
Croftbank Av. Both —6F 125
Croftbank Cres. Both —6F 125
Croftbank Cres. Udd —1D 124
Croftbank St. G21 —5B 64
Croftburn Dri. G44 —3H 119
Croftcot Av. Bell —4B 126
Croftcroighn Rd. G33 —2B 86
Croftend Av. G44 —1A 120
Croftend La. Ruth —2B 120
Croftfoot Cres. G45 —3C 120
Croftfoot Dri. G45 —3B 120
Croftfoot Quad. G45 —3A 120
Croftfoot Rd. G44 —3H 119
Croftfoot Rd. G45 —3B 120
CROFTFOOT STATION. Ruth —1A 120
Croftfoot St. G45 —3C 120
Croftfoot Ter. G45 —3B 120
Crofthead Cres. Bell —4B 126
Crofthead Dri. Len —2E 7
Crofthead Pl. Bell —4B 126
Crofthead Pl. Newt M —6E 133
Crofthead St. Udd —2D 124
Crofthill Av. Udd —1D 124
Crofthill Rd. G44 —1H 119
Crofthouse Dri. G44 —3A 120
Croftmont Av. G44 —3A 120
Croftmoraig Av. Chry —3E 53
Crofton Av. G44 —3H 119
Croftpark Av. G44 —3G 119
Croftpark Cres. Blan —3C 140
Croftpark Rd. Clyd —6D 22
Croftpark St. Bell —1C 126
Croft Pl. Lark —2D 160
Croft Rd. Camb —2B 122
Croft Rd. E Kil —4G 149
Croft Rd. Lark —3D 160
Croft Rd. Torr —5A 28
Croftside Av. G44 —3A 120
Croftspar Av. G32 —5C 86
Croftspar Dri. G32 —5C 86
Croftspar Pl. G32 —5C 86
Croftwood. B'rig —3C 48
Croftwood Av. G44 —3H 119
Croftwood Rd. Ham —2H 153
Croft Wynd. Udd —1E 126
Crogal Cres. Chap —3D 112
Cromalt Cres. Bear —5C 24
Cromarty Av. G43 —1D 118
Cromarty Av. B'rig —5F 49
Cromarty Cres. Bear —6F 25
Cromarty Gdns. Clar —6E 119
Cromarty Pl. Chry —6B 52
Cromarty Pl. E Kil —6C 138
Cromarty Rd. Air —6H 91
Crombie Gdns. Bail —2F 107
Cromdale St. G51 —4E 81
Cromer St. G20 —4D 62
Cromer Way. Pais —4H 77
Crompton Av. G44 —2F 119
Cromwell La. G20 —1E 83
(off Cromwell St.)
Cromwell St. G20 —1E 83
Crona Dri. Ham —5C 140
Cronberry Quad. G52 —2H 99
Cronberry Ter. G52 —2H 99
Cronin Pl. Bell —6D 110
Cronulla Pl. Kils —3B 12
Crookedshields Rd. E Kil —2A 138
Crookfur Cottage Homes. Newt M —4D 132
Crookfur Rd. Newt M —3B 132
Crookston Av. G52 —1A 100
Crookston Ct. G52 —1A 100
Crookston Dri. Pais & G52 —1H 99
Crookston Gdns. G52 —1H 99
Crookston Gro. G52 —1A 100
Crookstonhill Path. G52 —1H 99
(off Crookston Quad.)
Crookston Path. G52 —1H 99
(off Crookston Quad.)
Crookston Pl. G52 —1H 99
Crookston Quad. G52 —1H 99
Crookston Rd. G52 —2H 99
Crookston Rd. G53 —6A 100
CROOKSTON STATION. G52 —1H 99
Crookston Ter. G52 —1A 100
Crosbie Dri. Pais —6C 96
Crosbie La. G20 —1A 62
Crosbie St. G20 —1A 62
Crosbie Wood. Pais —4F 97
Cross Arthurlie St. Barr —4D 114
Crossbank Av. G42 —4A 104
Crossbank Dri. G42 —4H 103
Crossbank Rd. G42 —4H 103
Crossbank Ter. G42 —4H 103
Crossburn Av. Miln —4F 25
Cross Ct. B'rig —6B 48
Crossdykes. Kirk —6G 31
Crossen La. Carl —4H 165
(off Kilcadzow Rd.)
Crossflat Cres. Pais —6C 78
Crossford Dri. G23 —6C 46
Crossgate. Kirk —4D 30
Cross Gates. Bell —3C 126
Crossgates. B'ton —3F 39
Crossgates Av. Cle —4H 129
Crossgates St. Lark —1D 160
Crosshill Av. G42 —4F 103
Crosshill Av. Kirk —1D 50
Crosshill Dri. Cle —4H 129
Crosshill Dri. Ruth —1D 120
Crosshill Rd. B'rig —2E 49
Crosshill Rd. Kirk —4B 50
CROSSHILL STATION. G42 —4F 103
Crosshill St. Air —4H 91
Crosshill St. Coat —1F 109
Crosshill St. Len —2F 7
Crosshill St. Moth —3H 143
Crosshouse Rd. E Kil —6B 148
Crosslee Cres. Hous —2C 74
Crosslee Pk. C'lee —3C 74
Crosslee Rd. Bri W —5H 73
Crosslees Dri. T'bnk —4F 117
Crosslees Pk. T'bnk —4F 117
Crosslees Rd. T'bnk —5F 117
Crosslee St. G52 —6D 80
Crosslet Av. Dumb —1C 18
Crosslet Ct. Dumb —2C 18
Crosslet Pl. Dumb —4H 17
Crosslet Rd. Dumb —3G 17
Crossloan Rd. G51 —4F 81
Crossloan Ter. G51 —4F 81
Crossmill Av. Barr —3F 115
Crossmount Ct. Carl —3E 165
Crossmyloof Gdns. G41 —4B 102
CROSSMYLOOF STATION. G41 —4B 102
Cross Orchard Way. Bell —2C 126
Crosspoint Dri. G23 —6C 46
Cross Rd. Pais —3F 97
Cross St. G32 —4C 106
Cross St. Pais —1G 97
Cross, The. Kilb —2A 94
Cross, The. Pais —6A 78
Crosstobs Rd. G53 —4A 100
Crossveggate. Miln —4H 25
Crossview Av. Bail —6B 88
Crossview Pl. Bail —6B 88
Crossways. Hous —1D 74
Crovie Rd. G53 —6A 100
Crow Av. Moth —2B 128
Crowflats Rd. Udd —1C 124
Crowfoot View. Udd —4G 109
Crowhill Cres. Air —1H 91
Crowhill Rd. B'rig —2B 64
Crowhill St. G22 —3G 63
Crow La. G13 —4F 61
Crowlin Cres. G33 —3B 86
Crown Av. Clyd —4C 42
Crown Cir. G12 —6A 62
Crown Gdns. G12 —6A 62
Crownpoint Rd. G40 —6B 84
Crown Rd. N. G12 —6H 61
Crown Rd. S. G12 —6H 61
Crown St. G5 —1F 103
Crown St. Bail —2F 107
Crown St. C'bnk —2B 112
Crown St. Coat —4E 91
Crown Ter. G12 —6H 61
Crow Rd. G11 —5F 61
Crow Rd. G13 —3F 61
Crow Rd. Len —1F 7
Crow-Wood Cres. C'bnk —3B 112
Crow-Wood Dri. Air —4D 92
Crow-Wood Rd. C'bnk —3B 112
Crow Wood Rd. Chry —2H 67
Crow Wood Ter. Chry —2H 67
Croy. E Kil —6F 137
Croy Av. Newt M —4G 133
Croy Pl. G21 —4E 65
Croy Rd. G21 —4E 65
Croy Rd. Coat —1A 110
CROY STATION. Cumb —2B 34
Cruachan Av. Renf —2E 79
Cruachan Dri. Barr —6E 115
Cruachan Dri. Newt M —6F 133
Cruachan Rd. Bear —6B 24
Cruachan Rd. Ruth —4F 121
Cruachan St. T'bnk —3F 117
Cruachan Way. Barr —6E 115
Cruden St. G51 —5F 81
Crum Av. T'bnk —4G 117
Crusader Av. G13 —6D 44
Cubie St. G40 —6B 84
Cuckoo Way. Moth —2B 128
Cuilhill Rd. Bail —3D 88
Cuillins, The. Mood —3E 53
Cuillin Way. Barr —5E 115
Cuilmuir Ter. Kils —1B 34
Cuilmuir View. Kils —6B 12
Culbin Dri. G13 —1H 59
Cullen. Ersk —4E 41
Cullen La. E Kil —4G 149
Cullen Pl. Udd —5E 109
Cullen Rd. E Kil —4F 149
Cullen Rd. Moth —4E 143
Cullen St. G32 —1A 106
Cullin Gdns. G22 —5H 63
(in two parts)
Cullins Rd. Ruth —4F 121
Cullins, The. Udd —4C 108
Cullion Way. Moth —2G 129
Cullochrig Rd. Rigg —5G 55
Culloch Rd. Bear —5C 24
Culloden St. G31 —3D 84
Culrain Gdns. G32 —6A 86
Culrain St. G32 —6A 86
Culross Hill. E Kil —2F 149
Culross La. G32 —1C 106
Culross Pl. Coat —4B 90
Culross Pl. E Kil —2F 149
Culross St. G32 —1C 106
Culross Way. Mood —4E 53
Culterfell Path. Cle —5H 129
Cult Rd. Lenz —3E 51
Cults St. G51 —5F 81
Culvain Av. Bear —6B 24
Culzean. Glenm —4H 71
Culzean Av. Coat —6A 90
Culzean Ct. Coat —6A 90
(off Torriden St.)
Culzean Cres. Bail —1G 107
Culzean Cres. Newt M —4G 133
Culzean Dri. G32 —1D 106
Culzean Dri. E Kil —6F 137
Culzean Dri. N'hill —4D 128
Culzean Pl. E Kil —6F 137
Cumberland Arc. G5 —1G 103
Cumberland Pl. G5 —1G 103
Cumberland Pl. Coat —6G 89
Cumberland St. G5 —6F 83
(in two parts)
Cumbernauld Cen., The. Cumb —3H 35
Cumbernauld Rd. G31 & G33 —4D 84
Cumbernauld Rd. Cumb —3H 53
Cumbernauld Rd. Longc —1F 15
Cumbernauld Rd. Muir —2G 67
CUMBERNAULD STATION. Cumb —5A 36
Cumbrae. E Kil —2C 150
Cumbrae Ct. Clyd —5D 42
Cumbrae Cres. Coat —6G 91
Cumbrae Cres. N. Dumb —2C 16
Cumbrae Cres. S. Dumb —2B 16
Cumbrae Dri. Moth —1E 143
Cumbrae Pl. Coat —1G 111
Cumbrae Rd. Pais —6A 98
Cumbrae Rd. Renf —2F 79
Cumbrae St. G33 —3A 86
Cumlodden Dri. G20 —2A 62
Cumming Dri. G42 —5F 103
Cummock Dri. Barr —6F 115
Cumnock Dri. Ham —2B 152
Cumnock Rd. G33 —3G 65
Cumroch Rd. Len —2E 7
Cunard Ct. Clyd —1D 58
Cunard St. Clyd —1D 58
Cunningair Dri. Moth —5G 143
Cunningham Dri. Clyd —1B 42
Cunningham Dri. Giff —4C 118
Cunninghame Rd. E Kil —2G 149
Cunninghame Rd. Kilb —2B 94
Cunninghame Rd. Ruth —5E 105
Cunningham Rd. G52 —3H 79
Cunningham St. Moth —3F 143
Cuparhead Av. Coat —1H 109
Curfew Rd. G13 —6D 44
Curle St. G14 —1D 80
(in three parts)
Curlew Pl. John —6C 94
Curling Cres. G44 —6G 103
Curlinghaugh Cres. Wis —6A 146
Curlingmire. E Kil —4G 149
Curran Av. Wis —2E 157
Currie Ct. John —4E 95
(off Tannahill Cres.)
Currie St. G20 —3C 62
Curtis Av. G44 —5G 103
Curzon St. G20 —3C 62
Cuthberton St. G42 —2E 103
Cuthbert St. Udd —6F 109
Cuthelton Dri. G31 —1G 105
Cuthelton St. G31 —1F 105
Cuthelton Ter. G31 —1F 105
Cypress Av. Blan —6A 124
Cypress Av. Udd —5F 109
Cypress Ct. E Kil —6E 149
Cypress Ct. Ham —1A 154
Cypress Ct. Kirk —1B 50
Cypress Cres. E Kil —6E 149
Cypress Pl. E Kil —6E 149
Cypress St. G22 —4H 63
Cyprus Av. Eld —3H 95
Cyril St. Pais —1C 98

Daer Av. Renf —2G 79
Daer Wlk. Lark —5E 161

Daer Way. Ham —6E 141
Daffodil Way. Moth —1G 143
Dairsie Gdns. B'rig —1F 65
Dairsie St. G44 —3D 118
Daisy St. G42 —4F 103
Dakota Way. Renf —2F 79
Dalbeth Pl. G32 —3H 105
Dalbeth Rd. G32 —3H 105
Dalbowie Rd. Udd —3G 107
Dalcharn Path. G34 —3G 87
(off Kildermorie Rd.)
Dalcharn Pl. G34 —3G 87
Dalcraig Cres. Blan —5A 124
Dalcross St. G11 —1A 82
Dalcruin Gdns. Mood —3E 53
Daldowie Av. G32 —2D 106
Daldowie St. Coat —2A 110
(in two parts)
Dale Av. E Kil —4E 149
Dale Ct. Wis —1C 156
Dale Dri. Moth —3A 128
Dale Path. G40 —1B 104
(off Main St.)
Dale St. G40 —1B 104
(in two parts)
Daleswinton Path. G34 —3B 88
Daleview Av. G12 —3H 61
Daleview Dri. Clar —3B 134
Daleview Gro. Clar —3B 134
Dale Way. Ruth —3D 120
Dalfoil Ct. Pais —1H 99
Dalgarroch Av. Clyd —1G 59
Dalgleish Av. Clyd —1A 42
Dalhousie Gdns. B'rig —5B 48
Dalhousie La. G3 —2E 83 (2B 4)
Dalhousie Rd. Mill P —3B 94
Dalhousie St. G3 —3E 83 (3B 4)
Dalilea Dri. G34 —2B 88
Dalilea Path. G34 —2B 88
Dalilea Pl. G34 —2B 88
Dalintober St. G5 —5E 83
Dalkeith Av. G41 —1H 101
Dalkeith Av. B'rig —4D 48
Dalkeith Rd. B'rig —3D 48
Dalmacoulter Rd. Air —1B 92
Dalmahoy Cres. Bri W —5D 72
Dalmahoy St. G32 —4G 85
Dalmally St. G20 —6D 62
Dalmarnock Bri. Ruth —3D 104
Dalmarnock Ct. G40 —2D 104
Dalmarnock Rd. G40 —1B 104
Dalmarnock Rd. Ruth —3D 104
DALMARNOCK STATION. G40 —2C 104
Dalmary Dri. Pais —5D 78
Dalmellington Ct. E Kil —1G 149
(off Dalmellington Dri.)
Dalmellington Ct. Ham —2B 152
Dalmellington Dri. E Kil —1F 149
Dalmeny Av. Giff —4A 118
Dalmeny Dri. Barr —5C 114
Dalmeny Rd. Ham —1H 153
Dalmeny St. G5 —3A 104
Dalmuir Ct. Clyd —4A 42
Dalnair Pl. Miln —4D 24
Dalnair St. G3 —2A 82
Dalness Pas. G32 —1A 106
(off Ochil St.)
Dalness St. G32 —2A 106
Dalnottar Av. Old K —1F 41
Dalnottar Dri. Old K —2F 41
Dalnottar Gdns. Old K —2F 41
Dalnottar Hill Rd. Old K —2F 41
Dalnottar Ter. Old K —1F 41
Dalreoch Av. Bail —6A 88
Dalreoch Ct. Dumb —3D 16
Dalreoch Path. Bail —6A 88
DALREOCH STATION. Dumb —3E 17
Dalriada Cres. Moth —5F 127
Dalriada Dri. Torr —5E 29
Dalriada St. G40 —1E 105
Dalry Gdns. Ham —1B 152
Dalrymple Dri. E Kil —6G 137
Dalrymple Dri. Newt M —5G 133
Dalry Rd. Udd —6F 109
Dalry St. G32 —1B 106
Dalserf Cres. Giff —6H 117
Dalserf Path. Lark —4G 161
(off Donaldson Rd.)
Dalserf St. G31 —6D 84
Dalsetter Av. G15 —5H 43
Dalsetter Pl. G15 —5A 44
Dalshannon Pl. Cumb —6C 34
Dalshannon Rd. Cumb —6D 34
Dalshannon View. Cumb —6C 34
Dalshannon Way. Cumb —6C 34
Dalsholm Ind. Est. G20 —2H 61
Dalsholm Rd. G20 —2H 61
Dalskeith Av. Pais —6E 77
Dalskeith Cres. Pais —6E 77
Dalskeith Rd. Pais —1E 97
Dalswinton St. G34 —3A 88
Dalton Av. Clyd —6G 43
Dalton Hill. Ham —1C 152
Dalton St. G31 —6G 85
Dalveen Ct. Barr —6E 115
Dalveen Dri. Udd —5C 108
Dalveen Quad. Coat —6F 91
Dalveen St. G32 —6H 85
Dalveen Way. Ruth —4E 121
Dalwhinnie Av. Blan —5A 124
Daly Gdns. Blan —6C 124
Dalzell Av. Moth —5A 144
Dalzell Dri. Moth —5A 144
Dalziel Dri. G41 —2A 102
Dalziel Quad. G41 —2A 102
Dalziel Rd. H'ton I —3H 79
Dalziel St. Ham —4F 141
Dalziel St. Moth —2H 143
Dalziel Tower. Moth —6B 144
Damshot Cres. G53 —5D 100
Damshot Rd. G53 —6D 100
Danby Rd. Bail —1F 107
Danes Cres. G14 —4B 60
Danes Dri. G14 —4B 60
Danes La. S. G14 —5C 60
Daniel McLaughlin Pl. Kirk —4E 31
Dargarvel Av. G41 —1H 101
Dargavel Av. B'ton —4H 39
Dargavel Path. G41 —2G 101
(off Dumbreck Pl.)
Dargavel Rd. B'ton —6A 40
(in two parts)
Darkwood Ct. Pais —5F 77
Darkwood Cres. Pais —5F 77
Darkwood Dri. Pais —5F 77
Darleith St. G32 —6H 85
Darley Pl. Ham —3F 153
Darley Rd. Cumb —6G 13
Darluith Rd. Lin —5E 75
Darnaway Av. G33 —1D 86
Darnaway Dri. G33 —1D 86
Darnaway St. G33 —1D 86
Darngavel Ct. Air —3F 91
(off Monkscourt Av.)
Darnick St. G21 —6C 64
Darnley Cres. B'rig —4B 48
Darnley Gdns. G41 —3C 102
Darnley Ind. Est. G53 —3B 116
Darnley Mains Rd. G53 —4C 116
Darnley Path. T'bnk —2E 117
Darnley Pl. G41 —3C 102
Darnley Rd. G41 —3C 102
Darnley Rd. Barr —4F 115
Darnley St. G41 —3D 102
Darroch Dri. Ersk —4D 40
Darroch Way. Cumb —2A 36
Dartford St. G22 —6F 63
Darvel Cres. Pais —1F 99
Darvel Dri. Newt M —4G 133
Darvel St. G53 —1H 115
Darwin Pl. Clyd —3H 41
Darwin Rd. E Kil —3E 149
Davaar. E Kil —2C 150
Davaar Dri. Coat —4H 89
Davaar Dri. Moth —5E 127
Davaar Dri. Pais —6A 98
Davaar Pl. Newt M —3C 132
Davaar Rd. Renf —2F 79
Davaar St. G40 —1D 104
Davan Loan. Newm —3D 146
(off Isla Av.)
Dava St. G51 —4G 81
Dave Barrie Av. Lark —6H 155
Daventry Dri. G12 —4G 61
David Gray Dri. Kirk —4G 31
David Pl. Bail —1F 107
David Pl. Pais —4D 78
Davidson Cres. Twe —2D 32
Davidson Gdns. G14 —5E 61
Davidson La. Carl —4H 165
(off Kilcadzow Rd.)
Davidson Pl. G32 —5C 86
Davidson Quad. Clyd —1C 42
Davidson St. G40 —3C 104
Davidson St. Air —3H 91
Davidson St. Clyd —1G 59
Davidson St. Coat —1D 110
Davidston Pl. Kirk —3F 31
David St. G40 —6C 84
David St. Coat —4E 91
David Way. Pais —4D 78
Davieland Rd. Giff —6G 117
Davie's Acre. E Kil —5C 136
Davies Quad. Moth —5F 127
Davie's Sq. Clyd —1C 42
Davington Dri. Ham —1B 152
Daviot St. G51 —5D 80
Dawson Av. E Kil —2D 148
Dawson Pl. G4 —6F 63
Dawson Rd. G4 —6F 63
Deacons Rd. Kils —3A 12
Dealston Rd. Barr —3D 114
Deanbrae St. Udd —1D 124
Dean Cres. Chry —6B 52
Dean Cres. Ham —2G 153
Deanfield Quad. G52 —5H 79
Dean Pk. Av. Udd —5E 125
Dean Pk. Dri. Camb —3D 122
Dean Pk. Rd. Renf —1G 79
Deans Av. Camb —3D 122
Deanside Rd. G52 —3A 80
Deanside Transit Depot. G52 —2A 80
Deanston Dri. G41 —5B 102
Dean St. Bell —2D 126
Dean St. Clyd —6E 43
Deanwood Av. G44 —4D 118
Deanwood Rd. G44 —4D 118
Dechmont. E Kil —6F 149
Dechmont Av. Camb —4D 122
Dechmont Av. Moth —2E 143
Dechmont Cotts. Camb —4F 123
Dechmont Gdns. Blan —6A 124
Dechmont Pl. Camb —4D 122
Dechmont St. G31 —1E 105
Dechmont St. Ham —1G 153
Dechmont View. Bell —4B 126
Dechmont View. Udd —6E 109
Dee Av. Pais —3D 96
Dee Av. Renf —6G 59
Deedes St. Air —5F 91
Dee Dri. Pais —4D 96
Dee Path. Lark —5E 161
Dee Path. Moth —2B 128
Deep Dale. E Kil —6E 137
Deepdene Rd. Bear —4D 44
Deepdene Rd. Chry —5D 52
Dee Pl. E Kil —4A 148
Dee Pl. John —5C 94
Deerdykes Ct. N. Cumb —1A 54
Deerdykes Ct. S. Cumb —2A 54
Deerdykes Pl. Cumb —1A 54
Deerdykes Rd. Cumb —2H 53
Deerdykes View. Cumb —2H 53
Deer Pk. Ct. Ham —4H 153
Deer Pk. Pl. Ham —4A 154
Deeside Dri. Carl —2G 165
Dee St. G33 —2F 85
Dee St. Coat —1H 89
Dee Ter. Ham —3F 153
Delhi Av. Clyd —3G 41
Dellburn St. Moth —4A 144
Dell, The. Bell —4F 127
Delny Pl. G33 —4E 87
Delvin Rd. G44 —1E 119
Dempsey Rd. Bell —4B 126
Denbak Av. Ham —1E 153
Denbeck St. G32 —6H 85
Denbrae St. G32 —6H 85
Dene Wlk. B'rig —1E 65
Denewood Av. Pais —5H 97
Denham St. G22 —6F 63
Denholm Cres. E Kil —3G 149
Denholm Dri. Giff —6A 118
Denholm Dri. Wis —3A 146
Denholm Grn. E Kil —3H 149
Denholm Ter. Ham —6C 140
Denmark St. G22 —5G 63
Denmark St. Ind. Cen. G22 —4G 63
Denmilne Gdns. G34 —4A 88
Denmilne Path. G34 —4A 88
Denmilne Rd. Bail —4B 88
Denmilne St. G34 —4A 88
Dennison Av. Ham —1G 143
Dennistoun St. Bell —2C 126
Dentdale. E Kil —6E 137
Deramore Av. Giff —2G 133
Derby St. G3 —3C 82
Derby Ter. La. G3 —3C 82
(off Derby St.)
Derrywood Rd. Milt C —5C 8
Derwent Dri. Coat —1G 89
Derwent St. G22 —5F 63
Derwentwater. E Kil —5B 148
Despard Av. G32 —1D 106
Despard Gdns. G32 —1E 107
Deveron Av. Giff —5B 118
Deveron Cres. Ham —5B 140
Deveron Rd. Bear —5C 44
Deveron Rd. E Kil —2A 150
Deveron Rd. Moth —1B 128
Deveron St. G33 —2F 85
Deveron St. Coat —2G 89
Deveron Way. Cumb —3H 35
(off Cumbernauld Cen., The)
Deveron Way. Pais —4D 96
Devine Gro. Newm —2E 147
Devlin Gro. Blan —2C 140
Devol Cres. G53 —5D 100
Devondale Av. Blan —6A 124
Devon Dri. B'ton —4A 40
Devon Gdns. B'rig —4B 48
Devon Gdns. Carl —3E 165
Devonhill Av. Ham —4H 153
Devon Pl. G41 —1F 103
Devonport Pk. E Kil —4C 148
Devonshire Gdns. La. G12 —5H 61
Devonshire Ter. G12 —5H 61
Devonshire Ter. La. G12 —5H 61
Devon St. G5 —1F 103
Devonview Pl. Air —5H 91
Devonview St. Air —4H 91
Devon Wlk. Cumb —5A 34
Devon Way. Moth —3D 142
Dewar Clo. Udd —4E 109
Diamond St. Bell —3C 126
Diana Av. G13 —1B 60
Diana Quad. Moth —2A 128
Dickens Av. Clyd —3B 42
Dickson Sq. Cle —6H 129
Dickson St. Lark —4G 161
Dicks Pk. E Kil —3F 149
Dick St. G20 —6D 62
Differ Av. Twe —3D 32
Dilwara Av. G14 —1E 81
Dimity St. John —3F 95
Dimsdale Cres. Wis —2A 158
Dimsdale Rd. Wis —2A 158
Dinard Dri. Giff —3A 118
Dinart St. G33 —2F 85
Dinduff St. G34 —2A 88
Dinmont Av. Pais —4D 96
Dinmont Cres. Moth —5E 127
Dinmont Pl. G41 —4C 102
(off Dinmont Rd.)
Dinmont Rd. G41 —4B 102
Dinmont Way. Pais —4C 96
Dinnet Way. Newm —3D 146
(off Isla Av.)
Dinwiddie St. G21 —1E 85
Dinyra Pl. Glenb —3G 69
Dipple Pl. G15 —5B 44
Dirleton Dri. G41 —5C 102
Dirleton Dri. Pais —4E 97
Dirleton Ga. Bear —4D 44
Dirleton Pl. G41 —5C 102
Divernia Way. Barr —6E 115
Dixon Av. G42 —3E 103
Dixon Av. Dumb —4E 17
Dixon Dri. Dumb —5D 16
Dixon Pl. E Kil —6D 136
Dixon Rd. G42 —4F 103
Dixons Blazes Ind. Est. G5 —2G 103
Dixon St. G1 —5F 83
Dixon St. Coat —1D 110
Dixon St. Ham —6H 141
Dixon St. Pais —1B 98
Dobbies Ct. Law —5E 159
Dobbie's Loan. G4 —2F 83 (1D 4)
Dobbies Loan Pl. G4 —3H 83
Dochart Av. Renf —2G 79
Dochart Dri. Coat —1G 89
Dochart St. G33 —1G 85
Dock St. Clyd —2F 59
Dodhill Pl. G13 —3B 60
Dodside Gdns. G32 —1C 106
Dodside Pl. G32 —1C 106
Dodside Rd. Newt M —4A 132
Dodside St. G32 —1C 106
Dolan St. Bail —6H 87
Dollar Pk. Moth —6B 144
Dollar Ter. G20 —1A 62
(off Crosbie St.)
Dolley Rd. Wis —6G 145
Dolphin Rd. G41 —3B 102
Dominica Grn. E Kil —2C 148
Donaldfield Rd. Bri W —4D 72
Donaldson Av. Kils —4H 11
Donaldson Cres. Kirk —6C 30
Donaldson Dri. Renf —6E 59
Donaldson Grn. Udd —5E 109
Donaldson Pl. Kirk —5D 30
Donaldson Rd. Lark —4G 161
Donaldson St. Ham —4E 141
Donaldson St. Kirk —6C 30
Donaldswood Pk. Pais —5G 97
Donaldswood Rd. Pais —5G 97
Donald Ter. Ham —2G 153
Donald Way. Udd —6E 109
Don Av. Renf —1G 79
Doncaster St. G20 —6E 63
Don Ct. Ham —3E 153
Don Dri. Pais —4D 96
Donnelly Way. Wis —5C 144
Donnie Clo. Udd —5F 109
Donnies Brae. Barr —1F 131
Don Path. Lark —5E 161
Don Pl. John —5C 94
Don St. G33 —3F 85
Doon Cres. Bear —4D 44
Doonfoot Ct. E Kil —1F 149
Doonfoot Gdns. E Kil —1F 149
Doonfoot Rd. G43 —1B 118
Doon Pl. Kirk —3F 31
Doon Rd. Kirk —4F 31
Doonside. Cumb —3B 36
Doonside Tower. Moth —5B 144
Doon St. Clyd —4F 43
Doon Ct. Lark —3C 161
Doon St. Moth —5A 144
Doon Way. Kirk —4G 31
Dorain Rd. Moth —4D 128
Dora St. G40 —2C 104
Dorchester Av. G12 —3G 61
Dorchester Pl. G12 —3G 61
Dorian Dri. Clar —1H 133
Dorlin Rd. G33 —4E 67
Dormanside Ct. G53 —2B 100
Dormanside Gro. G53 —2B 100
Dormanside Rd. G53 —2B 100
Dornal Av. G13 —2G 59
Dornford Av. G32 —3D 106
Dornford Rd. G32 —3D 106
Dornie Dri. G32 —5B 106
Dornie Path. Newm —3D 146
(off Isla Av.)
Dornoch Av. Giff —6A 118
Dornoch Ct. Bell —1C 126
Dornoch Pl. B'rig —5F 49
Dornoch Pl. Chry —6B 52
Dornoch Pl. E Kil —1E 149
Dornoch Rd. Bear —5D 44
Dornoch Rd. Moth —3B 128
Dornoch St. G40 —6B 84
Dornoch Way. Air —6H 91
Dornoch Way. Cumb —6A 14
Dorset Sq. G3 —3D 82
(off Dorset St.)
Dorset St. G3 —3D 82
Dosk Av. G13 —1H 59
Dosk Pl. G13 —1H 59
Double Edge Rd. Neil —3D 130
Dougalston Av. Miln —4H 25
Dougalston Cres. Miln —4H 25
Dougalston Gdns. N. Miln —4H 25
Dougalston Gdns. S. Miln —4H 25
Dougalston Rd. G23 —6C 46
Douglas Av. G32 —4B 106
Douglas Av. Eld —3H 95
Douglas Av. Giff —6A 118
Douglas Av. Lenz —2D 50
Douglas Av. Ruth —2E 121
Douglas Ct. Lenz —2D 50
Douglas Cres. Air —5A 92
Douglas Cres. Ersk —4D 40
Douglas Cres. Ham —5H 153
Douglas Cres. Udd —5F 109
Douglasdale. E Kil —1F 149
Douglas Dri. G15 —6H 43
Douglas Dri. Ashg —5B 162
Douglas Dri. Bail —6F 87
Douglas Dri. Bell —3E 127
Douglas Dri. Both —6E 125
Douglas Dri. Camb —2H 121
Douglas Dri. E Kil —4A 148
Douglas Dri. Newt M —3E 133
Douglas Gdns. Bear —3F 45
Douglas Gdns. Giff —6A 118
Douglas Gdns. Lenz —2D 50
Douglas Gdns. Udd —2D 124
Douglas Ho. Cumb —3H 35
Douglas La. G2 —3E 83 (4B 4)
(off Pitt St.)
Douglas Muir Dri. Miln —2C 24
Douglas Muir Gdns. Miln —2C 24
Douglas Muir Pl. Miln —2C 24
Douglasmuir Rd. Clyd —6F 23
Douglas Muir Rd. Miln —3C 24
Douglas Pk. Cres. Bear —1G 45
Douglas Pk. La. Ham —5G 141
Douglas Pl. Bear —2E 45
Douglas Pl. Coat —5B 90
Douglas Pl. Ham —5H 153
Douglas Pl. Kirk —2D 50
Douglas Rd. Dumb —4H 17
Douglas Rd. Renf —3C 78
Douglas St. G2 —4E 83 (5B 4)
Douglas St. Air —5A 92
Douglas St. Blan —3A 140
Douglas St. Carl —3E 165
Douglas St. Ham —4G 141
(in two parts)
Douglas St. Lark —1E 161
Douglas St. Miln —4G 25
Douglas St. Moth —2F 143
Douglas St. Pais —6G 77
Douglas St. Udd —5F 109
Douglas St. Wis —4B 158
Douglas Ter. G41 —3D 102
Douglas Tower. Udd —3B 124
Douglas View. Coat —2B 110
Dougrie Dri. G45 —4H 119
Dougrie Pl. G45 —4A 120
Dougrie Rd. G45 —5G 119
Dougrie St. G45 —4H 119
Dougrie Ter. G45 —4H 119
Doune Cres. B'rig —3D 48
Doune Cres. Chap —4D 112
Doune Cres. Newt M —4F 133
Doune Gdns. G20 —6C 62
Doune Gdns. La. G20 —6C 62
Doune Quad. G20 —6C 62
Doune Ter. Coat —2H 89
Dovcothall St. Barr —4F 115
Dovecot. G43 —5A 102
Dovecotte View. Kirk —6F 31
Dovecotwood. Kils —2H 11
Doveholm. Dumb —2G 17
Doveholm Av. Dumb —2H 17
Dove Pl. E Kil —5B 148
Dover St. G3 —3C 82
Dover St. Coat —1H 89
Dove St. G53 —2A 116
Dove Wynd. Stra B —6A 110
Dowanfield Rd. Cumb —4F 35
Dowanhill St. G11 & G12 —1A 82
Dowan Rd. Miln —6C 26
Dowanside La. G12 —6B 62
Dowanside Rd. G12 —6A 62
Downcraig Dri. G45 —5H 119
Downcraig Rd. G45 —6G 119
Downcraig Ter. G45 —5H 119
Downfield Dri. Ham —4F 153
Downfield Gdns. Both —5D 124
Downfield St. G32 —2G 105
Downiebrae Rd. Ruth —3D 104
Downie St. Ham —2H 153
Downs St. G21 —4D 64
Dowrie Cres. G53 —4B 100
Draffan Tower. Moth —2H 143
Draffen Ct. Moth —2H 143
Draffen St. Moth —2H 143
Drakemire Av. G45 —3G 119
Drakemire Dri. G45 & G44 —5F 119
Drake St. G40 —6A 84
Dreghorn St. G31 —4E 85
Drimmin Rd. G33 —4F 67
Drive Rd. G51 —3E 81
Drochil St. G34 —2G 87
Dromore St. Kirk —6D 30
Drove Hill. Cumb —2D 34
Drumaling Ter. Len —3H 7

Drumbathie Rd. Air —3B 92
Drumbathie Ter. Air —3C 92
Drumbeg Dri. G53 —1A 116
Drumbeg Pl. G53 —1A 116
Drumbeg Ter. Miln —3D 24
Drumbottie Rd. G21 —4C 64
Drumbreck Pl. Kirk —3E 51
Drumby Cres. Clar —6B 118
Drumby Dri. Clar —1B 134
Drumcarn Dri. Miln —4F 25
Drumcavel Rd. Muir —2B 68
Drumchapel Gdns. G15 —5A 44
Drumchapel Rd. G15 —5A 44
DRUMCHAPEL STATION. G15 —6A 44
Drumclair Pl. Air —4D 92
Drumclog Av. Miln —1G 25
Drumclog Gdns. G33 —3H 65
Drumcross Rd. G53 —4C 100
Drumcross Rd. B'ton —4B 40
Drumduff. E Kil —6F 149
DRUMGELLOCH STATION. Air —4D 92
Drumgelloch St. Air —2D 92
Drumglass View. Croy —1B 34
Drumhead Pl. G32 —4H 105
Drumhead Rd. G32 —4H 105
Drumhill. Kirk —3H 31
Drumilaw Cres. Ruth —2C 120
Drumilaw Rd. Ruth —2C 120
Drumilaw Way. Ruth —2C 120
Drumlaken Av. G23 —6A 46 (off Drumlaken St.)
Drumlaken Ct. G23 —6B 46
Drumlaken Pl. G23 —6B 46 (off Drumlaken Ct.)
Drumlaken St. G23 —6A 46
Drumlanrig Av. G34 —2A 88
Drumlanrig Pl. G34 —3B 88
Drumlanrig Quad. G34 —2B 88
Drumlin Dri. Miln —5F 25
Drumloch Gdns. E Kil —6G 149
Drumlochy Rd. G33 —2A 86
Drum Mains Pk. Cumb —6G 33
Drummond Av. Ruth —5B 104
Drummond Dri. Pais —1F 99
Drummond Dri. Wis —1H 157
Drummond Hill. E Kil —6B 138
Drummond Ho. Cumb —2A 36
Drummond Pl. E Kil —6B 138
Drummore Rd. G15 —2A 44
Drumnessie Ct. Cumb —5B 34
Drumnessie Rd. Cumb —5B 34
Drumnessie View. Cumb —5B 34
Drumore Av. Chap —4D 112
Drumover Dri. G31 —1G 105
Drumoyne Av. G51 —4E 81
Drumoyne Cir. G51 —5E 81
Drumoyne Dri. G51 —4E 81
Drumoyne Pl. G51 —5E 81
Drumoyne Quad. G51 —5E 81
Drumoyne Rd. G51 —5E 81
Drumoyne Sq. G51 —4E 81
Drumpark St. Coat —1F 109
Drumpark St. T'bnk —3F 117
Drumpellier Av. Bail —2H 107
Drumpellier Av. Coat —4G 89
Drumpellier Av. Cumb —1C 55
Drumpellier Ct. Cumb —6E 35
Drumpellier Cres. Coat —5H 89
Drumpellier Gdns. Cumb —6E 35
Drumpellier Gro. Cumb —6E 35
Drumpellier Pl. Bail —1H 107
Drumpellier Pl. Coat —4H 89
Drumpellier Pl. Cumb —6E 35
Drumpellier Rd. Bail —2G 107
Drumpellier St. G33 —1F 85
Drumreoch Dri. G42 —5A 104
Drumreoch Pl. G42 —5A 104
Drumry Rd. Clyd —4D 42
Drumry Rd. E. G15 —5G 43
Drumsack Av. Chry —1A 68
Drumsargard Rd. Ruth —2F 121
Drums Av. Pais —5G 77
Drums Cres. Pais —6G 77
Drumshangie St. Air —1A 92
Drumshaw Dri. G32 —5C 106
Drums Rd. G53 —2A 100
Drumtrocher St. Kils —3H 11
Drumvale Dri. Chry —5C 52
Drury La. Ct. E Kil —5C 138 (off Bosworth Rd.)
Drury St. G2 —4F 83 (5D 4)
Dryad St. T'bnk —2E 117
Dryburgh Av. Pais —4E 97
Dryburgh Av. Ruth —6D 104
Dryburgh Gdns. G20 —6D 62
Dryburgh Hill. E Kil —2F 149
Dryburgh La. E Kil —2F 149
Dryburgh Pl. Coat —4B 90
Dryburgh Pl. Kirk —5F 31
Dryburgh Rd. Bear —1C 44
Dryburgh Rd. Wis —6G 145
Dryburgh St. Ham —3F 141
Dryburgh Wlk. Mood —4E 53
Dryburn Av. G52 —6A 80
Dryden St. Ham —3F 141
Drygate. G4 —4A 84
Drygate St. Lark —1E 161
Drygrange Rd. G33 —1C 86
Drymen Pl. Lenz —4D 50
Drymen Rd. Bear —1D 44
Drymen St. G52 —6E 81
Drynoch Pl. G22 —2F 63
Drysdale St. G14 —4H 59
Duart Dri. E Kil —6F 137
Duart Dri. Eld —4H 95
Duart Dri. Newt M —4G 133
Duart St. G20 —1A 62
Dubs Rd. Barr —4G 115
Dubton Path. G34 —2H 87
Dubton St. G34 —2H 87
Duchall Pl. G14 —5B 60
Duchess Ct. Ham —1C 154
Duchess Pl. Ruth —5E 105
Duchess Rd. Ruth —4E 105
Duchess Way. Bail —6D 88 (off Park Rd.)
Duchray Dri. Pais —2G 99
Duchray La. G33 —2F 85
Duchray St. G33 —2F 85
Ducraig St. G32 —6A 86
Dudhope St. G33 —1D 86
Dudley Dri. G12 —6G 61
Dudley Dri. Coat —1G 89
Dudley La. G12 —6G 61
Duffus Pl. G32 —5C 106
Duffus St. G34 —2G 87
Duffus Ter. G32 —5C 106
Duich Gdns. G23 —5C 46
Duisdale Rd. G32 —5C 106
Dukes Ga. Both —3C 124
Dukes Pl. Ham —5H 153
Dukes Rd. Bail —6D 88
Duke's Rd. Ruth —2E 121
Duke St. G1 —5F 83
Duke St. G4 —4A 84 (5H 5)
Duke St. G31 —5D 84
Duke St. Ham —6A 142
Duke St. Lark —1E 161
Duke St. Moth —1G 143
Duke St. Newm —3D 146
Duke St. Pais —3A 98
DUKE ST. STATION. G31 —4D 84
Dullatur Roundabout. Cumb —6H 13
Dulnain St. Camb —2D 122
Dulsie Rd. G21 —3E 65
DUMBARTON CENTRAL STATION. Dumb —3F 17
DUMBARTON EAST STATION. Dumb —4H 17
Dumbarton Rd. G11 —1F 81
Dumbarton Rd. G14 —3G 59
Dumbarton Rd. Bowl —5H 19
Dumbarton Rd. Dun —1B 42
Dumbarton Rd. Milt —4E 19
Dumbarton Rd. Old K —6D 20
Dumbreck Av. G41 —1G 101
Dumbreck Ct. G41 —2G 101
Dumbreck Path. G41 —2G 101 (off Dumbreck Pl.)
Dumbreck Pl. G41 —2G 101
Dumbreck Rd. G41 —6G 81
Dumbreck Sq. G41 —1G 101
DUMBRECK STATION. G41 —1A 102
Dumbreck Ter. Kils —3D 10
Dumbrock Rd. Miln —4D 24
Dumbuck Cres. Dumb —5H 17
Dumbuck Rd. Dumb —2C 18 (Crosslet)
Dumbuck Rd. Dumb —2H 17 (in two parts)
Dumbuie Av. Dumb —3H 17
Dumfries Cres. Air —6H 91
Dumgoyne Av. Miln —4F 25
Dumgoyne Ct. Air —1A 92 (off Thrushbush Rd.)
Dumgoyne Dri. Bear —6D 24
Dumgoyne Gdns. Miln —4F 25
Dumgoyne Pl. Clar —2A 134
Dunagoil Rd. G45 —5H 119
Dunagoil St. G45 —5A 120
Dunagoil Ter. G45 —5A 120
Dunalastair Dri. G33 —4B 66
Dunan Pl. G33 —4E 87
Dunard Ct. Carl —2F 165 (off Carranbute Rd.)
Dunard Rd. Ruth —6D 104
Dunard St. G20 —5D 62
Dunard Way. Pais —4H 77
Dunaskin St. G11 —2A 82
Dunbar Av. Coat —1H 109
Dunbar Av. John —5E 95
Dunbar Av. Ruth —6E 105
Dunbar Dri. Moth —5A 144
Dunbar Dri. Pais —4E 97
Dunbar Hill. E Kil —2E 149
Dunbar Pl. E Kil —2E 149
Dunbar St. Ham —4F 141
Dunbeath Av. Newt M —4F 133
Dunbeith Pl. G20 —4B 62
Dunbeth Av. Coat —4D 90
Dunbeth Ct. Coat —4D 90
Dunbeth Rd. Coat —3D 90
Dunblane Dri. E Kil —6H 137
Dunblane Pl. Coat —1B 110
Dunblane Pl. E Kil —1H 149
Dunblane St. G4 —2F 83 (1D 4)
Dunbrach Rd. Cumb —2D 34
Dunbritton Rd. Dumb —2C 18
Duncan Av. G14 —6C 60
Duncan Graham St. Lark —1F 161
Duncan La. N. G14 —5C 60 (off Norse La. N.)
Duncan Macintosh Rd. Ward N —4C 14
Duncansby Rd. G33 —5D 86
Duncarnock Av. Neil —2E 131
Duncarnock Cres. Neil —2E 131
Dunchatten St. G31 —4B 84
Dunchurch Rd. Pais —6F 79
Dunclutha Dri. Both —6E 125
Dunclutha St. G40 —3D 104
Duncolm Pl. Miln —3D 24
Duncombe Av. Clyd —6D 22
Duncombe St. G20 —2B 62
Duncombe View. Clyd —4E 43
Duncraig Cres. John —5D 94
Duncrub Dri. B'rig —6A 48
Duncruin St. G20 —2A 62
Duncruin Ter. G20 —2B 62
Duncryne Av. G32 —1D 106
Duncryne Gdns. G32 —1E 107
Duncryne Pl. B'rig —1A 64
Dundaff Hill. Cumb —3E 35
Dundas Av. Torr —5D 28
Dundas Cotts. Alla —1G 15
Dundas Ct. E Kil —1G 149
Dundashill. G4 —1F 83
Dundas La. G1 —3G 83 (4E 5)
Dundas Pl. E Kil —1G 149
Dundas St. G1 —3G 83 (4E 5)
Dundasvale Ct. G4 —2F 83 (1C 4)
Dundee Dri. G52 —1B 100
Dundee Path. G52 —2C 100
Dundonald Av. John —4D 94
Dundonald Cres. Newt M —5G 133
Dundonald Dri. Ham —4H 153
Dundonald Pl. Neil —2D 130
Dundonald Rd. G12 —6A 62
Dundonald Rd. Pais —4C 78
Dundonald St. Blan —1A 140
Dundrennan Rd. G42 —6D 102
Dundyvan Gdns. Coat —6C 90
Dundyvan Ga. Coat —6C 90
Dundyvan Ind. Est. Coat —6C 90
Dundyvan La. Wis —1G 157
Dundyvan Rd. Coat —5B 90
Dundyvan St. Wis —1G 157
Dundyvan Way. Coat —6B 90
Dunearn Pl. Pais —2C 98
Dunearn St. G4 —1D 82
Duneaton Wynd. Lark —5F 161
Dunedin Ct. E Kil —3C 148
Dunedin Dri. E Kil —2C 148
Dunedin Rd. Lark —4F 161
Dunellan Dri. Clyd —6D 22
Dunellan Rd. Miln —3D 24
Dunellan St. G52 —6E 81
Dungavel Gdns. Ham —3A 154
Dungavel La. Carl —4H 165 (off Kelso Dri.)
Dungeonhill Rd. G34 —3B 88
Dunglass Av. G14 —5C 60
Dunglass Av. E Kil —6H 137
Dunglass La. G14 —5C 60 (off Norse Rd.)
Dunglass La. N. G14 —5C 60 (off Danes Dri.)
Dunglass Pl. Miln —2E 25
Dunglass Rd. B'ton —5A 40
Dunglass Sq. E Kil —6H 137
Dungoil Av. Cumb —2D 34
Dungoil Rd. Lenz —3E 51
Dungoyne St. G20 —1A 62
Dunholme Pk. Clyd —4H 41
Dunira St. G32 —2H 105
Duniston Rd. Chap —1H 113
Dunkeld Av. Ruth —6D 104
Dunkeld Dri. Bear —3H 45
Dunkeld Gdns. B'rig —5D 48
Dunkeld La. Chry —5E 53
Dunkeld Pl. Coat —1B 110
Dunkeld Pl. Ham —6C 140
Dunkeld St. G31 —1E 105
Dunkenny Pl. G15 —3H 43
Dunkenny Rd. G15 —4H 43
Dunkenny Sq. G15 —4H 43
Dunlin. E Kil —5G 137
Dunlin Ct. Stra B —5A 110
Dunlin Cres. C'lee —2C 74
Dunlop Ct. Ham —4A 154
Dunlop Cres. Both —6F 125
Dunlop Cres. Renf —5F 59
Dunlop Gro. Udd —4E 109
Dunlop Pl. Ashg —5C 162
Dunlop Pl. Miln —2F 25
Dunlop St. G1 —5G 83 (in two parts)
Dunlop St. Camb —1E 123
Dunlop St. Lin —5A 76
Dunlop St. Renf —5F 59 (off Dunlop Cres.)
Dunlop Tower. E Kil —3G 149 (off Denholm Cres.)
Dunmore Dri. Miln —5A 26
Dunmore St. Clyd —1E 59
Dunnachie Dri. Coat —1F 109
Dunnachie Pl. Coat —1G 109
Dunnegan Dri. B'rig —3C 48
Dunnet Av. Glenm —4H 71
Dunnet Dri. C'lee —2B 74
Dunnichen Gdns. B'rig —6F 49
Dunnikier Wlk. Cumb —4A 34
Dunning St. G31 —2F 105
Dunnolly St. G21 —2C 84
Dunnotar Wlk. Newm —3D 146 (off Tiree Cres.)
Dunnottar Ct. E Kil —6E 137
Dunnottar Cres. E Kil —6E 137
Dunnottar St. G33 —1B 86
Dunnottar St. B'rig —5F 49
Dunn Sq. Pais —1A 98
Dunn St. G40 —2B 104
Dunn St. Clyd —4A 42
Dunn St. Dun —1B 42
Dunn St. Pais —6C 78
Dunns Wood Rd. Ward S —5D 14
Dunolly Dri. Newt M —4F 133
Dunottar Av. Coat —3D 110
Dunottar Pl. Coat —2D 110
Dunphail Dri. G34 —3B 88
Dunphail Rd. G34 —3B 88
Dunragit St. G31 —4E 85
Dunrobin Av. Eld —4A 96
Dunrobin Ct. Clyd —5C 42
Dunrobin Ct. E Kil —6F 137
Dunrobin Cres. E Kil —6F 137
Dunrobin Dri. E Kil —6F 137
Dunrobin Gdns. Air —5E 93
Dunrobin Pl. Coat —4B 90
Dunrobin Rd. Air —4E 93
Dunrobin St. G31 —5D 84
Dunrod Hill. E Kil —6H 137
Dunrod St. G32 —1B 106
Dunscore Brae. Ham —1C 152
Duns Cres. Wis —3A 146
Dunside Dri. G53 —1A 116
Dunskaith Pl. G34 —4B 88
Dunskaith St. G34 —3B 88
Dunsmore Rd. B'ton —3G 39
Dunsmuir St. G51 —4H 81
Duns Path. Coat —2F 111
Dunster Gdns. B'rig —3D 48
Dunswin Av. Clyd —4A 42
Dunswin Ct. Clyd —4A 42
Dunsyre Pl. G23 —6C 46
Dunsyre St. G33 —3G 85
Duntarvie Cres. G34 —3A 88
Duntarvie Pl. G34 —3H 87
Duntarvie Quad. G34 —3A 88
Duntarvie Rd. G34 —3H 87
Dunterlie Av. G13 —3A 60
Dunterlie Ct. Barr —4E 115
Duntiblae Rd. Kirk —6G 31
Duntiglennan Rd. Clyd —1C 42
Duntocher Rd. Clyd & Bear —6G 23
Duntocher Rd. Dun —2C 42
Duntocher Rd. Dun —4A 42
Duntreath Av. G13 —1G 59
Duntreath Av. G15 —6H 43
Duntreath Dri. G15 —6H 43
Duntreath Gdns. G15 —5H 43
Duntreath Gro. G15 —5A 44
Duntreath Ter. Kils —3H 11
Duntroon Pl. Bell —4D 126 (off Glencalder Cres.)
Duntroon St. G31 —3D 84
Dunure Dri. Ham —1B 152
Dunure Dri. Newt M —4G 133
Dunure Dri. Ruth —2B 120
Dunure Pl. Coat —2A 110
Dunure Pl. Newt M —5G 133
Dunure St. G20 —2B 62
Dunure St. Coat —2A 110
Dunvaig St. G33 —4D 86
Dunvegan. Glenm —5G 71
Dunvegan Av. Coat —2H 89
Dunvegan Av. Eld —4H 95
Dunvegan Dri. Newt M —4G 133
Dunvegan Pl. E Kil —6F 137
Dunvegan Pl. Udd —5B 108
Dunvegan Quad. Renf —5D 58
Dunwan Av. G13 —2H 59
Dunwan Pl. G13 —2H 59
Durban Av. Clyd —3G 41
Durham St. G41 —6B 82
Durisdeer Dri. Ham —2C 152
Durne Path. G33 —4E 87
Durness Av. Bear —2H 45
Duror St. G32 —6A 86
Durris Gdns. G32 —2D 106
Durrockstock Cres. Pais —6D 96
Durrockstock Rd. Pais —6D 96
Durrockstock Way. Pais —6D 96
Durward. E Kil —5E 139
Durward Av. G41 —4B 102
Durward Ct. G41 —4B 102
Durward Ct. Moth —5F 127
Durward Cres. Pais —4D 96
Durward Way. Pais —4D 96
Duthil St. G51 —5D 80
Dyce La. G11 —1G 81
Dyer's La. G1 —5H 83
Dyer's Wynd. Pais —6A 78
Dyfrig St. Blan —1A 140
Dykebar Av. G13 —3B 60
Dykebar Cres. Pais —3D 98
Dykehead Cres. Air —1H 91
Dykehead La. G33 —4D 86
Dykehead Rd. Air —1H 91
Dykehead Rd. Bail —6D 88
Dykehead Rd. Dull —5E 13
Dykehead Rd. Kils —2C 10
Dykehead Sq. Ham —6D 140
Dykehead St. G33 —4D 86
Dykemuir Pl. G21 —5D 64
Dykemuir Quad. G21 —5C 64
Dykemuir St. G21 —5C 64
Dyke Rd. G13 —1A 60
Dyke Rd. G14 —4H 59
Dyke St. Bail —6A 88
Dyke St. Coat —1F 109
Dysart Ct. Cumb —4A 34
Dysart Way. Air —5G 93

Eagle Cres. Bear —1B 44
Eaglesham Ct. G51 —5C 82
Eaglesham Path. Glenb —3G 69
Eaglesham Pl. G51 —5C 82
Eaglesham Rd. Clar —6B 134
Eaglesham Rd. E Kil —3A 148
Eaglesham Rd. Newt M —5D 132
Eagle St. G4 —1G 83
Earlbank Av. G14 —5C 60
Earlbank La. G14 —5C 60 (off Earlbank Av.)
Earlbank La. N. G14 —5C 60
Earlbank La. S. G14 —5C 60
Earl Haig Rd. G52 —4H 79
Earl La. G14 —6C 60
Earl Pl. G14 —5C 60
Earl Pl. Bri W —5F 73
Earlsburn Rd. Lenz —3E 51
Earlscourt. Mood —6D 52
Earl's Ga. Both —4C 124
Earl's Hill. Cumb —3D 34
Earlspark Av. G43 —1D 118
Earlston Cres. Coat —2F 111
Earlston St. Wis —3A 146
Earl St. G14 —5A 60
Earl View. Moth —4A 128
Earn Av. Bear —3H 45
Earn Av. Renf —1G 79
Earn Av. Rig I —1A 126
Earn Cres. Wis —2H 157
Earn Gdns. Lark —5E 161
Earn La. Moth —2A 128 (off Howden Pl.)
Earnock Av. Moth —3E 143
Earnock Rd. Ham —1B 152
Earnock St. G33 —5F 65
Earnock St. Ham —5E 141
Earn Rd. Newt M —2D 132
Earnside St. G32 —6B 86
Earn St. G33 —2G 85
Easdale. E Kil —4B 150
Easdale Dri. G32 —1A 106
Easdale Path. Glenb —3G 69
Easdale Pl. Newt M —4B 132
Easdale Rise. Ham —6C 140
E. Academy St. Wis —1H 157
East Av. Blan —4B 140
East Av. Carl —3D 164
East Av. Moth —5A 128
East Av. Plain —1G 93
East Av. Renf —6F 59
East Av. Udd —1G 125
E. Barns St. Clyd —1F 59
E. Bath La. G2 —3G 83 (4E 5)
E. Buchanan St. Pais —6B 78
Eastburn Rd. G21 —4D 64
E. Burnside St. Kils —3H 11
E. Campbell St. G1 —5A 84
Eastcote Av. G14 —5E 61
Eastcroft. Ruth —5D 104
Eastcroft Ter. G21 —5C 64
E. Dean St. Bell —2D 126
Eastend Av. Moth —6B 128
Easter Craigs. G31 —3D 84
Easter Cres. Wis —5C 146
Easter Garngaber Rd. Lenz —2E 51
Eastergreens Av. Kirk —6C 30
Easterhill Pl. G32 —2H 105
Easterhill St. G32 —2H 105
Easterhouse Path. G34 —3A 88
Easterhouse Pl. G34 —3A 88
Easterhouse Quad. G34 —4A 88
Easterhouse Rd. Bail & G34 —6H 87
EASTERHOUSE STATION. Bail —5A 88
Easterhouse Township Cen. G34 —3G 87
Eastermains. Kirk —3H 31
Easter M. Udd —2C 124
Easter Queenslie Rd. G33 —3E 87
Easter Rd. Clar —3E 135
Easterton Av. Clar —4E 135
Easter Wood Cres. Udd —4H 109
Eastfield Av. Camb —1G 121
Eastfield Cres. Dumb —5H 17
Eastfield Pl. Dumb —5H 17
Eastfield Rd. G21 —5A 64
Eastfield Rd. Carl —4G 165
Eastfield Rd. Cumb —3C 34
Eastfield Ter. Bell —3F 127
E. Gartferry Rd. Bail —5C 52
Eastgate. G'csh —4E 69
East Ga. Glenb —2H 69
East Ga. Wis —6B 146
E. George St. Coat —3D 90

E. Glebe Ter. *Ham* —1H **153**
E. Greenlees Av. *Camb* —4C **122**
E. Greenlees Cres. *Camb* —4B **122**
E. Greenlees Dri. *Camb* —4C **122**
E. Greenlees Rd. *Camb* —4A **122**
E. Hallhill Rd. *Bail* —5F **87**
E. Hamilton St. *Wis* —1H **157**
E. High St. *Air* —3A **92**
E. High St. *Kirk* —4C **30**
E. Kilbride Rd. *Clar* —3E **135**
E. Kilbride Rd. *Ruth* —2E **121**
EAST KILBRIDE STATION. *E Kil* —1G **149**
East La. *Pais* —1C **98**
Eastlea Pl. *Air* —5B **92**
E. Machen St. *Lark* —4F **161**
E. Mains Rd. *E Kil* —1G **149**
E. Milton Gro. *E Kil* —2D **148**
Eastmuir St. *G32* —6B **86**
Eastmuir St. *Wis* —5C **146**
Easton Pl. *Coat* —6D **90**
East Rd. *Kilb* —1A **94**
East Rd. *Moth* —3A **128**
E. Scott Ter. *Ham* —2H **153**
Eastside. *Kirk* —4D **30**
E. Springfield Ter. *B'rig* —1D **64**
E. Station Ind. Est. *Lark* —1F **161**
E. Stewart Pl. *Coat* —4E **91**
E. Stewart St. *Coat* —5E **91**
E. Thomson St. *Clyd* —4D **42**
E. Thornlie St. *Wis* —1H **157**
Eastvale Pl. *G3* —3A **82**
E. Wellbrae Cres. *Ham* —2F **153**
E. Wellington St. *G31* —6F **85**
Eastwood Av. *G41* —5B **102**
Eastwood Av. *Giff* —4A **118**
Eastwood Cres. *T'bnk* —3F **117**
Eastwood Dri. *Newm* —3E **147**
Eastwoodmains Rd. *Giff* —6H **117**
Eastwood Rd. *Chry* —5D **52**
Eastwood Toll. *T'bnk* —6H **117**
Eastwood View. *Camb* —1E **123**
*Eastwood Way. Lark —1F **161***
(off Antrim La.)
Easwald Bank. *Mill P* —3B **94**
Ebroch Dri. *Kils* —3A **12**
Ebroch Pk. *Kils* —3A **12**
Eccles St. *G22* —4A **64**
Eckford St. *G32* —1A **106**
*Eck Path. Moth —2A **128***
(off Howden Pl.)
Eday St. *G22* —3H **63**
Edderton Pl. *G34* —4G **87**
Eddington Dri. *Newt M* —6C **132**
Eddleston Pl. *Camb* —2E **123**
Eddlewood Path. *G33* —4F **87**
Eddlewood Rd. *G33* —4F **87**
Eden Dri. *E Kil* —5B **148**
Eden Gdns. *E Kil* —4B **148**
Eden La. *G33* —2F **85**
Eden Pk. *Both* —5D **124**
Eden Pl. *Camb* —2D **122**
Eden Pl. *Renf* —1G **79**
Edenside. *Cumb* —4B **14**
Eden St. *G33* —2F **85**
Edenwood St. *G31* —6G **85**
Edgam Dri. *G52* —6C **80**
Edgefauld Av. *G21* —6B **64**
Edgefauld Dri. *G21* —5B **64**
Edgefauld Pl. *G21* —4B **64**
Edgefauld Rd. *G21* —4B **64**
Edgehill La. *G11* —5G **61**
Edgehill Rd. *G11* —5F **61**
Edgehill Rd. *Bear* —1E **45**
Edgemont Pk. *Ham* —3G **153**
Edgemont St. *G41* —5C **102**
Edinbeg Av. *G42* —5A **104**
Edinbeg Pl. *G42* —5A **104**
Edinburgh Rd. *G33 & Bail* —1F **86**
Edinburgh Rd. *Ham* —5B **142**
Edinburgh Rd. *Moth* —1C **128**
Edington Gdns. *Chry* —4D **52**
Edington St. *G4* —1F **83**
Edison St. *G52* —3G **79**
(in three parts)
Edmiston Dri. *G51* —5F **81**
Edmiston Dri. *Lin* —5F **75**
Edmonstone Ct. *Clyd* —2F **59**
Edmonstone Dri. *Kils* —4H **11**
Edmonton Ter. *E Kil* —3E **149**
Edmund Kean. *E Kil* —4C **138**
*Edrick Ct. Coat —5B **90***
(off Kirk St.)
Edrom Ct. *G32* —6H **85**
Edrom Path. *G32* —6H **85**
Edrom St. *G32* —1H **105**
(in two parts)
Edward Av. *Renf* —5G **59**
Edward St. *Bail* —6D **88**
Edward St. *Clyd* —2F **59**
Edward St. *Ham* —1H **153**
Edward St. *Kils* —2H **11**
Edward St. *Moth* —4H **143**
Edwin St. *G51* —6B **82**
Edzell Ct. *G14* —1D **80**
Edzell Dri. *Eld* —3B **96**
Edzell Dri. *Newt M* —5E **133**
Edzell Gdns. *B'rig* —1E **65**
Edzell Pl. *G14* —6D **60**
Edzell St. *G14* —1D **80**
Edzell St. *Coat* —1H **109**
Egidia Av. *Giff* —5A **118**
Egilsay Cres. *G22* —1G **63**
Egilsay Pl. *G22* —1G **63**
Egilsay St. *G22* —1G **63**
Egilsay Ter. *G22* —1G **63**
Eglinton Ct. *G5* —6F **83**
Eglinton Dri. *Giff* —5A **118**
Eglinton St. *G41 & G5* —1E **103**
Eglinton St. *Coat* —3D **90**
Egmont Pk. *E Kil* —4C **148**
Eider Av. *E Kil* —6C **148**
Eider Gro. *E Kil* —6C **148**
Eider Pl. *E Kil* —6C **148**
Eighth St. *Udd* —4C **108**
Eildon Dri. *Barr* —6E **115**
Eildon Rd. *Kirk* —5F **31**
Eileen Gdns. *B'rig* —5D **48**
Elcho St. *G40* —5B **84**
Elderbank. *Bear* —4E **45**
Elder Gro. *Udd* —5F **109**
Elderpark Gdns. *G51* —4F **81**
Elderpark Gro. *G51* —4F **81**
Elderpark St. *G51* —4F **81**
Elderslea Rd. *Carl* —5G **165**
Elderslie St. *G3* —2D **82**
Elder St. *G51* —4F **81**
(in two parts)
Eldin Pl. *Bri W* —5G **73**
Eldin Pl. *Eld* —3H **95**
Eldon Ct. *G11* —1H **81**
Eldon Gdns. *B'rig* —6A **48**
Eldon St. *G3* —1C **82**
Elgin Av. *E Kil* —6H **137**
Elgin Gdns. *Clar* —1D **134**
Elgin Pl. *Air* —6G **91**
Elgin Pl. *Coat* —2D **110**
Elgin Pl. *E Kil* —6H **137**
Elgin Pl. *Kils* —2H **11**
Elgin Rd. *Bear* —6F **25**
Elgin Ter. *Ham* —5C **140**
Elgin Way. *Bell* —1C **126**
Elibank St. *G33* —2A **86**
Elie St. *G11* —1A **82**
Eliot Cres. *Ham* —2H **153**
Eliot Ter. *Ham* —1H **153**
Elizabethan Way. *Renf* —2E **79**
Elizabeth Av. *Milt C* —5B **8**
Elizabeth Cres. *T'bnk* —4G **117**
Elizabeth Quad. *Moth* —2A **128**
Elizabeth St. *G51* —6A **82**
Elizabeth Wynd. *Ham* —4H **153**
Ella Gdns. *Bell* —3E **127**
Ellangowan Rd. *G41* —5A **102**
Ellangowan Rd. *Miln* —3G **25**
Ellergreen Rd. *Bear* —3E **45**
Ellerslie St. *John* —2G **95**
Ellesmere St. *G22* —6E **63**
Ellinger Ct. *Clyd* —3A **42**
Elliot Av. *Giff* —5A **118**
Elliot Av. *Pais* —6C **96**
Elliot Cres. *E Kil* —1B **150**
Elliot Dri. *Giff* —4A **118**
Elliot Pl. *G3* —4C **82**
Elliot St. *G3* —4C **82**
(in two parts)
Ellisland. *E Kil* —6D **138**
Ellisland. *Kirk* —3H **31**
Ellisland Av. *Clyd* —4E **43**
Ellisland Cres. *Ruth* —2B **120**
Ellisland Dri. *Blan* —3H **139**
Ellisland Dri. *Kirk* —3G **31**
Ellisland Rd. *G43* —1B **118**
Ellisland Rd. *Clar* —4C **134**
Ellisland Rd. *Cumb* —3B **36**
Ellisland Wynd. *Moth* —4C **128**
Ellismuir Farm Rd. *Bail* —1B **108**
Ellismuir Pl. *Bail* —1A **108**
Ellismuir Rd. *Bail* —1A **108**
Ellismuir St. *Coat* —2H **109**
(in two parts)
Ellis St. *Coat* —4C **90**
Elliston Av. *G53* —2C **116**
Elliston Cres. *G53* —2C **116**
Elliston Dri. *G53* —2C **116**
Ellis Way. *Moth* —4H **143**
Ellon Dri. *Lin* —6G **75**
Ellon Way. *Pais* —4C **78**
Ellrig. *E Kil* —6F **149**
Elm Av. *Lenz* —1C **50**
Elm Av. *Renf* —5E **59**
Elm Bank. *B'rig* —6D **48**
Elm Bank. *Kirk* —4D **30**
Elmbank Av. *Udd* —6F **109**
Elmbank Cres. *G2* —3E **83**
Elmbank Cres. *Ham* —5E **141**
Elmbank Dri. *Lark* —4G **161**
Elmbank St. *G2* —3E **83** (4A **4**)
Elmbank St. *Bell* —2C **126**
Elmbank St. *Carl* —5G **165**
*Elmbank St. La. G2 —3E **83** (4A **4**)*
(off Elmbank St.)
Elm Cres. *Udd* —6H **109**
Elm Dri. *Camb* —2C **122**
Elm Dri. *Cumb* —1F **37**
Elm Dri. *John* —5F **95**
Elmfoot St. *G5* —3H **103**
Elm Gdns. *Bear* —1E **45**
Elmhurst. *Moth* —5F **143**
Elmira Rd. *Muirh* —2B **68**
*Elm La. W. G14 —6D **60***
(off Lime St.)
Elmore Av. *G44* —2F **119**
Elmore La. *G44* —2F **119**
Elm Pl. *E Kil* —5E **149**
Elm Quad. *Air* —4D **92**
Elm Rd. *Bri W* —2G **73**
Elm Rd. *Broad I* —3F **17**
Elm Rd. *Clyd* —2C **42**
Elm Rd. *Moth* —2B **128**
Elm Rd. *Pais* —4C **98**
Elm Rd. *Ruth* —3D **120**
Elmslie Ct. *Bail* —1A **108**
Elms, The. *G44* —3F **119**
Elm St. *G14* —6D **60**
Elm St. *Blan* —2C **140**
Elm St. *Clar* —3D **134**
Elm St. *Coat* —6E **91**
Elm St. *Len* —3G **7**
Elm St. *Moth* —2F **143**
*Elm St. E. G14 —6D **60***
(off Elm St.)
Elmvale Rd. *G21* —4A **64**
Elmvale St. *G21* —4A **64**
Elm View Ct. *Bell* —3F **127**
Elm Wlk. *Bear* —1E **45**
Elm Way. *Lark* —6A **156**
Elmwood Av. *G11* —5F **61**
Elmwood Av. *Newt M* —3F **133**
Elmwood Ct. *Both* —5E **125**
Elmwood Gdns. *Kirk* —2A **50**
*Elmwood La. G11 —5F **61***
(off Elmwood Av.)
Elphinstone Cres. *E Kil* —4H **149**
Elphinstone Pl. *G51* —4A **82**
Elphinstone Rd. *Giff* —2G **133**
Elphin St. *G23* —6B **46**
Elrig Rd. *G44* —2D **118**
Elsinore Path. *E Kil* —6G **149**
Elspeth Gdns. *B'rig* —5E **49**
Eltham St. *G22* —6F **63**
Elvan Ct. *Moth* —3F **143**
Elvan Pl. *E Kil* —4A **148**
Elvan St. *G32* —6H **85**
Elvan St. *Moth* —2F **143**
Elvan Tower. *Moth* —4G **143**
Embo Dri. *G13* —3B **60**
Emerald Ter. *Bell* —3C **126**
Emerson Rd. *B'rig* —6C **48**
Emerson Rd. W. *B'rig* —6C **48**
Emerson St. *G20* —3E **63**
Emily Dri. *Moth* —5G **143**
Emma Jay Rd. *Bell* —2D **126**
Endfield Av. *G12* —3H **61**
Endrick Bank. *B'rig* —3C **48**
Endrick Dri. *Bear* —4F **45**
Endrick Dri. *Pais* —5D **78**
Endrick Gdns. *Miln* —3E **25**
Endrick St. *G21* —6H **63**
English St. *Wis* —6D **144**
Ennerdale. *E Kil* —5B **148**
Ennisfree Rd. *Blan* —1B **140**
Ensay St. *G22* —2H **63**
Enterkin St. *G32* —1H **105**
Eriboll Pl. *G22* —2F **63**
Eriboll St. *G22* —2F **63**
Eribol Wlk. *Moth* —4D **128**
Ericht Rd. *G43* —2A **118**
Eriska Av. *G14* —4A **60**
Eriskay Av. *Ham* —1D **152**
Eriskay Av. *Newt M* —4B **132**
Eriskay Cres. *Newt M* —4B **132**
Eriskay Dri. *Old K* —1G **41**
Eriskay Pl. *Old K* —1G **41**
Erradale St. *G22* —2E **63**
Errogie St. *G34* —3H **87**
Erskine Av. *G41* —1H **101**
Erskine Bri. *B'ton* —3D **40**
*Erskine Ct. Air —3E **93***
(off Katherine St.)
Erskine Cres. *Air* —6H **91**
Erskinefauld Rd. *Lin* —5G **75**
Erskine Ferry Rd. *Old K* —2F **41**
Erskine Rd. *Giff* —3H **133**
Erskine Sq. *G52* —4H **79**
Erskine View. *Clyd* —4D **42**
Erskine View. *Old K* —1E **41**
Ervie St. *G34* —4A **88**
Escarp Rd. *Carl* —2F **165**
Esdaile Ct. *Moth* —4A **128**
Esk Av. *Renf* —1G **79**
Eskbank St. *G32* —5A **86**
Eskdale. *E Kil* —6E **137**
Eskdale. *Newt M* —4H **133**
Eskdale Dri. *Ruth* —6F **105**
Eskdale Rd. *Bear* —5D **44**
Eskdale St. *G42* —4F **103**
Esk Dri. *Pais* —4C **96**
Esk St. *G14* —4H **59**
*Esk Wlk. Cumb —3H **35***
(off Cumbernauld Cen., The)
Esk Way. *Pais* —4C **96**
Esmond St. *G3* —2A **82**
Espedair St. *Pais* —2A **98**
Espieside Cres. *Coat* —3H **89**
Essenside Av. *G15* —5B **44**
Essex Dri. *G14* —5D **60**
Essex La. *G14* —5D **60**
Esslemont Av. *G14* —4B **60**
Esslemont La. *G14* —4C **60**
Estate Quad. *G32* —4C **106**
Estate Rd. *G32* —4C **106**
Etive Av. *Bear* —3H **45**
Etive Av. *Ham* —2E **153**
Etive Ct. *Clyd* —2E **43**
Etive Ct. *Coat* —2D **110**
Etive Ct. *Cumb* —1D **54**
Etive Cres. *B'rig* —6D **48**
Etive Cres. *Cumb* —1D **54**
Etive Cres. *Wis* —3H **157**
Etive Dri. *Air* —6C **92**
Etive Dri. *B'ton* —5A **40**
Etive Dri. *Cumb* —1D **54**
Etive Dri. *Giff* —6B **118**
Etive Pl. *Cumb* —1E **55**
Etive St. *G32* —6A **86**
Etive St. *Wis* —2H **157**
Etna Ind. Est. *Wis* —5C **144**
Etna St. *Wis* —5C **144**
*Eton La. G12 —1C **82***
(off Gt. George St.)
Etrick Av. *Bell* —6C **110**
*Etterick Wynd. Blan —2A **140***
(off Winton Cres.)
Ettrick Av. *Renf* —1H **79**
Ettrick Ct. *Camb* —2D **122**
Ettrick Ct. *Coat* —2E **111**
Ettrick Cres. *Ruth* —6E **105**
Ettrick Dri. *Bear* —6C **24**
Ettrick Dri. *B'ton* —5A **40**
Ettrick Hill. *E Kil* —6A **138**
Ettrick Oval. *Pais* —5C **96**
Ettrick Pl. *G41* —6B **102**
*Ettrick Sq. Cumb —3H **35***
(off Cumbernauld Cen., The)
Ettrick St. *Wis* —4G **145**
Ettrick Ter. *John* —5C **94**
*Ettrick Wlk. Cumb —3H **35***
(off Cumbernauld Cen., The)
*Ettrick Way. Cumb —3H **35***
(off Cumbernauld Cen., The)
Eurocentral Ind. Est. *Moth* —6H **111**
Evan Cres. *Giff* —5B **118**
Evan Dri. *Giff* —5B **118**
Evanton Dri. *Giff* —5E **117**
Evanton Pl. *T'bnk* —4E **117**
Everall Dri. *Wis* —4E **147**
Everard Ct. *G21* —2A **64**
Everard Dri. *G21* —3A **64**
Everard Pl. *G21* —2A **64**
Everard Quad. *G21* —3A **64**
Everglades, The. *Chry* —1H **67**
Eversley St. *G32* —2A **106**
Everton Rd. *G53* —3C **100**
Ewart Cres. *Ham* —1E **153**
Ewart Ter. *Ham* —1F **153**
Ewing Ct. *Ham* —4G **153**
Ewing Pl. *G31* —6E **85**
Ewing St. *Kilb* —2A **94**
Ewing St. *Ruth* —6C **104**
Ewing Wlk. *Miln* —4A **26**
Excelsior St. *Wis* —6D **144**
*Exchange Pl. G1 —4G **83** (5E **5**)*
(off Buchanan St.)
Exchange Pl. *Coat* —5C **90**
Exeter Dri. *G11* —1G **81**
*Exeter La. G11 —1G **81***
(off Dumbarton Rd.)
Exeter St. *Coat* —6C **90**
EXHIBITION CENTRE STATION. *G3* —3C **82**
Exhibition Way. *G3* —4C **82**
Eynort St. *G22* —2E **63**

Factory Rd. *Moth* —4G **143**
Fagan Ct. *Blan* —6C **124**
Faifley Rd. *Clyd* —6F **23**
Fairbairn Cres. *T'bnk* —5G **117**
Fairbairn St. *G40* —1C **104**
Fairburn St. *G32* —1H **105**
Fairfax Av. *G44* —2G **119**
Fairfield Ct. *Clar* —4C **134**
Fairfield Dri. *Clar* —4C **134**
Fairfield Gdns. *G51* —3F **81**
Fairfield Pl. *G51* —3F **81**
Fairfield Pl. *Both* —5F **125**
Fairfield Pl. *E Kil* —1D **148**
Fairfield Pl. *Ham* —2A **154**
Fairfield St. *G51* —3F **81**
Fairford Dri. *Cumb* —6F **35**
Fairhaven Rd. *G23* —1C **62**
Fairhill Av. *G53* —6C **100**
Fairhill Av. *Ham* —2G **153**
Fairhill Cres. *Ham* —2G **153**
Fairhill Pl. *Ham* —4F **153**
Fairholm Av. *Ham* —2F **155**
Fairholm St. *G32* —1H **105**
Fairholm St. *Lark* —1D **160**
Fairley St. *G51* —5H **81**
Fairlie. *E Kil* —6F **107**
Fairlie Pk. Dri. *G11* —1G **81**
Fair Oaks. *Crmck* —1A **136**
Fairway. *Bear* —2B **44**
Fairway Av. *Pais* —5H **97**
Fairways. *Lark* —2G **161**
Fairways View. *Hard* —1F **43**
Fairweather Pl. *Newt M* —5C **132**
Fairyknowe Gdns. *Both* —5F **125**
Faith Av. *Bri W* —1A **72**
Falconbridge Rd. *E Kil* —5C **138**
Falcon Cres. *Pais* —5F **77**
Falconer Ter. *Ham* —2G **153**
Falcon Rd. *John* —6D **94**
Falcon Ter. *G20* —1A **62**
Falfield St. *G5* —1E **103**
Falkland Av. *Newt M* —4G **133**
Falkland Cres. *B'rig* —1F **65**
Falkland Dri. *E Kil* —2E **149**
Falkland La. *G12* —6H **61**
Falkland Pk. *E Kil* —2F **149**
Falkland Pl. *Coat* —2D **110**
Falkland Pl. *E Kil* —2F **149**
Falkland St. *G12* —6H **61**
Falloch Pl. *Newm* —3D **146**
Falloch Rd. *G42* —6E **103**
Falloch Rd. *Bear* —5C **44**
Falloch Rd. *Miln* —3D **24**
Fallside Av. *Udd* —1G **125**
Fallside Rd. *Both* —5E **125**
Falside Av. *Pais* —4A **98**
Falside Rd. *G32* —3A **106**
Falside Rd. *Pais* —4H **97**
Falstaff. *E Kil* —4C **138**
Fancett Sq. *E Kil* —3H **149**
Faraday Av. *Wis* —6A **146**
Faraday Retail Pk. *Coat* —5C **90**
Fara St. *G23* —1D **62**
Farie St. *Ruth* —5B **104**
Farm Ct. *Both* —3F **125**
Farm Cres. *Moth* —3F **129**
Farme Cross. *Ruth* —4D **104**
Farmeloan Rd. *Ruth* —5D **104**
Farmgate Sq. *Bell* —3B **126**
Farmington Av. *G32* —6D **86**
Farmington Gdns. *G32* —6D **86**
Farmington Ga. *G32* —1D **106**
Farmington Gro. *G32* —6D **86**
Farm La. *Bell* —4B **126**
Farm Pk. *Lenz* —3D **50**
Farm Rd. *G41* —6H **81**
Farm Rd. *Blan* —6B **124**
Farm Rd. *Dalm* —4H **41**
Farm Rd. *Dun* —6C **22**
Farm Rd. *Ham* —5D **140**
Farm St. *Moth* —2F **143**
Farm Ter. *Ham* —5D **140**
Farndale. *E Kil* —6E **137**
Farne Dri. *G44* —3F **119**
Farnell St. *G4* —1F **83**
Farrier Ct. *John* —2F **95**
Faskally Wlk. *Newm* —3D **146**
Faskin Cres. *G53* —6H **99**
Faskine Av. *Air* —5H **91**
Faskine Av. *C'bnk* —3B **112**
Faskine Cres. *Air* —5H **91**
Faskin Pl. *G53* —6H **99**
Faskin Rd. *G53* —6H **99**
Faskley Av. *B'rig* —4A **48**
Fasque Pl. *G15* —3G **43**
Fastnet St. *G33* —3A **86**
Fauldhouse St. *G5* —2H **103**
Faulds. *Bail* —6A **88**
Faulds Gdns. *Bail* —6A **88**
Fauldshead Rd. *Renf* —6E **59**
Faulds La. *Coat* —2B **110**
Fauldspark Cres. *Bail* —5A **88**
Faulds St. *Coat* —2A **110**
Fauldswood Cres. *Pais* —3F **97**
Fauldswood Dri. *Pais* —3F **97**
Fearnmore Rd. *G20* —2B **62**
Fells, The. *Len* —3G **7**
Fellsview Av. *Kirk* —4F **31**
Felton Pl. *G13* —2H **59**
Fendoch St. *G32* —1A **106**
Fenella St. *G32* —6B **86**
Fennsbank Av. *Ruth* —4F **121**
Fenwick Dri. *Barr* —6E **115**
Fenwick Dri. *Ham* —4A **154**
Fenwick Pl. *Giff* —6H **117**
Fenwick Rd. *Giff* —6H **117**
Ferclay St. *Clyd* —6F **23**
Fereneze Av. *Barr* —4D **114**
Fereneze Av. *Clar* —1A **134**
Fereneze Av. *Renf* —1C **70**
Fereneze Cres. *G13* —2A **60**
Fereneze Cres. *Ham* —6D **140**
Fereneze Dri. *Pais* —5F **97**
Fereneze Rd. *Neil* —2A **130**
Fergus Av. *Pais* —6E **77**
Fergus Ct. *G20* —5C **62**
Fergus Dri. *G20* —5C **62**
Fergus Dri. *Pais* —6E **77**
Fergus Gdns. *Ham* —1B **154**
Fergus La. *G20* —5D **62**
Ferguslie. *Pais* —2D **96**
Ferguslie Pk. Av. *Pais* —6E **77**
Ferguslie Pk. Oval. *Pais* —6E **77**
Ferguslie Wlk. *Pais* —1F **97**
(in two parts)
Ferguson Av. *Miln* —3F **25**
Ferguson Av. *Renf* —6F **59**
Ferguson Dri. *Moth* —6G **143**
Ferguson St. *John* —2E **95**
Ferguson St. *Renf* —5F **59**
Fergusson Pl. *E Kil* —4D **138**
Fergusson Rd. *Cumb* —3H **35**
Fergusson Ter. *Milt C* —5C **8**
Ferguston Rd. *Bear* —3F **45**
Fernan St. *G32* —6H **85**
Fern Av. *B'rig* —1D **64**
Fern Av. *Ersk* —2F **57**
Fern Av. *Lenz* —3C **50**
Fernbank Av. *Camb* —3C **122**
Fernbank St. *G21* —4A **64**

Fernbrae Av. Ruth —4D 120
Fernbrae Way. Ruth —4D 120
Fern Cotts. G13 —4F 61
Ferncroft Dri. G44 —2H 119
Ferndale. Lark —4E 161
Ferndale Ct. G23 —1B 62
Ferndale Dri. G23 —1B 62
Ferndale Gdns. G23 —1B 62
Ferndale Pl. G23 —1B 62
Fern Dri. Barr —3D 114
Ferness Oval. G21 —2E 65
Ferness Pl. G21 —2E 65
Ferness Rd. G21 —3E 65
Ferngrove Av. G12 —3H 61
Fernhill Grange. Both —6E 125
Fernhill Rd. Ruth —2C 120
Fern La. G13 —4F 61
Fernlea. Bear —4E 45
Fernleigh Pl. Chry —5D 52
Fernleigh Rd. G43 —2B 118
Fernside Wlk. Ham —2A 154
Fernslea Av. Blan —1A 140
Fern St. Moth —5A 144
Ferry Rd. G3 —3H 81
Ferry Rd. B'ton —4G 39
Ferry Rd. Both —5E 125
Ferry Rd. Renf —5F 59
Ferry Rd. Udd —1B 124
Fersit St. G43 —1A 118
Fetlar Dri. G44 —2G 119
Fetlar Rd. Bri W —3E 73
Fettercairn Av. G15 —4G 43
Fettercairn Gdns. B'rig —6E 49
Fettes St. G33 —3H 85
Fiddoch Ct. Newm —2D 146
Fidra St. G33 —3H 85
Fielden Pl. G40 —6C 84
Fielden St. G40 —6C 84
Field Gro. Clar —4D 134
Fieldhead Dri. G43 —2G 117
Fieldhead Sq. G43 —2G 117
Field Rd. Clar —4D 134
Field Rd. Clyd —5F 23
Field Rd. Lark —3F 161
Fields La. Hous —1B 74
Field St. Ham —2H 153
Fife Av. G52 —1B 100
Fife Av. Air —6A 92
Fife Cres. Both —6E 125
Fife Dri. Moth —5F 127
Fife Way. B'rig —1F 65
Fifth Av. G12 —4F 61
Fifth Av. Air —3C 92
Fifth Av. Blan —4C 140
Fifth Av. Renf —1E 79
Fifth Av. Step —4B 66
Fifty Pitches Pl. G52 —4B 80
Fifty Pitches Rd. G52 —4B 80
Finart Dri. Pais —4D 98
Finaven Gdns. Bear —5B 24
Finch Dri. G13 —1H 59
Finch Pl. John —6D 94
Findhorn. Ersk —4E 41
Findhorn Av. Pais —4D 96
Findhorn Av. Renf —6G 59
Findhorn Ct. E Kil —3A 148
Findhorn Pl. E Kil —3A 148
Findhorn St. G33 —3F 85
Findlay St. Kils —3H 11
Findlay St. Moth —4H 143
Findochty. Ersk —4E 41
Findochty St. G33 —2D 86
Fingal La. G20 —2A 62
Fingal St. G20 —2B 62
Fingalton Rd. Newt M —4A 132
Fingask St. G32 —1C 106
Finglas Av. Pais —4D 98
Finglen Gdns. Miln —3E 25
Finglen Pl. G53 —3B 116
Fingleton Av. Barr —6F 115
Finhaven St. G32 —2G 105
Finlarig St. G34 —4A 88
Finlas St. G22 —5H 63
Finlay Dri. G31 —4C 84
Finlay Dri. Lin —6F 75
Finlay Rise. Miln —5H 25
Finlayson Dri. Air —4E 93
Finlayson Quad. Air —4E 93
Finlaystone St. Coat —4A 90
Finnart Sq. G40 —2B 104
Finnart St. G40 —2B 104
Finnieston Sq. G3 —3C 82
Finnieston St. G3 —4C 82
Finnie Wynd. Moth —5B 144
Finsbay St. G51 —5D 80
Fintrie Ter. Ham —5C 140
Fintry Av. Pais —5A 98
Fintry Ct. Coat —2E 111
Fintry Cres. Barr —6E 115
Fintry Cres. B'rig —6E 49
Fintry Dri. G44 —6G 103
Fintry Gdns. Bear —5C 24
Fir Bank Av. Lark —3F 161
Firbank Av. Torr —5D 28
Firbank Ter. Barr —6G 115
Fir Ct. Coat —1A 110
Firdon Cres. G15 —6A 44
Fir Dri. E Kil —6D 148
Fir Gro. Udd —5F 109
Firhill Av. Air —5H 91
Firhill Rd. G20 —5D 62
Firhill St. G20 —5E 63
Firlee. E Kil —3B 148
Firpark Rd. B'rig —1D 64
Firpark St. G31 —3B 84
Fir Pk. St. Moth —5H 143
Firpark Ter. G31 —4B 84
Fir Pl. Bail —2G 107
Fir Pl. Camb —1C 122
Fir Pl. Cle —6H 129
Fir Pl. John —4G 95
First Av. G44 —5D 118
First Av. Bear —4G 45
First Av. Dumb —3C 18
First Av. Kirk —6D 50
First Av. Mille —4B 66
First Av. Renf —1E 79
First Av. Udd —5C 108
First Gdns. G41 —1G 101
Firs, The. G44 —2F 119
First Rd. Blan —4C 140
First St. Udd —5D 108
First Ter. Clyd —4C 42
Firthview Ter. Dumb —4C 16
Firtree Pl. Newm —3F 147
Firtree Rd. Newm —3F 147
Fir View. C'bnk —3B 112
Firwood Ct. Newt M —5E 133
Firwood Dri. G44 —1G 119
Firwood Rd. Newt M —4E 133
Fischer Gdns. Pais —1D 96
Fisher Av. Kils —3H 11
Fisher Av. Pais —1D 96
Fisher Ct. G31 —4B 84
Fisher Cres. Clyd —1D 42
Fisher Dri. Pais —1D 96
Fishers Rd. Renf —3E 59
Fisher St. Lark —4F 161
Fisher Way. Pais —1D 96
Fishescoates Av. Ruth —3E 121
(in two parts)
Fishescoates Gdns. Ruth —2F 121
Fitzalan Dri. Pais —5C 78
Fitzalan Rd. Renf —2C 78
Fitzroy La. G3 —3C 82
Fitzroy Pl. G3 —3C 82
(off Royal Cres.)
Flakefield. E Kil —1D 148
Flanders St. Clyd —6E 23
Flaxford Gro. Moth —5F 127
Flaxmill Av. Wis —5D 144
Flax Rd. Udd —2E 125
Fleet Av. Renf —2G 79
Fleet St. G32 —1B 106
Fleming Av. Chry —1A 68
Fleming Av. Clyd —1F 59
Fleming Ct. Carl —4E 165
Fleming Ct. Clyd —5D 42
Fleming Ct. Ham —5C 140
Fleming Ct. Moth —5A 144
Fleming Pl. E Kil —3G 149
Fleming Rd. Bell —1D 126
Fleming Rd. B'ton —4H 39
Fleming Rd. Cumb —3H 35
Fleming Rd. Hous —1A 74
Fleming St. G31 —5D 84
Fleming St. Pais —4A 78
Flemington Ind. Est. Camb —3E 123
Flemington Rd. G21 —6A 64
Flemington Rd. Camb —2E 139
Fleming Way. Ham —5B 140
Fleming Way. Lark —4G 161
(off Donaldson Rd.)
Flenders Av. Clar —3A 134
Flenders Rd. Clar —3A 134
Fleurs Av. G41 —1H 101
Fleurs Rd. G41 —1H 101
Flinders Pl. E Kil —3D 148
Flloyd St. Coat —4B 90
Floorsburn Cres. John —3E 95
Floors St. John —3E 95
Flora Gdns. B'rig —5E 49
Florence Dri. Giff —5A 118
Florence Gdns. Ruth —3E 121
Florence St. G5 —1G 103
Florida Av. G42 —5F 103
Florida Cres. G42 —5F 103
Florida Dri. G42 —5E 103
Florida Gdns. Bail —6G 87
Florida Sq. G42 —5F 103
Florida St. G42 —5F 103
Flowerdale Pl. G53 —4B 116
Flowerhill Ind. Est. Air —3B 92
Flowerhill St. Air —3B 92
Flures Av. Ersk —1A 58
Flures Cres. Ersk —2A 58
Flures Dri. Ersk —1A 58
Flures Pl. Ersk —1A 58
Fochabers Dri. G52 —5C 80
Fogo Pl. G20 —3B 62
Footfield Rd. Bell —3B 126
Forbes Dri. G40 —6B 84
Forbes Dri. Moth —5D 126
Forbes Pl. Pais —1A 98
Forbes St. G40 —5B 84
Fordneuk St. G40 —6C 84
Fordoun St. G34 —3B 88
Ford Rd. G12 —5B 62
Ford Rd. Newt M —6D 132
Fordyce Ct. Newt M —5D 132
Fordyce St. G11 —1H 81
Forehouse Rd. Kilb —1A 94
Foremount Ter. La. G12 —6H 61
(off Hyndland Rd.)
Fore Row. Ham —5A 142
Forest Av. Ham —5H 153
Forestburn Ct. Air —4F 91
(off Monkscourt Av.)
Forest Dri. Both —4E 125
Forest Gdns. Kirk —3A 50
Foresthall Dri. G21 —6C 64
Foresthall Gdns. G21 —6C 64
Forest Kirk. Carl —5H 165
Forest La. Ham —5H 153
Forest Pk. Wis —4B 146
Forest Pl. Kirk —3A 50
Forest Pl. Pais —3A 98
Fore St. G14 —6C 60
Forest Rd. Cumb —4C 36
Forest Rd. Lark —3F 161
Forest View. Cumb —2C 36
Forfar Av. G52 —1B 100
Forfar Cres. B'rig —1E 65
Forgan Gdns. B'rig —1F 65
Forge Dri. Coat —4B 90
Forge Pl. G21 —1D 84
Forge Rd. Air —5F 93
Forge Shopping Cen., The. G31 —6E 85
Forge St. G21 —1D 84
Forgewood Path. Air —5F 93
Forgewood Rd. Moth —5E 127
Forglen St. G34 —2H 87
Formby Dri. G23 —6B 46
Forres Av. Giff —4A 118
Forres Cres. Bell —1C 126
Forres Ga. Giff —5B 118
Forres Quad. Wis —4H 145
Forres St. G23 —6C 46
Forres St. Blan —3A 140
Forrest Cres. Ham —2F 153
Forrest Dri. Bear —4B 24
Forrest Dri. Bell —4E 127
Forrester Ct. B'rig —1B 64
Forrestfield Cres. Newt M —4E 133
Forrestfield Gdns. Newt M —4D 132
Forrestfield St. G21 —2C 84
Forrest Ga. Udd —4F 109
Forrestlea Rd. Carl —5G 165
Forrest St. G40 —6C 84
Forrest St. Air —3C 92
Forrest St. Blan —2D 140
Forsyth St. Air —3B 92
Forteviot Av. Bail —6A 88
Forteviot Pl. Bail —6A 88
Forth Av. Pais —4D 96
Forth Ct. E Kil —4A 148
Forth Cres. E Kil —3A 148
Forth Gro. E Kil —4A 148
Forth Pl. John —5C 94
Forth Pl. Lark —5F 161
Forth Rd. Bear —5D 44
Forth Rd. Torr —5D 28
Forth St. G41 —2D 102
Forth St. Clyd —1E 59
Forth Ter. Ham —3F 153
Forth Wlk. Cumb —3H 35
(off Cumbernauld Cen., The)
Forties Ct. T'bnk —2G 117
Forties Cres. T'bnk —2G 117
Forties Rd. Hous —3C 74
Fortieth Av. E Kil —6H 149
Fortingale Av. G12 —3A 62
Fortingale Pl. G12 —3A 62
Fortingall Rd. Blan —3D 140
Fortrose St. G11 —1H 81
Fort St. Moth —1D 142
Fossil Gro. Kirk —4G 31
Foswell Pl. G15 —2H 43
Fotheringay La. G41 —3B 102
Fotheringay Rd. G41 —3B 102
Foulis La. G13 —3F 61
Foulis St. G13 —3F 61
Foulsykes Rd. Wis —5C 146
Foundry La. Barr —5E 115
Foundry Rd. Cle —5H 129
Fountain Av. Inch —5F 57
Fountain Cres. Inch —4F 57
Fountain Dri. Inch —5G 57
Fountainwell Av. G21 —1H 83
Fountainwell Dri. G21 —1H 83
Fountainwell Pl. G21 —1H 83
Fountainwell Rd. G21 —1H 83
Fountainwell Sq. G21 —1A 84
Fountainwell Ter. G21 —1A 84
Fourth Av. G33 —4B 66
Fourth Av. Dumb —2C 18
Fourth Av. Kirk —6D 50
Fourth Av. Renf —1E 79
Fourth Gdns. G41 —1G 101
Fourth Rd. Blan —4C 140
Fourth St. Udd —4D 108
Four Windings. Hous —1B 74
Fowlis Dri. Newt M —3C 132
Foxbar Cres. Pais —6C 96
Foxbar Dri. G13 —3B 60
Foxbar Dri. Pais —6C 96
Foxbar Rd. Eld & Pais —6B 96
Foxes Gro. Lenz —2E 51
Foxglove Pl. G53 —4B 116
Fox Gro. Moth —2D 142
Foxhills Pl. G23 —6C 46
Foxley St. G32 —4C 106
Fox St. G1 —5F 83
Foyers Ter. G21 —5C 64
Francis St. G5 —1E 103
Franconia Sq. Clyd —6D 42
Frankel Ter. E Kil —1C 150
Frankfield Rd. G33 —4E 67
Frankfield St. G33 —1F 85
Frankfort St. G41 —4C 102
Franklin Pl. E Kil —2D 148
Franklin St. G40 —2B 104
Fraser Av. B'ton —3H 39
Fraser Av. Dumb —1C 18
Fraser Av. John —3G 95
Fraser Av. Newt M —3E 133
Fraser Av. Ruth —5E 105
Fraser Ct. Air —3E 93
(off Katherine St.)
Fraser Cres. Ham —1F 153
Fraser Gdns. Kirk —5B 30
Fraser St. Camb —1G 121
Fraser St. Cle —5H 129
Frazer River Tower. E Kil —3F 149
Frazer St. G40 —6C 84
Frederick St. Coat —3A 90
Freeland Brae. E Kil —3H 149
(off Telford Rd.)
Freeland Ct. G53 —1C 116
Freeland Cres. G53 —1B 116
Freeland Dri. G53 —1B 116
Freeland Dri. Bri W —2F 73
Freeland Dri. Inch —3G 57
Freeland La. E Kil —3H 149
(off Telford Rd.)
Freeland Pl. Kirk —5D 30
Freeland Rd. Ersk —2F 57
Freelands Ct. Old K —3G 41
Freelands Cres. Old K —2G 41
Freelands Pl. Old K —3G 41
Freelands Rd. Old K —3G 41
Freesia Ct. Moth —4G 143
French St. G40 —2B 104
French St. Clyd —4A 42
French St. Renf —1D 78
French St. Wis —6H 145
Freuchie St. G34 —4H 87
Frew St. Air —3A 92
Friar Av. B'rig —4D 48
Friarscourt Av. G13 —6D 44
Friarscourt Rd. Chry —6H 51
Friars Croft. Kirk —5E 31
Friars Pl. G13 —1D 60
Friars Way. Air —1C 112
Friarton Rd. G43 —2D 118
Friendship Way. Renf —2F 79
Frood St. Moth —6E 127
Fruin Av. Newt M —3E 133
Fruin Dri. Wis —6C 146
Fruin Pl. G22 —5G 63
Fruin Rise. Ham —1C 152
Fruin Rd. G15 —6H 43
Fruin St. G22 —5G 63
Fulbar Av. Pais —3D 96
Fulbar Av. Renf —5E 59
Fulbar Ct. Renf —5F 59
Fulbar La. Renf —5F 59
Fulbar Rd. G51 —4C 80
Fulbar Rd. Pais —3D 96
Fulbar St. Renf —5F 59
Fulfar Cres. Pais —3D 96
Fullarton Av. G32 —3A 106
Fullarton La. G32 —3A 106
Fullarton Pl. Coat —2A 110
Fullarton Rd. G32 —5H 105
Fullarton Rd. Cumb —6G 13
Fullarton St. Coat —2A 110
Fullers Ga. Clyd —6E 23
Fullerton St. Pais —4H 77
Fullerton Ter. Pais —4A 78
Fullwood Ind. Est. Ham —5F 141
Fulmar Ct. B'rig —1B 64
Fulmar Pk. E Kil —6F 137
Fulmar Pl. John —6C 94
Fulton Cres. Kilb —2A 94
Fulton Dri. Hous —4E 75
Fulton Gdns. Hous —3E 75
Fulton Rd. Miln —4H 25
Fulton St. G13 —2D 60
Fulwood Av. G13 —2H 59
Fulwood Av. Lin —5H 75
Fulwood Pl. G13 —2H 59
Furlongs, The. Ham —4A 142
Fyneart St. Wis —5C 146
Fyne Av. Rig I —6A 110
Fyne Ct. Ham —2E 153
Fyne Way. Moth —2A 128
(off Howden Pl.)
Fynloch Pl. Clyd —6A 22
Fyvie Av. G43 —2G 117

Gadie Av. Renf —1G 79
Gadie St. G33 —3F 85
Gadloch Av. Kirk —5D 50
Gadloch Gdns. Kirk —4D 50
Gadloch St. G22 —3G 63
Gadloch View. Kirk —5D 50
Gadsburn Ct. G21 —3E 65
Gadshill St. G21 —2B 84
Gailes Pk. Both —5D 124
Gailes Rd. Cumb —6H 13
Gailes St. G40 —1D 104
Gainburn Ct. Cumb —1B 54
Gainburn Cres. Cumb —2B 54
Gainburn Gdns. Cumb —2B 54
Gainburn Pl. Cumb —1B 54
Gainburn View. Cumb —1C 54
Gain Rd. Anna —6B 54
Gain & Shankburn Rd. Rigg —6D 54
Gainside Rd. Glenb —3G 69
Gairbraid Av. G20 —3A 62
Gairbraid Ct. G20 —3A 62
Gairbraid Pl. G20 —3B 62
Gairbraid Ter. Bail —6E 89
Gair Cres. Carl —2G 165
Gair Cres. Wis —2H 157
Gairloch Gdns. Kirk —4H 31
Gair Rd. Carl —1G 165
Gala Av. Renf —1G 79
Gala Cres. Wis —4G 145
Gala St. G33 —1G 85
Galbraith Cres. Law —5E 159
Galbraith Dri. G51 —3D 80
Galbraith Dri. Miln —5F 25
Galdenoch St. G33 —1B 86
Gallacher Av. Pais —4E 97
Gallacher Ct. Moth —6B 144
Gallacher Ct. Pais —6G 77
Gallan Av. G23 —6C 46
Galloway Av. Ham —4G 153
Galloway Dri. Ruth —4D 120
Galloway Rd. Air —6H 91
Galloway Rd. E Kil —6C 138
Galloway St. G21 —3B 64
Gallowflat St. Ruth —5D 104
Gallowgate. G1, G4, G40 & G31 —5H 83
Gallowhill. Lark —3E 161
Gallowhill Av. Lenz —1C 50
Gallowhill Ct. Pais —3C 78
Gallowhill Gro. Kirk —6C 30
Gallowhill Rd. Crmck —1H 135
Gallowhill Rd. Kirk —1C 50
Gallowhill Rd. Pais —5B 78
Galston Av. Newt M —4G 133
Galston Ct. Ham —4A 154
Galston St. G53 —1H 115
Galt Pl. E Kil —4F 149
Gamrie Dri. G53 —6A 100
Gamrie Gdns. G53 —6A 100
Gamrie Rd. G53 —5A 100
Gannochy Dri. B'rig —6E 49
Gantock Cres. G33 —4B 86
Gardenhall. E Kil —3A 148
Gardenhall Ct. E Kil —3A 148
Gardenside. Bell —3C 126
Gardenside Av. G32 —5B 106
Gardenside Av. Udd —1C 124
Gardenside Cres. G32 —5B 106
Gardenside Gro. G32 —5B 106
Gardenside Pl. G32 —5B 106
Gardenside Rd. Ham —1H 153
Gardenside St. Udd —1C 124
Garden Sq. Wlk. Air —3F 91
Gardner Gro. Udd —5E 109
Gardner St. G11 —1H 81
Gardyne St. G34 —2G 87
Gareloch Av. Air —1H 91
Gareloch Av. Pais —3E 97
Garfield Av. Bell —2E 127
Garfield Dri. Bell —3E 127
Garfield St. G31 —5C 84
Garforth Rd. Bail —1F 107
Gargrave Av. Bail —1F 107
Garion Dri. G13 —4B 60
Garlieston Rd. G33 —5F 87
Garliston Ter. Bail —6E 89
Garmouth Ct. G51 —3G 81
Garmouth Gdns. G51 —3G 81
Garmouth St. G51 —3F 81
Garnethill St. G3 —2E 83 (2B 4)
Garnet St. G3 —2E 83 (2A 4)
Garngaber Av. Lenz —2D 50
Garngaber Ct. Kirk —2E 51
Garngrew Rd. Hag —1F 15
Garnhall Farm Rd. Cumb —3E 15
Garnie Av. Ersk —6H 41
Garnieland Rd. Ersk —6H 41
Garnie La. Ersk —6H 41
Garnie Oval. Ersk —6A 42
Garnie Pl. Ersk —6H 41
Garnkirk La. G33 —4E 67
Garnock Pl. E Kil —2B 150
Garnock St. G21 —2B 84
Garrell Av. Kils —2H 11
Garrell Gro. Kils —1H 11
Garrell Pl. Kils —3G 11
Garrell Rd. Kils —4G 11
Garrell Way. Cumb —3G 35
Garrell Way. Kils —3G 11
Garrioch Cres. G20 —4B 62
Garrioch Dri. G20 —4B 62
Garrioch Ga. G20 —4B 62
Garriochmill Rd. G20 —6C 62
(in two parts)
Garrioch Quad. G20 —4B 62
Garrioch Rd. G20 —5B 62
Garrion Bus. Pk. Wis —3H 157
Garrion Pl. Ashg —4B 162
Garrion St. Wis —5A 158

Garrochmill Rd. G20 —6D 62
Garrochmill Way. G20 —6D 62
(off Henderson St.)
Garrowhill Dri. Bail —6F 87
GARROWHILL STATION. Bail —6F 87
Garry Av. Bear —5H 45
Garry Dri. Pais —3E 97
Garry St. G44 —6E 103
Garscadden Rd. G15 —4H 43
Garscadden Rd. S. G13 —1A 60
GARSCADDEN STATION. G14 —3A 60
Garscadden View. Clyd —4F 43
Garscube Rd. G4 —2F 83 (1C 4)
Garscube Rd. G20 & G4 —6E 63
Garshake Av. Dumb —1C 18
Garshake Rd. Dumb —3H 17
Garshake Ter. Dumb —1C 18
Garside Ct. Ham —1D 152
Gartartan Rd. Pais —6H 79
Gartcarron Hill. Cumb —2E 35
Gartcloss Rd. Coat —1G 89
Gartconnell Dri. Bear —1E 45
Gartconnell Gdns. Bear —1E 45
Gartconnell Rd. Bear —1E 45
Gartconner Av. Kirk —5H 31
Gartcosh Rd. Bail —5D 88
Gartcosh Rd. G'csh —1E 89
Gartcosh Wlk. Bell —2B 126
Gartcraig Path. G33 —2A 86
(off Gartcraig Rd.)
Gartcraig Pl. G33 —2A 86
Gartcraig Rd. G33 —3G 85
Gartferry Av. Chry —5D 52
Gartferry Rd. Mood —5B 52
Gartferry St. G21 —5C 64
Gartfield St. Air —5B 92
Gartgill Rd. Coat —1A 90
Garthamlock Rd. G33 —2E 87
Garthland Dri. G31 —4C 84
Garthland La. Pais —6B 78
Garth St. G1 —4G 83 (6F 5)
Gartlea Av. Air —4A 92
Gartlea Gdns. Air —4B 92
Gartleahill. Air —5A 92
Gartlea Rd. Air —4A 92
Gartliston Rd. Coat —6B 70
Gartloch Cotts. Bail —6C 68
Gartloch Rd. G33 & G34 —1H 85
Gartloch Rd. G'csh —6H 67
Gartly St. G44 —3D 118
Gartmore Gdns. Udd —5C 108
Gartmore La. Chry —5E 53
Gartmore Rd. Pais —1D 98
Gartmore Ter. Camb —4G 121
Gartness Dri. Air —6E 93
Gartness Rd. Air —2G 113
Gartocher Rd. G32 —6C 86
Gartocher Ter. G32 —6C 86
Gartons Rd. G21 —4E 65
Gartsherrie Av. Glenb —4B 70
Gartsherrie Ind. Est. Coat —2B 90
Gartsherrie Rd. Coat —3A 90
Gartshore Cres. Twe —3D 32
Gartshore Gdns. Cumb —4A 34
Garturk St. G42 —3F 103
Garturk St. Coat —1D 110
Garvald Ct. G40 —2D 104
Garvald St. G40 —2D 104
Garve Av. G44 —3E 119
Garvel Cres. G33 —5E 87
Garvel Pl. Miln —3D 24
Garvel Rd. G33 —5E 87
Garvel Rd. Miln —3E 25
Garvin Lea. Bell —5C 110
Garvock Dri. G43 —2H 117
Garwhitter Dri. Miln —3H 25
Gascoyne. E Kil —4E 149
Gaskin Path. G33 —4E 67
Gask Pl. G13 —1H 59
Gas St. John —2G 95
Gasworks Rd. Carl —2C 164
Gatehouse St. G32 —6B 86
Gateside Av. Camb —2D 122
Gateside Av. Kils —3F 11
Gateside Ct. Barr —5C 114
Gateside Cres. Air —3A 92
Gateside Cres. Barr —6C 114
Gateside Pk. Kils —2F 11
Gateside Pl. Kilb —2A 94
Gateside Rd. Barr —6B 114
Gateside Rd. Wis —5E 145
Gateside St. G31 —5D 84
Gateside St. Ham —1A 154
Gateway, The. E Kil —5A 138
Gauldry Av. G52 —2C 100
Gauze St. Pais —6B 78
Gavell Rd. Kils —4D 10
Gavinburn Gdns. Old K —6E 21
Gavinburn Pl. Old K —6E 21
Gavinburn St. Old K —6E 21
Gavin's Mill Rd. Miln —4G 25
Gavins Rd. Clyd —2D 42
Gavin St. Moth —4G 143
Gavinton St. G44 —2D 118
Gayne Dri. Glenb —3G 69
Gean Ct. Cumb —1F 37
Geary St. G23 —6B 46
Geddes Hill. E Kil —5B 138
Geddes Rd. G21 —2E 65
Geelong Gdns. Len —2F 7
Geils Av. Dumb —2C 18
Geils Quadrant. Dumb —2C 18
Gelston St. G32 —1B 106
Gemini Gro. Moth —2B 128
Gemmel Pl. Newt M —5B 132
Generals Ga. Udd —1C 124
Gentle Row. Clyd —1B 42
George Av. Clyd —4E 43
George Ct. Ham —4E 141
George Ct. Pais —1H 97
George Cres. Clyd —4E 43
George IV Bri. G5 —5F 83
George Gray St. Ruth —5E 105
George La. Ham —1B 154
George La. Pais —1A 98
George Mann Ter. Ruth —3C 120
George Pl. Pais —1A 98
George Reith Av. G12 —4F 61
George Sq. G2 —4G 83 (5E 5)
George St. G1 —4G 83 (5F 5)
George St. Air —4G 91
George St. Bail —1H 107
George St. Barr —4D 114
George St. Bell —2B 126
George St. Chap —2D 112
George St. Ham —4E 141
George St. John —2F 95
George St. Moth —5G 143
George St. New S —3B 128
George St. Pais —1G 97
George Way. Lark —1F 161
(off Duncan Graham St.)
Gerard Pl. Bell —6D 110
Gertrude Pl. Barr —5C 114
Ghillies La. Moth —6E 127
Gibbon Cres. E Kil —6C 138
Gibb St. Chap —2D 112
Gibb St. Cle —6H 129
Gibson Av. Dumb —3H 17
Gibson Cres. John —3E 95
Gibson Quad. Moth —6E 127
Gibson Rd. Renf —3D 78
Gibson St. G12 —1B 82
Gibson St. G40 —5A 84
Gibson St. Dumb —3G 17
Giffnock Pk. Av. Giff —3A 118
GIFFNOCK STATION. Giff —4A 118
Gifford Dri. G52 —6A 80
Gigha Gdns. Carl —5G 165
Gigha Quad. Wis —2E 157
Gilbertfield Path. G33 —1B 86
Gilbertfield Pl. G33 —1B 86
Gilbertfield Rd. Camb —4C 122
Gilbertfield St. G33 —1B 86
Gilbert St. G3 —3A 82
Gilchrist Ct. John —4E 95
(off Tannahill Cres.)
Gilchrist Gdns. Udd —6F 125
Gilchrist St. Coat —3D 90
Gilderdale. E Kil —1E 149
Gilfillan Pl. Over —4A 158
Gilfillan Way. Pais —5C 96
Gilhill St. G20 —2B 62
Gillbank Av. Carl —3D 164
Gillbank La. Lark —4G 161
(off Donaldson Rd.)
Gillburn St. Wis —5A 158
Gillies Ct. Air —3E 93
Gillies Cres. E Kil —4D 138
Gillies La. Bail —1A 108
Gill Rd. Wis —4A 158
Gilmartin Rd. Lin —5E 75
Gilmerton St. G32 —1A 106
Gilmour Av. Clyd —2D 42
Gilmour Av. T'hall —6F 135
Gilmour Cres. Ruth —5B 104
Gilmour Dri. Ham —1D 152
Gilmour Pl. G5 —1G 103
Gilmour Pl. Bell —2A 126
Gilmour Pl. Coat —3B 90
Gilmour St. Clyd —3E 43
Gilmour St. Pais —6A 78
Gilmourton Cres. Newt M —6D 132
Gimmerscroft Cres. Air —5F 93
Girthon St. G32 —1C 106
Girvan St. G33 —2F 85
Glade, The. Lark —3F 161
Gladney Av. G13 —1G 59
Gladsmuir Rd. G52 —5A 80
Gladstone Av. Barr —5D 114
Gladstone Av. John —6D 94
Gladstone Ct. Ham —4E 141
Gladstone St. G4 —1E 83
Gladstone St. Bell —2D 126
Glaive Rd. G13 —6D 44
Glamis Av. Carl —3F 165
Glamis Av. Eld —4H 95
Glamis Av. Newt M —4F 133
Glamis Dri. E Kil —6H 137
Glamis Gdns. B'rig —3D 48
Glamis Rd. G31 —1F 105
Glanderston Av. Newt M —3B 132
Glanderston Dri. G13 —2A 60
Glanderston Ga. Newt M —3B 132
Glanderston Rd. Barr —3H 131
Glandston Av. Barr —5G 115
Glasgow Airport. Abb —1H 77
Glasgow Bri. G5 —5F 83
Glasgow & Edinburgh Rd. Bail —6B 88
Glasgow & Edinburgh Rd. Moth —5E 113
Glasgow Fish Mkt. G21 —2D 84
Glasgow Fruit Mkt. G21 —2C 84
Glasgow Rd. Bail —1F 107
Glasgow Rd. Barg & Coat —5F 89
Glasgow Rd. Barr —4F 115
Glasgow Rd. Blan —6H 123
Glasgow Rd. Camb —6G 105
Glasgow Rd. Clar —6B 134
Glasgow Rd. Clyd —1D 58
Glasgow Rd. Cumb —5E 35
Glasgow Rd. Cumb —1B 36
(Cumbernauld Village)
Glasgow Rd. Dumb —3E 17
Glasgow Rd. Ham —4E 141
Glasgow Rd. Hard —1D 42
Glasgow Rd. Kils —3E 11
Glasgow Rd. Kirk —5A 30
Glasgow Rd. Miln —5G 25
Glasgow Rd. Pais —6B 78
Glasgow Rd. Renf —6G 59
Glasgow Rd. Ruth —3B 104
Glasgow Rd. Ruth —5G 121
(Cathkin)
Glasgow Rd. Udd —4A 108
Glasgow Rd. Wis —6D 144
Glasgow St. G12 —6C 62
Glassel Rd. G34 —2B 88
Glasserton Pl. G43 —2D 118
Glasserton Rd. G43 —2D 118
Glassford St. G1 —4G 83 (6F 5)
Glassford St. Miln —3H 25
Glassford St. Moth —5A 144
Glassford Tower. Moth —5A 144
(off Burnside Ct.)
Glaudhall Av. G'csh —2C 68
Glazert Meadow. Len —4G 7
Glazert Pk. Dri. Len —4G 7
Glazert Pl. Milt C —6B 8
Glebe Av. Both —5F 125
Glebe Av. Clar —2H 135
Glebe Av. Coat —1H 109
Glebe Ct. G4 —3H 83 (3H 5)
Glebe Cres. Air —3D 92
Glebe Cres. E Kil —2H 149
Glebe Cres. Ham —1G 153
Glebe Gdns. Hous —1B 74
Glebe Hollow. Both —5F 125
Glebe La. Newt M —5D 132
Glebe Pk. Dumb —2H 17
Glebe Pl. Camb —2B 122
Glebe Pl. Ruth —5B 104
Glebe Rd. Newt M —5D 132
Glebe St. G4 —2H 83 (2H 5)
(in three parts)
Glebe St. Bell —2B 126
Glebe St. E Kil —1H 149
Glebe St. Ham —1G 153
Glebe St. Renf —6F 59
Glebe, The. Both —5F 125
Glebe Wynd. Both —5F 125
Gleddoch Rd. G52 —5G 79
Gledstane Rd. B'ton —5H 39
Glenacre Cres. Udd —5C 108
Glenacre Dri. G45 —4H 119
Glenacre Dri. Air —5D 92
Glenacre Quad. G45 —4H 119
Glenacre Rd. Cumb —5H 35
Glenacre St. G45 —4H 119
Glenacre Ter. G45 —4H 119
Glenafeoch Rd. Carl —4F 165
Glen Affric. E Kil —2B 150
Glen Affric Av. G53 —3C 116
Glen Affric Dri. G53 —3D 116
Glen Affric Way. Chap —4D 112
(off Glen Avon Dri.)
Glenafton View. Ham —3F 153
Glen Alby Pl. G53 —3C 116
Glenallan Way. Pais —6B 96
Glen Almond. E Kil —1D 150
Glenalmond Rd. Ruth —4F 121
Glenalmond St. G32 —1A 106
Glenapp Av. Pais —4D 98
Glenapp Pl. Mood —4D 52
Glenapp Rd. Pais —4D 98
Glenapp St. G41 —2D 102
Glenarklet Dri. Pais —4C 98
Glen Arroch. E Kil —3B 150
Glenartney. Hous —1A 74
Glenartney Rd. Chry —6A 52
Glenashdale Way. Pais —4C 98
Glen Av. G32 —5B 86
Glen Av. Lark —5D 160
Glen Av. Mood —5D 52
Glen Av. Neil —2E 131
Glenavon Ct. Ham —2F 153
Glen Avon Dri. Air —4D 112
Glenavon Rd. G20 —2B 62
Glenbank Av. Lenz —3D 50
Glenbank Dri. T'bnk —5F 117
Glenbank Rd. Lenz —3D 50
Glenbarr St. G21 —2B 84
Glen Bervie. E Kil —1B 150
Glenbervie Cres. Cumb —1H 35
Glenbervie Pl. G23 —6B 46
Glenboig Farm Rd. Glenb —3A 70
Glenboig New Rd. Glenb —3B 70
Glenboig Rd. G'csh —1F 69
Glen Brae. Bri W —3E 73
Glenbrittle Dri. Pais —4C 98
Glenbrittle Way. Pais —4C 98
Glenbuck Av. G33 —3H 65
Glenbuck Dri. G33 —3H 65
Glenburn Av. Bail —6A 88
Glenburn Av. Camb —2F 121
Glenburn Av. Chry —5D 52
Glenburn Av. Moth —3C 128
Glenburn Cres. Milt C —6C 8
Glenburn Cres. Pais —5H 97
Glenburn Cres. Udd —5G 109
Glenburn Gdns. B'rig —5B 48
Glenburn Gdns. Glenb —3G 69
Glenburnie Pl. G34 —4F 87
Glenburn Rd. Bear —2D 44
Glenburn Rd. E Kil —6C 136
Glenburn Rd. Giff —6H 117
Glenburn Rd. Ham —6F 141
Glenburn Rd. Pais —5F 97
Glenburn St. G20 —2C 62
Glenburn Ter. Carl —5E 165
Glenburn Ter. Moth —6C 128
Glenburn Wlk. Bail —6A 88
Glenburn Way. E Kil —6B 136
Glenburn Wynd. Lark —1F 161
(off Muirshot Rd.)
Glencairn Av. Wis —5D 144
Glencairn Ct. Pais —3D 78
(off Montgomery Rd.)
Glencairn Dri. G41 —3B 102
Glencairn Dri. Chry —5C 52
Glencairn Dri. Ruth —5B 104
Glencairn Gdns. G41 —3C 102
Glencairn Gdns. Camb —2D 122
Glencairn La. G41 —3C 102
Glencairn Path. G32 —5C 86
(off Mansionhouse Dri.)
Glencairn Rd. Cumb —3C 36
Glencairn Rd. Dumb —4C 16
Glencairn Rd. Pais —4C 78
Glencairn St. Kirk —6D 30
Glencairn St. Moth —4G 143
Glencairn Tower. Moth —4G 143
Glen Calder Ct. Air —6D 92
Glencalder Cres. Bell —4D 126
Glen Cally. E Kil —1B 150
Glencally Av. Pais —4D 98
Glen Cannich. E Kil —2B 150
Glen Carron. E Kil —2B 150
Glencart Gro. Mill P —4C 94
Glencleland Rd. Wis —5D 144
Glenclora Dri. Pais —4C 98
Glencloy St. G20 —2A 62
Glen Clunie. E Kil —1D 150
Glen Clunie Av. G53 —3C 116
Glen Clunie Dri. G53 —3C 116
Glen Clunie Pl. G53 —3C 116
Glencoats Cres. Pais —6F 77
Glencoats Dri. Pais —6E 77
Glencoe Dri. Moth —2A 128
Glencoe Pl. G13 —2F 61
Glencoe Pl. Ham —3F 153
Glencoe Rd. Carl —5G 165
Glencoe Rd. Ruth —4F 121
Glencoe St. G13 —2F 61
Glen Cona Dri. G53 —2C 116
Glenconner Way. Kirk —4G 31
Glencorse Rd. Pais —3G 97
Glencorse St. G32 —4G 85
Glen Ct. Coat —6H 89
Glen Ct. Moth —5B 144
Glen Cova. E Kil —1B 150
Glencraig St. Air —4G 91
Glen Crerand Clo. Neil —3C 130
Glen Cres. G13 —2G 59
Glencroft Av. G44 —1H 119
Glencroft Av. Udd —5C 108
Glencroft Rd. G44 —2H 119
Glencryan Rd. Cumb —5A 36
Glendale Av. Air —5D 92
Glendale Cres. B'rig —1E 65
Glendale Dri. B'rig —1E 65
Glendale Pl. B'rig —2E 65
Glendale St. G31 —5D 84
Glendaruel Av. Bear —3H 45
Glendarvel Rd. Ruth —5G 121
Glendee Gdns. Renf —1F 79
Glendee Rd. Renf —1F 79
Glendentan Rd. Bri W —4F 73
Glendermott Ct. Carl —2F 165
Glen Derry. E Kil —6D 138
Glen Dessary. E Kil —3B 150
Glen Devon. E Kil —2D 150
Glendevon Pl. Clyd —4B 42
Glendevon Pl. Ham —3F 153
Glendevon Sq. G33 —1B 86
Glendinning Rd. G13 —6E 45
Glen Doll. E Kil —1B 150
Glendoll Rd. Neil —3B 130
Glendorch Av. Wis —2A 146
Glendore St. G14 —1E 81
Glen Douglas Dri. Cumb —1E 35
Glendoune Rd. Clar —4C 134
Glendower Way. Pais —5C 96
Glen Dri. Moth —2B 128
Glenduffhill Rd. Bail —6F 87
Glen Dye. E Kil —1B 150
Glen Eagles. E Kil —2C 150
Gleneagles Av. Cumb —6A 14
Gleneagles Dri. B'rig —4C 48
Gleneagles Dri. Newt M —5H 133
Gleneagles Gdns. B'rig —4B 48
Gleneagles La. N. G14 —5C 60
Gleneagles La. S. G14 —6C 60
Gleneagles Pk. Both —5D 124
Glenelg Cres. Kirk —4G 31
Glenelg Path. Glenb —3G 69
Glenelg Quad. G34 —2B 88
Glenelm Pl. Bell —1C 126
Glen Esk. E Kil —1C 150
Glen Esk Cres. G53 —3C 116
Glen Esk Dri. G53 —3C 116
Glen Etive Pl. Ruth —5G 121
Glen Falloch. E Kil —2C 150
Glen Falloch Cres. Neil —4D 130
Glen Farg. E Kil —2D 150
Glenfarg Ct. Ham —3F 153
Glenfarg Cres. Bear —3H 45
Glenfarg Rd. Ruth —3D 120
Glenfarg St. G20 —1E 83
Glenfarm Rd. Moth —3E 129
Glen Farrar. E Kil —2B 150
Glen Feshie. E Kil —3B 150
Glenfield Av. Pais —6H 97
Glenfield Cres. Pais —6H 97
Glenfield Gro. E Kil —5A 150
Glenfield Rd. Pais —6G 97
Glen Finlet Rd. Neil —3C 130
Glenfinnan Dri. G20 —3B 62
Glenfinnan Dri. Bear —4H 45
Glenfinnan Pl. G20 —3B 62
(off Glenfinnan Rd.)
Glenfinnan Rd. G20 —3B 62
Glenfruin Cres. Pais —4D 98
Glen Fruin Dri. Lark —4G 161
Glen Fruin Pl. Chap —3D 112
(off Glen Rannoch Dri.)
Glenfruin Rd. Blan —1A 140
Glen Fyne Rd. Cumb —1D 34
Glen Gairn. E Kil —1D 150
Glen Gairn Cres. Neil —3C 130
Glen Gdns. Eld —2A 96
Glen Garrell Pl. Kils —2F 11
Glengarriff Rd. Bell —5D 110
Glen Garry. E Kil —3B 150
Glengarry Dri. G52 —6C 80
Glengavel Cres. G33 —3H 65
Glengavel Gdns. Wis —2A 146
Glengonnar St. Lark —5E 161
Glengowan Rd. Bri W —3E 73
Glen Gro. E Kil —4F 149
Glen Gro. Kils —1H 11
Glengyre St. G34 —2A 88
Glenhead Cres. G22 —3G 63
Glenhead Cres. Clyd —6C 22
Glenhead Rd. Clyd —2B 42
Glenhead Rd. Lenz —3D 50
Glenhead St. G22 —3G 63
Glenholme Av. Pais —4F 97
Glenhove Rd. Cumb —3A 36
Gleniffer Av. G13 —3A 60
Gleniffer Ct. Air —1B 92
Gleniffer Ct. Pais —6F 97
Gleniffer Cres. Eld —4A 96
Gleniffer Dri. Barr —2C 114
Gleniffer Rd. Pais —6D 96
Gleniffer Rd. Renf —3D 78
Gleniffer View. Clyd —4F 43
Gleniffer View. Neil —1D 130
Glen Isla. E Kil —1C 150
Glenisla Av. Chry —3E 53
Glen Isla Av. Neil —4C 130
Glenisla St. G31 —2F 105
Glenkirk Dri. G15 —5B 44
Glen La. Pais —6A 78
Glen Lednock Dri. Cumb —1D 34
Glen Lee. E Kil —1C 150
Glenlee St. Ham —4D 140
Glen Lethnot. E Kil —1C 150
Glen Livet Pl. G53 —3C 116
Glenlivet Rd. Neil —3C 130
Glen Lochay Gdns. Cumb —1D 34
Glenlora Dri. G53 —6A 100
Glenlora Ter. G53 —6B 100
Glen Loy Pl. G53 —3C 116
Glenluce Dri. G32 —2D 106
Glenluce Gdns. Mood —4E 53
Glenluce Ter. E Kil —1E 149
Glenluggie Rd. Kirk —6G 31
Glenlui Av. Ruth —2D 120
Glen Luss Gdns. Cumb —1D 34
Glen Luss Pl. Coat —6F 91
Glen Lyon. E Kil —2C 150
Glen Lyon Ct. Cumb —1D 34
Glenlyon Ct. Ham —3F 153
Glenlyon Pl. Ruth —4E 121
Glen Lyon Rd. Neil —3C 130
Glen Mair Rd. Neil —3C 130
Glen Mallie. E Kil —2C 150
Glenmalloch Pl. Eld —2A 96
Glenmanor Av. Mood —5C 52
Glenmanor Rd. Chry —5C 52
Glenmare Av. Kirk —6G 31
Glen Mark. E Kil —1C 150
Glen Markie Dri. G53 —3C 116
Glen Mark Rd. Neil —3C 130
Glenmavis Cres. Carl —4G 165
Glenmavis Rd. Glenm —6G 71
Glenmavis St. G4 —2F 83 (1D 4)
Glen More. E Kil —2A 150
Glenmore Av. G42 —5A 104
Glenmore Av. Bell —4D 126
Glenmore Rd. Moth —4C 128

Glen Moriston Rd. G53 —4C 116
Glen Morriston. E Kil —2C 150
Glen Morriston Rd. Cumb —1D 34
Glenmoss Av. Ersk —6D 40
Glen Moy. E Kil —2B 150
Glenmuir Dri. G53 —2B 116
Glen Nevis. E Kil —3B 150
Glen Nevis Pl. Ruth —5E 121
Glen Ochil Rd. Chap —4D 112
Glen Ogilvie. E Kil —1C 150
Glenogle St. G32 —1D 106
Glenoran La. Lark —1F 161
Glenorchard Rd. Torr —3H 27
Glen Orchy Ct. Cumb —6D 12
Glen Orchy Dri. G53 —3C 116
Glen Orchy Dri. Cumb —1D 34
Glen Orchy Pl. G53 —3D 116
Glen Orchy Pl. Chap —4D 112
(off Glen Rannoch Dri.)
Glen Orchy Pl. Cumb —1D 34
Glen Orrin Way. Neil —3C 130
Glenpark. Air —5E 93
Glenpark Av. T'bnk —5F 117
Glenpark Gdns. Camb —6G 105
Glenpark Ind. Est. G31 —5D 84
Glenpark Rd. G31 —5D 84
Glenpark St. G31 —5D 84
Glenpark St. Wis —5G 145
Glenpark Ter. Camb —6G 105
Glenpath. Dumb —2C 18
Glenpatrick Rd. Eld —5A 96
Glen Prosen. E Kil —1C 150
Glen Quoich. E Kil —6D 138
Glenraith Path. G33 —6B 66
Glenraith Rd. G33 —6B 66
Glenraith Sq. G33 —6B 66
Glenraith Wlk. G33 —6C 66
Glen Rannoch Dri. Chap —4D 112
Glen Rinnes Dri. Neil —4D 130
Glen Rd. G32 —4B 86
Glen Rd. Air —5E 93
Glen Rd. B'ton —3G 39
Glen Rd. Dull —4F 13
Glen Rd. E Kil —4B 136
(in two parts)
Glen Rd. Len —1C 6
Glen Rd. Moth —6D 112
Glen Rd. Old K —1F 41
Glen Rd. Wis —5G 145
Glen Roy Dri. Neil —3C 130
Glen Sax Dri. Renf —2G 79
Glen Shee. E Kil —1C 150
Glen Shee Av. Neil —3C 130
Glen Shee Cres. Air —4D 112
Glenshee St. G31 —1F 105
Glenshee Ter. Ham —3F 153
Glenshiel Av. Pais —4C 98
Glenshira Av. Pais —4C 98
Glen Shirva Rd. Kils —1C 32
Glenside Av. G53 —3B 100
Glenside Dri. Ruth —1F 121
Glenside Rd. Dumb —1H 17
Glen Spean Pl. Coat —6F 91
Glenspean St. G43 —1A 118
Glen St. Barr —5E 115
Glen St. Camb —3D 122
Glen St. Moth —6G 127
Glen St. N'hill —3D 128
Glen St. Pais —6H 77
Glentanar Pl. G22 —2F 63
Glentanar Rd. G22 —2F 63
Glen Tanner. E Kil —1D 150
Glentarbert Rd. Ruth —4F 121
Glen Tarbet Dri. Neil —3C 130
Glen Tennet. E Kil —1C 150
Glentore Quad. Air —1A 92
Glen Tower. Moth —5B 144
(off Glen Ct.)
Glentrool Gdns. Mood —4E 53
Glen Turret. E Kil —1C 150
Glenturret St. G32 —1A 106
Glentyan Av. Kilb —1A 94
Glentyan Dri. G53 —6A 100
Glentyan Ter. G53 —6A 100
Glen Urquhart. E Kil —2B 150
Glenview. Air —5D 92
Glen View. Cumb —2C 36
Glen View. Ham —5H 153
Glenview. Kirk —5D 30
Glenview. Lark —1D 160
Glenview Av. Bank —1E 15
Glenview Cres. Chry —4D 52
Glenview Pl. Blan —6B 124
Glenview St. Glenm —5G 71
Glenville Av. Giff —4H 117
Glenville Ga. Clar —4E 135
Glenville Ter. Clar —4E 135
Glenward Av. Len —3G 7
Glenwell St. Glenm —6G 71
Glenwood Av. Air —1C 112
Glenwood Bus. Cen. G45 —4B 120
Glenwood Ct. Kirk —2A 50
Glenwood Dri. T'bnk —5F 117
Glenwood Gdns. Kirk —2A 50
Glenwood Pl. Kirk —2A 50
Glenwood Rd. Kirk —2A 50
Glidden Ct. Over —4A 158
Glorat Av. Len —3G 7
Gloucester Av. Clar —2B 134
Gloucester Av. Ruth —2F 121
Gloucester St. G5 —6E 83
Gockston Rd. Pais —4H 77
Goddard Pl. Wis —4F 147
Gogar Pl. G33 —3G 85
Gogar St. G33 —3G 85
Goil Av. Rig I —1H 125
Goil Way. Moth —2A 128
(off Howden Pl.)
Goldberry Av. G14 —4B 60
Goldenhill Ct. Clyd —1D 42
Goldie Rd. Udd —3E 125
Golf Av. Bell —4C 126
Golf Course Rd. Balm —5A 28
Golf Course Rd. Bri W —3D 72
Golf Dri. G15 —6H 43
Golf Dri. Pais —1E 99
Golf Gdns. Lark —3G 161
Golfhill Dri. G31 —3C 84
Golfhill Quad. Air —1A 92
Golfhill Rd. Wis —5D 144
Golf Pl. Bell —4D 126
Golf Rd. Clar —2B 134
Golf Rd. Ruth —3D 120
Golfview. Bear —2B 44
Golf View. Clyd —3B 42
Golfview Dri. Coat —4G 89
Golfview Pl. Coat —5G 89
Golsbie Av. Air —1G 111
Golspie St. G51 —3G 81
Gonval Way. Pais —3H 77
Goodfellow M. Wis —2E 157
Goodview Gdns. Lark —3G 161
Goosedubs. G1 —5G 83
(off Bridgegate)
Gooseholm Cres. Dumb —2G 17
Gooseholm Rd. Dumb —2G 17
Gopher Av. Udd —5F 109
Gorbals Cross. G5 —6G 83
Gorbals Cross. Lark —2E 161
Gorbals St. G5 —6F 83
Gordon Av. G44 —5C 118
Gordon Av. G52 —4G 79
Gordon Av. Bail —6F 87
Gordon Av. B'ton —3G 39
Gordon Ct. Air —3E 93
Gordon Cres. Newt M —3E 133
Gordon Dri. G44 —5C 118
Gordon Dri. E Kil —6B 138
Gordon La. G1 —4F 83 (5D 4)
Gordon Pl. Bell —4B 126
Gordon Rd. G44 —5C 118
Gordon Rd. Ham —5D 140
Gordon St. G2 & G1 —4F 83 (5D 4)
Gordon St. Pais —1A 98
Gordon Ter. Blan —5A 124
Gordon Ter. Ham —6D 140
Gorebridge St. G32 —4G 85
Goremire Rd. Carl —6G 165
Gorget Av. G13 —6C 44
Gorget Pl. G13 —6C 44
Gorget Quad. G13 —6B 44
Gorse Cres. Bri W —4G 73
Gorse Dri. Barr —3D 114
Gorsehall St. Cle —5H 129
Gorse Pl. Udd —5F 109
Gorsewood. B'rig —6A 48
Gorstan Pl. G20 —4A 62
Gorstan St. G23 —1B 62
Gosford La. G14 —5A 60
Goudie St. Pais —4H 77
Gough St. G33 —3F 85
Gourlay. E Kil —4D 138
Gourlay Dri. Wis —5A 158
Gourlay St. G21 —6H 63
(in two parts)
Gourlock St. G41 —1E 103
Govanhill St. G42 —3F 103
Govan Rd. G51 —2D 80
GOVAN STATION. G51 —3G 81
Gowanbank Gdns. John —3E 95
Gowanbrae. Kirk —1C 50
Gowanlea Av. G15 —6A 44
Gowanlea Dri. Giff —3B 118
Gowanlea Ter. Udd —6F 109
Gowanside Pl. Carl —3D 164
Gower St. G51 —1A 102
Gower Ter. G41 —6A 82
Gowkhall Av. Moth —4F 129
Goyle Av. G15 —4C 44
Goy Pl. Law —6E 159
Grace Av. Bail —6D 88
Grace St. G3 —4D 82
Graeme Ct. Moth —5F 127
Graffham Av. Giff —4B 118
Grafton Pl. G1 —3G 83 (3F 5)
Graham Av. Camb —2D 122
Graham Av. Clyd —4D 42
Graham Av. E Kil —1G 149
Graham Av. Ham —3H 153
(in two parts)
Graham Dri. Miln —3E 25
Graham Ho. Cumb —3G 35
Graham Pl. Ashg —4B 162
Graham Pl. Kils —1G 11
Graham Rd. Dumb —3D 16
Grahamsdyke Rd. Kirk —4E 31
Grahamshill Av. Air —3D 92
Grahamshill St. Air —3C 92
Graham Sq. G40 —5B 84
Grahamston Ct. Pais —5E 99
Grahamston Cres. Pais —5E 99
Grahamston Pk. Barr —2D 114
Grahamston Rd. Barr & Pais —2D 114
Graham St. Air —4A 92
(in two parts)
Graham St. Barr —4D 114
Graham St. Ham —6A 142
Graham St. John —3E 95
Graham St. Moth —2A 128
Graham St. Wis —1H 157
Grahamstson Pl. Pais —5E 99
Graham Ter. B'rig —2D 64
Graignestock Pl. G40 —6A 84
Graignestock St. G40 —6A 84
Grainger Rd. B'rig —6F 49
Grampian Av. Pais —5H 97
Grampian Cres. G32 —1B 106
Grampian Pl. G32 —1B 106
Grampian Rd. Wis —5F 145
Grampian St. G32 —1B 106
Grampian Way. Barr —6E 115
Grampian Way. Bear —6B 24
Grampian Way. Cumb —3C 34
Granby La. G12 —6B 62
Grandtully Dri. G12 —3A 62
Grange Av. Miln —3H 25
Grange Av. Wis —2E 157
Grange Gdns. Both —6F 125
Grangeneuk Gdns. Cumb —4E 35
Granger Av. Lark —2F 161
Grange Rd. G42 —5E 103
Grange Rd. Bear —2F 45
Grange St. Moth —5A 144
Grange Tower. Moth —1B 156
Gran St. Clyd —1G 59
Grant Ct. Air —3E 93
Grant Ct. Ham —5G 153
Grantholm Av. Moth —1B 128
Grantlea Gro. G32 —1D 106
Grantlea Ter. G32 —1D 106
Grantley Gdns. G41 —5B 102
Grantley St. G41 —5B 102
Grantoften Path. E Kil —5F 149
Granton St. G5 —3A 104
Grantown Gdns. Glenm —4H 71
Grant St. G3 —2D 82
Granville St. G3 —3D 82
Granville St. Clyd —4D 42
Grasmere. E Kil —6B 148
Grathellen Ct. Moth —1A 144
Gray Dri. Bear —4F 45
Grayshill Rd. Cumb —6H 33
Gray's Rd. Udd —2F 125
Gray St. G3 —2B 82
Gray St. Cle —6H 129
Gray St. Kirk —6H 31
Gray St. Lark —1E 161
Gt. George La. G12 —6B 62
Gt. George St. G12 —6B 62
Gt. Hamilton St. Pais —3A 98
Gt. Kelvin La. G12 —1C 82
(off Glasgow St.)
Gt. Western Retail Pk. G15 —6H 43
Gt. Western Rd. G15, G13, G12 & G4 —6H 43
Gt. Western Ter. G12 —5A 62
Gt. Western Ter. La. G12 —5A 62
Gt. West Rd. Old K —5H 19
Greenacres. Moth —4E 143
Greenacres View. Moth —4E 143
Greenan Av. G42 —6A 104
Greenbank. Blan —2A 140
Greenbank Av. Giff —2G 133
Greenbank Dri. Pais —6H 97
Green Bank Rd. Cumb —3E 35
Greenbank Rd. Wis —6A 146
Greenbank St. Ruth —5C 104
Greenbank Ter. Carl —3F 165
Green Dale. Wis —4B 146
Greendyke St. G1 —5H 83
Greenend Av. John —5D 94
Greenend Pl. G32 —4C 86
Greenend View. Bell —3B 126
Green Farm Rd. Lin —5H 75
Greenfarm Rd. Newt M —4B 132
Greenfaulds Cres. Cumb —5A 36
Greenfaulds Rd. Cumb —6F 35
Greenfaulds Rd. Cumb —5A 36
(Lenziemill)
GREENFAULDS STATION. Cumb —6H 35
Greenfield Av. G32 —5B 86
Greenfield Cres. Wis —5B 146
Greenfield Dri. Wis —5B 146
Greenfield Pl. G32 —5B 86
Greenfield Quad. Moth —3F 129
Greenfield Rd. G32 —4C 86
Greenfield Rd. Carl —2F 165
Greenfield Rd. Clar —3C 134
Greenfield Rd. Ham —3E 141
Greenfield St. G51 —4F 81
Greenfield St. Wis —5B 146
Greengairs Av. G51 —3D 80
Green Gdns. Cle —5H 129
Greenhall Pl. Blan —3A 140
Greenhead Av. Dumb —4H 17
Greenhead Gdns. Dumb —3C 18
Greenhead Rd. Bear —3F 45
Greenhead Rd. Dumb —4H 17
Greenhead Rd. Inch —2G 57
Greenhead Rd. Len —3G 7
Greenhead Rd. Wis —1A 158
Greenhead St. G40 —6A 84
Greenhill. B'rig —1E 65
Greenhill Av. G'csh —2C 68
Greenhill Av. Giff —6H 117
Greenhill Ct. Ruth —5C 104
Greenhill Cres. Eld —3B 96
Greenhill Cres. Lin —5H 75
Greenhill Dri. Lin —5A 76
Greenhill Rd. Pais —5G 77
Greenhill Rd. Ruth —5C 104
Greenhills Cres. E Kil —6D 148
Greenhills Rd. E Kil —3A 148
Greenhills Sq. E Kil —5C 148
Greenhill St. Ruth —6C 104
Greenhills Way. E Kil —5F 149
Greenholm Av. Clar —2C 134
Greenholm Av. Udd —6C 108
Greenholme Ct. G44 —1F 119
Greenholme St. G44 —1F 119
Greenknowe Dri. Law —5D 158
Greenknowe Rd. G43 —1H 117
Greenknowe St. Wis —5H 157
Greenlaw Av. Pais —6C 78
Greenlaw Av. Wis —4A 146
Greenlaw Cres. Pais —5C 78
Greenlaw Dri. Newt M —4C 132
Greenlaw Dri. Pais —6C 78
Greenlaw Ind. Est. Pais —5B 78
Greenlaw Rd. G14 —3F 59
Greenlaw Rd. Newt M —4C 132
Greenlea Rd. Chry —1H 67
Greenlea St. G13 —3E 61
Greenlees Gdns. Camb —4H 121
Greenlees Pk. Camb —4A 122
Greenlees Rd. Camb —5H 121
Greenless Gro. Coat —6F 91
Green Loan. Moth —4A 128
Greenloan Av. G51 —3D 80
Greenloan View. Lark —4F 161
(off Keir Hardie Rd.)
Greenlodge Ter. G40 —1B 104
Greenmoss Pl. Bell —2D 126
Greenmount. G22 —2E 63
Greenock Av. G44 —2F 119
Greenock Rd. B'ton & Inch —1A 38
Greenock Rd. Pais —4H 77
Green Pl. Both —5F 125
Green Pl. C'bnk —3B 112
Greenrig. Udd —1D 124
Greenrigg Rd. Cumb —4A 36
Greenrig St. G33 —6F 65
Greenrig St. Udd —1D 124
Green Rd. Pais —2D 96
Green Rd. Ruth —5C 104
Greens Av. Kirk —6C 30
Greens Cres. Kirk —6C 30
Greenshields Rd. Bail —6H 87
Greenside Cres. G33 —6G 65
Greenside Pl. Bear —5C 24
Greenside Rd. Clar —1A 136
Greenside Rd. Clyd —6D 22
Greenside Rd. Moth —6C 112
Greenside Rd. Wis —1A 158
Greenside St. G33 —6G 65
Greenside St. Coat —2D 90
Greenside St. Moth —3F 129
Greens Rd. Cumb —1H 55
Green St. G40 —6A 84
Green St. Both —5F 125
Green St. Clyd —4C 42
Green, The. G40 —1A 104
Greentree Dri. Bail —2F 107
Greenview St. G43 —5A 102
Greenway La. Blan —3A 140
Greenways Av. Pais —3E 97
Greenways Ct. Pais —3E 97
Greenwood Av. Camb —1E 123
Greenwood Av. Chry —5D 52
Greenwood Ct. Clar —2C 134
Greenwood Cres. Coat —6E 91
Greenwood Dri. Bear —3G 45
Greenwood Quad. Clyd —6F 43
Greenwood Rd. Clar —2B 134
Greenyards Interchange. Cumb —4C 36
Greer Quad. Clyd —3D 42
Grenada Pl. E Kil —2C 148
Grenadier Gdns. Moth —6F 143
Grenville Dri. Camb —3H 121
Greta Meek La. Milt C —5C 8
Gretna St. G40 —1D 104
Greyfriars Rd. Udd —5A 108
Greyfriars St. G32 —4H 85
Greystone Av. Ruth —1E 121
Greywood St. G13 —2E 61
Grier Path. G31 —6F 85
Grier Pl. Lark —3D 160
Grierson St. G33 —3F 85
Grieve Croft. Both —6E 125
Grieve Rd. Cumb —2A 36
Griffin Pl. Bell —5C 110
Griffin Pl. Law —1H 163
Griffiths Way. Law —1H 163
Griqua Ter. Both —5F 125
Grogan Ct. G32 —5C 86
Grogarry Rd. G15 —3A 44
Grosvenor Cres. G12 —6B 62
Grosvenor Cres. La. G12 —6B 62
Grosvenor La. G12 —6B 62
Grosvenor Ter. G12 —6B 62
Groveburn Av. T'bnk —3G 117
Grove Cres. Lark —3G 161
Grove Pk. Lenz —3D 50
Grovepark Ct. G20 —1E 83
Grove Pk. Gdns. G20 —1E 83
Grovepark St. G20 —6E 63
Grove, The. B'ton —4G 39
Grove, The. Bri W —5G 73
Grove, The. Giff —1H 133
Grove, The. Kilb —1A 94
Grove, The. Neil —3C 130
Grove Way. Bell —2B 126
Grovewood Bus. Cen. Bell —5A 110
Grove Wood N. Udd —4H 109
Grove Wynd. Moth —4A 128
Grudie St. G34 —3G 87
Gryfebank Av. Hous —2E 75
Gryfebank Clo. Hous —2E 75
Gryfee St. G44 —6E 103
Gryfewood Cres. Hous —2E 75
Gryfewood Way. Hous —2E 75
Gryffe Av. Bri W —2E 73
Gryffe Av. Renf —4D 58
Gryffe Cres. Pais —4D 96
Gryffe Gro. Bri W —3F 73
Gryffe Pk. Bri W —2E 73
Gryffe Rd. Bri W —4F 73
Guildford St. G33 —2C 86
Gullane Ct. Ham —3F 153
Gullane Cres. Cumb —5H 13
Gullane St. G11 —2H 81
Gunderson Rd. G2 —4F 83
Gunn Quad. Bell —4A 126
Guthrie Dri. Udd —4E 109
Guthrie Pl. E Kil —1H 149
Guthrie Pl. Torr —5E 29
Guthrie St. G20 —3B 62
Guthrie St. Ham —5H 141

Haberlea Av. G53 —4C 116
Haberlea Gdns. G53 —5C 116
Haddow Gro. Udd —5E 109
Haddow St. Ham —6A 142
Hadrian Ter. Moth —1E 143
Hagart Rd. Hous —1B 74
Hagg Cres. John —2E 95
Hagg Pl. John —2E 95
Hagg Rd. John —3E 95
Haggs La. G41 —3A 102
Haggs Rd. G41 —4A 102
Haggswood Av. G41 —3A 102
Haghill Rd. G31 —5E 85
Hagmill Cres. Coat —3E 111
Hagmill Rd. Coat —3C 110
Haig Dri. Bail —1F 107
Haig St. G21 —5B 64
Hailes Av. G32 —6D 86
Haining Rd. Renf —6F 59
Haining, The. Renf —1F 79
Hairmyres Dri. E Kil —3A 148
Hairmyres La. E Kil —2A 148
Hairmyres Pk. E Kil —3B 148
Hairmyres Roundabout. E Kil —2B 148
HAIRMYRES STATION. E Kil —2B 148
Hairmyres St. G42 —3G 103
Hairst St. Renf —5F 59
Halbeath Av. G15 —4H 43
Halbert St. G41 —4C 102
Haldane La. G14 —6D 60
(off Haldane St.)
Haldane Pl. E Kil —4H 149
Haldane St. G14 —6D 60
Halfmerk N. E Kil —1A 150
Halfmerk St. E Kil —1A 150
Halgreen Av. G15 —4G 43
Halifax Way. Renf —2E 79
(off Three Av.)
Hallbrae St. G33 —1G 85
Hallburton Cres. G34 —4F 87
Hallburton Ter. G34 —4G 87
Hallcraig Pl. Carl —3D 164
Hallcraig St. Air —3A 92
Halley Dri. G13 —2G 59
Halley Pl. G13 —3G 59
Halley Sq. G13 —2H 59
Halley St. G13 —2G 59
Hallforest St. G33 —1B 86
Hallhill Cres. G33 —5E 87
Hallhill Rd. G32 —6B 86
Hallhill Rd. Bail —5G 87
Hallhill Rd. John —6C 94
Hallidale Cres. Renf —1H 79
Hallinan Gdns. Wis —2F 157
Hallrule Dri. G52 —6C 80
Hallside Av. Camb —2E 123
Hallside Cres. Camb —2E 123
Hallside Dri. Camb —2E 123
Hallside Gdns. Wis —5C 146
Hallside Pl. G5 —1G 103
Hallside Rd. Camb —3E 123
Hall St. Clyd —6C 42
Hall St. Ham —2H 153
Hall St. Moth —3A 128
Hallydown Dri. G13 —4C 60
Halpin Clo. Bell —2H 125
Halston St. Pais —1C 98
Halton Gdns. Bail —1F 107
Hamersley Pl. E Kil —4D 148
Hamilcomb Rd. Bell —4C 126

Hamill Dri. *Kils* —3B **12**
Hamilton Av. *G41* —2H **101**
Hamilton Bus. Pk. *Ham* —4H **141**
HAMILTON CENTRAL STATION. *Ham* —6A **142**
Hamilton Ct. *Pais* —3A **98**
Hamilton Cres. *Bear* —6E **25**
Hamilton Cres. *B'ton* —4F **39**
Hamilton Cres. *Camb* —3B **122**
Hamilton Cres. *Coat* —6C **90**
Hamilton Cres. *Renf* —4F **59**
Hamilton Dri. *G12* —6C **62**
Hamilton Dri. *Air* —2B **92**
Hamilton Dri. *Blan* —4H **139**
Hamilton Dri. *Both* —6F **125**
Hamilton Dri. *Camb* —2A **122**
Hamilton Dri. *Ersk* —4D **40**
Hamilton Dri. *Giff* —5B **118**
Hamilton Dri. *Moth* —5H **143**
Hamiltonhill Cres. *G22* —5F **63**
Hamiltonhill Rd. *G22* —6F **63**
Hamilton International Technology Pk. *Ham* —4A **140**
Hamilton Pk. Av. *G12* —6C **62**
Hamilton Pl. *Carf* —3C **128**
Hamilton Pl. *E Kil* —4G **149**
Hamilton Pl. *Ham* —5H **153**
Hamilton Pl. *New S* —3B **128**
Hamilton Rd. *G32* —2B **106**
Hamilton Rd. *Bell* —4B **126**
Hamilton Rd. *Both* —6F **125**
Hamilton Rd. *Camb* —1A **122**
Hamilton Rd. *E Kil* —4C **138**
Hamilton Rd. *Lark* —6H **155**
Hamilton Rd. *Moth* —4D **142**
Hamilton Rd. *Ruth* —5D **104**
Hamilton St. *G42* —4G **103**
Hamilton St. *Carl* —4F **165**
Hamilton St. *Clyd* —2F **59**
Hamilton St. *Dumb* —3G **17**
Hamilton St. *Lark* —1E **161**
Hamilton St. *Pais* —6B **78**
Hamilton Ter. *Clyd* —2F **59**
Hamilton Tower. *Udd* —3B **124**
Hamilton View. *Udd* —6E **109**
HAMILTON WEST STATION. *Ham* —5G **141**
Hamlet. *E Kil* —5B **138**
Hampden Dri. *G42* —6F **103**
Hampden La. *G42* —5F **103**
Hampden Ter. *G42* —5F **103**
Hampden Way. *Renf* —2F **79**
Hangingshaw Pl. *G42* —5G **103**
Hanover Clo. *G42* —5E **103**
Hanover Ct. *G1* —3G **83** (4F **5**)
Hanover Ct. *G11* —1G **81**
Hanover Ct. *Pais* —6C **78**
Hanover Gdns. *B'rig* —6C **48**
Hanover Gdns. *Pais* —1G **97**
Hanover St. *G1* —4G **83** (5E **5**)
Hanson St. *G31* —4B **84**
Hapland Av. *G53* —3C **100**
Hapland Rd. *G53* —3C **100**
Harbour La. *Pais* —6A **78**
Harbour Rd. *Pais* —4A **78**
Harburn Pl. *G14* —3H **59**
Harburn Pl. *G23* —6C **46**
Harcourt Dri. *G31* —3D **84**
Hardgate Dri. *G51* —3C **80**
Hardgate Gdns. *G51* —3C **80**
Hardgate Pl. *G51* —3C **80**
Hardgate Rd. *G51* —3C **80**
Hardie Av. *Ruth* —5E **105**
Hardie St. *Blan* —2B **140**
Hardie St. *Ham* —1F **153**
Hardie St. *Moth* —1G **143**
Hardmuir Gdns. *Kirk* —4E **31**
Hardmuir Rd. *Kirk* —4E **31**
Hardridge Av. *G52* —3E **101**
Hardridge Pl. *G52* —3E **101**
Hardridge Rd. *G52* —3D **100**
Harefield Dri. *G14* —4B **60**
Harelaw Av. *G44* —3C **118**
Harelaw Av. *Barr* —6F **115**
Harelaw Av. *Neil* —3D **130**
Harelaw Cres. *Pais* —6G **97**
Hareleeshill Rd. *Lark* —3F **161**
Harestanes Gdns. *Kirk* —4G **31**
Harestone Cres. *Wis* —1A **158**
Harestone Rd. *Wis* —1A **158**
Harhill St. *G51* —4F **81**
Harkins Av. *Blan* —2A **140**
Harkness Av. *Milt C* —6B **8**
Harland Cotts. *G14* —6C **60**
Harland St. *G14* —6C **60**
Harlaw Gdns. *B'rig* —5F **49**
Harley St. *G51* —5A **82**
Harmetray St. *G22* —3H **63**
Harmony Pl. *G51* —4G **81**
Harmony Row. *G51* —4G **81**
(in two parts)
Harmony Sq. *G51* —4G **81**
Harmsworth St. *G11* —1E **81**
Harper Cres. *Wis* —5C **146**
Harport St. *T'bnk* —2E **117**
Harriet Pl. *G43* —1H **117**
Harriet St. *Ruth* —6C **104**
Harrington Rd. *E Kil* —2G **149**
Harris Clo. *Newt M* —6D **102**
Harris Cres. *Old K* —2F **41**
Harris Dri. *Old K* —2F **41**
Harris Gdns. *Old K* —2G **41**
Harrison Dri. *G51* —5H **81**
Harrison Quad. *Wis* —4C **146**
Harris Rd. *G23* —6C **46**
Harris Rd. *Old K* —2F **41**
Harrow Ct. *G15* —4H **43**
Harrow Pl. *G15* —4H **43**
Hartfield Ct. *Dumb* —3G **17**
Hartfield Cres. *Neil* —2E **131**
Hartfield Gdns. *Dumb* —3G **17**
Hartfield Ter. *Pais* —3B **98**
Hartlaw Cres. *G52* —5A **80**
Hartree Av. *G13* —1G **59**
Hartstone Pl. *G53* —6B **100**
Hartstone Rd. *G53* —6B **100**
Hartstone Ter. *G53* —6B **100**
Hart St. *G31* —6G **85**
Hart St. *Lin* —6H **75**
Harvest Dri. *Moth* —5F **143**
Harvey St. *G4* —1G **83**
Harvey Way. *Bell* —6E **111**
Harvie Av. *Newt M* —4C **132**
Harvie St. *G51* —5B **82**
Harwood Gdns. *Mood* —4E **53**
Harwood St. *G32* —4G **85**
Hastie St. *G3* —2B **82**
Hastings. *E Kil* —4D **148**
Hatchard Gdns. *Lin* —5H **75**
Hatfield Dri. *G12* —4F **61**
Hathaway Dri. *Giff* —5H **117**
Hathaway La. *G20* —4C **62**
Hathaway St. *G20* —4C **62**
Hathersage Av. *Bail* —6H **87**
Hathersage Dri. *Bail* —6H **87**
Hathersage Gdns. *Bail* —6H **87**
Hatton Gdns. *G52* —1A **100**
Hattonhill. *Moth* —5C **128**
Hatton Path. G52 —1A 100
(off Hatton Gdns.)
Hatton Pl. *Moth* —5C **128**
Hattonrigg Rd. *Bell* —1D **126**
Hatton Ter. *Moth* —5C **128**
Haughburn Pl. *G53* —6B **100**
Haughburn Rd. *G53* —6B **100**
Haughburn Ter. *G53* —6C **100**
Haughhead Bri. *Udd* —5A **108**
Haugh Pl. *Ham* —2A **154**
Haugh Rd. *G3* —3B **82**
Haugh Rd. *Kils* —3G **11**
Haughton Av. *Kils* —3A **12**
Haughview Rd. *Moth* —3D **142**
Havelock La. G11 —1A 82
(off Havelock St.)
Havelock Pk. *E Kil* —2C **148**
Havelock St. *G11* —1A **82**
Haven Pl. *E Kil* —5B **148**
Havoc Rd. *Dumb* —4B **16**
Hawbank Rd. *E Kil* —6C **136**
Hawbank Roundabout. *E Kil* —1D **148**
Hawick Av. *Pais* —4F **97**
Hawick Cres. *Lark* —3E **161**
Hawick Dri. *Coat* —2F **111**
Hawick St. *G13* —3G **59**
Hawick St. *Wis* —4A **146**
Hawkhead Av. *Pais* —3D **98**
Hawkhead Rd. *Pais* —1D **98**
HAWKHEAD STATION. *Pais* —1D **98**
Hawksland Wlk. *Ham* —2A **154**
Hawkwood. *E Kil* —6F **149**
Hawkwood Rd. *Glenm* —5H **71**
Hawthorn Av. *Bear* —6G **25**
Hawthorn Av. *B'rig* —1D **64**
Hawthorn Av. *Dumb* —2B **16**
Hawthorn Av. *Ersk* —1A **58**
Hawthorn Av. *John* —4G **95**
Hawthorn Av. *Lenz* —2C **50**
Hawthorn Av. *Newm* —3G **147**
Hawthorn Ct. *Clar* —3C **134**
Hawthorn Cres. *Ersk* —1A **58**
Hawthornden Gdns. *G23* —5C **46**
Hawthorn Dri. *Air* —4D **92**
Hawthorn Dri. *Bank* —1E **15**
Hawthorn Dri. *Barr* —6F **115**
Hawthorn Dri. *Coat* —6F **91**
Hawthorn Dri. *Moth* —4B **128**
Hawthorn Dri. *Wis* —1A **158**
Hawthorn Gdns. *Bell* —3E **127**
Hawthorn Gdns. *Clar* —3C **134**
Hawthorn Gdns. *Lark* —3G **161**
Hawthorn Gro. *Law* —5D **158**
Hawthorn Hill. *Ham* —2A **154**
Hawthornhill Rd. *Dumb* —2B **16**
Hawthorn Pl. *Blan* —2C **140**
Hawthorn Quad. *G22* —4G **63**
Hawthorn Rd. *Clar* —3C **134**
Hawthorn Rd. *Cumb* —1F **37**
Hawthorn Rd. *Ersk* —1A **58**
Hawthorn St. *G22* —4G **63**
Hawthorn St. *Clyd* —3C **42**
Hawthorn St. *Torr* —4E **29**
Hawthorn Ter. *E Kil* —5D **148**
Hawthorn Ter. *Udd* —6F **109**
Hawthorn Wlk. *B'rig* —1F **65**
Hawthorn Wlk. *Camb* —2F **121**
Hawthorn Way. *Ersk* —1A **58**
Hawthorn Way. *Milt C* —6C **8**
Hay Av. *B'ton* —4A **40**
Hayburn Cres. *G11* —6G **61**
Hayburn Ga. *G11* —1H **81**
Hayburn La. *G12* —6G **61**
Hayburn St. *G11* —2G **81**
Hay Dri. *John* —2H **95**
Hayfield St. *G5* —1H **103**
Hayle Gdns. *Chry* —4D **52**
Haylynn St. *G14* —1E **81**
Haymarket St. *G32* —4G **85**
Haystack Pl. *Lenz* —3D **50**
Hayston Cres. *G22* —4F **63**
Hayston Rd. *Kirk* —5A **30**
Hayston St. *G22* —4F **63**
Haywood St. *G22* —3F **63**
Hazel Av. *G44* —3D **118**
Hazel Av. *Bear* —6G **25**
Hazel Av. *Dumb* —2B **16**
Hazel Av. *John* —4G **95**
Hazel Av. *Lenz* —1D **50**
Hazel Bank. *Milt C* —1B **30**
Hazelbank. *Moth* —2B **128**
Hazelbank Wlk. *Air* —3F **91**
Hazeldean Cres. *Wis* —4A **146**
Hazel Dene. *B'rig* —6D **48**
Hazeldene La. Lark —4G 161
(off Donaldson Rd.)
Hazel Gdns. *Moth* —6G **143**
Hazel Gro. *Kirk* —1D **50**
Hazel Gro. *Law* —5D **158**
Hazelhead. *E Kil* —1B **150**
Hazellea Dri. *Giff* —3C **118**
Hazel Pk. *Ham* —1A **154**
Hazel Path. *Cle* —6H **129**
Hazel Rd. *Bank* —1E **15**
Hazel Rd. *Cumb* —2D **36**
Hazel Ter. *Udd* —6F **109**
Hazelton. *Moth* —4F **143**
Hazel Wood. *Wis* —4B **146**
Hazelwood Av. *Bri W* —4G **73**
Hazelwood Av. *Newt M* —5E **133**
Hazelwood Av. *Pais* —6C **96**
Hazelwood Gdns. *Ruth* —3E **121**
Hazelwood La. *Bri W* —4F **73**
Hazelwood Rd. *G41* —1A **102**
Hazelwood Rd. *Bri W* —4F **73**
Hazlewood Dri. *Blan* —1A **140**
Hazlitt St. *G20* —3F **63**
Headhouse Ct. *E Kil* —3F **149**
Headhouse Grn. *E Kil* —3G **149**
Headsmuir Av. *Carl* —3D **164**
Hearn Pl. *Bail* —4D **68**
Heath Av. *B'rig* —1D **64**
Heath Av. *Lenz* —3C **50**
Heathcliffe Av. *Blan* —6A **124**
Heathcot Av. *G15* —5G **43**
Heathcot Pl. *G15* —5G **43**
Heather Av. *Barr* —2C **114**
Heather Av. *Bear* —5D **24**
Heather Av. *Clyd* —6C **22**
Heather Av. *Moth* —2A **128**
Heatherbank Wlk. *Air* —3F **91**
Heatherbrae. *B'rig* —6A **48**
Heather Dri. *Kirk* —3A **50**
Heather Gdns. *Kirk* —3A **50**
Heather Gro. E Kil —4G 149
(off Heathery Knowe)
Heather Pl. *John* —3G **95**
Heather Pl. *Kirk* —2A **50**
Heather Row. *Carl* —1E **165**
Heather View. *Len* —2G **7**
Heather Way. *Moth* —3A **128**
Heathery Knowe. *E Kil* —4G **149**
Heatheryknowe Rd. *Barg* —4C **88**
Heathery Rd. *Wis* —6F **145**
Heathfield. *Wis* —4G **157**
Heathfield Av. *Mood* —5D **52**
Heathfield Dri. *Miln* —2H **25**
Heathfield St. *G33* —3C **86**
Heath Rd. *Lark* —2F **161**
Heathside Rd. *Giff* —4B **118**
Heathwood Dri. *T'bnk* —4G **117**
Hecla Av. *G15* —4H **43**
Hecla Pl. *G15* —4H **43**
Hecla Sq. *G15* —5H **43**
Hector Rd. *G41* —5B **102**
Helena Pl. *Clar* —1C **134**
Helena Ter. *Clyd* —1C **42**
Helensburgh Dri. *G13* —3D **60**
Helenslea. *Camb* —3D **122**
Helenslea Pl. *Bell* —3B **126**
Helenslee Ct. *Dumb* —4D **16**
Helenslee Cres. *Dumb* —4D **16**
Helenslee Rd. *Dumb* —4D **16**
Helen St. *G51* —4G **81**
Helen St. *G52* —6F **81**
Helenvale Ct. *G31* —6F **85**
Helenvale St. *G31* —1E **105**
Helmsdale Av. *Blan* —4A **124**
Helmsdale Ct. *Camb* —2D **122**
Hemlock St. *G13* —2F **61**
Hemmingen Ct. *Carl* —2E **165**
Henderland Ga. *Bear* —5E **45**
Henderland Rd. *Bear* —5E **45**
Henderson Av. *Camb* —1D **122**
Henderson St. *G20* —6D **62**
Henderson St. *Air* —3B **92**
Henderson St. *Clyd* —1G **59**
Henderson St. *Coat* —5B **90**
Henderson St. *Pais* —6H **77**
Hendy Ct. *Clyd* —5C **42**
Henrietta St. *G14* —6C **60**
Henry Bell Grn. E Kil —3H 149
(off Telford Rd.)
Henry St. *Barr* —4D **114**
Hepburn Hill. *Ham* —3F **153**
Hepburn Rd. *G52* —4B **80**
Herald Av. *G13* —6D **44**
Herald Gro. *Moth* —5F **143**
Herald Way. *Renf* —2E **79**
Herbertson Gro. *Blan* —6A **124**
Herbertson St. *G5* —6F **83**
Herbertson St. *Blan* —2C **140**
Herbert St. *G20* —6D **62**
Hercules Way. *Renf* —2F **79**
Heriot Av. *Pais* —5C **96**
Heriot Ct. *Pais* —5D **96**
Heriot Cres. *B'rig* —4C **48**
Heriot Rd. *Lenz* —4C **50**
Heritage Ct. *Newt M* —4E **133**
Heritage View. *Coat* —3B **90**
Heritage Way. *Coat* —4B **90**
Herma St. *G23* —1C **62**
Hermes Way. *Bell* —2H **127**
Hermiston Av. *G32* —5C **86**
Hermiston Pl. *G32* —5C **86**
Hermiston Pl. Moth —2A 128
(off Windsor Rd.)
Hermiston Rd. *G32* —4B **86**
Hermitage Av. *G13* —2C **60**
Hermitage Cres. *Coat* —2D **110**
Herndon Ct. *Newt M* —3G **133**
Heron Ct. *Clyd* —2D **42**
Heron Pl. *John* —6D **94**
Heron St. *G40* —1B **104**
Heron Way. *Renf* —2E **79**
Herries Rd. *G41* —4A **102**
Herriet St. *G41* —2D **102**
Herriot St. *Coat* —3A **90**
Herschell St. *G13* —3F **61**
Hertford Av. *G12* —3H **61**
Hewett Cres. *C'lee* —2C **74**
Hexham Gdns. *G41* —4B **102**
Heys St. *Barr* —5E **115**
Hickman St. *G42* —4F **103**
Hickory Cres. *Udd* —4G **109**
Hickory St. *G22* —4A **64**
High Avon St. *Lark* —1D **160**
High Barholm. *Kilb* —2A **94**
High Barrwood Rd. *Kils* —3A **12**
High Beeches. *Crmck* —1A **136**
High Blantyre Rd. *Ham* —4D **140**
Highburgh Dri. *Ruth* —2D **120**
Highburgh Rd. *G12* —6A **62**
High Burnside Av. *Coat* —6A **90**
High Calside. *Pais* —2H **97**
High Coats. *Coat* —4D **90**
High Comn. Rd. *E Kil* —4B **150**
Highcraig Av. *John* —4D **94**
High Craigends. *Kils* —3H **11**
High Craighall Rd. *G4* —1F **83**
Highcroft Av. *G44* —2H **119**
Highcross Av. *Coat* —1H **109**
Highfield Av. *Kirk* —4E **31**
Highfield Av. *Pais* —6H **97**
Highfield Ct. *Kirk* —5F **31**
Highfield Cres. *Moth* —1A **144**
Highfield Cres. *Pais* —6H **97**
Highfield Dri. *G12* —3H **61**
Highfield Dri. *Clar* —2B **134**
Highfield Dri. *Ruth* —4E **121**
Highfield Gro. *Kirk* —4E **31**
Highfield Pl. *G12* —3H **61**
Highfield Pl. *E Kil* —6H **137**
Highfield Rd. *Kirk* —4E **31**
Highfield Rd. *Lark* —2F **161**
High Flender Rd. *Clar* —3A **134**
High Kirk View. *John* —3F **95**
Highland Av. *Blan* —1A **140**
Highland La. *G51* —3A **82**
Highland Pk. *Kils* —2G **11**
Highland Pl. *Kils* —1G **11**
High Mains Av. *Dumb* —2C **18**
High Meadow. *Carl* —5H **165**
(in two parts)
High Mill Rd. *Carl* —3G **165**
High Parksail. *Ersk* —1G **57**
High Parks Cres. *Ham* —5H **153**
High Patrick St. *Ham* —1A **154**
High Pleasance. *Lark* —2E **161**
High Rd. *Cast* —2G **97**
High Rd. *Moth* —2F **143**
High Row. *B'rig* —2D **48**
Highstonehall Rd. *Ham* —4C **152**
High St. Airdrie, *Air* —3H **91**
High St. Carluke, *Carl* —3F **165**
High St. Dumbarton, *Dumb* —4E **17**
High St. Glasgow, *G1 & G4* —5H **83** (6G **5**)
High St. Johnstone, *John* —2E **95**
High St. Neilston, *Neil* —2D **130**
High St. Newarthill, *N'hill* —3E **129**
High St. Paisley, *Pais* —1H **97**
High St. Renfrew, *Renf* —5F **59**
High St. Rutherglen, *Ruth* —5C **104**
HIGH ST. STATION. *G1* —4H **83** (6H **5**)
High Whitehills Rd. *E Kil* —6F **149**
Hilary Dri. *Bail* —6F **87**
Hilda Cres. *G33* —5G **65**
Hillary Av. *Ruth* —1F **121**
Hill Av. *Newt M* —5C **132**
Hill Cres. *Clar* —3C **134**
Hillcrest. *Crmck* —1H **135**
Hillcrest. *Chry* —1B **68**
Hillcrest Av. *Clyd* —6C **22**
Hillcrest Av. *Coat* —5E **91**
Hillcrest Av. *Cumb* —5H **35**
Hillcrest Av. *Mt V* —5B **106**
Hillcrest Av. *Muir* —3C **118**
Hillcrest Av. *Pais* —6G **97**
Hillcrest Av. *Wis* —6E **145**
Hillcrest Ct. *Cumb* —4H **35**
Hillcrest Dri. *Newt M* —4G **133**
Hillcrest Rd. *G32* —4C **106**
Hillcrest Rd. *Bear* —3F **45**
Hillcrest Rd. *Kils* —3C **10**
Hillcrest Rd. *Udd* —6E **109**
Hillcrest St. *Miln* —3G **25**
Hillcrest Ter. *Both* —4F **125**
Hillcrest View. *Lark* —3F **161**
Hillcroft Ter. *B'rig* —1B **64**
Hillend Cres. *Clar* —3A **134**
Hillend Cres. *Clyd* —1B **42**
Hillend Rd. *G22* —2E **63**
Hillend Rd. *Clar* —3A **134**
Hillend Rd. *Ruth* —2D **120**
Hillfoot. *Hous* —3D **74**
Hillfoot Av. *Dumb* —1C **18**
Hillfoot Av. *Ruth* —6C **104**
Hillfoot Av. *Wis* —2B **146**
Hillfoot Cres. *Wis* —2B **146**
Hillfoot Dri. *Bear* —2F **45**
Hillfoot Dri. *Coat* —5H **89**
Hillfoot Dri. *Wis* —2B **146**
Hillfoot Gdns. *Udd* —5C **108**
Hillfoot Gdns. *Wis* —2B **146**
Hillfoot Rd. *Air* —5A **92**
HILLFOOT STATION. *Bear* —2G **45**
Hillfoot St. *G31* —4C **84**
Hillfoot Ter. *Carl* —4G **165**
Hillhead Av. *Bank* —1E **15**
Hillhead Av. *Carl* —3G **165**
Hillhead Av. *Chry* —5D **52**
Hillhead Av. *Moth* —5A **128**
Hillhead Av. *Ruth* —3D **120**
Hillhead Cres. *Ham* —6C **140**
Hillhead Cres. *Moth* —5A **128**
Hillhead Dri. *Air* —5A **92**
Hillhead Dri. *Moth* —6A **128**
Hillhead Pl. *Ruth* —3D **120**
Hillhead Rd. *G21* —2F **65**
Hillhead Rd. *Kirk* —4D **30**
HILLHEAD STATION. *G12* —6B **62**
Hillhead St. *G12* —1B **82**
Hillhead St. *Miln* —3G **25**
Hillhead Ter. *Ham* —6C **140**
Hillhouse Cres. *Ham* —6D **140**
Hillhouse Ga. *Carl* —5H **165**
Hillhouse Pk. Ind. Est. *Ham* —5E **141**
Hillhouse Rd. *Ham* —4H **139**
Hillhouse St. *G21* —5C **64**
Hillhouse Ter. *Ham* —6D **140**
HILLINGTON EAST STATION. *G52* —5B **80**
Hillington Gdns. *G52* —1C **100**
Hillington Ind. Est. G52 —3H 79
(off Lothian St.)
Hillington Pk. Cir. *G52* —6C **80**
Hillington Quad. *G52* —6A **80**
Hillington Rd. *H'ton I* —4A **80**
Hillington Rd. S. *G52* —5A **80**
Hillington Ter. *G52* —6A **80**
HILLINGTON WEST STATION. *G52* —4H **79**
Hillkirk La. G21 —5B 64
(off Hillkirk St.)
Hillkirk Pl. *G21* —5B **64**
Hillkirk St. *G21* —5B **64**
Hillneuk Av. *Bear* —2F **45**
Hillneuk Dri. *Bear* —2G **45**
Hillpark Av. *Pais* —4H **97**
Hillpark Dri. *G43* —1H **117**
Hill Pl. *Bell* —4B **126**
Hill Pl. *Moth* —5C **128**
Hillrigg Av. *Air* —3C **92**
Hill Rd. *Cumb* —3G **35**
Hill Rd. *Kils* —1H **11**
Hillsborough Rd. *Bail* —6F **87**
Hillside. *Croy* —6B **12**
Hillside. *Hous* —3E **75**
Hillside Av. *Bear* —2F **45**
Hillside Av. *Clar* —2B **134**
Hillside Cotts. *Glenb* —3A **70**
Hillside Ct. *T'bnk* —4F **117**
Hillside Cres. *Coat* —1B **110**
Hillside Cres. *Ham* —1H **153**
Hillside Cres. *Moth* —3D **128**
Hillside Cres. *Neil* —2D **130**
Hillside Dri. *Barr* —4C **114**
Hillside Dri. *Bear* —2G **45**
Hillside Dri. *B'rig* —5C **48**
Hillside Gro. *Barr* —5C **114**
Hillside Gro. *B'rig* —1E **65**
Hillside La. *Ham* —1G **153**
Hillside Pk. *Hard* —1D **42**
Hillside Pl. *Moth* —4D **128**
Hillside Quad. *G43* —2H **117**
Hillside Rd. *G43* —2H **117**
Hillside Rd. *Barr* —5B **114**
Hillside Rd. *Neil* —2D **130**
Hillside Rd. *Pais* —3C **98**
Hillside Ter. *Ham* —1G **153**
Hillside Ter. *Milt C* —6B **8**
Hillside Ter. *Old K* —1F **41**
Hill St. *G3* —2E **83** (2A **4**)

Hill St. Chap —3D 112
Hill St. Dumb —4D 16
Hill St. Ham —6D 140
Hill St. Wis —1G 157
Hillswick Cres. G22 —1F 63
Hill Ter. Moth —5C 128
Hilltop Av. Bell —6C 110
Hilltop Ter. Bail —5D 52
Hill View. E Kil —3G 149
Hill View. Milt —4F 19
Hillview Av. Kils —4H 11
Hillview Av. Len —3G 7
Hillview Cres. Bell —5C 110
Hillview Cres. Lark —3F 161
Hillview Cres. Udd —5C 108
Hillview Dri. Blan —5A 124
Hillview Dri. Clar —2B 134
Hill View Gdns. B'rig —1F 65
Hillview Pl. Clar —2C 134
Hillview Pl. Newt M —5D 132
Hillview Rd. Bri W —4G 73
Hillview Rd. Eld —3H 95
Hillview St. G32 —6H 85
Hillview Ter. Old K —2F 41
Hiltonbank St. Ham —5F 141
Hilton Ct. B'rig —4C 48
Hilton Gdns. G13 —2F 61
Hilton Gdns. La. G13 —2F 61
Hilton Pk. B'rig —3B 48
Hilton Rd. B'rig —4B 48
Hilton Rd. Miln —3E 25
Hilton Ter. G13 —2E 61
Hilton Ter. B'rig —3B 48
Hilton Ter. Camb —4G 121
Hindsland Rd. Lark —4F 161
Hinshaw St. G20 —6E 63
Hinshelwood Dri. G51 —5G 81
Hinshelwood Pl. G51 —6H 81
Hirsel Pl. Both —5F 125
Hobart Cres. Clyd —2H 41
Hobart Quad. Wis —6C 146
Hobart Rd. E Kil —4E 149
Hobart St. G22 —5F 63
Hobden St. G21 —6C 64
Hoddam Av. G45 —4B 120
Hoddam Ter. G45 —4C 120
Hoey Dri. Wis —4A 158
Hogan Ct. Clyd —1B 42
Hogarth Av. G32 —4F 85
Hogarth Cres. G32 —4F 85
Hogarth Dri. G32 —4F 85
Hogarth Gdns. G32 —4F 85
Hogganfield St. G33 —1F 85
Hogg Av. John —4E 95
Hogg Rd. Chap —1D 112
Hogg St. Air —4A 92
Holeburn La. G43 —1A 118
Holeburn Rd. G43 —1A 118
Holehills Dri. Air —1B 92
Holehills Pl. Air —1B 92
Holehouse Brae. Neil —2C 130
Holehouse Dri. G13 —3A 60
Holehouse Ter. Neil —2C 130
Hollandbush Cres. Bank —1F 15
Hollandbush Gro. Ham —3H 153
Hollandhurst Rd. Coat —2B 90
Holland St. G2 —3E 83 (4A 4)
Hollinwell Rd. G23 —1B 62
Hollowglen Rd. G32 —5B 86
Hollows Av. Pais —6D 96
Hollows Cres. Pais —6D 96
Holly Av. Milt C —6B 8
Hollybank Pl. Camb —3B 122
Hollybank St. G21 —2C 84
Hollybrook St. G42 —3F 103
(in two parts)
Hollybush Av. Pais —6F 97
Hollybush Rd. G52 —6H 79
Holly Dri. G21 —6C 64
Holly Dri. Dumb —2B 16
Holly Gro. Bank —1F 15
Holly Gro. Bell —2H 127
Hollymount. Bear —5F 45
Holly Pl. John —5G 95
Holly St. Air —4C 92
Holly St. Clyd —3C 42
Holm Av. Pais —3B 98
Holm Av. Udd —6C 108
Holmbank Av. G41 —6B 102
Holmbrae Av. Udd —6D 108
Holmbrae Rd. Udd —6D 108
Holmbyre Rd. G45 —6F 119
Holmbyre Ter. G45 —5G 119
Holmes Av. Renf —2E 79
Holmes Quad. Bell —4D 126
Holmfauldhead Pl. G51 —3E 81
Holmfauld Pl. G51 —3E 81
Holmfauld Rd. G51 —3E 81
Holmfield. Kirk —6E 31
Holm Gdns. Bell —3E 127
Holmhead Cres. G44 —1E 119
Holmhead Pl. G44 —1E 119
Holmhead Rd. G44 —2E 119
Holmhill Av. Camb —3A 122
Holmhills Dri. Camb —4H 121
Holmhills Gdns. Camb —3H 121
Holmhills Gro. Camb —3H 121
Holmhills Pl. Camb —3H 121
Holmhills Rd. Camb —3H 121
Holmhills Ter. Camb —3H 121
Holm La. E Kil —2G 149
Holmlea Rd. G42 & G44 —6E 103
Holmpark. B'ton —4G 39
Holm Pl. Lark —3C 160
Holm Pl. Lin —4H 75
Holms Cres. Ersk —5D 40
Holms Pl. G'csh —2C 68
Holm St. G2 —4E 83 (6B 4)
Holm St. Carl —3E 165
Holm St. Moth —4A 128
Holmswood Av. Blan —1B 140
Holmwood Av. Udd —6D 108
Holmwood Gdns. Udd —1D 124
Holmwood Gro. G44 —3E 119
Holyknowe Cres. Len —3G 7
Holyknowe Rd. Len —4G 7
Holyrood Cres. G20 —1D 82
Holyrood Quad. G20 —1D 82
(off Holyrood Cres.)
Holyrood St. Ham —4E 141
Holytown Rd. Bell & Moth —2G 127
HOLYTOWN STATION. Holy —4A 128
Holywell St. G31 —6D 84
Homeblair Ho. Giff —2A 118
Homeglen Ho. Giff —5A 118
Homer Pl. Bell —2G 127
Homeston Av. Both —4E 125
Honeybank Cres. Carl —2F 165
Honeybog Rd. G52 —5G 79
Honeywell Cres. Chap —4E 113
Hood St. Clyd —5E 43
Hope Av. Bri W —1A 72
Hope Cres. Lark —2F 161
Hopefield Av. G12 —4A 62
Hopehill Rd. G20 —6E 63
(in two parts)
Hopeman. Ersk —4E 41
Hopeman Av. T'bnk —3E 117
Hopeman Dri. Giff —3E 117
Hopeman Path. T'bnk —2E 117
Hopeman Rd. T'bnk —3E 117
Hopeman St. T'bnk —3E 117
Hope St. G2 —4F 83 (6C 4)
Hope St. Ham —6A 142
Hope St. Moth —2G 143
Hope St. Newm —5E 147
Hopetoun Pl. G23 —6C 46
Hopkins Brae. Kirk —4D 30
Horatius St. Moth —6D 126
Hornal Rd. Udd —3E 125
Hornbeam Dri. Clyd —3C 42
Hornbeam Rd. Cumb —6E 15
Hornbeam Rd. Udd —5F 109
Horndeak Ct. B'rig —3C 48
Horndean Cres. G33 —2D 86
Horne St. G22 —4A 64
Hornock Rd. Coat —2B 90
Hornshill Dri. Cle —5H 129
Hornshill Farm Rd. Step —3E 67
Hornshill St. G21 —5C 64
Horsbrugh Av. Kils —2H 11
Horsburgh St. G33 —1D 86
Horse Shoe Rd. Bear —2E 45
Horsewood Rd. Bri W —4E 73
Horslethill Rd. G12 —5A 62
Horslet St. Coat —1G 109
Horsley Brae. Wis —2C 162
Hospital Rd. Wis —3H 157
Hospital St. G5 —6G 83
Hospital St. Coat —1C 110
Hotspur St. G20 —4C 62
Houldsworth La. G3 —3C 82
(off Elliot St.)
Houldsworth St. G3 —3C 82
Househillmuir Cres. G53 —1C 116
Househillmuir Pl. G53 —6C 100
Househillmuir Rd. G53 —2A 116
Househillwood Cres. G53 —6B 100
Househillwood Rd. G53 —1A 116
Housel Av. G13 —2B 60
Houston Ct. John —2F 95
(off Houston Sq.)
Houstonfield Quad. Hous —1A 74
Houstonfield Rd. Hous —1A 74
Houston Pl. G5 —5D 82
Houston Pl. Eld —3A 96
Houston Rd. B'ton —5B 38
Houston Rd. Bri W —3F 73
Houston Rd. Hous —1B 74
Houston Rd. Inch —5D 56
Houston St. G5 —6D 82
Houston St. Ham —2H 153
Houston St. Renf —5F 59
Houston St. Wis —2B 158
Houston Ter. E Kil —1F 149
Houstoun Sq. John —2F 95
Howard Av. E Kil —4A 138
Howard Ct. E Kil —4A 138
Howard St. G1 —5F 83
Howard St. Lark —4G 161
Howard St. Pais —6C 78
Howatshaws Rd. Dumb —1H 17
Howat St. G51 —3G 81
Howcraigs Ct. Clyd —2F 59
(off Clydeholm Ter.)
Howden Av. Moth —5D 112
Howden Dri. Lin —6G 75
Howden Pl. Moth —2A 128
Howe Rd. Kils —4H 11
Howes St. Coat —1D 110
Howe St. Pais —1D 96
Howford Rd. G52 —1B 100
Howgate Av. G15 —4H 43
Howgate Rd. Ham —3F 153
Howie Bldgs. Clar —1C 134
Howieshill Av. Camb —2B 122
Howieshill Rd. Camb —3B 122
Howie St. Lark —4F 161
Howletnest Rd. Air —5C 92
Howlet Pl. Ham —2A 154
Howson Lea. Moth —5B 144
Howson View. Moth —2D 142
Howth Dri. G13 —1F 61
Howth Ter. G13 —1F 61
Hoylake Pk. Both —5D 124
Hoylake Pl. G23 —6C 46
Hozier Cres. Udd —5D 108
Hozier Loan. Lark —1F 161
(off Duncan Graham St.)
Hozier Pl. Both —4F 125
Hozier St. Carl —3F 165
Hozier St. Coat —6C 90
Hudson Ter. E Kil —3D 148
Hudson Way. E Kil —3E 149
Hughenden Dri. G12 —5H 61
Hughenden Gdns. G12 —5G 61
Hughenden La. G12 —5H 61
Hughenden Rd. G12 —5H 61
Hughenden Ter. G12 —5H 61
Hugh Murray Dri. Camb —2C 122
Hugo St. G20 —4D 62
Humbie Ct. Newt M —6E 133
Humbie Ga. Newt M —6E 133
Humbie Gro. Newt M —6E 133
Humbie Lawns. Newt M —6E 133
Humbie Rd. Newt M —6E 133
Hume Dri. Both —4E 125
Hume Dri. Udd —6C 108
Hume Pl. E Kil —3F 149
Hume Rd. Cumb —2A 36
Hume St. Clyd —6D 42
Hunterfield Dri. Camb —2G 121
Hunterhill Av. Pais —2B 98
Hunterhill Rd. Pais —2B 98
Hunter Pl. Kilb —3A 94
Hunter Pl. Miln —4E 25
Hunter Rd. Ham —3F 141
Hunter Rd. Miln —3E 25
Hunter Rd. Ruth —4E 105
Hunter's Av. Dumb —2D 18
Huntersfield Rd. John —4C 94
Hunters Hill Ct. G21 —3B 64
Huntershill Rd. B'rig —1B 64
Hunter St. G4 —4A 84
Hunter St. Air —2H 91
Hunter St. Bell —2C 126
Hunter St. E Kil —1H 149
Hunter St. Pais —6A 78
Hunthill La. Blan —3H 139
Hunthill Pl. Clar —4E 135
Hunthill Rd. Blan —2H 139
Huntingdon Rd. G21 —1A 84
Huntingdon Sq. G21 —1A 84
Hunting Lodge Gdns. Ham —1C 154
Huntingtower Rd. Bail —1F 107
Huntly Av. Bell —1C 126
Huntly Av. Giff —5B 118
Huntly Ct. B'rig —1C 64
Huntly Dri. Bear —6E 25
Huntly Dri. Camb —3B 122
Huntly Dri. Coat —1H 109
Huntly Gdns. G12 —6B 62
Huntly Ga. Giff —4B 118
Huntly Path. Chry —5E 53
Huntly Quad. Wis —4H 145
Huntly Rd. G12 —6A 62
Huntly Rd. H'ton I —3H 79
Huntly Ter. Pais —4C 98
Huntshill St. G21 —3A 64
Hurlawcrook Rd. E Kil —6A 150
Hurlet Rd. Pais & G53 —4E 99
Hurley Hawkin. B'rig —1F 65
Hurlford Av. G13 —2H 59
Hutcheson Rd. T'bnk —5G 117
Hutcheson St. G1 —4G 83 (6F 5)
Hutchinson Pl. Camb —4E 123
Hutchinson Town Ct. G5 —1G 103
Hutchison Ct. Giff —6H 117
Hutchison Dri. Bear —5G 45
Hutchison Pl. Coat —5B 90
Hutchison St. Ham —3H 153
Hutchison St. Wis —4B 158
Hutton Av. C'lee —3C 74
Hutton Dri. G51 —3E 81
Huxley St. G20 —3D 62
Hyacinth Way. Carl —5F 165
Hydepark St. G3 —4D 82
Hyndal Av. G53 —4C 100
Hyndland Av. G11 —1H 81
Hyndland Rd. G12 —6H 61
HYNDLAND STATION. G11 —5G 62
Hyndland St. G11 —1A 82
Hyndlee Dri. G52 —6C 80
Hyndshaw Rd. Carl —2F 165
Hyndshaw View. Law —1A 164
Hyslop Pl. Clyd —4C 42
Hyslop St. Air —3G 91

Iain Dri. Bear —1C 44
Iain Rd. Bear —2C 44
Ian Smith Ct. Clyd —1F 59
Ibroxholm Av. G51 —6H 81
Ibroxholm Oval. G51 —5H 81
Ibroxholm Pl. G51 —6H 81
Ibrox Ind. Est. G51 —5H 81
IBROX STATION. G51 —5H 81
Ibrox St. G51 —5A 82
Ibrox Ter. G51 —5H 81
Ida Quad. Bell —2B 126
Iddesleigh Av. Miln —3G 25
Ilay Av. Bear —1G 61
Ilay Ct. Bear —1G 61
Ilay Rd. Bear —1G 61
Imperial Dri. Air —6H 91
Inchbrae Rd. G52 —1C 100
Inchcolm Gdns. Mood —4E 53
Inchcolm Pl. E Kil —1E 149
Inchfad Dri. G15 —4G 43
Inch Garvie. E Kil —2D 150
Inchinnan Ind. Est. Inch —5F 57
Inchinnan Rd. Bell —6B 110
Inchinnan Rd. Pais —4A 78
Inchinnan Rd. Renf —5D 58
Inch Keith. E Kil —2D 150
Inchkeith Pl. G32 —4B 86
Inchlee St. G14 —1E 81
Inch Marnock. E Kil —3C 150
Inch Murrin. E Kil —2D 150
Inchmurrin Av. Kirk —5H 31
Inchmurrin Dri. Ruth —5F 121
Inchmurrin Gdns. Ruth —5F 121
Inchmurrin Pl. Ruth —5F 121
Inchneuk Rd. Glenb —3A 70
Inchoch St. G33 —1E 87
Incholm La. G11 —1E 81
(off Incholm St.)
Incholm St. G11 —1E 81
Inchrory Pl. G15 —3G 43
Inchwood Ct. Cumb —6B 34
Inchwood Pl. Cumb —6B 34
Inchwood Rd. Cumb —6B 34
Incle St. Pais —6B 78
India Dri. Inch —3G 57
India St. G2 —3E 83
Industry St. Kirk —6D 30
Inga St. G20 —2C 62
Ingerbreck Av. Ruth —3F 121
Ingleby Dri. G31 —4C 84
Ingleby Pl. Neil —2E 131
Inglefield Ct. Air —4A 92
Inglefield St. G42 —3F 103
Ingleneuk Av. G33 —4B 66
Ingleside. Kirk —1C 50
Inglestone Av. T'bnk —5G 117
Inglewood Cres. E Kil —3C 148
Inglis Pl. E Kil —4H 149
Inglis St. G31 —5C 84
Inglis St. Wis —1D 156
Ingliston Dri. B'ton —4F 39
Ingram St. G1 —4G 83 (5E 5)
Inishail Rd. G33 —2C 86
Inkerman Rd. G52 —6H 79
Innerleithen Dri. Wis —3A 146
Innermanse Quad. Moth —2F 129
Innerwick Dri. G52 —6B 80
Innes Ct. Air —3E 93
Innes Ct. E Kil —5G 137
Innspark. Kils —2H 11
International Av. Ham —5B 140
Inveraray Dri. B'rig —3D 48
Inveravon Dri. Moth —4D 142
Inverbervie. Ersk —5E 41
Invercanny Dri. G15 —3H 43
Invercanny Pl. G15 —3A 44
Invercargill. E Kil —4C 148
Inverclyde Gdns. Ruth —4F 121
Invercree Wlk. Glenb —3G 69
(off Dinyra Pl.)
Inveresk Pl. Coat —3C 90
Inveresk Quad. G32 —5A 86
Inveresk St. G32 —5H 85
Inverewe Av. T'bnk —5D 116
Inverewe Dri. T'bnk —5D 116
Inverewe Gdns. T'bnk —5D 116
Inverewe Pl. T'bnk —4D 116
Inverewe Way. Newt M —4B 132
Invergarry Av. T'bnk —6D 116
Invergarry Ct. T'bnk —6E 117
Invergarry Dri. T'bnk —5D 116
Invergarry Gdns. T'bnk —6D 116
Invergarry Gro. T'bnk —5D 116
Invergarry Pl. T'bnk —5E 117
Invergarry Quad. T'bnk —5E 117
Invergarry View. T'bnk —5E 117
Inverglas Av. Renf —2H 79
Invergordon Av. G43 —6D 102
Invergyle Dri. G52 —6B 80
Inverkar Dri. Pais —3E 97
Inverlair Av. G43 & G44 —1D 118
Inverleith St. G32 —5F 85
Inverlochy St. G33 —2D 86
Inverness St. G51 —5D 80
Invernia Sq. Clyd —5D 42
Inveroran Dri. Bear —3H 45
Inver Rd. G33 —4E 87
Invershiel Rd. G23 —6B 46
Invershin Dri. G20 —4B 62
Inverurie St. G21 —6H 63
Invervale Av. Air —5F 93
Inzievar Ter. G32 —4B 106
Iona. Air —6D 92
Iona Av. E Kil —5A 138
Iona Ct. G51 —4H 81
Iona Cres. Old K —2G 41
Iona Dri. Pais —6H 97
Iona Gdns. Old K —2G 41
Iona La. Chry —5E 53
Iona Path. Blan —2A 140
Iona Pl. Coat —2H 89
Iona Pl. Old K —2G 41
Iona Quad. Wis —4C 146
Iona Ridge. Ham —2C 152
Iona Rd. Newm —3D 146
Iona Rd. Renf —2E 79
Iona Rd. Ruth —4G 121
Iona St. G51 —4H 81
Iona St. Moth —6F 127
Iona Way. G33 —5E 67
Iona Way. Kirk —5G 31
Iris Av. G45 —4C 120
Irongray St. G31 —4E 85
Irvine Cres. Coat —4E 91
Irvine Dri. Lin —4F 75
Irvine Gdns. Milt C —6B 8
Irvine Pl. Kils —2F 11
Irvine St. G40 —2D 104
Irvine St. Glenm —5H 71
Irvine Ter. Ham —3H 153
Irving Av. Clyd —1D 42
Irving Ct. Clyd —1D 42
Irving Quad. Clyd —1D 42
Isabella Gdns. Ham —2D 154
Iser La. G41 —5C 102
Isla Av. Newm —3D 146
Island Rd. Cumb —5F 35
Islay. Air —5E 93
Islay Av. Bear —1F 61
Islay Av. Ruth —4G 121
Islay Ct. Ham —1D 152
Islay Cres. Old K —2G 41
Islay Cres. Pais —6H 97
Islay Dri. Newt M —4B 132
Islay Dri. Old K —2G 41
Islay Gdns. Carl —5F 165
Islay Gdns. Lark —2F 161
Islay Quad. Wis —2E 157
Islay Rd. Kirk —5G 31
Ivanhoe. E Kil —5D 138
Ivanhoe Ct. Carl —4D 164
Ivanhoe Cres. Wis —6H 145
Ivanhoe Dri. Kirk —5E 31
Ivanhoe Pl. Moth —2B 128
Ivanhoe Rd. G13 —1D 60
Ivanhoe Rd. Cumb —5G 35
Ivanhoe Rd. Pais —4D 96
Ivanhoe Way. Pais —5D 96
Ivybank Av. Camb —3C 122
Ivy Gro. Coat —5D 90
Ivy Pl. Blan —1A 140
Ivy Pl. Moth —4A 128
Ivy Rd. Udd —5G 109
Ivy Ter. Moth —2A 128

Jackson Ct. Coat —5D 90
Jackson Pl. Carl —2E 165
Jackson St. Coat —4D 90
Jack St. Ham —3H 153
Jack St. Moth —5B 144
Jackton Rd. E Kil —6A 148
Jacob's Ladder. Wis —5B 158
Jacob's Ladder Way. Wis —4A 158
Jade Ter. Bell —3C 126
Jagger Gdns. Bail —1F 107
Jamaica Dri. E Kil —2C 148
Jamaica St. G1 —4F 83 (6D 4)
James Dempsey Ct. Coat —5B 90
James Dempsey Gdns. Coat —5B 90
James Dunlop Gdns. B'rig —2D 64
James Gray St. G41 —5C 102
James Hamilton Dri. Bell —2D 126
James Healy Dri. Ham —4G 153
James Hemphill Ct. Len —3G 7
James Leeson Ct. Milt C —5C 8
James Morrison St. G1 —5H 83
James Nisbet St. G21 —2B 84
James St. G40 —1A 104
James St. Carl —4F 165
James St. Moth —2F 143
James St. Rig I —1A 126
James View. Moth —4H 127
James Watt Av. E Kil —3H 149
James Watt La. G2 —4E 83
James Watt Pl. E Kil —6D 136
James Watt Rd. Miln —2F 25
James Watt St. G2 —4E 83 (6B 4)
Jamieson Ct. G42 —3F 103
Jamieson Ct. Clyd —6D 22
Jamieson Dri. E Kil —1A 150
Jamieson St. G42 —3F 103
(in two parts)
Janebank Av. Camb —3C 122
Jane Ct. Lark —3E 161
Janefield Av. John —3E 95
Janefield Pl. Blan —3A 140
Janefield Pl. Len —2F 7
Janefield St. G31 —6D 84
Jane's Brae. Cumb —5H 35
Jane's Brae Interchange. Cumb —5H 35
Janesmith St. Wis —5C 144

Janetta St. Clyd —4C 42
Jardine St. G20 —6D 62
Jardine Ter. G'csh —4D 68
Jarvie Av. Plain —1G 93
Jarvie Cres. Kils —4H 11
Jarvie Way. Pais —5C 96
Jasmine Pl. Cumb —6D 34
Jasmine Way. Carl —5E 165
Java St. Moth —6E 127
Jean Armour Dri. Clyd —4E 43
Jeanette Av. Ham —4H 153
Jean Maclean Pl. B'rig —2D 48
Jedburgh Av. Ruth —6D 104
Jedburgh Dri. Pais —4E 97
Jedburgh Gdns. G20 —6D 62
Jedburgh Pl. Coat —2B 110
Jedburgh Pl. E Kil —1H 149
Jedburgh St. Blan —2B 140
Jedburgh St. Wis —4A 146
Jedworth Av. G15 —4B 44
Jedworth Rd. G15 —4B 44
Jeffrey Pl. Kils —2G 11
Jellicoe St. Clyd —4A 42
Jennie Lee Dri. Over —4H 157
Jennys Well Ct. Pais —3E 99
Jennys Well Rd. Pais —3D 98
Jervis Ter. E Kil —4D 148
Jerviston Ct. Moth —6A 128
Jerviston Rd. G33 —1C 86
Jerviston Rd. Moth —5A 128
Jerviston St. Moth —1H 143
Jerviston St. New S —4A 128
(in two parts)
Jerviswood. Moth —6A 128
Jessie St. G42 —3H 103
Jessiman Sq. Renf —2D 78
Jimmy Sneddon Way. Moth —5F 127
Joanna Ter. Blan —1B 140
John Bassy Dri. Bank —1D 14
John Brannan Way. Bell —1H 125
John Brown Pl. Chry —1A 68
John Burnside Dri. Clyd —6E 23
John Ewing Gdns. Lark —1E 161
John Hendry Rd. Udd —3E 125
John Jarvis Sq. Kils —2H 11
John Knox La. Ham —5B 140
John Knox St. G4 —4A 84
John Knox St. Clyd —1E 59
John Lang St. John —2G 95
John McEwan Way. Torr —5D 28
John Murray Ct. Moth —6G 143
Johnsburn Dri. G53 —1B 116
Johnsburn Rd. G53 —1B 116
Johnshaven. Ersk —5E 41
Johnshaven St. G43 —6A 102
John Smith Ct. Air —3H 91
John Smith Gdns. Coat —6F 91
Johnson Dri. Camb —2A 122
Johnston Av. Clyd —1F 59
Johnston Av. Kils —4H 11
Johnstone Av. H'ton I —5B 80
Johnstone By-Pass. How & John —6A 94
Johnstone Dri. Ruth —6C 104
Johnstone La. Carl —4H 165
(off Kilcadzow Rd.)
Johnstone Rd. Ham —1A 154
JOHNSTONE STATION. John —3G 95
Johnstone St. Bell —2E 127
Johnstone Ter. Kils —2D 32
Johnston Rd. G'csh —3D 68
Johnston St. Air —3B 92
Johnston St. Pais —1A 98
John St. G1 —4G 83 (5F 5)
John St. Barr —4D 114
John St. Bell —2C 126
John St. Blan —2C 140
John St. Carl —4F 165
John St. Ham —6A 142
John St. Kirk —4D 30
John St. Lark —3E 161
John St. Wis —5C 144
John Wilson Dri. Kils —2F 11
Jones Wynd. Moth —6E 129
Jonquil Way. Carl —5F 165
Joppa St. G33 —4G 85
Jordanhill Cres. G13 —4D 60
Jordanhill Dri. G13 —4C 60
Jordanhill La. G13 —4E 61
(off Munro Rd.)
JORDANHILL STATION. G11 —5F 61
Jordan St. G14 —1D 80
Jordanvale Av. G14 —1D 80
Jowitt Av. Clyd —6F 43
Joycelyn Sq. G1 —5G 83
Jubilee Bank. Kirk —4C 50
Jubilee Gdns. Bear —3E 45
Jubilee Ter. John —3D 94
Julian Av. G12 —5A 62
Julian La. G12 —5A 62
Juniper Av. E Kil —5F 149
Juniper Ct. Kirk —2B 50
Juniper Dri. Milt C —1B 30
Juniper Gro. Ham —1B 154
Juniper Pl. G32 —1E 107
Juniper Pl. John —5G 95
Juniper Pl. Udd —5H 109
Juniper Rd. Udd —6H 109
Juniper Ter. G32 —1E 107
Juniper Wynd. Moth —2B 128
(off Dornoch Rd.)
Juno St. Moth —6F 127
Jupiter St. Moth —6F 127
Jura. E Kil —4B 150
Jura Av. Renf —2F 79
Jura Ct. G52 —6E 81
Jura Dri. Blan —4A 124
Jura Dri. Kirk —5G 31
Jura Dri. Newt M —3B 132
Jura Dri. Old K —2G 41
Jura Gdns. Carl —5G 165
Jura Gdns. Ham —1E 153
Jura Gdns. Lark —2G 161
Jura Gdns. Old K —2G 41
Jura Pl. Old K —2G 41
Jura Quad. Wis —2E 157
Jura Rd. Old K —2G 41
Jura Rd. Pais —6H 97
Jura St. G52 —6F 81
Jura Wynd. Glenb —3G 69

Kaim Dri. G53 —1C 116
Karadale Gdns. Lark —3E 161
Karol Path. G4 —1E 83
Katewell Av. G15 —3G 43
Katherine St. Air —3E 93
Kathkin Dri. Clar —1A 134
Katrin Ct. G20 —1E 83
(off Cedar St.)
Katrine Av. B'rig —6D 48
Katrine Av. Rig I —1H 125
Katrine Cres. Air —2H 91
Katrine Dri. Newt M —5H 133
Katrine Dri. Pais —3D 96
Katrine Pl. Camb —1A 122
Katrine Pl. Coat —2H 89
Katrine Wynd. Moth —2A 128
(off Glencoe Dri.)
Katriona Path. Lark —4G 161
(off Donaldson Rd.)
Kay Gdns. Moth —3D 142
Kaystone Rd. G15 —6A 44
Kay St. G21 —5B 64
Keal Av. G15 —1A 60
Keal Cres. G15 —1A 60
Keal Dri. G15 —1A 60
Keal Pl. G15 —1A 60
Kearn Av. G15 —6B 44
Kearn Pl. G15 —6B 44
Keats Pk. Both —4F 125
Keil Cres. Dumb —4D 16
Keir Cres. Wis —5H 145
Keir Dri. B'rig —5B 48
Keir Hardie Av. Moth —2B 128
Keir Hardie Ct. B'rig —6C 48
Keir Hardie Dri. Bell —3B 126
Keir Hardie Dri. Kils —4H 11
Keir Hardie Pl. Bell —3B 126
Keir Hardie Rd. Lark —4F 161
Keir St. G41 —2D 102
Keir's Wlk. Camb —1A 122
Keith Av. Giff —4B 118
Keith Ct. G11 —2A 82
Keith Quad. Wis —4H 145
Keith St. G11 —1A 82
Keith St. Bell —1C 126
Keith St. Ham —5B 142
Kelbourne Cres. Bell —2B 126
Kelbourne St. G20 —5C 62
Kelburne Dri. Pais —6D 78
Kelburne Gdns. Bail —2G 107
Kelburne Gdns. Pais —6C 78
Kelburne Oval. Pais —6C 78
Kelburn St. Barr —6C 114
Kelhead Av. G52 —6H 79
Kelhead Dri. G52 —6H 79
Kelhead Path. G52 —6H 79
Kelhead Pl. G52 —6H 79
Kellas St. G51 —5G 81
Kellock Av. Coat —1H 109
Kellock Cres. Coat —1H 109
Kells Pl. G15 —3G 43
Kelly's La. Carl —4H 165
(off Kelso Dri.)
Kelso Av. Bri W —4F 73
Kelso Av. Pais —4E 97
Kelso Av. Ruth —6D 104
Kelso Cres. Wis —3H 145
Kelso Dri. Carl —4H 165
Kelso Dri. E Kil —6A 138
Kelso Gdns. Mood —4D 52
Kelso Pl. G14 —3G 59
Kelso Quad. Coat —3B 90
Kelso St. G14 & G13 —3G 59
Kelton St. G32 —1B 106
Kelvie Gro. E Kil —6F 137
Kelvin Av. H'ton I —2H 79
Kelvinbridge Roundabout. B'rig —5D 28
KELVINBRIDGE STATION. G4 —1C 82
Kelvin Ct. G12 —4G 61
Kelvin Cres. Bear —5F 45
Kelvindale. Torr —4E 29
Kelvindale Bldgs. G12 —4A 62
Kelvindale Gdns. G20 —3A 62
Kelvindale Pl. G20 —3B 62
Kelvindale Rd. G12 & G20 —4H 61
Kelvin Dri. G20 —5B 62
Kelvin Dri. Air —2B 92
Kelvin Dri. Barr —6F 115
Kelvin Dri. B'rig —5C 48
Kelvin Dri. Chry —5C 52
Kelvin Dri. E Kil —4H 149
Kelvin Dri. Kirk —5A 30
Kelvin Gdns. Ham —5C 140
Kelvin Gdns. Kils —4H 11
Kelvingrove St. G3 —3C 82
KELVINHALL STATION. G11 —1A 82
Kelvinhaugh Pl. G3 —3B 82
Kelvinhaugh St. G3 —3A 82
Kelvinhead Rd. Kils —1G 13
Kelvin Pk. S. E Kil —6A 150
Kelvin Pl. E Kil —4A 150
Kelvin Rd. Bell —6D 110
Kelvin Rd. Cumb —5A 36
Kelvin Rd. E Kil —4H 149
Kelvin Rd. Miln —2E 25
Kelvin Rd. Udd —6C 108
Kelvin Rd. N. Cumb —5A 36
Kelvinside Av. G20 —5C 62
Kelvinside Dri. G20 —5D 62
Kelvinside Gdns. G20 —5C 62
Kelvinside Gdns. E. G20 —6D 62
Kelvinside Gdns. La. G20 —6C 62
Kelvinside Ter. S. G20 —6C 62
Kelvinside Ter. W. G20 —6C 62
Kelvin S. Business Pk. E Kil —6A 150
Kelvin St. Coat —6E 91
Kelvin Ter. Kils —3D 32
Kelvinvale. Kirk —4D 30
Kelvin View. Torr —5E 29
Kelvin View. Twe —3D 32
Kelvinview Av. Bank —1E 15
Kelvin Way. G3 —2B 82
Kelvin Way. Kils —2G 11
Kelvin Way. Kirk —5A 30
Kemp Av. Pais —2C 78
Kemp Ct. Ham —6A 142
Kempock St. G40 —1E 105
Kempsthorn Cres. G53 —4B 100
Kempsthorn Path. G53 —4B 100
(off Kempsthorn Cres.)
Kempsthorn Rd. G53 —4A 100
Kemp St. G21 —5A 64
Kemp St. Ham —6H 141
Kenbank Cres. Bri W —3F 73
Kenbank Rd. Bri W —3F 73
Kendal Av. G12 —3G 61
Kendal Av. Giff —4A 118
Kendal Dri. G12 —3G 61
Kendal Rd. E Kil —5B 148
Kendoon Av. G15 —4G 43
Kenilburn Av. Air —1B 92
Kenilburn Cres. Air —1B 92
Kenilworth. E Kil —5D 138
Kenilworth Av. G41 —5B 102
Kenilworth Av. Pais —5D 96
Kenilworth Av. Wis —6H 145
Kenilworth Ct. Carl —4E 165
Kenilworth Ct. Moth —2B 128
(off Rowantree Ter.)
Kenilworth Cres. Bear —1C 44
Kenilworth Cres. Bell —1C 126
Kenilworth Cres. Ham —5D 140
Kenilworth Dri. Air —3C 92
Kenilworth Rd. Kirk —5E 31
Kenilworth Way. Pais —4D 96
Kenmar Gdns. Udd —5C 108
Kenmar Rd. Ham —4F 141
Kenmar Ter. Ham —4F 141
Kenmore Gdns. Bear —2H 45
Kenmore Rd. Cumb —3B 36
Kenmore St. G32 —6A 86
Kenmore Way. Carl —2F 165
Kenmuiraid Pl. Bell —4B 126
Kenmuir Av. G32 —2E 107
Kenmuirhill Rd. G32 —3D 106
Kenmuir Rd. G32 —5C 106
(in two parts)
Kenmuir St. Coat —1F 109
Kenmure Av. B'rig —6A 48
Kenmure Cres. B'rig —6B 48
Kenmure Dri. B'rig —6B 48
Kenmure Gdns. B'rig —6A 48
Kenmure La. B'rig —6B 48
Kenmure Rd. Giff —3H 133
Kenmure St. G41 —2D 102
Kenmure Way. Ruth —1D 120
Kennedar Dri. G51 —3E 81
Kennedy Ct. Giff —3A 118
Kennedy Dri. Air —4G 91
Kennedy Gdns. Over —4H 157
Kennedy Path. G4 —3H 83 (3G 5)
Kennedy St. G4 —3G 83 (3F 5)
Kennedy St. Wis —6A 146
Kennelburn Rd. Chap —4D 112
Kenneth Rd. Moth —4E 143
Kennihill. Air —1A 92
Kennihill St. Air —2A 92
Kennishead Av. T'bnk —2E 117
Kennishead Path. T'bnk —2E 117
(off Kennisholm Av.)
Kennishead Pl. T'bnk —3E 117
Kennishead Rd. G53 —3B 116
Kennishead Rd. T'bnk —3F 117
KENNISHEAD STATION. T'bnk —2E 117
Kennisholm Av. Giff —2E 117
Kennisholm Path. T'bnk —2E 117
(off Kennisholme Av.)
Kennisholm Pl. T'bnk —2E 117
Kennoway Dri. G11 —1F 81
Kennoway La. G11 —1F 81
(off Thornwood Av.)
Kennyhill Sq. G31 —3D 84
Kenshaw Av. Lark —5E 161
Kenshaw Pl. Lark —5E 161
Kensington Dri. Giff —6B 118
Kensington Ga. G12 —5A 62
Kensington Ga. La. G12 —5A 62
Kensington Rd. G12 —5A 62
Kentallen Rd. G33 —5E 87
Kent Dri. Ruth —2F 121
Kentigern Ter. B'rig —1D 64
Kentmere Clo. E Kil —5C 148
Kentmere Dri. E Kil —5C 148
Kentmere Pl. E Kil —5C 148
Kent Pl. E Kil —5B 148
Kent Rd. G3 —3C 82
Kent St. G40 —5A 84
Keppel Dri. G44 —6A 104
Keppochill Rd. G21 —6G 63
Keppoch St. G21 —6H 63
Kerfield Pl. G15 —3G 43
Kerr Cres. Ham —2G 153
Kerr Dri. Moth —3E 143
Kerrera Pl. G33 —5D 86
Kerrera Rd. G33 —5D 86
Kerr Gdns. Udd —5E 109
Ker Rd. Miln —2E 25
Kerr Pl. G40 —6B 84
Kerr St. G40 —6B 84
Kerr St. Barr —5C 114
Kerr St. Blan —1C 140
Kerr St. Kirk —5C 30
Kerr St. Pais —6H 77
Kerrycroy Av. G42 —6H 103
Kerrycroy Pl. G42 —5H 103
Kerrycroy St. G42 —5H 103
Kerrydale St. G40 —1D 104
Kerrylamont Av. G42 —6A 104
Kerry Pl. G15 —4G 43
Kershaw St. Wis —4A 158
Kersland Dri. Miln —3H 25
Kersland La. G12 —6B 62
(off Kersland St.)
Kersland La. Miln —3H 25
Kersland St. G12 —6B 62
Kessington Dri. Bear —3G 45
Kessington Rd. Bear —4G 45
Kessock Dri. G22 —6F 63
Kessock Pl. G22 —6F 63
Kestrel Ct. Clyd —2C 42
Kestrel Pl. John —6D 94
Kestrel Rd. G13 —3C 60
Keswick Rd. E Kil —5B 148
Kethers La. Moth —2E 143
Kethers St. Moth —2E 143
Kew Gdns. Udd —6F 109
Kew La. G12 —6B 62
Kew Ter. G12 —6B 62
Keynes Sq. Bell —3F 127
Keystone Av. Miln —5G 25
Keystone Quad. Miln —5F 25
Keystone Rd. Miln —5G 25
Kibbleston Rd. Kilb —2A 94
Kidston St. G5 —1G 103
Kierhill. Cumb —3E 35
Kilallan Av. Bri W —2F 73
Kilbarchan Rd. Bri W —4G 73
Kilbarchan Rd. John —4D 94
Kilbarchan Rd. Mill P —3C 94
Kilbarchan St. G5 —6F 83
Kilbeg Ter. T'bnk —4D 116
Kilberry St. G21 —2C 84
Kilbirnie Pl. G5 —1E 103
Kilbirnie St. G5 —1E 103
Kilbowie Ct. Clyd —4D 42
Kilbowie Rd. Cumb —4A 36
Kilbowie Rd. Hard —2D 42
Kilbreck Gdns. Bear —5C 24
Kilbreck La. Moth —3C 128
Kilbrennan Dri. Moth —2D 142
Kilbrennan Rd. Lin —5H 75
Kilbride St. G5 —3H 103
Kilbride View. Udd —6E 109
Kilburn Gro. Blan —6B 124
Kilburn Pl. G13 —3B 60
Kilcadzow Rd. Carl —4H 165
Kilchattan Dri. G44 —6G 103
Kilchoan Rd. G33 —1C 86
Kilcloy Av. G15 —3A 44
Kildale Way. Ruth —5B 104
Kildary Av. G44 —2E 119
Kildary Rd. G44 —2E 119
Kildermorie Path. G34 —3G 87
Kildermorie Rd. G34 —3F 87
Kildonan Ct. Newm —2D 146
Kildonan Dri. G11 —1G 81
Kildonan Pl. Moth —2E 143
Kildonan St. Coat —4D 90
Kildrostan St. G41 —3D 102
Kildrummy Pl. E Kil —6F 137
Kildrum Rd. Cumb —2B 36
Kildrum S. Interchange. Cumb —4D 30
Kildrum S. Roundabout. Cumb —4B 36
Kilearn Rd. Pais —4D 78
Kilearn Sq. Pais —4D 78
Kilearn Way. Pais —4D 78
(in two parts)
Kilfinan St. G22 —2F 63
Kilgarth St. Coat —1F 109
Kilgraston Rd. Bri W —5E 73
Kilkerran Dri. G33 —3H 65
Killearn Dri. Pais —1H 99
Killearn St. G22 —5F 63
Killermont Ct. Bear —4H 45
Killermont Meadows. Both —5C 124
Killermont Rd. Bear —4F 45
Killermont St. G2 —3G 83 (3E 5)
Killermont View. G20 —5G 45
Killiegrew Rd. G41 —3B 102
Killin Ct. Coat —2D 110
Killin Dri. Lin —6F 75
Killin St. G32 —2B 106
Killoch Av. Pais —6E 77
Killoch Dri. G13 —2A 60
Killoch Dri. Barr —6F 115
Killoch Rd. Pais —6E 77
Kilmacolm Rd. Bri W —1C 72
Kilmacolm Rd. Hous —1B 74
Kilmailing Rd. G44 —2F 119
Kilmair Pl. G20 —4B 62
Kilmaluag Ter. T'bnk —4D 116
Kilmannan Gdns. Miln —2D 24
Kilmany Dri. G32 —6H 85
Kilmany Gdns. G32 —6H 85
Kilmardinny Av. Bear —2F 45
Kilmardinny Cres. Bear —1F 45
Kilmardinny Dri. Bear —1F 45
Kilmardinny Ga. Bear —2F 45
Kilmardinny Gro. Bear —1F 45
Kilmarnock Rd. G43 & G41 —2B 118
Kilmartin La. Carl —2F 165
Kilmartin Pl. T'bnk —3E 117
Kilmartin Pl. Udd —4E 109
Kilmaurs Dri. Giff —4C 118
Kilmaurs St. G51 —5F 81
Kilmeny Cres. Wis —4A 146
Kilmichael Av. Newm —3E 147
Kilmorie Dri. Ruth —6A 104
Kilmory Av. Udd —6E 109
Kilmory Dri. Newt M —3E 133
Kilmory Gdns. Carl —2F 165
Kilmory Rd. Carl —5H 165
Kilmuir Cres. T'bnk —3D 116
Kilmuir Dri. T'bnk —3E 117
(in two parts)
Kilmuir Rd. T'bnk —4D 116
Kilmuir Rd. Udd —4D 108
Kilmun St. G20 —2A 62
Kilnburn Rd. Moth —2E 143
Kilncroft La. Pais —4A 98
Kilnside Rd. Pais —6B 78
Kilnwell Quad. Moth —2F 143
Kiloran St. T'bnk —3F 117
Kilpatrick Av. Pais —3F 97
Kilpatrick Ct. Old K —1E 41
Kilpatrick Cres. Pais —4H 97
Kilpatrick Dri. Bear —5C 24
Kilpatrick Dri. Renf —3D 78
Kilpatrick Gdns. Clar —1H 133
KILPATRICK STATION. Old K —1F 41
Kilpatrick View. Dumb —3H 17
Kilpatrick Way. Udd —5E 109
Kilsyth Rd. Bank —1C 14
Kilsyth Rd. Kirk —4D 30
Kilsyth Rd. Queen —5B 10
Kiltarie Cres. Air —4F 93
Kiltearn Rd. G33 —4F 87
Kiltongue Cotts. Air —3F 91
(off Monkscourt Av.)
Kilvaxter Dri. T'bnk —3E 117
Kilwinning Cres. Ham —2C 152
Kilwynet Way. Pais —4C 78
Kimberley Gdns. E Kil —3E 149
Kimberley St. Clyd —2H 41
Kimberley St. Wis —5C 144
Kinalty Rd. G44 —2E 119
Kinarvie Cres. G53 —6H 99
Kinarvie Gdns. G53 —6H 99
Kinarvie Pl. G53 —6H 99
Kinarvie Rd. G53 —6H 99
Kinarvie Ter. G53 —6H 99
Kinbuck Pas. G22 —5H 63
Kinbuck St. G22 —5H 63
Kincaid Dri. Len —2E 7
Kincaid Field. Milt C —6C 8
Kincaid Gdns. Camb —1A 122
Kincaid Way. Milt C —6B 8
Kincardine Dri. B'rig —1D 64
Kincardine Pl. B'rig —2E 65
Kincardine Pl. E Kil —6C 138
Kincardine Sq. G33 —2D 86
Kincath Av. Ruth —4F 121
Kinclaven Av. G15 —4A 44
Kincraig St. G51 —5D 80
Kinellan Rd. Bear —6F 45
Kinellar Dri. G14 —3A 60
Kinfauns Dri. G15 —3H 43
Kinfauns Dri. Newt M —4F 133
Kingarth St. G42 —3F 103
Kingarth St. Ham —3H 153
King Edward La. G13 —4E 61
(off Woodend Dri.)

King Edward Rd. G13 —4F 61
Kingfisher Dri. G13 —2H 59
Kinghorn Dri. G44 —1G 119
Kinghorn La. G44 —6G 103
Kinglas Rd. Bear —5C 44
King Pl. Bail —6E 89
Kingsacre Rd. G44 —6G 103
Kingsacre Rd. Ruth —1A 120
Kingsbarns Dri. G44 —6F 103
Kingsborough Gdns. G12 —6H 61
Kingsborough Ga. G12 —6H 61
Kingsborough La. G12 —6H 61
Kingsborough La. E. G12 —6H 61
Kingsbrae Av. G44 —6G 103
King's Bri. G5 —1H 103
Kingsbridge Cres. G44 —1H 119
Kingsbridge Dri. G44 —1H 119
Kingsbridge Dri. Ruth —1A 120
Kingsburgh Dri. Pais —6D 78
Kingsburn Dri. Ruth —1C 120
Kingsburn Gro. Ruth —1B 120
Kingscliffe Av. G44 —1G 119
Kingscourt Av. G44 —6H 103
Kings Cres. Camb —2B 122
King's Cres. Carl —3G 165
Kings Cres. Eld —2A 96
Kingsdale Av. G44 —6G 103
King's Dri. G40 —1A 104
King's Dri. Cumb —5H 13
Kings Dri. Moth —4H 127
Kings Dri. Newt M —6F 133
Kingsdyke Av. G44 —6G 103
Kingsford Av. G44 —3C 118
Kingsford Ct. Newt M —3B 132
King's Gdns. Newt M —6G 133
Kingsgate Retail Pk. E Kil —3H 137
Kingsheath Av. Ruth —1A 120
Kingshill Av. Cumb —4A 34
Kingshill Dri. G44 —1G 119
Kingshill View. Law —1A 164
Kingshouse Av. G44 —6G 103
Kingshurst Av. G44 —6G 103
King's Inch Rd. Renf —4F 59
Kingsknowe Dri. Ruth —1A 120
Kingsland Cres. G52 —5B 80
Kingsland Dri. G52 —5B 80
Kingsland La. G52 —5C 80
Kingslea Rd. Hous —1B 74
Kingsley Av. G42 —4F 103
Kingsley Ct. Udd —6E 109
Kingslynn Dri. G44 —1H 119
Kingsmuir Dri. Ruth —1A 120
King's Pk. Torr —4E 29
King's Pk. Av. G44 —1F 119
King's Pk. Rd. G44 —6F 103
KING'S PK. STATION. G44 —1G 119
King's Pl. G22 —3F 63
King's Rd. Eld —3H 95
Kingston Av. Air —4C 92
Kingston Av. Neil —3D 130
Kingston Av. Udd —5E 109
Kingston Bri. G5 —5D 82
Kingston Flats. Kils —2H 11
Kingston Gro. B'ton —4H 39
Kingston Pl. Clyd —3H 41
Kingston Rd. B'ton —5H 39
(in two parts)
Kingston Rd. Kils —2H 11
Kingston Rd. Neil —5C 130
Kingston St. G5 —5E 83
King St. G1 —5G 83
King St. Clyd —1F 59
King St. Coat —5A 90
King St. Ham —4D 140
King St. Kils —3H 11
King St. Lark —2E 161
King St. Newm —4D 146
King St. Pais —6G 77
King St. Ruth —5C 104
King St. Wis —1H 157
King St. La. Kils —3H 11
(off King St.)
King St. La. Ruth —5C 104
King's View. Cumb —5H 13
Kingsway. G14 —4A 60
King's Way. Dumb —2C 16
Kingsway. E Kil —4A 138
Kingsway. Kils —2H 11
Kingsway. Kirk —3H 31
Kingsway Ct. G14 —4A 60
Kingswood Dri. G44 —1G 119
Kingswood Rd. B'ton —3F 39
Kingussie Dri. G44 —1G 119
Kiniver Dri. G15 —6A 44
Kinkell Gdns. Kirk —4H 31
Kinloch Av. Camb —3B 122
Kinloch Av. Lin —6G 75
Kinloch Dri. Moth —5F 127
Kinloch Rd. Newt M —3C 132
Kinloch Rd. Renf —3D 78
Kinloch St. G40 —1E 105
Kinloss Pl. E Kil —1H 149
Kinmount Av. G44 —6F 103
Kinnaird Av. Newt M —4G 133
Kinnaird Cres. Bear —3H 45
Kinnaird Dri. Lin —5H 75
Kinnaird Pl. B'rig —2D 64
Kinnear Rd. G40 —2C 104
Kinneil Ho. Ham —4A 142
Kinneil Pl. Ham —1D 152
Kinnell Av. G52 —2C 100
Kinnell Cres. G52 —2C 100
Kinnell Path. G52 —2C 100
Kinnell Pl. G52 —2D 100
Kinnell Sq. G52 —2C 100
Kinning Pk. Ind. Est. G5 —6D 82
KINNING PK. STATION. G41 —6B 82
Kinning St. G5 —6E 83
Kinnoul Gdns. Bear —6D 24
Kinnoull Pl. Blan —2B 140
Kinpurnie Rd. Pais —6F 79
Kinross Av. G52 —1B 100
Kinross Pk. E Kil —6D 138
Kinsail Dri. G52 —5H 79
Kinstone Av. G14 —4A 60
Kintail Gdns. Kirk —4H 31
Kintessack Pl. B'rig —5F 49
Kintillo Dri. G13 —3B 60
Kintore Pk. Ham —4F 153
Kintore Rd. G43 —1D 118
Kintore Tower. Camb —4G 121
Kintra St. G51 —5H 81
(in two parts)
Kintyre Av. Lin —1G 95
Kintyre Cres. Newt M —3C 132
Kintyre Cres. Plain —1F 93
Kintyre Gro. Kirk —4H 31
Kintyre Rd. Blan —1A 140
Kintyre St. G21 —2C 84
Kintyre Wynd. Carl —2F 165
Kipland Wlk. Coat —6F 91
Kippen Dri. Clar —4E 135
Kippen St. G22 —3H 63
Kippen St. Air —5F 91
Kipperoch Rd. Dumb —1B 16
Kippford St. G32 —1C 106
Kipps Av. Air —3G 91
Kippsbyre Ct. Air —4F 91
(off Monkscourt Av.)
Kirkaig Av. Renf —1H 79
Kirk Bean Av. Ruth —3C 120
Kirkburn Av. Camb —3A 122
Kirkcaldy Rd. G41 —3B 102
Kirkconnel Av. G13 —3H 59
Kirkconnel Av. Cumb —4A 34
Kirkconnel Dri. Ruth —2B 120
Kirk Cres. Old K —6E 21
Kirkcudbright Pl. E Kil —6D 138
Kirkdale Dri. G52 —1E 101
Kirkdene Av. Newt M —4H 133
Kirkdene Bank. Newt M —4H 133
Kirkdene Cres. Newt M —4H 133
Kirkdene Gro. Newt M —5H 133
Kirkdene Pl. Newt M —4H 133
Kirkfieldbank Way. Ham —6E 141
Kirkfield Rd. Both —4E 125
Kirkford Rd. Chry —5C 52
Kirk Glebe. Neil —2E 131
Kirkhall Rd. Moth —3D 128
Kirkhill Av. Camb —4A 122
Kirkhill Cres. Neil —1F 131
Kirkhill Dri. G20 —4B 62
Kirkhill Gdns. Camb —4A 122
Kirkhill Ga. Newt M —5H 133
Kirkhill Gro. Camb —4A 122
Kirkhill Pl. G20 —4B 62
Kirkhill Pl. Wis —1C 156
Kirkhill Rd. G'csh —4D 68
Kirkhill Rd. Newt M —4H 133
Kirkhill Rd. Udd —5C 108
Kirkhill Rd. Wis —2B 156
KIRKHILL STATION. Camb —2A 122
Kirkhill St. Wis —2D 156
Kirkhill Ter. Camb —4A 122
Kirkhope Dri. G15 —6B 44
Kirkinner Rd. G32 —2D 106
Kirkintilloch Ind. Est. Kirk —3C 30
Kirkintilloch Rd. B'rig —2B 64
Kirkintilloch Rd. Kils —2H 20
Kirkintilloch Rd. Kirk —2C 50
Kirkland Gro. John —2F 95
Kirklandneuk Cres. Renf —5C 58
Kirklandneuk Rd. Renf —5C 58
Kirklands Cres. Both —4E 125
Kirklands Cres. Kils —4H 11
Kirkland St. G20 —6D 62
Kirkland St. Moth —2F 143
Kirk La. G43 —6A 102
Kirk La. Bear —2E 45
Kirklea Av. Pais —6E 77
Kirkle Dri. Newt M —4H 133
Kirklee Cir. G12 —5B 62
Kirklee Gdns. G12 —4B 62
Kirklee Gdns. La. G12 —4B 62
Kirklee Pl. G12 —5B 62
Kirklee Quad. G12 —5B 62
Kirklee Quad. La. G12 —5B 62
Kirklee Rd. G12 —5A 62
Kirklee Rd. Bell —3F 127
Kirklee Rd. Moth —6G 127
Kirklee Ter. G12 —5A 62
Kirklee Ter. La. G12 —5B 62
Kirklee Ter. Rd. G12 —5A 62
Kirkliston St. G32 —5H 85
Kirkmichael Av. G11 —6G 61
Kirkmichael Gdns. G11 —6G 61
Kirkmuir Dri. Ruth —4D 120
Kirkness St. Air —3A 92
Kirknethan. Wis —2C 156
Kirknewton St. G32 —5B 86
Kirkoswald. E Kil —6D 138
Kirkoswald Dri. Clyd —4E 43
Kirkoswald Rd. G43 —1B 118
Kirkoswald Rd. Moth —3E 129
Kirkpatrick St. G40 —6C 84
Kirk Pl. Bear —2E 45
Kirk Pl. Cumb —6C 34
Kirk Pl. Udd —2C 124
Kirkriggs Av. Ruth —2D 120
Kirkriggs Gdns. Ruth —2D 120
Kirkriggs Way. Ruth —2D 120
(off Kirkriggs Gdns.)
Kirk Rd. Bear —2E 45
Kirk Rd. Carl —3E 165
Kirk Rd. Crmck —2H 135
Kirk Rd. Dals —3D 162
Kirk Rd. Hous —1B 74
Kirk Rd. Moth —6D 112
Kirk Rd. Wis —6H 145
Kirkshaws Av. Coat —2A 110
Kirkshaws Pl. Coat —2B 110
Kirkshaws Rd. Coat —2H 109
Kirkstall Gdns. B'rig —3D 48
Kirkstone. Newt M —4H 133
Kirkstone Clo. E Kil —5B 148
Kirk St. Carl —3E 165
Kirk St. Coat —5B 90
(in two parts)
Kirk St. Miln —3E 25
Kirk St. Moth —2G 143
Kirkstyle Av. Carl —4E 165
Kirkstyle Cres. Air —1H 91
Kirkstyle Cres. Neil —2D 130
Kirkstyle La. Barr —2E 131
Kirkstyle Pl. Glenm —5F 71
Kirksyde Av. Kirk —6D 30
Kirkton. Ersk —4E 41
Kirkton. Old K —6E 21
Kirkton Av. G13 —3A 60
Kirkton Av. Barr —5D 114
Kirkton Av. Blan —4A 140
Kirkton Av. Carl —3E 165
Kirkton Ct. Carl —4E 165
Kirkton Cres. G13 —3A 60
Kirkton Cres. Coat —2F 111
Kirkton Cres. Milt C —6C 8
Kirktonfield Rd. Neil —2E 131
Kirkton Ga. E Kil —1G 149
Kirktonholme Cres. E Kil —1F 149
Kirktonholme Rd. E Kil —1D 148
Kirkton Ho. Blan —3B 140
Kirkton Pk. E Kil —1H 149
Kirkton Pl. Blan —3B 140
Kirkton Pl. Coat —1F 111
Kirkton Pl. E Kil —1H 149
(in two parts)
Kirkton Rd. Camb —2B 122
Kirkton Rd. Dumb —4D 16
Kirkton Rd. Neil —3D 130
Kirkton Side. Barr —6D 114
Kirkton St. Carl —4F 165
Kirkton Ter. Cam G —1B 6
Kirkvale Ct. Newt M —4H 133
Kirkvale Cres. Newt M —4H 133
Kirkvale Dri. Newt M —4H 133
Kirkview. Cumb —1C 54
Kirkview Ct. Cumb —1C 54
Kirkview Cres. Newt M —6E 133
Kirkview Gdns. Udd —5D 108
Kirkwall. Cumb —6A 14
Kirkwall Av. Blan —5A 124
Kirkwell Rd. G44 —2F 119
Kirkwood Av. Clyd —6F 43
Kirkwood Pl. Coat —6A 90
Kirkwood Quad. Clyd —6F 43
Kirkwood Rd. Udd —5D 108
KIRKWOOD STATION. Coat —6H 89
Kirkwood St. G51 —6A 82
Kirkwood St. Coat —5A 90
Kirkwood St. Ruth —5C 104
Kirn St. G20 —1A 62
Kirriemuir. E Kil —4D 138
Kirriemuir Av. G52 —2C 100
Kirriemuir Gdns. B'rig —5E 49
Kirriemuir Pl. G52 —1C 100
(off Bucklaw Gdns.)
Kirriemuir Rd. B'rig —6E 49
Kirtle Dri. Renf —1G 79
Kirtle Pl. E Kil —4A 148
Kishorn Pl. G33 —2C 86
Kitchener St. Wis —6G 145
Kittoch Pl. E Kil —1H 149
Kittochside Rd. Crmck —2A 136
Kittoch St. E Kil —1G 149
Knapdale St. G22 —2E 63
Knightsbridge St. G13 —2D 60
Knightscliffe Av. G13 —1D 60
Knights Ga. Both —2C 124
Knightswood Cross. G13 —2D 60
Knightswood Rd. G13 —6C 44
Knightswood Ter. Blan —6C 124
Knivysbridge Pl. Bell —4B 126
Knockburnie Rd. Both —3E 125
Knockhall St. G33 —1D 86
Knockhill Dri. G44 —6F 103
Knockhill Rd. Renf —2D 78
Knockside Av. Pais —6H 97
Knock Way. Pais —4C 78
Knollpark Dri. Clar —2B 134
Knowe Cres. Moth —3D 128
Knowehead Dri. Udd —1C 124
Knowehead Gdns. Udd —1C 124
Knowehead Rd. Wis —1A 158
Knowe Rd. Chry —1A 68
Knowe Rd. Pais —4D 78
Knowes Av. Newt M —4E 133
Knowes Rd. Newt M —4F 133
Knowe St. Miln —3F 25
Knowetap St. G20 —2C 62
Knowetop Av. Moth —4H 143
Knowetop Cres. Dumb —2C 16
Knowhead Gdns. G41 —2C 102
Knowhead Ter. G41 —2C 102
Knownoble St. Moth —5H 129
Knox Av. Bri W —4E 73
Knoxland Sq. Dumb —5G 17
Knoxland St. Dumb —5G 17
Knox Pl. Newt M —5B 132
Knox St. Air —3B 92
Knox St. Pais —1F 97
Kronberg Way. E Kil —6F 149
Kyleakin Gdns. Blan —5H 123
Kyleakin Rd. T'bnk —4D 116
Kyleakin Ter. T'bnk —4D 116
Kyle Ct. Camb —1A 122
Kyle Dri. Giff —4C 118
Kyle Gro. Moth —4A 128
Kylemore Cres. Moth —5F 127
Kylepark Av. Udd —1B 124
Kylepark Cres. Udd —6B 108
Kylepark Dri. Udd —6B 108
Kyle Quad. Moth —3C 128
Kyle Quad. Wis —2E 157
Kylerhea Rd. T'bnk —4D 116
Kyle Rd. Cumb —2B 36
Kyle Sq. Ruth —2B 120
Kyle St. G4 —2G 83 (2F 5)
Kyle St. Moth —2D 142
Kyle Ter. Dumb —2B 16

La Belle Allee. G3 —2C 82
(off Claremont St.)
La Belle Pl. G3 —2C 82
Laburnam Cres. Wis —4H 145
Laburnum Av. E Kil —5E 149
Laburnum Ct. E Kil —5E 149
Laburnum Gdns. Kirk —2B 50
Laburnum Gro. Coat —6D 90
Laburnum Gro. Kirk —2B 50
Laburnum Lea. Ham —2A 154
Laburnum Pl. John —5G 95
Laburnum Rd. G41 —1A 102
Laburnum Rd. Bank —1E 15
Laburnum Rd. Moth —3D 36
Laburnum Rd. Udd —4G 109
Lachlan Cres. Ersk —6C 40
La Crusse Ter. G12 —6C 62
Lacy St. Pais —6C 78
Ladeside Clo. Newt M —3C 132
Ladeside Dri. John —3D 94
Ladeside Dri. Kils —2A 12
Lade Ter. G52 —1A 100
Ladhope Pl. G13 —1G 59
Ladyacres. Inch —3H 57
Ladyacres Way. Inch —3H 57
Lady Ann Cres. Air —5C 92
Lady Anne St. G14 —3H 59
Ladybank. Cumb —5H 13
Ladybank Ct. E Kil —1G 149
Ladybank Dri. G52 —1E 101
Ladybank Gdns. E Kil —1H 149
Ladybank Pl. E Kil —1G 149
Ladyburn Dri. Kils —6B 8
Ladyburn St. Pais —1C 98
Ladyhill Dri. Bail —1G 107
Lady Isle Cres. Udd —1C 124
Lady Jane Ga. Both —3B 124
Ladykirk Cres. G52 —5B 80
Ladykirk Cres. Pais —2B 98
Ladykirk Dri. G52 —5B 80
Lady La. Pais —1H 97
Ladyloan Av. G15 —3G 43
Ladyloan Pl. G15 —3G 43
Lady Mary Wlk. Ham —2A 154
Ladymuir Circ. Ersk —6D 40
Ladymuir Cres. G53 —3C 100
Ladysmith Av. Mill P —3B 94
Ladysmith St. Wis —5C 144
Lady Watson Gdns. Ham —1E 153
Ladywell Rd. Moth —3D 142
Ladywell St. G4 —4A 84
Lady Wilson St. Air —5B 92
Ladywood. Miln —3H 25
Lagan Rd. Carl —4F 165
Laggan Quad. Air —2G 91
Laggan Rd. G43 —2C 118
Laggan Rd. Air —2H 91
Laggan Rd. B'rig —6D 48
Laggan Rd. Newt M —2D 132
Laggan Ter. Renf —5D 58
Laggan Way. Newm —2D 146
Lagholm Dri. Lin —6A 76
Laidlaw Av. Moth —4H 127
Laidlaw Gdns. Udd —4D 108
Laidlaw St. G5 —6E 83
(in three parts)
Laidon Rd. Air —2H 91
Laidon Wlk. Newm —3D 146
(off Murdostoun View)
Laighcartside St. John —2G 95
Laighlands Rd. Both —5F 125
Laighmuir St. Udd —2D 124
Laighpark Av. B'ton —4H 39
Laigh Rd. Newt M —4H 133
Laighstonehall Rd. Ham —1F 153
Laightoun Ct. Cumb —1C 54
Laightoun Dri. Cumb —1C 54
Laightoun Gdns. Cumb —1C 54
Lainshaw Dri. G45 —5E 119
Laird Gro. Udd —5E 109
Laird Pl. G40 —1B 104
Lairds Ga. Udd —2B 124
Lairds Hill. Cumb —3G 35
Laird's Hill Ct. Kils —3E 11
Laird's Hill Pl. Kils —3E 11
Laird St. Coat —4D 90
Lairhills Rd. E Kil —4G 149
Lamberton Dri. G52 —5B 80
Lambhill Quad. G41 —6C 82
LAMBHILL STATION. G23 —2C 62
Lambhill St. G41 —6B 82
Lambie Cres. Newt M —4C 132
Lamb St. G22 —3F 63
Lamb St. Ham —6A 142
Lamerton Rd. Cumb —3C 36
Lamington Rd. G52 —1B 100
Lamlash Cres. G33 —3B 86
Lamlash Pl. G33 —3B 86
Lamlash Pl. Moth —2E 143
Lamlash Sq. G33 —3C 86
Lammermoor. E Kil —5E 139
Lammermoor Av. G52 —1C 100
Lammermoor Cres. Kirk —5F 31
Lammermoor Dri. Cumb —6G 35
Lammermoor Gdns. Kirk —5F 31
Lammermoor Rd. Kirk —5F 31
Lammermoor Ter. Wis —6H 145
Lammermuir Ct. Pais —5A 98
Lammermuir Dri. Pais —5H 97
Lammermuir Gdns. Bear —6C 24
Lammermuir Pl. Moth —3B 128
(off Cherry Pl.)
Lammer Wynd. Lark —4G 161
(off Donaldson Rd.)
Lamont Av. B'ton —4A 40
Lamont Rd. G21 —3D 64
Lanark Av. Air —1A 112
Lanark Rd. Carl —4F 165
Lanark Rd. Lark —4H 155
Lanark Rd. End. Lark —4G 155
Lanark St. G1 —5H 83
Lancaster Av. Chap —4D 112
Lancaster Cres. G12 —5A 62
Lancaster Cres. La. G12 —5A 62
Lancaster Rd. B'rig —3D 48
Lancaster Ter. G12 —5A 62
Lancaster Ter. La. G12 —5A 62
Lancaster Way. Renf —2E 79
Lancefield Quay. G3 —4C 82
Lancefield St. G3 —4D 82
Landemer Dri. Ruth —1B 120
Landressy Pl. G40 —1B 104
Landressy St. G40 —6B 84
Landsdowne Gdns. Ham —6B 142
Landsdowne Rd. Lark —3G 161
Lane Gdns. G11 —6H 61
(off Partickhill Av.)
Lane, The. Dull —5F 13
Lanfine Rd. Pais —1D 98
Langa Gro. G20 —2C 62
(off Lochburn Cres.)
Langa St. G20 —2C 62
Lang Av. B'ton —4A 40
Lang Av. Renf —1E 79
Langbank St. G5 —6F 83
Langbar Cres. G33 —4D 86
Langbar Path. G33 —4D 86
(off Langbar Cres.)
Langcraigs. Dumb —2G 17
Langcraigs Ct. Pais —5G 97
Langcraigs Dri. Pais —6G 97
Langcraigs Ter. Pais —6G 97
Langcroft Dri. Camb —3C 122
Langcroft Pl. G51 —4C 80
Langcroft Rd. G51 —4C 80
Langcroft Ter. G51 —4D 80
Langdale. E Kil —6E 137
Langdale. Newt M —4H 133
Langdale Av. G33 —6G 65
Langdale Rd. Chry —5D 52
Langdales Av. Cumb —3F 35
Langdale St. G33 —6G 65
Langfaulds Cres. Clyd —6F 23
Langford Dri. G53 —4A 116
Langford Pl. G53 —4B 116
Langhill Dri. Cumb —2F 35
Langholm Ct. Chry —5E 53
Langholm Cres. Wis —3H 145
Langholme. E Kil —5B 148
Langholm Path. Blan —2A 140
Langlands Av. G51 —4D 80
Langlands Av. E Kil —6H 149
Langlands Ct. G51 —3F 81
Langlands Dri. G51 —3C 80
Langlands Dri. E Kil —6H 149
Langlands Rd. G51 —4D 80
(in two parts)
Langlands-Seafar Interchange. Cumb —5H 35
Langlands Ter. Dumb —1H 17
Langlea Av. Camb —3F 121
Langlea Rd. Camb —3G 121
Langlees Av. Newt M —4H 133

G13 —1B **60**
. *Camb* —3G **121**
Cres. *Coat* —6A **90**
Pl. *Coat* —5A **90**
Langloan St. *Coat* —6A **90**
Langmuir Av. *Kirk* —4E **31**
Langmuirhead Rd. *Kirk* —1H **65**
Langmuir Rd. *Barg* —6E **89**
Langmuir Rd. *Kirk* —4F **31**
Langmuir Way. *Bail* —6E **89**
Langness Rd. *G33* —3B **86**
Langoreth Av. *Ham* —1D **152**
Langrig Rd. *G21* —4C **64**
Langrig Rd. *Newt M* —6C **132**
Langshaw Cres. *Carl* —3F **165**
Langshot St. *G51* —6B **82**
Langside Av. *G41* —4C **102**
Langside Av. *Udd* —1G **125**
Langside Ct. *Both* —6F **125**
Langside Dri. *G43* —3C **118**
Langside Dri. *Kilb* —3A **94**
Langside La. *G42* —4E **103**
Langside Pk. *Kilb* —3A **94**
Langside Pl. *G41* —5D **102**
Langside Rd. *G42* —5D **102**
Langside Rd. *Both* —6F **125**
LANGSIDE STATION. *G43* —1C **118**
Langside St. *Clyd* —1G **43**
Langstile Pl. *G52* —6H **79**
Langstile Rd. *G52* —6H **79**
Lang St. *Pais* —1C **98**
Langton Cres. *G53* —4C **100**
Langton Cres. *Barr* —6F **115**
Langton Gdns. *Bail* —1F **107**
Langton Ga. *Newt M* —4C **132**
Langton Pl. *Newt M* —4C **132**
Langton Rd. *G53* —4C **100**
Langtree Av. *Giff* —6G **117**
Lanrig Pl. *Chry* —1A **68**
Lanrig Rd. *Chry* —6A **52**
Lansbury Gdns. *Pais* —4H **77**
Lansbury Ter. *Lark* —4G **161**
Lansdowne Cres. *G20* —1D **82**
Lansdowne Cres. La. G20 —1D ***82***
(off Gt. Western Rd.)
Lansdowne Dri. *Cumb* —6H **13**
Lantana Gro. *Moth* —1F **143**
Lanton Dri. *G52* —6B **80**
Lanton Rd. *G43* —2C **118**
Lappin St. *Clyd* —1F **59**
Larbert St. *G4* —2F **83** (2D **4**)
Larch Av. *B'rig* —1D **64**
Larch Av. *Lenz* —1C **50**
Larch Ct. *Blan* —1A **140**
Larch Ct. *Cumb* —1D **36**
Larch Ct. *E Kil* —6D **148**
Larch Cres. *Kirk* —1C **50**
Larch Dri. *Bank* —1E **15**
Larch Dri. *E Kil* —6D **148**
Larches, The. *Mood* —3E **53**
Larchfield Av. *G14* —5B **60**
Larchfield Av. *Newt M* —5E **133**
Larchfield Ct. *Newt M* —5D **132**
Larchfield Cres. *Wis* —3A **146**
Larchfield Dri. *Ruth* —3D **120**
Larchfield Gdns. *Wis* —3B **146**
Larchfield Gro. *Wis* —2B **146**
Larchfield Pl. *G14* —5B **60**
Larchfield Pl. *Wis* —3B **146**
Larchfield Rd. *Bear* —6F **45**
Larch Gro. *Cumb* —1D **36**
Larch Gro. *Ham* —1A **154**
Larch Gro. *Milt C* —6B **8**
Larch Gro. *Moth* —2B **128**
Larchgrove Av. *G32* —5C **86**
Larchgrove Pl. *G32* —4C **86**
Larchgrove Rd. *G32* —4C **86**
Larch Pl. *E Kil* —6D **148**
Larch Pl. *John* —5G **95**
Larch Pl. *Udd* —5H **109**
Larch Rd. *G41* —1H **101**
Larch Rd. *Cumb* —1D **36**
Larchwood Ter. *Barr* —6F **115**
Larg Dri. *Blan* —5A **124**
Largie Rd. *G43* —2D **118**
Largo Pl. *G51* —4E **81**
Larkfield Ct. *Blan* —3A **140**
Larkfield Dri. *Blan* —3B **140**
Larkfield Rd. *Lenz* —1E **51**
Larkfield St. *G42* —2F **103**
Larkhall Ind. Est. *Lark* —5G **161**
Larkin Gdns. *Pais* —4H **77**
Larkin Way. *Bell* —[illegible] **110**
Larksfield Dri. *Carl* —5G **165**
Larkspur Dri. *E Kil* —5E **137**
Larkspur Way. *Carl* —5F **165**
Lashley Gro. *Over* —4A **158**
Lasswade St. *G14* —3G **59**
Latherton Dri. *G20* —4B **62**
Latimer Gdns. *G52* —1A **100**
Latimer Path. G52 —1A ***100***
(off Hatton Gdns.)
Latta St. *Dumb* —3G **17**
Lauchlin Pl. *Kirk* —6H **31**
Lauchope Rd. *Moth* —6D **112**
Lauchope St. *Chap* —3E **113**
Lauder Cres. *Wis* —3H **145**
Lauderdale Dri. *Newt M* —6C **132**
Lauderdale Gdns. *G12* —6H **61**
Lauderdale La. *G12* —6H **61**
Lauder Dri. *Lin* —6H **75**
Lauder Dri. *Ruth* —1F **121**
Lauder Gdns. *Blan* —5A **124**
Lauder Gdns. *Coat* —2F **111**
Lauder Grn. *E Kil* —5B **138**
Lauder La. *Ham* —6C **140**
Lauder St. *G5* —1E **103**
Laughland Dri. *Moth* —4D **128**
Laundry La. *G33* —4C **66**
Lauranne Pl. *Bell* —2A **126**
Laurel Av. *Clyd* —3H **41**
Laurel Av. *Lenz* —1D **50**
Laurelbank. *Coat* —3C **90**
Laurel Bank. *Ham* —3G **153**
Laurelbank Rd. *G32* —5C **106**
Laurelbank Rd. *Chry* —2H **67**
Laurel Clo. *E Kil* —6F **149**
Laurel Dri. *E Kil* —6E **149**
Laurel Dri. *Lark* —3G **161**
Laurel Dri. *Wis* —5D **144**
Laurel Gdns. *Chap* —3E **113**
Laurel Gdns. *Udd* —5D **108**
Laurel La. Lark —4G ***161***
(off Donaldson Rd.)
Laurel Pl. *G11* —1G **81**
Laurel Sq. *Bank* —1E **15**
Laurels, The. *Newt M* —4D **132**
Laurel St. *G11* —1G **81**
Laurel Wlk. *Ruth* —4E **121**
Laurel Way. *Barr* —4D **114**
Laurence Dri. *Bear* —1D **44**
Laurenstone Ter. E Kil —1B ***150***
(off Capelrig Dri.)
Lauren View. *Air* —4H **91**
Laurie Ct. *Udd* —6E **109**
Laurieston Rd. *G5* —1F **103**
Lauriston Way. *Ruth* —3D **120**
Lavelle Dri. *Coat* —4E **91**
Lavender Dri. *E Kil* —6F **149**
Lavender La. *Carl* —5E **165**
Laverock Av. *Ham* —1C **154**
Laverockhall St. *G21* —6B **64**
Laverock Rd. *Air* —1B **92**
Laverock Ter. *Chry* —6D **52**
Law Dri. *Moth* —3C **128**
Lawers Dri. *Bear* —1C **44**
Lawers La. *Moth* —3C **128**
Lawers Rd. *G43* —2H **117**
Lawers Rd. *Renf* —2E **79**
Lawfield Av. *Newt M* —4H **133**
Lawhill Av. *G45* —3H **119**
Lawhill Rd. *Law* —6D **158**
Lawhope Mill Rd. *Chap* —2F **113**
Lawmarnock Cres. *Bri W* —4E **73**
Lawmarnock Rd. *Bri W* —5E **73**
Lawmoor Av. *Dix B* —3G **103**
Lawmoor Pl. *G5* —3G **103**
Lawmoor Rd. *G5* —2G **103**
Lawmoor St. *G5* —2G **103**
Lawmuir Cres. *Clyd* —6G **23**
Lawmuir Pl. *Bell* —5C **126**
Lawmuir Rd. *Bell* —4C **126**
Lawmuir Rd. *Law* —6D **158**
Lawn Pk. *Miln* —4A **26**
Lawn St. *Pais* —6B **78**
Law Pl. *E Kil* —5G **137**
Lawrence Av. *Giff* —6A **118**
Lawrence St. *G11* —1A **82**
Lawrie St. *G11* —1H **81**
Lawrie St. *Newm* —4D **146**
Lawrie Way. *Lark* —4G **161**
Law Roundabout. *E Kil* —5G **137**
Lawson Av. *Moth* —6G **143**
Law St. *G40* —6C **84**
Law View. *Wis* —5A **158**
Laxford Av. *G44* —3E **119**
Laxford Pl. *Coat* —1F **111**
Laxford Rd. *Ersk* —6C **40**
Laxford Way. *Moth* —3C **128**
Laxton Dri. *Lenz* —3E **51**
Lea Av. *Neil* —2D **130**
Leabank Av. *Pais* —5A **98**
Leadburn Rd. *G21* —5E **65**
Leadburn St. *G32* —4G **85**
Leader St. *G33* —2F **85**
Leaend Rd. *Air* —2G **91**
Leander Cres. *Bell* —2G **127**
Leander Cres. *Renf* —1G **79**
Learigg Rd. *Plain* —1H **93**
Learmouth Pl. *Miln* —3F **25**
Leathem Pl. *Wis* —2C **156**
Leathen Pl. *Ersk* —6C **40**
Leckethill Av. *Cumb* —6B **34**
Leckethill Ct. *Cumb* —[illegible] **34**
Leckethill Pl. *Cumb* —6A **34**
Leckethill View. *Cumb* —6B **34**
Leckie Dri. *Ham* —5G **141**
Leckie St. *G43* —5A **102**
Ledaig St. *G31* —4E **85**
Ledard Rd. *G42* —5D **102**
Ledcameroch Cres. *Bear* —3D **44**
Ledcameroch Pk. *Bear* —3D **44**
Ledcameroch Rd. *Bear* —3D **44**
Ledgate. *Kirk* —4D **30**
Ledgowan Pl. *G20* —1B **62**
Ledi Dri. *Bear* —6B **24**
Ledi Path. *Moth* —4C **128**
Ledl Rd. *G43* —2A **118**
Ledmore Dri. *G15* —3H **43**
Lednock Rd. *G52* —6A **80**
Lednock Rd. *Step* —4C **66**
Lee Av. *G33* —2G **85**
Leebank Dri. *G44* —6D **118**
Leeburn Av. *C'lee* —2C **74**
Leechlee St. *Ham* —6A **142**
Lee Cres. *B'rig* —1C **64**
Leefield Dri. *G44* —5D **118**
Leehill Rd. *G21* —2A **64**
Lee Pl. *Bell* —3F **127**
Leesburn Pl. *E Kil* —5H **137**
Leeside Rd. *G21* —2A **64**
Leesland. *Udd* —5E **109**
Leeward Circ. *E Kil* —2C **148**
Leewood Dri. *G44* —5E **119**
Le Froy Gdns. *E Kil* —3E **149**
Le Froy La. *E Kil* —3E **149**
Lefroy St. *Coat* —4A **90**
Legbrannock Av. *Moth* —6D **112**
Legbrannock Cres. *Moth* —3D **128**
Legbrannock Rd. *Moth* —1E **129**
Leicester Av. *G12* —4H **61**
Leighton St. *G20* —3C **62**
Leighton St. *Wis* —1H **157**
Leitchland Rd. *Eld & Pais* —5B **96**
Leithington Rd. *Giff* —2G **133**
Leithland Av. *G53* —4B **100**
Leithland Rd. *G53* —4B **100**
Leith St. *G33* —3F **85**
Leman Dri. *Hous* —3D **74**
Leman Gro. *Hous* —3D **74**
Lembert Dri. *Clar* —1B **134**
Lendale La. *B'rig* —3C **48**
Lendalfoot Gdns. *Ham* —1B **152**
Lendal Pl. *E Kil* —5A **148**
Lendel Pl. *G51* —5B **82**
Lenihall Dri. *G45* —5A **120**
Lenihall Ter. *G45* —5A **120**
Lennox Av. *G14* —6C **60**
Lennox Av. *B'ton* —4H **39**
Lennox Av. *Coat* —4A **90**
Lennox Av. *Miln* —4G **25**
Lennox Ct. Kirk —5E ***31***
(off Highfield Rd.)
Lennox Cres. *B'rig* —1B **64**
Lennox Dri. *Bear* —1F **45**
Lennox Dri. *Clyd* —6E **23**
Lennox Gdns. *G14* —5D **60**
Lennox La. E. *G14* —6D **60**
Lennox La. W. G14 —5D ***60***
(off Norse La. N.)
Lennox Pl. *Clyd* —4A **42**
Lennox Rd. *Cumb* —3H **35**
Lennox Rd. *Dumb* —4H **17**
Lennox Rd. *Len* —2E **7**
Lennox Rd. *Milt* —4E **19**
Lennox St. *G20* —2A **62**
Lennox St. *Dumb* —4G **17**
Lennox St. *Wis* —5C **146**
Lennox Ter. *Pais* —3C **78**
Lennox View. *Clyd* —4D **42**
Lentran St. *G34* —4A **88**
Leny St. *G20* —5D **62**
Lenziemill Rd. *Cumb* —6H **35**
Lenzie Pl. *G21* —3B **64**
Lenzie Rd. *Kirk* —6D **30**
Lenzie Rd. *Step* —2D **66**
LENZIE STATION. *Lenz* —3C **50**
Lenzie St. *G21* —4B **64**
Lenzie Ter. *G21* —3A **64**
Lesley Quad. *Bell* —5B **126**
Leslie Av. *B'ton* —4H **39**
Leslie Av. *Newt M* —2E **133**
Leslie Rd. *G41* —3C **102**
Leslie St. *G41* —2D **102**
Leslie St. *Moth* —2H **143**
Lesmuir Dri. *G14* —4H **59**
Lesmuir Pl. *G14* —4H **59**
Letham Ct. *G43* —2C **118**
Letham Dri. *G43* —2C **118**
Letham Dri. *B'rig* —1E **65**
Lethame Grange. *Cumb* —1H **35**
Lethamhill Cres. *G33* —2H **85**
Lethamhill Pl. *G33* —2G **85**
Lethamhill Rd. *G33* —2G **85**
Lethbridge Pl. *E Kil* —3E **149**
Letherby Dri. *G44* —6F **103**
Letheron Dri. *Wis* —4H **145**
Lethington Av. *G41* —5C **102**
Lethington Pl. *G41* —5D **102**
Letterfearn Dri. *G23* —6C **46**
Letterickhills Cres. *Camb* —4E **123**
Lettoch St. *G51* —5G **81**
Leven Av. *B'rig* —6D **48**
Leven Ct. *Barr* —2D **111**
Leven Ct. *Dumb* —3E **17**
Leven Dri. *Bear* —3F **45**
Leven Dri. *Ham* —3F **153**
Levenford Ter. *Dumb* —4E **17**
Levengrove Ct. *Dumb* —4E **17**
Levengrove Ter. *Dumb* —4E **17**
Leven Path. Moth —2A ***128***
(off Graham St.)
Leven Pl. *Ersk* —6C **40**
Leven Quad. *Air* —1H **91**
Leven Rd. *Coat* —2G **89**
Leven Sq. *Renf* —5D **58**
Leven St. *G41* —2D **102**
Leven St. *Dumb* —4G **17**
Leven St. *Moth* —4G **143**
Leven Ter. *Moth* —5C **128**
Leven Valley Enterprise Cen. *Dumb* —3D **16**
Leven View. *Clyd* —4D **42**
Leven Way. Cumb —3H ***35***
(off Cumbernauld Cen., The)
Leven Way. *E Kil* —5B **148**
Leven Way. *Pais* —4C **96**
Levern Cres. *Barr* —5D **114**
Leverndale Ind. Cen. *G53* —5H **99**
Levern Rd. *G53* —1G **115**
Levernside Av. *G53* —5C **100**
Levernside Av. *Barr* —5C **114**
Levernside Cres. *G53* —4B **100**
Levernside Rd. *G53* —4B **100**
Lewis Av. *Renf* —2F **79**
Lewis Av. *Wis* —4C **146**
Lewis Cres. *Mill P* —3C **94**
Lewis Cres. *Old K* —2G **41**
Lewis Dri. *Old K* —2F **41**
Lewis Gdns. *Bear* —1B **44**
Lewis Gdns. *Old K* —2G **41**
Lewis Gro. *Old K* —2G **41**
Lewis Pl. *Newt M* —3B **132**
Lewis Pl. *Old K* —2G **41**
Lewiston Dri. G23 —6B ***46***
(off Lewiston Rd.)
Lewiston Pl. G23 —6B ***46***
(off Lewiston Rd.)
Lewiston Rd. *G23* —6B **46**
Lexwell Av. *Eld* —2B **96**
Lexwell Rd. *Pais* —3D **96**
Leyden Ct. *G20* —4C **62**
Leyden Gdns. *G20* —4D **62**
Leyden St. *G20* —4C **62**
Leys Pk. *Ham* —5E **141**
Leys, The. *B'rig* —6C **48**
Libberton Way. *Ham* —6E **141**
Liberton St. *G33* —3F **85**
Liberty Av. *Bail* —6E **89**
Liberty Path. *Blan* —2B **140**
Liberty Rd. *Bell* —3C **126**
Libo Av. *G53* —4D **100**
Libo Pl. *Ersk* —5C **40**
Library La. *Giff* —4F **117**
Library Rd. *Wis* —6H **145**
Lickprivick Rd. *E Kil* —6D **148**
Liddel Gro. *E Kil* —4F **149**
Liddells Ct. *B'rig* —2C **64**
Liddell St. *G32* —4C **106**
Liddel Rd. *Cumb* —4G **35**
Liddel Rd. *Cumb* —4A **36**
(Carbrain)
Liddesdale Pass. *G22* —2G **63**
Liddesdale Pl. *G22* —2A **64**
Liddesdale Rd. *G22* —2F **63**
Liddesdale Sq. *G22* —2H **63**
Liddesdale Ter. *G22* —2A **64**
Liddoch Way. *Ruth* —5B **104**
Liff Gdns. *B'rig* —1F **65**
Liff Pl. *G34* —2A **88**
Lightburn Pl. *G32* —4B **86**
Lightburn Rd. *G31* —5E **85**
Lightburn Rd. *Camb* —3D **122**
Lilac Av. *Clyd* —2H **41**
Lilac Av. *Cumb* —6E **15**
Lilac Ct. *Cumb* —6F **15**
Lilac Cres. *Udd* —5F **109**
Lilac Gdns. *B'rig* —1D **64**
Lilac Hill. *Cumb* —6F **15**
Lilac Hill. *Ham* —1B **154**
Lilac Pl. *Cumb* —6F **15**
Lilac Way. *Moth* —2B **128**
Lillyburn Pl. *G15* —3G **43**
Lilybank Av. *Air* —1B **92**
Lilybank Av. *Camb* —3B **122**
Lilybank Av. *Muirh* —2A **68**
Lilybank Gdns. *G12* —1B **82**
Lilybank Gdns. La. G12 —1B ***82***
(off Lilybank Gdns.)
Lilybank La. G12 —1B ***82***
(off Lilybank Gdns.)
Lilybank St. *Ham* —5G **141**
Lilybank Ter. *G12* —1B **82**
Lilybank Ter. La. G12 —1B ***82***
(off Gt. George St.)
Lily St. *G40* —2D **104**
Limdores St. *G42* —5F **103**
Limecraigs Av. *Pais* —6G **97**
Limecraigs Cres. *Pais* —6G **97**
Limecraigs Rd. *Pais* —6F **97**
Lime Cres. *Air* —4C **92**
Lime Cres. *Cumb* —2E **37**
Lime Gro. *Blan* —6A **124**
Lime Gro. *Lenz* —2D **50**
Lime Gro. *Moth* —6C **143**
Limegrove St. *Bell* —6C **110**
Limekilns Rd. *Cumb* —1H **55**
Limekilns St. *Clyd* —6F **23**
Lime La. G14 —6D ***60***
(off Dumbarton Rd.)
Lime Loan. *Moth* —3B **128**
Lime Rd. *Broad I* —3F **17**
Limeside Av. *Ruth* —6D **104**
Limeside Gdns. *Ruth* —6E **105**
Limes, The. *G44* —3F **119**
Lime St. *G14* —6D **60**
Limetree Av. *Udd* —5F **109**
Limetree Ct. *Ham* —4E **141**
Limetree Cres. *Newt M* —5D **132**
Limetree Dri. *Clyd* —3C **42**
Limetree Quad. *Udd* —5G **109**
Limetree Wlk. *Milt C* —1B **30**
Limeview Av. *Pais* —6F **97**
Limeview Cres. *Pais* —6F **97**
Limeview Rd. *Pais* —6F **97**
Limeview Way. *Pais* —6F **97**
Linacre Dri. *G32* —6C **86**
Linacre Gdns. *G32* —6D **86**
Linburn Pl. *G52* —5A **80**
Linburn Rd. *G52* —4G **79**
Linburn Rd. *Ersk* —6C **40**
Linclive Interchange. *Lin* —6B **76**
Linclive Spur. *Lin* —6B **76**
Linclive Ter. *Lin* —6B **76**
Lincoln Av. *G13* —2C **60**
Lincoln Av. *Udd* —4D **108**
Lincuan Av. *Giff* —6A **118**
Lindams. *Udd* —2D **124**
Lindcres Av. *Ruth* —6D **104**
Linden Av. *Wis* —3A **146**
Linden Ct. *Clyd* —1C **42**
Linden Dri. *Bank* —1E **15**
Linden Dri. *Clyd* —1C **42**
Linden Lea. *Ham* —5F **141**
Linden Lea. *Milt C* —6B **8**
Linden Pl. *G13* —2F **61**
Linden St. *G13* —2F **61**
Linden Way. *G13* —2F **61**
Lindores Dri. *E Kil* —1D **148**
Lindores Pl. *E Kil* —2E **149**
Lindrick Dri. *G23* —6C **46**
Lindsaybeg Rd. *Chry* —5H **51**
Lindsaybeg Rd. *Lenz* —3D **50**
Lindsay Dri. *G12* —3H **61**
Lindsayfield Rd. *E Kil* —6D **148**
Lindsay Gro. *E Kil* —1H **149**
Lindsay Pl. *G12* —3H **61**
Lindsay Pl. *E Kil* —2A **150**
Lindsay Pl. John —2G ***95***
(off John Lang St.)
Lindsay Pl. *Lenz* —4D **50**
Lindsay Rd. *E Kil* —2H **149**
Lindsay Ter. *Len* —3G **7**
Lindum Cres. *Moth* —1D **142**
Lindum St. *Moth* —1D **142**
Linfern Rd. *G12* —6A **62**
Linghope Pl. *Wis* —3F **157**
Lingley Av. *Air* —5A **92**
Linhope Pl. *E Kil* —4A **148**
Links Rd. *G32* —2D **106**
Links Rd. *G44* —3F **119**
Links, The. *Cumb* —5B **14**
Links View. *Lark* —3G **161**
Linksview Rd. *Moth* —6B **128**
Linkwood Av. *G15* —4H **43**
Linkwood Cres. *G15* —4A **44**
Linkwood Dri. *G15* —4H **43**
Linkwood Pl. *G15* —4H **43**
Linlithgow Gdns. *G32* —6D **86**
Linn Cres. *Pais* —6G **97**
Linn Dri. *G44* —4D **118**
Linnet Av. *John* —6C **94**
Linnet Pl. *G13* —2H **59**
Linnet Rd. *Bell* —3D **126**
Linn Gdns. *Cumb* —3B **34**
Linn Glen. *Len* —3H **7**
Linnhead Dri. *G53* —1B **116**
Linnhead Pl. *G14* —5B **60**
Linnhe Av. *G44* —3E **119**
Linnhe Av. *B'rig* —6D **48**
Linnhe Av. *Ham* —2E **153**
Linnhe Cres. *Wis* —2H **157**
Linnhe Dri. *Barr* —2D **114**
Linnhe Pl. *Blan* —5A **124**
Linnhe Pl. *Ersk* —6C **40**
Linnpark Av. *G44* —5D **118**
Linnpark Ct. *G44* —5D **118**
Linn Pk. Gdns. *John* —3G **95**
Linnpark Ind. Est. *G45* —5F **119**
Linside Av. *Pais* —1C **98**
Lint Butts. *Blan* —2A **140**
Linthaugh Rd. *G53* —3A **100**
Linthaugh Ter. *G53* —4D **100**
Linthouse Rd. *G51* —2E **81**
Lintie Rd. *Moth* —3C **128**
Lintlaw. *Blan* —5B **124**
Lintlaw Dri. *G52* —5B **80**
Lintmill Ter. *Neil* —3C **130**
Linton St. *G33* —3G **85**
Lintwhite Cres. *Bri W* —3G **73**
Linwell Cres. *Pais* —6H **97**
Linwood Av. *Clar* —2D **134**
Linwood Av. *E Kil* —1B **148**
Linwood Ct. *G44* —2E **119**
Linwood Ind. Est. *Lin I* —1H [illegible]
Linwood Rd. *Lin* —6B **76**
Linwood Ter. *Ham* —5F **141**
Lion Bank. *Kirk* —4D **30**
Lismore. *E Kil* —3C **150**
Lismore Av. *Moth* —1D **142**
Lismore Av. *Renf* —2F **79**
Lismore Dri. *Lin* —6F **75**
Lismore Dri. *Pais* —6H **97**
Lismore Gdns. *Mill P* —3C **94**
Lismore Hill. *Ham* —6B **140**
Lismore Pl. *Chry* —4E **53**
Lismore Pl. *Newt M* —4B **132**
Lismore Rd. *G12* —4H **61**
Lister Gdns. *Clar* —4E **135**
Lister Pl. *H'ton I* —4A **80**
Lister Rd. *G52* —4H **79**
(in two parts)
Lister St. *G4* —2H **83** (2H **5**)
Lister Tower. E Kil —3H ***149***
(off Sinclair Pl.)

Lister Wlk. Bell —6E 111
Lithgow Av. Kirk —6E 31
Lithgow Cres. Pais —3C 98
Lithgow Dri. Cle —6H 129
Lithgow Pl. E Kil —1D 148
Lit. Dovehill. G1 —5H 83
Lit. Drum Rd. Cumb —5F 33
Littlehill Av. Cumb —4A 34
Littlehill St. G21 —5C 64
Littleholm Pl. Clyd —3A 42
Lit. John Gdns. Newm —5D 146
Littlesdale Av. Pais —6B 96
Littleston Gdns. Ersk —6D 40
Little St. G3 —4D 82
Littleton Dri. G23 —6B 46
(off Littleton St.)
Littleton St. G23 —6B 46
Livingston Dri. Plain —1G 93
Livingstone Av. G52 —3A 80
Livingstone Boulevd. Ham —5B 140
Livingstone Clo. E Kil —4F 149
Livingstone Cres. Blan —6B 124
Livingstone Dri. E Kil —3F 149
Livingstone Gdns. Lark —2F 161
Livingstone Pk. Kils —1F 11
Livingstone Pl. Air —4B 92
Livingstone St. Clyd —6E 43
Livingstone St. Ham —5D 140
Lloyd Av. G32 —3A 106
Lloyd Dri. Moth —6A 128
Lloyds St. Coat —6C 90
Lloyd St. G31 —3C 84
Lloyd St. Moth —6A 128
Lloyd St. Ruth —4D 104
Loanbank Pl. G51 —4G 81
Loanbank Quad. G51 —4F 81
Loancroft Av. Bail —2A 108
Loancroft Gdns. Udd —2C 124
Loancroft Ga. Udd —2C 124
Loancroft Ho. Bail —2H 107
Loancroft Pl. Bail —2H 107
Loanend Cotts. Camb —6F 123
Loanfoot Av. G13 —2A 60
Loanfoot Av. Neil —3D 130
Loanfoot Rd. Blan —4B 140
Loanhead Av. Lin —5G 75
Loanhead Av. Moth —4D 128
Loanhead Av. Renf —6F 59
Loanhead Cres. Moth —4D 128
Loanhead La. Lin —5G 75
Loanhead Rd. Lin —5G 75
Loanhead Rd. Moth —4C 128
Loanhead St. G32 —4H 85
Loanhead St. Coat —2A 110
Loaning. Lark —4G 161
(off Donaldson Rd.)
Loaninghead Dri. Dumb —1H 17
Loaning, The. Bear —2E 45
Loaning, The. Giff —1G 133
Loaning, The. Kirk —6C 30
Loaning, The. Moth —2E 143
Loan Lea Cres. Lark —4F 161
Loan, The. Miln —1C 24
Lobnitz Av. Renf —6F 59
Lochaber Dri. Kils —5C 8
Lochaber Dri. Ruth —3F 121
Lochaber Pl. Blan —2B 140
Lochaber Pl. E Kil —6H 137
Lochaber Rd. Bear —5G 45
Lochaber Wlk. Milt C —4C 8
Lochachray Gdns. G32 —1C 106
Lochachray St. G32 —1C 106
Lochaline Av. Pais —3E 97
Lochaline Dri. G44 —3E 119
Lochalsh Cres. Milt C —5C 8
Lochalsh Dri. Pais —3E 97
Lochalsh Pl. Blan —5H 123
Lochar Cres. G53 —3D 100
Lochard Dri. Pais —1E 97
Lochar Pl. E Kil —4A 148
Lochart Pl. Wis —5C 146
Loch Assynt. E Kil —3B 150
Loch Awe. E Kil —3A 150
Loch Awe Pl. Coat —5B 90
Lochay St. G32 —1C 106
Lochbrae Dri. Ruth —3E 121
Lochbridge Rd. G34 —4G 87
Lochbroom Dri. Newt M —3F 133
Lochbroom Dri. Pais —3E 97
Loch Brora Cres. Coat —5A 90
Lochbuie La. Glenm —5G 71
Lochburn Cres. G20 —2C 62
Lochburn Gro. G20 —2C 62
(off Lochburn Cres.)
Lochburn Pas. G20 —2C 62
Lochburn Rd. G20 —3B 62
Lochdochart Path. G34 —4B 88
(off Lentran St.)
Lochdochart Rd. G34 —3A 88
Lochearn Cres. Air —1H 91
Lochearn Cres. Pais —3E 97
Lochearnhead Rd. G33 —4B 66
Lochend Av. G'csh —2C 68
Lochend Cres. Bear —4D 44
Lochend Dri. Bear —4D 44
Lochend Path. G34 —2H 87
Lochend Rd. G34 —2H 87
Lochend Rd. Bear —4E 45
Lochend Rd. G'csh —2D 68
Lochend St. Moth —3H 143
Locher Av. Hous —2E 75
Locherburn Av. Hous —4D 74
Locherburn Gro. Hous —3D 74
Locherburn Pl. Hous —3D 74
Locher Cres. Hous —3E 75
Locher Gdns. Hous —3E 75
Locher Rd. Kilb & Bri W —6H 73
Locher Way. Hous —2E 75
Lochfauld Rd. G23 —5E 47
Lochfield Cres. Pais —4B 98
Lochfield Dri. Pais —4C 98
Lochfield Rd. Pais —4A 98
Lochgilp St. G20 —2A 62
Loch Goil. E Kil —2A 150
Lochgoin Av. G15 —3G 43
Lochgreen Pl. Coat —1G 89
Lochgreen Pl. Ham —3F 153
Lochgreen St. G33 —6F 65
Lochhead Av. Lin —6H 75
Lochiel Ct. Air —4F 91
(off Monkscourt Av.)
Lochiel La. Ruth —3F 121
Lochiel Rd. T'bnk —3F 117
Lochinvar Rd. Cumb —6F 35
Lochinver Cres. Pais —3E 97
Lochinver Dri. G44 —3E 119
Lochinver Gro. Camb —2C 122
Loch Laidon Ct. G32 —1D 106
Loch Laidon St. G32 —1D 106
Loch Laxford. E Kil —3B 150
Lochlea. E Kil —5D 138
Loch Lea. Kirk —3F 31
Lochlea Av. Clyd —4E 43
Lochlea Loan. Lark —3G 161
(off Catrine St.)
Lochlea Rd. G43 —1B 118
Lochlea Rd. Clar —4C 134
Lochlea Rd. Cumb —2B 36
Lochlea Rd. Ruth —2B 120
Lochlea Rd. Ruth —2G 121
(Burnside)
Lochlea Way. Moth —3E 129
Lochlee Loan. Lark —4G 161
(off Donaldson Rd.)
Lochleven La. G42 —6E 103
Lochleven Rd. G42 —6E 103
Lochlibo Av. G13 —3H 59
Lochlibo Cres. Barr —6C 114
Lochlibo Rd. Barr —3A 130
Lochlibo Ter. Barr —6C 114
Loch Long. E Kil —3A 150
Loch Loyal. E Kil —3B 150
Lochmaben Rd. G52 —1H 99
Lochmaddy Av. G44 —3E 119
Loch Maree. E Kil —3B 150
Loch Meadie. E Kil —3B 150
Lochnagar Dri. Bear —6B 24
Lochnagar Way. Lark —4G 161
(off Donaldson Rd.)
Loch Naver. E Kil —3B 150
Lochore Av. Pais —4B 78
Loch Pk. Wis —6A 146
Loch Pk. Av. Carl —5E 165
Loch Pk. Pl. Lark —4E 161
Loch Pl. Bri W —3F 73
Loch Rd. G33 —4D 66
Loch Rd. Bri W —3F 73
Loch Rd. Chap —3D 112
Loch Rd. Kirk —6D 30
Loch Rd. Miln —2H 25
Loch Shin. E Kil —3B 150
Lochside. Bear —4F 45
Lochside. G'csh —3D 68
Lochside St. G41 —4C 102
Loch St. C'bnk —3B 112
Loch Striven. E Kil —2A 150
Loch Torridon. E Kil —3B 150
Loch View. C'bnk —3B 112
Lochview Cotts. Bail —6C 68
Lochview Cres. G33 —6H 65
Lochview Dri. G33 —6H 65
Lochview Gdns. G33 —6H 65
Lochview Pl. G33 —6H 65
Lochview Quad. Bell —4B 126
Lochview Rd. Bear —4E 45
Lochview Rd. Coat —2G 89
Lochview Ter. G'csh —4D 68
Loch Voil St. G32 —1D 106
Lochwood Cotts. Bail —1C 88
Lochwood Loan. Mood —4E 53
Lochwood St. G33 —1G 85
Lochy Av. Renf —2H 79
Lochy Gdns. B'rig —6D 48
Lochy Pl. Ersk —6C 40
Lochy St. Wis —2G 157
Lockerbie Av. G43 —1D 118
Locket Yett View. Bell —2A 126
Lockhart Av. Camb —1D 122
Lockhart Dri. Camb —1D 122
Lockhart St. G21 —1D 84
Lockhart St. Carl —3F 165
Lockhart St. Ham —5G 153
Lockhart Ter. E Kil —1B 150
Locksley Av. G13 —1C 60
Locksley Av. Cumb —1G 55
Locksley Ct. Cumb —1G 55
Locksley Cres. Cumb —1G 55
Locksley Pl. Cumb —1G 55
Locksley Rd. Cumb —1G 55
Locksley Rd. Pais —4D 96
Locksley Way. Pais —4D 96
Locks St. Coat —5F 91
Lodge Tower. Moth —5A 144
(off Burnside Ct.)
Logan Av. Newt M —3C 132
Logandale Av. Newm —3D 146
Logan Dri. Cumb —2F 35
Logan Dri. Pais —5G 77
Logan Gdns. Cle —1H 145
Loganlea Dri. Moth —6A 128
Logans Rd. Moth —2D 142
Logan St. G5 —3H 103
Logan St. Blan —2C 140
Loganswell Dri. T'bnk —5E 117
Loganswell Gdns. T'bnk —5E 117
Loganswell Pl. T'bnk —5E 117
Loganswell Rd. T'bnk —5E 117
Logan Tower. Camb —3E 123
Logie Pk. E Kil —6A 138
Logie Sq. E Kil —6A 138
Lomax St. G33 —3F 85
Lomnay Rd. G33 —3D 86
Lomond. E Kil —6G 149
Lomond Av. Renf —2D 78
Lomond Ct. Barr —5E 115
Lomond Ct. Cumb —6E 35
Lomond Ct. Dumb —3E 17
Lomond Cres. Bri W —3E 73
Lomond Cres. Cumb —6E 35
Lomond Cres. Pais —5H 97
Lomond Dri. Air —1G 91
Lomond Dri. Barr —3D 114
Lomond Dri. B'rig —4B 48
Lomond Dri. Both —4F 125
Lomond Dri. Cumb —6D 34
Lomond Dri. Dumb —1H 17
Lomond Dri. Newt M —2D 132
Lomond Dri. Wis —1G 157
Lomond Gdns. Eld —3A 96
Lomond Gro. Cumb —6E 35
Lomond Pl. G33 —5D 66
Lomond Pl. Coat —2A 90
Lomond Pl. Cumb —6D 34
Lomond Pl. Ersk —6C 40
(in two parts)
Lomond Rd. Bear —5E 45
Lomond Rd. Coat —1G 89
Lomond Rd. Kirk —2D 50
Lomond Rd. Udd —4D 108
Lomondside Av. Clar —1A 134
Lomond St. G22 —4F 63
Lomond View. Clyd —4D 42
(off Church St.)
Lomond View. Cumb —6E 35
Lomond View. Ham —1D 152
Lomondview Ind. Est. John —1F 95
Lomond Wlk. Lark —1F 161
(off Duncan Graham St.)
Lomond Wlk. Moth —3C 128
Lomond Way. Moth —2A 128
(off Graham St.)
London Rd. G1 —5H 83
London Rd. G32 —4A 106
London Rd. G40 & G31 —1C 104
London St. Lark —1E 161
London St. Renf —4F 59
Lonend. Pais —1B 98
Longay Pl. G22 —1G 63
Longay St. G22 —1G 63
Long Calderwood Cotts. E Kil
(off Maxwellton Rd.) —5C 138
Long Crags. Dumb —1H 17
Longcroft Dri. Renf —5E 59
Longden St. Clyd —1F 59
Long Dri. E Kil —4A 150
Longford St. G33 —3F 85
Longlee. Bail —1H 107
Longmeadow. John —4D 94
Long Row. Bail —5A 88
Longstone Pl. G33 —3B 86
Longstone Rd. G33 —3B 86
Longwill Ter. Cumb —1B 36
Lonsdale Av. Giff —4A 118
Loom Wlk. Kilb —2A 94
(in two parts)
Lora Dri. G52 —1E 101
Lord Way. Bail —6D 88
Loretto Pl. G33 —3H 85
Loretto St. G33 —3H 85
Lorimer Cres. E Kil —4F 149
Lorn Av. Chry —1B 68
Lorne Cres. B'rig —5F 49
Lorne Dri. Lin —6G 75
Lorne Dri. Moth —5F 127
Lorne Pl. Coat —6F 91
Lorne Rd. H'ton I —3H 79
Lorne St. G51 —5B 82
Lorne St. Ham —5G 141
Lorne Ter. Camb —4H 121
Lorn Pl. Kirk —4A 32
Lorraine Gdns. G12 —5A 62
Lorraine Gdns. La. G12 —5A 62
(off Lorraine Gdns.)
Lorraine Rd. G12 —5A 62
Loskin Dri. G22 —2F 63
Lossie Cres. Renf —1H 79
Lossie St. G33 —2F 85
Lothian Cres. Pais —4H 97
Lothian Dri. Clar —1B 134
Lothian Gdns. G20 —6C 62
Lothian St. G52 —3G 79
(in five parts)
Lothian Way. E Kil —6D 138
Louden St. Air —4A 92
Loudon. E Kil —6G 149
Loudon Gdns. John —2G 95
Loudonhill Av. Ham —3A 154
Loudon Rd. G33 —5B 66
Loudon St. Wis —3H 145
Loudon Ter. Bear —6D 24
(off Grampian Way)
Louise Gdns. Holy —2H 127
Louisville Av. Wis —4B 146
Lounsdale Cres. Pais —3E 97
Lounsdale Dri. Pais —3F 97
Lounsdale Ho. Pais —4E 97
Lounsdale Pl. G14 —5B 60
Lounsdale Rd. Pais —3F 97
Lourdes Av. G52 —1D 100
Lourdes Ct. G52 —1D 100
Lovat Av. Bear —6E 25
Lovat Dri. Kirk —5B 30
Lovat Path. Lark —4G 161
(off Donaldson Rd.)
Lovat Pl. Ruth —3F 121
Love Av. Bri W —1A 72
Love St. Pais —5A 78
Low Barholm. Kilb —3B 94
Low Broadlie Rd. Neil —1D 130
Low Craigends. Kils —3A 12
Low Cres. Clyd —1G 59
Lwr. Admiralty Rd. Old K —2F 41
Lwr. Auchingramont Rd. Ham —5A 142
Lwr. Bourtree Dri. Ruth —3E 121
Lwr. Hill Rd. Clar —3D 134
Lwr. Millgate. Udd —1D 124
Low Flender Rd. Clar —4B 134
Lowndes St. Barr —5E 115
Low Parksail. Ersk —2G 57
Low Patrick St. Ham —6B 142
Low Pleasance. Lark —2F 161
Low Rd. Cast —2G 97
Lowther Av. Bear —6C 24
Lowther Ter. G12 —5A 62
Low Waters Rd. Ham —3H 153
Loyal Av. Ersk —6D 40
Loyal Gdns. Bear —6B 24
Loyal Pl. Ersk —6D 40
Loyne Dri. Renf —1H 79
Luath St. G51 —3G 81
Lubas Av. G42 —6H 103
Lubas Pl. G42 —6H 103
Lubnaig Dri. Ersk —6D 40
Lubnaig Gdns. Bear —6C 24
Lubnaig Pl. Air —1G 91
Lubnaig Rd. G43 —2C 118
Lubnaig Wlk. Moth —2A 128
Luckiesfauld. Neil —3D 130
Luckingsford Av. Inch —2H 57
Luckingsford Dri. Inch —2G 57
Luckingsford Rd. Inch —2G 57
Lucy Brae. Udd —5C 108
Ludovic Sq. John —2F 95
Luffnoco Gdns. G32 —3B 106
Lugar Dri. G52 —1E 101
Lugar Pl. G44 —2A 120
Lugar St. Coat —3D 90
Luggiebank Pl. Bail —1E 109
Luggiebank Rd. Kirk —5D 30
(in two parts)
Luggie Rd. Carl —3D 164
Luggie View. Cumb —6C 34
Luing. Air —5E 93
Luing Rd. G52 —6E 81
Lumloch St. G21 —5C 64
Lumsden La. G3 —2B 82
(off Lumsden St.)
Lumsden St. G3 —3B 82
Lunan Dri. B'rig —1E 65
Lunan Pl. G51 —4E 81
Luncarty Pl. G32 —2A 106
Luncarty St. G32 —2A 106
Lunderston Dri. G53 —6A 100
Lundie Gdns. B'rig —1F 65
Lundie St. G32 —2G 105
Luss Brae. Ham —1C 152
Lusset Glen. Old K —1F 41
Lussett Rd. Old K —1F 41
Lusset View. Clyd —4D 42
Lusshill Ter. Udd —3H 107
Luss Rd. G51 —4F 81
Lybster Cres. Ruth —4F 121
Lye Brae. Cumb —3B 36
Lyell Gro. E Kil —6G 137
Lyell Pl. E Kil —6G 137
Lyle Cres. B'ton —3F 39
Lyle Pl. Pais —3B 98
Lyle Rd. Air —4F 93
Lyle's Land. Hous —1B 74
Lylesland Ct. Pais —3A 98
Lyle Sq. Miln —3E 25
Lyman Dri. Wis —2A 146
Lymburn St. G3 —3B 82
Lymekilns Rd. E Kil —1F 149
Lyndale Pl. G20 —1B 62
Lyndale Rd. G20 —1B 62
Lyndhurst Gdns. G20 —6D 62
Lyndhurst Gdns. La. G20 —6C 62
(off Lothian Gdns.)
Lyne Croft. B'rig —3C 48
Lynedoch Cres. G3 —2D 82
Lynedoch Pl. G3 —2D 82
Lynedoch St. G3 —2D 82
Lynedoch Ter. G3 —2D 82
Lyne St. Wis —4G 145
Lynnburn Av. Bell —1C 126
Lynn Ct. Lark —3E 161
Lynn Dri. Miln —3A 26
Lynne Dri. G23 —6C 46
Lynnhurst. Udd —6D 108
Lynton Av. Giff —6G 117
Lynwood Rd. Newm —3G 147
Lyoncross Av. Barr —5F 115
Lyoncross Cres. Barr —4F 115
Lyoncross Rd. G53 —3B 100
Lyon Rd. Ersk —6C 40
Lyon Rd. Pais —4D 96
Lyons Quad. Wis —5D 144
Lysander Way. Renf —2F 79
Lysa Vale Pl. Bell —2A 126
Lytham Dri. G23 —6C 46
Lytham Meadows. Both —5C 124
Lyttelton. E Kil —5D 148

M8 Food Pk. G21 —1H 83
Mabel St. Moth —4G 143
Macadam Gdns. Bell —1C 126
Macadam Pl. E Kil —3G 149
McAllister Av. Air —3D 92
McAlpine St. G2 —4E 83 (6A 4)
McAlpine St. Wis —1H 157
McArdle Av. Moth —2D 142
Macarthur Av. Glenm —6F 71
Macarthur Ct. E Kil —6E 137
Macarthur Cres. E Kil —5E 137
Macarthur Dri. E Kil —6E 137
Macarthur Gdns. E Kil —6E 137
McArthur Pk. Kirk —6C 30
McArthur St. G43 —6A 102
McAslin Ct. G4 —3H 83 (3H 5)
McAslin St. G4 —3A 84
Macbeth. E Kil —4B 138
Macbeth Pl. G31 —1F 105
Macbeth St. G31 —1F 105
MacCabe Gdns. Len —4H 7
McCallum Av. Ruth —6D 104
McCallum Ct. E Kil —5D 136
McCallum Gdns. Bell —5B 126
McCallum Gro. E Kil —5D 136
McCallum Pl. E Kil —5D 136
McCallum Rd. Lark —4F 161
McCarrison Rd. Wis —3E 147
McCash Pl. Kirk —6C 30
McClue Av. Renf —6D 58
McClue Rd. Renf —5E 59
McClurg Ct. Moth —4G 143
McConnell Gdns. Kils —3A 12
McCormack Gdns. Moth —3E 129
McCracken Av. Renf —1D 78
McCracken Dri. Udd —5G 109
McCreery St. Clyd —1F 59
Maccrimmon Pk. E Kil —5D 136
McCulloch Av. Udd —1G 125
McCulloch St. G41 —1D 102
Macdairmid Dri. Ham —4F 153
Macdonald Av. E Kil —5C 136
McDonald Av. John —4E 95
McDonald Cres. Clyd —1F 59
Macdonald Cres. Twe —2D 32
MacDonald Gro. Bell —5B 126
McDonald Pl. Barr —2E 131
McDonald Pl. Moth —2A 128
Macdonald St. Moth —4H 143
Macdonald St. Ruth —6C 104
Macdougal Quad. Bell —5B 126
Macdougal St. G43 —6A 102
Macdowall St. John —2F 95
Macdowall St. Pais —5H 77
Macduff. Ersk —5E 41
Macduff Pl. G31 —1F 105
Macduff St. G31 —1F 105
Mace Rd. G13 —6C 44
McEwan Gdns. E Kil —5C 136
Macfarlane Rd. Bear —4G 45
McFarlane St. G4 —5A 84
McFarlane St. Pais —4G 77
Macfie Pl. E Kil —5D 136
McGarvey Pl. Kirk —5E 31
McGhee St. Clyd —3D 42
McGowan Pl. Ham —4E 141
McGown St. Pais —5H 77
McGregor Av. Air —3D 92
McGregor Av. Renf —1D 78
McGregor Dri. Dumb —1C 18
McGregor Path. Glenb —3G 69
McGregor Rd. Cumb —4G 35
McGregor St. G51 —5F 81
McGregor St. Clyd —1F 59
McGregor St. Wis —5D 144
McGrigor Rd. Miln —2F 25
Machan Av. Lark —2E 161
Machanhill. Lark —2F 161
Machanhill View. Lark —3F 161
Machan Rd. Lark —3E 161
Machrie Dri. G45 —3B 120
Machrie Dri. Newt M —3E 133
Machrie Rd. G45 —3A 120
Machrie Rd. Moth —2D 142
Machrie St. G45 —4A 120
McInnes Ct. Wis —1H 157
McInnes Pl. Wis —4H 157
McIntosh Pl. G31 —4B 84
Macintosh Pl. E Kil —4E 149

...uad. Bell —5B 126
...osn St. G31 —4B 84
McIntosh Way. Moth —4E 143
McIntyre Pl. Pais —3A 98
Macintyre St. G3 —4D 82
McIntyre Ter. Camb —1A 122
McIver St. Camb —1D 122
Macivor Cres. E Kil —5C 136
McKay Cres. John —3G 95
McKay Gro. Bell —2B 126
McKay Pl. E Kil —5C 136
MacKean St. Pais —5G 77
McKechnie St. G51 —3G 81
MacKeith St. G40 —1B 104
McKenna Dri. Air —4G 91
McKenzie Av. Clyd —3D 42
Mackenzie Dri. Mill P —4B 94
Mackenzie Gdns. E Kil —5C 136
McKenzie St. Pais —6G 77
Mackenzie Ter. Bell —6C 110
McKerrell St. Pais —6C 78
Mackie's Mill Rd. Eld —5B 96
Mackinlay St. G5 —1F 103
McKinley Pl. Newt M —5D 132
Mack St. Air —3A 92
McLaren Ct. Giff —6H 117
McLaren Gro. E Kil —5C 136
McLaren Pl. G44 —5D 118
McLaurin Cres. John —4D 94
Maclay Av. Kilb —3A 94
McLean Av. Renf —2E 79
Maclean Ct. E Kil —5D 136
McLean Dri. Bell —5B 126
Maclean Gro. E Kil —5D 136
Maclean Pl. Cumb —6C 34 (off Airdrie Rd.)
McLean Pl. Pais —4H 77
Maclean Rd. Barr —3E 131
Maclean Rd. E Kil —5D 136
Maclean Sq. G51 —5B 82
Maclean St. G51 —5B 82
Mclean St. Clyd —1G 59 (off Wood Quad.)
McLees La. Moth —2D 142
Maclehose Rd. Cumb —2C 36
McLelland Dri. Plain —1H 93
Maclellan St. G41 —6B 82
McLennan St. G42 —5F 103
Macleod Pl. E Kil —6B 138
McLeod Rd. Dumb —1C 18
Macleod St. G4 —4A 84
McMahon Rd. Newm —3E 147
Macmillan Gdns. Udd —5E 109
McMillan Rd. Wis —1D 156
Macmillan St. Lark —3D 160
McMillan Way. Law —6D 158
McNair St. G32 —6A 86
McNeil Av. Clyd —6G 43
McNeil Dri. Moth —6G 111
McNeil Gdns. G5 —1H 103
Macneill Dri. E Kil —5D 136
Macneill Gdns. E Kil —5D 136
Macneill St. Lark —2D 160
McNeil Pl. Over —4A 158
McNeil St. G5 —1H 103
Macneish Way. E Kil —5D 136
Macnicol Ct. E Kil —5C 136
Macnicol Pk. E Kil —5C 136
Macnicol Pl. E Kil —5C 136
McPhail St. G40 —1A 104
McPhater St. G4 —2F 83 (2D 4)
McPherson Cres. Chap —4E 113
McPherson Dri. Both —4F 125
Macpherson Pk. E Kil —6E 137
McPherson St. Bell —2F 127
Macphie Rd. Dumb —1C 18
Macquisten Bri. G41 —6B 102
Macrae Ct. John —4E 95 (off Tannahill Cres.)
Macrae Gdns. E Kil —6E 137
Macrimmon Pl. E Kil —3G 149
McSparran Rd. Kils —1B 34
MacTaggart Rd. Cumb —5G 35
Madison Av. G44 —2F 119
Madison Pl. Blan —2B 140
Madras Pl. G40 —2B 104
Madras Pl. Neil —2E 131
Madras St. G40 —2B 104
Mafeking St. G51 —5H 81
Mafeking St. Wis —5D 144
Mafeking Ter. Neil —2C 130
Magdalen Way. Pais —6B 96
Magna St. Moth —1D 142
Magnolia Gdns. Moth —4C 128
Magnolia Pl. Udd —5G 109
Magnolia St. Wis —4H 145
Magnus Cres. G44 —3F 119
Magnus Rd. Hous —3C 74
Mahon Ct. Mood —6D 52
Maidens. E Kil —6F 137
Maidens Av. Newt M —4G 133
Maidland Rd. G53 —5C 100
Mailerbeg Gdns. Chry —4D 52
Mailie Wlk. Moth —4C 128
Mailing Av. B'rig —5D 48
Mainhead Ter. Cumb —6B 14
Mainhill Av. Bail —6B 88
Mainhill Dri. Bail —6A 88
Mainhill Pl. Bail —5B 88
Mainhill Rd. Bail —6C 88
Main Rd. Cast —1H 97
Main Rd. Cumb —2B 54
Main Rd. Eld & Milla —3H 95
Mains Av. Giff —6H 117
Mainscroft. Ersk —6G 41
Mains Dri. Ersk —6G 41
Mains Hill. Ersk —6F 41
Mainshill Av. Ersk —6F 41
Mainshill Gdns. Ersk —6F 41
Mains Pl. Bell —4C 126
Mains River. Ersk —6G 41
Mains Rd. E Kil —6G 137
Mains Rd. E Kil —4G 137 (Nerston)
Main St. G40 —2B 104
Main St. Bail —1H 107
Main St. Barr —5D 114
Main St. Bell —2B 126
Main St. Blan —3A 140
Main St. Bog —6E 147
Main St. Both —5E 125
Main St. Bri W —3F 73
Main St. C'bnk —2C 112
Main St. Camb —1A 122
Main St. Chap —2E 113
Main St. Chry —1A 68
Main St. Clar —3D 134
Main St. Cle —1H 145
Main St. Coat —4C 90 (in two parts)
Main St. Cumb —6B 14
Main St. E Kil —1H 149
Main St. Glenb —3H 69
Main St. Holy —2A 128
Main St. Hous —1A 74
Main St. Kils —2H 11
Main St. Len —3F 7
Main St. Miln —4G 25 (in two parts)
Main St. Neil —2D 130
Main St. Over —5A 158
Main St. Plain —1G 93
Main St. Ruth —5C 104
Main St. T'bnk —4F 117
Main St. Torr —5D 28
Main St. Twe —1D 32
Main St. Udd —1D 124
Main St. Wis —5F 145
Mains Wood. Ersk —6H 41
Mair St. G51 —5C 82
Maitland Bank. Lark —2G 161
Maitland Dri. Torr —4D 28
Maitland Pl. Renf —1D 78
Maitland St. G4 —2F 83 (1D 4)
Malcolm Gdns. E Kil —1E 149
Malcolm St. Moth —3E 143
Mal Fleming's Brae. Kils —4B 12
Malin Pl. G33 —3H 85
Mallaig Pl. G51 —4D 80
Mallaig Rd. G51 —4D 80
Mallard Cres. E Kil —6C 148
Mallard Pl. E Kil —6C 148
Mallard Rd. Clyd —2D 42
Mallard Ter. E Kil —6C 148
Malleable Gdns. Moth —5E 127
Malletsheugh Rd. Newt M —6A 132
Malloch Cres. Eld —3H 95
Malloch Pl. E Kil —1B 150
Malloch St. G20 —4C 62
Malov Ct. E Kil —6G 149
Mal Plaquet Ct. Carl —4H 165
Maltbarns St. G20 —6E 63
Malvaig La. Blan —2A 140
Malvern Ct. G31 —5C 84
Malvern Way. Pais —3H 77
Mambeg Dri. G51 —3E 81
Mamore Pl. G43 —1A 118
Mamore St. G43 —1A 118
Manchester Dri. G12 —3G 61
Mandora Ct. Carl —4H 165
Manitoba Cres. E Kil —2D 148
Mannering. E Kil —5D 138
Mannering Ct. G41 —5A 102
Mannering Rd. G41 —5A 102
Mannering Rd. Pais —6C 96
Mannering Way. Pais —5C 96
Mannofield. Bear —3D 44
Manor Dri. Air —3G 91
Manor Pk. Ham —1H 153
Manor Rd. G14 —5E 61
Manor Rd. Drum —6H 43
Manor Rd. G'csh —4D 68
Manor Rd. Pais —4D 96
Manor View. C'bnk —3B 112
Manor View. Lark —3G 161
Manor Way. Ruth —3E 121
Manot Ga. Newt M —6F 133
Manresa Pl. G4 —1F 83
Manse Av. Bear —2F 45
Manse Av. Both —5E 125
Manse Av. Coat —1H 109
Manse Brae. G44 —1F 119
Manse Brae. Lark —6D 162
Manse Bri. Carl —4G 165
Manse Ct. Barr —4F 115
Manse Ct. Kils —4H 11
Manse Ct. Law —1A 164
Manse Cres. Hous —1B 74
Mansefield Av. Camb —3A 122
Mansefield Cres. Clar —3B 134
Mansefield Cres. Old K —6E 21
Mansefield Dri. Udd —1D 124
Mansefield Rd. Clar —3B 134
Mansefield Rd. Ham —5H 153
Mansel St. G21 —4B 64
Manse Pl. Air —4A 92
Manse Rd. G32 —1D 106
Manse Rd. Barg —5C 88
Manse Rd. Bear —2E 45
Manse Rd. Bowl —5B 20
Manse Rd. Crmck —2H 135
Manse Rd. Kils —4H 11
Manse Rd. Moth —1G 155
Manse Rd. Neil —2D 130
Manse Rd. Newm —5D 146
Manse St. Coat —5B 90
Manse St. Renf —5F 59
Manse View. Lark —3F 161
Manse View. Moth —3F 129
Mansewood Dri. Dumb —2H 17
Mansewood Rd. G43 —1H 117
Mansfield Rd. G52 —4H 79
Mansfield Rd. Bell —3B 126
Mansfield St. G11 —1A 82
Mansion Ct. Camb —1A 122
Mansionhouse Av. G32 —5C 106
Mansionhouse Dri. G32 —5C 86
Mansionhouse Gdns. G41 —6C 102
Mansionhouse Gro. Mt V —2E 107
Mansionhouse Rd. G41 —6C 102
Mansionhouse Rd. Mt V —1E 107
Mansionhouse Rd. Pais —6C 78
Mansion St. G22 —4G 63
Mansion St. Camb —1A 122
Manson Pl. E Kil —6B 150
Maple Av. Dumb —2B 16
Maple Av. Milt C —6B 8
Maple Av. Newt M —5D 132
Maple Bank. Ham —1B 154
Maple Ct. Coat —1B 110 (off Ailsa Rd.)
Maple Ct. Cumb —6F 15
Maple Dri. Barr —6F 115
Maple Dri. Clyd —2B 42
Maple Dri. John —5F 95
Maple Dri. Kirk —2A 50
Maple Dri. Lark —6A 156
Maple Gro. E Kil —6D 148
Maple Pl. Bank —1E 15
Maple Pl. E Kil —5D 148
Maple Pl. Udd —5H 109
Maple Quad. Air —5D 92
Maple Rd. G41 —1H 101
Maple Rd. Cumb —6F 15
Maple Rd. Moth —2B 128
Maple Ter. E Kil —5D 148
Maple Way. Blan —2A 140
Maple Way. Milt C —6B 8
Mar Av. B'ton —4H 39
Marchbank Gdns. Pais —1F 99
Marchfield. B'rig —4A 48
Marchfield Av. Pais —3H 77
Marchglen Pl. G51 —4D 80
Marchmont Gdns. B'rig —4B 48
Marchmont Ter. G12 —6A 62 (off Observatory Rd.)
March St. G41 —3D 102
Mardale. E Kil —6E 137
Mar Dri. Bear —6F 25
Maree Dri. G52 —1E 101
Maree Dri. Cumb —6D 34
Maree Gdns. B'rig —6D 48
Maree Rd. Pais —3E 97
Maree Wlk. Newm —3D 146 (off Banavie Rd.)
Maree Way Houses. Blan —1B 140
Marfield St. G32 —4G 85
Mar Gdns. Ruth —3F 121
Margaret Av. Hag —1G 15
Margaret Pl. Bell —2A 126
Margaret Rd. Ham —3F 141
Margaret's Pl. Lark —2E 161
Margaret St. Coat —1C 110
Margaretvale Dri. Lark —3E 161
Marguerite Av. Lenz —1C 50
Marguerite Dri. Kirk —1C 50
Marguerite Gdns. Both —5F 125
Marguerite Gdns. Kirk —1C 50
Marguerite Gro. Kirk —1C 50
Marguerite Pl. Milt C —5B 8
Marian Dri. Moth —5C 128
Maric La. Plain —1G 93
Marigold Av. Moth —1G 143
Marigold Way. Carl —5F 165
Marine Cres. G51 —5C 82
Marine Gdns. G51 —5C 82
Mariner Ct. Clyd —5C 42
Mariscat Rd. G41 —3C 102
Marjory Dri. Pais —4C 78
Marjory Rd. Pais —2C 78
Market Clo. Kils —3H 11 (off Market St.)
Market Ct. Kils —3H 11 (off Market St.)
Markethill Rd. E Kil —3F 137
Markethill Roundabout. E Kil —6G 137
Market Pl. Carl —3F 165
Market Pl. Kils —3H 11
Market Pl. Udd —6G 109
Market Rd. Carl —3F 165
Market Rd. Kirk —6G 31
Market Rd. Udd —6G 109
Market Sq. Kils —3H 11
Market St. Air —3A 92
Market St. Kils —3H 11
Market St. Udd —6G 109
Marlborough Av. G11 —6F 61
Marlborough La. S. G11 —6F 61 (off Broomhill Dri.)
Marlborough Pk. E Kil —4C 148
Marldon La. G11 —6F 61
Marley Way. Milt C —5B 8
Marlfield Gdns. Bell —6C 110
Marlinford Rd. G51 —6A 60
Marlow St. G41 —1C 102
Marlow Ter. G41 —1C 102
Marmion Ct. Pais —5D 96
Marmion Cres. Moth —5F 127
Marmion Dri. Kirk —5F 31
Marmion Pl. Cumb —6G 35
Marmion Rd. Cumb —6G 35
Marmion Rd. Pais —5C 96
Marne St. G31 —4D 84
Marnoch Dri. Glenb —3H 69
Marnoch Way. Chry —5D 52
Marnock Ter. Pais —2C 98
Marrswood Grn. Ham —5E 141
Marrwood Av. Kirk —1H 51
Marshall Gro. Ham —6F 141
Marshall La. Wis —6G 145
Marshall's La. Pais —1A 98
Marshall St. Coat —1H 109
Marshall St. Lark —2E 161
Marshall St. Wis —6F 145
Martha Pl. Lark —3F 161
Martha St. G1 —3G 83 (4F 5)
Martin Ct. Ham —6G 141
Martin Cres. Bail —6A 88
Martin Pl. Moth —4C 128
Martinside. E Kil —6G 149
Martin St. G40 —2B 104
Martin St. Coat —4F 91
Martlet Dri. John —6C 94
Mart St. G1 —5G 83
Martyn St. Air —4G 91
Martyrs Pl. B'rig —1C 64
Marwick St. G31 —4D 84
Mary Dri. Bell —4A 126
Mary Glen. Wis —4B 146
Maryhill Rd. G20 —3B 62
Maryhill Rd. Bear —5F 45
Maryhill Shopping Cen. G20 —4C 62
MARYHILL STATION. G20 —1A 62
Maryknowe Rd. Moth —5C 128
Maryland Dri. G52 —6E 81
Maryland Gdns. G52 —6E 81
Maryland Rd. Dumb —1H 17
Mary Rae Rd. Bell —4A 126
Mary Sq. Bail —6D 88
Maryston St. G33 —1F 85
Mary St. Ham —1G 153
Mary St. John —2G 95
Mary St. Pais —3A 98
Maryville Av. Giff —5A 118
Maryville La. Udd —5B 108
Maryville View. Udd —4B 108
Marywood Sq. G41 —3D 102
Mary Young Pl. Clar —3D 134
Masonfield Av. Cumb —3F 35
Mason La. Moth —3G 143 (in two parts)
Mason St. Lark —4G 161
Mason St. Moth —3G 143
Masterton St. G21 —6G 63
Matherton Av. Newt M —4H 133
Mathieson Rd. Ruth —4E 105
Mathieson St. Pais —6D 78
Matilda Rd. G41 —2C 102
Matthew McWhirter Pl. Lark —1F 161
Mauchline. E Kil —6D 138
Mauchline Av. Kirk —3G 31
Mauchline Ct. Ham —1B 152
Mauchline Ct. Kirk —3G 31
Mauchline St. G5 —1E 103
Maudslie St. Bell —3C 126
Maudslie St. Coat —6C 90
Maukinfauld Ct. G32 —2F 105
Maukinfauld Rd. G32 —2G 105
Mauldslie Dri. Law —5D 158
Mauldslie Pl. Ashg —5B 162
Mauldslie Rd. Carl —2F 163
Mauldslie St. G40 —1D 104
Maule Dri. G11 —1G 81
Mavis Bank. B'rig —1B 64
Mavis Bank. Blan —2A 140 (off Moorfield Rd.)
Mavisbank Gdns. G51 —5C 82
Mavisbank Gdns. Bell —1C 126
Mavisbank Rd. G51 —4B 82
Mavisbank St. Air —3G 91
Mavisbank St. Newm —4G 147
Mavisbank Ter. John —3F 95
Mavisbank Ter. Pais —2B 98
Mavis Valley Rd. B'rig —3A 48
Mavor Av. E Kil —5H 137
Mavor Roundabout. E Kil —6H 137
Maxton Av. Barr —4C 114
Maxton Cres. Wis —3A 146
Maxton Ter. Camb —4H 121
Maxwell Av. G41 —1D 102
Maxwell Av. Bail —1G 107
Maxwell Av. Bear —4E 45
Maxwell Ct. G41 —1C 102
Maxwell Cres. Blan —3B 140
Maxwell Dri. G41 —1A 102
Maxwell Dri. Bail —6F 87
Maxwell Dri. E Kil —1H 149
Maxwell Dri. Ersk —4D 40
Maxwell Gdns. G41 —1B 102
Maxwell Gro. G41 —1B 102
Maxwell Oval. G41 —1D 102
MAXWELL PK. STATION. G41 —3B 102
Maxwell Path. Lark —4G 161 (off Donaldson Rd.)
Maxwell Pl. G41 —2E 103
Maxwell Pl. Coat —5B 90
Maxwell Pl. Kils —2H 11
Maxwell Rd. G41 —1D 102
Maxwell Rd. B'ton —4H 39
Maxwell St. G1 —5G 83
Maxwell St. Bail —1H 107
Maxwell St. Clyd —3B 42
Maxwell St. Pais —6A 78
Maxwell Ter. G41 —1D 102
Maxwellton Av. E Kil —1A 150
Maxwellton Ct. Pais —1G 97
Maxwellton Pl. E Kil —6B 138
Maxwellton Rd. E Kil —6B 138
Maxwellton Rd. Pais —1F 97
Maxwellton St. Pais —1G 97
Maxwelton Rd. G33 —1F 85
Maybank La. G42 —4E 103
Maybank St. G42 —4E 103
Mayberry Cres. G32 —6D 86
Mayberry Gdns. G32 —6D 86
Mayberry Gro. G32 —6D 86
Mayberry Pl. Blan —1B 140
Maybole Cres. Newt M —5G 133
Maybole Gdns. Ham —1B 152
Maybole Gro. Newt M —5G 133
Maybole Pl. Coat —2F 111
Maybole St. G53 —1H 115
Mayfield Av. Clar —2C 134
Mayfield Gdns. Carl —6G 165
Mayfield Pl. Carl —6G 165
Mayfield Rd. Ham —5D 140
Mayfield St. G20 —4D 62
May Gdns. Ham —4G 141
May Rd. Pais —6A 98
May St. Ham —4H 141
May Ter. G42 —5F 103
May Ter. Giff —4A 118
Meadow Av. Blan —3B 140
Meadowbank La. Udd —1C 124
Meadowbank Pl. Newt M —4D 132
Meadowbank St. Dumb —3E 17
Meadowburn. B'rig —3C 48
Meadowburn Av. Lenz —2E 51
Meadowburn Av. Newt M —4D 132
Meadowburn Rd. Wis —6A 146
Meadow Ct. Dumb —2F 17
Meadowfield Pl. Newm —3G 147
Meadowhead Av. Chry —5D 52
Meadowhead Rd. Plain —1F 93
Meadowhead Rd. Wis —5C 144
Meadowhill. Newt M —4D 132
Meadowhill St. Lark —2F 161
Meadow La. Both —5F 125
Meadow La. Renf —4F 59
Meadowpark St. G31 —4D 84 (in two parts)
Meadow Path. Chap —4D 112
Meadow Rd. G11 —1G 81
Meadow Rd. Dumb —3F 17
Meadow Rd. Moth —4H 143
Meadows Av. Lark —2F 161
Meadow Side. Ham —5H 153
Meadowside Av. Eld —3B 96
Meadowside Gdns. Air —4D 92
Meadowside Ind. Est. Renf —3F 59
Meadowside Pl. Air —4D 92
Meadowside Rd. Kils —3C 10
Meadowside St. G11 —2G 81
Meadowside St. Renf —4F 59
Meadows, The. Hous —2D 74
Meadow St. Coat —1D 110
Meadow View. Cumb —1C 36
Meadow View. Plain —1G 93
Meadow Wlk. Coat —5D 90
Meadow Way. Newt M —4D 132
Meadowwell St. G32 —6B 86
Meadside Av. Kilb —1A 94
Meadside Rd. Kilb —1A 94
Mealkirk St. Clyd —6E 23
Mearns Ct. Ham —4A 154
Mearnscroft Gdns. Newt M —6F 133
Mearnscroft Rd. Newt M —6F 133
Mearns Rd. Moth —1E 143
Mearns Rd. Newt M —6E 133
Mearns Way. B'rig —5F 49
Medlar Rd. Cumb —3D 36
Medrox Gdns. Cumb —2B 54
Medwin Ct. E Kil —4A 148
Medwin Gdns. E Kil —4A 148
Medwin St. Camb —2D 122
Medwyn St. G14 —6D 60 (in two parts)
Meek Pl. Camb —2B 122
Meetinghouse La. Pais —6A 78
Megan Ga. G40 —1B 104
Megan St. G40 —1B 104

Meikle Av. Renf —1E 79
Meikle Bin Brae. Len —3G 7
Meikle Cres. Ham —4G 153
Meikle Earnock Rd. Ham —5D 152
Meiklehill Ct. Kirk —4E 31
(in two parts)
Meiklehill Rd. Kirk —4E 31
Meiklem St. Bell —2E 127
Meiklerig Cres. G53 —3B 100
Meikleriggs Dri. Pais —4E 97
Meikle Rd. G53 —5C 100
Meiklewood Rd. G51 —5D 80
Melbourne Av. Clyd —2H 41
Melbourne Av. E Kil —4E 149
Melbourne Ct. Giff —4B 118
Melbourne Grn. E Kil —3E 149
Melbourne St. G31 —5B 84
Meldon Pl. G51 —4D 80
Meldrum Gdns. G41 —3B 102
Meldrum Mains. Glenm —5G 71
Meldrum St. Clyd —1F 59
Melford Av. Giff —5B 118
Melford Av. Kirk —5B 30
Melford Gdns. Mill P —4C 94
Melford Rd. Rig I —1H 125
Melford Way. Pais —3D 78
Melfort Av. G41 —1H 101
Melfort Av. Clyd —4D 42
Melfort Path. Newm —2D 146
(off Kildonan Ct.)
Melfort Quad. Moth —4D 128
(off Glenmore Rd.)
Melfort Rd. Ham —6C 140
Mellerstain Rd. G14 —3G 59
Melness Pl. G51 —4D 80
Melrose Av. Chap —3D 112
Melrose Av. Lin —6H 75
Melrose Av. Moth —1B 128
Melrose Av. Pais —4E 97
Melrose Av. Ruth —6D 104
Melrose Ct. Ruth —6D 104
(off Dunard Rd.)
Melrose Cres. Wis —4G 145
Melrose Gdns. G20 —6D 62
Melrose Gdns. Kils —1C 32
(off Glen Shirva Rd.)
Melrose Gdns. Udd —4D 108
Melrose Pl. Blan —6A 124
Melrose Pl. Coat —4B 90
Melrose Pl. Lark —4E 161
Melrose Rd. Cumb —6G 35
Melrose St. G4 —1E 83
Melrose St. Ham —4F 141
Melrose Ter. E Kil —6H 137
Melrose Ter. Ham —3F 141
Melvaig Pl. G20 —4B 62
Melvick Pl. G51 —4D 80
Melville Dri. Moth —3G 143
Melville Gdns. B'rig —5C 48
Melville Pk. E Kil —6B 138
Melville Pl. Carl —3E 165
Melville St. G41 —2D 102
Memel St. G21 —4A 64
Memus Av. G52 —1C 100
Mennock Ct. Ham —1C 152
Mennock Dri. B'rig —3C 48
Mennock St. Cle —5H 129
Menock Rd. G44 —1F 119
Menteith Av. B'rig —6D 48
Menteith Dri. Ruth —5F 121
Menteith Gdns. Bear —5C 24
Menteith Loan. Moth —2A 128
Menteith Pl. Ruth —5F 121
Menteith Rd. Moth —2G 143
Menteith St. Moth —2G 143
Menzies Dri. G21 —4C 64
Menzies Pl. G21 —4C 64
Menzies Rd. G21 —4D 64
Merchant La. G1 —5G 83
Merchants Clo. Kilb —2A 94
Merchiston Av. Lin —6F 75
Merchiston Dri. Brkfld —6D 74
Merchiston St. G32 —4G 85
Merkins Av. Dumb —1H 17
Merkland Ct. G11 —2H 81
Merkland Dri. Kirk —4G 31
Merkland Rd. Coat —1G 89
Merkland St. G11 —1H 81
Merksworth Way. Pais —4H 77
(off Mosslands Rd.)
Merlewood Av. Both —3F 125
Merlin Av. Bell —6C 110
Merlinford Av. Renf —6G 59
Merlinford Cres. Renf —6G 59
Merlinford Dri. Renf —6G 59
Merlinford Way. Renf —6G 59
Merlin Way. Pais —4D 78
Merrick Ct. Air —1B 92
Merrick Gdns. G51 —6H 81
Merrick Gdns. Bear —6C 24
Merrick Path. G51 —6H 81
(off Merrick Gdns.)
Merrick Ter. Udd —6F 109
Merrick Way. Ruth —4D 120
Merryburn Av. Giff —2B 118
Merrycrest Av. Giff —3A 118
Merrycroft Av. Giff —3B 118
Merryflats. Twe —1D 32
Merryland Pl. G51 —4A 82
Merryland St. G51 —4H 81
(in two parts)
Merrylee Cres. Giff —2A 118
Merrylee Pk. Av. Giff —3A 118
Merrylee Pk. M. Giff —2A 118
Merrylee Rd. G43 & G44 —2B 118
Merrylees Rd. Blan —2A 140
Merryston Ct. Coat —5A 90
Merrystone St. Coat —4B 90
Merry St. Moth —2G 143
(in two parts)
Merryton Av. G15 —4B 44
Merryton Av. Giff —3A 118
Merryton Rd. Lark —5H 155
Merryton Rd. Moth —1B 156
Merryton St. Lark —6H 155
Merryton Tower. Moth —1B 156
Merryvale Av. Giff —2B 118
Merryvale Pl. Giff —2A 118
Merton Dri. G52 —6A 80
Meryon Gdns. G32 —3D 106
Meryon Rd. G32 —2D 106
Methil St. G14 —6C 60
Methlan Pk. Dumb —5D 16
Methlick Av. Air —1G 111
Methuen Rd. Pais —2B 78
Methven Av. Bear —2H 45
Methven Pl. E Kil —1E 149
Methven Rd. Giff —3G 133
Methven St. G31 —2F 105
Methven St. Clyd —3B 42
Metropole La. G1 —5G 83
Mews La. Pais —4B 78
Michael McParland Dri. Torr —5D 28
Michael Ter. Chap —4D 112
Micklehouse Oval. Bail —5H 87
Micklehouse Pl. Bail —5H 87
Micklehouse Rd. Bail —5H 87
Micklehouse Wynd. Bail —5H 87
Midas Pl. Bell —2G 127
Mid Barrwood Rd. Kils —4A 12
Mid Carbarns. Wis —2D 156
Midcroft. B'rig —4A 48
Midcroft Av. G44 —2H 119
Middlefield. E Kil —6G 149
Middlehouse Ct. Carl —3D 164
Middlemuir Av. Kirk —2D 50
Middlemuir Rd. Lenz —1D 50
Middle Pk. Pais —3H 97
Middlerigg Rd. Cumb —3F 35
Middlesex St. G41 —6C 82
Middleton Av. Stru I —5F 161
Middleton Cres. Pais —5F 77
Middleton Dri. Miln —3H 25
Middleton Rd. Lin —5A 76
Middleton Rd. Pais —5F 77
Middleton St. G51 —5A 82
Middleward St. Clyd —6F 23
Midland St. G1 —4F 83 (6C 4)
Midlem Dri. G52 —6C 80
Midlem Oval. G52 —6C 80
Midlock St. G51 —6A 82
Midlothian Dri. G41 —4B 102
Mid Park. E Kil —3G 149
Mid Rd. Cumb —1H 55
Midton Rd. How —6B 94
Midton St. G21 —6B 64
Mid Wharf St. G4 —1G 83
Migvie Pl. G20 —4B 62
Milford. E Kil —4D 148
Milford St. G33 —3A 86
Millands Av. Blan —6A 124
Millarbank St. G21 —5A 64
Millars Pl. Lenz —3D 50
Millarston Av. Pais —1E 97
Millarston Ct. Pais —1F 97
Millarston Dri. Pais —1E 97
Millarston Ind. Est. Pais —2E 97
Millar St. Pais —6B 78
Millar Ter. Ruth —1D 104
Millbank Av. Bell —4D 126
Millbank Rd. Wis —2F 157
Millbeg Cres. G33 —5E 87
Millbeg Pl. G33 —6E 87
Mill Brae. Bri W —3F 73
Millbrae Av. Chry —1B 68
Millbrae Ct. G42 —6D 102
Millbrae Ct. Coat —6H 89
Millbrae Cres. G42 —6C 102
Millbrae Cres. Clyd —2F 59
Millbrae Gdns. G42 —6D 102
Millbrae Rd. G43 & G42 —6C 102
Millbrix Av. G14 —4A 60
Millbrook. E Kil —1D 148
Millburn Av. Clyd —1G 59
Millburn Av. Renf —6F 59
Millburn Av. Ruth —1C 120
Millburn Ct. E Kil —4A 148
Millburn Cres. Dumb —4H 17
Millburn Dri. Renf —6G 59
Millburn Gdns. E Kil —4A 148
Millburn La. Lark —3G 161
Millburn Pl. Lark —5F 161
Millburn Rd. Ashg —4B 162
Millburn Rd. Dumb —4H 17
Millburn Rd. Renf —6F 59
Millburn St. G21 —2C 84
Millburn St. Len —3F 7
Millburn St. Moth —2G 143
Millburn Way. E Kil —4A 148
Millburn Way. Renf —6G 59
Mill Ct. Ham —1G 153
Mill Ct. Ruth —5C 104
Mill Cres. G40 —2B 104
Mill Cres. Torr —4E 29
Millcroft Rd. Cumb —3G 55
Millcroft Rd. Cumb —4B 36
(Carbrain)
Millcroft Rd. Ruth —3B 104
Milldam Rd. Clyd —6E 23
Miller Ct. Dumb —3H 17
Millerfield Pl. G40 —2D 104
Millerfield Pl. Ham —6B 142
Millerfield Rd. G40 —2D 104
Millersneuk Av. Lenz —3D 50
Millersneuk Ct. Lenz —3D 50
Millersneuk Cres. G33 —4A 66
Millersneuk Dri. Lenz —3D 50
Millersneuk Rd. Lenz —3D 50
Miller's Pl. Air —4B 92
Millerston St. G40 —5C 84
Miller St. G1 —4G 83 (6E 5)
Miller St. Bail —1H 107
Miller St. Carl —3F 165
Miller St. Clyd —6D 42
Miller St. Coat —6D 90
Miller St. Dumb —3H 17
Miller St. Ham —6B 142
Miller St. John —2H 95
Miller St. Lark —2E 161
Miller St. Wis —6G 145
Millfield Av. Ersk —6D 40
Millfield Av. Moth —1H 143
Millfield Cres. Ersk —6E 41
Millfield Dri. Ersk —6E 41
Millfield Gdns. Ersk —6D 40
(East Craigend)
Millfield Gdns. Ersk —6E 41
(West Craigend)
Millfield Hill. Ersk —6D 40
Millfield La. Ersk —6D 40
Millfield Pl. Ersk —6D 40
Millfield View. Ersk —6D 40
Millfield Wlk. Ersk —1E 57
Millfield Wynd. Ersk —6D 40
Millford Dri. Lin —6H 75
Millgate. Udd —5D 108
Millgate Av. Udd —5D 108
Millgate Ct. Udd —6D 108
Millgate Rd. Ham —2G 153
Mill Gro. Ham —1G 153
Millheugh. Lark —3C 160
Millheugh Brae. Lark —3C 160
Millheugh Pl. Blan —3A 140
Millheugh Rd. Ham —6C 160
Millheugh Rd. Lark —3C 160
Millholm Rd. G44 —3F 119
Millhouse Cres. G20 —2A 62
Millhouse Dri. G20 —2H 61
Millichen Rd. G23 —3B 46
Milliken Dri. Mill P —3C 94
Milliken Pk. Rd. Mill P —4C 94
MILLIKENPARK STATION. John —5C 94
Milliken Rd. Mill P —3C 94
Mill Loan. Air —3A 92
Mill of Gryffe Rd. Bri W —3F 73
Mill Pk. Ham —1G 153
Mill Pl. Lin —5G 75
Millport Av. G44 —6G 103
Millrig. E Kil —6F 149
Mill Rise. Lenz —3D 50
Mill Rd. Air —2A 92
Mill Rd. Both —6E 125
Mill Rd. Camb —1C 122
Mill Rd. Carl —4E 165
Mill Rd. Clyd —2F 59
Mill Rd. Moth —2H 143
Mill Rd. Queen —4C 10
Mill Rd. Wis —6G 147
Millroad Dri. G40 —5A 84
Millroad Gdns. G40 —5B 84
(off Millroad Dri.)
Millroad St. G40 —5A 84
(in two parts)
Millstream Ct. Pais —1B 98
Mill St. G40 —2B 104
Mill St. Pais —1B 98
Mill St. Ruth —5C 104
(in two parts)
Millview. Barr —4F 115
Millview Meadows. Neil —2C 130
Millview Pl. G53 —3B 116
Millview Ter. Neil —2C 130
Mill Way. Kirk —6G 31
Millwood St. G41 —5C 102
Milnbank St. G31 —3C 84
Milncroft Pl. G33 —2A 86
Milncroft Rd. G33 —2A 86
Milner La. G13 —4E 61
Milner Rd. G13 —4E 61
Milngavie Rd. Bear —4F 45
MILNGAVIE STATION. Miln —4H 25
Milnpark Gdns. G41 —6B 82
Milnpark St. G41 —6C 82
Milnwood Dri. Bell —3E 127
Milnwood Dri. Moth —5E 127
Milovaig Av. G23 —6B 46
Milovaig St. G23 —6B 46
Milrig Rd. Ruth —6B 104
Milroy Gdns. Bell —5C 110
Milton Av. Camb —2G 121
Milton Brae. Milt —1F 19
Milton Ct. Air —3A 92
Milton Ct. Kirk —5E 31
(off Highfield Rd.)
Milton Ct. Milt —3F 19
Milton Cres. Carl —4F 165
Milton Douglas Rd. Clyd —2C 42
Milton Dri. B'rig —2B 64
Milton Gdns. Udd —5C 108
Milton Hill. Milt —4F 19
Milton Mains Rd. Dun —2C 42
Milton Rd. Carl —5B 164
Milton Rd. E Kil —1C 148
Milton Rd. Kirk —3C 30
Milton Rd. Len —4G 7
Milton St. G4 —2F 83 (2D 4)
Milton St. Air —3A 92
Milton St. Carl —3E 165
Milton St. Ham —5E 141
Milton St. Moth —1G 143
Milton Ter. Ham —4E 141
Milverton Av. Bear —1C 44
Milverton Rd. Giff —6G 117
Mimosa Rd. Bri W —3F 73
Minard Rd. G41 —4C 102
Minard Way. Udd —6E 109
Mincher Cres. Moth —5G 143
Minch Way. Air —6C 92
Minella Gdns. Bell —5C 110
Minerva Ct. G3 —3C 82
(off Houldsworth St.)
Minerva St. G3 —3C 82
Minerva Way. G3 —3B 82
Mingarry La. G20 —5C 62
Mingarry St. G20 —5C 62
Mingulay Cres. G22 —1H 63
Mingulay Pl. G22 —1A 64
Mingulay St. G22 —1H 63
Minister's Pk. E Kil —5B 136
Minmoir Rd. G53 —6H 99
Minster Wlk. Bail —6D 88
Minstrel Rd. G13 —6D 44
Minto Av. Ruth —3F 121
Minto Cres. G52 —6F 81
Minto Pk. Wis —3A 146
Minto St. G52 —6F 81
Mireton St. G22 —4F 63
Mirren Dri. Clyd —6B 22
Mirrlees Dri. G12 —5A 62
Mirrlees La. G12 —5A 62
Mitchell Arc. Ruth —5D 104
Mitchell Av. Camb —1E 123
Mitchell Av. Renf —1D 78
Mitchell Ct. E Kil —1E 149
Mitchell Dri. Miln —4A 26
Mitchell Dri. Ruth —1D 120
Mitchell Gro. E Kil —1E 149
Mitchell Hill Rd. G45 —5B 120
Mitchell La. G1 —4F 83 (5D 4)
Mitchell Rd. Cumb —3A 36
Mitchell St. G1 —4F 83 (6D 4)
Mitchell St. Air —3H 91
Mitchell St. Coat —1F 109
Mitchison Rd. Cumb —2A 36
Mitre Ct. G11 —5F 61
Mitre La. G14 —5E 61
Mitre La. W. G14 —5D 60
Mitre Rd. G11 —5F 61
Mitre Rd. G14 —5D 60
Moat Av. G13 —2C 60
Mochrum Rd. G43 —1C 118
Moffat Ct. E Kil —4A 148
Moffat Gdns. E Kil —4A 148
Moffathill. Air —6E 93
Moffat Pl. Air —3F 93
Moffat Pl. Blan —6B 124
Moffat Pl. Coat —1F 111
Moffat Pl. E Kil —4A 148
Moffat Rd. Air —4F 93
Moffat St. G5 —1H 103
Moffat View. Plain —1C 93
Mogarth Av. Pais —5D 96
Moidart Av. Renf —5D 58
Moidart Ct. Barr —3D 114
Moidart Cres. G52 —6F 81
Moidart Gdns. Kirk —4H 31
Moidart Gdns. Newt M —3E 133
Moidart Pl. G52 —6F 81
Moidart Rd. G52 —6E 81
Moir St. G1 —5H 83
Molendinar St. G1 —5H 83
Molendinar Ter. Neil —3C 130
Mollinsburn Rd. Cumb —3A 54
Mollinsburn Rd. Glenb —6B 54
Mollinsburn St. G21 —6A 64
Mollins Ct. Cumb —1E 53
Mollins Rd. Cumb —1G 53
Mollins Roundabout. Cumb —3H 53
Monach Rd. G33 —3C 86
Monar Dri. G22 —6F 63
Monar Pl. G22 —6F 63
Monar St. G22 —6F 63
Monart Pl. G20 —5D 62
Monar Way. Newm —3D 146
(off Murdostoun View)
Moncrieff Av. Lenz —2C 50
Moncrieffe Rd. Chap —1D 112
Moncrieff St. Pais —6A 78
Moncur St. G40 —5A 84
(in two parts)
Moness Dri. G52 —1E 101
Money Gro. Moth —5B 144
Moniebrugh Cres. Kils —2A 12
Moniebrugh Rd. Kils —2A 12
Monifieth Av. G52 —2D 100
Monkcastle Dri. Camb —1A 122
Monkie Gdns. B'rig —6F 49
Monkland Av. Kirk —6D 30
Monkland La. Coat —1A 110
Monklands Ind. Est. Coat —3B 110
Monkland St. Air —4B 92
Monkland Ter. Glenb —3H 69
Monkland View. C'bnk —3B 112
Monkland View. Udd —4E 109
Monkland View Cres. Barg —1D 108
Monksbridge Av. G13 —6C 44
Monkscourt Av. Air —3G 91
Monkscroft Av. G11 —6G 61
Monkscroft Ct. G11 —1G 81
Monkscroft Gdns. G11 —6G 61
Monks Rd. Air —1C 112
Monkton Dri. G15 —5B 44
Monkton Gdns. Newt M —5G 133
Monmouth Av. G12 —3G 61
Monreith Av. Bear —5D 44
Monreith Rd. G43 —1B 118
Monreith Rd. E. G44 —2E 119
Monroe Dri. Udd —4D 108
Monroe Pl. Udd —4D 108
Montague La. G12 —5H 61
Montague St. G4 —1D 82
Montalto Av. Moth —6A 128
Montclair Pl. Lin —5H 75
Montego Grn. E Kil —2C 148
Monteith Dri. Clar —1D 134
Monteith Gdns. Clar —1D 134
Monteith Pl. G40 —6A 84
Monteith Pl. Blan —1C 140
Monteith Row. G40 —5H 83
Montford Av. G44 —6H 103
Montford Av. Ruth —6A 104
Montgomery Av. Coat —4B 90
Montgomery Av. Pais —4D 78
Montgomery Cres. Wis —2E 157
Montgomery Dri. Giff —6A 118
Montgomery Dri. Kilb —1A 94
Montgomery Pl. E Kil —1H 149
Montgomery Pl. Lark —3F 161
Montgomery Rd. Pais —3C 78
Montgomery St. Camb —2D 122
Montgomery St. E Kil —1H 149
Montgomery St. Lark —1E 161
Montgomery Ter. G40 —1C 104
Montgomery Ter. Milt C —6B 8
Montraive St. Ruth —4E 105
Montrave St. G52 —1D 100
Montreal Pk. E Kil —2E 149
Montrose Av. G32 —4B 106
Montrose Av. G52 —3G 79
Montrose Ct. Pais —5D 96
Montrose Cres. Ham —5G 141
Montrose Dri. Bear —6E 25
Montrose Gdns. Blan —5A 124
Montrose Gdns. Kils —2G 11
Montrose Gdns. Miln —2H 25
Montrose Pl. Lin —5G 75
Montrose Rd. Pais —5D 96
Montrose St. G1 —4H 83 (5G 5)
Montrose St. Clyd —5D 42
Montrose St. Moth —6F 127
Montrose Ter. B'rig —2E 65
Montrose Ter. Bri W —4F 73
Montrose Way. Pais —5D 96
Monymusk Gdns. B'rig —5F 49
Monymusk Pl. G15 —2G 43
Moodiesburn St. G33 —1F 85
Moorburn Av. Giff —4H 117
Moorburn Pl. Lin —5E 75
Moorcroft Dri. Air —4E 93
Moorcroft Rd. Newt M —6C 132
Moore Dri. Bear —4F 45
Moore Gdns. Ham —4A 154
Moore St. G40 —5B 84
Moore St. Moth —4A 128
Moorfield Rd. Blan —3A 140
Moorfoot. B'rig —5E 49
Moorfoot Av. Pais —4H 97
Moorfoot Av. T'bnk —4G 117
Moorfoot Dri. Wis —6F 145
Moorfoot Path. Pais —5H 97
Moorfoot St. G32 —5G 85
Moorfoot Way. Bear —5B 24
Moorhill Cres. Newt M —6C 132
Moorhill Rd. Newt M —5C 132
Moorhouse Av. G13 —3H 59
Moorhouse Av. Pais —3F 97
Moorhouse St. Barr —5E 115
Moorings, The. Pais —2F 97
Moorland Dri. Air —4F 93
Moorpark Av. G52 —5H 79
Moorpark Av. Air —4E 93
Moorpark Av. Muirh —2A 68
Moorpark Sq. Renf —1D 78
Moor Rd. Miln —3H 25
Moorside St. Carl —3G 165
Morag Av. Blan —6A 124
Moraine Av. G15 —6A 44
Moraine Cir. G15 —6A 44
Moraine Dri. G15 —6A 44
Moraine Dri. Clar —1B 134
Moraine Pl. G15 —6B 44
Morar Av. Clyd —3D 42
Morar Ct. Clyd —3D 42

Cumb —5D 34
Ham —2E 153
...ar Cres. Air —1G 91
Morar Cres. B'rig —5B 48
Morar Cres. B'ton —5A 40
Morar Cres. Clyd —3D 42
Morar Cres. Coat —2H 89
Morar Dri. Bear —4H 45
Morar Dri. Clyd —3D 42
Morar Dri. Cumb —6D 34
Morar Dri. Lin —6G 75
Morar Dri. Pais —3D 96
Morar Dri. Ruth —4D 120
Morar Pl. E Kil —6H 137
Morar Pl. Newt M —2D 132
Morar Pl. Renf —5D 58
Morar Rd. G52 —6E 81
Morar Rd. Clyd —3D 42
Morar St. Wis —2G 157
Morar Ter. Ruth —4F 121
Morar Ter. Udd —6F 109
Morar Way. Moth —4C 128
Moravia Av. Both —4E 125
Moray Av. Air —6A 92
Moray Dri. Clar —2D 134
Moray Dri. Torr —4D 28
Moray Gdns. Clar —1D 134
Moray Gdns. Cumb —6H 13
Moray Gdns. Udd —5D 108
Moray Ga. Both —3C 124
Moray Pl. G41 —3C 102
Moray Pl. B'rig —6E 49
Moray Pl. Blan —3A 140
Moray Pl. Chry —1B 68
Moray Pl. Kirk —4G 31
Moray Pl. Lin —5G 75
Moray Quad. Bell —2C 126
Moray Way. Moth —2A 128
Mordaunt St. G40 —2C 104
Moredun Cres. G32 —4C 86
Moredun Dri. Pais —4F 97
Moredun Rd. Pais —4F 97
Moredun St. G32 —4C 86
Morefield Rd. G51 —4D 80
Morgan M. G42 —2F 103
Morgan St. Ham —1H 153
Morgan St. Lark —2D 160
Morina Gdns. G53 —4C 116
Morion Rd. G13 —1D 60
Morison Ho. Cumb —3A 36
(off Burns Rd.)
Moriston Ct. Newm —3D 146
Morland. E Kil —4D 138
Morley St. G42 —6E 103
Morna La. G14 —1E 81
(off Glendore St.)
Morningside Rd. Newm —4E 147
Morningside St. G33 —3F 85
Morrin Path. G21 —6A 64
Morrin St. G21 —5A 64
Morris Cres. Blan —2B 140
Morris Cres. Moth —6E 129
Morrishall Rd. E Kil —5C 138
Morrison Dri. Len —4G 7
Morrison Gdns. Torr —5E 29
Morrison Quad. Clyd —6G 43
Morrison St. G5 —5E 83
Morrison St. Clyd —1B 42
Morris St. Ham —2H 153
Morris St. Lark —4G 161
Morriston Cres. Renf —2H 79
Morriston Pk. Dri. Camb —6A 106
Morriston St. Camb —1A 122
Morton Gdns. G41 —4A 102
Morton St. Moth —1G 143
Morvan St. G52 —6E 81
Morven Av. B'rig —6E 49
Morven Av. Blan —6A 124
Morven Av. Pais —5H 97
Morven Ct. Air —1B 92
Morven Dri. Clar —1B 134
Morven Dri. Lin —6G 75
Morven Gait. Ersk —1A 58
Morven Gdns. Udd —5D 108
Morven La. Blan —6A 124
Morven Rd. Bear —1E 45
Morven Rd. Camb —4H 121
Morven St. Coat —3C 90
Morven Way. Both —4F 125
Mosesfield St. G21 —4B 64
Mossacre Rd. Wis —5A 146
Moss Av. Lin —5H 75
Mossbank. Blan —2B 110
Mossbank. E Kil —3B 148
Mossbank Av. G33 —5H 65
Mossbank Cres. Moth —3F 129
Mossbank Dri. G33 —5H 65
Mossbank Rd. Wis —5A 146
Mossbell Rd. Bell —1A 126
Mossblown St. Lark —2D 160
Mossburn Rd. Wis —6B 146
Mossburn St. Wis —2B 158
Mosscastle Rd. G33 —1C 86
Mossdale. E Kil —6E 137
Mossdale Ct. Bell —2F 127
Mossdale Gdns. Ham —1C 152
Moss Dri. Barr —2C 114
Moss Dri. Ersk —2F 57
Mossedge Ind. Est. Lin —5A 76
Mossend La. G33 —3D 86
Mossend St. G33 —3D 86
Mossgeil Ter. Blan —5A 124
Mossgiel. E Kil —4D 148
Mossgiel Av. Ruth —2C 120
Mossgiel Cres. Clar —4D 134
Mossgiel Dri. Clyd —4E 43
Mossgiel Gdns. Kirk —4F 31
Mossgiel Gdns. Udd —5C 108
Mossgiel La. Lark —4G 161
(off Donaldson Rd.)
Mossgiel Rd. G43 —1B 118
(in two parts)
Mossgiel Rd. Cumb —2B 36
(in two parts)
Mossgiel Way. Moth —3C 128
Mosshall Gro. Moth —3F 129
Mosshall Rd. Moth —6D 112
Mosshall St. Moth —3F 129
Mosshead Rd. Bear —6F 25
Moss Heights Av. G52 —6D 80
Mosshill Rd. Bell —5D 110
Moss Knowe. Cumb —3C 36
Mossland Dri. Wis —5A 146
Mossland Rd. G52 —3F 79
Mossland Rd. Renf —2H 79
Mosslands Rd. Pais —3H 77
Mosslingal. E Kil —6G 149
Mossmulloch. E Kil —6G 149
Mossneuk Av. E Kil —4A 148
Mossneuk Cres. Wis —5B 146
Mossneuk Dri. E Kil —4B 148
Mossneuk Dri. Pais —5G 97
Mossneuk Dri. Wis —5A 146
Mossneuk Pk. Wis —5A 146
Mossneuk Rd. E Kil —3B 148
Mossneuk St. Coat —2B 110
Mosspark Av. G52 —2F 101
Mosspark Av. Miln —2G 25
Mosspark Boulevd. G52 —1E 101
Mosspark Dri. G52 —1C 100
Mosspark La. G52 —2E 101
Mosspark Oval. G52 —2E 101
Mosspark Rd. Coat —3H 89
Mosspark Rd. Miln —2G 25
Mosspark Sq. G52 —2E 101
MOSSPARK STATION. G52 —2C 100
Moss Path. Bail —2F 107
Moss Rd. G51 —3D 80
Moss Rd. Air —5A 92
Moss Rd. Bail —2A 68
Moss Rd. Bri W —3G 73
Moss Rd. Cumb —2E 37
Moss Rd. Hous & Lin —6A 56
Moss Rd. Kirk —1B 50
Moss Rd. Waters —6H 31
Moss Rd. Wis —6C 146
Moss Side Av. Air —3G 91
Moss Side Av. Carl —3D 164
Mossside Rd. G41 —4B 102
Moss St. Pais —6A 78
Mossvale Cres. G33 —1C 86
Mossvale La. Pais —5H 77
Mossvale Path. G33 —6C 66
Mossvale Rd. G33 —6B 66
Mossvale Sq. G33 —1B 86
Mossvale Sq. Pais —5H 77
Mossvale St. Pais —4H 77
Mossvale Ter. Bail —4E 53
Mossvale Wlk. G33 —1C 86
Mossvale Way. G33 —1C 86
Mossview Cres. Air —5A 92
Mossview La. G52 —6C 80
Mossview Quad. G52 —6D 80
Mossview Rd. G33 —4E 67
Mosswell Rd. Miln —2H 25
Mossywood Ct. Cumb —6B 34
Mossywood Pl. Cumb —6B 34
Mossywood Rd. Cumb —6B 34
Mote Hill. Ham —4A 142
Mote Hill Rd. Pais —5C 78
Motherwell Bus. Cen. Moth —2H 143
Motherwell Food Pk. Bell —1B 126
Motherwell Rd. Bell —2C 126
Motherwell Rd. Carf —6C 128
Motherwell Rd. Ham —5B 142
Motherwell Rd. Moth —2G 129
MOTHERWELL STATION. Moth —2G 143
Motherwell St. Air —2C 92
Moulin Cir. G52 —1A 100
Moulin Pl. G52 —1A 100
Moulin Rd. G52 —1A 100
Moulin Ter. G52 —1A 100
Mountainblue St. G31 —6D 84
Mt. Annan Dri. G44 —6F 103
Mountblow Rd. Clyd —1H 41
Mt. Cameron Dri. N. E Kil —3A 150
Mt. Cameron Dri. S. E Kil —3A 150
MT. FLORIDA STATION. G42 —5E 103
Mountgarrie Rd. G51 —4D 80
Mt. Harriet Av. Step —3E 67
Mt. Harriet Dri. Step —3D 66
Mountherrick. E Kil —6G 149
Mt. Pleasant Cres. Milt C —5B 8
Mt. Pleasant Pl. Old K —1F 41
(off Mt. Pleasant Rd.)
Mt. Pleasant Rd. Old K —6F 21
Mt. Stewart St. Carl —3E 165
Mount St. G20 —6D 62
Mt. Stuart St. G41 —5C 102
Mount, The. Moth —3F 143
Mt. Vernon Av. G32 —3E 107
Mt. Vernon Av. Coat —4A 90
MOUNT VERNON STATION. Udd —3F 107
Mournian Way. Ham —2H 153
Mowbray. E Kil —5C 138
Mowbray Av. G'csh —4D 68
Moyne Rd. G53 —3A 100
Moy Path. Newm —3D 146
(off Murdostoun View)
Muckcroft Rd. Bail —3H 51
Mugdock Rd. Miln —3G 25
Muirbank Av. Ruth —6B 104
Muirbank Gdns. Ruth —6B 104
Muirbrae Rd. Ruth —3D 120
Muirbrae Way. Ruth —3D 120
Muirburn Av. G44 —3C 118
Muir Ct. G44 —5D 118
Muircroft Dri. Cle —5H 129
Muirdrum Av. G52 —2D 100
Muirdyke Rd. Coat —3H 89
Muirdyke Rd. Glenb —5B 70
Muirdykes Av. G52 —6A 80
Muirdykes Cres. Pais —5F 77
Muirdykes Rd. G52 —6A 80
Muirdykes Rd. Pais —4F 77
Muiredge Ct. Udd —1D 124
Muiredge Ter. Bail —1H 107
Muirend Av. G44 —3D 118
Muirend Rd. G44 —3C 118
MUIREND STATION. G44 —3D 118
Muirfield Ct. G44 —3D 118
Muirfield Cres. G23 —6C 46
Muirfield Meadows. Both —5C 124
Muirfield Rd. Cumb —6A 14
Muirhead-Braehead Interchange. Cumb —2A 36
Muirhead Ct. Bail —1A 108
Muirhead Dri. Lin —6G 75
Muirhead Dri. Moth —3F 129
Muirhead Gdns. Bail —1A 108
Muirhead Ga. Udd —5F 109
Muirhead Gro. Bail —1A 108
Muirhead Rd. Bail —2H 107
Muirhead Rd. Neil —4A 130
Muirhead Roundabout. Cumb —2B 36
Muirhead St. Kirk —6C 30
Muirhead Ter. Moth —5G 143
Muirhead Way. B'rig —6F 49
Muirhill Av. G44 —3C 118
Muirhill Cres. G13 —2A 60
Muirhouse Av. Moth —6B 144
Muirhouse Av. Newm —3F 147
Muirhouse Dri. Moth —1C 156
Muirhouse La. E Kil —3H 149
Muirhouse Pk. Bear —5D 24
Muirhouse Rd. Moth —1B 156
Muirhouse St. G41 —2E 103
Muirhouse Tower. Moth —6B 144
Muirkirk Dri. G13 —2F 61
Muirkirk Dri. Ham —1B 152
Muirlee Rd. Carl —4H 165
Muirlees Cres. Miln —3E 25
Muirmadkin Rd. Bell —2D 126
Muirpark Av. Renf —1E 79
Muirpark Dri. G52 —5A 80
Muirpark Dri. B'rig —1C 64
Muirpark St. G11 —1H 81
Muirpark Ter. B'rig —1B 64
Muir Rd. Dumb —1H 17
Muirshiel Av. G53 —1C 116
Muirshill Cres. G53 —1C 116
Muirshot Rd. Lark —1F 161
Muirside Av. G32 —2E 107
Muirside Av. Kirk —5G 31
Muirside Pl. Wis —3D 146
Muirside Rd. Bail —1H 107
Muirside Rd. Pais —4F 77
Muirside St. Bail —1H 107
Muirskeith Cres. G43 —1D 118
Muirskeith Pl. G43 —1D 118
Muirskeith Rd. G43 —1D 118
Muir St. B'rig —6C 48
Muir St. Blan —3B 140
Muir St. Coat —4A 90
Muir St. Ham —5H 141
Muir St. Lark —2E 161
Muir St. Law —5D 158
Muir St. Moth —1F 143
Muir St. Renf —5F 59
Muir Ter. Pais —4C 78
Muirton Dri. B'rig —4B 48
Muiryfauld Dri. G31 —1G 105
Muiryhall St. Coat —4C 90
Muiryhall St. E. Coat —4D 90
Mulben Cres. G53 —6H 99
Mulben Pl. G53 —6H 99
Mulben Ter. G53 —5H 99
Mulberry Dri. E Kil —6E 149
Mulberry Rd. G43 —2B 118
Mulberry Rd. Udd —4G 109
Mulberry Way. E Kil —6E 149
Mull. Air —6D 92
Mull. E Kil —3C 150
Mullardoch St. G23 —6B 46
(off Rothes Dri.)
Mull Av. Pais —6A 98
Mull Av. Renf —2E 79
Mull Quad. Wis —4C 146
Mull St. G21 —1D 84
Mulvey Cres. Air —4G 91
Mungo Pk. E Kil —3F 149
Munlochy Rd. G51 —4D 80
Munro Ct. Clyd —1B 42
Munro Dri. Milt C —6B 8
Munro La. G13 —4E 61
Munro La. E. G13 —4E 61
Munro Pl. G13 —2E 61
Munro Pl. E Kil —6B 138
Munro Rd. G13 —4E 61
Murano St. G20 —4D 62
Murchison Dri. E Kil —4D 148
Murchison Rd. C'lee —2C 74
Murdoch Ct. John —4E 95
(off Tannahill Cres.)
Murdoch Dri. Miln —5B 26
Murdoch Pl. Moth —4H 127
Murdoch Sq. Bell —6E 111
Murdock Rd. E Kil —3G 149
Murdostoun Gdns. Wis —4H 145
Murdostoun Rd. Wis —1G 147
Murdostoun View. Newm —3D 146
Muriel La. Barr —4E 115
Muriel St. Barr —4E 115
Murray Av. Kils —4H 11
Murrayfield. B'rig —4C 48
Murrayfield Dri. Bear —6E 45
Murrayfield St. G32 —4G 85
Murray Gdns. Milt C —5C 8
Murray Gro. Bear —5B 24
Murrayhill. E Kil —3F 149
Murray Path. Udd —1C 124
Murray Pl. Barr —3F 115
Murray Pl. Dumb —1C 18
Murray Pl. Rig I —6A 110
Murray Rd. Both —4E 125
Murray Rd. Law —1H 163
Murray Rd., The. E Kil —3E 149
Murray Roundabout, The. E Kil —3H 149
Murray Sq., The. E Kil —4G 149
Murray St. Pais —5G 77
Murray St. Renf —6E 59
Murray Ter. Moth —2D 142
Murrin Av. B'rig —6F 49
Murroch Av. Dumb —1H 17
Murroes Rd. G51 —4D 80
Murtonhole Rd. Ham —3H 151
Musgrove Pl. E Kil —3E 149
Muslin St. G40 —1B 104
Muttonhole Rd. Ham —3H 151
Mybster Pl. G51 —4D 80
Myers Cres. Udd —2E 125
Myreside Pl. G32 —5F 85
Myreside St. G32 —5F 85
Myres Rd. G53 —5D 100
Myrie Gdns. B'rig —5D 48
Myroch Pl. G34 —2A 88
Myrtle Av. Lenz —2C 50
Myrtle Dri. Moth —2B 128
Myrtle Dri. Wis —5D 144
Myrtle Hill La. G42 —5G 103
Myrtle La. Lark —4F 161
Myrtle Pk. G42 —4F 103
Myrtle Pl. G42 —4G 103
Myrtle Rd. Clyd —3H 41
Myrtle Rd. Udd —5F 109
Myrtle Sq. B'rig —1C 64
Myrtle St. Blan —6B 124
Myrtle View Rd. G42 —5G 103
Myrtle Wlk. Camb —1H 121
Myvot Av. Cumb —1D 54
Myvot Rd. Cumb —1D 54
(Condorrat)
Myvot Rd. Cumb —3A 54
(Mollinsburn)

Nairn Av. Bell —1C 126
Nairn Av. Blan —5A 124
Nairn Cres. Air —6A 92
Nairn Pl. Clyd —4B 42
Nairn Pl. E Kil —6C 138
Nairn Quad. Wis —4H 145
Nairnside Rd. G21 —2E 65
Nairn St. G3 —2B 82
Nairn St. Blan —3A 140
Nairn St. Clyd —4B 42
Nairn St. Lark —3D 160
Nairn Way. Cumb —6A 14
Naismith St. G32 —5C 106
Naismith Wlk. Bell —6E 111
Nansen St. G20 —6E 63
Napier Ct. Old K —2G 41
Napier Ct. Ward N —3D 14
Napier Cres. Dumb —3C 16
Napier Dri. G51 —3H 81
Napier Gdns. Lin —5A 76
Napier Hill. E Kil —3G 149
Napier La. E Kil —3G 149
Napier Pk. Ward N —4C 14
Napier Pl. G51 —3H 81
Napier Pl. Old K —2G 41
Napier Pl. Ward N —3C 14
Napier Rd. G51 —3H 81
Napier Rd. H'ton I —2H 79
Napier Rd. Ward N —4C 14
Napiershall La. G20 —1D 82
(off Napiershall St.)
Napiershall Pl. G20 —1D 82
Napiershall St. G20 —1D 82
Napier Sq. Bell —6D 110
Napier St. G51 —3H 81
Napier St. Clyd —2E 59
Napier St. John —2E 95
Napier St. Lin —5A 76
Napier Ter. G51 —3H 81
Napier Way. Ward N —4C 14
Naproch Pl. Newt M —4A 134
Naseby Av. G11 —6F 61
Naseby La. G11 —6F 61
Nasmyth Av. Bear —5B 24
Nasmyth Av. E Kil —4H 149
Nasmyth Bank. E Kil —4H 149
Nasmyth Pl. H'ton I —4A 80
Nasmyth Rd. N. H'ton I —4A 80
(in two parts)
Nasmyth Rd. S. H'ton I —4A 80
Nassau Pl. E Kil —2C 148
National Bank La. G1 —4F 83 (5D 4
Navar Pl. Pais —3C 98
Naver St. G33 —2G 85
Naylor La. Air —3B 92
Needle Grn. Carl —3F 165
Neidpath. Bail —1G 107
Neidpath Av. Coat —2D 110
Neidpath E. E Kil —1F 149
Neidpath Pl. Coat —2C 110
Neidpath Rd. Carl —2E 165
Neidpath Rd. E. Giff —3G 133
Neidpath Rd. W. Giff —2G 133
Neidpath W. E Kil —1F 149
Neilsland Dri. Ham —4G 153
Neilsland Dri. Moth —3D 142
Neilsland Oval. G53 —5D 100
Neilsland Rd. Ham —2F 153
Neilsland Sq. G53 —4D 100
Neilsland Sq. Ham —2G 153
Neilsland St. Ham —2G 153
Neilson St. Bell —2C 126
Neilston Av. G53 —2C 116
(in two parts)
Neilston Pl. Kils —2F 11
Neilston Rd. Barr —1E 131
Neilston Rd. Pais —2A 98
NEILSTON STATION. Neil —2D 130
Neilston Wlk. Kils —2G 11
Neil St. Renf —4F 59
Neilvaig Dri. Ruth —4D 120
Nelson Av. Coat —1A 110
Nelson Cres. Moth —5B 144
Nelson Mandela Pl. G2 —3G 83 (4E 5)
Nelson Pl. Bail —1H 107
Nelson St. G5 —5E 83
Nelson St. Bail —1H 107
Nelson Ter. E Kil —3A 150
Neptune St. G51 —4H 81
Neptune Way. Bell —2G 127
Nerston Rd. E Kil —3G 137
Ness Av. John —5C 94
Ness Dri. Blan —6C 124
Ness Dri. E Kil —2B 150
Ness Gdns. B'rig —6D 48
Ness Gdns. Lark —5E 161
Ness Rd. Renf —5D 58
Ness St. G33 —2G 85
Ness St. Wis —3H 157
Ness Ter. Ham —2E 153
Ness Way. Moth —2A 128
Nethan Av. Wis —1C 156
Nethan Ga. Ham —6G 141
Nethan Path. Lark —5E 161
Nethan Pl. Ham —5H 153
Nethan St. G51 —3G 81
Nethan St. Moth —5E 127
Nether Auldhouse Rd. G43 —1H 117
Netherbank Rd. Wis —1D 156
Netherbog Av. Dumb —3H 17
Netherbog Rd. Dumb —3H 17
Netherburn Av. G44 —5D 118
Netherburn Av. Hous —3E 75
Netherburn Gdns. Hous —3E 75
Netherburn Rd. Ashg —5C 162
Netherby Dri. G41 —1B 102
Nethercairn Pl. Newt M —4A 134
Nethercairn Rd. G43 —3A 118
Nethercliffe Av. G44 —5D 118
Nethercommon Ind. Est. Pais —3A 78
Nethercraigs Ct. Pais —6F 97
Nethercraigs Dri. Pais —5G 97
Nethercraigs Rd. Pais —6F 97
Nethercroy Rd. Kils —6A 12
Netherdale. Newt M —4H 133
Netherdale Cres. Wis —1C 156
Netherdale Dri. Pais —1H 99
Netherdale Rd. Wis —1E 157
Nethergreen Wynd. Renf —6D 58
Netherhall Rd. Wis —1D 156
Netherhill Av. G44 —6D 118
Netherhill Cotts. Pais —4C 78
(off Netherhill Rd.)
Netherhill Cres. Pais —5C 78
Netherhill Rd. Chry —6D 52
Netherhill Rd. Pais —5B 78
Netherhill Way. Pais —4D 78
Netherhouse Av. Coat —2B 110

Netherhouse Av. *Lenz* —3E **51**
Netherhouse Pl. *G34* —3C **88**
Netherhouse Rd. *Bail & G34* —4B **88**
Netherlee Rd. *G44* —2E **119**
Nethermains Rd. *Miln* —5G **25**
Netherpark Av. *G44* —6D **118**
Netherplace Cres. *G53* —5B **100**
Netherplace Cres. *Newt M* —5C **132**
Netherplace Rd. *G53* —5B **100**
Netherplace Rd. *Newt M* —5A **132**
Netherton Ct. *G45* —5B **120**
Netherton Ct. *Newt M* —3F **133**
Netherton Dri. *Barr* —5F **115**
Netherton Hill. *Len* —3C **6**
Netherton Ind. Est. *Wis* —1E **157**
Netherton Oval. *Len* —3D **6**
Netherton Rd. *G13* —1E **61**
Netherton Rd. *E Kil* —5E **149**
Netherton Rd. *E Kil* —6C **148**
(Greenhills)
Netherton Rd. *Newt M* —3F **133**
Netherton Rd. *Wis* —1C **156**
Netherton St. *G13* —2F **61**
Netherton St. *Wis* —1F **157**
Nethervale Av. *G44* —6D **118**
Netherview Rd. *G44* —6E **119**
Netherway. *G44* —6D **118**
Netherwood Av. *Cumb* —5C **34**
Netherwood Ct. *Cumb* —5C **34**
Netherwood Gro. *Cumb* —5C **34**
Netherwood Pl. *Cumb* —5B **34**
Netherwood Rd. *Cumb* —5B **34**
Netherwood Rd. *Moth* —6B **144**
Netherwood Tower. *Moth* —1B **156**
Netherwood Way. *Cumb* —5C **34**
Nethy Way. *Renf* —2H **79**
Neuk Av. *Hous* —2C **74**
Neuk Av. *Muirh* —2A **68**
Neuk Cres. *Hous* —1C **74**
Neuk, The. *Wis* —6E **145**
Neuk Way. *G32* —5C **106**
Neville. *E Kil* —4C **138**
Nevis Av. *Ham* —1E **153**
Nevis Ct. *Coat* —2E **111**
Nevis Dri. *Torr* —4D **28**
Nevison St. *Lark* —3F **161**
Nevis Rd. *G43* —2H **117**
Nevis Rd. *Bear* —6B **24**
Nevis Rd. *Renf* —2D **78**
Nevis Way. *Glas A* —2A **78**
Newall Rd. *Pais* —3B **78**
Newark Dri. *G41* —2B **102**
Newark Dri. *Pais* —5G **97**
Newark Dri. *Wis* —3A **146**
Newark Pl. *Wis* —3B **146**
Newarthill Rd. *Moth* —5C **128**
New Ashtree St. *Wis* —6E **145**
Newbarns St. *Carl* —2F **165**
Newbattle Av. *C'bnk* —3B **112**
Newbattle Ct. *G32* —3B **106**
Newbattle Gdns. *G32* —3B **106**
Newbattle Pl. *G32* —3B **106**
Newbattle Rd. *G32* —3A **106**
Newbold Av. *G21* —2A **64**
Newburgh. *Ersk* —4E **41**
Newburgh St. *G43* —6B **102**
Newcastleton Dri. *G23* —6C **46**
New City Rd. *G4* —1E **83** (1A **4**)
(in two parts)
Newcroft Dri. *G44* —2H **119**
Newdyke Av. *Kirk* —5E **31**
Newdyke Rd. *Kirk* —5E **31**
New Edinburgh Rd. *Udd* —6C **108**
Newfield Cres. *Ham* —5F **141**
Newfield La. *Both* —4F **125**
Newfield Pl. *Ruth* —6A **104**
Newfield Pl. *T'bnk* —5F **117**
Newfield Sq. *G53* —1A **116**
Newhall St. *G40* —2B **104**
Newhaven Rd. *G33* —3B **86**
Newhaven St. *G32* —4A **86**
Newhills Rd. *G33* —4E **87**
Newhouse Ind. Est. *Moth* —6C **112**
Newhousemill Rd. *E Kil* —4C **150**
Newhousemill Rd. *Ham* —3H **151**
Newhut Rd. *Moth* —1F **143**
New Inchinnan Rd. *Pais* —4A **78**
Newington St. *G32* —5H **85**
New Kirk Rd. *Bear* —2E **45**
New Lairdsland Rd. *Kirk* —4C **30**
Newlands Dri. *Ham* —3H **153**
Newlandsfield Rd. *G43* —6B **102**
Newlands Gdns. *Eld* —4A **96**
Newlandsmuir Rd. *E Kil* —5B **148**
Newlands Pl. *E Kil* —2G **149**
Newlands Rd. *G43 & G44* —6B **102**
Newlands Rd. *E Kil* —6A **148**
Newlands Rd. *Udd* —5D **108**
Newlands St. *Coat* —1C **110**
Newlands Ter. *Carl* —3F **165**
Newlands Ter. *Milt C* —5C **8**
New La. *C'bnk* —3B **112**
New Luce Dri. *G32* —2D **106**
Newmains Av. *Inch* —4F **57**
Newmains Rd. *Renf* —1D **78**
Newmill Rd. *G21* —4E **65**
Newnham Rd. *Pais* —1G **99**
Newpark Cres. *Camb* —6A **106**
New Pk. St. *Ham* —4G **141**
New Plymouth. *E Kil* —4C **148**
New Rd. *Camb* —3E **123**
Newrose Av. *Bell* —6D **110**
Newshot Ct. Clyd —2F 59
(off Clydeholm Ter.)
Newshot Dri. *Ersk* —5F **41**
New Sneddon St. *Pais* —5A **78**
(in two parts)
Newstead Gdns. *G23* —6C **46**
New Stevenston Rd. *Moth* —5B **128**
New St. *Blan* —2A **140**
New St. *Clyd* —1C **42**
New St. *Kilb* —2A **94**
New St. *Pais* —1A **98**
Newton Av. *Barr* —6F **115**
Newton Av. *Camb* —1D **122**
Newton Av. *Eld* —2C **96**
Newton Av. *Pais* —4D **78**
Newton Brae. *Camb* —1F **123**
Newton Ct. *Newt M* —6D **132**
Newton Dri. *Eld* —2C **96**
Newton Dri. *Newm* —4E **147**
Newton Dri. *Udd* —6E **109**
Newton Farm Rd. *Camb* —6F **107**
Newtongrange Av. *G32* —2B **106**
Newtongrange Gdns. *G32* —3B **106**
Newton Gro. *Newt M* —6D **132**
Newtonlea Av. *Newt M* —5E **133**
Newton Pl. *G3* —2D **82**
Newton Pl. *Newt M* —6E **133**
Newton Rd. *B'ton* —4F **39**
Newton Rd. *Lenz* —3E **51**
NEWTON STATION. *Camb* —2E **123**
Newton Sta. Rd. *Camb* —3E **123**
Newton St. *G3* —3E **83** (3A **4**)
Newton St. *Coat* —1A **110**
Newton St. *Pais* —1G **97**
Newton Ter. G3 —3D 82
(off Sauchiehall St.)
Newton Ter. *Pais* —2D **96**
Newton Ter. La. G3 —3D 82
(off Elderslie St.)
Newton Way. *Pais* —4D **78**
Newtown St. *Kils* —3H **11**
Newtyle Pl. *B'rig* —6F **49**
Newtyle Rd. *Pais* —1D **98**
New View Cres. *Bell* —4C **126**
New View Dri. *Bell* —4C **126**
New View Pl. *Bell* —4C **126**
New Wynd. *G1* —5G **83**
Nicholas St. *G1* —4H **83** (5H **5**)
Nicholson St. *G5* —6F **83**
(in two parts)
Nicklaus Way. *Moth* —6E **113**
Nicolson Ct. *Step* —4D **66**
Nicol St. *Air* —2C **92**
Niddrie Rd. *G42* —3D **102**
Niddrie Sq. *G42* —3D **102**
Niddry St. *Pais* —6B **78**
Nigel Gdns. *G41* —4B **102**
Nigel St. *Moth* —3F **143**
Nigg Pl. *G34* —3G **87**
Nightingale Pl. *John* —6D **94**
Nikitas Av. *Lark* —6F **161**
Nimmo Dri. *G51* —4E **81**
Nimmo Pl. *Carl* —2E **165**
Nimmo Pl. *Wis* —6A **146**
Ninian Av. *Hous* —3C **74**
Ninian Rd. *Air* —6B **92**
Ninian's Rise. *Kirk* —6F **31**
Nisbet St. *G31* —6F **85**
Nisbett Pl. *Chap* —2E **113**
Nisbett St. *Chap* —3E **113**
Nith Av. *Pais* —3D **96**
Nith Dri. *Ham* —3E **153**
Nith Dri. *Renf* —1G **79**
Nith La. Newm —3D 146
(off King St.)
Nith Path. *Cle* —5H **129**
Nith Pl. *John* —5C **94**
Nith Quad. *Moth* —4C **128**
Nithsdale. *E Kil* —6D **138**
Nithsdale Cres. *Bear* —1C **44**
Nithsdale Dri. *G41* —3D **102**
Nithsdale Pl. *G41* —2D **102**
Nithsdale Rd. *G41* —1H **101**
Nithsdale St. *G41* —3D **102**
Nith St. *G33* —2F **85**
Nith Way. *Renf* —1G **79**
Nitshill Rd. *G53 & G46* —1H **115**
NITSHILL STATION. *G53* —2A **116**
Niven St. *G20* —3A **62**
Noble Rd. *Bell* —2C **126**
Nobles Pl. *Bell* —3B **126**
Nobles View. *Bell* —3B **126**
Noldrum Av. *G32* —5C **106**
Noldrum Gdns. *G32* —5C **106**
Norbreck Dri. *Giff* —3A **118**
Norby Rd. *G11* —6F **61**
Noremac Way. *Bell I* —6B **110**
Norfolk Ct. *G5* —6F **83**
Norfolk Cres. *B'rig* —4A **48**
Norfolk St. *G5* —6F **83**
Norham St. *G41* —4C **102**
Norman St. *G40* —2B **104**
Norse La. N. *G14* —5C **60**
Norse La. S. *G14* —5C **60**
Norse Rd. *G14* —5C **60**
Northfield Dri. *G44* —6F **103**
Northall Quad. *Moth* —6A **128**
Northampton Dri. *G12* —3H **61**
Northampton La. G12 —3H 61
(off Northampton Dri.)
North Av. *Camb* —1H **121**
North Av. *Carl* —3D **164**
North Av. *Clyd B* —4C **42**
North Av. *Moth* —5A **128**
Northbank Av. *Camb* —1D **122**
Northbank Av. *Kirk* —5C **30**
N. Bank Pl. *Clyd* —1E **59**
Northbank Rd. *Kirk* —5C **30**
Northbank St. *Camb* —1D **122**
N. Bank St. *Clyd* —1E **59**
N. Barr Av. *Ersk* —4E **41**
N. Berwick Av. *Cumb* —6H **13**
N. Berwick Cres. *E Kil* —5C **148**
N. Berwick Gdns. *Cumb* —6H **13**
N. Biggar Rd. *Air* —3B **92**
N. Birbiston Rd. *Len* —3F **7**
Northbrae Pl. *G13* —3B **60**
North Bri. St. *Air* —3H **91**
N. British Rd. *Udd* —1D **124**
Northburn Av. *Air* —2B **92**
Northburn Pl. *Air* —1B **92**
Northburn Rd. *Coat* —2E **91**
Northburn St. *Plain* —1H **93**
N. Bute St. *Coat* —1D **110**
N. Caldean Rd. *Coat* —6E **91**
N. Calder Dri. *Air* —5D **92**
N. Calder Rd. *Udd* —4G **109**
N. Campbell Av. *Miln* —4F **25**
N. Canal Bank St. *G4* —1G **83**
N. Carbrain Rd. *Cumb* —5G **35**
N. Claremont La. *Miln* —3G **25**
N. Claremont St. *G3* —2C **82**
N. Corsebar Rd. *Pais* —3G **97**
North Ct. *G1* —4G **83** (5E **5**)
North Ct. La. *G1* —4G **83** (5E **5**)
Northcroft Rd. *Chry* —5C **52**
N. Croft St. *Pais* —6B **78**
N. Dean Pk. Av. *Both* —4E **125**
N. Douglas St. *Clyd* —1E **59**
North Dri. *Lin* —5H **75**
N. Dryburgh Rd. *Wis* —4G **145**
N. Dumgoyne Av. *Miln* —2F **25**
N.E.L. Technology Pk. *E Kil* —4A **150**
N. Elgin Pl. *Clyd* —2E **59**
N. Elgin St. *Clyd* —1E **59**
N. Erskine Pk. *Bear* —2D **44**
Northfield. *E Kil* —4B **148**
Northfield Rd. *Kils* —2F **11**
Northfield St. *Moth* —1G **143**
N. Frederick St. *G1* —4G **83** (5F **5**)
N. Gardinar St. *G11* —6H **61**
Northgate Quad. *G21* —2E **65**
Northgate Rd. *G21* —2E **65**
N. Gower St. *G51* —6A **82**
N. Grange Rd. *Bear* —1E **45**
N. Hanover St. *G1* —3G **83** (5F **5**)
Northinch St. *G14* —1D **80**
N. Iverton Pk. Rd. *John* —2G **95**
N. Kilmeny Cres. *Wis* —3A **146**
Northland Av. *G14* —4C **60**
Northland Dri. *G14* —4C **60**
Northland Gdns. *G14* —4C **60**
Northland La. G14 —5C 60
(off Northland Dri.)
North La. *Lin* —5A **76**
N. Lodge Av. *Moth* —5G **143**
N. Lodge Rd. *Renf* —5E **59**
N. Moraine La. *G15* —5C **44**
Northmuir Dri. *Wis* —5B **146**
Northmuir Rd. *G15* —3B **44**
N. Orchard St. *Moth* —2F **143**
North Pk. Av. *T'bnk* —3F **117**
Northpark St. *G20* —5D **62**
N. Portland St. *G1* —4H **83** (5G **5**)
North Rd. *Bell* —2C **126**
North Rd. *Cumb* —5C **34**
North Rd. *John* —3E **95**
North & South Rd. *Moth* —6G **113**
North & South Rd. *Newm* —1C **146**
North Sq. *Coat* —3A **90**
North St. *G3* —2D **82**
North St. *Hous* —1B **74**
North St. *Lark* —1E **161**
North St. *Moth* —1H **143**
North St. *Pais* —5A **78**
Northumberland St. *G20* —5C **62**
North View. *Bear* —5D **44**
N. View Rd. *Bri W* —5H **73**
N. Wallace St. *G4* —2H **83** (2G **5**)
Northway. *Blan* —6A **124**
Northwood Dri. *Newm* —3E **147**
N. Woodside Rd. *G20* —6D **62**
Norval St. *G11* —1G **81**
Norwich Dri. *G12* —4H **61**
Norwood Av. *Kirk* —5B **30**
Norwood Dri. *Giff* —6G **117**
Norwood Pk. *Bear* —4F **45**
Norwood Ter. *Udd* —6E **109**
Nottingham Av. *G12* —3H **61**
Nottingham La. G12 —3H 61
(off Northampton Dri.)
Novar Dri. *G12* —5G **61**
Novar Gdns. *B'rig* —5A **48**
Novar St. *Ham* —1H **153**
Nuneaton St. *G40* —2C **104**
Nuneaton St. Ind. Est. *G40* —2C **104**
Nurseries Rd. *Bail* —5F **87**
Nursery Av. *Ersk* —3C **40**
Nursery Ct. *Carl* —2E **165**
Nursery Dri. *Ashg* —5C **162**
Nursery La. *G41* —3D **102**
Nursery Pl. *Blan* —3B **140**
Nursery St. *G41* —2E **103**
Nutberry Ct. *G42* —4F **103**

Oak Av. *Bear* —6F **25**
Oak Av. *E Kil* —5D **148**
Oakbank Av. *Wis* —2E **157**
Oakbank Dri. *Barr* —6F **115**
Oakbank Ind. Est. *G20* —6F **63**
Oakbank St. *Air* —4D **92**
Oakburn Av. *Miln* —4F **25**
Oakburn Cres. *Miln* —3F **25**
Oak Cres. *Bail* —1G **107**
Oakdene Av. *Bell* —6C **110**
Oakdene Av. *Udd* —6F **109**
Oakdene Cres. *N'hill* —4C **128**
Oak Dri. *Camb* —3C **122**
Oak Dri. *Kirk* —2B **50**
Oak Fern Dri. *E Kil* —5F **137**
Oak Fern Gro. *E Kil* —5F **137**
Oakfield Av. *G12* —1C **82**
Oakfield Dri. *Moth* —3G **143**
Oakfield La. G12 —1C 82
(off Gibson St.)
Oakfield Rd. *Moth* —3G **143**
Oakfield Tower. *Moth* —4G **143**
Oakhill Av. *Bail* —2F **107**
Oak Lea. *Ham* —1B **154**
Oaklea Cres. *Blan* —1A **140**
Oakley Dri. *G44* —4D **118**
Oakley Ter. *G31* —4B **84**
Oak Pk. *B'rig* —6D **48**
Oak Pk. *Moth* —5F **143**
Oak Pl. *Coat* —6E **91**
Oak Pl. *E Kil* —5D **148**
Oak Pl. *Udd* —6G **109**
Oak Rd. *Clyd* —2B **42**
Oak Rd. *Cumb* —1E **37**
Oak Rd. *Pais* —4C **98**
Oakshaw Brae. *Pais* —6H **77**
Oakshawhead. *Pais* —6H **77**
Oakshaw La. W. *Pais* —6H **77**
Oakshaw St. E. *Pais* —6H **77**
Oakside Pl. *Ham* —4H **153**
Oaks, The. *G44* —3F **119**
Oaks, The. *John* —3E **95**
Oakwood Av. *Pais* —4F **97**
Oakwood Dri. *Newt M* —5F **133**
Oakwood View. *Moth* —2B **128**
Oates Gdns. *Moth* —5B **144**
Oatfield St. *G21* —5D **64**
Oban Ct. *G20* —5C **62**
Oban Dri. *G20* —5C **62**
Oban La. *G20* —5C **62**
Observatory La. *G12* —6B **62**
Observatory Rd. *G12* —6A **62**
Ochil Dri. *Barr* —6E **115**
Ochil Dri. *Pais* —5H **97**
Ochil Pl. *G32* —1A **106**
Ochil Rd. *Bear* —6D **24**
Ochil Rd. *B'rig* —6E **49**
Ochil Rd. *Renf* —2D **78**
Ochil St. *G32* —1A **106**
Ochil St. *Wis* —5F **145**
Ochiltree Av. *G13* —2F **61**
Ochiltree Dri. *Ham* —2C **152**
Ochil View. *Udd* —5E **109**
Odence Ct. *E Kil* —5G **149**
Ogilvie Ct. Air —3E 93
(off Katherine St.)
Ogilvie Pl. *G31* —1F **105**
Ogilvie St. *G31* —1F **105**
Old Aisle Rd. *Kirk* —6F **31**
Old Avon Rd. *Ham* —1C **154**
Old Bore Rd. *Air* —3E **93**
Old Bothwell Rd. *Both* —6F **125**
Old Bridgend. *Carl* —4F **165**
Old Bridge of Weir Rd. *Hous* —1A **74**
Old Castle Rd. *G44* —3F **119**
Old Castle St. *G44* —1E **119**
Old Church Gdns. *Barg* —6E **89**
Old Coach Rd. *E Kil* —6H **137**
Old Dalmarnock Rd. *G40* —1B **104**
Old Dalnottar Rd. *Old K* —2F **41**
Old Dumbarton Rd. *G3* —2A **82**
Old Edinburgh Rd. *Udd* —4B **108**
Old Ferry Rd. *Ersk* —3D **40**
Old Gartloch Rd. *G'csh* —5D **68**
Old Glasgow Rd. *Cumb* —1H **35**
Old Glasgow Rd. *Udd* —6B **108**
(in two parts)
Old Govan Rd. *Renf* —6H **59**
Old Greenock Rd. *B'ton & Ersk* —2A **38**
Old Greenock Rd. *Inch* —1F **57**
Oldhall Rd. *Pais* —6E **79**
Old Humbie Rd. *Newt M* —6E **133**
Old Inns Interchange. *Cumb* —6C **14**
Old Inns Roundabout. *Cumb* —5B **14**
Old Lanark Rd. *Carl* —4F **165**
(in two parts)
Old Manse Rd. *G32* —1D **106**
Old Manse Rd. *Wis* —3E **157**
Old Mill Pk. Ind. Est. *Kirk* —4C **30**
Old Mill Rd. *Both* —6E **125**
Old Mill Rd. *Clyd* —1C **42**
Old Mill Rd. *E Kil* —1H **149**
Old Mill Rd. *Udd* —2D **124**
(in two parts)
Old Mill View. *Croy* —1B **34**
Old Monkland Rd. *Coat* —2H **109**
Old Moor Rd. *Pais* —2F **97**
Old Playfield Rd. *Crmck* —1H **135**
Old Quarry Rd. *Cumb* —2H **53**
Old Renfrew Rd. *G51* —1A **80**
Old Rd. *Eld* —2H **95**
Old Rutherglen Rd. *G5* —6G **83**
Old Schoolhouse La. *Hous* —1B **74**
Old Shettleston Rd. *G32* —6H **85**
Old Sneddon St. *Pais* —6A **78**
Old Stable Row. *Coat* —4D **90**
Old St. *Clyd* —1B **42**
Old Union St. *Air* —4B **92**
Old Vic Ct. E Kil —5B 138
(off Bosworth Rd.)
Old Wishaw Rd. *Carl* —2E **165**
Old Wishaw Rd. *Law* —5F **159**
Old Wood Rd. *Bail* —2G **107**
Old Wynd. *G1* —5G **83**
Olifard Av. *Both* —4F **125**
Oliphant Ct. *Pais* —5D **96**
Oliphant Cres. *Clar* —4C **134**
Oliphant Cres. *Pais* —5C **96**
Oliphant Oval. *Pais* —5C **96**
Olive Bank. *Udd* —4G **109**
Olive Ct. Moth —2B 128
(off Elm Rd.)
Olive St. *G33* —5F **65**
Olympia. *E Kil* —2H **149**
Olympia Arc. E Kil —3H 149
(off Olympia Ct.)
Olympia Ct. *E Kil* —2H **149**
Olympia St. *G40* —6B **84**
Olympia, The. E Kil —3H 149
(off Olympia Ct.)
Omoa Rd. *Cle* —6G **129**
O'Neill Av. *B'rig* —1D **64**
Onslow. *E Kil* —4E **149**
Onslow Dri. *G31* —4C **84**
Onslow Rd. *Clyd* —5E **43**
Onslow Sq. *G31* —4C **84**
Ontario Pk. *E Kil* —2D **148**
Ontario Pl. *E Kil* —2D **148**
Onyx St. *Bell* —3C **126**
Oran Gdns. *G20* —4C **62**
Oran Ga. *G20* —4C **62**
Oran Pl. *G20* —5C **62**
Oran St. *G20* —4C **62**
Orbiston Ct. *Moth* —4A **144**
Orbiston Dri. *Bell* —4D **126**
Orbiston Dri. *Clyd* —6F **23**
Orbiston Gdns. *G32* —6A **86**
Orbiston Pl. *Clyd* —6F **23**
Orbiston Rd. *Bell* —5D **126**
(Community Rd.)
Orbiston Rd. *Bell* —3B **126**
(Hamilton Rd.)
Orbiston Sq. *Bell* —4B **126**
Orbiston St. *Moth* —3H **143**
Orb Ter. *Neil* —3C **130**
Orcades Dri. *G44* —3F **119**
Orchard Av. *Both* —6F **125**
Orchard Brae. *Kirk* —3E **51**
Orchard Ct. *G32* —5B **106**
Orchard Ct. *T'bnk* —4G **117**
Orchard Dri. *Blan* —1A **140**
Orchard Dri. *Giff* —4H **117**
Orchard Dri. *Ruth* —5B **104**
Orchard Field. *Lenz* —3E **51**
Orchard Ga. *Lark* —3E **161**
Orchard Grn. *E Kil* —5B **138**
Orchard Gro. *Coat* —5D **90**
Orchard Gro. *Giff* —3H **117**
Orchard Pk. *Giff* —4A **118**
Orchard Pk. Av. *T'bnk* —3G **117**
Orchard Pk. Trad. Est. *Giff* —5A **118**
Orchard Pl. *Bell* —4B **126**
Orchard Pl. *Ham* —6H **141**
Orchard Pl. *Kirk* —6G **31**
Orchard St. *Bail* —2F **107**
Orchard St. *Carl* —4F **165**
Orchard St. *Ham* —6A **142**
Orchard St. *Moth* —2F **143**
Orchard St. *Pais* —1A **98**
Orchard St. *Renf* —5F **59**
Orchard St. *Wis* —5H **157**
Orchardton Rd. *Cumb* —2H **53**
(Mollinsburn)
Orchardton Rd. *Cumb* —1G **53**
(Westfield Ind. Area)
Orchardton Woods Ind. Pk. *Cumb* —5G **33**
Orchy Av. *Clar* —6D **118**
Orchy Ct. *Clyd* —2E **43**
Orchy Cres. *Air* —6C **92**
Orchy Cres. *Bear* —5D **44**
Orchy Cres. *Pais* —4D **96**
Orchy Dri. *Clar* —6D **118**
Orchy Gdns. *Clar* —6D **118**
Orchy St. *G44* —1E **119**
Orchy Ter. *E Kil* —2B **150**
Orefield Pl. *E Kil* —6G **137**
Oregon Pl. *G5* —1G **103**
Orion Pl. *Bell* —2G **127**
Orion Way. *Camb* —1A **122**
Orion Way. *Carl* —3D **164**

Orkney Pl. G51 —4H 81
Orkney Quad. Wis —5B 146
Orkney St. G51 —4H 81
Orlando. E Kil —4C 138
Orleans Av. G14 —6E 61
Orleans La. G14 —6E 61
(off Victoria Pk. Dri. N.)
Orlington Ct. Coat —3B 90
Ormiston Av. G14 —5C 60
Ormiston Dri. Ham —3G 153
Ormiston La. G14 —5C 60
(off Earlbank Av.)
Ormiston La. N. G14 —5C 60
(off Norse La. N.)
Ormonde Av. G44 —4D 118
Ormonde Ct. G44 —4C 118
Ormonde Cres. G44 —4D 118
Ormonde Dri. G44 —4D 118
Ornsay St. G22 —2H 63
Oronsay Ct. Old K —1G 41
Oronsay Cres. Bear —4H 45
Oronsay Cres. Old K —1G 41
Oronsay Gdns. Old K —1G 41
Oronsay Pl. Old K —1G 41
Oronsay Sq. Old K —1G 41
Orr Sq. Pais —6A 78
Orr St. G40 —6B 84
(in two parts)
Orr St. Pais —2A 98
(Neilston Rd.)
Orr St. Pais —6A 78
(Oakshaw St.)
Orton St. G51 —5G 81
Osborne Cres. T'hall —6F 135
Osborne St. G1 —5G 83
Osborne St. Clyd —4C 42
Osprey Dri. Udd —6E 109
Ossian Av. Pais —6H 79
Ossian Rd. G43 —1C 118
Oswald St. G1 —5F 83 (6C 4)
Oswald Wlk. Miln —5A 26
Otago La. G12 —1C 82
Otago La. N. G12 —1C 82
(off Otago St.)
Otago Pk. E Kil —2C 148
Otago St. G12 —1C 82
Othello. E Kil —4B 138
Ottawa Cres. Clyd —3H 41
Otterburn Dri. Giff —6A 118
Otterswick Pl. G33 —1C 86
Oudenarde Ct. Carl —4H 165
Oval, The. Clar —6D 118
Oval, The. Glenb —3G 69
Overbrae Pl. G15 —2H 43
Overburn Av. Dumb —3F 17
Overburn Cres. Dumb —2F 17
Overburn Ter. Dumb —2G 17
Overcroy Rd. Kils —1B 34
Overdale Av. G42 —5D 102
Overdale Gdns. G42 —5D 102
Overdale Pl. Wis —5A 158
Overdale St. G42 —5D 102
Overjohnstone Dri. Wis —5D 144
Overlea Av. Ruth —1F 121
Overlee Rd. Clar —2D 134
Overnewton Pl. G3 —3B 82
Overnewton Sq. G3 —2B 82
Overnewton St. G3 —2B 82
Overton Cres. John —2H 95
Overton Rd. Camb —3D 122
Overton Rd. John —3G 95
Overton St. Camb —3D 122
Overtoun Av. Dumb —4H 17
Overtoun Dri. Clyd —3B 42
Overtoun Dri. Ruth —6C 104
Overtoun Rd. Clyd —3A 42
Overtown Av. G53 —1A 116
Overtown Ct. Clyd —4A 42
Overtown Rd. Waterl —4B 158
Overtown St. G40 —6C 84
Overwood Dri. G44 —1G 119
Overwood Dri. Dumb —3H 17
Overwood Gro. Dumb —3H 17
Owen Av. E Kil —4E 149
Owendale Av. Bell —6D 110
Owen Pl. E Kil —4F 149
Owen St. Moth —1G 143
O'Wood Av. Moth —1B 128
Oxford Dri. Lin —5H 75
Oxford La. G5 —6F 83
Oxford Rd. Renf —6E 59
Oxford St. G5 —5F 83
Oxford St. Coat —5B 90
Oxford St. Kirk —5C 30
Oxgang Pl. Kirk —6E 31
Oxhill Pl. Dumb —4D 16
Oxhill Rd. Dumb —3D 16
Oxton Dri. G52 —6B 80

Paddock St. Coat —1F 111
Paddock, The. Clar —4E 135
Paidmyre Cres. Newt M —6D 132
Paidmyre Rd. Newt M —6C 132
PAISLEY CANAL STATION. Pais —2A 98
Paisley Cen., The. Pais —1A 98
PAISLEY GILMOUR ST. STATION. Pais —6A 78
Paisley Rd. G51 —5D 82
Paisley Rd. Barr —2D 114
Paisley Rd. Renf —3C 78
Paisley Rd. W. G51 —6G 81
Paisley Rd. W. G52 & G5 —1H 99
PAISLEY ST JAMES STATION. Pais —5G 77
Palacecraig St. Coat —2C 110
Paladin Av. G13 —1B 60
Paldmyre Gdns. Newt M —6D 132
Palermo St. G21 —5A 64
Palladium Pl. White —6D 60
Palmer Av. G1 —4G 83 (6F 5)
Palmer Av. G13 —6D 44
Palmerston. E Kil —4C 148
Palmerston Pl. G3 —3B 82
Palmerston Pl. John —5C 94
Palm Pl. Udd —4F 109
Pandora Way. Udd —6E 109
Pankhurst Pl. E Kil —1H 149
Panmure St. G20 —5E 63
Parkandarroch Cres. Carl —4G 165
Park Av. G3 —1D 82
Park Av. Barr —6D 114
Park Av. B'rig —4C 48
Park Av. Carl —2F 165
Park Av. Dumb —4H 17
Park Av. Eld —3A 96
Park Av. Kils —1D 32
Park Av. Kirk —5C 30
Park Av. Miln —4G 25
Park Av. Moth —2A 128
Park Av. Pais —4G 97
Park Bank. Ersk —6F 41
Park Brae. Ersk —1G 57
Parkburn Av. Kirk —1C 50
Park Burn Ct. Ham —3D 140
Park Burn Ind. Est. Ham —3E 141
Parkburn Rd. Kils —2H 11
Park Cir. G3 —2C 82
Park Cir. Carl —2F 165
Park Cir. La. G3 —2C 82
Park Cir. Pl. G3 —2D 82
Park Ct. B'rig —4D 48
Park Ct. Clyd —3A 42
Park Ct. Giff —4H 117
Park Cres. Air —3G 91
Park Cres. Bear —2B 44
Park Cres. B'rig —5C 48
Park Cres. Blan —3A 140
Park Cres. Dumb —2F 17
Park Cres. Inch —2G 57
Park Cres. Torr —4E 29
Park Dri. G3 —1C 82
Park Dri. Ersk —1F 57
Park Dri. Ham —2E 155
Park Dri. Newm —4E 147
Park Dri. Ruth —6C 104
Park Dri. T'hall —6G 135
Parker Pl. Kils —3H 11
Parker Pl. Lark —2F 161
Parkfield. E Kil —6G 149
Parkfoot St. Kils —2H 11
Park Gdns. G3 —2C 82
Park Gdns. Kilb —1B 94
Park Gdns. La. G3 —2C 82
(off Clifton St.)
Park Ga. G3 —2C 82
Park Ga. Ersk —1F 57
Park Ga. Pl. Bell —2B 126
Park Glade. Ersk —1F 57
Park Grn. Ersk —1F 57
Park Gro. Ersk —1G 57
Parkgrove Av. Giff —3B 118
Parkgrove Ter. G3 —2C 82
Parkgrove Ter. La. G3 —2C 82
(off Derby St.)
Parkhall Rd. Clyd —3B 42
Parkhall St. E Kil —1H 149
Parkhall Ter. Clyd —2B 42
Parkhead Cross. G31 —6F 85
Parkhead La. Air —3A 92
Parkhead St. Air —3A 92
Parkhead St. Moth —4H 143
Park Hill. Ersk —6F 41
Parkhill Dri. Ruth —6C 104
Parkhill Rd. G43 —5B 102
Parkholm La. G51 —5D 82
Park Ho. Ham —4H 141
Parkhouse Path. G53 —3B 116
Parkhouse Rd. Barr & G53 —3H 115
Parkinch. Ersk —1G 57
Parklands Rd. G44 —4D 118
Park La. G40 —6B 84
Park La. Blan —1B 140
Park La. Carl —4E 165
Park La. Kils —3H 11
Parklea. B'rig —4A 48
Parklee Dri. Crmck —2A 136
Park Moor. Ersk —1F 57
Parkneuk Rd. G43 —3H 117
Parkneuk Rd. Blan —1G 151
Parkneuk St. Moth —1F 143
Parknook Way. Lark —1F 161
(off Muirshot Rd.)
Park Pl. Bell —4A 126
Park Pl. Coat —1F 111
Park Pl. John —3F 95
Park Pl. T'hall —6G 135
Park Quad. G3 —2C 82
Park Quad. Wis —2E 157
Park Ridge. Ersk —1F 57
Park Rd. G2 —1C 82
Park Rd. Bail —6D 88
Park Rd. Bell —3C 126
Park Rd. B'rig —5C 48
Park Rd. Bri W —2F 73
Park Rd. C'bnk —3B 112
Park Rd. Carf —4A 128
Park Rd. Carm —5C 106
Park Rd. Chry —1A 68
Park Rd. Clyd —4B 42
Park Rd. Giff —5A 118
Park Rd. Ham —6H 141
Park Rd. Inch —2H 57
Park Rd. John —3F 95
Park Rd. Mill P —4C 94
Park Rd. Miln —4G 25
Park Rd. Pais —5H 97
Parksail. Ersk —2G 57
Parksail Dri. Ersk —1G 57
Parkside Rd. Moth —3D 142
Park St. Air —3G 91
Park St. Carl —4F 165
Park St. Cle —4H 129
Park St. Coat —3D 90
Park St. Dumb —4G 17
Park St. Kirk —6H 31
Park St. Moth —2G 143
Park St. New S —4A 128
Park St. S. G3 —2C 82
Parks View. Ham —5H 153
Park Ter. G3 —2C 82
Park Ter. E Kil —2G 149
Park Ter. La. G3 —2C 82
Park Ter. La. E. G3 —2D 82
Park Top. Ersk —6G 41
Parkvale Cres. Ersk —1H 57
Parkvale Dri. Ersk —1H 57
Parkvale Gdns. Ersk —1H 57
Parkvale Pl. Ersk —1H 57
Parkvale Way. Ersk —1H 57
Park View. Kilb —1A 94
Park View. Lark —3F 161
Park View. Pais —3H 97
Parkview Av. Kirk —6D 30
Parkview Ct. Kirk —6D 30
Parkview Cres. Newm —5E 147
Parkview Dri. Coat —4A 90
Parkview Dri. Step —3E 67
Parkville Dri. Blan —3C 140
(in two parts)
Parkville Rd. Bell —6E 111
Parkway. G32 —5C 106
Park Way. Cumb —1B 36
Parkway Ct. Coat —5A 90
Parkway Pl. Coat —6A 90
Park Winding. Ersk —1G 57
Park Wood. Ersk —6G 41
Parnell St. Air —6H 91
Parnie St. G1 —5G 83
Parrish Dri. Kils —3G 7
Parry Ter. E Kil —2D 148
Parsonage Row. G1 —4H 83 (6H 5)
Parsonage Sq. G1 —4H 83 (6H 5)
Parson St. G4 —3A 84
Partick Bri. St. G11 —2A 82
Partickhill Av. G11 —6H 61
Partickhill Ct. G11 —6H 61
Partickhill Rd. G11 —6H 61
PARTICK STATION. G11 —1H 81
Partick St. Coat —6E 91
Patchy Pk. Lark —5E 161
Paterson Pl. Bear —5C 24
Paterson St. G5 —6E 83
(in three parts)
Paterson St. Moth —2G 143
Paterson Ter. E Kil —4F 149
Pather St. Wis —1H 157
Pathhead Gdns. G33 —3H 65
Pathhead Rd. Crmck —2H 135
Patna Ct. Ham —2C 152
Patna St. G40 —2D 104
Paton St. G31 —4D 84
Patrick St. Pais —2B 98
Patterson Dri. Law —5E 159
Patterton Dri. Barr —6F 115
PATTERTON STATION. Newt M —1D 132
Pattison St. Clyd —4A 42
Payne St. G4 —1G 83
Peace Av. Bri W —1B 72
Peacock Av. Pais —3D 96
Peacock Cross. Ham —5G 141
Peacock Cross Ind. Est. Ham —5G 141
Peacock Dri. Ham —5G 141
Peacock Dri. Pais —3D 96
Peacock Loan. Carl —2F 165
(off Carranbute Rd.)
Peacock M. Miln —4G 25
Pearce La. G51 —3G 81
Pearl St. Bell —4D 126
Pearson Dri. Renf —1F 79
Pearson Pl. Lin —6H 75
Peathill Av. Chry —6H 51
Peathill St. G21 —6G 63
Peat Pl. G53 —2A 116
Peat Rd. G53 —2A 116
Peat Rd. Bri W —4G 73
Pedmyre La. Crmck —2G 135
Peebles Dri. Ruth —6F 105
Peebles Path. Coat —2F 111
Peel Brae. Kirk —4C 30
Peel Ct. Camb —1A 122
Peel Glen Rd. G15 —3A 44
Peel La. G11 —1G 81
Peel Pk. Ind. Est. E Kil —1A 148
Peel Pk. Pl. E Kil —2B 148
Peel Pl. Both —4E 125
Peel Pl. Coat —6H 89
Peel Rd. T'hall —6F 135
Peel St. G11 —1H 81
Peel View. Clyd —4F 43
Pegasus Av. Carl —3E 165
Pegasus Rd. Bell —2G 127
Pembroke. E Kil —5D 138
Pembroke St. G3 —3D 82
Pencaitland Dri. G32 —2A 106
Pencaitland Gdns. G32 —3A 106
Pencaitland Pl. G23 —6C 46
Pendeen Cres. G33 —6E 87
Pendeen Pl. G33 —5F 87
Pendeen Rd. G33 —6E 87
Pendicle Cres. Bear —4D 44
Pendicle Rd. Bear —4D 44
Penfold Cres. E Kil —3F 149
Penicuik St. G32 —5F 85
Penilee Rd. H'ton I & Pais —3F 79
Penilee Ter. G52 —4G 79
Peninver Dri. G51 —3C 81
Penman Av. Ruth —5B 104
Pennan. Ersk —5E 41
Pennan Pl. G14 —4A 60
Penneld Rd. G52 —6H 79
Penniecroft Av. Dumb —2H 17
Pennyroyal Ct. E Kil —5F 137
Penrith Av. Giff —4A 118
Penrith Dri. G12 —3G 61
Penrith Pl. E Kil —5B 148
Penryn Gdns. G32 —2D 106
Penston Rd. G33 —3D 86
Pentland Av. Lin —6G 75
Pentland Ct. Air —1B 92
Pentland Ct. Barr —6D 114
Pentland Ct. Coat —2E 111
Pentland Cres. Pais —5H 97
Pentland Dri. Barr —6D 114
Pentland Dri. B'rig —5F 49
Pentland Dri. Renf —3D 78
Pentland Pl. Bear —6B 24
Pentland Rd. G43 —2A 118
Pentland Rd. Chry —1B 68
Pentland Rd. Wis —5E 145
Penzance Way. Chry —4C 52
Peockland Gdns. John —2G 95
Peockland Pl. John —2G 95
Peploe Dri. E Kil —4D 138
Percy Dri. Giff —6A 118
Percy Rd. Renf —3C 78
Percy St. G51 —6B 82
Percy St. Lark —1E 161
Perran Gdns. Chry —5C 52
Perray Av. Dumb —2B 16
Perrays Dri. Dumb —3A 16
Perth Av. Air —1A 112
Perth Cres. Clyd —2H 41
Perth St. G3 —4D 82
Peter Coats Building. Pais —2A 98
Peter Dri. Kirk —4D 30
Petersburn Pl. Air —5D 92
Petersburn Rd. Air —6C 92
Petershill Ct. G21 —6D 64
Petershill Dri. G21 —5D 64
Petershill Pl. G21 —5D 64
Petershill Rd. G21 —6B 64
Peterson Dri. G13 —1G 59
Peterson Gdns. G13 —1G 59
Petition Pl. Udd —2E 125
Pettigrew St. G32 —6A 86
Peveril Av. G41 —4B 102
Peveril Av. Ruth —2E 121
Peveril Ct. Ruth —3E 121
Pharonhill St. G31 —6F 85
Philip Murray Rd. Bell —1H 125
Philipshill Ga. Clar —6A 136
Philipshill Rd. Clar —6A 136
Phipp La. Dumb —1D 18
Phoenix Cres. Stra B —5A 110
Phoenix Ind. Est. Pais —3H 77
Phoenix Pl. Eld —2B 96
Phoenix Pl. Moth —4A 128
Phoenix Retail Pk., The. Lin —6C 76
Phoenix Rd. Bell —2G 127
Piazza Shopping Cen. Pais —6B 78
Picadilly St. G3 —4D 82
Pickerston Hill. Moth —3C 129
Picketlaw Dri. Crmck —2H 135
Picketlaw Farm Rd. Clar —2G 135
Piershill St. G32 —4H 85
Pikeman Rd. G13 —3C 60
Pilmuir Av. G44 —3D 118
Pilrig St. G32 —4G 85
Pilton Rd. G15 —3A 44
Pine Clo. Cumb —1E 37
Pine Ct. Coat —1A 110
(off Ailsa Rd.)
Pine Ct. Cumb —1E 37
Pine Ct. E Kil —6D 148
Pine Cres. Cumb —1E 37
Pine Cres. E Kil —6D 148
Pine Cres. John —4G 95
Pine Gro. C'bnk —3B 112
Pine Gro. Cumb —1E 37
Pine Gro. Moth —2B 128
Pine Gro. Udd —5F 109
Pinelands. B'rig —3C 48
Pine Lawn. Wis —4B 146
Pine Pk. Ham —2A 154
Pine Pl. G5 —1G 103
Pine Pl. Cumb —1E 37
Pine Rd. Clyd —3H 41
Pine Rd. Cumb —6E 15
Pine Rd. Dumb —3F 17
Pines, The. G44 —3F 119
Pine St. Air —4D 92
Pine St. Len —3G 7
Pine St. Pais —3C 98
Pinewood Av. Kirk —2A 50
Pinewood Ct. Dumb —2H 17
Pinewood Ct. Kirk —2A 50
Pinewood Pl. Kirk —2A 50
Pinewood Sq. G15 —4B 44
Pinkerton Av. Ruth —5A 104
Pinkston Dri. G21 —1H 83 (1H 5)
Pinkston Rd. G21 & G4 —6H 63 (1H 5)
Pinmore Pl. G53 —2H 115
Pinmore St. G53 —2H 115
Pinwherry Dri. G33 —3H 65
Pinwherry Pl. Both —4E 125
Piper Av. Hous —3C 74
Piper Rd. Air —6C 92
Piper Rd. Hous —3C 74
Pirnie Pl. Kils —3H 11
Pirnmill Av. Moth —2D 142
Pitcairn Cres. E Kil —3B 148
Pitcairn Gro. E Kil —3C 148
Pitcairn Pl. E Kil —3B 148
Pitcairn St. G31 —1F 105
Pitcairn Ter. Ham —5E 141
Pitcaple Dri. G43 —1H 117
Pitlochry Dri. G52 —1B 100
Pitlochry Dri. Lark —4G 161
Pitmedden Rd. B'rig —5F 49
Pitmilly Rd. G15 —3C 44
Pitreavie Ct. Ham —3F 153
Pitreavie Pl. G33 —2C 86
Pit Rd. Bell I —1B 126
Pit Rd. Kirk —6A 32
Pitt St. G2 —4E 83 (5B 4)
Pladda Rd. Renf —2F 79
Pladda St. Moth —2D 142
Plaintrees Ct. Pais —4A 98
Plane Pl. Udd —4G 109
Planetree Pl. John —4G 95
Planetree Rd. Clyd —2C 42
Plantation Av. Moth —1B 128
Plantation Pk. Gdns. G51 —6B 82
Plantation Sq. G51 —5C 82
Plant St. G31 —5E 85
Platthorn Dri. E Kil —2H 149
Platthorn Rd. E Kil —2H 149
Playfair St. G40 —2C 104
Plaza, The. E Kil —2G 149
Pleaknowe Cres. Chry —5C 52
Pleamuir Pl. Cumb —4E 35
Plean St. G14 —4A 60
Pleasance La. G43 —6A 102
Pleasance St. G43 —5A 102
Plotcock Rd. Ham —4A 160
Plover Dri. E Kil —6C 148
Plover Pl. John —6C 94
Plusgarten Loan. Newm —2D 146
Poet's View. Kirk —6F 31
Poindfauld Ter. Dumb —3G 17
Pointhouse Rd. G3 —3A 82
Pollock Gdns. B'rig —5A 48
Pollock Rd. Bear —4G 45
Pollock Rd. Newt M —5C 132
Pollockshields Sq. G41 —3C 102
Pollock St. Bell —2E 127
Pollock St. Moth —2G 143
Pollok Av. G43 —5H 101
Pollok La. E Kil —6B 138
Pollok Pl. E Kil —6B 138
POLLOKSHAWS EAST STATION. G43 —6B 102
Pollokshaws Rd. G41 —4C 102
Pollokshaws Rd. G43 —6H 101
POLLOKSHAWS WEST STATION. G43 —6H 101
POLLOKSHIELDS EAST STATION. G41 —2E 103
POLLOKSHIELDS WEST STATION. G41 —3D 102
Pollok Township Cen. G53 —6C 100
Polmadie Av. G5 —3H 103
Polmadie Ind. Est. G5 —3A 104
Polmadie Rd. G42 —4G 103
Polmadie St. G42 —4G 103
Polnoon Av. G13 —3A 60
Polson Dri. John —3E 95
Polsons Cres. Pais —3H 97
Polwarth La. G12 —6H 61
Polwarth St. G12 —6H 61
Pomona Pl. Ham —1D 152
Poplar Av. G11 —5F 61
Poplar Av. B'ton —5H 39
Poplar Av. John —4G 95
Poplar Av. Newt M —6D 132
Poplar Ct. Coat —1A 110
Poplar Cres. B'ton —5H 39
Poplar Dri. Clyd —2B 42

Poplar Dri. Kirk —2A 50
Poplar Dri. Milt C —6C 8
Poplar Gdns. E Kil —6E 149
Poplar Pl. Blan —6A 124
Poplar Pl. Moth —3B 128
Poplar Pl. Udd —5H 109
Poplar Rd. Dumb —3F 17
Poplars, The. Bear —5D 24
Poplar St. Air —4D 92
Poplin St. G40 —2B 104
Porchester St. G33 —1D 86
Portal Rd. G13 —1C 60
Port Dundas Ind. Est. G4 —1G 83
Port Dundas Pl. G2 —3G 83 (3E 5)
Port Dundas Rd. G4 —2F 83 (1D 4)
Porterfield Rd. Renf —6C 58
Porters La. Chap —3D 112
Porter St. G51 —6A 82
Porters Well. Udd —2C 124
Portessie. Ersk —5E 41
Portland Pk. Ham —1A 154
Portland Pl. Ham —1A 154
Portland Rd. Cumb —6H 13
Portland Rd. Pais —2D 98
Portland Sq. Ham —1A 154
Portland St. Coat —3D 90
Portland Wynd. Lark —1F 161 (off Muirshot Rd.)
Portlethen. Ersk —5E 41
Portman St. G41 —6C 82
Portmarnock Dri. G23 —1C 62
Porton Pl. B'ton —4G 39
Portpatrick Rd. Old K —6D 20
Portreath Rd. Chry —4D 52
Portsoy. Ersk —5E 41
Portsoy Av. G13 —1H 59
Portsoy Pl. G13 —1G 59
Port St. G3 —4D 82
Portugal St. G5 —6F 83
Portwell. Ham —5A 142
POSSILPARK & PARKHOUSE STATION. G22 —3F 63
Possil Pk. Trading Cen. G22 —4G 63
Possil Rd. G4 —1F 83
Postgate. Ham —5A 142
Potassels Rd. Muirh —2A 68
Potrail Pl. Ham —6E 141
Potter Clo. G32 —2G 105
Potter Gro. G32 —2G 105
Potterhill Av. Pais —5A 98
Potterhill Rd. G53 —3A 100
Potter Path. G32 —2G 105
Potter Pl. G32 —2G 105
Potter St. G32 —2G 105
Potts Way. Moth —6E 127
Powbrone. E Kil —6G 149
Powburn Cres. Udd —6B 108
Powfoot St. G31 —6F 85
Powforth Clo. Lark —2C 160
Powrie St. G33 —6C 66
Prentice La. Udd —5E 109
Prentice Rd. Moth —4D 142
Prestonfield. Miln —4E 25
Preston Pl. G42 —3F 103
Prestwick Ct. Cumb —1H 35
Prestwick Pl. Newt M —5G 133
Prestwick St. G53 —1A 116
Priestfield Ind. Est. Blan —4B 140
Priestfield St. Blan —3A 140
Priesthill Av. G53 —1C 116
Priesthill Cres. G53 —1C 116
PRIESTHILL & DARNLEY STATION. G53 —2C 116
Priesthill Rd. G53 —1B 116
Priestknowe Roundabout. E Kil —2H 149
Prieston Rd. Bri W —4E 73
Primrose Av. Bell —6C 110
Primrose Av. Lark —5E 161
Primrose Ct. G14 —6D 60
Primrose Cres. Moth —4G 143
Primrose Pl. Cumb —6D 34
Primrose Pl. Udd —5G 109
Primrose St. G14 —6C 60
Primrose Way. Carl —5E 165
Prince Albert Rd. G12 —6H 61
Prince Edward St. G42 —3E 103
Prince of Wales Gdns. G20 —1A 62
Prince Pl. Wis —3E 147
Prince's Gdns. G12 —6H 61
Princes Ga. Both —3C 124
Princes Ga. Ruth —5C 104
Princes Mall. E Kil —2G 149
Princes Pk. B'ton —3C 40
Prince's Pl. G12 —6A 62
Princess Anne Quad. Moth —2H 127 (off Sherry Av.)
Princess Cres. Pais —6D 78
Princess Dri. Bail —6E 89
Princes Sq. E Kil —2G 149 (off Cornwall St.)
Princes Sq. Shopping Cen. G1 —4G 83 (6E 5) (off Buchanan Sq.)
Princess Rd. Moth —3H 127
Princess Sq. Barr —4F 115
Princess Sq. E Kil —2G 149
Princess Sq. Newm —4D 146
Princes St. Moth —1G 143
Princes St. Ruth —5C 104
Prince's Ter. G12 —6A 62
Printers Land. Clar —3E 135
Priory Av. Pais —4C 78
Priory Dri. Udd —6B 108
Priory Ga. Over —4H 157
Priory Pl. G13 —2D 60
Priory Pl. Cumb —4A 34
Priory Rd. G13 —2D 60
Priory St. Blan —1B 140
Priory Ter. Wis —1C 156
Procession Rd. Pais —1A 114
Professors Sq. G12 —1B 82
Prosen St. G32 —2G 105
Prospect Av. Camb —1H 121
Prospect Av. Udd —1C 124
Prospect Ct. Blan —4B 140
Prospect Dri. Ashg —5B 162
Prospecthill Cir. G42 —4H 103
Prospecthill Cres. G42 —5A 104
Prospect Hill Dri. G42 —5G 103
Prospecthill Pl. G42 —5A 104
Prospecthill Rd. G42 —5E 103
Prospecthill Sq. G42 —4H 103
Prospect Rd. G43 —5B 102
Prospect Rd. Dull —5E 13
Provandhall Cres. Bail —2H 107
Provanhill St. G21 —2B 84
Provanmill Pl. G33 —6F 65
Provanmill Rd. G33 —6F 65
Provan Rd. G33 —2E 85
Provost Clo. John —2F 95
Provost Ga. Lark —2E 161
Purdie. E Kil —4D 138
Purdie St. Ham —4E 141
Purdon St. G11 —1H 81
Pyatshaw Rd. Lark —4F 161

Quadrant Rd. G43 —1C 118
Quadrant Shopping Cen. Coat —4C 90
Quadrant, The. Clar —1C 134
Quarrelton Rd. John —3E 95
Quarreton Gro. John —4F 95
Quarry Av. Camb —4D 122
Quarrybank. Mill P —3C 94
Quarrybrae Av. Clar —2B 134
Quarrybrae Gdns. Udd —1G 125
Quarrybrae St. G31 —6G 85
Quarry Dri. Kirk —5F 31
Quarry Knowe. Dumb —2D 16
Quarryknowe. Ruth —6B 104
Quarry Knowe Pl. Bell —4B 126
Quarryknowe St. G31 —6G 85
Quarryknowe St. Clyd —6F 23
Quarry La. Dumb —4E 17
Quarry La. Len —2F 7
Quarry Pk. E Kil —3G 149
Quarry Pl. Camb —1G 121
Quarry Pl. Dumb —2D 16
Quarry Pl. Ham —6A 142
Quarry Pl. Wis —3H 147
Quarry Rd. Air —2H 91
Quarry Rd. Barr —3D 114
Quarry Rd. E Kil —6F 149
Quarry Rd. Lark —3E 161
Quarry Rd. Law —3H 163
Quarry Rd. Pais —4B 98
Quarryside St. Glenm —5G 71
Quarry St. Coat —5F 91
Quarry St. Ham —6A 142
Quarry St. John —2F 95
Quarry St. Lark —4F 161
Quarry St. Moth —3A 128
Quarry St. Wis —6G 145
Quarrywood Av. G21 —5E 65
Quarrywood Rd. G21 —5E 65
Quay Pend. Dumb —4E 17
Quay Rd. Ruth —4C 104
Quay Rd. N. Ruth —4C 104
Quay St. Dumb —4F 17
Quebec Dri. E Kil —3E 149
Quebec Grn. E Kil —2E 149
Quebec Wynd. G32 —5C 106
Queen Elizabeth Av. H'ton I —4G 79
Queen Elizabeth Ct. Moth —2F 143
Queen Elizabeth Sq. G5 —1G 103
Queen Margaret Ct. G20 —5C 62 (off Fergus Dri.)
Queen Margaret Dri. G12 & G20 —6B 62
Queen Margaret Rd. G20 —5C 62
Queen Mary Av. G42 —4E 103
Queen Mary Av. Clyd —5F 43
Queen Mary St. G40 —1C 104
Queen's Av. Camb —1B 122
Queensbank Av. G'csh —2C 68
Queensberry Av. Bear —6E 25
Queensberry Av. Clar —2C 134
Queensborough Gdns. G12 —5G 61
Queensby Av. Bail —6H 87
Queensby Dri. Bail —5H 87
Queensby Pl. Bail —5A 88
Queensby Rd. Bail —5H 87
Queen's Ct. Miln —5G 25
Queen's Cres. G4 —1D 82 (1A 4)
Queen's Cres. Bail —6D 88
Queen's Cres. Bell —3B 126
Queen's Cres. Carl —3G 165
Queen's Cres. Chap —2D 112
Queens Cres. Moth —4H 127
Queensdale Av. Lark —5F 161
Queensdale Rd. Lark —5F 161
Queen's Dri. G42 —3D 102
Queens Dri. B'ton —4H 39
Queen's Dri. Cumb —5H 13
Queens Dri. Ham —5H 153
Queen's Dri. La. G42 —4E 103
Queensferry St. G5 —3A 104
Queen's Gdns. G12 —6A 62
Queen's Ga. Clar —1C 134
Queenside Cres. Ersk —6D 40
Queensland Ct. G52 —5C 80
Queensland Dri. G52 —5C 80
Queensland Gdns. G52 —5C 80
Queensland La. E. G52 —5C 80
Queensland La. W. G52 —5C 80
Queenslie Ind. Est. G33 —3D 86
Queenslie St. G33 —1F 85
Queen's Pk. Av. G42 —4F 103
QUEEN'S PK. STATION. G42 —3E 103
Queens Pl. G12 —6A 62
Queen Sq. G41 —3D 102
Queen's Rd. Eld —3A 96
Queen's St. Moth —5H 129
Queen St. G1 —4G 83 (6E 5)
Queen St. Ham —4E 141
Queen St. Kirk —5C 30
Queen St. Moth —2G 143
Queen St. Newm —3D 146
Queen St. Pais —1G 97
Queen St. Renf —6F 59
Queen St. Ruth —5C 104
QUEEN ST. STATION. G1 —3G 83 (4E 5)
Queens Way. B'rig —5D 28
Queensway. E Kil —6B 136
Queen Victoria Dri. G14 & G13 —5C 60
Queen Victoria Ga. G13 —4C 60
Queen Victoria St. Air —4H 91
Queenzieburn Ind. Est. Kils —3D 10
Quendale Dri. G32 —2H 105
Quentin St. G41 —4C 102
Quinton Gdns. Bail —6G 87

Raasay Cres. Air —5E 93
Raasay Dri. Pais —6H 97
Raasay Gdns. Newt M —4B 132
Raasay Pl. G22 —1G 63
Raasay St. G22 —1G 63
Racecourse View. Ham —4A 142
Rachan St. G34 —2B 88
Radnor St. G3 —2B 82
Radnor St. Clyd —4C 42 (in two parts)
Raeberry St. G20 —6D 62
Raebog Cres. Air —1H 91
Raebog Rd. Glenm —5G 71
Raeburn Av. E Kil —5B 138
Raeburn Cres. Ham —6C 140
Raeburn Pl. E Kil —5B 138
Raeburn Wlk. Bell —6D 110
Raeside Av. Newt M —6D 132
Raes Rd. Carl —5B 164
Raeswood Dri. G53 —5H 99
Raeswood Gdns. G53 —5H 99
Raeswood Pl. G53 —5H 99
Raeswood Rd. G53 —5H 99
Raewell Cres. Bell —4B 126
Rafford St. G51 —4G 81
Raglan St. G4 —1E 83
Railway Rd. Air —4F 91
Raith Av. G45 —3H 119
Raithburn Av. G45 —3G 119
Raithburn Rd. G45 —4G 119
Raith Dri. Bell —3D 126
Ralston Av. Pais & G52 —2H 99
Ralston Ct. G52 —1H 99
Ralston Dri. G52 —1H 99
Ralston Path. G52 —1H 99
Ralston Pl. G52 —1H 99
Ralston Rd. Barr —5E 115
Ralston Rd. Bear —2E 45
Ralston St. Air —4G 91
Ramage Rd. Carl —5H 165
Ramillies Ct. Carl —4G 165
Rampart Av. G13 —1A 60
Ramsay Av. John —4E 95
Ramsay Ct. Newt M —6E 133
Ramsay Cres. Mill P —3B 94
Ramsay Hill. E Kil —6A 138
Ramsay Ind. Est. Kirk —4B 30
Ramsay Pl. Coat —6G 89
Ramsay Pl. John —4E 95
Ramsay St. Clyd —4F 43
Ramsey Wynd. Bell —6D 110
Ram St. G32 —6H 85
Ranaldard Gdns. Ruth —4F 121
Randolph Av. Clar —6E 119
Randolph Dri. Clar —6D 118
Randolph Gdns. Clar —6D 118
Randolph La. G11 —6F 61
Randolph Rd. G11 —5F 61
Ranfurly Ct. Bri W —4F 73
Ranfurly Pl. Bri W —4F 73
Ranfurly Rd. G52 —6H 79
Ranfurly Rd. Bri W —5F 73
Range Av. Moth —5C 144
Range Pl. Ham —2A 154
Rangerhouse Rd. E Kil —6H 149
Range Rd. Moth —5B 144
Range Rd. Ind. Est. Moth —5B 144
Range St. Moth —5B 144
Rankin Dri. Newt M —3C 132
Rankine Av. E Kil —4A 150
Rankine Pl. John —2F 95
Rankine St. John —2F 95
Rankin Rd. Wis —5C 146
Rankin St. Carl —3F 165
Rannoch Av. B'rig —6D 48
Rannoch Av. Coat —2H 89
Rannoch Av. Ham —2E 153
Rannoch Av. Newt M —2D 132
Rannoch Ct. Blan —4D 140
Rannoch Ct. Cumb —1D 54
Rannoch Dri. Bear —2H 45
Rannoch Dri. Cumb —1D 54
Rannoch Dri. Kirk —4H 31
Rannoch Dri. Renf —5E 59
Rannoch Dri. Wis —2H 157
Rannoch Gdns. B'rig —6E 49
Rannoch Grn. E Kil —6H 137
Rannoch Pl. Pais —2C 98
Rannoch Rd. Air —2H 91
Rannoch Rd. John —4E 95
Rannoch Rd. Udd —4C 108
Rannoch St. G44 —1E 119
Rannoch Ter. Lark —4G 161
Rannock La. Chry —5E 53
Ranson Way. B'rig —6E 49
Raploch Av. G14 —5B 60
Raploch Cres. Clyd —6F 23
Raploch La. G14 —5B 60
Raploch Rd. Lark —2D 160
Raploch St. Lark —2D 160
Rashieburn. Ersk —5E 41
Rashieglen. Ersk —5E 41
Rashiehill. Ersk —5E 41
Rashielee Rd. Ersk —5E 41
Rashiewood. Ersk —5F 41
Rashilee Av. Ersk —5F 41
Rathlin St. G51 —3G 81
Rathlin Ter. Dumb —2C 16
Ratho Dri. G21 —5A 64
Ratho Pk. Ham —4F 153
Rattray. Ersk —4E 41
Rattray St. G32 —2G 105
Ravelston Rd. Bear —5E 45
Ravelston St. G32 —5F 85
Ravel Wynd. Udd —5F 109
Ravenscliffe Dri. Giff —4H 117
Ravens Ct. B'rig —1B 64
Ravenscourt. T'hall —6G 135
Ravenscraig Av. Pais —4G 97
Ravenscraig Ct. Bell —2D 126
Ravenscraig Dri. G53 —1B 116
Ravenscraig Ter. G53 —2C 116
Ravenshall Rd. G41 —5A 102
Ravenshill Dri. Cle —6H 129
Ravenstone Dri. Giff —2A 118
Ravenswood Av. Pais —6C 96
Ravenswood Dri. G41 —4B 102
Ravenswood Rd. Bail —6A 88
Raven Wynd. Wis —5H 145
Rawyards Av. Air —1B 92
Raymond Pl. E Kil —2E 149
Rayne Pl. G15 —3B 44
Ream Av. Air —5F 93
Reay Av. E Kil —1D 148
Reay Gdns. E Kil —1D 148
Redan St. G40 —6B 84
Redbrae Rd. Kirk —4D 30
Red Bri. Ct. Coat —3C 90
Redburn Av. Giff —1H 133
Redburn Ct. Cumb —5F 15
Redburn Pl. Cumb —5F 15
Redburn Rd. Cumb —5F 15
Redcastle Sq. G33 —2D 86
Redcliffe Dri. E Kil —3D 148
Reddeer Rd. E Kil —3C 149
Rederech Cres. Ham —1D 152
Redford St. G33 —3F 85
Redgate Pl. G14 —5B 60
Redgrave. E Kil —4C 138
Redhill Rd. Cumb —2F 35
Redhills View. Len —4G 7
Redholme. Lark —4F 161 (off Keir Hardie Rd.)
Redhouse La. Carl —2F 165
Redhurst Cres. Pais —6F 97
Redhurst La. Pais —6F 97
Redhurst Way. Pais —6F 97
Redlands La. G12 —5A 62 (off Kirklee Rd.)
Redlands Rd. G12 —5A 62
Redlands Ter. G12 —5A 62
Redlands Ter. La. G12 —5A 62
Redlawood Pl. Camb —1G 123
Redlawood Rd. Camb —1G 123
Redmoss Rd. Clyd —1B 42
Redmoss Rd. Kils —6B 8
Redmoss St. G22 —4F 63
Rednock St. G22 —5G 63
Redpath Dri. G52 —5B 80
Red Rd. G21 —5D 64
Red Rd. Ct. G21 —6D 64
Redwing Gdns. Wis —2F 157
Redwood Av. E Kil —2A 148
Redwood Ct. E Kil —3A 148
Redwood Cres. B'ton —4A 40
Redwood Cres. E Kil —6A 136
Redwood Cres. Udd —5G 109
Redwood Dri. G21 —6C 64
Redwood Dri. T'hall —3A 148
Redwood Gro. Coat —5D 90
Redwood Pl. E Kil —1A 148
Redwood Pl. Kirk —2B 50
Redwood Pl. Udd —5G 109
Redwood Rd. Cumb —3D 36
Redwood Rd. Moth —2C 128
Reelick Av. G13 —1G 59
Reelick Quad. G13 —1G 59
Reema Rd. Bell —1D 126
Reen Pl. Both —3F 125
Regency Way. Ham —1C 154
Regency Way. Moth —3H 127
Regent Moray St. G3 —2B 82
Regent Pk. Sq. G41 —3D 102
Regent Pl. Clyd —3A 42
Regents Ga. Both —3B 124
Regent Shopping Cen. Kirk —5C 30
Regent Sq. Lenz —3C 50
Regent St. Clyd —3A 42
Regent St. Kirk —5C 30
Regent St. Pais —6D 78
Regent Way. Ham —6A 142
Register Av. Bell —4C 126
Register Rd. Kils —3A 12
Regwood St. G41 —5B 102
Reid Av. Bear —1G 45
Reid Av. Lin —6H 75
Reid Gro. Moth —5B 144
Reid Pl. G40 —1B 104
Reid St. G40 —2B 104
Reid St. Air —2B 92
Reid St. Coat —3C 90
Reid St. Ham —4D 140
Reid St. Ruth —5D 104
Reidvale St. G31 —5B 84
Reilly Rd. Hous —6B 38
Reith Dri. E Kil —4F 149
Remus Pl. Bell —2G 127
Renfield La. G2 —4F 83 (5D 4)
Renfield St. G2 —4F 83 (5D 4)
Renfield St. Renf —5F 59
Renfrew Ct. G2 —3G 83 (3E 5)
Renfrew La. G2 —3F 83 (3D 4)
Renfrew Pl. Coat —1G 109
Renfrew Rd. G51 —3B 80
Renfrew Rd. Pais —5B 78
Renfrew Rd. Renf —1A 80
Renfrew St. G3 & G2 —2E 83 (2A 4)
Renfrew St. Coat —1G 109
Rennie Pl. E Kil —6C 136
Rennie Rd. Kils —2F 11
Renshaw Dri. G52 —5B 80
Renshaw Rd. B'ton —4H 39
Renshaw Rd. Eld —4A 96
Renton Rd. Dumb —1D 16
Renton St. G4 —2G 83 (1E 5)
Resipol Rd. G33 —4E 67
Reston Dri. G52 —5B 80
Reuther Av. Ruth —6D 104
Revoch Dri. G13 —2A 60
Reynolds Av. E Kil —4A 150
Reynolds Path. Wis —2B 158
Rhannan Rd. G44 —2E 119
Rhannan Ter. G44 —2E 119
Rhindhouse Pl. Bail —6B 88
Rhindhouse Rd. Bail —6B 88
Rhindmuir Av. Bail —6A 88
Rhindmuir Ct. Bail —5A 88
Rhindmuir Cres. Bail —5A 88
Rhindmuir Dri. Bail —5A 88
Rhindmuir Gdns. Bail —5A 88
Rhindmuir Gro. Bail —5B 88
Rhindmuir Path. Bail —5B 88
Rhindmuir Pl. Bail —5A 88
Rhindmuir Rd. Bail —5A 88
Rhindmuir View. Bail —5B 88
Rhindmuir Wynd. Bail —5B 88
Rhinds St. Coat —1F 109
Rhinsdale Cres. Bail —6A 88
Rhumor. Mill P —3C 94
Rhu Quad. Wis —5A 158
Rhymer St. G21 —2A 84
Rhymie Rd. G32 —2D 106
Rhynie Dri. G51 —6H 81
Riach Gdns. Moth —6E 127
Ribblesdale. E Kil —6E 137
Riccarton. E Kil —4D 148
Riccarton St. G42 —3G 103
Riccartsbar Av. Pais —2G 97
Rice Way. Moth —5B 144
Richmond Av. Clar —2C 134
Richmond Ct. Ruth —5E 105
Richmond Dri. B'rig —3D 48
Richmond Dri. Camb —2G 121
Richmond Dri. Lin —4G 75
Richmond Dri. Ruth —6E 105
Richmond Gdns. Chry —6H 51
Richmond Gro. Ruth —6E 105
Richmond Pl. Ruth —5E 105
Richmond Rd. Ruth —6F 105
Richmond St. G1 —4H 83 (5G 5)
Richmond St. Clyd —6E 43
Riddell St. Clyd —4E 43
Riddell St. Coat —4E 91
Riddon Av. G13 —1G 59
Riddon Pl. G13 —1G 59

Riddrie Cres. G33 —3G 85
Riddrie Knowes. G33 —3G 85
Riddrievale Ct. G33 —2G 85
Riddrievale St. G33 —2G 85
Rigby St. G32 —6G 85
Rigghead Av. Cumb —6B 14
Rigg Pl. G33 —4E 87
Riggside Rd. G33 —1C 86
Riggs, The. Miln —2G 25
Righead Ga. E Kil —2G 149
Righead Ind. Est. Bell —6A 110
Righead Roundabout. E Kil —2F 149
Riglands Way. Renf —6E 59
Riglaw Pl. G13 —2A 60
Rigmuir Rd. G51 —4C 80
Rimsdale St. G40 —6C 84
Ringford St. G21 —6B 64
Ripon Dri. G12 —3G 61
Risk St. Clyd —3B 42
Risk St. Dumb —4E 17
Ristol Rd. G13 —4B 60
Ritchie Cres. Eld —2A 96
Ritchie Pk. John —2H 95
Ritchie St. G5 —1E 103
Ritchie St. Wis —6D 144
Riverbank Dri. Bell —4E 127
Riverbank St. G43 —6A 102
Riverdale Gdns. Ham —2A 154
Riverdale La. G14 —5A 60
Riverford Rd. G43 —6A 102
Riverford Rd. Ruth —4E 105
River Rd. G32 —6B 106
Riverside. Hous —2D 74
Riverside. Miln —3G 25
Riverside Ct. G44 —5D 118
Riverside Gdns. Clar —4D 134
Riverside La. Dumb —4E 17
Riverside Pk. G44 —5E 119
Riverside Pl. Camb —1E 123
Riverside Rd. G43 —6C 102
Riverside Rd. Lark —5E 161
Riverside Ter. Clar —4D 134
Riverside Wlk. Moth —1H 143
Riverton Dri. E Kil —3D 148
(off Tasman Dri.)
Riverview Dri. G5 —5E 83
Riverview Gdns. G5 —5E 83
Riverview Pl. G5 —5E 83
Roaden Av. Pais —6D 96
Roaden Rd. Pais —6D 96
Roadside. Cumb —6A 14
Robb Ter. Kirk —1G 51
Robert Burns Av. Clyd —4E 43
Robert Burns Av. Moth —3E 129
Robert Burns Quad. Bell —2B 126
Roberton St. Chap —2E 113
Robert Smillie Cres. Lark —4E 161
Robertson Av. G41 —3A 102
Robertson Cres. Neil —2D 130
Robertson Dri. Bell —3C 126
Robertson Dri. E Kil —1B 150
Robertson La. G2 —4F 83 (6B 4)
Robertson St. G2 —5F 83 (6C 4)
Robertson St. Air —4G 91
Robertson St. Barr —5D 114
Robertson St. Ham —4D 140
Robertson Ter. Bail —6A 88
Roberts Quad. Bell —4D 126
Roberts St. Clyd —4A 42
Roberts St. Wis —6G 145
Robert St. G51 —4G 81
Robert Templeton Dri. Camb —2B 122
Robet Gilson Gdns. Coat —6D 90
Robin Pl. Wis —6H 145
Robin Way. G32 —5C 106
Robroyston Av. G33 —6G 65
Robroyston Rd. G33 —5F 65
Robroyston Rd. B'rig —6H 49
Robshill Ct. Newt M —5D 132
Robslee Dri. Giff —4H 117
Robslee Rd. T'bnk —5G 117
Robson Gro. G42 —2F 103
Rochdale Pl. Kirk —5C 30
(off New Lairdsland Rd.)
Rochsoles Dri. Air —1H 91
Rochsolloch Farm Cotts. Air —4G 91
Rochsolloch Rd. Air —5F 91
Rockall Dri. G44 —3F 119
Rockbank Pl. G40 —6C 84
Rockbank Pl. Clyd —1E 43
Rockbank St. G40 —6C 84
Rockburn Cres. Bell —6C 110
Rockburn Dri. Clar —1A 134
Rockcliffe St. G40 —2B 104
Rock Dri. Kilb —3B 94
Rockfield Pl. G21 —4E 65
Rockfield Rd. G21 —4E 65
Rockhampton Av. E Kil —4D 148
Rockmount Av. Barr —6F 115
Rockmount Av. T'bnk —3G 117
Rock St. G4 —6F 63
Rockwell Av. Pais —5G 97
Roddinghead Rd. Giff —3G 133
Rodger Av. Newt M —4C 132
Rodger Dri. Ruth —1C 120
…odger Pl. Ruth —1C 120
…il Av. G44 —3G 119
… St. G4 —1F 83

Roebank Dri. Barr —6E 115
Roebank St. G31 —3D 84
Roffey Pk. Rd. Pais —6F 79
Rogart St. G40 —6B 84
(in two parts)
Rogerfield Rd. Bail —4A 88
Roland Cres. Newt M —6F 133
Roman Av. G15 —6A 44
Roman Av. Bear —2F 45
Roman Ct. Bear —2F 45
Roman Cres. Old K —6D 20
Roman Dri. Bear —2F 45
Roman Dri. Bell —3D 126
Roman Gdns. Bear —2F 45
Roman Hill Rd. Clyd —6D 22
Roman Pl. Bell —4A 126
Roman Rd. Bear —2E 45
Roman Rd. Clyd —1C 42
Roman Rd. Kirk —5B 30
Roman Rd. Moth —1F 143
(in two parts)
Roman Way. Udd —1G 125
Romney Av. G44 —2G 119
Ronaldsay Dri. B'rig —5F 49
Ronaldsay Pass. G22 —2H 63
Ronaldsay Pl. Cumb —5F 35
Ronaldsay St. G22 —2G 63
Rona St. G21 —1D 84
Rona Ter. Camb —4H 121
Ronay St. G22 —2H 63
Ronay St. Wis —4C 146
Rooksdell Av. Pais —4G 97
Ropework La. G1 —5G 83
Rorison Pl. Ashg —4B 162
Rosa Burn Av. E Kil —6D 148
Rosebank Av. Blan —6C 124
Rosebank Av. Kirk —4E 31
Rosebank Dri. Camb —3C 122
Rosebank Dri. Udd —6G 109
Rosebank Pl. Ham —6E 141
Rosebank Rd. Bell —5D 110
Rosebank Rd. Wis —5A 158
Rosebank St. Air —3E 93
Rosebank Ter. Bail —1D 108
Roseberry La. Chap —2E 113
Roseberry Pl. Ham —5E 141
Roseberry Rd. Chap —1D 112
Rosebery St. G5 —2A 104
Roseburn Ct. Cumb —5F 15
Rose Cres. Ham —5D 140
Rose Dale. B'rig —1D 64
Rosedale. E Kil —6E 137
Rosedale Av. Pais —6B 96
Rosedale Dri. Bail —1G 107
Rosedale Gdns. G20 —1A 62
Rosedene Ter. Bell —1C 126
Rosefield Gdns. Udd —6C 108
Rosegreen Cres. Bell —5C 110
Rosehall Av. Coat —1D 110
Rosehall Ind. Est. Coat —2C 110
Rosehall Rd. Bell I —1B 126
Rosehall Ter. Wis —2E 157
Rosehill Dri. Cumb —1C 54
Rosehill Pl. Cumb —1C 54
Rosehill Rd. Torr —5D 28
Rose Knowe Rd. G42 —5H 103
Roselea Dri. Miln —2H 25
Roselea Gdns. G13 —2F 61
Roselea Pl. Blan —6A 124
Roselea Rd. Udd —5C 108
Roselea St. Lark —1F 161
Rosemary Cres. E Kil —5F 137
Rosemary Pl. E Kil —5F 137
Rosemount. Cumb —6H 13
Rose Mt. Ct. Air —3C 92
Rosemount La. Bri W —5D 72
Rosemount La. Lark —4G 161
(off Donaldson Rd.)
Rosemount Meadows. Both —5D 124
Rosemount St. G21 —2B 84
Rosendale Way. Blan —2C 140
Roseneath Ga. E Kil —1E 149
Rosepark Av. Udd —1G 125
Rosepark Cotts. Coat —2B 110
Rose St. G3 —3F 83 (3C 4)
Rose St. Cumb —6D 34
Rose St. Kirk —5D 30
Rose St. Moth —4A 144
Rosevale Cres. Bell —3E 127
Rosevale Gdns. Ham —1F 153
Rosevale Rd. Bear —3E 45
Rosevale St. G11 —1G 81
Rosewood Av. Bell —6D 110
Rosewood Av. Pais —4F 97
Rosewood Path. Bell —2A 126
Rosewood St. G13 —2E 61
Roslea Dri. G31 —4C 84
Roslin Tower. Camb —4G 121
Roslyn Dri. Bail —6D 88
Rosneath St. G51 —3G 81
Ross Av. Kirk —5F 31
Ross Av. Renf —2C 78
Ross Cres. Moth —4E 143
Ross Dri. Air —1G 111
Ross Dri. Moth —4E 143
Ross Dri. Udd —4G 109
Rossendale Ct. G43 —5A 102
Rossendale Rd. G43 & G41 —5A 102
Ross Gdns. Moth —4E 143

Rosshall Av. Pais —1E 99
Ross Hall Pl. Renf —6F 59
Rosshill Av. G52 —6H 79
Rosshill Rd. G52 —6H 79
Rossie Cres. B'rig —1E 65
Rossland Cres. B'ton —4G 39
Rossland Pl. B'ton —5H 39
Rosslea Dri. Giff —5A 118
Rosslee Cres. Giff —4G 117
Rosslyn Av. E Kil —6H 137
Rosslyn Av. Ruth —6D 104
Rosslyn Ct. Ham —5E 141
Rosslyn Rd. Ashg —5B 162
Rosslyn Rd. Bear —1B 44
Rosslyn Ter. G12 —6B 62
Ross Pl. E Kil —6C 138
Ross Pl. Ruth —3F 121
Ross St. G40 —5H 83
Ross St. Coat —4C 90
Ross St. Pais —2C 98
Ross Ter. Ham —2E 155
Rostan Rd. G43 —2A 118
Rosyth Rd. G5 —3A 104
Rosyth St. G5 —3A 104
Rotherwick Dri. Pais —1G 99
Rotherwood Av. G13 —6C 44
Rotherwood Av. Pais —5D 96
Rotherwood Pl. G13 —1D 60
Rotherwood Way. Pais —5D 96
Rothesay Cres. Coat —1D 110
Rothesay Pl. Coat —1D 110
Rothesay Pl. E Kil —2G 149
Rothesay St. E Kil —2G 149
Rothes Dri. G23 —6A 46
Rothes Pl. G23 —6A 46
Rottenrow. G1 —3H 83 (4G 5)
Rottenrow. G4 —4A 84
Rottenrow E. G4 —4H 83 (5H 5)
Roughcraig St. Air —1A 92
Roughrigg Rd. Air —5G 93
Roukenburn St. T'bnk —3E 117
Rouken Glen Rd. T'bnk —5F 117
Roundel, The. Wis —1A 158
Roundhill Dri. Eld —2C 96
Roundknowe Rd. Udd —4A 108
Round Riding Rd. Dumb —3G 17
Rowallan Gdns. G11 —6G 61
Rowallan La. G11 —6F 61
Rowallan La. Clar —2C 134
Rowallan Rd. T'bnk —5F 117
Rowallan Ter. G33 —5B 66
Rowan Av. Milt C —6B 8
Rowan Av. Renf —5E 59
Rowanbank Pl. Air —3F 91
Rowan Ct. Pais —3A 98
Rowan Ct. Wis —1D 156
Rowan Cres. Lenz —2C 50
Rowandale Av. Bail —1G 107
Rowand Av. Giff —4A 118
Rowanden Av. Bell —1C 126
Rowan Dri. Bank —1E 15
Rowan Dri. Bear —6F 25
Rowan Dri. Clyd —3B 42
Rowan Dri. Dumb —3A 16
Rowan Gdns. G41 —1H 101
Rowan Ga. Pais —3B 98
Rowan La. Moth —5A 128
Rowanlea. John —3E 95
Rowanlea Av. Pais —6B 96
Rowanlea Dri. Giff —3B 118
Rowanpark Dri. Barr —2C 114
Rowan Pl. Blan —1B 140
Rowan Pl. Camb —1C 122
Rowan Pl. Coat —1A 110
Rowan Rise. Ham —1A 154
Rowan Rd. G41 —1H 101
Rowan Rd. Cumb —2D 36
Rowan Rd. Lin —4F 75
Rowans Gdns. Both —3F 125
Rowans, The. B'rig —5B 48
Rowan St. Pais —3A 98
Rowan St. Wis —4H 145
Rowantree Av. N'hse —6C 112
Rowantree Av. Ruth —2D 120
Rowantree Av. Udd —6G 109
Rowantree Gdns. Ruth —2D 120
Rowantree Pl. John —4F 95
(off Rowantree Rd.)
Rowan Tree Pl. Lark —3H 161
Rowantree Pl. Len —4G 7
Rowantree Rd. John —4F 95
Rowantree Ter. Moth —2B 128
Rowena Av. G13 —6D 44
Roxburgh Dri. Bear —6E 25
Roxburgh Dri. Coat —1F 111
Roxburgh Pk. E Kil —2H 149
Roxburgh Rd. Pais —6B 96
Roxburgh St. G12 —6B 62
Royal Bank Pl. G1 —4G 83 (5E 5)
(off Buchanan St.)
Royal Cres. G3 —3C 82
Royal Dri. Ham —1C 154
Royal Exchange Ct. G1
(off Buchanan St.) —4G 83 (6E 5)
Royal Exchange Sq. G1 —4G 83 (5E 5)
Royal Inch Ter. Renf —4F 59
Royal Ter. G3 —2C 82
Royal Ter. Wis —2A 146
Royal Ter. La. G3 —2C 82
Royellon Av. Ham —1D 152

Roystonhill. G21 —2B 84
Royston Rd. G21 & G33 —2A 84
Royston Sq. G21 —2A 84
Roy St. G21 —6H 63
Rozelle Av. G15 —4B 44
Rubislaw Dri. Bear —4E 45
Ruby St. G40 —1C 104
Ruchazie Pl. G33 —3H 85
Ruchazie Rd. G33 & G32 —3H 85
Ruchill Pl. G20 —4D 62
Ruchill St. G20 —4C 62
Ruel St. G44 —6E 103
Rufflees Av. Barr —3F 115
Rugby Av. G13 —1B 60
Rullion Pl. G33 —3H 85
Rumford St. G40 —2B 104
Runciman Pl. E Kil —5B 138
Rundell Dri. Milt C —6C 8
Rupert St. G4 —1D 82
Rushyhill St. G21 —5C 64
Ruskin La. G12 —6C 62
Ruskin Pl. G12 —6C 62
Ruskin Pl. Kils —3H 11
Ruskin Sq. B'rig —6C 48
Ruskin Ter. G12 —6C 62
Rusling Pl. Cumb —1E 37
Russell Colt St. Coat —3C 90
Russell Dri. Bear —1E 45
Russell Gdns. Newt M —5C 132
Russell Gdns. Udd —5E 109
Russell La. Wis —1G 157
Russell Pl. Clar —4E 135
Russell Pl. E Kil —4E 149
Russell Pl. Lin —5F 75
Russell Rd. Clyd —6A 22
Russell St. Bell —2F 127
Russell St. Chap —3E 113
Russell St. Ham —4D 140
Russell St. John —2G 95
Russell St. Pais —4H 77
Russell St. Wis —1G 157
Rutherford Av. Bear —5B 24
Rutherford Av. Kirk —1H 51
Rutherford Ct. Clyd —5C 42
Rutherford La. E Kil —3H 149
Rutherford Sq. E Kil —3G 149
Rutherglen Bri. G5 —2B 104
Rutherglen Ind. Est. Ruth —4C 104
RUTHERGLEN STATION. Ruth —5D 104
Ruthven Av. Giff —6B 118
Ruthven La. G12 —6B 62
Ruthven La. Glenb —3G 69
Ruthven Pl. B'rig —1E 65
Ruthven St. G12 —6B 62
Rutland Cres. G51 —5C 82
Rutland Pl. G51 —5C 82
Ryan Rd. B'rig —6D 48
Ryan Way. Ruth —4E 121
Ryat Dri. Newt M —3C 132
Ryat Grn. Newt M —3C 132
(in two parts)
Ryatt Linn. Ersk —6D 40
Rydal Gro. E Kil —5B 148
Rydal Pl. E Kil —5B 148
Ryden Mains Rd. Glenm —5F 71
Ryde Rd. Wis —6A 146
Ryebank Rd. G21 —4E 65
Rye Cres. G21 —4D 64
Ryecroft Dri. Bail —6H 87
Ryedale Pl. G15 —3A 44
Ryefield Av. Coat —4H 89
Ryefield Av. John —4D 94
Ryefield Pl. John —4D 94
Ryefield Rd. G21 —4D 64
Ryehill Pl. G21 —4E 65
Ryehill Rd. G21 —4E 65
Ryemount Rd. G21 —4E 65
Rye Rd. G21 —4D 64
Ryeside Rd. G21 —4D 64
Rye Way. Pais —4C 96
Rylands Dri. G32 —1D 106
Rylands Gdns. G32 —1E 107
Rylees Cres. G52 —5G 79
Rylees Pl. G52 —5G 79
Rylees Rd. G52 —5G 79
Rysland Av. Newt M —4E 133
Rysland Cres. Newt M —4E 133
Ryvra Rd. G13 —3D 60

Sachelcourt Av. B'ton —5H 39
Sackville Av. G13 —4F 61
Sackville La. G13 —4F 61
Saddell Rd. G15 —3B 44
Sadlers Wells Ct. E Kil —5B 138
(off Bosworth Rd.)
Saffronhall Cres. Ham —5H 141
Saffronhall La. Ham —5H 141
St Abb's Dri. Pais —4E 97
St Andrew's Av. B'rig —5A 48
St Andrews Av. Both —6E 125
St Andrew's Brae. Dumb —1H 17
St Andrews Ct. Carl —3E 165
St Andrew's Ct. E Kil —5E 149
St Andrews Ct. Moth —1A 128
St Andrew's Cres. G41 —1C 102
St Andrew's Cres. Dumb —2H 17
St Andrew's Cres. Pais —2G 77
St Andrew's Dri. G41 —3A 102
St Andrew's Dri. Abb —3H 77

St Andrew's Dri. Bri W —4E 73
St Andrew's Dri. Cumb —5B 14
St Andrew's Dri. Ham —5B 140
St Andrew's Dri. W. Glas A —2G 77
St Andrew's Gdns. Air —3B 92
St Andrew's Ga. Bell —2B 126
St Andrew's Path. Lark —4G 161
(off Donaldson Rd.)
St Andrews Pl. Kils —2G 11
St Andrew's Rd. G41 —1D 102
St Andrew's Rd. Renf —6E 59
St Andrew's Sq. G1 —5H 83
St Andrew's St. G1 —5H 83
St Andrews St. Moth —2A 128
St Ann's Dri. Giff —5A 118
St Blanes Dri. Ruth —1A 120
St Boswell's Cres. Pais —4E 97
St Boswells Dri. Coat —1F 111
St Bride's Av. Udd —6G 109
St Bride's Rd. G43 —6B 102
St Brides Way. Both —3E 125
St Bryde St. E Kil —1H 149
St Catherine's Rd. Giff —5A 118
St Clair Av. Giff —4A 118
St Clair St. G20 —1D 82
St Columba Dri. Kirk —6E 31
St Cyrus Gdns. B'rig —6E 49
St Cyrus Rd. B'rig —6E 49
St Davids Dri. Air —1C 112
St David's Pl. Lark —2E 161
St Denis Way. Coat —3B 90
St Edmunds Gro. Miln —2G 25
St Enoch Av. Udd —5G 109
St Enoch Pl. G1 —5F 83 (6D 4)
St Enoch Shopping Cen. G1 —5G 83
St Enoch Sq. G1 —5F 83
ST ENOCH ST. STATION. G1 —4F 83
St Fillans Dri. Hous —1A 74
St Fillans Rd. G33 —4C 66
St Flanan Rd. Kirk —4B 32
ST GEORGES CROSS STATION. G20 —1E 83
St George's Pl. G2 —1E 83
(off St George's Rd.)
St George's Rd. G3 —2D 82 (1A 4)
St Germains. Bear —3E 45
St Giles Pk. Ham —1F 153
St Giles Way. Ham —1F 153
St Helena Cres. Clyd —1E 43
St Ives Rd. Mood —4D 52
St James Av. Pais —4F 77
St James Ct. Coat —1A 110
St James Rd. G4 —3H 83 (3G 5)
St James' St. Pais —6A 78
St James Way. Coat —2A 110
St John's Ct. G41 —1C 102
St John's Quad. G41 —1C 102
St John's Rd. G41 —2C 102
St John St. Coat —4C 90
St Kenneth Dri. G51 —3D 80
St Kilda Dri. G14 —5E 61
St Kilda Way. Wis —4C 146
St Lawrence Pk. E Kil —2E 149
St Leonard's Dri. Giff —4A 118
St Leonards Rd. E Kil —1B 150
St Leonards Sq. E Kil —2C 150
St Leonards Wlk. Coat —2E 111
St Lukes's Av. Carl —5E 165
St Machan's Way. Len —2F 7
St Machars Rd. Bri W —4G 73
St Margaret's Av. Bant —1G 13
St Margarets Dri. Wis —2E 157
St Margaret's Pl. G1 —5G 83
(off Bridgegate)
St Mark Gdns. G32 —6H 85
St Mark St. G32 —6G 85
(in two parts)
St Marnock St. G40 —6C 84
St Mary's Ct. Wis —1H 157
St Mary's Cres. Barr —5E 115
St Mary's Gdns. Barr —5F 115
St Mary's Rd. Bell —2A 126
St Mary's Rd. B'rig —5A 48
St Mary's Way. Dumb —4F 17
St Maurice's Roundabout. Cumb —4C 34
St Michael Rd. Wis —2C 156
St Mirren's Rd. Kils —3A 12
St Mirren St. Pais —1A 98
St Monance St. G21 —4B 64
St Mungo Av. G4 —3G 83 (3F 5)
St Mungo Ct. Bri W —3G 73
St Mungo Pl. G4 —3H 83 (3H 5)
St Mungo Pl. Ham —5B 140
St Mungo's Rd. Cumb —4H 35
St Mungo St. B'rig —1B 64
St Mungo's Wlk. Cumb —3H 35
(off Cumbernauld Cen., The)
St Ninian's Cres. Pais —3B 98
St Ninian's Pl. Ham —6D 140
St Ninian's Rd. Ham —6D 140
St Ninian's Rd. Pais —3B 98
St Ninians Ter. G5 —6G 83
St Ninian St. G5 —6G 83
St Peters La. G2 —4E 83
St Peter's Path. G4 —1E 83
St Peter's St. G4 —1E 83 (1B 4)
St Rollox Brae. G21 —1A 84
St Rollox Bus. & Retail Pk. G21 —1B 84

St Ronan's Dri. G41 —4B 102
St Ronan's Dri. Ham —3G 153
St Ronans Dri. Ruth —1E 121
St Stephen's Av. Ruth —4F 121
St Stephen's Cres. Ruth —4G 121
St Vigean's Av. Newt M —6B 132
St Vincent Cres. G3 —3B 82
St Vincent Cres. La. G3 —3B 82
St Vincent La. G2 —3E 83 (4B 4)
St Vincent Pl. G1 —4G 83 (5E 5)
St Vincent Pl. E Kil —3C 148
St Vincent Pl. Moth —2G 143
St Vincent St. G2 —3E 83 (4B 4)
St Vincent St. G3 —3D 82
St Vincent Ter. G3 —3D 82
St Winifred's Way. Wis —5G 145
Salamanca St. G31 —6F 85
Salen St. G52 —6F 81
Saline St. Air —5F 91
Salisbury. E Kil —5D 138
Salisbury Cres. Moth —1D 142
Salisbury La. G41 —1F 103
Salisbury Pl. Clyd —2H 41
Salisbury St. G5 —1F 103
Salkeld St. G5 —1E 103
Salmona St. G22 —5F 63
Saltaire Av. Udd —2E 125
Salterland Rd. G53 —2G 115
Saltire Cres. Lark —3G 161
Saltmarket. G1 —5G 83
Saltmarket Pl. G1 —5G 83
Saltoun La. G12 —6B 62
Saltoun St. G12 —6A 62
Salvia St. Camb —1H 121
Sandaig Rd. G33 —6E 87
Sandale Path. Blan —3A 140
Sandalwood Av. E Kil —5F 137
Sandalwood Ct. E Kil —5F 137
Sanda St. G20 —5C 62
Sandbank Av. G20 —2B 62
Sandbank Cres. G20 —3B 62
Sandbank Dri. G20 —2B 62
Sandbank St. G20 —1B 62
Sandbank Ter. G20 —2B 62
Sandend. Ersk —4E 41
Sandend Rd. G53 —6A 100
Sanderling Pl. John —6D 94
Sanderling Rd. Pais —3H 77
Sanderson Av. Udd —1H 125
Sanderson La. Kirk —5F 51
Sandfield Av. Miln —2G 25
Sandfield St. G20 —4C 62
Sandford Gdns. Bail —6H 87
Sandgate Av. G32 —2D 106
Sandhaven Pl. G53 —6A 100
Sandhaven Rd. G53 —6A 100
Sandhead Cres. Chap —4E 113
Sandholes Rd. Brkfld & Hous —6C 74
Sandholes St. Pais —1G 97
Sandholm Pl. G14 —4H 59
Sandholm Ter. G14 —4H 59
Sandiefield Rd. G5 —1G 103
Sandielands Av. Ersk —2H 57
Sandilands Cres. Moth —4D 142
Sandilands St. G32 —6B 86
Sandmill St. G21 —2C 84
Sandpiper Dri. E Kil —6C 148
Sandpiper Pl. E Kil —6C 148
Sandra Rd. B'rig —5E 49
Sandringham Av. Newt M —3G 133
Sandringham Ct. Newt M —4G 133
Sandringham Dri. Eld —4H 95
Sandwood Cres. G52 —6A 80
Sandwood Path. G52 —6A 80
Sandwood Rd. G52 —1A 100
Sandyfaulds Sq. G5 —1G 103
Sandyfaulds St. G5 —1H 103
Sandyford Av. Moth —5D 112
Sandyford Pl. G3 —3C 82
(off Claremont St.)
Sandyford Pl. Moth —6D 112
Sandyford Pl. La. G3 —3C 82
Sandyford Rd. G3 —3A 82
Sandyford Rd. Moth —6D 112
Sandyford Rd. Pais —3C 78
Sandyhills Cres. G32 —2B 106
Sandyhills Dri. G32 —2B 106
Sandyhills Gro. G32 —3B 106
Sandyhills Pl. G32 —2B 106
Sandyhills Rd. G32 —2B 106
Sandyknowes Rd. Cumb —5A 36
Sandy Rd. G11 —1G 81
Sandy Rd. Carl —3F 165
Sandy Rd. Renf —2E 79
Sannox Dri. Moth —2D 142
Sannox Gdns. G31 —3D 84
Sanquhar Gdns. Blan —5H 123
Sapphire Rd. Bell —4C 126
Saracen St. G22 —6G 63
Sardinia La. G12 —6B 62
Saskatoon Pl. E Kil —2D 148
Saucel Hill Ter. Pais —2A 98
Saucel St. Pais —1A 98
Sauchiehall La. G2 —3E 83 (3D 4)
Sauchiehall St. G3 & G2 —2B 82 (3A 4)
Sauchiehall St. Shopping Cen. G2 —3F 83 (3C 4)
Sauchiemuir Rd. Carl —5G 165
Saughs Av. G33 —3H 65
Saughs Dri. G33 —3H 65
Saughs Ga. G33 —3H 65
Saughs Pl. G33 —3H 65
Saughs Rd. G33 —4G 65
Saughton St. G32 —4G 85
Saunders Ct. Barr —4D 114
Savoy St. G40 —1B 104
Sawmillfield St. G4 —1F 83
Sawmill Rd. G11 —1F 81
Saxon Rd. G13 —2D 60
Scadlock Rd. Pais —5F 77
Scalpay. E Kil —2C 150
Scalpay Pass. G22 —2H 63
Scalpay Pl. G22 —2H 63
Scalpay St. G22 —2G 63
Scapa St. G23 —1C 62
Scaraway Dri. G22 —1H 63
Scaraway Pl. G22 —1H 63
Scaraway St. G22 —1G 63
Scaraway Ter. G22 —1H 63
Scarba Dri. G43 —2H 117
Scarba Quad. Wis —2E 157
Scarffe Av. Lin —6F 75
Scarhill Av. Air —6H 91
Scarhill La. Air —6A 92
Scarhill St. Cle —5H 129
Scarhill St. Coat —2B 110
Scarrel Dri. G45 —3C 120
Scarrel Gdns. G45 —3C 120
Scarrel Rd. G45 —3C 120
Scarrel Ter. G45 —3C 120
Schaw Ct. Bear —1E 45
Schaw Dri. Bear —1D 44
Schaw Dri. Clyd —6G 23
Schaw Rd. Pais —5C 78
Scholar's Ga. E Kil —5F 149
School Av. Camb —2B 122
Schoolhouse La. Blan —3A 140
School La. Carl —4E 165
School La. Dumb —3D 16
School La. Len —3F 7
School La. Milt C —5C 8
School Quad. Air —1H 91
School Rd. Morn —5F 147
School Rd. Newm —5E 147
School Rd. Newt M —5D 132
School Rd. Pais —6G 79
School Rd. Step —3E 67
School Rd. Torr —4E 29
School St. Chap —3D 112
School St. Coat —1C 110
School St. Ham —2H 153
School Wynd. Pais —6A 78
Scioncroft Av. Ruth —6E 105
Scone Pl. E Kil —6F 137
Scone St. G21 —6G 63
Scone Wlk. Bail —2G 107
Sconser St. G23 —6C 46
Scorton Gdns. Bail —1F 107
Scotia Cres. Lark —4E 161
Scotia Gdns. Ham —4G 153
Scotia St. Moth —2E 143
Scotland St. G5 —6C 82
Scotland St. W. G41 —6B 82
Scotsblair Av. Kirk —1C 50
Scotsburn Rd. G21 —5E 65
SCOTSTOUNHILL STATION. G14 —4B 60
Scotstoun St. G14 —6C 60
Scot St. G3 —3E 83
Scott Av. Bowl —5B 20
Scott Av. John —5E 95
Scott Av. Milt C —5C 8
Scott Cres. Cumb —6F 35
Scott Dri. Bear —1C 44
Scott Dri. Cumb —6F 35
Scott Gro. Ham —1H 153
Scott Hill. E Kil —6A 138
Scott Ho. Cumb —2A 36
Scott Pl. Bell —6D 110
Scott Pl. John —5E 95
Scott Rd. G52 —3H 79
Scott's Pl. Air —3B 92
Scott's Rd. Pais —2D 98
Scott St. Bail —1H 107
Scott St. Clyd —3A 42
Scott St. Ham —2H 153
Scott St. Lark —3F 161
Scott St. Moth —2G 143
Seafar Rd. Cumb —5G 35
Seafar Roundabout. Cumb —5G 35
Seafield Av. Bear —6F 25
Seafield Cres. Cumb —4A 34
Seaford Dri. Ruth —4F 121
Seaforth Cres. Barr —2D 114
Seaforth La. Chry —5E 53
Seaforth Pl. Bell —4B 126
Seaforth Rd. Clyd —6D 42
Seaforth Rd. N. H'ton I —4A 80
Seaforth Rd. S. G52 —4A 80
Seagrove St. G32 —5F 85
Seamill Gdns. E Kil —1F 149
Seamill Path. G53 —2H 115
Seamill St. G53 —2H 115
Seamore St. G20 —1D 82
Seath Av. Air —4G 91
Seath Rd. Ruth —4C 104
Seath St. G42 —3G 103
Seaton Ter. Ham —5E 141
Seaward St. G41 —6C 82
(in two parts)
Second Av. G44 —1F 119
Second Av. Bear —4F 45
Second Av. Clyd —4B 42
Second Av. Dumb —3C 18
Second Av. Kirk —6C 50
Second Av. Renf —2E 79
Second Av. Step —4B 66
Second Av. Udd —4C 108
Second Gdns. G41 —1G 101
Second Rd. Blan —4C 140
Second St. Udd —5D 108
Seedhill. Pais —1B 98
Seedhill Rd. Pais —1B 98
Seggielea La. G13 —3D 60
(off Helensburgh Dri.)
Seggielea Rd. G13 —3D 60
Seil Dri. G44 —3F 119
Selborne Pl. La. G13 —4E 61
Selborne Rd. G13 —4E 61
Selby Gdns. G32 —6D 86
Selby Pl. Coat —1H 89
Selby St. Coat —1H 89
Selkirk Av. G52 —1C 100
Selkirk Av. Pais —4E 97
Selkirk Dri. Ruth —6E 105
Selkirk Pl. E Kil —6D 138
Selkirk Pl. Ham —1A 154
Selkirk St. Blan —2B 140
Selkirk St. Ham —1A 154
Selkirk St. Wis —4A 146
Selkirk Way. Bell —6D 110
Selkirk Way. Coat —2G 111
Sella Rd. B'rig —5F 49
Selvieland Rd. G52 —6H 79
Semphill Gdns. E Kil —1B 150
Sempill Av. Ersk —5D 40
Semple Av. B'ton —4H 39
Semple Pl. Lin —4H 75
Senga Cres. Bell —6C 110
Seres Rd. Clar —1B 134
Sergeantlaw Rd. Pais —6E 97
Service St. Len —2E 7
Seton Ter. G31 —4B 84
Settle Gdns. Bail —1F 107
Seven Sisters. Kirk —2E 51
Seventh Av. Udd —5D 108
Seventh Rd. Blan —4C 140
Severn Rd. E Kil —4B 148
Seymour Grn. E Kil —3D 148
Seyton Av. Giff —6A 118
Seyton La. E Kil —6G 137
Shaftesbury Av. Clyd —5B 42
Shaftesbury Cres. Moth —4D 128
Shaftesbury St. G3 —3D 82
Shafton Pl. G13 —1E 61
Shafton Rd. G13 —1E 61
Shakespeare Av. Clyd —3B 42
Shakespeare St. G20 —4C 62
Shamrock St. G4 —2E 83 (1B 4)
Shamrock St. Kirk —5D 30
Shandon Cres. Bell —6C 110
Shandon Ter. Ham —6D 140
Shand Pl. Carl —2F 165
Shand St. Wis —6H 145
Shandwick St. G34 —3G 87
Shanks Av. Barr —5E 115
Shanks Cres. John —3E 95
Shanks St. G20 —4C 62
Shanks St. Air —2A 92
Shannon St. G20 —4D 62
Shapinsay St. G22 —1H 63
Sharp Av. Coat —1G 109
Sharp St. Moth —2D 142
Shaw Av. B'ton —4A 40
Shawbridge Arc. G43 —5A 102
Shawbridge Ind. Est. G43 —6A 102
Shawbridge St. G43 —6H 101
Shawburn Cres. Ham —5F 141
Shawburn St. Ham —5F 141
Shaw Ct. Ersk —4D 40
Shawfield Cres. Law —6D 158
Shawfield Dri. G5 —3A 104
Shawfield Ind. Est. Ruth —3B 104
Shawfield Rd. Ruth —3B 104
Shawgill Ct. Law —1H 163
Shawhead Av. Coat —1D 110
Shawhead Cotts. Coat —3D 110
Shawhead Ind. Est. Coat —2E 111
Shawhill Cres. Newt M —6E 133
Shawhill Rd. G43 & G41 —5A 102
Shawholm Cres. G43 —6H 101
(in two parts)
Shawlands Arc. G41 —5B 102
SHAWLANDS STATION. G41 —5B 102
Shawmoss Rd. G41 —4A 102
Shawpark St. G20 —3C 62
Shaw Pl. Lin —6H 75
Shawrigg Rd. Lark —3G 161
Shaw Rd. Miln —5G 25
Shaw Rd. Newt M —5E 133
Shaws Rd. Lark —6F 161
Shaw St. G51 —3G 81
Shaw St. Lark —5F 161
Shawwood Cres. Newt M —6E 133
Shearer Dri. Ham —4G 153
Sheddens Pl. G32 —6G 85
Sheepburn Rd. Udd —6C 108
Sheila St. G33 —5G 65
Sheldaig Rd. G22 —1F 63
Sheldrake Pl. John —6D 94
Shelley Ct. G12 —4G 61
Shelley Dri. Both —4F 125
Shelley Dri. Clyd —3C 42
Shelley Rd. G12 —4F 61
Shells Rd. Kirk —4E 31
Sherbrooke Av. G41 —2A 102
Sherbrooke Dri. G41 —1A 102
Sherbrooke Gdns. G41 —2A 102
Sherbrooke Pl. E Kil —2E 149
Sherburn Gdns. Bail —2F 107
Sherdale Av. Chap —3D 112
Sheriff Pk. Av. Ruth —6C 104
Sherry Av. Moth —2H 127
Sherry Dri. Ham —2E 153
Sherwood Av. Pais —5C 78
Sherwood Av. Udd —2E 125
Sherwood Dri. T'bnk —4G 117
Sherwood Pl. G15 —4B 44
Shetland Dri. G44 —3F 119
Shettleston Rd. G31 & G32 —5E 85
SHETTLESTON STATION. G32 —6B 86
Shiel Av. E Kil —6H 137
Shielbridge Gdns. G23 —6C 46
Shiel Ct. Barr —2D 114
Shieldaig Dri. Ruth —3D 120
Shieldburn Rd. G51 —4C 80
Shieldhall Gdns. G51 —4C 80
Shieldhall Rd. G51 —3B 80
Shieldhill. E Kil —4H 149
Shieldhill Rd. Carl —5E 165
SHIELDMUIR STATION. Moth —5C 144
Shieldmuir St. Wis —5C 144
Shields Dri. Moth —6B 144
Shields Rd. G41 —3C 102
Shields Rd. E Kil —6E 149
Shields Rd. Moth —5A 144
SHIELDS RD. STATION. G5 —6D 82
Shields Tower. Moth —6B 144
Shiel Pl. Coat —6F 91
Shiel Pl. E Kil —6H 137
Shiel Rd. B'rig —6D 48
Shiel Ter. Newm —3D 146
Shilford Av. G13 —2A 60
Shillay St. G22 —1A 64
Shillingworth Pl. Bri W —5F 73
Shilton Dri. G53 —2C 116
Shilton La. B'ton —3C 40
Shinwell Av. Clyd —6F 43
Shira Ter. E Kil —2B 150
Shirley Quad. Moth —6F 143
Shirrel Av. Bell —6C 110
Shirrel Rd. Moth —3A 128
Shirva Lea. Twe —1D 32
Shiskine Pl. G20 —1A 62
Shiskine St. G20 —1A 62
Sholto Cres. Bell —6H 109
Shore St. G40 —3B 104
Shortroods Av. Pais —4H 77
Shortroods Cres. Pais —4H 77
Shortroods Rd. Pais —4H 77
Shotts St. G33 —3D 86
Shuna Pl. G20 —4C 62
Shuna Pl. Newt M —3B 132
Shuna St. G20 —3C 62
Shuttle St. G1 —4H 83 (6G 5)
Shuttle St. Kilb —1A 94
Shuttle St. Kils —3H 11
Shuttle St. Pais —1A 98
Sidland Rd. G21 —4E 65
Sidlaw Av. Barr —6E 115
Sidlaw Av. Ham —1D 152
Sidlaw Ct. Coat —2E 111
Sidlaw Dri. Wis —6F 145
Sidlaw Rd. Bear —1B 44
Sielga Pl. G34 —3G 87
Siemens Pl. G21 —1D 84
Siemens St. G21 —1D 84
Sievewright St. Ruth —4E 105
Sighthill Loan. Lark —1F 161
(off Muirshot Rd.)
Sikeside Pl. Coat —6F 91
Sikeside St. Coat —6F 91
Silkin Av. Clyd —6F 43
Silk St. Pais —6B 78
Silvan Pl. Clar —4E 135
Silverburn Cres. Moth —4D 128
Silverburn St. G33 —3G 85
Silverdale. E Kil —6E 137
Silverdale St. G40 —1E 105
Silverfir Ct. G5 —1H 103
Silver Firs. Moth —4C 128
Silverfir St. G5 —2H 103
Silvergrove St. G40 —6A 84
Silverton Av. Dumb —4H 17
Silvertonhill Av. Ham —3A 154
Silvertonhill Pl. Ham —4H 153
Silverwells. Both —6F 125
Silverwells Cres. Both —6E 125
Silverwood Ct. Both —6F 125
Simons Cres. Renf —4F 59
Simpson Ct. Clyd —5C 42
Simpson Ct. Udd —1D 124
Simpson Dri. E Kil —4F 149
Simpson Pl. E Kil —4F 149
Simpson St. G20 —6D 62
Simpson Way. Bell —6E 111
Simshill Rd. G44 —4F 119
Sinclair Av. Bear —1E 45
Sinclair Dri. G42 —6D 102
Sinclair Dri. Coat —4H 89
Sinclair Gdns. B'rig —1D 64
Sinclair Gro. Bell —5B 126
Sinclair Pk. E Kil —3H 149
Sinclair Pl. E Kil —3H 149
Sinclair St. Clyd —1F 59
Sinclair St. Miln —3G 25
Singer Rd. Clyd —4B 42
Singer Rd. E Kil —5H 149
Singer St. Clyd —4D 42
Sir Michael Pl. Pais —1H 97
Sixth Av. Renf —2E 79
Sixth St. Udd —4C 108
Skaethorn Rd. G20 —2H 61
Skara Wlk. Newm —2D 146
(off Kildonan Ct.)
Skaterigg Dri. G13 —4F 61
Skaterigg Gdns. G13 —4F 61
Skaterigg La. G13 —4E 61
(off Chamberlain Rd.)
Skelbo Path. G34 —2B 88
Skelbo Pl. G34 —2B 88
Skellyton Cres. Lark —3F 161
Skene Rd. G51 —6H 81
Skerne Gro. E Kil —5B 148
Skerray Quad. G22 —1G 63
Skerray St. G22 —1G 63
Skerryvore Pl. G33 —3B 86
Skerryvore Rd. G33 —3B 86
Skibo La. Giff —4E 117
Skipness Av. Carl —5G 165
Skipness Dri. G51 —4D 80
Skirsa Ct. G23 —1E 63
Skirsa Pl. G23 —2D 62
Skirsa Sq. G23 —2E 63
Skirsa St. G23 —1D 62
Skirving St. G41 —5C 102
Skovlunde Way. E Kil —5G 149
Skye. E Kil —2C 150
Skye Av. Renf —2E 79
Skye Ct. Cumb —5F 35
Skye Cres. Old K —2G 41
Skye Cres. Pais —6H 97
Skye Dri. Cumb —5F 35
Skye Dri. Old K —2G 41
Skye Gdns. Bear —1B 44
Skye Pl. Cumb —5F 35
Skye Quad. Wis —4C 146
Skye Rd. Cumb —5F 35
Skye Rd. Ruth —4F 121
Slakiewood Av. G'csh —2C 68
Slatefield. Len —3F 7
Slatefield Ct. G31 —5C 84
(off Slatefield St.)
Slatefield St. G31 —5C 84
Sleaford Av. Moth —5F 143
Slenavon Av. Ruth —4F 121
Slessor Dri. E Kil —4G 149
Slioch Sq. Moth —3C 128
Sloy St. G22 —5H 63
Sloy St. Wis —2G 157
Small Cres. Blan —2B 140
Smeaton Av. Torr —5D 28
Smeaton St. G20 —3D 62
Smith Av. Wis —4G 157
Smith Cres. Clyd —2D 42
Smithhills St. Pais —6A 78
Smith Quad. Coat —4E 91
Smith's La. Pais —5A 78
Smithstone Cres. Kils —6A 12
Smith St. G14 —1E 81
(in two parts)
Smith Ter. Ruth —4D 104
Smithview. Over —4A 158
Smith Wlk. G14 —3G 59
Smithycroft. Ham —1C 154
Smithycroft Rd. G33 —3F 85
Smithyends. Cumb —6B 14
Smollett Rd. Dumb —4H 17
Snaefell Av. Ruth —3E 121
Snaefell Cres. Ruth —2E 121
Sneddon Av. Wis —2A 158
Sneddon St. Ham —3D 140
Sneddon Ter. Ham —3D 140
Snowdon Pl. G5 —1H 103
Snowdon St. G5 —1H 103
Snuff Mill Rd. G44 —2E 119
Society St. G31 —6D 84
Solar Ct. Lark —5F 161
Sollas Pl. G13 —1G 59
Solsgirth Gdns. Kirk —4H 31
Solway Ct. Ham —3F 153
Solway Pl. Chry —6B 52
Solway Rd. B'rig —5F 49
Solway St. G40 —3B 104
Somerford Rd. Bear —6F 45
Somerled Av. Pais —2B 78
Somerset Av. Ham —5F 141
Somerset Pl. G3 —2D 82
Somerset Pl. Meuse. G3 —2D 82
(off Elderslie St.)
Somervell St. Camb —1H 121
Somerville Dri. G42 —5F 103
Somerville Dri. E Kil —4G 149
Sommerville La. E Kil —4H 149
Sommerville Ter. E Kil —4G 149
Sorby St. G31 —6F 85
Sorley St. G11 —1F 81
Sorn St. G40 —2D 104
Souterhouse Path. Coat —6B 90
Souterhouse Rd. Coat —6B 90

Southampton Dri. G12 —3H 61
Southampton La. G12 —3H 61
(off Burlington Av.)
S. Annandale St. G42 —3F 103
South Av. Blan —4B 140
South Av. Carl —4E 165
South Av. Clyd B —5C 42
South Av. Pais —5B 98
South Av. Renf —6F 59
Southbank Dri. Kirk —6C 30
Southbank Rd. Kirk —6B 30
Southbank St. G31 —6F 85
S. Bank St. Clyd —2E 59
Southbar Av. G13 —2A 60
Southbar Rd. Inch —3E 57
S. Barrwood Rd. Kils —4A 12
S. Biggar Rd. Air —4B 92
South Brae. Kils —5E 7
Southbrae Av. Bri W —4D 72
Southbrae Dri. G13 —4C 60
Southbrae La. G13 —4E 61
(off Selborne Rd.)
South Bri. St. Air —3A 92
S. Burn Rd. Air —4F 91
S. Caldean Rd. Coat —6D 90
S. Campbell St. Pais —2A 98
S. Carbrain Rd. Cumb —5H 35
S. Chester St. G32 —6A 86
S. Circular Rd. Coat —4C 90
S. Claremont La. Miln —4G 25
S. Commonhead Av. Air —2H 91
Southcroft Rd. Ruth —4A 104
Southcroft St. G51 —4H 81
S. Crosshill Rd. B'rig —6C 48
S. Dean Pk. Av. Both —5E 125
Southdeen Av. G15 —4A 44
Southdeen Rd. G15 —4A 44
S. Douglas St. Clyd —1E 59
South Dri. Lin —5H 75
S. Dumbreck Rd. Kils —3F 11
S. Elgin Pl. Clyd —2E 59
S. Elgin St. Clyd —2E 59
Southend Pl. Bell —3B 126
Southend Rd. Clyd —2D 42
Southern Av. Ruth —2D 120
Southerness Dri. Cumb —6A 14
S. Erskine Pk. Bear —2D 44
Southesk Av. B'rig —4B 48
Southesk Gdns. B'rig —4B 48
S. Exchange Ct. G1 —4G 83 (6E 5)
(off Buchanan St.)
Southfield Av. Pais —5A 98
Southfield Cres. G53 —5C 100
Southfield Cres. Coat —6E 91
Southfield Rd. Cumb —4E 35
S. Frederick St. G1 —4G 83 (5F 5)
Southgate. E Kil —2G 149
S. Glassford St. Miln —4H 25
Southhill Av. Ruth —1E 121
Southinch Av. G14 —3G 59
Southlea Av. T'bnk —4G 117
South Loan. Chry —1B 68
Southloch Gdns. G21 —6B 64
Southloch St. G21 —6B 64
S. Mains Rd. Miln —4F 25
S. Medrox St. Glenb —2G 69
S. Moraine La. G15 —5C 44
S. Mound. Hous —1A 74
S. Muirhead Rd. Cumb —3A 36
Southmuir Pl. G20 —4B 62
S. Nimmo St. Air —4B 92
South Pk. Ham —1H 153
Southpark Av. G12 —1B 82
South Pk. Dri. Pais —3A 98
South Pk. Gro. Ham —6H 141
South Pk. La. G12 —1C 82
South Pk. Ter. G12 —1C 82
South Pl. Bell —3B 126
S. Portland St. G5 —6F 83
(in two parts)
South Rd. Clar —4E 135
S. Robertson Pl. Air —4G 91
S. Scott St. Bail —1H 107
S. Spiers Wharf. G4 —1F 83
South St. G14 & G11 —5A 60
South St. Hous —1A 74
South St. Inch —5F 57
S. Vesalius St. G32 —6A 86
Southview. Bear —2C 44
South View. Bell —3A 126
South View. Blan —6A 124
South View. Clyd —4B 42
Southview Av. Clar —1D 134
Southview Ct. B'rig —2B 64
Southview Cres. Bri W —2F 73
Southview Pl. G'csh —3C 68
Southview Ter. B'rig —2B 64
S. William St. John —3F 95
Southwold Rd. Pais —6G 79
Southwood Dri. G44 —2G 119
S. Woodside Rd. G4 —1C 82
S. Woodside Rd. G20 —6D 62
Soutra Pl. G33 —3B 86
Spaehouse Wynd. Carl —4H 165
Spalehall Dri. Moth —4F 129
Spateston Rd. John —6C 94
Spean Av. E Kil —2B 150
Spean St. G44 —6E 103
Speirsfield Gdns. Pais —2A 98
...hall Clo. G14 —4H 59
... Ter. G14 —3G 59
Speirs Rd. Bear —4G 45
Speirs Rd. John —2H 95
Spencer Dri. Pais —5B 96
Spencerfield Gdns. Ham —6B 142
Spencer St. G13 —2F 61
Spencer St. Clyd —4C 42
Spence St. G20 —1A 62
Spey Av. Pais —5C 96
Spey Ct. Air —6C 92
Spey Ct. Newm —3D 146
Spey Dri. Renf —1G 79
Spey Gdns. Ham —3F 153
Spey Gro. E Kil —4A 148
Spey Pl. John —5C 94
Spey Rd. Bear —5C 44
Spey St. G33 —3H 85
Spey Ter. E Kil —4B 148
Spey Wlk. Cumb —3H 35
(off Cumbernauld Cen., The)
Spey Wlk. Moth —1C 128
Spey Wynd. Lark —5E 161
Spiersbridge Av. T'bnk —5E 117
(in two parts)
Spiersbridge La. Giff —4E 117
Spiersbridge Rd. T'bnk —5F 117
Spiersbridge Ter. T'bnk —4E 117
Spiers Gro. T'bnk —4F 117
Spiers Pl. Lin —4A 76
Spiers Rd. Bear —4H 45
Spiers Rd. Hous —1B 74
Spindlehowe Rd. Udd —2D 124
Spindlehowe Rd. Udd —6E 109
(Tannochside)
Spinners Gdns. Pais —2F 97
Spinners La. Clyd —6D 22
Spittal Rd. Ruth —3B 120
Spoutmouth. G1 —5H 83
Springbank Rd. Pais —4H 77
Springbank St. G20 —5D 62
Springbank Ter. Pais —4H 77
Springboig Av. G32 —5C 86
Springboig Rd. G32 —4C 86
Springburn Pl. E Kil —6C 136
Springburn Rd. G21 —4A 64
Springburn Shopping Cen. G21 —5B 64
SPRINGBURN STATION. G21 —5B 64
Springburn Way. G21 —5A 64
Springcroft Av. Bail —5H 87
Springcroft Cres. Bail —5H 87
Springcroft Dri. Bail —5G 87
Springcroft Gdns. Bail —5A 88
Springcroft Gro. Bail —5H 87
Springcroft Rd. Bail —5G 87
Springcroft Wynd. Bail —5H 87
Springfield Av. B'rig —1C 64
Springfield Av. Pais —1D 98
Springfield Av. Udd —2D 124
Springfield Ct. G1 —4G 83 (6E 5)
Springfield Ct. B'rig —6D 48
Springfield Cres. B'rig —1C 64
Springfield Cres. Blan —2A 140
Springfield Cres. Carl —5F 165
Springfield Cres. Udd —2D 124
Springfield Dri. Barr —6G 115
Springfield Pk. John —3G 95
Springfield Pk. Rd. Ruth —1E 121
Springfield Quay. G51 —5D 82
Springfield Rd. G31 —1E 105
Springfield Rd. G40 —2C 104
Springfield Rd. Air —3E 93
Springfield Rd. Barr —2F 131
Springfield Rd. B'rig —6C 48
Springfield Rd. Cumb —1A 36
Springfield Sq. B'rig —1C 64
Springfield Woods. John —3G 95
Springhall Ct. Ruth —4F 121
(off Slenavon Av.)
Springhill Av. Air —3B 92
Springhill Av. Coat —1G 109
Springhill Gdns. G41 —4C 102
Springhill Pl. Coat —1G 109
Springhill Rd. Bail —6F 87
Springhill Rd. Barr —5D 114
Springhill Rd. Clar —2D 134
Springholm Dri. Air —1H 91
Springkell Av. G41 —2H 101
Springkell Dri. G41 —3H 101
Springkell Gdns. G41 —3B 102
Springkell Ga. G41 —3B 102
Springside Pl. G15 —3A 44
Springvale Ter. G21 —5A 64
Springwell Cres. Blan —2D 140
Springwells Av. Air —3C 92
Springwells Cres. Air —3C 92
Spruce Av. Blan —1A 140
Spruce Av. Ham —1A 154
Spruce Av. John —4G 95
Spruce Ct. Coat —1B 110
Spruce Ct. Ham —2A 154
Spruce Dri. Kirk —2A 50
Spruce Rd. Cumb —1D 36
Spruce Rd. Udd —4G 109
Spruce St. G22 —4H 63
Spruce Way. Moth —3B 128
Spynie Pl. B'rig —5F 49
Spynie Way. Newm —3D 146
(off Iona Rd.)
Squire St. G14 —1D 80
Stable Pl. Miln —2F 25
Stable Rd. Miln —2F 25
Staffa. E Kil —3C 150
Staffa Av. Renf —2E 79
Staffa Dri. Air —4F 93
Staffa Dri. Kirk —5H 31
Staffa Dri. Pais —6A 98
Staffa Rd. Camb —4H 121
Staffa St. G31 —3D 84
Staffin Dri. G23 —6B 46
Staffin Path. G23 —6C 46
(off Staffin St.)
Staffin St. G23 —6C 46
Stafford St. G4 —2G 83 (2G 5)
Stafford St. Bell —3B 126
Stag Ct. Udd —1G 125
Stag St. G51 —4H 81
Staig Wynd. Moth —5A 144
Staineybraes Pl. Air —1H 91
Stalker St. Wis —5C 144
Stamford St. G40 & G31 —6D 84
Stamperland Av. Clar —2D 134
Stamperland Cres. Clar —1C 134
Stamperland Dri. Clar —2D 134
Stamperland Gdns. Clar —6D 118
Stamperland Hill. Clar —1C 134
Stanalane St. T'bnk —3F 117
Standburn Rd. G21 —2F 65
Staneacre Pk. Ham —6B 142
Stanecraigs Pl. Newm —3D 146
Stanefield Dri. Moth —3E 129
Stanely Av. Pais —5F 97
Stanely Ct. Pais —5F 97
Stanely Cres. Pais —5F 97
Stanely Dri. Pais —4G 97
Stanely Rd. Pais —4G 97
Stanford St. Clyd —6E 43
Stanhope Dri. Ruth —2F 121
Stanhope Pl. Wis —4G 157
Stanistone Rd. Carl —3G 165
Stanka Av. Pais —2G 97
Stanley Dri. Bell —1C 126
Stanley Dri. B'rig —5D 48
Stanley Dri. Brkfld —6C 74
Stanley La. Brkfld —6C 74
Stanley Pk. Air —3B 92
Stanley Pl. Blan —6B 124
Stanley St. G41 —6C 82
Stanley St. Ham —5D 140
Stanley St. La. G41 —6C 82
Stanmore Rd. G42 —5F 103
Stanrigg St. Plain —1G 93
Stark Av. Clyd —1A 42
Starling Way. Stra B —5A 110
Startpoint St. G33 —3A 86
Stathers Yd. G12 —5A 62
Station Brae. Neil —1C 130
Station Cres. Renf —5F 59
Station Pl. Law —5E 159
Station Rd. G20 —1A 62
Station Rd. Air —3E 93
Station Rd. Bail —1A 108
Station Rd. Bard —6E 27
Station Rd. Bear —3C 44
Station Rd. B'ton —5H 39
Station Rd. Blan —1C 140
Station Rd. Both —5E 125
Station Rd. Carl —4E 165
Station Rd. Clar —4E 135
Station Rd. Cle —6H 129
Station Rd. Dumb —3E 17
Station Rd. Giff —4A 118
Station Rd. Ham —6A 142
Station Rd. Kilb —3A 94
Station Rd. Kils —2H 11
Station Rd. Lark —1F 161
Station Rd. Law —6D 158
Station Rd. Len —3F 7
Station Rd. Mille —4A 66
Station Rd. Miln —4G 25
Station Rd. Moth —4B 128
Station Rd. Muirh —2A 68
Station Rd. Neil —2D 130
Station Rd. Old K —1F 41
Station Rd. Pais —2E 97
Station Rd. Plain —1H 93
Station Rd. Renf —5F 59
Station Rd. Step —4D 66
Station Rd. Udd —1C 124
Station Rd. Wis —1G 157
Station Row. Law —5E 159
Station Way. Udd —1D 124
Station Wynd. Kilb —3B 94
Steading, The. Wis —4H 145
Steel St. G1 —5H 83
Steele St. Wis —1H 157
Steeple Sq. Kilb —2A 94
Steeple St. Kilb —2A 94
Stemac La. Plain —1G 93
Stenhouse Av. Muirh —2A 68
Stenton Cres. Wis —2D 156
Stenton Pl. Wis —2D 156
Stenton St. G32 —4G 85
Stepends Rd. Air —5H 93
Stepford Path. G33 —4G 87
Stepford Pl. G33 —4F 87
Stepford Rd. G33 —4F 87
Stephen Cres. Bail —6F 87
Stephenson Pl. E Kil —3F 149
Stephenson Sq. E Kil —3F 149
Stephenson St. H'ton I —3G 79
Stephenson Ter. E Kil —3F 149
Steppshill Ter. G33 —4C 66
Stepps Rd. G33 —2B 86
Stepps Rd. Kirk —5E 51
STEPPS STATION. Step —4E 67
Stevens La. Moth —4A 128
Stevenson Pl. Bell —6D 110
Stevenson St. G40 —5A 84
(in two parts)
Stevenson St. Carl —3E 165
Stevenson St. Clyd —3B 42
Stevenson St. Pais —2A 98
Stevens Pas. Pais —2A 98
Stevenston Ct. New S —3A 128
Stevenston St. Moth —3A 128
Stewart Av. Blan —2A 140
Stewart Av. Newt M —3E 133
Stewart Av. Renf —2D 78
Stewart Ct. Barr —3E 115
Stewart Ct. Coat —5E 91
(off Clifton Pl.)
Stewart Ct. Ruth —6E 105
Stewart Cres. Newm —3E 147
Stewart Dri. Bail —5F 89
Stewart Dri. Clar —1B 134
Stewart Dri. Clyd —1D 42
Stewartfield Rd. E Kil —6E 137
Stewartfield Way. E Kil —6A 136
Stewart Gill Pl. Ashg —4B 162
Stewarton Dri. Camb —2G 121
Stewarton Rd. T'bnk —6E 117
Stewarton St. Wis —1H 157
Stewarton Ter. Wis —1H 157
Stewart Pl. Barr —3F 115
Stewart Pl. Carl —3F 165
Stewart Quad. Holy —1B 128
Stewart Rd. Pais —5B 98
Stewarts La. Wis —6A 146
Stewart St. G4 —2F 83 (1D 4)
Stewart St. Barr —3F 115
Stewart St. Bell —2E 127
Stewart St. Carl —2E 165
Stewart St. Clyd —4A 42
Stewart St. Coat —3C 90
Stewart St. Ham —4E 141
(in two parts)
Stewart St. Miln —4G 25
Stewartville St. G11 —1H 81
Stirling Av. Bear —5E 45
Stirling Dri. Bear —1D 44
Stirling Dri. B'rig —4A 48
Stirling Dri. E Kil —6A 138
Stirling Dri. Ham —5C 140
Stirling Dri. John —3D 94
Stirling Dri. Lin —6F 75
Stirling Dri. Ruth —2D 120
Stirlingfauld Pl. G5 —6F 83
Stirling Gdns. B'rig —4A 48
Stirling Pl. Len —3G 7
Stirling Rd. G4 —3H 83 (4H 5)
Stirling Rd. Air —1B 92
Stirling Rd. Carl —1E 165
Stirling Rd. Chap —1D 112
Stirling Rd. Dumb —1G 17
Stirling Rd. Kils —2A 12
Stirling Rd. Kirk —4D 30
Stirling Rd. Ind. Est. Air —1B 92
Stirling St. Air —4H 91
Stirling St. Coat —1H 109
Stirling St. Cumb —1B 36
Stirling St. Moth —5B 144
Stirling Way. Bail —1G 107
Stirling Way. Renf —2F 79
Stirrat St. G20 —3A 62
Stirrat St. Pais —4F 77
Stobcross Rd. G3 —3A 82
Stobcross St. G3 —4C 82
Stobcross St. Coat —5C 90
Stobhill Rd. G21 —2B 64
Stobo. E Kil —5C 138
Stobo Ct. E Kil —5C 138
Stobo St. Wis —4A 146
Stobs Dri. Barr —2D 114
Stobs Pl. G34 —2A 88
Stock Av. Pais —2A 98
Stockholm Cres. Pais —2A 98
Stockiemuir Av. Bear —6D 24
Stockiemuir Ct. Bear —6E 25
Stockiemuir Rd. Bear —1D 44
Stockiemuir Rd. Miln —3C 24
Stocks Rd. Moth —1D 146
Stock St. Pais —3A 98
Stockwell Pl. G1 —5G 83
Stockwell St. G1 —5G 83
Stoddard Sq. Eld —2B 96
Stonebyres Ct. Ham —6E 141
Stonecraig Rd. Wis —1H 157
Stonedyke Rd. Carl —2G 165
Stonefield Av. G12 —3A 62
Stonefield Av. Pais —4B 98
Stonefield Cres. Blan —3A 140
Stonefield Cres. Clar —1A 134
Stonefield Cres. Pais —4B 98
Stonefield Dri. Pais —4B 98
Stonefield Gdns. Carl —2F 165
Stonefield Gdns. Pais —4B 98
Stonefield Grn. Pais —4A 98
Stonefield Pk. Pais —5A 98
Stonefield Pk. Gdns. Blan —1C 140
Stonefield Pl. Blan —3H 139
Stonefield Rd. Blan —2A 140
Stonefield St. Air —2A 92
Stonehall Av. Ham —1F 153
Stonelaw Dri. Ruth —6D 104
Stonelaw Rd. Ruth —6D 104
Stonelaw Towers. Ruth —1E 121
Stoneside Dri. G43 —1G 117
Stoneside Sq. G43 —1G 117
Stoney Brae. Pais —5A 98
(in two parts)
Stoneydyke Cres. Carl —2G 165
Stoneyetts Rd. Chry —4D 52
Stoneymeadow Rd. E Kil —5B 138
Stony Brae. Pais —6A 78
Stonyflatt Av. Dumb —2H 17
Stonyflatt Rd. Dumb —2H 17
Stonyhurst St. G22 —5F 63
(in two parts)
Stonylee Rd. Cumb —4A 36
Storie St. Pais —1A 98
Stormyland Way. Barr —5E 115
Stornaway St. G22 —1G 63
Stornoway Cres. Wis —4C 146
Stow Brae. Pais —1A 98
Stow St. Pais —1A 98
Strachan St. Bell —3C 126
Strachur St. G22 —2E 63
Strain Cres. Air —5B 92
Straiton Dri. Ham —1B 152
Straiton St. G32 —4G 85
Stranraer Dri. G15 —5C 44
Stratford. E Kil —4D 138
Stratford St. G20 —4B 62
Strathallan Gdns. Kirk —5D 30
(off Willowbank Gdns.)
Strathallon Pl. Ruth —4F 121
(off St Stephen's Av.)
Strathaven Rd. E Kil —3A 150
Strathaven Rd. Ham —6G 153
Strathavon Cres. Air —1A 92
Strathblane Cres. Air —6H 71
Strathblane Rd. Kils —1A 6
Strathblane Rd. Miln —3H 25
Strathbran St. G31 —1F 105
Strathcairn Cres. Air —6H 71
Strath Carron. Law —6E 159
Strathcarron Pl. G20 —3B 62
Strathcarron Rd. Pais —5D 98
Strathclyde Bus. Pk. Bell —5B 110
Strathclyde Dri. Ruth —6C 104
Strathclyde Path. Udd —1C 124
Strathclyde Rd. Dumb —2G 17
Strathclyde Rd. Moth —3D 142
Strathclyde St. G40 —3C 104
Strathclyde View. Both —6F 125
Strathcona Dri. G13 —2F 61
Strathcona Gdns. G13 —2G 61
Strathcona La. E Kil —4G 149
Strathcona Pl. E Kil —4G 149
Strathcona Pl. Ruth —3F 121
Strathcona St. G13 —2F 61
Strathconon Gdns. E Kil —2A 148
(off Strathnairn Dri.)
Strath Dearn. Law —6E 159
Strathdearn Gro. E Kil —3A 148
Strathdee Av. Clyd —2D 42
Strathdee Rd. G44 —5C 118
Strathdon Av. G44 —5C 118
Strathdon Av. Pais —3G 97
Strathdon Dri. G44 —5D 118
Strathdon Pl. E Kil —3A 148
(off Strathnairn Dri.)
Strathearn Gro. Kirk —4H 31
Strathearn Rd. Clar —3C 134
Strath Elgin. Law —6D 158
Strathendrick Dri. G44 —3C 118
Strathfillan Rd. E Kil —1F 149
Strath Halladale. Law —6E 159
Strathkelvin Av. B'rig —2B 64
Strathkelvin Retail Pk. B'rig —3E 49
Strathlachan Av. Carl —4G 165
Strathleven Pl. Dumb —4F 17
Strathmore Av. Blan —6A 124
Strathmore Av. Pais —1F 99
Strathmore Cres. Air —1A 92
Strathmore Gdns. Ruth —3F 121
Strathmore Pl. Coat —6F 91
Strathmore Rd. G22 —2F 63
Strathmore Rd. Ham —6A 142
Strathmore Wlk. Coat —6F 91
Strathmungo Cres. Air —1H 91
Strath Nairn. Law —6E 159
Strathnairn Av. E Kil —3A 148
Strathnairn Ct. E Kil —3A 148
Strathnairn Dri. E Kil —3A 148
Strathnairn Way. E Kil —3A 148
Strath Naver. Law —6E 159
Strathnaver Gdns. E Kil —3A 148
Strathord Pl. Chry —3E 53
Strathord St. G32 —2A 106
Strath Peffer. Law —6D 158
Strathpeffer Cres. Air —1A 92
Strathpeffer Dri. E Kil —2A 148
(off Strathnairn Dri.)
Strathspey Cres. Air —6H 71
Strathtay Av. G44 —5C 118
Strathtummel Cres. Air —6H 71
Strathview Gro. G44 —5C 118
Strathview Pk. G44 —5C 118
Strathview Rd. Bell —4A 126
Strathy Pl. G20 —3B 62
Strathyre Gdns. Bear —2H 45
Strathyre Gdns. Chry —4E 53

Strathyre Gdns. Glenm —4H 71
Strathyre Rd. Blan —3D 140
Strathyre St. G41 —5C 102
Stratton Dri. Giff —5H 117
Strauss Av. Clyd —6G 43
Stravaig Path. Pais —6E 97
Stravaig Wlk. Pais —6E 97
Stravanan Rd. G45 —6H 119
Stravannan St. G45 —5H 119
Stravenhouse Rd. Law —1G 163
Strawberry Field Rd. C'lee —2B 74
Strawhill Rd. Clar —2C 134
Strenabey Av. Ruth —3F 121
Striven Ct. Coat —2D 110
Striven Cres. Wis —2G 157
Striven Gdns. G20 —6D 62
Striven Ter. Ham —2E 153
Stroma St. G21 —1D 84
Stromness St. G5 —1E 103
Strone Gdns. Kils —3F 11
Stronend St. G22 —4F 63
Strone Path. Glenb —3G 69
Strone Rd. G33 —4B 86
Stronsay Pl. B'rig —5F 49
Stronsay St. G21 —1D 84
Stronvar Dri. G14 —5B 60
Stroud Rd. E Kil —6E 149
Strowan Cres. G32 —1B 106
Strowan's Rd. Dumb —2C 18
Strowan St. G32 —1B 106
Strowan's Well Rd. Dumb —2C 18
Struan Av. Giff —4A 118
Struan Gdns. G44 —2E 119
Struan Rd. G44 —2E 119
Struie St. G34 —3G 87
Struma Dri. Clar —1A 134
Strutherhill Ind. Est. Lark —5G 161
Struthers Cres. E Kil —5B 138
Struther St. Lark —5F 161
Struther & Swinhill Rd. Lark —6G 161
Stuart Av. Old K —2F 41
Stuart Av. Ruth —2D 120
Stuart Dri. B'rig —1A 64
Stuart Dri. Lark —4G 161
Stuart Ho. Cumb —2B 36
Stuarton Pk. E Kil —1G 149
Stuart Quad. Wis —2E 157
Stuart Rd. B'ton —3H 39
Stuart Rd. Crmck —1H 135
Stuart Rd. Dumb —1C 18
Stuart St. E Kil —1H 149
Stuart St. Old K —2F 41
Succoth St. G13 —2F 61
Sudbury Cres. E Kil —2D 148
Sugworth Av. Bail —6H 87
Sumburgh St. G33 —4H 85
Summerfield Rd. Cumb —1C 54
Summerfield St. G40 —2D 104
Summerhill Av. Lark —3E 161
Summerhill & Garngibbock Rd. Cumb —4E 55
Summerhill Rd. G15 —3A 44
Summerhill Rd. Clar —2D 134
Summerhill Way. Bell —3B 126
Summerlea Rd. T'bnk —3F 117
Summerlee Cotts. Coat —4B 90
Summerlee Rd. Lark —6H 155
Summerlee Rd. Wis —5C 144
Summerlee St. G33 —3C 86
Summerlee St. Coat —4B 90
SUMMERSTON STATION. G23 —1B 62
Summer St. G40 —6B 84
Summertown Rd. G51 —4H 81
Sunart Av. Renf —5D 58
Sunart Ct. Ham —2E 153
Sunart Gdns. B'rig —6E 49
Sunart Rd. G52 —6E 81
Sunart Rd. B'rig —6E 49
Sunart St. Wis —2G 157
Sunbury Av. Clar —2A 134
Sundale Av. Clar —3B 134
Sunderland Av. Dumb —3C 16
Sunflower Gdns. Moth —1F 143
Sunningdale Av. Newt M —4F 133
Sunningdale Dri. Bri W —5E 73
Sunningdale Rd. G23 —1B 62
Sunningdale Wynd. Both —4C 124
Sunnybank Dri. Clar —3B 134
Sunnybank Gro. Clar —3B 134
Sunnybank St. G40 —2D 104
Sunnyhill. Twe —2D 32
Sunnylaw Dri. Pais —3F 97
Sunnylaw St. G22 —5F 63
Sunnyside Av. Moth —2B 128
Sunnyside Av. Udd —2D 124
Sunnyside Cres. Moth —2A 128
Sunnyside Dri. G15 —6A 44
Sunnyside Dri. Bail —6D 88
Sunnyside Dri. Clar —1B 134
Sunnyside Pl. G15 —6A 44
Sunnyside Pl. Barr —5D 114
Sunnyside Pl. Moth —2A 128
Sunnyside Rd. Cle —1H 145
Sunnyside Rd. Coat —4C 90
Sunnyside Rd. Ham & Lark —3A 160
Sunnyside Rd. Pais —4H 97
Sunnyside St. Lark —1D 160
Sunnyside Ter. Moth —2A 128
Surrey St. G5 —1F 103
Sussex St. G41 —6C 82
Sutcliffe Ct. G13 —2E 61
Sutcliffe Rd. G13 —2E 61
Sutherland Av. G41 —2H 101
Sutherland Av. Bear —6E 25
Sutherland Dri. Air —6G 91
Sutherland Dri. Dumb —2C 18
Sutherland Dri. Giff —6B 118
Sutherland La. G12 —1B 82
Sutherland Pl. Bell —5B 126
Sutherland Rd. Clyd —5D 42
Sutherland St. Blan —4A 140
Sutherland St. Pais —6H 77
Sutherland Way. E Kil —6C 138
Swaledale. E Kil —6E 137
Swallow Gdns. G13 —2H 59
Swallow Rd. Clyd —6F 23
Swallow Rd. Wis —6H 145
Swan Pl. John —6C 94
Swanston St. G40 —3C 104
Swan St. G4 —2G 83 (1F 5)
Swan St. Clyd —4B 42
Swan Way. Law —1H 163
Sween Av. G44 —3E 119
Sween Dri. Ham —2E 153
Sween Path. Bell —4E 127
(off Millbank Av.)
Sweethill Ter. Coat —2F 111
Sweethill Wlk. Bell —6E 111
Sweethope Gdns. Both —5F 125
Sweethope Pl. Both —4E 125
Swift Bank. Ham —2C 152
Swift Cres. G13 —1H 59
Swift Pl. E Kil —5A 148
Swift Pl. John —6D 94
Swindon St. Clyd —4A 42
Swinstie Rd. Cle —1A 146
Swinton Av. Bail —6A 88
Swinton Cres. Bail —6A 88
Swinton Cres. Coat —1F 109
Swinton Dri. G52 —6B 80
Swinton Gdns. Bail —6B 88
Swinton Path. Bail —6B 88
Swinton Pl. G52 —6B 80
Swinton Pl. Coat —1F 109
(off Swinton Cres.)
Swinton Rd. Bail —6A 88
Swinton View. Bail —6B 88
Swisscot Av. Ham —3F 153
Swisscot Wlk. Ham —3F 153
Switchback Rd. Bear —5F 45
Swordale Path. G34 —3G 87
(off Kildermorie Rd.)
Swordale Pl. G34 —3G 87
Sword St. G31 —5C 84
Sword St. G40 —5B 84
Sword St. Air —4H 91
Sycamore Av. John —4G 95
Sycamore Av. Lenz —2D 50
Sycamore Av. Udd —6G 109
Sycamore Ct. Coat —1B 110
(off Ailsa Rd.)
Sycamore Ct. E Kil —5F 149
Sycamore Cres. Air —5D 92
Sycamore Cres. E Kil —5E 149
Sycamore Dri. Air —5D 92
Sycamore Dri. Clyd —3C 42
Sycamore Dri. Ham —1B 154
Sycamore Gro. Blan —1A 140
Sycamore Pl. E Kil —5F 149
Sycamore Pl. Moth —4C 128
Sycamore Way. Clar —2H 135
Sycamore Way. Milt C —6C 8
Sydenham Ct. G12 —5A 62
(off Westbourne Gdns. La.)
Sydenham La. G12 —6H 61
Sydenham Rd. G12 —6A 62
Sydes Brae. Blan —5H 139
Sydney Dri. E Kil —4E 149
Sydney Pl. E Kil —3E 149
Sydney St. G31 —5A 84
Sydney St. Clyd —3H 41
Sykehead Av. Bell —2D 126
Sykeside Rd. Coat —1G 111
Sykes Ter. Neil —2F 131
Sylvania Way. Clyd —5D 42
Sylvania Way S. Clyd —6D 42
Symington Dri. Clyd B —5C 42
Symington Sq. E Kil —3H 149
Syrett Cotts. Coat —5B 90
Syriam Pl. G21 —5B 64
Syriam St. G21 —4B 64

Tabard Pl. G13 —1C 60
Tabard Rd. G13 —1C 60
Tabernacle La. Camb —2A 122
Tabernacle St. Camb —2A 122
Taggart Rd. Kils —2B 34
Taig Rd. Kirk —6H 31
Tait Av. Barr —3F 115
Takmadoon Rd. Kils —2A 12
Talbot. E Kil —5C 138
Talbot Dri. G13 —4B 60
Talbot Pl. G13 —4B 60
Talbot Ter. G13 —4B 60
Talbot Ter. Udd —5C 108
Talisman Av. Dumb —3C 16
Talisman Cres. Moth —5F 127
Talisman Rd. G13 —3C 60
Talisman Rd. Pais —6C 96
Tallant Rd. G15 —4B 44
Tallant Ter. G15 —4C 44
Talla Rd. G52 —5A 80
Tamarack Cres. Udd —4G 109
Tamar Dri. E Kil —5B 148
Tambowie Av. Miln —3F 25
Tambowie Cres. Miln —3F 25
Tambowie St. G13 —1E 61
Tamshill St. G20 —3D 62
Tanar Av. Renf —2G 79
Tanar Way. Renf —1G 79
Tandlehill Rd. Mill P —4A 94
Tanera Av. G44 —2G 119
Tanfield Pl. G32 —4C 86
Tanfield St. G32 —4C 86
Tankerland Rd. G44 —1E 119
Tannadice. G52 —1C 100
(off Tannadice Av.)
Tannadice Av. G52 —2C 100
Tanna Dri. G52 —2F 101
Tannahill Cen. Pais —5E 77
Tannahill Cres. John —4E 95
(in two parts)
Tannahill Dri. E Kil —6C 138
Tannahill Rd. G43 —1D 118
Tannahill Rd. Pais —5F 77
Tannahill Ter. Pais —5F 77
Tannoch Dri. Cumb —6H 35
Tannoch Dri. Miln —2G 25
Tannoch Pl. Cumb —6H 35
Tannochside Dri. Udd —4E 109
Tannochside Pk. Udd —4F 109
Tannock St. G22 —5F 63
Tantallon Ct. Carl —2E 165
Tantallon Dri. Coat —2G 89
Tantallon Dri. Pais —4E 97
Tantallon Pk. E Kil —1F 149
Tantallon Rd. G41 —5C 102
Tantallon Rd. Bail —2G 107
Tanzieknowe Av. Camb —4B 122
Tanzieknowe Dri. Camb —4B 122
Tanzieknowe Pl. Camb —4A 122
Tanzieknowe Rd. Camb —4A 122
Taransay St. G51 —3G 81
Tarbert Av. Blan —5A 124
Tarbert Av. Wis —2G 157
Tarbert Ct. Ham —2E 153
Tarbet Pl. Carl —4G 165
Tarbolton. E Kil —6D 138
Tarbolton Dri. Clyd —4E 43
Tarbolton Pl. Lark —2D 160
Tarbolton Rd. G43 —1B 118
Tarbolton Rd. Cumb —3B 36
Tarbolton Sq. Clyd —4E 43
Tarbrax Way. Ham —6E 141
Tarfside Av. G52 —1C 100
Tarfside Gdns. G52 —1D 100
Tarfside Oval. G52 —1D 100
Target Rd. Air —5B 92
Tarland St. G51 —5F 81
Tarras Dri. Renf —2G 79
Tarras Pl. Camb —2D 122
Tasman Dri. E Kil —4D 148
Tasmania Quad. Wis —6C 146
Tassie Pl. E Kil —1A 150
Tassie St. G41 —5B 102
Tattershall Rd. G33 —1C 86
Tavistock Dri. G43 —2B 118
Tay Av. Pais —4D 96
Tay Av. Renf —6G 59
Tay Ct. E Kil —4A 148
Tay Cres. G33 —2G 85
Tay Cres. B'rig —6D 48
Tay Gdns. Ham —3F 153
Tay Gro. E Kil —4A 148
Tayinloan Dri. Carl —5H 165
Tay La. Newm —4E 147
Tay Loan. Moth —2A 128
(off Windsor Rd.)
Taylor Av. Kilb —2A 94
Taylor Av. Moth —5D 128
Taylor Pl. G4 —3H 83 (3H 5)
Taylor St. G4 —3H 83 (4H 5)
(in two parts)
Taylor St. Clyd —1E 59
Taymouth St. G32 —2B 106
Taynish Dri. G44 —3F 119
Tay Pl. Dumb —1H 17
Tay Pl. E Kil —4A 148
Tay Pl. John —5C 94
Tay Pl. Lark —5E 161
Tay Rd. Bear —5D 44
Tay Rd. B'rig —6D 48
Tayside. Air —2H 91
Tay St. Coat —2G 89
Tay Ter. E Kil —3A 148
Tay Wlk. Cumb —3H 35
(off Cumbernauld Cen., The)
Teak Pl. Udd —4H 109
Teal Ct. Stra B —5A 110
Teal Cres. E Kil —6B 148
Teal Dri. G13 —2A 60
Tealing Av. G52 —1C 100
Tealing Cres. G52 —1C 100
Teasel Av. G53 —4B 116
Teawell Rd. Newt M —4D 132
Teesdale. E Kil —6E 137
Teign Gro. E Kil —5B 148
Teith Av. Renf —1H 79
Teith Dri. Bear —4D 44
Teith Pl. Camb —2D 122
Teith St. G33 —2G 85
Telephone La. G12 —1A 82
(off Highburgh Rd.)
Telford Ct. Clyd —5C 42
Telford Pl. Cumb —5A 36
Telford Rd. Cumb —5A 36
Telford Rd. E Kil —3F 149
Telford St. Bell —1C 126
Telford Ter. E Kil —3H 149
(off Telford Rd.)
Teme Pl. E Kil —4B 148
Templar Av. G13 —6D 44
Temple Gdns. G13 —2F 61
Templeland Av. G53 —3C 100
Templeland Rd. G53 —3C 100
Temple Rd. G13 —2G 61
Templeton Bus. Cen. G40 —6A 84
Templeton St. G40 —6A 84
Tennant Av. E Kil —1C 148
Tennant Rd. Pais —5F 77
Tennant St. Renf —5F 59
Tennent St. Coat —6D 90
Tennyson Dri. G31 —1G 105
Tern Pl. John —6D 94
Terregles Av. G41 —3H 101
Terregles Cres. G41 —3A 102
Terregles Dri. G41 —3A 102
Teviot Av. B'rig —4C 48
Teviot Av. Pais —5C 96
Teviot Cres. Bear —5D 44
Teviotdale. E Kil —1F 149
(off Strathfillan Rd.)
Teviotdale. Newt M —4H 133
Teviot Dri. B'ton —5A 40
Teviot Path. Blan —2A 140
Teviot Pl. Camb —2E 123
Teviot Sq. Cumb —3H 35
(off Cumbernauld Cen., The)
Teviot St. G3 —3A 82
Teviot St. Coat —1H 89
Teviot Ter. John —5C 94
Teviot Wlk. Cumb —3H 35
(off Cumbernauld Cen., The)
Teviot Way. Cumb —3H 35
(off Cumbernauld Cen., The)
Tewkesbury Rd. E Kil —4D 138
Thane Rd. G13 —3C 60
Thanes Ga. Udd —2C 124
Thankerton Av. Moth —2H 127
Thankerton Rd. Lark —4F 161
Tharsis St. G21 —2B 84
Third Av. G44 —6F 103
Third Av. Blan —4C 140
Third Av. Dumb —3C 18
Third Av. Kirk —5D 50
Third Av. Mille —4B 66
Third Av. Renf —1E 79
Third Gdns. G41 —1G 101
Thirdpart Cres. G13 —2G 59
Third St. Udd —5D 108
Thirlmere. E Kil —6B 148
Thistle Bank. Lenz —3D 50
Thistle Cres. Lark —3F 161
Thistledown Gro. Coat —5E 91
Thistle Gdns. Moth —2A 128
Thistleneuk. Old K —6E 21
Thistle Pl. E Kil —6G 137
Thistle Quad. Air —2B 92
Thistle Rd. Moth —4A 128
Thistle St. G5 —1F 103
(in two parts)
Thistle St. Air —2B 92
Thistle St. Kirk —5D 30
Thistle St. Moth —6H 129
Thistle St. Pais —3G 97
Thomas Muir Av. B'rig —1C 64
Thomas St. Pais —1F 97
Thompson Av. Kirk —5E 31
Thompson Dri. Air —5H 91
Thompson Pl. Clyd —1E 43
Thompson St. Renf —1E 79
Thomson Av. John —2E 95
Thomson Av. Wis —2D 156
Thomson Dri. Bear —1F 45
Thomson Dri. Bell —2H 125
Thomson Gro. Camb —6A 106
Thomson St. G31 —5C 84
Thomson St. Carl —3F 165
Thomson St. John —3E 95
Thorn Av. T'hall —6G 135
Thornbank St. G3 —3A 82
Thornbridge Av. G12 —4A 62
Thornbridge Av. Bail —6H 87
Thornbridge Gdns. Bail —6G 87
Thornbridge Rd. Bail —6G 87
Thorncliffe Gdns. G41 —3C 102
Thorncroft Dri. G44 —3H 119
Thorndale Gdns. Alla —1H 15
Thorndean Av. Bell —3D 126
Thorndean Cres. Bell —3D 126
Thorndene. Eld —2H 95
Thorndene Av. Moth —5C 128
Thornden La. G14 —5A 60
Thorn Dri. Bear —1D 44
Thorn Dri. Ruth —3E 121
Thorndyke. E Kil —4C 138
Thorne Brae. John —2G 95
Thornhill. John —3H 95
Thornhill Av. Blan —1B 140
Thornhill Av. Eld —3H 95
Thornhill Dri. Eld —3H 95
Thornhill Gdns. John —2G 95
Thornhill Path. G31 —6F 85
Thornhill Rd. Ham —5C 140
Thornhill Way. Coat —2F 111
Thorniecroft Dri. Cumb —1E 55
Thorniecroft Pl. Cumb —1E 55
Thornielee. E Kil —1B 150
Thorniewood Gdns. Udd —6E 109
Thorniewood Rd. Udd —5D 108
Thornkip Pl. Coat —6F 91
Thornlea Dri. Giff —3B 118
Thornlea St. Carl —5G 165
Thornley Av. G13 —3B 60
Thornliebank Ind. Est. T'bnk —4E 117
Thornliebank Rd. G43 & G46 —1H 117
Thornliebank Rd. Newt M —2C 132
THORNLIEBANK STATION. T'bnk —3G 117
Thornlie Gill. Wis —1H 157
Thornly Pk. Av. Pais —5B 98
Thornly Pk. Dri. Pais —5B 98
Thornly Pk. Gdns. Pais —4B 98
Thornly Pk. Rd. Pais —5B 98
Thorn Rd. Bear —2C 44
Thorn Rd. Bell —2D 126
Thornside Rd. John —2G 95
THORNTONHALL STATION. E Kil —6F 135
Thornton La. G20 —2C 62
Thornton Pl. Ham —5H 153
Thornton Rd. T'hall —6G 135
Thornton St. G20 —2B 62
Thornton St. Coat —1H 89
Thorntree Av. Ham —4D 140
Thorntree Way. Both —4F 125
Thornwood Av. G11 —1G 81
Thornwood Av. Kirk —2A 50
Thornwood Cres. G11 —6F 61
Thornwood Dri. G11 —1F 81
Thornwood Dri. Bri W —4D 72
Thornwood Dri. Pais —3F 97
Thornwood Gdns. G11 —1F 81
Thornwood Pl. G11 —6G 61
Thornwood Rd. G11 —1F 81
Thornwood Ter. G11 —1F 81
Thornyburn Dri. Bail —1B 108
Thornyburn Pl. Bail —1A 108
Thorp Ct. John —3G 95
Thrashbush Av. Wis —5B 146
Thrashbush Cres. Wis —5B 146
Thrashbush Rd. Wis —5B 146
Threave Ct. Carl —2E 165
Three Queens Sq. Clyd —6D 42
Three Rivers Wlk. E Kil —3D 148
Threestonehill Av. G32 —5B 86
Threshold Pk. E Kil —1A 150
Threshold Rd. E Kil —1A 150
Thriplee Rd. Bri W —3E 73
Thrums. E Kil —4D 138
Thrums Av. B'rig —6E 49
Thrums Gdns. B'rig —6E 49
Thrushbush La. Air —1B 92
Thrushbush Quad. Air —1A 92
Thrushbush Rd. Air —1A 92
Thrushcraig Cres. Pais —3B 98
Thrush Pl. John —6D 94
Thurso St. G11 —2A 82
Thurston Rd. G52 —6A 80
Thyme Sq. Moth —1G 143
Tibbermore Rd. G11 —6G 61
Tighnasheen Way. Blan —1B 140
Tillanburn Rd. Moth —4F 129
Tillet Oval. Pais —4H 77
Tillie St. G20 —6D 62
Till St. Wis —3H 145
Tillycairn Av. G33 —1D 86
Tillycairn Dri. G33 —1D 86
Tillycairn Pl. G33 —1E 87
Tillycairn Rd. G33 —1E 87
Tillycairn St. G33 —1E 87
Tilt Rd. Newm —3D 146
Tilt St. G33 —1G 85
Timmons Ter. Chap —4D 112
Tinker's La. Moth —3E 143
Tintagel Gdns. Chry —4D 52
Tintock Dri. Kirk —4F 31
Tintock Rd. Kirk —3H 31
Tinto Ct. Coat —2E 111
Tinto Cres. Wis —1A 158
Tinto Dri. Barr —6D 114
Tinto Rd. G43 —2A 118
Tinto Rd. Air —5B 92
Tinto Rd. Bear —1B 44
Tinto Rd. B'rig —6F 49
Tinto Sq. Renf —2D 78
Tinto St. Wis —1A 158
Tinto View. Ham —3A 154
Tinto Way. Cle —5H 129
Tinto Way. E Kil —6D 148
Tinwald Path. G52 —6A 80
Tiree. E Kil —4C 150
Tiree Av. Pais —6H 97
Tiree Av. Renf —3E 79
Tiree Ct. Cumb —5F 35
Tiree Cres. Newm —2D 146
Tiree Dri. Cumb —5F 35
Tiree Gdns. Bear —1B 44
Tiree Gdns. Glenm —4H 71

Tiree Gdns. Old K —1G 41
Tiree Pl. Newt M —4B 132
Tiree Pl. Old K —1G 41
Tiree Rd. Cumb —5F 35
Tiree St. G21 —1E 85
Tirry Av. Renf —1H 79
Tirry Way. Renf —1H 79
Titwood Rd. G41 —3A 102
(in two parts)
Tiverton Av. G32 —2D 106
Tivoli Ct. E Kil —5G 149
Tobago Pl. G40 —6B 84
Tobago Pl. E Kil —2C 148
Tobago St. G40 —6A 84
Tobermory Rd. Ruth —4F 121
Todburn Dri. Pais —6B 98
Todd St. G31 —4E 85
Todhills. E Kil —3H 149
Todhills N. E Kil —3H 149
Todhills S. E Kil —3H 149
Todholm Cres. Pais —3D 98
Todholm Rd. Pais —3D 98
Todholm Ter. Pais —3D 98
Tofthill Av. B'rig —5B 48
Tofthill Gdns. B'rig —5B 48
Tollbrae Av. Air —4B 92
Tollcross Rd. G31 & G32 —6F 85
Tollhouse Gdns. Bell —4E 127
Toll La. G51 —5C 82
Tollpark Cres. Newm —4E 147
Tollpark Pl. Ward E —3E 15
Tollpark Rd. Ward E —3D 14
Toll St. Moth —4H 143
Toll, The. Clar —1C 134
Toll Wynd. Ham —4G 153
Tolsta St. G23 —6C 46
Tomtain Brae. Cumb —6B 34
Tomtain Ct. Cumb —6B 34
Toner Gdns. Wis —4H 157
Tonge Pl. Air —1B 92
Tontine La. G1 —5H 83
Tontine Pl. Ruth —3G 121
Topaz Ter. Bell —4C 126
Toppersfield. Mill P —3C 94
Torbreck St. G52 —6F 81
Torbrex Rd. Cumb —4A 36
Torburn Av. Giff —3H 117
Tordene Path. Cumb —2F 35
Torgyle St. G23 —6B 46
Tormeadow Rd. Newt M —4D 132
Tormore St. G51 —5D 80
Tormusk Dri. G45 —3C 120
Tormusk Gdns. G45 —3C 120
Tormusk Rd. G45 —3B 120
Torness St. G11 —1A 82
Torogay Pl. G22 —1A 64
Torogay St. G22 —1G 63
Torogay Ter. G22 —1G 63
Toronto Wlk. G32 —5C 106
Torphin Cres. G32 —5A 86
Torphin Wlk. G32 —5B 86
Torrance Av. Air —4D 92
Torrance Rd. E Kil —1G 149
Torrance Rd. Torr —5D 28
Torrance Roundabout. E Kil —6B 150
Torran Rd. G33 —4F 87
Torranyard Ter. Ham —2C 152
Torr Av. Quar H —1A 72
Torr Gdns. Bear —6D 24
Torriden Pl. Coat —6A 90
Torriden St. Coat —6A 90
Torridon Av. G41 —2G 101
Torridon Av. Moth —4D 128
Torridon Ct. G20 —1E 83
(off Cedar St.)
Torridon Ct. Coat —6H 89
Torridon Gdns. Newt M —5H 133
Torridon Path. G41 —2G 101
(off Dumbreck Pl.)
Torrington Av. Giff —1G 133
Torrington Cres. G32 —2D 106
Torrin Rd. G23 —6B 46
Torrisdale Pl. Coat —4A 90
Torrisdale St. G42 —3D 102
Torrisdale St. Coat —4A 90
Torr La. Bri W —1A 72
Torr Rd. B'rig —6F 49
Torr Rd. Bri W —2C 72
Torr St. G22 —5H 63
Torryburn Rd. G21 —5E 65
Torwood Brae. Ham —1D 152
Torwood La. Chry —5F 53
Toryglen Rd. Ruth —5B 104
Toryglen St. G5 —3H 103
Tourmaline Ter. Bell —4D 126
Tournan Path. Blan —2B 140
Toward Ct. Blan —6C 124
Toward Rd. G33 —4C 86
Tower Av. Barr —3F 115
Tower Cres. Renf —1D 78
Tower Dri. Renf —1D 78
Towerhill Rd. G13 —6C 44
Tower Pl. G20 —3B 62
T[illegible] John —4G 95
[illegible]Miln —3H 25
[illegible] —2G 27
[illegible]b —1H 55
[illegible] —4F 95
[illegible]53 —3A 100
[illegible] 3A 100
Towers Pl. Air —4F 93
Towers Rd. Air —3E 93
Tower St. G41 —6C 82
Tower Ter. Pais —1H 97
Towie Pl. Udd —1D 124
Townend Rd. Dumb —3F 17
Townhead. Kirk —5D 30
Townhead Dri. Moth —4F 129
Townhead Pl. Udd —5E 109
Townhead Rd. Coat —1E 89
Townhead Rd. Newt M —5D 132
Townhead St. Ham —6B 142
Townhead St. Kils —3H 11
Townhead Ter. Pais —1H 97
Townhill Rd. Ham —6B 140
Townhill Ter. Ham —6C 140
Townmill Rd. G31 —3B 84
Townsend St. G4 —1G 83 (1E 5)
Tradeston Ind. Est. G5 —1E 103
Tradeston St. G5 —6E 83
Trafalgar St. G40 —2B 104
Trafalgar St. Clyd —5B 42
Trainard Av. G32 —1H 105
Tranent Path. Moth —5H 129
Tranent Pl. G33 —3G 85
Tranent Pl. Cle —5H 129
Traquair Av. Pais —5C 96
Traquair Av. Wis —4A 146
Traquair Dri. G52 —1B 100
Traquair Wynd. Blan —2B 140
Treeburn Av. Giff —4H 117
Treemain Rd. Giff —1G 133
Trees Pk. Av. Barr —3D 114
Trefoil Av. G41 —5B 102
Trent Pl. E Kil —5A 148
Trent St. Coat —1H 89
Tresta Rd. G23 —1C 62
Triangle, The. B'rig —6C 48
Tribboch St. Lark —2D 160
Trident Way. Renf —2E 79
Trigg St. Pais —2E 97
Trinidad Grn. E Kil —2C 148
Trinidad Way. E Kil —2C 148
Trinity Av. G52 —1C 100
Trinity Dri. Camb —4C 122
Trinity Way. Lark —4G 161
Trinley Rd. G13 —6D 44
Triton Pl. Bell —2H 127
Tronda Path. G34 —3F 87
Trondra Pl. G34 —3F 87
Trongate. G1 —5G 83
Troon Av. E Kil —5C 148
Troon Ct. E Kil —5D 148
Troon Dri. Bri W —4E 73
Troon Gdns. Cumb —5H 13
Troon Pl. Newt M —5G 133
Troon St. G40 —2D 104
Trossachs Av. Moth —2A 128
Trossachs Ct. G20 —6E 63
Trossachs Rd. Ruth —5F 121
Trossachs St. G20 —6E 63
Troubridge Av. Mill P —4B 94
Troubridge Cres. Mill P —3B 94
Trows Rd. Wis —5H 157
Truce Rd. G13 —1B 60
Truro Av. Chry —4D 52
Tryst Rd. Cumb —4H 35
(in two parts)
Tryst Wlk. Cumb —3A 36
Tudor La. S. G14 —6E 61
Tudor St. Bail —2F 107
Tulliallan Pl. E Kil —3A 150
Tullis St. G40 —1A 104
Tulloch Gdns. Moth —5B 144
Tulloch Pl. Ruth —4F 121
Tulloch St. G44 —1E 119
Tullymet Rd. Ham —3H 153
Tummel Dri. Air —1H 91
Tummel Grn. E Kil —6G 137
Tummell Way. Pais —4D 96
Tummel St. G33 —1G 85
Tummel Wlk. Cumb —3H 35
(off Cumbernauld Cen., The)
Tummel Way. Cumb —3H 35
(off Cumbernauld Cen., The)
Tunnel St. G3 —4C 82
Tuphall Rd. Ham —1H 153
Turnberry Av. G11 —6H 61
Turnberry Cres. Chap —4E 113
Turnberry Dri. Bri W —5E 73
Turnberry Dri. Ham —1B 152
Turnberry Dri. Newt M —5G 133
Turnberry Dri. Ruth —2B 120
Turnberry Gdns. Cumb —6H 13
Turnberry Pl. Dumb —3C 16
Turnberry Pl. E Kil —5D 148
Turnberry Rd. G11 —6G 61
Turnberry Wynd. Both —4C 124
Turnbull St. G1 —5H 83
Turner Rd. Pais —3B 78
Turner Rd. St R —1B 84
Turner St. Coat —5B 90
Turnhill Av. Ersk —2F 57
Turnhill Cres. Ersk —2F 57
Turnhill Dri. Ersk —2F 57
Turnhill Gdns. Ersk —2F 57
Turnlaw. E Kil —6F 149
Turnlaw Rd. Camb —6A 122
Turnlaw St. G5 —1H 103
Turnyland Meadows. Ersk —2F 57
Turquoise Ter. Bell —4D 126
Turret Cres. G13 —1C 60
Turret Rd. G13 —6C 44
Turriff St. G5 —1F 103
Tweed Av. Pais —3D 96
Tweed Ct. Air —6C 92
Tweed Cres. G33 —2F 85
Tweed Cres. Renf —6G 59
Tweed Cres. Wis —4A 146
Tweed Dri. Bear —4D 44
Tweed La. Moth —2B 128
Tweedmuir Pl. Coat —2F 111
Tweed Pl. John —5C 94
Tweedsmuir. B'rig —5E 49
Tweedsmuir Cres. Bear —6E 25
Tweedsmuir Pk. Ham —3G 153
Tweedsmuir Rd. G52 —1B 100
Tweed St. Coat —2D 110
Tweed St. E Kil —4B 148
Tweed St. Lark —4E 161
Tweedvale Av. G14 —3G 59
Tweedvale Pl. G14 —3G 59
Tweed Wlk. Cumb —3H 35
(off Cumbernauld Cen., The)
Twinlaw St. G34 —2B 88
Tylney Rd. Pais —6F 79
Tyndrum Rd. Bear —2H 45
Tyndrum St. G4 —2G 83 (1E 5)
Tynecastle Cres. G32 —4B 86
Tynecastle Path. G32 —4B 86
Tynecastle Pl. G32 —4B 86
Tynecastle St. G32 —4B 86
Tyne Pl. E Kil —5A 148
Tynron Ct. Ham —2C 152
Tynwald Av. Ruth —3F 121

Uddingston Rd. Both —4D 124
UDDINGSTON STATION. Udd —1C 124
Udston Rd. Ham —5C 140
Udston Ter. Ham —4D 140
Uig Pl. G33 —6E 87
Uist Cres. G33 —5E 67
Uist Dri. Kirk —5G 31
Uist St. G51 —4F 81
Uist Way. Wis —4C 146
Ullswater. E Kil —6B 148
Ulundi Rd. John —3D 94
Ulva St. G52 —6F 81
Underwood La. Pais —6H 77
Underwood Rd. Pais —6G 77
Underwood Rd. Ruth —1E 121
Underwood St. G41 —5C 102
Union Pl. G1 —4F 83 (5D 4)
Union St. G1 —4F 83 (5D 4)
Union St. Carl —4F 165
Union St. Ham —5G 141
Union St. Kirk —5C 30
Union St. Lark —2E 161
Union St. Moth —3A 128
Union St. Pais —3A 98
Unitas Cres. Carl —4E 165
Unitas Rd. Bell —2E 127
Unity Pl. G4 —1E 83
University Av. G12 —1B 82
University Gdns. G12 —1B 82
University Pl. G12 —1A 82
Unsted Pl. Pais —1C 98
Unthank Rd. Bell —2E 127
Uphall Pl. G33 —4G 85
Upland Rd. G14 —5C 60
U. P. Lane. Kils —3H 11
Uplawmoor Rd. Neil —4A 130
Up. Bourtree Ct. Ruth —3E 121
Up. Bourtree Dri. Ruth —3D 120
Up. Glenburn Rd. Bear —2C 44
Up. Mill St. Air —3A 92
U. P. Road. Kils —3H 11
Urquhart Cres. Renf —1E 79
Urquhart Dri. E Kil —6A 138
Urrdale Rd. G41 —6H 81
Usmore Pl. G33 —6E 87

Vaila Pl. G23 —2E 63
Vaila St. G23 —1D 62
Valence Tower. Udd —3B 124
Valerio Ct. Blan —1B 140
Valetta Pl. Clyd —4H 41
Valeview Ter. G42 —5E 103
Valeview Ter. Dumb —1G 17
Vale Wlk. B'rig —1E 65
Vallantine Cres. Udd —5E 109
Valley St. G22 —1H 63
Valleybank. Bant —1F 13
Valley Ct. Ham —1G 153
Valleyfield. E Kil —2F 149
Valleyfield. Milt C —5A 8
Valleyfield Dri. Cumb —4A 34
Valleyfield St. G21 —6A 64
Valley View. Camb —1C 122
Vancouver Ct. E Kil —2D 148
Vancouver Dri. E Kil —2D 148
Vancouver La. G14 —5C 60
(off Norse La. S.)
Vancouver La. N. G14 —5C 60
(off Norse La. N.)
Vancouver Pl. Clyd —4H 41
Vancouver Rd. G14 —5C 60
Vanguard St. Clyd —5E 43
Vanguard Way. Renf —2E 79
Vardar Av. Clar —1A 134
Vardon Lea. Moth —6E 129
Varna La. G14 —6E 61
Varna Rd. G14 —5E 61
Varnsdorf Way. Air —5D 92
Vasart Pl. G20 —5D 62
Veir Ter. Dumb —4E 17
Veitch Dri. G53 —4C 100
Veitches Ct. Clyd —1C 42
Veitch Pl. Len —3F 7
Vennacher Rd. Renf —5C 58
Vennard Gdns. G41 —3C 102
Vermont Av. Ruth —6C 104
Vermont St. G41 —6B 82
Vernon Bank. E Kil —6G 137
Vernon Dri. Lin —5G 75
Verona Av. G14 —5C 60
Verona La. G14 —5C 60
Vesalius St. G32 —6A 86
Viaduct Rd. Clar —2D 134
Vicarfield St. G51 —4H 81
Vicarland Pl. Camb —3A 122
Vicarland Rd. Camb —2A 122
Vicars Wlk. Camb —2B 122
Vickers St. Moth —1D 142
Victoria Av. Carl —4E 165
Victoria Bri. G5 —5G 83
Victoria Cir. G12 —6A 62
Victoria Ct. Lark —1E 161
Victoria Cres. Air —5G 91
Victoria Cres. Clar —2D 134
Victoria Cres. Kils —3F 11
Victoria Cres. Wis —5D 144
Victoria Cres. La. G12 —6A 62
Victoria Cres. Pl. G12 —6A 62
Victoria Cres. Rd. G12 —6A 62
Victoria Cross. G42 —3E 103
Victoria Dri. E. Renf —1E 79
Victoria Dri. W. Renf —6D 58
Victoria Gdns. Air —4H 91
Victoria Gdns. Barr —3D 114
Victoria Gdns. Pais —3G 97
Victoria Pk. Kils —3F 11
Victoria Pk. Corner. G14 —6D 60
Victoria Pk. Dri. N. G14 —5D 60
Victoria Pk. Dri. S. G14 —6D 60
Victoria Pk. Gdns. N. G11 —6F 61
Victoria Pk. Gdns. S. G11 —6F 61
Victoria Pk. La. S. G14 —6D 60
(off Westland Dri.)
Victoria Pk. St. G14 —6D 60
Victoria Pl. Air —5G 91
Victoria Pl. Bell —3B 126
Victoria Pl. Kils —3G 11
Victoria Pl. Miln —4H 25
Victoria Pl. Ruth —5C 104
(off King St.)
Victoria Quad. Moth —2H 127
Victoria Rd. G42 —4E 103
Victoria Rd. Barr —3D 114
Victoria Rd. Brkfld —6D 74
Victoria Rd. Dull —5F 13
Victoria Rd. Ham —3F 141
Victoria Rd. Lenz —3C 50
Victoria Rd. Pais —3G 97
Victoria Rd. Ruth —1D 120
Victoria Rd. Step —4D 66
Victoria St. Blan —3B 140
Victoria St. Dumb —5G 17
Victoria St. Kirk —5C 30
Victoria St. Lark —2E 161
Victoria St. Newm —5E 147
Victoria St. Ruth —5C 104
Victoria Ter. Dull —5F 13
Victor St. Plain —1G 93
Victory Dri. Kilb —1A 94
Victory Way. Bail —1H 107
Viewbank. T'bnk —4G 117
Viewbank Av. C'bnk —3B 112
Viewbank St. Glenb —4B 70
Viewfield. Air —5G 91
Viewfield Av. Bail —6F 87
Viewfield Av. B'rig —1A 64
Viewfield Av. Blan —6C 124
Viewfield Av. Lenz —2C 50
Viewfield Av. Milt C —6B 8
Viewfield Dri. Bail —6F 87
Viewfield Dri. B'rig —1A 64
Viewfield La. G12 —1C 82
Viewfield Rd. Bank —1D 14
Viewfield Rd. Bell —4B 126
Viewfield Rd. B'rig —1A 64
Viewfield Rd. Coat —1F 109
Viewmount Dri. G20 —2D 62
Viewpark. Miln —4H 25
Viewpark Av. G31 —3D 84
Viewpark Dri. Ruth —1D 120
Viewpark Pl. Moth —3E 143
Viewpark Rd. Moth —3E 143
Viewpark Shopping Cen. Udd —1H 125
Viewpoint Pl. G21 —3B 64
Viewpoint Rd. G21 —3B 64
Viking Cres. Hous —3D 74
Viking Rd. Air —6B 92
Viking Ter. E Kil —5G 149
Viking Way. Giff —2F 117
Viking Way. Renf —2E 79
Villafield Av. B'rig —4C 48
Villafield Dri. B'rig —4C 48
Villafield Loan. B'rig —4C 48
Village Gdns. Blan —6C 124
Village Rd. Camb —2E 123
Vinegarhill St. G31 —5D 84
Vine St. G11 —1H 81
Vinicombe La. G12 —6B 62
(off Vinicombe St.)
Vinicombe St. G12 —6B 62
Vintner St. G4 —1G 83
Viola Pl. Torr —5E 29
Violet Gdns. Carl —5E 165
Violet Pl. Moth —1B 128
Violet St. Pais —1C 98
Virginia Ct. G1 —4G 83 (6F 5)
Virginia Gdns. Miln —5A 26
Virginia St. G1 —4G 83 (6F 5)
Viscount Av. Renf —2E 79
Viscount Ga. Both —2C 124
Vivian Av. Miln —4F 25
Voil Dri. G44 —3E 119
Vorlich Ct. Barr —6E 115
Vorlich Gdns. Bear —6C 24
Vorlich Wynd. Moth —3C 128
Vulcan St. G21 —5B 64
Vulcan St. Moth —1G 143

Waddell Av. Glenm —5F 71
Waddell Ct. G5 —6H 83
Waddell St. G5 —1H 103
Waddell St. Air —2A 92
Waid Av. Newt M —3C 132
Waldemar Rd. G13 —2C 60
Waldo St. G13 —2F 61
Walkerburn Dri. Wis —3A 146
Walkerburn Rd. G52 —1B 100
Walker Ct. G11 —2H 81
Walker Dri. Eld —3H 95
Walker Path. Udd —5E 109
Walker St. G11 —2H 81
Walker St. Pais —1H 97
Walkinshaw Cres. Pais —5F 77
Walkinshaw Rd. Renf —6F 57
Walkinshaw St. G40 —1C 104
Walkinshaw St. John —2G 95
Walkinshaw Way. Pais —4A 78
Wallace Av. B'ton —4H 39
Wallace Av. Eld —2A 96
Wallace Dri. Lark —3G 161
Wallace Gdns. Torr —4D 28
Wallace Ho. Cumb —3G 35
Wallace Pl. Blan —6C 124
Wallace Pl. Ham —1C 154
Wallace Rd. Moth —5B 128
Wallace Rd. Renf —2C 78
Wallace St. G5 —5E 83
Wallace St. Clyd —6D 42
Wallace St. Coat —6C 90
Wallace St. Dumb —5G 17
Wallace St. Moth —2F 143
Wallace St. Pais —5A 78
Wallace St. Plain —1G 93
Wallace St. Ruth —6C 104
Wallacewell Cres. G21 —4D 64
Wallacewell Pl. G21 —4D 64
Wallacewell Quad. G21 —3E 65
Wallacewell Rd. G21 —4C 64
Wallbrae Rd. Cumb —5A 36
Waller Gdns. G41 —4B 102
Wallneuk. Pais —6B 78
Wallneuk Rd. Pais —6B 78
Walls St. G1 —4H 83 (6G 5)
Walmer Cres. G51 —5A 82
Walnut Ct. Milt C —6B 8
Walnut Cres. G22 —4H 63
Walnut Cres. John —4H 95
Walnut Dri. Kirk —1B 50
Walnut Pl. G22 —4G 63
Walnut Rd. G22 —4G 63
Walpole Pl. John —6D 94
Walter St. G31 —4D 84
Walter St. Wis —6B 146
Walton Av. Newt M —3C 132
Walton Ct. Giff —5A 118
Walton St. G41 —5C 102
Walton St. Barr —4E 115
Wamba Av. G13 —1E 61
Wamba Pl. G13 —1E 61
Wamphray Pl. E Kil —4A 148
Wandilla Av. Clyd —5F 43
Wanlock St. G51 —3G 81
Wardend Rd. Torr —4D 28
Warden Rd. G13 —2D 60
Wardhill Rd. G21 —4D 64
Wardhouse Rd. Pais —6G 97
Wardie Path. G33 —4F 87
Wardie Pl. G33 —4F 87
Wardie Rd. G33 & G34 —4F 87
Wardlaw Av. Ruth —6D 104
Wardlaw Cres. E Kil —4H 149
Wardlaw Dri. Ruth —5D 104
Wardlaw Rd. Bear —6F 45
Wardpark Ct. Cumb —5D 14
Wardpark E. Ind. Est. Cumb —3E 15
Wardpark N. Ind. Est. Cumb —4C 14
Wardpark Pl. Cumb —5D 14
Wardpark Rd. Ward S —5C 14
Wardpark Roundabout. Cumb —4C 14
Wardpark S. Ind. Est. Cumb —5D 14

Wardrop Pl. E Kil —6H 137
Wardrop St. G51 —3G 81
Wardrop St. Pais —1A 98
Wards Cres. Coat —6A 90
Ware Path. G34 —4G 87
Ware Rd. G34 —3F 87
Warilda Av. Clyd —5E 43
Warlock Dri. Bri W —2F 73
Warlock Rd. Bri W —2F 73
Warnock Cres. Bell —3D 126
Warnock Rd. Newt M —3C 132
Warnock St. G31 —3A 84
Warren Rd. Ham —3H 153
Warren St. G42 —4F 103
Warren Wlk. Len —4G 7
Warriston Cres. G33 —3F 85
Warriston Pl. G32 —4B 86
Warriston St. G33 —3F 85
Warriston Way. Ruth —3F 121
(off Kilbride Rd.)
Warroch St. G3 —4D 82
Warwick. E Kil —5C 138
Warwick Gro. Ham —5C 140
Warwick Vs. Clyd —2G 59
(off Edward St.)
Washington Rd. Kirk —5B 30
Washington Rd. Pais —3B 78
Washington St. G3 —4E 83 (6A 4)
Watchmeal Cres. Clyd —6E 23
Waterbank Rd. Clar —3H 135
Waterfoot Av. G53 —5C 100
Waterfoot Rd. Newt M —6F 133
Waterfoot Row. Clar —6B 134
Waterfoot Ter. G53 —5C 100
(off Waterfoot Av.)
Waterford Rd. Giff —4H 117
Waterlands Gdns. Carl —2G 165
Waterlands Pl. Law —1A 164
Waterloo Gdns. Kirk —4D 30
(off John St.)
Waterloo La. G2 —4F 83 (5C 4)
Waterloo St. G2 —4E 83 (5B 4)
Watermill Av. Lenz —3D 50
Water Rd. Barr —4E 115
Water Row. G51 —3G 81
Watershaugh Dri. Cle —5H 129
Waterside Av. Newt M —5C 132
Waterside Ct. Crmck —2A 136
Waterside Dri. Newt M —5C 132
Waterside Gdns. Crmck —2H 135
Waterside Gdns. Ham —2A 154
Waterside La. Mill P —3C 94
Waterside Rd. Crmck —4H 135
Waterside Rd. Kirk —6E 31
Waterside St. G5 —1H 103
Watling Pl. E Kil —2C 148
Watling St. Moth —6D 126
Watling St. Udd —4C 108
Watson Av. Lin —5H 75
Watson Av. Ruth —6B 104
Watson Cres. Kils —3A 12
Watson Pl. Blan —2H 139
Watson St. G1 —5H 83
Watson St. Blan —2H 139
Watson St. Lark —2D 160
Watson St. Moth —4G 143
Watson St. Udd —2D 124
Watsonville Pk. Moth —3G 143
Watt Cres. Bell —6D 110
Watt La. Bri W —4G 73
Watt Low Av. Ruth —1B 120
Watt Pl. Miln —2F 25
Watt Rd. G52 —4H 79
Watt Rd. Bri W —4F 73
Watt St. G5 —5D 82
Watt St. Air —2C 92
Waukglen Av. G53 —5B 116
Waukglen Cres. G53 —4C 116
Waukglen Dri. G53 —4B 116
Waukglen Path. G53 —4B 116
Waukglen Pl. G53 —4B 116
Waukglen Rd. G53 —4B 116
Waulking Mill Rd. Clyd —6E 23
Waulkmill Av. Barr —3F 115
Waulkmill St. T'bnk —3E 117
Waulkmill Way. Barr —3F 115
Waverley. Clyd —5E 43
Waverley. E Kil —5D 138
Waverley Ct. Both —5E 125
Waverley Ct. Pais —5D 96
Waverley Cres. Cumb —6F 35
Waverley Cres. Ham —5D 140
Waverley Cres. Kirk —5E 31
Waverley Dri. Air —2B 92
Waverley Dri. Ruth —6E 105
Waverley Dri. Wis —5H 145
Waverley Gdns. G41 —4C 102
Waverley Gdns. Eld —3B 96
Waverley Rd. Lark —5E 161
Waverley Rd. Pais —6D 96
Waverley St. G41 —4C 102
Waverley St. Coat —2D 90
Waverley St. Ham —5D 140
Waverley Ter. Blan —4A 140
Waverley Ter. Dumb —3B 16
Waverley Way. Pais —6D 96
Weardale La. G33 —3C 86
Weardale St. G33 —3C 86
Weaver Av. Newt M —2C 132
Weaver Cres. Air —6A 92
Weaver La. Kilb —1A 94
Weaver Pl. E Kil —4A 148
Weavers Av. Pais —2F 97
Weavers Ct. E Kil —1H 149
(off Parkhall St.)
Weavers Rd. Pais —2F 97
Weaver St. G4 —4H 83 (5H 5)
Weaver Ter. Pais —2C 98
Webster Groves. Wis —4B 146
Webster St. G40 —2C 104
Webster St. Clyd —1G 59
Wedderlea Dri. G52 —6A 80
Weensmoor Rd. G53 —3H 115
Weeple Dri. Lin —5G 75
Weighhouse Clo. Pais —1A 98
Weigh Ho. Rd. Carl —2E 165
Weir Av. Barr —5E 115
Weir Pl. Law —1H 163
Weir St. Coat —4C 90
Weir St. Pais —6B 78
Weirwood Av. Bail —1F 107
Weirwood Gdns. Bail —6F 87
Welbeck Rd. G53 —2B 116
Weldon Pl. Kils —2B 34
Welfare Av. Camb —3D 122
Welland Pl. E Kil —4A 148
Wellbank Pl. Udd —2D 124
Wellbeck Ho. E Kil —1H 149
(off Stuart St.)
Wellbrae Hill. Lark —3E 161
Wellbrae Rd. Ham —2F 153
Wellbrae Ter. Chry —5D 52
Wellcroft Pl. G5 —1F 103
Wellcroft Rd. Ham —6C 140
Wellcroft Ter. Ham —6C 140
Wellesley Cres. E Kil —4B 148
Wellesley Dri. E Kil —3B 148
Wellfield Av. Giff —4H 117
Wellfield St. G21 —5B 64
Wellgate St. Lark —1E 161
Well Grn. G43 —5A 102
Wellhall Ct. Ham —5F 141
Wellhall Rd. Ham —1C 152
Wellhouse Cres. G33 —4E 87
Wellhouse Path. G34 —4F 87
Wellhouse Rd. G33 —3F 87
Wellington. E Kil —4D 148
Wellington La. G2 —4E 83 (5B 4)
Wellington Pl. Clyd —4H 41
Wellington Pl. Coat —6G 89
Wellington Pl. Wis —3B 158
Wellington Rd. B'rig —3D 48
Wellington St. G2 —4F 83 (6C 4)
Wellington St. Air —2A 92
Wellington St. Pais —5H 77
Wellington St. Wis —4C 144
Wellington Way. Renf —2E 79
Wellknowe Av. T'hall —6G 135
Wellknowe Pl. T'hall —6G 135
Wellknowe Rd. T'hall —6G 135
Well La. Len —3F 7
Wellmeadow Clo. Newt M —4D 132
Wellmeadow Grn. Newt M —3D 132
Wellmeadow Rd. G43 —1H 117
Wellmeadow St. Pais —1H 97
Wellmeadow Way. Newt M —4D 132
Wellpark La. Neil —3D 130
Wellpark Rd. Bank —1D 14
Wellpark Rd. Moth —3E 143
Wellpark St. G31 —4A 84
Wellpark Ter. Neil —3D 130
Well Rd. Kilb —2A 94
Wellshot Dri. Camb —2H 121
Wellshot Rd. G32 —2H 105
Wellside Av. Air —2A 92
Wellside Dri. Camb —3C 122
Wellside La. Air —2B 92
Wellside Quad. Air —2A 92
Wellsquarry Rd. Clar —5E 137
Wells St. Clyd —4B 42
Well St. Pais —6G 77
Wellview Dri. Moth —3F 143
Wellwynd. Air —3H 91
Wellwynd Gdns. Air —3H 91
Welsh Dri. Blan —3B 140
Welsh Dri. Ham —4G 153
Wemyss Av. Newt M —2C 132
Wemyss Dri. Cumb —4A 34
Wemyss Gdns. Bail —2G 107
Wendur Way. Pais —3A 78
Wenlock Rd. Pais —3B 98
Wensleydale. E Kil —6E 137
Wentworth Dri. G23 —6C 46
Wesley St. Air —4H 91
W. Academy St. Wis —6E 145
West Av. Blan —4C 140
West Av. Carl —4D 164
West Av. Moth —5A 128
West Av. Plain —1G 93
West Av. Renf —6F 59
West Av. Step —4D 66
West Av. Udd —1F 125
W. Balgrochan Rd. Torr —4D 28
Westbank Ct. G12 —1C 82
(off Westbank Quad.)
Westbank La. G12 —1C 82
(off Gibson St.)
Westbank Quad. G12 —1C 82
Westbourne Cres. Bear —1C 44
Westbourne Dri. Bear —2C 44
Westbourne Gdns. La. G12 —5A 62
Westbourne Gdns. N. G12 —5A 62
Westbourne Gdns. S. G12 —5A 62
Westbourne Gdns. W. G12 —5H 61
Westbourne Rd. G12 —5H 61
Westbourne Ter. La. N. G12 —5H 61
Westbourne Ter. La. S. G12 —5H 61
West Brae. Pais —1H 97
Westbrae Dri. G14 —5E 61
Westbrae Rd. Newt M —3F 133
W. Bridgend. Dumb —3E 17
W. Buchanan Pl. Pais —1H 97
Westburn Av. Camb —1D 122
Westburn Av. Pais —6F 77
Westburn Cres. Clyd —6D 22
Westburn Cres. Ruth —6B 104
Westburn Farm Rd. Camb —1B 122
Westburn Rd. Camb —2B 122
W. Burnside St. Kils —3H 11
Westburn Way. Pais —6F 77
W. Campbell St. G2 —4E 83 (6B 4)
W. Campbell St. Pais —1F 97
W. Canal St. Coat —5B 90
W. Chapelton Av. Bear —3F 45
W. Chapelton Cres. Bear —3F 45
W. Chapelton Dri. Bear —3F 45
W. Chapelton La. Bear —3F 45
Westcliff. Dumb —3B 16
W. Clyde St. Lark —3F 161
Westclyffe St. G41 —4C 102
W. Coats Rd. Camb —2H 121
West Ct. Clyd —3A 42
West Ct. Pais —1E 97
West Dri. Air —5E 93
Westend. Bear —5G 45
W. End Dri. Bell —3A 126
Westend Pk. St. G3 —2D 82
West End Pl. Bell —3B 126
Westerburn St. G32 —5H 85
Wester Carriagehill. Pais —3H 97
Wester Cleddens Rd. B'rig —5C 48
Wester Cochno Holdings. Clyd —5C 22
Wester Comn. Dri. G22 —5E 63
Wester Comn. Rd. G22 —5E 63
Westercraigs. G31 —4B 84
Westercraigs Ct. G31 —4B 84
Westerdale. E Kil —6E 137
Westerfield Rd. Clar —5H 135
Westergreens Av. Kirk —1B 50
Westerhill Rd. B'rig —3D 48
Westerhouse Ct. Carl —3D 164
Westerhouse Path. G34 —3G 87
(off Arnisdale Rd.)
Westerhouse Rd. G34 —3F 87
Westerkirk Dri. G23 —6C 46
Westermains Av. Kirk —5B 30
Wester Mavisbank Av. Air —3G 91
Wester Moffat Av. Air —3E 93
Wester Moffat Cres. Air —4E 93
Wester Myvot Rd. Cumb —3C 54
Western Av. Ruth —5B 104
Western Isles Rd. Old K —1G 41
Western Rd. Camb —3G 121
Wester Rd. G32 —1D 106
Westerton. Len —3H 7
Westerton Av. Bear —1F 61
Westerton Av. Clar —4E 135
Westerton Av. Lark —4E 161
Westerton Ct. Clar —4E 135
Westerton La. Clar —4E 135
WESTERTON STATION. Bear —6E 45
W. Fairholm St. Lark —6H 155
Westfield. Dumb —3C 16
Westfield Av. Ruth —6B 104
Westfield Ct. Law —1H 163
Westfield Cres. Bear —5E 45
Westfield Dri. G52 —6A 80
Westfield Dri. Bear —5E 45
Westfield Dri. Cumb —6A 34
Westfield Ind. Area. Cumb —1H 53
Westfield Ind. Est. Cumb —2A 54
Westfield Pl. Cumb —1H 53
Westfield Rd. Cumb —4C 34
Westfield Rd. Cumb —1H 53
(Westfield Ind. Area)
Westfield Rd. Kils —2F 11
Westfield Rd. Moth —6C 112
Westfield Rd. T'bnk —5G 117
Westfields. B'rig —4A 48
Westgarth Pl. E Kil —6C 136
West Ga. Wis —6B 146
Westgate Way. Bell —3B 126
W. George La. G2 —3E 83 (4A 4)
W. George St. G2 —3E 83 (4B 4)
W. George St. Coat —3C 90
W. Glebe Ter. Ham —1G 153
W. Graham St. G4 —2E 83 (2B 4)
W. Greenhill Pl. G3 —3C 82
W. Hamilton St. Moth —3G 143
W. High St. Kirk —4C 30
Westhouse Av. Ruth —6A 104
Westhouse Gdns. Ruth —6A 104
W. Kirk St. Air —4H 91
Westknowe Gdns. Ruth —2D 120
Westland Dri. G14 —6D 60
Westlands Gdns. Pais —3H 97
West La. Pais —1F 97
Westlea Pl. Air —5B 92
W. Lodge Rd. Renf —5D 58
W. Mains Rd. E Kil —1D 148
Westminster Ter. G3 —3C 82
(off Royal Cres.)
Westmoreland St. G42 —3E 103
Westmuir Pl. Ruth —5B 104
Westmuir St. G31 —6F 85
W. Nile St. G1 —3F 83 (5D 4)
West Pk. Miln —5G 25
Westpark Dri. Pais —6F 77
West Pl. Newm —4E 147
Westport. E Kil —2C 148
W. Porton Pl. B'ton —3F 39
Westport St. Kils —3H 11
W. Prince's La. G4 —1C 82
W. Prince's St. G4 —1D 82 (1A 4)
Westray Av. Newt M —2C 132
Westray Cir. G22 —3G 63
Westray Ct. Cumb —5G 35
Westray Pl. G22 —2H 63
Westray Pl. B'rig —5F 49
Westray Rd. Cumb —5G 35
Westray Sq. G22 —2G 63
Westray St. G22 —2G 63
Westray Wynd. Newm —3D 146
(off Iona Rd.)
W. Regent La. G2 —3F 83 (4C 4)
W. Regent St. G2 —3E 83 (3B 4)
West Rd. Kilb —1A 94
West Rd. Torr —4D 28
W. Scott Ter. Ham —2H 153
Westside Gdns. G11 —1H 81
W. Stewart St. Ham —5G 141
West St. G5 —1E 103
West St. Clyd —1G 59
West St. Pais —1G 97
WEST ST. STATION. G5 —6E 83
W. Thomson St. Clyd —3C 42
W. Thornlie St. Wis —1G 157
W. Westbrae Cres. Ham —2F 153
Westwood Av. Giff —4H 117
Westwood Cres. Ham —1F 153
Westwood Gdns. Pais —6F 77
Westwood Hill. E Kil —3D 148
Westwood Quad. Clyd —6F 43
Westwood Rd. G43 —1H 117
Westwood Rd. E Kil —2D 148
Westwood Rd. Newm —2D 146
Westwood Sq. E Kil —3D 148
Weymouth Dri. G12 —3G 61
Whamflet Av. Bail —4A 88
Whamond Tower. Moth —4G 143
Wheatfield Rd. Bear —4D 44
Wheatholm Cres. Air —2B 92
Wheatholm St. Air —2B 92
Wheatland Av. Blan —1A 140
Wheatlandhead Ct. Blan —1A 140
Wheatlands Dri. Kilb —1A 94
Wheatlands Farm Rd. Kilb —1A 94
Wheatley Cres. Kils —4H 11
Whifflet Ct. Coat —6D 90
(off Whifflet St.)
WHIFFLET STATION. Coat —6D 90
Whifflet St. Coat —2C 110
Whin Av. Barr —3D 114
Whinfell Dri. E Kil —5C 148
Whinfell Gdns. E Kil —5C 148
Whinfield Av. Camb —6G 105
Whinfield Rd. G53 —3A 116
Whinhall Av. Air —2G 91
Whinhall Rd. Air —2G 91
Whin Hill. E Kil —5B 138
Whinhill Rd. G53 —2A 100
Whinhill Rd. Pais —3D 98
Whinknowe. Ashg —5B 162
Whin Loan. Kils —2A 10
Whinney Gro. Wis —5C 146
Whinnie Knowe. Lark —4D 160
Whinpark Av. Bell —4B 126
Whin Pl. E Kil —4B 138
Whins Rd. G41 —4A 102
Whin St. Clyd —3C 42
Whirlie Dri. C'lee —3B 74
Whirlie Rd. C'lee —2B 74
Whirlies Roundabout, The. E Kil —5A 138
Whirlow Gdns. Bail —6G 87
Whirlow Rd. Bail —6G 87
Whistleberry Cres. Ham —2F 141
Whistleberry Dri. Ham —2E 141
Whistleberry Ind. Pk. Ham —2E 141
Whistleberry Rd. Blan —2D 140
Whistlefield Ct. Bear —4E 45
Whitacres Path. G53 —3A 116
Whitacres Rd. G53 —3H 115
Whitburn St. G32 —4H 85
Whitby St. G31 —1E 105
Whiteadder Pl. E Kil —4A 148
White Av. Dumb —4H 17
Whitebill Rd. Ham —4F 141
Whitebridge Av. Pais —1D 96
Whitebridge Clo. Pais —6D 76
White Cart Rd. Glas A —2A 78
White-Cart Tower. E Kil —4B 150
(off Easdale)
Whitecraigs Pl. G23 —1C 62
WHITECRAIGS STATION. Giff —1G 133
Whitecrook St. Clyd —1D 58
Whitefield. Len —2E 7
Whitefield Av. Camb —3A 122
Whitefield Rd. G51 —6A 82
Whitefield Ter. Camb —2B 122
Whitefield Ter. Len —2E 7
Whiteford Av. Dumb —1H 17
Whiteford Ct. Ham —5G 153
Whiteford Cres. Dumb —2H 17
Whiteford Pl. Dumb —2H 17
Whiteford Rd. Pais —3C 98
White Gro. Ruth —5C 104
Whitehall St. G3 —4D 82
Whitehaugh Av. Pais —6D 78
Whitehaugh Cres. G53 —3A 116
Whitehaugh Dri. Pais —6D 78
Whitehaugh Rd. G53 —3A 116
Whitehill Av. Air —2A 92
Whitehill Av. Cumb —3F 35
Whitehill Av. Kirk —4F 31
Whitehill Av. Step —3D 66
Whitehill Ct. Kirk —4F 31
Whitehill Cres. Carl —2F 165
Whitehill Cres. Clyd —6G 23
Whitehill Cres. Kirk —4F 31
Whitehill Farm Rd. Step —4D 66
Whitehill Gdns. G31 —4C 84
Whitehill Gro. Newt M —6F 133
Whitehill Rd. Bear —2D 44
Whitehill Rd. Ham —3F 141
Whitehills. Ersk —5E 41
Whitehills Dri. E Kil —4G 149
Whitehills Pl. E Kil —4G 149
Whitehills Ter. E Kil —5G 149
Whitehill St. G31 —4C 84
(in two parts)
Whitehill St. La. G31 —4C 84
Whitehill Ter. G'csh —5D 68
Whitehorse Wlk. E Kil —3D 148
Whitehurst. Bear —1C 44
Whitekirk Pl. G15 —5A 44
Whitelaw Av. Glenb —4B 70
Whitelaw Cres. Bell —3F 127
Whitelaw St. G20 —2A 62
Whitelaw Ter. Kils —1D 32
Whitelee. E Kil —6F 149
Whitelee Cres. Newt M —3B 132
Whitelee Ga. Newt M —3B 132
Whitelees Rd. Cumb —5F 15
Whitelees Roundabout. Cumb —6F 15
Whiteloans. Both —4F 125
Whitemoss Av. G44 —3D 118
Whitemoss Av. E Kil —2H 149
Whitemoss Gro. E Kil —1A 150
Whitemoss Rd. E Kil —2H 149
Whitemoss Roundabout. E Kil —2A 150
Whitepond Av. Bell —4B 126
Whiterigg Ct. Air —3F 91
(off Monkscourt Av.)
Whiteshaw Av. Carl —3D 164
Whiteshaw Dri. Carl —3D 164
Whiteshaw Rd. Carl —2B 164
Whitestone Av. Cumb —3D 34
White St. G11 —1H 81
White St. Clyd —2F 59
Whitevale St. G40 —5C 84
Whithope Rd. G53 —3H 115
Whithope Ter. G53 —3H 115
Whithorn Cres. Mood —4D 52
Whitlawburn Av. Camb —3G 121
Whitlawburn Rd. Camb —3G 121
Whitlawburn Shopping Cen. Camb
(off Western Rd.) —4G 121
Whitlawburn Ter. Camb —3G 121
Whitriggs Rd. G53 —2H 115
Whitslade St. G34 —2G 87
Whitsun Dale. E Kil —6E 137
Whittagreen Av. Moth —4D 128
Whittagreen Ct. Moth —4D 128
Whittagreen Cres. Moth —4D 128
Whittinghame Dri. G13 & G12 —4F 61
Whittinghame La. G13 —4F 61
Whittington St. Coat —5C 90
Whittlemuir Av. G44 —3D 118
Whitton Dri. Giff —3B 118
Whitton St. G20 —1A 62
Whitworth Dri. Clyd —5C 42
Whitworth St. G20 —3E 63
Whyte Av. Camb —1G 121
Whyte Corner. Milt —4F 19
Wick Av. Air —1G 111
Wickets, The. Pais —2C 98
Wickham Av. Newt M —3D 132
Wigton Av. Newt M —2C 132
Wigton St. G4 —6F 63
Wigtoun Pl. Cumb —1B 36
Wildman Rd. Law —5F 159
Wilfred Av. G13 —2D 60
Wilkie Cres. Lark —3F 161
Wilkie Loan. Bell —1D 126
Wilkie Rd. Udd —2E 125
William Dri. Ham —4H 153
William Mann Dri. Newt M —5B 132
Williamsburgh Ct. Pais —1C 98
(off Ladyburn St.)
Williamsburgh Ter. Pais —6C 78
Williamson Av. Dumb —3G 17
Williamson Pl. John —3H 95
Williamson St. G40 —1E 105
Williamson St. Clyd —3D 42

William Spiers Pl. Lark —4F 161
William St. G2 —3E 83
William St. G3 —3D 82
William St. Clyd —1C 42
William St. Coat —1D 110
William St. Ham —4F 141
William St. John —2F 95
William St. Kils —3H 11
William St. Pais —1G 97
William Ure Pl. B'rig —2D 48
Williamwood Dri. G44 —5C 118
Williamwood Pk. G44 —5D 118
Williamwood Pk. Way. G44 —5D 118
WILLIAMWOOD STATION. Giff —6B 118
Willoughby Dri. G13 —3F 61
Willow Av. B'rig —1C 64
Willow Av. Eld —3A 96
Willow Av. Lenz —2C 50
Willow Av. New S —5A 128
Willowbank. Lark —6A 156
Willowbank Cres. G3 —1D 82
Willowbank Gdns. Kirk —5D 30
Willowbank St. G3 —1D 82
Willow Ct. E Kil —5D 148
Willow Cres. Coat —1C 110
Willowdale Cres. Bail —1G 107
Willowdale Gdns. Bail —1G 107
Willow Dri. Air —4C 92
Willow Dri. Bank —1E 15
Willow Dri. Blan —1A 140
Willow Dri. John —4F 95
Willow Dri. Milt C —6C 8
Willowford Rd. G53 —3H 115
Willow Gro. Moth —2B 128
Willow La. G32 —3B 106
Willow Pl. John —3G 95
Willow Pl. Udd —5H 109
Willows, The. Crmck —1H 135
Willow St. G13 —2F 61
Willow Way. Ham —2A 154
Willwood Dri. Wis —2A 146
Wilmot Rd. G13 —3D 60
Wilsgait St. Cle —5H 129
Wilson Av. Lin —5G 75
Wilson Pl. E Kil —5A 138
Wilson Pl. Newt M —5C 132
Wilson Rd. Bri W —3E 73
Wilson St. G1 —4G 83 (6F 5)
Wilson St. Air —2H 91
Wilson St. Coat —4E 91
Wilson St. Ham —4E 141
Wilson St. Lark —4F 161
Wilson St. Moth —2H 143
Wilson St. Pais —1G 97
Wilson St. Renf —5F 59
Wiltonburn Path. G53 —3A 116
Wiltonburn Rd. G53 —3A 116
Wilton Ct. G20 —6C 62
(off Wilton St.)
Wilton Cres. La. G20 —6D 62
Wilton Dri. G20 —6D 62
Wilton Rd. Carl —5G 165
Wilton St. G20 —5C 62
Wilton St. Coat —1H 89
Wilverton Rd. G13 —1E 61
Winburne Cres. Ham —5F 141
Winchester Dri. G12 —3H 61
Windermere. E Kil —6B 148
Windermere St. Bell —3B 126
Windhill Cres. G43 —2H 117
Windhill Pl. G43 —2A 118
Windhill Rd. G43 —2H 117
Windlaw Ct. G45 —5H 119
Windlaw Gdns. G44 —4D 118
Windlaw Pk. Gdns. G44 —3D 118
Windlaw Rd. Clar —6H 119
Windmill Ct. Moth —4H 143
Windmillhill St. Moth —3H 143
Windmill Rd. Ham —5H 141
Windrow Ter. Wis —2A 146
Windsor Av. Newt M —4F 133
Windsor Ct. Carl —3F 165
Windsor Cres. Clyd —4C 42
Windsor Cres. Eld —4H 95
Windsor Cres. Pais —5C 78
Windsor Dri. Glenm —5H 71
Windsor Gdns. Ham —3E 141
Windsor Path. Bail —5D 88
(off Park Rd.)
Windsor Path. Lark —4G 161
(off Donaldson Rd.)
Windsor Quad. Carl —3F 165
Windsor Rd. Moth —2A 128
Windsor Rd. Renf —1E 79
Windsor St. G20 —1E 83
Windsor St. Coat —2A 110
Windsor St. Spri —5C 86
Windsor Ter. G20 —1E 83
Windsor Wlk. Udd —6F 109
Windward Rd. E Kil —2C 148
Windyedge Cres. G13 —4C 60
Windyedge & Hareshaw Rd. Moth —4H 129
Windyedge Pl. G13 —4C 60
Windyridge. Ham —2A 154
Windyridge Pl. Blan —2A 140
Windy Yetts. Twe —2D 32
Wingate Cres. E Kil —5C 138
Wingate Dri. E Kil —5C 138
Wingate Pk. E Kil —5C 138
Wingate St. Wis —5D 144
Wingfield Gdns. Both —6F 125
Winifred St. G33 —5F 65
Winning Ct. Blan —6C 124
Winning Quad. Wis —6D 144
Winning Row. G31 —6F 85
Winnipeg Dri. E Kil —3D 148
Winston Cres. Len —3F 7
Wintergreen Ct. E Kil —5F 137
Wintergreen Dri. E Kil —5F 137
Winton Av. Giff —5A 118
Winton Cres. Blan —2A 140
Winton Dri. G12 —4A 62
Winton Gdns. Udd —6D 108
Winton La. G12 —4A 62
Winton Pk. E Kil —2C 148
Wirran Pl. G13 —1G 59
Wishart Av. Clyd —6E 23
Wishart St. G31 —4A 84
Wishaw High Rd. Cle —1H 145
Wishawhill St. Wis —6F 145
Wishaw Low Rd. Cle —3G 145
Wishaw Rd. Wis —2B 158
WISHAW STATION. Wis —1G 157
Wisner Ct. T'bnk —3F 117
Wisteria La. Carl —5F 165
Wiston St. Camb —2E 123
Witchwood Ct. Coat —1H 89
Witcutt Way. Wis —2E 157
Wolcott Dri. Blan —1B 140
Wolfe Av. Newt M —2C 132
Wolseley St. G5 —2H 103
Wood Aven Dri. E Kil —5F 137
Woodbank Cres. Clar —3C 134
Woodbank Cres. John —3F 95
Woodburn Av. Air —5H 91
Woodburn Av. Blan —1C 140
Woodburn Av. Clar —3C 134
Woodburn Pl. Hous —4E 75
Woodburn Rd. G43 —2B 118
Woodburn Rd. Moth —6D 112
Woodburn St. Moth —1G 143
Woodburn Ter. Lark —3G 161
Woodburn Way. Cumb —3E 35
Woodburn Way. Miln —4G 25
Wood Cres. Moth —1G 143
Woodcroft Av. G11 —6F 61
Wooddale. Moth —5F 143
Woodend. Lark —4G 161
(off Donaldson Rd.)
Woodend Ct. G32 —3E 107
Woodend Dri. G13 —4E 61
Woodend Dri. Air —2C 92
Woodend Dri. Pais —1F 99
Woodend Gdns. G32 —3D 106
Woodend La. G13 —4E 61
Woodend Pl. Eld —3H 95
Woodend Rd. G32 —3D 106
Woodend Rd. Carl —3G 165
Woodend Rd. Ruth —3C 120
Wood Farm Rd. T'bnk —5G 117
Woodfield. Udd —1G 125
Woodfield Av. B'rig —6D 48
Woodfoot Pl. G53 —3B 116
Woodfoot Quad. G53 —3B 116
Woodfoot Rd. G53 —3A 116
Woodfoot Rd. Ham —1E 153
Woodford Pl. Lin —5G 75
Woodford St. G41 —6C 102
Woodgreen Av. G44 —1F 119
Woodhall Av. C'bnk —3B 112
Woodhall Av. Coat —2A 110
Woodhall Av. Ham —5F 141
Woodhall Av. Moth —2H 127
Woodhall Cottage Rd. C'bnk —4C 112
Woodhall Mill Rd. C'bnk —4B 112
Woodhall Pl. Coat —2B 110
Woodhall Rd. C'bnk —3B 112
Woodhall Rd. Wis —5D 146
Woodhall St. G40 —3D 104
Woodhall St. Chap —4D 112
Woodhams Way. Carl —4G 165
Woodhead Av. Both —6F 125
Woodhead Av. Cumb —6B 34
Woodhead Av. Kirk —6D 30
Woodhead Ct. Cumb —6B 34
Woodhead Cres. Ham —3E 153
Woodhead Cres. Udd —6D 108
Woodhead Gdns. Both —1F 141
Woodhead Gro. Cumb —6B 34
Woodhead Ind. Est. Muir —3H 67
Woodhead La. Ham —3F 153
Woodhead Pl. Cumb —6B 34
Woodhead Rd. G53 —2H 115
Woodhead Rd. Cumb —6B 34
Woodhead Rd. Muir —3H 67
Woodhead Ter. Chry —2H 67
Woodhead View. Cumb —6B 34
Woodhill Gro. B'rig —1E 65
Woodhill Rd. G21 —3D 64
Woodhill Rd. B'rig —6E 49
Woodholm Av. G44 —1G 119
Woodhouse Ct. Clar —4E 135
Woodhouse St. G13 —2E 61
Woodilee Rd. Kirk —6E 31
Woodilee Rd. Moth —3E 129
Woodland Av. Air —1C 112
Woodland Av. Kirk —5B 30
Woodland Av. Pais —5A 98
Woodland Cres. Camb —3C 122
Woodland Gdns. Clar —2H 135
Woodland Gdns. Ham —1B 154
Woodlands Av. Both —4E 125
Woodlands Av. G'csh —2C 68
Woodlands Av. Law —5D 158
Woodlands Ct. T'bnk —5F 117
Woodlands Cres. Both —4D 124
Woodlands Cres. John —4D 94
Woodlands Cres. T'bnk —4F 117
Woodlands Dri. G2 —1D 82
Woodlands Dri. Coat —4H 89
Woodlands Dri. Moth —2H 127
Woodlands Gdns. Both —3D 124
Woodlands Ga. G3 —2D 82
Woodlands Ga. T'bnk —4F 117
Woodlands Gro. Miln —2G 25
Woodlands Pk. T'bnk —5F 117
Woodlands Rd. G3 —1D 82
Woodlands Rd. Moth —6H 143
Woodlands Rd. N'hse —6D 112
Woodlands Rd. T'bnk —5F 117
Woodlands St. Miln —3G 25
Woodlands St. Moth —5H 143
Woodlands Ter. G3 —2C 82
Woodlands Ter. Both —4E 125
Woodlands, The. Bell —4F 127
Woodland Ter. Lark —4G 161
Woodland Way. Cumb —2B 36
Wood La. B'rig —1E 65
Woodlea Av. Air —1C 112
Woodlea Dri. Giff —3B 118
Woodlea Dri. Ham —3H 153
Woodlea Pl. Air —2C 92
Woodlinn Av. G44 —2F 119
Woodmill Dri. Torr —4E 29
Woodmill Gdns. Cumb —1B 54
Woodneuk Ct. Pais —1E 97
Woodneuk La. G'csh —4D 68
Woodneuk Rd. G53 —3B 116
Woodneuk Rd. G'csh —4D 68
Woodneuk St. Chap —4D 112
Woodneuk Ter. G'csh —4D 68
Wood Quad. Clyd —1G 59
Wood Rd. Giff —5G 117
Woodrop St. G40 —3D 104
Woodrow Av. Moth —5B 128
Woodrow Cir. G41 —1B 102
Woodrow Pl. G41 —1A 102
Woodrow Rd. G41 —1B 102
Woodside. Hous —2D 74
Woodside Av. Bri W —2F 73
Woodside Av. Ham —1A 154
Woodside Av. Kils —3B 12
Woodside Av. Lenz —1D 50
Woodside Av. Ruth —6E 105
Woodside Av. T'bnk —4G 117
Woodside Ct. Coat —6H 89
(off Woodside St.)
Woodside Cres. G3 —2D 82
Woodside Cres. Barr —5F 115
Woodside Cres. Newm —3F 147
Woodside Cres. Pais —1G 97
Woodside Dri. C'bnk —3A 112
Woodside Dri. Eag —6B 134
Woodside Gdns. Crmck —2H 135
Woodside Gdns. Clar —2A 134
Woodside Gdns. Coat —1H 109
Woodside La. Brkfld —5D 74
Woodside Pl. G3 —2D 82
Woodside Pl. Udd —5G 109
Woodside Pl. La. G3 —2D 82
Woodside Rd. Brkfld —5C 74
Woodside Rd. Crmck —2H 135
Woodside St. Chap —3D 112
Woodside St. Coat —2H 109
(in two parts)
Woodside St. Moth —5B 144
Woodside St. New S —4A 128
Woodside Ter. G3 —2D 82
Woodside Ter. La. G3 —2D 82
(off Lynedoch Ter.)
Woodside Tower. Moth —5B 144
Woodside Wlk. Ham —1A 154
Woods La. Renf —6E 59
Woodstock Av. G41 —4B 102
Woodstock Av. Kirk —5F 31
Woodstock Av. Pais —5C 96
Woodstock Dri. Wis —5A 146
Woodstock Way. Pais —5C 96
Wood St. G31 —3D 84
Wood St. Air —2B 92
Wood St. Coat —4A 90
Wood St. Moth —1H 143
Wood St. Pais —2D 98
Woodvale Av. Air —1D 112
Woodvale Av. Bear —5H 45
Woodvale Av. Giff —1H 133
Woodvale Dri. Pais —6E 77
Woodview. Udd —5H 109
Woodview Dri. Air —6A 92
Woodview Dri. Bell —6E 111
Woodview La. Air —6A 92
Woodview Rd. Lark —5E 161
Woodview Ter. Ham —5F 141
Woodville Pk. G51 —5H 81
Woodville Pk. Ind. Est. G51 —5H 81
(off Woodville Pk.)
Woodville St. G51 —5H 81
Woodyard Rd. Dumb —4E 17
Woodyett Pk. Clar —4D 134
Woodyett Rd. Clar —4D 134
Wordsworth Way. Both —4F 125
Works Av. Camb —2E 123
Worsley Cres. Newt M —3C 132
Wraes Av. Barr —3F 115
Wraes View. Barr —6B 114
Wraisland Cres. B'ton —3F 39
Wrangholm Cres. Moth —4B 128
Wrangholm Dri. Moth —4A 128
Wren Ct. Stra B —5A 110
Wren Pl. John —6D 94
Wren Pl. Wis —6H 145
Wright Av. Barr —5C 114
Wrightlands Cres. Ersk —2A 58
Wright St. Renf —1B 78
Wright Way. Moth —4A 128
Wye Cres. Coat —2H 89
Wykeham Pl. G13 —3C 60
Wykeham Rd. G13 —3C 60
Wyler Tower. Ham —6A 142
Wylie. E Kil —4D 138
Wylie Av. Newt M —2D 132
Wylie St. Ham —1H 153
Wyndford Dri. G20 —4B 62
Wyndford Pl. G20 —4B 62
Wyndford Rd. G20 —4A 62
Wyndford Rd. Ward N —3D 14
Wyndford Ter. Udd —6F 109
Wyndham Ct. G12 —5B 62
(off Wyndham St.)
Wyndham St. G12 —5B 62
Wynd, The. Cumb —6B 14
Wynyard Grn. E Kil —3D 148
Wyper Pl. G31 —5C 84
Wyvil Av. G13 —6E 45
Wyvis Av. G13 —1H 59
Wyvis Av. Bear —6C 24
Wyvis Pl. G13 —1H 59
Wyvis Quad. G13 —1H 59

Yair Dri. G52 —5A 80
Yarrow Ct. Camb —2D 122
Yarrow Cres. B'ton —5A 40
Yarrow Cres. Wis —5H 145
Yarrow Gdns. G20 —6D 62
Yarrow Gdns. La. G20 —6D 62
(off Yarrow Gdns.)
Yarrow Pk. E Kil —2A 150
Yarrow Rd. B'rig —3C 48
Yate St. G40 —6D 84
Yetholm St. G14 —3G 59
Yetholm Ter. Ham —6C 140
Yett Rd. Moth —4D 128
Yetts Cres. Kirk —5F 31
Yetts Hole Rd. Air —6D 54
Yew Dri. G21 —6C 64
Yew Pl. John —4F 95
Yews Cres. Ham —4F 141
Yokerburn Ter. Clyd —2F 59
Yoker Ferry Rd. G14 —3G 59
Yoker Ind. Est. G14 —3H 59
Yoker Mill Gdns. G13 —2G 59
Yoker Mill Rd. G13 —2G 59
York Dri. Ruth —2F 121
Yorkhill Pde. G3 —2A 82
Yorkhill St. G3 —3B 82
York St. G2 —4E 83 (6B 4)
York St. Clyd —5F 43
York St. Wis —1H 157
York Way. Renf —2E 79
Younger Quad. B'rig —6C 48
Young Pl. E Kil —6A 150
Young Pl. Udd —5E 109
Young St. Clyd —3D 42
Young St. Wis —6H 145
Young Ter. G21 —5C 64
Young Wynd. Bell —5C 110
Yukon Ter. E Kil —3D 148
Yvetot Ct. Carl —2E 165

Zambesi Dri. Blan —6A 124
Zena Cres. G33 —5E 65
Zena Pl. G33 —5F 65
Zena St. G33 —5E 65
Zetland Rd. H'ton I —3H 79

AREAS COVERED BY THIS ATLAS

with their map square reference

Names in this Index shown in CAPITAL LETTERS followed by their Postcode District(s), are Postal Addresses.

Abronhill. —1E **37**
AIRDRIE. (ML6) —3H **91**
ALLANDALE. (FK4) —1H **15**
Allanton. —2E **155**
Anderston. —4D **82**
ANNATHILL. (ML5) —5B **54**
Anniesland. —3F **61**
Arden. —3D **116**
Arkleston. —3E **79**
Arthurlie. —6D **114**
Ashgillhead. —4A **162**
ASHGILL. (ML9) —4B **162**
Auchenback. —6F **115**
Auchenreoch. —5H **9**
Auchentibber. —6F **139**
Auchentorlie. —2D **98**
Auchinairn. —1D **64**
Auchinloch. —1C **14**
(nr. Banknock)
Auchinloch. —5D **50**
(nr. Lenzie)
Auchinraith. —3C **140**
Auchinstarry. —5A **12**

BAILLIESTON. (G69) —6A **88**
Baldernock. —3D **26**
BALLOCH. (G83) —3D **34**
Balmalloch. —2G **11**
BALMORE. (G64) —5A **28**
Balornock. —3D **64**
Bankhead. —1B **120**
BANKNOCK. (FK4) —1E **15**
BANTON. (G65) —1F **13**
BARDOWIE. (G62) —6F **27**
Bargarran. —5D **40**
BARGEDDIE. (G69) —6D **88**
Barlanark. —5E **87**
Barmulloch. —5E **65**
Barnellan. —4E **27**
Barnhill. —1H **139**
Barrachnie. —6E **87**
BARRHEAD. (G78) —5E **115**
Barrowfield. —1C **110**
(nr. Coatbridge)
Barrow Field. —6C **84**
(nr. Glasgow)
Barrwood. —3B **12**
Battlefield. —6E **103**
BEARSDEN. (G61) —2E **45**
Bellahouston. —1F **101**
BELLSHILL. (ML4) —2C **126**
Bellsmyre. —1H **17**
Biggar Road. —2G **129**
Birdston. —2C **30**
Birkenshaw. —5D **108**
BIRKENSHAW. (ML9) —6F **161**
Birniehill. —3H **149**
BISHOPBRIGGS. (G64) —6C **48**
BISHOPTON. (PA7) —4G **39**
Blackhall. —2C **98**
Blackhill. —1F **85**
Blackwood. —4A **34**
Blairhill. —4B **90**
Blairlinn. —1H **55**
Blairskaith. —2H **27**
Blantyreferme. —1B **124**
BLANTYRE. (G72) —3A **140**
Blythswood. —4F **59**
Boghead. —3H **49**
BOGSIDE. (ML2) —3G **159**
Bonkle. —3G **147**
BOTHWELL. (G71) —5E **125**
BOWLING. (G60) —5B **20**
Braedale. —3D **142**
Braehead. —6H **135**
Braidfauld. —2G **105**
Brankumhall. —6D **138**
Brediland. —4E **97**
Bridgend. —4C **52**
BRIDGE OF WEIR. (PA11) —3F **73**
Bridgeton. —1B **104**
BROOKFIELD. (PA5) —6D **74**
Broom. —4H **133**
Broomhill. —6F **61**
(nr. Glasgow)
Broomhill. —3E **31**
(nr. Kirkintilloch)
Broomhouse. —3H **107**
Brownsburn. —1C **112**
Brucehill. —3C **16**
Burnbank. —4E **141**
Burnfoot. —2G **91**
Burnhead. —2G **161**
Burnside. —2E **121**
Busby. —3D **134**

Cadder. —2D **48**
(nr. Bishopbriggs)
Cadder. —2D **62**
(nr. Glasgow)
Cairnhill. —6H **91**
Cairns. —3C **122**
CALDERBANK. (ML6) —3B **112**
Calderbraes. —4C **108**
Calderwood. —6B **138**
CAMBUSLANG. (G72) —1A **122**
Cambusnethan. —6C **146**
Camlachie. —6D **84**
Carbrain. —4A **36**
Cardonald. —6B **80**
CARFIN. (ML1) —5B **128**
Carlston. —3G **29**
CARLUKE. (ML8) —3F **165**
CARMUNNOCK. (G76) —2H **135**
CARMYLE. (G32) —5C **106**
CARNBROE. (ML5) —1E **111**
Carntyne. —4G **85**
Carnwadric. —3E **117**
Carriagehill. —4A **98**
Carrickstone. —6G **13**
Cartside. —4D **94**
CASTLECARY. (G68) —3E **15**
CASTLEHEAD. (PA2) —2H **97**
Castlehill. —1E **165**
(nr. Carluke)
Castlehill. —2C **16**
(nr. Dumbarton)
Castlemilk. —4A **120**
Cathcart. —1E **119**
Cathkin. —5F **121**
Chantinghall. —6F **141**
Chapel. —1G **159**
CHAPELHALL. (ML6) —3E **113**
Chapel Hill. —6D **20**
Charleston. —3A **98**
CHRYSTON. (G69) —6B **52**
Claddenys. —3E **51**
Clarkston. —3D **92**
CLARKSTON. (G76) —2C **134**
Cleddans. —4F **31**
Cleekhimin. —1B **144**
CLELAND. (ML1) —6H **129**
Cliftonville. —4E **91**
Clincarthill. —6C **104**
Clippens. —5G **75**
CLYDEBANK. (G81) —6D **42**
Clydesdale. —4H **127**
COATBRIDGE. (ML5) —4C **90**
Coatdyke. —5F **91**
Coatshill. —6A **124**
Cochrane Castle. —5E **95**
College Milton. —6D **136**
Colston. —2A **64**
Coltness. —3A **146**
Condorrat. —6C **34**
Corkerhill. —3D **100**
Corseford. —6B **94**
Cowcaddens. —2F **83** (2E **5**)
Cowlairs. —5A **64**
Craigend. —6C **66**
Craigendmuir. —5E **67**
Craigends. —3D **74**
Craighead. —1E **141**
Craiglinn. —4B **34**
Craigmarloch. —1E **35**
Craigneuk. —4D **92**
(nr. Airdrie)
Craigneuk. —5D **144**
(nr. Wishaw)
Craigton. —6D **80**
Cranhill. —3B **86**
Cranston Hill. —3D **82**
Crawforddyke. —4G **165**
Crindledyke. —4G **147**
Croftfoot. —2A **120**
Crookfur. —3C **132**
Crookston. —1A **100**
Crossbasket. —3F **139**
Crosshill. —6B **88**
(nr. Baillieston)
Crosshill. —4F **103**
(nr. Glasgow)
CROSSLEE. (PA6) —3B **74**
Crosslet. —1C **18**
Crossmill. —3F **115**
Crossmyloof. —4B **102**
Cross Stobs. —2C **114**
CROY. (G65) —1B **34**
CUMBERNAULD. (G67 & G68) —4H **35**
Cumbernauld Village. —6B **14**

Dalbeth. —3G **105**
Dalmarnock. —2C **104**
DALMUIR. (G81) —4A **42**
Dalreoch. —3D **16**
DALSERF. (ML9) —3D **162**
Dalshannon. —1B **54**
Dean Park. —1G **79**
Dennistoun. —4C **84**
Dennystown. —3D **16**
Dimsdale. —2A **158**
Dovecothall. —3G **115**
Dovecotwood. —2H **11**
Dowanhill. —6A **62**
DRUMCHAPEL. (G15) —4H **43**
Drumgelloch. —3D **92**
Drumgrew. —4F **33**
Drumoyne. —5E **81**
Drumpellier. —4H **89**
Drumry. —4E **43**
DULLATUR. (G68) —5F **13**
DUMBARTON. (G82) —4F **17**
Dumbreck. —2A **102**
Dumbuck. —4E **19**
Dunbeth. —4D **90**
Dundyvan. —6B **90**
Dunrobin. —4E **93**
Duntiblae. —6G **31**
DUNTOCHER. (G81) —1C **42**
Dykebar. —4D **98**

Earnock. —1C **152**
East Balgrochan. —3E **29**
East Craigend. —6D **40**
East Crindledyke. —3E **147**
Easterhouse. —3G **87**
Eastfield. —6F **105**
East Fulton. —5F **75**
EAST KILBRIDE. (G74, G75 & G79) —2H **149**
East Mains. —1A **150**
East Shawhead. —3E **111**
Eddlewood. —4H **153**
ELDERSLIE. (PA5) —2A **96**
ERSKINE. (PA8) —6F **41**

Faifley. —6E **23**
Fairhill. —3G **153**
Fallside. —1G **125**
Farme Cross. —4E **105**
Fauldhead. —1H **51**
Ferguslie Park. —5E **77**
Fernhill. —4D **120**
FERNIEGAIR. (ML3) —2D **154**
Finniestor. —3C **82**
Firhill. —5E **63**
Flemington. —3E **123**
(nr. Cambuslang)
Flemington. —5B **144**
(nr. Motherwell)
Fluchter. —3E **27**
Forgewood. —6F **127**
Foulsykes. —5C **146**
Foxbar. —4D **96**
Foxley. —3C **106**
Freeland. —2F **57**
Fullarton. —4A **106**

Gallowflat. —6E **105**
Gallowgate. —6C **84**
Gallowhill. —4D **78**
Gardenhall. —4A **148**
Garnethill. —2E **83** (2C **4**)
Garnick. —3H **67**
Garnqueen. —4H **69**
Garrowhill. —6F **87**
GARTCOSH. (G69) —4D **68**
Garthamlock. —1E **87**
Gartlea. —5B **92**
Gartness. —6E **93**
Gartsherrie. —2B **90**
Gateside. —6B **114**
Germiston. —1D **84**
GIFFNOCK. (G46) —4A **118**
Gilshochill. —2B **62**
Gladstone. —6H **39**
GLASGOW. (G1 to G7 & G9) —4G **83** (5F **5**)
GLENBOIG. (ML5) —4B **70**
Glenburn. —5H **97**
Glengowan. —2C **160**
GLENMAVIS. (ML6) —5G **71**
Gockston. —3H **77**
Golfhill. —1H **91**
Gorbals. —1G **103**
Govan. —3G **81**
Govanhill. —3F **103**
Gowkthrapple. —3G **157**
Greenend. —1F **111**
Greenfaulds. —6G **35**
Greenfield. —5B **86**
Greenfoot. —2C **70**
Greenhead. —1B **158**
Greenhill. —2D **90**
Greenhills. —6D **148**
Greenlees. —4B **122**
Greens, The. —6C **30**

HAGGS. (FK4) —1G **15**
Hairmyres. —3B **148**
Halfway. —3D **122**
Hallside. —3F **123**
Hamiltonhill. —5F **63**
HAMILTON. (ML3) —6A **142**
Hangingshaw. —5F **103**
HARDGATE (G81) —1E **43**
Hareleeshill. —3F **161**
Harestanes. —4H **31**
Hattonrig. —1D **126**
Haughhead. —1C **6**
Hawkhead. —3E **99**
Hayston. —5A **30**
Heatherbell. —6A **70**
High Balmalloch. —2G **11**
High Blantyre. —4A **140**
High Burnside. —3E **121**
High Crosshill. —2D **120**
High Gallowhill. —2B **50**
High Knightswood. —1D **60**
Highland Park. —1G **11**
Hillhead. —6B **62**
(nr. Glasgow)
Hillhead. —4D **30**
(nr. Kirkintilloch)
Hillhouse. —6D **140**
Hillington. —6A **80**
HILLINGTON INDUSTRIAL ESTATE. (G52) —3H **79**
Hillside. —5B **114**
Hogganfield. —1A **86**
Holehills. —2B **92**
Holehouse. —2C **130**
Holmpark. —4H **39**
HOLYTOWN. (ML1) —2A **128**
Househillwood. —6B **100**
HOUSTON. (PA6) —1A **74**
Howwood Road. —4E **95**
Hunterhill. —3C **98**
Hurlet. —6H **99**
Hutchesontown. —1H **103**
Hyndland. —6H **61**

Ibrox. —6H **81**
INCHINNAN. (PA4) —2H **57**

Jellyhill. —3C **48**
Jenny Lind. —5D **116**
Johnstone Castle. —4G **95**
JOHNSTONE. (PA5, PA6, PA9 & PA10) —2F **95**
Jordanhill. —4E **61**

Kelvin. —6A **150**
Kelvindale. —3H **61**
Kelvingrove. —2C **82**
Kelvinhaugh. —3B **82**
Kelvinhead. —1H **13**
Kelvinside. —4H **61**
Kennishead. —2E **117**
KILBARCHAN. (PA10) —2A **94**
Kilbowie. —4D **42**
Kildrum. —2B **36**
KILSYTH. (G65) —3H **11**
King's Park. —1H **119**
Kingston. —4A **40**
(nr. Bishopton)
Kingston. —6E **83**
(nr. Glasgow)
Kinning Park. —1C **102**
Kirkhill. —2B **122**
(nr. Cambuslang)
Kirkhill. —4G **133**
(nr. Newton Mearns)
KIRKINTILLOCH. (G66) —4C **30**
Kirklandneuk. —5D **58**
Kirkshaws. —2A **110**
Kirkton. —3E **131**
Kirktonhill. —4D **16**
Kirkwood. —2G **109**
Kittochside. —4C **136**
Knightswood. —2D **60**
Knowetop. —5H **143**
Knownoble. —5H **129**
Kylepark. —6B **108**

Laigh Park. —5A **78**
Laighstonehall. —1F **153**
Lambhill. —2E **63**
Langloan. —6A **90**
Langmuir. —4H **31**
Langside. —5D **102**
Lanrigg. —6A **52**
LARKHALL. (ML9) —2E **161**
Laurieston. —6G **83**
Law Hill. —1A **164**
LAW. (ML8) —6D **158**
Lawn Park. —4A **26**
Law of Mauldslie. —1H **163**
LENNOXTOWN. (G65) —3F **7**
LENZIE. (G66) —2C **50**
Lenziemill. —5A **36**
Lightburn. —4E **123**
(nr. Cambuslang)
Lightburn. —4A **86**
(nr. Glasgow)
Linburn. —6D **40**
Linthouse. —3E **81**
Linvale. —6G **43**
LINWOOD. (PA3) —6A **76**
Little Earnock. —2E **153**
Loanhead. —1E **79**
Lochfield. —4B **98**
Lochlibo. —6C **114**
LONGCROFT. (FK4) —1G **15**
Lounsdale. —3E **97**
Low Blantyre. —6C **124**
Low Waters. —2A **154**
Lumloch. —1G **65**

Machan. —4F **161**
Mansewood. —2A **118**
Marnock. —3G **69**
Maryhill. —1A **62**
Meadowhill. —2F **161**
Mearns. —6E **133**
Mearns Castle. —6G **133**
Meikle Earnock. —4G **153**
Meikleriggs. —3F **97**
Merkland. —4G **31**
Merrylee. —3B **118**
MILLARSTON. (PA1) —1E **97**
Millersneuk. —3E **51**

Areas covered by this atlas

Millerston. —5C **134**
MILLERSTON. (G33) —5B **66**
Millheugh. —3C **160**
Millikenpark. —4C **94**
Milnbank. —3C **84**
MILNGAVIE. (G62) —3H **25**
Milnwood. —3E **127**
Milton. —1G **63**
MILTON. (G82) —4F **19**
Milton of Campsie. —5C **8**
Moffat Mills. —5F **93**
MOLLINSBURN. (G67 & G68) —3H **53**
MOODIESBURN. (G69) —5D **52**
Moorpark. —1D **78**
MORNINGSIDE. (ML2) —6G **147**
Mossend. —2E **127**
Mossneuk. —4B **148**
Mosspark. —2E **101**
MOTHERWELL. (ML1) —3G **143**
Mountblow. —2G **41**
Mount Ellen. —2C **68**
Mount Florida. —5F **103**
MOUNT VERNON. (G32) —3C **106**
MUIREND. (G44) —3D **118**
Muirhead. —1H **107**
MUIRHEAD. (G69) —2A **68**
Muirhouse. —1B **156**
Murray, The. —4G **149**

NEILSTON. (G78) —2E **131**
Nerston. —3A **138**
Nether Kirkton. —1F **131**
Netherlee. —5D **118**
Netherton. —1E **61** (nr. Glasgow)
Netherton. —2E **157** (nr. Wishaw)
NEWARTHILL. (ML1) —3F **129**
Newbridge End. —5F **165**
NEWHOUSE. (ML1) —5H **113**
Newlands. —2C **118**
Newlandsmuir. —6A **148**
Newmains. —2E **79**
NEWMAINS. (ML2) —5E **147**
New Monkland. —5G **71**
NEW STEVENSTON. (ML1) —3A **128**
Newton. —1G **123**
NEWTON MEARNS. (G77) —5D **132**
Nitshill. —2A **116**
North Barr. —4E **41**
North Barrwood. —3A **12**
North Cardonald. —4B **80**
Northfield. —2F **11**
North Kelvin. —6C **62**
North Lodge. —5F **143**
North Motherwell. —2D **142**

Oatlands. —3H **103**
Old Balornock. —4D **64**
Oldhill. —6G **79**
OLD KILPATRICK. (G60) —1E **41**
Old Monkland. —1A **110**
ORBISTON. (ML4) —3C **126**
Orchard Park. —4E **51** (nr. Lenzie)
Orchard Park. —4H **117** (nr. Thornliebank)
OVERTOWN. (ML2) —5A **158**
Oxgang. —6F **31**

PAISLEY. (PA1 to PA3) —1H **97**
Parkhall. —2B **42**
Parkhead. —6F **85**
Parkhouse. —3H **115**
Park Mains. —2G **57**
Parkneuk. —1G **151**
Partick. —1H **81**
Partickhill. —1H **81**
Patner. —2H **157**
PATTERTON. (G77) —1D **132**
Peel Park. —1A **148**
Penilee. —5G **79**
Petersburn. —5E **93**
Petershill. —6D **64**
Philipshill. —5A **136**
Pickerstonhill. —2F **129**
PLAINS. (ML6) —1G **93**
Plantation. —5B **82**
Pollok. —6C **100**
Pollokshaws. —5A **102**
Pollokshields. —2D **102**
Polmaide. —3H **103**
Port Dundas. —1G **83**
Port Eglington. —1E **103**
Porter Field. —1D **78**
Possil Park. —4G **63**
Potterhill. —4H **97**
Powburn. —6C **108**
Priesthill. —1A **116**
Provanmill. —6G **65**

Quarrelton. —3E **95**
QUARRIER'S VILLAGE. (PA11) —1A **72**
QUEENZIEBURN. (G65) —3C **10**

Radnor Park. —3C **42**
Ralston. —1F **99**
Ranfurly. —5G **73**
Raploch. —2D **160**
Rashiebarn. —5E **41**
Rawyards. —2C **92**
RENFREW. (PA4) —5F **59**
Riddrie. —2F **85**
Riddrie Knowes. —3G **85**
Robroyston. —3G **65**
Rogerton. —3F **137**
Rosebank. —5G **31**
ROSEBANK. (ML8) —5E **163**
Rosehall. —2D **110**
Rosshall. —2A **100**
Rossland. —5H **39**
Royston. —2B **84**
Ruchazie. —2A **86**
Ruchill. —4D **62**
RUTHERGLEN. (G73) —5C **104**

St Leonards. —2C **150**
Sandyhills. —1D **106**
Scotstoun. —5B **60**
Scotstounhill. —3B **60**
Seafar. —3G **35**
Seedhill. —1C **98**
Shawfield. —3B **104**
Shawhead. —2B **110**
Shawlands. —5C **102**
SHAWSBURN. (ML9) —3A **162**
Shettleston. —6B **86**
Shieldhall. —3C **80**
Shirrel. —6C **110**
Shortroods. —4A **78**
Sighthill. —1A **84**
Sikeside. —6F **91**
Silverbank. —1G **121**
Silverton. —4H **17**
Silvertonhill. —1B **154**
Silverwells. —6E **125**
Smithstone. —2B **34**
Southbar. —1E **57**
South Barrwood. —4A **12**
South Cardonald. —1C **100**
South Nitshill. —3A **116**
Spateston. —6C **94**
Spittal. —2B **120**
SPRINGBOIG. (G32) —5C **86**
Springburn. —5B **64**
Springhall. —3F **121**
Springhill. —1G **131**
Springwell. —4D **122**
Springwells. —3D **140**
Stamperland. —6D **118**
Stanley. —4G **97**
STEPPS. (G33) —3D **66**
Stewartfield. —5E **137**
Stonefield. —1C **140**
Strathbungo. —3D **102**
Strutherhill. —5E **161**
Summerlee. —3B **90**
Summerston. —6B **46**
Sunnyside. —3C **90**
Swinhill. —6G **161**
Swinton. —5G **87**

Tandlehill. —3B **94**
Tannochside. —4F **109**
Temple. —2F **61**
THORNLIEBANK. (G46) —4F **117**
Thornly Park. —5B **98**
THORNTONHALL. (G72) —6G **135**
Thrashbush. —1A **92**
Tintock. —3A **32**
Tollcross. —2A **106**
Torbush. —5F **147**
TORRANCE. (G64) —5D **28**
Toryglen. —6A **104**
Townend. —2F **17**
Townhead. —2H **89** (nr. Coatbridge)
Townhead. —4G **83** (6F **5**) (nr. Glasgow)
Townhead. —5D **30** (nr. Kirkintilloch)
Tradeston. —6E **83**

UDDINGSTON. (G71) —2D **124**
Udston. —5E **141**

Vicarland. —2A **122**
Victory Gardens. —1E **79**
Viewfield. —4B **126**
Viewpark. —6G **109**

Wardpark. —4C **14**
Waterfoot. —6B **134**
WATERLOO. (ML2) —2B **158**
Waterside. —2G **115**
WATERSIDE. (G66) —6H **31**
Waverley Park. —4B **102**
Wellside. —3D **122**
West Arthurlie. —6C **114**
West Balgrochan. —3D **28**
Westburn. —1E **123**
West Craigend. —6E **41**
West Crindledyke. —3D **146**
West Drumoyne. —4D **80**
Wester Auchinloch. —6C **50**
Wester Holytown. —2G **127**
Westerwood. —6A **14**
Westfield. —6B **34** (nr. Cumbernauld)
Westfield. —2F **11** (nr. Kilsyth)
West Mains. —1D **148**
West Maryston. —4A **88**
West Porton. —3G **39**
Westwood. —3D **148**
Wheatlands. —1A **140**
Whifflet. —6D **90**
Whinhall. —2G **91**
Whinknowe. —5C **162**
Whitecraigs. —2G **133**
Whitecrook. —6E **43**
Whitehaugh. —6C **78**
Whitehill. —3F **141**
Whitehills. —5G **149**
WHITEINCH. (G14) —6C **60**
Whitestripe. —3F **147**
Whitlawburn. —4H **121**
Whittagreen. —4D **128**
Wildmanbridge. —4G **159**
Williamsburgh. —1C **98**
Williamwood. —1B **134**
Wishawhill. —5F **145**
WISHAW. (ML2) —5H **145**

Yett. —4C **128**
Yoker. —3G **59**

TOURIST INFORMATION CENTRES covered by this atlas

with their map square reference

Coatbridge T.I.C. —5B **90**
The Time Capsule,
Buchanan St.,
COATBRIDGE, ML5 1DL
Tel: (01236) 431133

Dumbarton T.I.C. —4F **19**
Milton Gateway, A82 Northbound,
Milton, DUMBARTON, G82 2TZ
Tel: (01389) 742306

Glasgow T.I.C. —5G **5**
35 St. Vincent Pl.,
GLASGOW, G1 2ER
Tel: (0141) 204 4400

Glasgow Airport T.I.C. —2H **77**
Tourist information desk,
International Arrivals Hall,
Glasgow Airport, Abbotsinch,
PAISLEY, PA3 2ST
Tel: (0141) 848 4440

Hamilton T.I.C. —3A **142**
Road Chef Services,
M74 Northbound,
HAMILTON, ML3 6JW
Tel: (01698) 285590

Paisley T.I.C. —1A **98**
Town Hall, Abbey Clo.,
PAISLEY, PA1 1LZ
Tel: (0141) 889 4000

PLACES OF INTEREST
covered by this atlas

with their map square reference

*Auld Kirk Museum. —4C **30***
(off Cowgate.)

Barons Haugh R.S.P.B. Nature Reserve. —1F **155**
*Barras, The. —5A **84***
(off Moncur St.)
*Barrhead Community Museum. —5E **115***
(off Main St.)
Bellahouston Park. —1F **101**
Bothwell Castle. —4B **124**
Burrell Collection. —4H **101**

Carfin Lourdes Grotto. —5D **128**
Chatelherault. —3D **154**
Clydebank District Museum. —6C **42**
Coats Observatory. —6H **77**
Collins Gallery. —5G **5**
Colzium House & Estate. —1B **12**
Compass Gallery. —4C **4**
Crookston Castle (NTS). —3B **100**
Cumbernauld Museum. —6F **37**

David Livingstone Centre. —5C **124**
Dumbarton Castle. —6G **17**

Finnieston Crane. —4C **82**
Fossil Grove. —6D **60**

*Gallery of Modern Art. —4G **83** (5E **5**)*
(off Queen St.)
George Sq. —4G **83** (5F **5**)
Glasgow Botanic Gardens. —5B **62**
Glasgow's Centre for Contemporary Arts. —3B **4**
Glasgow School of Art. —3E **83** (3B **4**)
Glasgow Zoo Park. —3A **108**
Greenbank Gardens (NTS). —4A **134**

Hamilton Mausoleum. —4A **142**
Heatherbank Museum of Social Work.
*(off Park Dri.) —1C **82***
House for an Art Lover. —6G **81**
*Hunter House Museum. —5C **138***
(off Maxwellton Rd.)
Hunterian Art Gallery. —1B **82**
Hunterian Museum. —1B **82**
Hutchesons' Hall (NTS). —6F **5**

International Stock Exchange, The. —5D **4**

James Hamilton Heritage Centre, The. —5F **137**

Kelvingrove Museum & Art Gallery. —2B **82**
Kilsyth Heritage Museum. —3A **12**
(Burngreen)

*Lillie Art Gallery. —3H **25***
(off Station Rd.)
Linn Park & Cathcart Castle. —4E **119**
Low Parks Museum. —5A **142**

McLellan Galleries. —3C **4**
M & D's Theme Park. —5H **125**
Merchant's House. —5E **5**
M.V. Gypsy Princess. —5A **12**
*Mitchell Library, The. —3D **82***
(off North St.)
Motherwell Heritage Centre. —3F **143**
Museum of 602 (City of Glasgow) Squadron
*(off Queen Elizabeth Av.) —4H **79***
*Museum of Transport. —2B **82***
(off Bunhouse Rd.)

*Paisley Museum & Art Gallery. —1H **97***
(off High St.)
People's Palace. —6A **84**
Pollok House. —5F **101**
Proven Hall (NTS). —2F **87**
P.S. Waverley. —5D **82**

Quarrier's Village. —1B **72**

Roman Bath House. —2F **45**
Rouken Glen Park. —6F **117**
Royal Highland Fusiliers Museum, The. —3E **83** (3A **4**)
Rutherglen Museum. —5D **104**

St Mungo Museum of Religious Life & Art.
*(off Castle St.) —4A **84***
*Scotland Street School Museum. —6D **82***
(off Scotland St.)
Scottish Maritime Museum. —4F **17**
Sma'Shot Cottages. —1A **98**
*Springburn Museum. —5B **64***
(off Ayr St.)
*Strathclyde Arts Centre. —4E **83** (6A **4**)*
(off Washington St.)
Summerlee Heritage Trust. —4B **90**

Tenement House , The (NTS). —6A **4**

University of Glasgow Visitor Centre. —1B **82**

Viewpark Gardens. —1F **125**

*Weaver's Cottage Museum, The. —3A **92***
(off Wellwynd)
Weaver's Cottage (NTS). —2A **94**
Willow Tearooms. —3C **4**

SPORTS and LEISURE FACILITIES covered by this atlas

with their map square reference

*ABC Cinema. —3D **118***
(off Clarkston Rd.)
ABC Film Centre. —3B **4**
Airdrie Golf Course. —1H **91**
Airdrie Leisure Centre. —2C **92**
Airdrieonians F.C. —4B **34**
(Shared ground with Clyde F.C.)
Albion Rovers F.C. —5E **91**
Alexandra Park Golf Course. —3D **84**
Alexandra Sports Hall. —3E **85**
Allander Sports Complex, The. —6H **25**
*All Saints Sports Centre. —5E **65***
(off Scotsburn Rd.)
Antonine Sports Centre, The. —1C **42**
Aquatec, The. —2G **143**
Arches Theatre. —6C **4**

Balmore Golf Course. —5H **27**
Barlia Sports Park. —4A **120**
*Barony Chambers. —4C **30***
(off W. High St.)
Barrhead Sports Centre. —4E **115**
Barshaw (Municipal) Golf Course. —6E **79**
Bearsden Golf Course. —2C **44**
Bearsden Ski Club. —6D **24**
Bellahouston Sports Centre —1F **101**
*Bellshill Cultural Centre. —2C **126***
(off John St.)
Bellshill Golf Course. —4D **126**
Birkenshaw Sports Hall. —4D **108**
Bishopbriggs Golf Course. —5B **48**
Blairbeth Golf Course. —5C **120**
Blantyre Sports Centre. —1C **140**
Bothwell Castle Golf Course. —5E **125**
Burnhill Sports Centre. —5B **104**

Calderbraes Golf Course. —4B **108**
Calderglen Children's Zoo. —5C **150**
Cambuslang Golf Course. —6B **106**
Campsie Golf Course. —1F **7**
*Campsie Recreation Centre. —3G **7***
(off Bencloich Rd.)
*Carlton Kelburne Cinema. —6C **78***
(off Glasgow Rd.)
Carluke Golf Course. —3B **164**
Carluke Leisure Centre. —3G **165**
*Castlemilk Sports Centre. —4A **120***
(off Dougrie Rd.)
*Castlemilk Swimming Pool. —4A **120***
(off Castlemilk Dri.)
Cathcart Castle Golf Course. —2A **134**
Cathkin Braes Golf Course. —6D **120**
Cawder Golf Course. —1B **48**
Celtic F.C. —1E **105**
*Church Street Swimming Pool. —1A **82***
(off Byres Rd.)
Citizens' Theatre. —6G **83**
City Hall. —4H **83** (6G **5**)
Civic Theatre. —4F **17**
Clober Golf Course. —2F **25**
Clydebank & District Golf Course. —1E **43**
Clydebank F.C. —3H **17**
(Shared ground with Dumbarton F.C.)
Clydebank Megabowl. —6E **43**
Clyde F.C. —4B **34**
*Coatbridge College Sports Centre. —4D **90***
(off Park St.)
Coatbridge Golf Course. —2G **89**
Coatbridge Outdoor Sports Complex. —6B **90**
Cochrane Castle Golf Course. —5E **95**
*Columba Sports Complex. —6C **90***
(off Wallace St.)
Colville Park Golf Course. —6H **127**
Cowglen Golf Course. —6F **101**
Crownpoint Sports Park. —5B **84**
Crow Wood Golf Course. —1G **67**
Cumbernauld Theatre. —1B **36**

Dalmuir (Clydebank) Municipal Golf Course. —3A **42**
David Lloyd Club, The. —3D **78**
Deaconsbank Golf Course. —5E **117**
Dollan Aqua Centre. —2G **149**
Dougalston Golf Course. —2B **26**
Douglas Park Golf Course. —2G **45**
Drumchapel Sports Centre. —5H **43**
*Drumchapel Swimming Pool. —5H **43***
(off Drumry Rd. E.)
Drumpellier Golf Course. —5H **89**
Dullatur Golf Course. —6E **13**
Dumbarton F.C. —3H **17**
Dumbarton Golf Course. —2F **17**
Duncanrig Sports Centre. —3D **148**

*Eastbank Sports Centre. —6B **86***
(off Academy St.)
*Easterhouse Pool. —3G **87***
(off Bogbain Rd.)
Easterhouse Sports Centre. —2F **87**
Easter Moffat Golf Course. —2H **93**
East Kilbride Arts Centre. —6H **137**
(Old Coach Rd.)
East Kilbride Golf Course. —3B **138**
*East Kilbride Ice Rink, The. —3H **149***
(off Olympia Shopping Centre, The)
*East Kilbride Village Theatre. —1H **149***
(off Maxwell Dri.)
Eddlewood Sports Barn. —4H **153**
Elderslie Golf Course. —2C **96**
Elderslie Leisure Centre. —2B **96**
Erskine Golf Course. —2H **39**
Erskine Pool. —5F **41**

Fereneze Golf Course. —4D **114**
Ferguslie Park Sports & Recreation Centre. —5E **77**
Fort Antonine Theatre. —6B **48**

Glasgow Academicals R.U.F.C. —3E **61**
*Glasgow Film Theatre. —3C **4***
(off Rose St.)
Glasgow High / Kelvinside R.U.F.C. —3E **61**
Glasgow (Killermont) Golf Course. —5A **46**
Glasgow Royal Concert Hall. —3G **83** (3E **5**)
*Glasgow's Grand Ole Opry. —5C **82***
(off Govan Rd.)
Glasgow Ski Centre. —1G **101**
Govan Fun Pool. —4F **81**
*Govanhill Pool. —3E **103***
(off Calder St.)
*Greenhills Sports Centre. —6E **149***
(off Stroud Rd.)
*Grosvenor Cinema. —1B **82***
(off Ashton La.)
GX Superbowl. —5B **78**

Haggs Castle Golf Course. —2G **101**
Hamilton Academical F.C. —5E **91**
(Shared ground with Albion Rovers)
Hamilton Golf Course. —3E **155**
*Hamilton Water Palace. —5H **141***
(off Almada St.)
Harehills Sports Barn. —4G **161**
Hayston Golf Course. —4A **30**
*Henry Wood Hall, The. —3C **82***
(off Claremont St.)
Hollywood Bowl (Cumbernauld). —3A **36**
*Hollywood Bowl (Glasgow). —3D **82***
(off Elliott Street)

Iain Nicholson Recreation Centre. —1B **68**

Jock Stein Sports Barn. —5C **140**
*John Smith Swimming Pool. —4H **91***
(off Stirling St.)
*Johnstone Swimming Pool. —2F **95***
(off Ludvic Sq.)
John Wright Sports Centre, The. —1A **150**

Keir Hardie Sports Centre. —1A **128**
*Kelvin Hall International Sports Arena. —2B **82***
(off Argyle St.)
Kilmardinney Art Centre. —1G **45**
Kilsyth Lennox Golf Course. —1A **12**
*Kilsyth Swimming Pool. —2G **11***
(off Airdrie Rd.)
King's Park Golf Course. —2H **119**
Kirkhill Golf Course. —5H **121**
Kirkintilloch Golf Course. —3B **30**
*Kirkintilloch Swimming Pool. —6D **30***
(off Woodhead Pk.)
Kirkwood Sports Barn. —1F **109**
Knightswood (Park) Golf Course. —3B **60**

*Lagoon Leisure Centre. —1B **98***
(off Mill St.)
*Lanarkshire Ice Rink. —5A **142***
(off Muir St.)
Larkhall Golf Course. —3H **161**
Larkhall Leisure Centre. —3E **161**
Leisuredome, The. —4A **48**
Lenzie Golf Course. —4D **50**
Lethamhill Golf Course. —6H **65**
Linn Park Golf Course. —4F **119**
Linwood Moss Sports Complex. —4G **75**
Littlehill Golf Course. —2C **64**

*Marcos Leisue Centre. —6A **84***
(off Templeton St.)
Meadow Centre, The. —3F **17**
*Mitchell Theatre, The. —3D **82***
(off Granville St.)
*Motherwell Concert Hall & Theatre Complex. —4H **143***
(off Windmill Hill St.)
Motherwell F.C. —5H **143**

Sports and Leisure Facilities

Mount Ellen Golf Course. —3F **69**
Mount Vernon Sports Centre. —3G **107**

*Neilston Leisure Centre. —2E **131***
(off Main St.)
*North Woodside Leisure Centre. —1E **83***
(off Braid Sq.)

*Odeon Cinema (Glasgow). —3F **83** (4D **4**)*
(off Renfield St.)
Odeon Cinema (Hamilton). —6B **142**
Old Athenaeum Theatre. —5E **5**
Old Ranfurly Golf Course. —4F **73**

*Paisley Arts Centre. —1A **98***
(off New St.)
Palacerigg (Cumbernauld) Golf Course. —6F **37**
Partick Thistle F.C. —5E **63**
Pavilion Theatre. —3D **4**
Pollok Golf Course. —6H **101**
*Pollok Leisure Pool. —6C **100***
(off Cowglen Rd.)
*Pollokshaws Sports Centre. —6A **102***
(off Ashtree Rd.)
Powerdrome Bowl. —5F **91**
Pro Bowl. —4D **30**
Pro Lane Bowl. —5A **150**

Queen's Park F.C. —6G **103**

Ralston Golf Course. —1F **99**
Ranfurly Castle Golf Course. —4E **73**
Rangers F.C. —5H **81**
Renfrew Golf Course. —4D **58**
Royal Scottish Academy of Music & Drama. (New Atheneaum) —3D **4**
Ruchill Golf Course. —3D **62**
*Rutherglen Swimming Pool. —5C **104***
(off Greenhill Rd.)

*St Andrews Sports Centre. —5F **149***
(off Scholars Ga.)
St Mirren F.C. —5A **78**
Sandyhills Golf Course. —2C **106**
Scotstoun Leisure Centre. —5D **60**
Scottish Exhibition & Conference Centre. —4B **82**
Shawfields Stadium. —3A **104**
*Shettleston Sports Centre. —6H **85***
(off Elvan St.)
Showcase Cinema. —2G **109**
Sir Matt Busby Sports Complex. —2B **126**
*Springburn Sports Centre. —5B **64***
(off Kay St.)
Strathclyde Park Golf Course. —4A **142**
Summit Centre Ice Rink. —3C **82**

Temple Swimming Pool. —1E **61**
*Theatre Royal. —2D **4***
(off Hope St.)
Time Capsule, The. —5B **90**
Torrance Park Golf Course. —5C **150**
Tramway. —2E **103**
Tryst Sports Centre. —3A **36**

*UCI (Clydebank). —6D **42***
(off Britannia Way)
*UCI (East Kilbride). —3H **149***
(off Olympia Shop. Cen.)

*Victoria Baths. —5F **59***
(off Inchinnan Rd.)
Virgin Cinema. —6E **85**

Westerwood Hotel Golf & Country Club. —5A **14**
West of Scotland R.U.F.C. —5H **25**
Whitecraigs Golf Course. —2G **133**
Whitehill Pool. —4D **84**
*Whitehill Sports Barn. —3F **141***
(off Hunter Rd.)
Williamwood Golf Course. —6D **118**
Windyhill Golf Course. —5A **24**
Wishaw Golf Course. —5G **145**
Wishaw Greyhound Stadium. —1F **157**
Wishaw Sports Centre. —1F **157**
*Woodfarm Sports Centre. —5G **117***
(off Burns Gro.)

*Yoker Sports Centre. —3H **59***
(off Spiershall Ter.)

HOSPITALS and HEALTH CENTRES covered by this atlas

with their map square reference

N.B. Where Hospitals and Health Centres are not named on the map, the reference given is for the road in which they are situated.

Abronhill Health Centre —1E **37**
Pine Rd., Abronhill,
Cumbernauld, G67 3BE
Tel: (01236) 731881

Accord Hospice —3E **99**
Hawkhead Hospital Grounds,
Hawkhead Rd., Paisley, PA2 7BL
Tel: (0141) 889 8169

Airbles Road Centre —4H **143**
59 Airbles Rd.,
Motherwell, ML1 2TJ
Tel: (01698) 261331

Airdrie Health Centre —4G **91**
Monkscourt Av.,
Airdrie, ML6 0JU
Tel: (01236) 769388

Alexander Hospital —3A **90**
Blair Rd., Coatbridge, ML5 2EW
Tel: (01236) 422661

Baillieston Health Centre —1H **107**
20 Muirside Rd., Glasgow, G69 7AD
Tel: (0141) 531 8008

Barrhead Health Centre —4E **115**
201 Main St., Barrhead,
Renfrewshire, G78 1SA
Tel: (0141) 880 6161

Bellshill Maternity Hospital —5C **110**
North Rd., Bellshill, ML4 3JN
Tel: (01689) 747292

Belvidere Hospital —1E **105**
1360-1432, London Rd.,
Glasgow, G31 4PG
Tel: (0141) 211 8500

Bishopton Health Centre —5H **39**
Greenock Rd., Bishopton,
Renfrewshire, PA7 5AW
Tel: (01505) 863223

Blantyre Health Centre —2B **140**
Victoria St., Blantyre, G72 0BS
Tel: (01698) 823583

Blarwarthill Hospital —3A **60**
129 Holehouse Dri., Knightswood,
Glasgow, G13 3TG
Tel: (0141) 211 9000

Bon Secours Hospital —5D **102**
36 Mansionhouse Rd.,
Glasgow, G41 3DW
Tel: (0141) 632 9231

Bridge of Weir Hospital —2B **72**
Torr Rd., Bridge of Weir, PA11 3RY
Tel: (01475) 633777

Bridgeton Health Centre —6B **84**
201 Abercromby St.,
Glasgow, G40 2DA
Tel: (0141) 531 6500

Canniesburn Hospital —5E **45**
Switchback Rd.,
Bearsden, G61 1QL
Tel: (0141) 211 5600

Carluke Health Centre —3F **165**
Market Pl., Carluke, ML8 4BP
Tel: (01555) 770635

Castlemilk Health Centre —4A **120**
Dougrie Dri., Glasgow, G45 9AW
Tel: (0141) 531 8500

Central Health Centre —4H **35**
North Carbrain Rd.,
Cumbernauld, G67 1BJ
Tel: (01236) 731771

Cleland Hospital —1A **146**
Bellside Rd., Cleland, ML1 5NR
Tel: (01698) 860293

Clydebank Health Centre —4D **42**
Kilbowie Rd., Clydebank, G81 2TQ
Tel: (0141) 533 6363

Coatbridge Health Centre —5C **90**
1 Centre Park Court,
Coatbridge, ML5 3AP
Tel: (01236) 432200

Coathill Hospital —1C **110**
Hospital St., Coatbridge, ML5 4DN
Tel: (01236) 421266

Condorrat Health Centre —1C **54**
16 Airdrie Rd., Condorrat,
Cumbernauld, G67 4DN
Tel: (01236) 723383

Cowglen Hospital —6D **100**
10 Boystone Rd., Glasgow, G53 6XJ
Tel: (0141) 211 9200

Dumbarton Cottage Hospital —2F **17**
Townend Rd., Dumbarton, G82 2AN
Tel: (01389) 763151

Dumbarton Joint Hospital —3C **16**
Cardross Rd., Dumbarton, G82 5JA
Tel: (01389) 762317

Drumchapel Health Centre —4H **43**
80/90 Kinfauns Dri., Drumchapel,
Glasgow, G15 7TS
Tel: (0141) 211 6070

Drumchapel Hospital —5B **44**
129 Drumchapel Rd.,
Glasgow, G15 6PX
Tel: (0141) 211 6000

Dykebar Hospital —6D **98**
Grahamston Rd.,
Paisley, PA2 7DE
Tel: (0141) 884 5122

Easterhouse Health Centre —3G **87**
9 Auchinlea Rd.,
Glasgow, G34 9HQ
Tel: (0141) 531 8100

Elderslie Hospital —3H **95**
Cherrywood Rd.,
Elderslie, PA5 9EE
Tel: (01505) 323301

Erskine Health Centre —4E **41**
Bargarran Sq., Erskine,
Renfrewshire, PA8 6BS
Tel: (0141) 812 6513

Ferguslie Clinic —5E **77**
Tannahill Centre, 76 Blackstoun Rd.,
Ferguslie Park, Paisley, PA3 1NT
Tel: (0141) 849 0554

Foxbar Clinic —4E **97**
Morar Dri., Paisley, PA2 9QR
Tel: (01505) 813119

Gartloch Hospital —6A **68**
2154 Gartloch Rd.,
Glasgow, G69 8EJ
Tel: (0141) 771 0771

Gartnavel General Hospital —5G **61**
1053 Gt. Western Rd.,
Glasgow, G12 0YN
Tel: (0141) 211 3000

Gartnavel Royal Hospital —5G **61**
1055 Gt. Western Rd.,
Glasgow, G12 0XH
Tel: (0141) 211 3600

Glasgow Dental Hospital —3E **83** (3B **4**)
378 Sauchiehall St.,
Glasgow, G2 3JZ
Tel: (0141) 211 9600

Glasgow Eye Infirmary —3C **82**
3 Sandyford Pl., Glasgow, G3 7JA
Tel: (0141) 211 6767

Glasgow Homoeopathic Hospital —4H **61**
1000 Gt. Western Rd.,
Glasgow, G12 0NR
Tel: (0141) 211 1600

Glasgow Nuffield Hospital, The —4H **61**
25 Beaconsfield Rd.,
Glasgow, G12 0PJ
Tel: (0141) 334 9441

Glasgow Royal Infirmary —3A **84**
84 Castle St., Glasgow, G4 0SF
Tel: (0141) 211 4000

Glasgow Royal Maternity Hospital —4H **83** (5G **5**)
147-163 Rottenrow,
Glasgow, G4 0NA
Tel: (0141) 211 3500

Glenburn Clinic —5H **97**
Fairway Av., Paisley, PA2 8DX
Tel: (0141) 884 3221

Gorbals Health Centre —1G **103**
45 Pine Pl., Glasgow, G5 0BQ
Tel: (0141) 429 6291

Govan Health Centre —3E **81**
5 Drumoyne Rd.,
Glasgow, G51 4BJ
Tel: (0141) 531 8400

Govanhill Health Centre —3F **103**
233 Calder St., Glasgow, G42 7DR
Tel: (0141) 531 8300

Greenhills Health Centre —6D **148**
Greenhills Sq.,
East Kilbride, G72 8TU
Tel: (013552) 34325

Hairmyres Hospital —3B **148**
Eaglesham Rd.,
East Kilbride, G75 8RG
Tel: (01355) 220292

Hawkhead Hospital —3E **99**
Hawkhead Rd., Hawkhead,
Paisley, PA2 7BL
Tel: (0141) 889 8151

Health Care International Hospital —5A **42**
Beardmore St.,
Clydebank, G81 4HX
Tel: (0141) 951 5000

Hunter Health Centre —2H **149**
Andrew St.,
East Kilbride, G74 1AD
Tel: (013552) 39111

Hunters Hill Marie Curie Centre —3B **64**
Belmont Rd., Glasgow, G21 3AY
Tel: (0141) 558 2555

Johnstone Health Centre —3F **95**
60 Quarry St., Johnstone,
Renfrewshire, PA5 8EY
Tel: (01505) 320278

Johnstone Hospital —6G **75**
Bridge of Weir Rd.,
Johnstone, PA5 8YX
Tel: (01505) 331471

Kildrum Health Centre —2B **36**
Afton Rd., Kildrum,
Cumbernauld, G67 2EU
Tel: (01236) 731711

Kilsyth Health Centre —3A **12**
Burngreen, Kilsyth, G65 0HU
Tel: (01236) 822151

Kirklands Hospital —3F **125**
Fallside Rd., Bothwell, G71 8BB
Tel: (01698) 852508

Knightswood Hospital —3D **60**
125 Knightswood Rd.,
Glasgow, G13 2XG
Tel: (0141) 211 6900

Langside Priory Hospital —5D **102**
38 Mansionhouse Rd.,
Glasgow, G41 3DW
Tel: (0141) 636 6116

Larkhall Health Institute —2F **161**
Low Pleasance, Larkhall, ML9 2HW
Tel: (01698) 884731

Law Hospital —4H **159**
Carluke, ML8 5ER
Tel: (01698) 361100

Lennox Castle Hospital —2C **6**
Glen Rd., Lennoxtown, G65 7LB
Tel: (01360) 329200

Lenzie Hospital —4E **51**
Auchinloch Rd., Kirkintilloch,
Glasgow, G66 5DE
Tel: (0141) 776 1208

Leverndale Hospital —3H **99**
510 Crookston Rd.,
Glasgow, G53 7TU
Tel: (0141) 211 6400

Lightburn Hospital —4B **86**
966 Carntyne Rd., Glasgow, G32 6ND
Tel: (0141) 774 5102

Linwood Health Centre —6A **76**
Ardlamont Sq., Linwood,
Renfrewshire, PA3 3DE
Tel: (01505) 324337

Maryhill Heath Centre —3C **62**
41 Shawpark St., Glasgow, G20 9DR
Tel: (0141) 531 8700

Mearnskirk Hospital —6D **132**
Mearns Rd., Newton Mearns,
Glasgow, G77 5RZ
Tel: (0141) 201 6000

Merchiston Hospital —6E **75**
Bridge of Weir Rd., Barrochan Rd.,
Brookfield, Johnstone, PA5 8TY
Tel: (01505) 328261

Hospitals and Health Centres

Monkland District General Hospital —4G **91**
Monkscourt Av., Airdrie, ML6 0JS
Tel: (01236) 748748

Motherwell Health Centre —4H **143**
138 Windmillhill St.,
Motherwell, ML1 1TB
Tel: (01698) 254601

Newmains Health Centre —5E **147**
17 Manse Rd., Newmains, ML2 9AX
Tel: (01698) 381006

New Sneddon Street Clinic —6A **78**
8 New Sneddon St.,
Paisley, PA3 2AD
Tel: (0141) 887 7771

Parkhead Health Centre —6F **85**
101 Salamanca St.,
Glasgow, G31 5BA
Tel: (0141) 531 9000

Parkhead Hospital —6F **85**
81 Salamanca St.,
Glasgow, G31 5ES
Tel: (0141) 211 8300

Pollock Health Centre —6C **100**
21 Cowglen Rd.,
Glasgow, G53 6EQ
Tel: (0141) 531 6800

Possilpark Health Centre —5G **63**
85 Denmark St., Glasgow, G22 5EG
Tel: (0141) 531 6120

Prince and Princess of Wales Hospice —5F **83**
71 Carlton Pl., Glasgow, G5 9TD
Tel: (0141) 429 5599

Princess Louise Scottish Hospital (Erskine Hospital) —1C **40**
Bishopton, Renfrewshire, PA7 5PU
Tel: (0141) 812 1100

Queen Mother's Maternity Hospital —2A **82**
Dalnair St., Yorkhill,
Glasgow, G3 8SH
Tel: (0141) 201 0550

Red Deer Day Hospital —3E **149**
Alberta Av., East Kilbride, G75 8NH
Tel: (01355) 244 254

Renfrew Health Centre —1E **79**
103 Paisley Rd., Renfrew,
Renfrewshire, PA4 8LL
Tel: (0141) 886 5921

Roadmeetings Hospital —5H **165**
Goremire Rd., Carluke, ML8 4PS
Tel: (01555) 77221

Ross Hall Hospital —2A **100**
221 Crookston Rd.,
Glasgow, G52 3NQ
Tel: (0141) 810 3151

Royal Alexandra Hospital —3H **97**
Corsebar Rd., Paisley, PA2 9PN
Tel: (0141) 887 9111

Royal Hospital For Sick Children —2A **82**
Dalnair St., Yorkhill,
Glasgow, G3 8SJ
Tel: (0141) 201 0000

Ruchill Hospital —4E **63**
520 Bilsland Dri.,
Glasgow, G20 9NB
Tel: (0141) 946 7120

Russel Institute —1A **98**
Causeyside St., Paisley, PA1 1UR
Tel: (0141) 889 8701

Rutherglen Health Centre —6D **104**
130 Stonelaw Rd.,
Glasgow, G73 2PQ
Tel: (0141) 531 6000

Rutherglen Maternity Hospital —6D **104**
120 Stonelaw Rd., Rutherglen,
Glasgow, G73 2PG
Tel: (0141) 201 6060

St Andrew's Hospice —3A **92**
Henderson St., Airdrie, ML6 6DJ
Tel: (01236) 766951

St Margaret's Hospice —2F **59**
East Barns St., Clydebank, G81 1EG
Tel: (0141) 952 1141

Shettleston Day Hospital —1H **105**
152 Wellshot Rd., Glasgow, G32 7AX
Tel: (0141) 778 8381

Shettleston Health Centre —6A **86**
420 Old Shettleston Rd.,
Glasgow, G32 7JZ
Tel: (0141) 531 6200

Southern General Hospital —3D **80**
1345 Govan Rd., Glasgow, G51 4TF
Tel: (0141) 201 1100

Springburn Health Centre —5B **64**
200 Springburn Way,
Glasgow, G21 1TR
Tel: (0141) 558 0101

Stobhill General Hospital —3C **64**
133 Balornock Rd., Glasgow, G21 3UW
Tel: (0141) 201 3000

Strathclyde Hospital —4F **143**
Airbles Rd., Motherwell, ML1 3BW
Tel: (01698) 258800

Thornliebank Health Centre —3F **117**
20 Kennishead Rd., Glasgow, G46 8NY
Tel: (0141) 531 6900

Townhead Health Centre —3A **84**
16 Alexandra Parade,
Glasgow, G31 2ES
Tel: (0141) 531 8900

Udston Hospital —5D **140**
Farm Rd., Hamilton, ML3 9LA
Tel: (01698) 823255

Victoria Infirmary —5E **103**
Langside Rd.,
Glasgow, G42 9TY
Tel: (0141) 201 6000

Victoria Geriatric Unit —5D **102**
100 Mansionhouse Rd.,
Glasgow, G41 3DX
Tel: (0141) 201 6161

Victoria Memorial Cottage Hospital —3F **11**
19 Glasgow Rd.,
Kilsyth, G65 9AG
Tel: (01236) 822172

Viewpark Health Centre —6G **109**
Burnhead St., Viewpark,
Uddingston, G71 5SU
Tel: (01698) 810171

Wester Moffat Hospital —3F **93**
Towers Rd.,
Airdrie, ML6 8LW
Tel: (01236) 763377

Western Infirmary —1B **82**
Dumbarton Rd.,
Glasgow, G11 6NT
Tel: (0141) 211 2000

Wishaw Health Centre —6H **145**
Kenilworth Av.,
Wishaw, ML2 7BQ
Tel: (01698) 355511

Woodilee Hospital —1F **51**
Lenzie, Glasgow, G66 3UG
Tel: (0141) 777 8000

Woodside Health Centre —6E **63**
Barr St., Glasgow, G20 7LR
Tel: (0141) 531 9200